(Continued on back endsheets)

British Children's Writers
Since 1960
First Series

British Children's Writers Since 1960
First Series

Edited by
Caroline C. Hunt
College of Charleston

A Bruccoli Clark Layman Book
Gale Research Inc.
Detroit, Washington, D.C., London

Printed in the United States of America

Published simultaneously in the United Kingdom
by Gale Research International Limited
(An affiliated company of Gale Research Inc.)

The paper used in this publication meets the minimum requirements
of American National Standard for Information Sciences–Permanence
Paper for Printed Library Materials, ANSI Z39.48-1984. ∞™

Library of Congress Cataloging-in-Publication Data

British children's writers since 1960. First series / edited by Caroline C. Hunt.
    p. cm. – (Dictionary of literary biography; v. 161)
"A Bruccoli Clark Layman book."
Includes bibliographical references and index.
ISBN 0-8103-9356-5 (alk. paper)
1. Children's literature, English – Bio-bibliography – Dictionaries. 2. English literature – 20th century
– Bio-bibliography – Dictionaries. 3. Authors, English – 20th century – Biography – Dictionaries.
I. Hunt, Caroline C. (Caroline Collins), 1941- . II. Series.
PR990.B753 1995
820.9'9287'09045 – dc20   95–25954
                                                                            CIP

[B]

For my family

Contents

Plan of the Series

. . . Almost the most prodigious asset of a country, and perhaps its most precious possession, is its native literary product – when that product is fine and noble and enduring.

Mark Twain*

The advisory board, the editors, and the publisher of the *Dictionary of Literary Biography* are joined in endorsing Mark Twain's declaration. The literature of a nation provides an inexhaustible resource of permanent worth. We intend to make literature and its creators better understood and more accessible to students and the reading public, while satisfying the standards of teachers and scholars.

To meet these requirements, *literary biography* has been construed in terms of the author's achievement. The most important thing about a writer is his writing. Accordingly, the entries in *DLB* are career biographies, tracing the development of the author's canon and the evolution of his reputation.

The purpose of *DLB* is not only to provide reliable information in a convenient format but also to place the figures in the larger perspective of literary history and to offer appraisals of their accomplishments by qualified scholars.

The publication plan for *DLB* resulted from two years of preparation. The project was proposed to Bruccoli Clark by Frederick C. Ruffner, president of the Gale Research Company, in November 1975. After specimen entries were prepared and typeset, an advisory board was formed to refine the entry format and develop the series rationale. In meetings held during 1976, the publisher, series editors, and advisory board approved the scheme for a comprehensive biographical dictionary of persons who contributed to North American literature. Editorial work on the first volume began in January 1977, and it was published in 1978. In order to make *DLB* more than a reference tool and to compile volumes that individually have claim to status as literary history, it was decided to organize volumes by topic, period, or genre. Each of these freestanding volumes provides a biographical-bibliographical guide and overview for a particular area of literature. We are convinced that this organization – as opposed to a single alphabet method – constitutes a valuable innovation in the presentation of reference material. The volume plan necessarily requires many decisions for the placement and treatment of authors who might properly be included in two or three volumes. In some instances a major figure will be included in separate volumes, but with different entries emphasizing the aspect of his career appropriate to each volume. Ernest Hemingway, for example, is represented in *American Writers in Paris, 1920–1939* by an entry focusing on his expatriate apprenticeship; he is also in *American Novelists, 1910–1945* with an entry surveying his entire career. Each volume includes a cumulative index of the subject authors and articles. Comprehensive indexes to the entire series are planned.

With volume ten in 1982 it was decided to enlarge the scope of *DLB*. By the end of 1986 twenty-one volumes treating British literature had been published, and volumes for Commonwealth and Modern European literature were in progress. The series has been further augmented by the *DLB Yearbooks* (since 1981) which update published entries and add new entries to keep the *DLB* current with contemporary activity. There have also been *DLB Documentary Series* volumes which provide biographical and critical source materials for figures whose work is judged to have particular interest for students. One of these companion volumes is entirely devoted to Tennessee Williams.

We define literature as the *intellectual commerce of a nation:* not merely as belles lettres but as that ample and complex process by which ideas are generated, shaped, and transmitted. *DLB* entries are not limited to "creative writers" but extend to other figures who in their time and in their way influenced the mind of a people. Thus the series encompasses historians, journalists, publishers, and screenwriters. By this means readers of *DLB* may be aided to perceive literature not as cult scripture in the keeping of intellectual high

*From an unpublished section of Mark Twain's autobiography, copyright by the Mark Twain Company

priests but firmly positioned at the center of a nation's life.

DLB includes the major writers appropriate to each volume and those standing in the ranks immediately behind them. Scholarly and critical counsel has been sought in deciding which minor figures to include and how full their entries should be. Wherever possible, useful references are made to figures who do not warrant separate entries.

Each DLB volume has a volume editor responsible for planning the volume, selecting the figures for inclusion, and assigning the entries. Volume editors are also responsible for preparing, where appropriate, appendices surveying the major periodicals and literary and intellectual movements for their volumes, as well as lists of further readings. Work on the series as a whole is coordinated at the Bruccoli Clark Layman editorial center in Columbia, South Carolina, where the editorial staff is responsible for accuracy of the published volumes.

One feature that distinguishes DLB is the illustration policy – its concern with the iconography of literature. Just as an author is influenced by his surroundings, so is the reader's understanding of the author enhanced by a knowledge of his environment. Therefore DLB volumes include not only drawings, paintings, and photographs of authors, often depicting them at various stages in their careers, but also illustrations of their families and places where they lived. Title pages are regularly reproduced in facsimile along with dust jackets for modern authors. The dust jackets are a special feature of DLB because they often document better than anything else the way in which an author's work was perceived in its own time. Specimens of the writers' manuscripts are included when feasible.

Samuel Johnson rightly decreed that "The chief glory of every people arises from its authors." The purpose of the *Dictionary of Literary Biography* is to compile literary history in the surest way available to us – by accurate and comprehensive treatment of the lives and work of those who contributed to it.

The *DLB* Advisory Board

Introduction

On 9 February 1964 four young Britons appearing on American television brought the Merseyside sound from the clubs of Liverpool to international prominence: the Beatles' now-legendary appearance on *The Ed Sullivan Show*. Newspapers and television newscasts ran pictures of screaming teenage fans. Less than a year later, on 30 January 1965, crowds of ordinary people along the streets of London watched the funeral procession of Winston Churchill, who for more than half a century had not only led his nation when called upon to do so but often seemed to personify it. Millions more watched on television and saw the somber parade pictured in the newspapers the next day – viewers more fortunate than those actually at the scene, for the overcast winter day was so cold that police horses were not used and reporters had to wrap papers around their legs to keep warm. Like their parents, British children in the 1960s were exposed to much that had remained unchanged for years – and simultaneously to much that was radically new and different. (The very fact that so many British families saw the Beatles or the Churchill funeral on television marks a dramatic change: in 1951, three British families in four had television, a figure that rose to nine families in ten by 1971.

The contrast between the new and the well known was clearly reflected in children's books of the 1960s and early 1970s, which range from the traditional (or even reactionary) to the experimental. Especially after 1975, some of the more nostalgic forms, such as school and pony stories of the most formulaic type, began to give way to "new" realism; experimentation became gradually more common, with the "problem novel" gaining ground just as in the United States at the same time. From 1960 to the present, competition from other media, especially television, has influenced the juvenile-book market both directly and indirectly. This introduction, focusing on the types of books written by authors included in this volume, concerns chiefly the earlier part of the decades since 1960: that is, from 1960 to approximately the middle 1970s. A separate introduction to the forthcoming Second Series will concentrate on the years after 1975.

It is easy to forget the atmosphere of austerity with which the 1960s opened. Having won the election of 1959 handily, Harold Macmillan (who at this time appeared in cartoons as "Supermac") and his Conservatives put in place various financial restraints that caused resentment and, on occasion, stoppages and strikes. In the summer of 1961 increases in bank rates and sales taxes, coupled with wage freezes, led teachers in British schools to hold walkouts, followed by a one-day strike of twenty-five thousand teachers on 20 September. The years 1963 and 1964, culminating in the narrow Labour victory of October 1964, marked the end of the long transition from the postwar period to something new and unfamiliar. No longer impoverished as in the 1930s and the immediate postwar years, British families still were not growing more prosperous at the rate of their peers in many other developed countries. Though ownership of household appliances and automobiles grew swiftly in the 1960s, so did labor unrest (along with trade union difficulties, especially from 1968 through 1974) and a sense of financial struggle for many. Two-income couples became more common (with obvious implications for child rearing and, thus, indirectly, for children's books).

Further, it became increasingly apparent during these years that Britain was no longer a major world power; the "wind of change," to quote Macmillan's famous speech about developing African countries, blew also through the rest of the former Empire. Eventually, the loss of Empire was to have an important influence on children's books; with no colonies to govern, the type of young hero presented by G. A. Henty and his literary descendants became, in a remarkably short time, "redundant" – to use the term applied to workers no longer needed. In fact, the entire social scheme represented by the Henty tradition, which had continued through the war both in popular children's books and in children's serials, became essentially irrelevant. Though she was older than sixty when she wrote *A Stranger at Green Knowe,* Lucy M. Boston caught the tone of this period as freshly as any angry young writer of the 1960s (and in better prose than most of them): the book critically portrays the plundering of the jungle for gain; the impossibility of accommodating a "stranger" from Africa, a gorilla, in any remotely tolerable manner in England; and the dubious advancement of material "progress."

One can easily forget the strange, uneasy feeling of those early transitional years. It is also easy to forget the relative conservatism of the early 1960s in custom and in law. In March 1961 Parliament was urged to consider raising the school-leaving age from fifteen (where it had been since 1944) to sixteen; the change was not implemented. Later the same year (29 June) the Wolfenden Report's recommendation that homosexual acts between consenting adults be legalized was defeated in the same Parliament. This was perhaps not surprising; until an Old Bailey jury's decision during the previous winter (2 November 1960), it had been illegal to sell the unexpurgated edition of *Lady Chatterley's Lover*. During the spring and summer of 1963, British tabloids widely publicized the association of John Profumo, secretary of state for war, with the call girl Christine Keeler — an affair that seriously embarrassed the Conservatives. Complicating the case was the presence of a Captain Ivanov, formerly of the Soviet embassy, and a Dr. Ward, accused of living off the earnings of the call girls. One of the girls, Mandy Rice-Davies, was only eighteen at the time. Ward committed suicide. Compulsory military conscription ended in 1962, the same year in which new immigration controls were imposed; in 1966 an Anti-Discrimination Act attempted to address the new problems of a society no longer racially homogeneous. The following year the Hunt Committee on Immigrants in the Youth Service noted the possibility of serious race conflicts if steps were not taken to improve relations. During the 1970s, particularly during the intermittent periods of high unemployment, race became a far more conspicuous issue than it had been.

Change, when it came about, came swiftly and in many areas. In a single year, 1967, the Sexual Offences Act was abolished (thus making homosexual activities legal between consenting adults); abortion also became legal; and contraceptives could be legally obtained, even through the National Health Service. A year later, theater censorship by the government ceased. In addition to their effect on the general public, these changes in social outlook strongly affected the youth culture that had begun to be conspicuous as a separate entity earlier in the decade. Carnaby Street became a household name around the world for offbeat new fashions aimed at the young. The Ginger Group fashions of Mary Quant and the androgynous image of Twiggy, a

waiflike model with huge eyes, anchored one version of the new look. Increasingly, drugs (notably marijuana, LSD, and heroin) also invaded the youth scene. Like clothing, phonograph records, and other consumer goods, books began to be produced specifically for the upper segment of the youth market; these young-adult books, dating from 1967 to 1968 in the United States and slightly later in Britain, often focused on subjects that had previously been taboo.

Political strife and violence also became more prominent in the early 1970s. In 1973–1974 there were many violent episodes in England, some connected with strikes but most involving bombs planted by the Irish Republican Army. (Meanwhile, the Scottish National Party achieved a surprising success in the 1974 election, and Welsh separatists also flourished.) These events, as well as the spread of television, contributed to the growing awareness of regions of the British Isles quite outside the traditional venues of children's books.

To return to the transitional early years of the 1960s, much in the juvenile publishing world was, not surprisingly, a good deal like the 1950s. Puffin Books, a leading publisher of children's paperbacks since 1940, continued its successful (and extensive) offerings. In 1968 the publisher Hamish Hamilton, also a longtime power in the juvenile market, added a fine new specialist children's editor, Julia Macrae. From Loughborough, beginning in 1964, came Ladybird Books, initially featuring a generic pair of children named Peter and Jane; these soon came to dominate the market, causing their publisher to expand Ladybird from graded readers to similarly formatted (but equally bland) volumes of fiction, fairy tales, and nonfiction. These small, attractively colored books showed precisely the same white, middle-class suburban children as readers of the 1940s and 1950s had done; it was another ten years before children who were not white appeared in the illustrations. (During the 1970s Ladybird also ran a parallel series showing children of color.)

Apart from mass-market series and other "checkout books," so called because they could be bought in the new supermarkets and at general outlets such as Marks and Spencer, some publishers were giving serious thought to the direction in which juvenile books should go. In 1962 a publishers' group was formed, which included on its board the influential editor Kaye Webb (Puffin Books) and other progressives, such as Anthony Kamm. This organization, the Children's Book Circle, encouraged interaction among professionals in the field, making possible discussion of a significant kind.

The 1960s ushered in an era of better-informed and generally more useful criticism of children's books than had previously been the case. One indicator was the rise of journals and reviews devoted to children's books. The earliest and most remarkable of the new review journals was Margery Fisher's *Growing Point,* begun in 1962 and continued for thirty years – a source of thoughtful, knowledgeable readings of new children's books, readings produced entirely by Fisher. Other review journals used the more traditional stable of reviewers. *Books for Your Children* appeared in 1965, and the year 1970 saw the beginning of another review journal, *Children's Book Review* (which ended its run in 1976), as well as the remarkable new departure *Signal,* under the leadership of Nancy Chambers and Aidan Chambers. This important journal will be discussed more fully in *British Children's Writers Since 1960, Second Series.* The third journal launched in 1970 was the Anglo-American cooperative production *Children's Literature in Education,* which publishes a variety of critical pieces (not necessarily about pedagogy) but no reviews as such.

To the analysis and promotion of good children's books came critics of a kind previously unknown. There had for years been librarians, gifted teachers, and editors in several major publishing houses, who knew the juvenile field thoroughly; most of these, however, did not write about it. The single magisterial exception, Harvey Darton's *Children's Books in England: Five Centuries of Social Life* (1932), surveys the publishing history of juveniles but does not pretend to offer the sort of detailed criticism for which there seemed, by the 1960s, to be a need. John Rowe Townsend 's *Written for Children* (1965), like Darton's book often revised to keep it current, was one of the earliest of the newer type, followed by several titles from Aidan Chambers and eventually by offerings from Peter Hunt and others, the last taking a somewhat more academic approach. Townsend and Chambers themselves wrote books for children and young adults, Townsend beginning in 1961 with *Gumble's Yard* and Chambers with *Cycle Smash* (1967, following some earlier children's plays); in addition, both had extensive reviewing careers, Townsend as editor of children's-book reviews for the *Guardian* and Chambers as coeditor of *Signal* and, from 1972 to 1984, as a columnist for the American *Horn Book Magazine.* Criticism of children's books on social grounds in addition to or instead of literary ones flourished toward the end of the 1960s and throughout the 1970s, spearheaded by Robert Leeson (who, like Townsend and Chambers, had been an editor and wrote children's books). Leeson's perception of the contemporary juvenile scene, expressed most forcefully in *Children's Books and Class Society* (1977), associated the newer type of children's book – treating class issues and formerly taboo subjects – with the emergence of a new type of author from a working-class background. Perceptive essays on contemporary children's writers came from David Rees; many of them (originally from *Horn Book* and other serials, beginning in 1971) appearing in the collected volume *The Marble in the Water* (1980). None of these four writer-critics came from a traditional middle-class Anglican background. In addition to their class background, special differences played a part in their outlook: Chambers spent nearly a decade as a monk; Leeson had edited the *Morning Star,* a paper put out by the British Communist Party; and Rees (though this was not widely known until the later 1970s) was homosexual.

Meanwhile, the serious study of children's literature was beginning in a few British universities and teacher-training colleges. Dennis Butts influenced a generation of classroom teachers and scholars in the field and later edited an important essay collection, *Good Writers for Young Readers* (1977). His associate at Reading, Tony Watkins, also had a widespread influence and has been cited (for instance, by Peter Hunt) as a model of the university teacher in this subject. Peter Hollindale at York and Fred Inglis at Bristol taught and published in the field. By 1976 there was a common text, or "set book," for a course given through the Open University, Britain's "distance learning" institution; the anthology, *Writers, Critics, and Children,* edited by Geoff Fox, included essays by practicing children's writers such as Joan Aiken and Peter Dickinson, literary criticism, and essays on children and their responses. The fact that both C. S. Lewis (at Cambridge) and J. R. R. Tolkien (at Oxford) had written for children and about children's books did not initially have much influence at those universities, though an increase of interest in the topic subsequently came about at Oxford with the acquisition of the Opie Collection of children's books.

In some ways the market for children's books and periodicals did not change as rapidly as the reviewing and criticism did; although distinctly iconoclastic books were being published for children, sales figures during the 1960s reflected the continuing success of traditional materials. Survivors from the past included many juvenile magazines: the venerable *Boy's Own Paper*, begun by the Religious Tract Society in 1879, was still being published on a monthly basis; it finally expired in 1967 and was memorialized by Philip Warner in *The Best of British Pluck* (1976) and later by its last editor in *Take a Cold Bath, Sir!* (1983). Its counterpart, *Girl's Own Paper*, founded in 1880, lingered on until 1965 under an updated title, *Heiress*. It, too, was memorialized — not in a history but in an anthology of selected advice columns edited by Roy Hindle, *Oh, No Dear! Advice to Girls a Century Ago* (1982). After the demise of *Boy's Own Paper*, its rival, *Eagle* (begun in 1950), experienced considerable success before it, too, vanished in 1969. D. C. Thomson's comic papers, *Beano* and *Dandy*, survived from prewar days. The main attraction in *Beano*, Dennis the Menace (not the same character as in Hank Ketchum's popular American comic strip), continued his popularity; indeed his clothing and habits remained those of many years earlier. Many other long-lived comics, however, like their magazine counterparts, disappeared during the mid to late 1960s — a demise hastened by the absorption of many of their publishers (for instance, Amalgamated Press) by larger firms.

A demise that showed no sign of occurring at the beginning of the decade was that of Enid Blyton (1897–1968) and her immensely successful publishing career. Though reduced by age and ill health to an output less than the thirty books a year she had written in her middle years, Blyton was still turning out the Noddy stories nearly up to her death in 1968. Blyton books — whether Famous Five, Secret Seven, or Noddy — still occupy an astounding amount of shelf space in bookstores. (As of the summer of 1995, for instance, Blyton books with their conspicuous cover signature took up almost an entire bookcase at Stockholm's largest department store, Ahléns.) Blyton's near-contemporary, Alison Uttley (1884–1976), similarly, was still producing Little Grey Rabbit books in a series begun in 1929; the last, *Hare and the Rainbow*, appeared in 1975. An older and even more prolific writer than Blyton, "Frank Richards" (Charles Hamilton) died in 1961, but his most popular creation, Billy Bunter, lived on in a series of BBC television adaptations that ran until 1962. Elinor Brent-Dyer (1895–1969) continued to publish in the 1960s books in a series she had begun in 1925 with *The School at the Chalet;* the last

title, *Prefects of the Chalet School,* appeared posthumously in 1970.

The type of school story represented by Talbot Baines Reed, Angela Brazil, and their imitators gradually faded away — partly, as historians of the genre have pointed out, because a smaller percentage of both its readers and its writers came from backgrounds of established residential ("public") schools. There has been speculation that the survival of Billy Bunter and his ilk into the 1960s was actually the result of middle-aged nostalgia: that these books were bought and the programs were watched by adults revisiting childhood favorites and not by children discovering them for the first time. As it turned out, the old formulas could be altered in several ways. "Though dead," as Marcus Crouch points out, "the conventional school story did not readily lie down." William Mayne, perhaps the most brilliant writer ever to attempt this genre, was able to use the residential tradition convincingly and freshly in his Cathedral School books, beginning with *A Swarm in May* (1955) and continuing through the 1960s. What Mayne brought to these books, in addition to a writing style more varied and more subtle than had ever been seen in school stories, was a clear-eyed examination of the nature and nuances of social class, along with a focus on music as a shared important experience. The substitution of choral music for sports as the unifying force of a group of schoolboys virtually guarantees the unique quality of these books. (A substantial entry for Mayne will appear in the Second Series.)

More often, in the 1960s and early 1970s, authors moved the school story into the realm of commuting children who live in a more complex world divided between home and school. Mary K. Harris and Antonia Forest depicted day schools for girls; K. M. Peyton set much of the action in the Pennington books on her unprepossessing but musically gifted hero's struggles at a day school. A distinction between the contemporary school story and earlier ones is of course the prevalence of coeducational schools, such as those in several decades of books by Geoffrey Trease. Eventually, the school setting in British fiction for children became what it had long been in the United States — a microcosm of the society around it. Jan Mark, Bernard Ashley, Jan Needle, Berlie Doherty, and many of the New Realists who dominated the later 1970s and early 1980s used schools in this way.

Like the school story, the pony story continued for a while unchanged, then altered with the times and quietly trotted away toward extinction as a separate form. The Jill series from Ruby Ferguson, along with many similar books with "gymkhana" in their titles, went on in the 1960s exactly as they had from their inception in 1950 – except that the poverty-stricken atmosphere of the immediate postwar Jill books moderates into a comfortable affluence by the mid 1960s. The Pullein-Thompson sisters (second-generation writers of pony books) continued their output for many years. The Romney Marsh and Devil's Punchbowl series by Monica Edwards, almost the only long-term survivors among pony books, began appearing in revised editions in the 1980s. There was a limit to how far this subgenre would stretch, however, and the difficulty of depicting in the gymkhana world a more mixed society (both in race and in class) meant that few new, younger authors took on the task.

In addition to the survival of highly traditional forms such as the school and pony story, there were specific character types and motifs that remained popular for a surprising length of time. The paradoxical figure of the golliwog, originally a doll-like black figure invented by Bertha Upton, continued to appeal, taking on villainous roles in at least one Blyton book (which was subsequently criticized as racist) and more positive roles in the Rufty Tufty series of Ruth Ainsworth, begun in the early 1950s and continued through the mid 1960s with such titles as *Rufty Tufty's Island* (1960) and *Rufty Tufty Makes a House* (1965). The grotesque image of the coal-black golliwog figure with its stand-out hair, whether in Blyton or in Ainsworth, attracted strong criticism from socially oriented critics. Less troublesome were the traditional animal stories, whether about anthropomorphized creatures wearing clothes or about realistic animals. The descendants of Beatrix Potter and Kenneth Grahame continued unabated in such uninspired (but marketable) books as *Pinny's Holiday* and many other short, brightly illustrated picture books by Racey Helps and other purveyors of cozy nursery tales about little furry creatures.

From books about talking, well-dressed animals to books that more overtly announce their identity as fantasy is but a short step. The nonrealistic form most comfortable for British writers and their child readers was fantasy. In the initial year of this survey, 1960, one of the most significant books published was a fantasy from a new author, Alan Garner – *The Weirdstone of Brisingamen*. This book, which like its sequel, *The Moon of Gomrath* (1963),

was extremely well received, shows several features common to the fantasy of the 1960s and 1970s. It uses generally familiar, but not too familiar, mythological material (Celtic and Norse) and adapts it to present-day uses. It also employs a favorite device of British fantasy writers, the time warp (or, as British writers usually call it, the time-slip). Both traditions apply equally to the popular five-volume series from Susan Cooper called "The Dark Is Rising" after its second volume; the first, *Over Sea, Under Stone* (1965), introduces the Grail motif and the Welsh setting that tie the books to their Arthurian origins. Time warps also anchor the plots of Clive King's *Stig of the Dump* (1963), a perennial favorite in which a modern-day boy meets a cave dweller from the Stone Age; Peter Dickinson's "Changes" trilogy (1968–1970); several books by Penelope Lively; and, perhaps most memorably, Philippa Pearce's instant classic *Tom's Midnight Garden* (1958).

A significant development in recent British fantasy for children has been the increasingly independent nature of the children: as Karen Patricia Smith says, "the young person was no longer a being happening upon some unusual magical experience, but rather an initiator of action." The image of the youthful hero as independent agent had, of course, long been a staple of science fiction; but science fiction, well established in the juvenile market in the United States for many years, did not succeed as well in Britain until John Christopher's *The White Mountains* (1967) helped to popularize the form. (Science-fiction writers, including Christopher, will be found in the Second Series.)

Last among the traditional forms that continued to succeed into the 1960s and beyond are historical fiction and family stories. A favorite with young readers since the time of Sir Walter Scott, the historical novel emerged in the twentieth century as a form with new, and often overt, political possibilities. Developing steadily since the pioneer work of Trease in the 1930s, this new type of novel often presented historical events from the standpoint of ordinary people – preferably, ordinary working-class people. Robert Leeson, among others, followed Trease's lead in presenting a more leftist view of historical events than had previously been the case. More-conventional political approaches (and in most cases not overtly political in their texts) came from Rosemary Sutcliff, Barbara Willard, Barbara Picard, Henry Treece, and others. Nearly all of these writers also differed from their predecessors in their caution about authentic speech, taking great pains to avoid the artificial re-creations of medieval or Renaissance speech found in older books. (Trease refers to this memorably as "the varlet-and-halidom type of language" and attributes its demise to Naomi Mitchison's earlier work.)

The family story also underwent considerable change in this period, but the results were more apparent after 1970 — certainly after 1975 — than before. Blended families, racially mixed families, single-parent or two-wage-earner families, and other variations began to appear. Even more significantly, perhaps, families from different sorts of class and regional backgrounds populated children's books. The Cheshire speech of some of Alan Garner's characters would probably have been normalized by almost any earlier publisher. And certainly, the type of family situation depicted in Michelle Magorian's horrific *Good Night, Mr. Tom* (1982) would have caused an editor of the early 1960s to reject the book outright. The most significant development in the family story, thus, is in the direction of the New Realism (as seen in the writers of the Second Series).

All but two of the authors in *British Children's Writers Since 1960, First Series* were born before World War II, most of them early enough to have clear memories of it. Two-thirds of them were born in the quarter century from 1920 to 1945; of those born well before 1920, all were still active well after 1960 and thus could not appropriately be included in *British Children's Writers, 1914–1960*. Although most of these writers began publishing before 1960, the bulk of their work falls in the 1960s, 1970s, and 1980s, in many cases continuing up to the present. For example, Barbara Willard began writing in the 1930s, but the Mantlemass series, for which she is best known, falls entirely in the 1970s. Similarly, the veteran writer Margery Sharp did not initiate her popular Rescuers series until 1959. Lucy M. Boston, born in 1908, did not begin bringing out her Green Knowe books until 1954; she won the 1961 Carnegie Medal for *A Stranger at Green Knowe*. All but four of the authors in the First Series were still living when work on it began in 1991, and three more died during the preparation of the volume: Ian Serraillier, Sharp, and Willard.

In addition to their chronology, the writers in the First Series share a tendency toward certain well-established forms: the family story, the animal story, variants on the school story, and the traditional types of high fantasy. Two poets are also included. The historical novel for young readers is represented both in this volume and its companion; in particular, it should be noted that two of the finest practitioners of the form, Rosemary Sutcliff and Geoffrey Trease, will appear in major articles in the Second Series despite being born before 1925. Illustrators, science-fiction writers, and writers of problem novels will be found in the forthcoming Second Series, where nearly all of them would fall chronologically except for some of the illustrators. Finally, writers who have published significant amounts of criticism in addition to their fiction — John Rowe Townsend, Aidan Chambers, Robert Leeson, David Rees, and others — will also be found in the Second Series.

— Caroline C. Hunt

Acknowledgments

This book was produced by Bruccoli Clark Layman, Inc. Karen L. Rood is senior editor for the *Dictionary of Literary Biography* series. Sam Bruce was the in-house editor.

Production coordinator is James W. Hipp. Photography editor is Bruce Andrew Bowlin. Photographic copy work was performed by Joseph M. Bruccoli. Layout and graphics supervisor is Penney L. Haughton. Copyediting supervisor is Laurel M. Gladden. Typesetting supervisor is Kathleen M. Flanagan. Systems manager is George F. Dodge. Julie E. Frick is editorial associate. The production staff includes Phyllis A. Avant, Ann M. Cheschi, Melody W. Clegg, Patricia Coate, Denise Edwards, Joyce Fowler, Stephanie C. Hatchell, Rebecca Mayo, Margaret Meriwether, Kathy Lawler Merlette, Jeff Miller, Pamela D. Norton, Delores Plastow, Laura Pleicones, Emily R. Sharpe, William L. Thomas Jr., and Allison Trussell.

Walter W. Ross and Robert S. McConnell did library research. They were assisted by the following librarians at the Thomas Cooper Library of the University of South Carolina: Linda Holderfield and the interlibrary-loan staff; reference-department head Virginia Weathers; reference librarians Marilee Birchfield, Stefanie Buck, Cathy Eckman, Rebecca Feind, Jill Holman, Karen Joseph, Jean Rhyne, Kwamine Washington, and Connie Widney; circulation-department head Caroline Taylor; and acquisitions-searching supervisor David Haggard.

The editor is indebted to the College of Charleston for ongoing support, including two grants from the faculty Research and Development Committee. The interlibrary loan and reference staffs of the Robert Scott Small Library provided help beyond any normal expectations, especially Marlene Barnola, Shirley Davidson, Tom Gilson, Michael Phillips, Phil Powell, Jerry Seay, and Alis Whitt. The editor's 1994 research assistant, C. P. Seabrook Wilkinson, did wonders with typescripts and textual problems. The Children's Literature Association helped in selecting qualified contributors; individual scholars, particularly Rod McGillis, Marilynn Olson, Elizabeth Overmyer, Barbara Rosen, John Stephens, and Donna White, advised on many matters. Michael Joseph's online discussion group, CHILDLIT, was a useful forum for discussion. Advice and encouragement came from editors of other volumes in the series: Don Hettinga, Meena Khorana, Gary Schmidt, and Laura Zaidman. The greatest debt is expressed in the dedication.

Dictionary of Literary Biography® • Volume One Hundred Sixty-One

British Children's Writers
Since 1960
First Series

Dictionary of Literary Biography

Joan Aiken

(4 September 1924 –   )

Sarah V. Clere
Mount Olive College

BOOKS: *All You've Ever Wanted and Other Stories* (London: Cape, 1953);

More Than You Bargained For and Other Stories (London: Cape, 1955; New York: Abelard-Schuman, 1957);

The Kingdom and the Cave (London: Abelard Schuman, 1960; Garden City, N.Y.: Doubleday, 1974);

The Wolves of Willoughby Chase (London: Cape, 1962; Garden City, N.Y.: Doubleday, 1963);

Black Hearts in Battersea (Garden City, N.Y.: Doubleday, 1964; London: Cape, 1965);

The Silence of Herondale (Garden City, N.Y.: Doubleday, 1964; London: Gollancz, 1965);

The Fortune Hunters (Garden City, N.Y.: Doubleday, 1965);

Nightbirds on Nantucket (London: Cape / Garden City, N.Y.: Doubleday, 1966);

Trouble with Product X (London: Gollancz, 1966); also published as *Beware of the Bouquet* (Garden City, N.Y.: Doubleday, 1966);

Hate Begins at Home (London: Gollancz, 1967); also published as *Dark Interval* (Garden City, N.Y.: Doubleday, 1967);

The Ribs of Death (London: Gollancz, 1967); republished as *The Crystal Crow* (Garden City, N.Y.: Doubleday, 1968);

The Whispering Mountain (London: Cape, 1968; Garden City, N.Y.: Doubleday, 1968);

The Necklace of Raindrops and Other Stories (London: Cape, 1968; Garden City, N.Y.: Doubleday, 1968);

Armitage, Armitage, Fly Away Home (Garden City, N.Y.: Doubleday, 1968);

A Small Pinch of Weather and Other Stories (London: Cape, 1969);

Joan Aiken

Night Fall (London: Macmillan, 1969; New York: Holt, 1971);

The Windscreen Weepers and Other Tales of Horror and Suspense (London: Gollancz, 1969); republished as *The Green Flash and Other Tales of Horror, Suspense, and Fantasy* (New York: Holt, Rinehart, 1971);

Died on a Rainy Sunday (London: Gollancz, 1970; New York: Holt, Rinehart & Winston, 1972);

Smoke From Cromwell's Time and Other Stories (Garden City, N.Y.: Doubleday, 1970);

The Embroidered Sunset (London: Gollancz, 1970; Garden City, N.Y.: Doubleday, 1970);

The Cuckoo Tree (London: Cape, 1971; Garden City, N.Y.: Doubleday, 1971);

The Kingdom Under the Sea and Other Stories (London: Cape, 1971);

Nightly Deadshade (New York: Macmillan, 1971);

The Butterfly Picnic (London: Gollancz, 1972); also published as *A Cluster of Separate Sparks* (Garden City, N.Y.: Doubleday, 1972);

Arabel's Raven (London: BBC Publications, 1972; Garden City, N.Y.: Doubleday, 1974);

Winterthing: A Child's Play (New York: Holt, 1972);

A Harp of Fishbones and Other Stories (London: Cape, 1972);

Arabel and the Escaped Black Mamba (London: BBC Publications, 1973);

The Mooncusser's Daughter (New York: Viking, 1973);

Winterthing, and The Mooncusser's Daughter (London: Cape, 1973);

All But A Few (London: Penguin, 1974);

The Bread Bin (London: BBC Publications, 1974);

Midnight Is a Place (London: Cape, 1974; New York: Viking, 1974);

Not What You Expected: A Collection of Short Stories (Garden City, N.Y.: Doubleday, 1974);

Voices in an Empty House (London: Gollancz, 1975; Garden City, N.Y.: Doubleday, 1975);

A Bundle of Nerves (London: Gollancz, 1976);

Castle Barebane (London: Gollancz, 1976; New York: Viking, 1976);

Mortimer's Tie (London: BBC Publications, 1976);

The Skin Spinners (New York: Viking, 1976);

Go Saddle the Sea (New York: Doubleday, 1977; London: Cape, 1978);

The Faithless Lollybird (London: Cape, 1977; Garden City, N.Y.; Doubleday, 1978);

Last Movement (Garden City, N.Y.: Doubleday, 1977; London: Gollancz, 1977);

The Five-Minute Marriage (London: Gollancz, 1977; Garden City, N.Y.: Doubleday, 1978);

The Far Forests: Tales of Romance, Fantasy, and Suspense (New York: Viking, 1977);

Mice and Mendelson (London: Cape, 1978);

The Smile of the Stranger (London: Gollancz, 1978; Garden City, N.Y.: Doubleday, 1978);

Tale of a One-Way Street, and Other Stories (London: Cape, 1978; Garden City, N.Y.: Doubleday, 1978);

The Spiral Stair (London: BBC, 1979);

Mortimer and the Sword Excalibur (London: BBC, 1979);

A Touch of Chill: Tales for Sleepless Nights (London: Gollancz, 1979; New York: Delacorte, 1980);

The Shadow Guests (London: Cape, 1980; New York: Delacorte, 1980);

The Lightning Tree (London: Gollancz, 1980); also published as *The Weeping Ash* (Garden City, N.Y.: Doubleday, 1980);

The Stolen Lake (London: Cape, 1981; New York: Delacorte, 1981);

The Girl From Paris (Garden City, N.Y.: Doubleday, 1982); also published as *The Young Lady from Paris* (London: Gollancz, 1982);

Mortimer's Portrait on Glass (London: BBC Publications, 1982);

The Mystery of Mr. Jones's Disappearing Taxi (London: BBC Publications, 1982);

The Way to Write for Children (London: Elm Tree Books, 1982; New York: St. Martin's Press, 1983);

A Whisper in the Night: Tales of Terror and Suspense (London: Gollancz, 1982; New York: Delacorte, 1983);

Bridle the Wind (New York: Delacorte, 1983; London: Cape, 1983);

Foul Matter (Garden City, N.Y.: Doubleday, 1983; London: Gollancz, 1983);

Mortimer's Cross (London: BBC/Cape, 1983; New York: Harper & Row, 1984) – includes *Mortimer's Portrait on Glass* and *The Mystery of Mr. Jones's Disappearing Taxi*;

The Kitchen Warriors (London: BBC, 1983; Garden City, N.Y.: Doubleday, 1985);

Mansfield Revisited (London: Gollancz, 1984; Garden City, N.Y.: Doubleday, 1985);

Up the Chimney Down and Other Stories (London: Cape, 1984; New York: Harper & Row, 1985);

Fog Hounds, Wind Cat, Sea Mice (New York: Macmillan, 1984);

Mortimer Says Nothing (London: Cape, 1985; New York: Harper & Row, 1986);

The Last Slice of Rainbow, and Other Stories (London: Cape, 1985; New York: Harper & Row, 1985);

Past Eight O'Clock (London: Cape, 1986; New York: Viking Kestrel, 1987);

Dido and Pa (New York: Delacorte, 1986);

If I Were You (Garden City, N.Y.: Doubleday, 1987);

Deception (London: Gollancz, 1987);

The Moon's Revenge (London: Cape, 1987; New York: Knopf, 1988);

The Teeth of the Gale (London: Cape, 1988; New York: Harper & Row, 1988);

Return to Harken House (New York: Delacorte, 1988); also published as *Voices* (London: Hippo Books, 1988);

Blackground (Garden City, N.Y.: Doubleday, 1989);

The Erl King's Daughter (New York: Barron's, 1989);

Give Yourself a Fright (New York: Delacorte, 1989);

A Goose on Your Grave (London: Lions Tracks, 1989);

A Fit of Shivers: Tales for Late at Night (London: Gollancz, 1990; New York: Delacorte, 1992);

Jane Fairfax (London: Gollancz, 1990; New York: St. Martin's Press, 1991);

A Foot in the Grave (London: Cape, 1991; New York: Viking, 1992);

The Haunting of Lamb House (London: Cape, 1991; New York: St. Martin's Press, 1993);

The Shoemaker's Boy (London & New York: Simon & Schuster, 1991);

A Creepy Companion (London: Gollancz, 1993);

Is Underground (New York: Delacorte, 1993);

The Midnight Moropus (Hemel Hempstead: Simon & Schuster, 1993);

Eliza's Daughter (New York: St. Martin's Press, 1994; London: Gollancz, 1994);

Mortimer's Mine (London: BBC, 1994);

Mortimer's Pocket (London: BBC, 1994);

The Winter Sleepwalker and Other Stories (London: Cape, 1994);

Dark Interval (London: Chivers, 1995).

Collections: *All and More* (London: Cape, 1971) — comprises *All You've Ever Wanted and Other Stories* and *More Than You Bargained For and Other Stories*;

Arabel and Mortimer (London: BBC / Cape, 1980; Garden City, N.Y.: Doubleday, 1981) — comprises *Mortimer's Tie, The Spiral Stair,* and *Mortimer and the Sword Excalibur.*

PLAY PRODUCTION: *The Mooncusser's Daughter,* London, The Unicorn Theatre for Young People, 7 April 1973.

OTHER: "A Free Gift," in *The Thorny Paradise: Writers on Writing for Children,* edited by Edward Blishen (Harmondsworth: Kestrel, 1975), pp. 36–52;

Sophie De Seger, *The Angle Inn,* translated from the French by Aiken (London: Cape, 1976; New York: Stemmer House, 1978);

Haunting Christmas Tales, edited by Aiken (New York: Scholastic, 1991);

Henry James, *Portrait of a Lady,* with an introductory essay by Aiken (London: Folio Society, 1994).

Joan Delano Aiken is one of the most prolific and energetic of living authors, with a body of works that includes novels, short stories, drama, and poetry. She is probably best known for the Wolves Chronicles, a series of loosely connected "unhistorical" novels set in a fictional England in which the Stuarts continue to reign into the nineteenth century and the Hanoverians are the pretenders. However, she also writes adult thrillers and Gothics, juvenile novels set in contemporary England, and modern fairy tales. Within the genre of the short story alone, her versatility is apparent. For example, the contents of *A Touch of Chill: Tales for Sleepless Nights* (1979) include examples of the classic tale of folk magic, domestic comedy shading into the bizarre, and modern psychological horror. The title suggests the only common factor in the collection: the touch of chill and horror lurking below the surface of even the comic tales.

Aiken's works for adults and children share a strong sense, not always of horror, but of the potential for danger and evil. Although a happy ending is usually achieved in her juvenile publications, it is often at a price. The titular heroine of *Is Underground* (1993) discovers only one of the two young men she is seeking because the other, the king's son, is dead; the two youngsters in *Midnight Is a Place* (1974) experience the evils of child labor in England's nineteenth-century sweatshops. Even in the comic stories of Mortimer the talking raven, whose audience could include preschoolers, Mortimer and Arabel confront adults unsympathetic to the point of cruelty in some of their adventures. Nevertheless, the dominant impression left by Aiken's books — at least the juveniles — is not one of foreboding but of high spirits, laughter, and imagination. Her characters respond to loss not just with courage but with a touch of defiance, a high-spirited determination not only to surmount the obstacle but to enjoy the climb. Dido Twite and her younger sister, Is, from the Wolves Chronicles, are the most obvious examples, but the gutsy kid is an Aiken staple.

Another characteristic of the Aiken canon is craftsmanship. All her books are gracefully written in an easy-to-read, fluent style, a skill remarkable but perhaps not surprising considering her lifelong involvement with books and writers. The daughter of American poet Conrad Aiken and Canadian Jessie MacDonald, Joan Delano Aiken was born in Rye, Sussex, on 4 September 1924. When her parents separated, Aiken remained in England with her mother, who taught her at home. She thus grew up in a rather isolated adult world filled with long walks, books, and storytelling. Her wide reading informs her own works, most notably the Dickensian *Midnight is a Place* and the Jane Austen–influenced *Mansfield Revisited* (1984), *Jane Fairfax* (1990), and

Eliza's Daughter (1994). Daughter of a poet and stepdaughter of writer Martin Armstrong, Aiken married another writer, journalist Ronald George Brown, in 1945. When he died ten years later, leaving her with a son (John Sebastian) and a daughter (Elizabeth Delano), Aiken turned to writing to support herself. Employed by *Argosy,* a short-story magazine, her first professional publications were collections of short stories, *All You Ever Wanted and Other Stories* (1953) and *More Than You Bargained For and Other Stories* (1955). She turned to longer fiction partly for economic reasons. Her first novel, *The Kingdom and the Cave* (1960), a revision of a work she had written in her teens, features the talking animals and intrepid youngsters that figure in her later work. Although imaginative, humorous, and fast-paced, *The Kingdom and the Cave* seems bland compared to her more mature work. The animals, though nicely differentiated by dialect and personality, lack the appeal of the exasperating and endearing raven Mortimer. The humor in the book tends to weaken the suspense rather than providing the needed release from tension. It remained for the next publication to reveal Aiken's real ability.

The Wolves of Willoughby Chase (1962) was not only Aiken's first notable children's book but her first fully successful novel. It includes all the elements of melodrama: the wicked governess; the house with secret passages; the boarding school inflicting physical privation and mental cruelty; and an atmosphere of terror provided by the wolves of the natural world and by human wickedness. All are coped with successfully by the intrepid heroine, Bonnie, who is rewarded not only by financial security and physical safety but by the return of her "dead" parents. Like many melodramas, the book sounds improbable and is cliché-ridden in plot summary, but Aiken's deft style sketches the admittedly flat characters quickly and satisfyingly. The book provides exciting adventures in which the endangered good triumphs resoundingly over evil, but the imaginative historical setting of a nineteenth-century England stalked by wolves and ruled over by the Stuarts (constantly threatened by the evil Hanoverians plotting to put the young pretender George on the throne) gives a new twist to an old form.

The Wolves of Willoughby Chase provides the name Wolves Chronicles for a series of loosely connected novels set in this alternative England. The wild plots of the Hanoverians or Georgians – to roll St. Paul's Cathedral into the Thames, for example, or to fire a cannon across the Atlantic and kill the king – provide the large-scale conflict in several of the books in this series. The more personal, small-scale conflicts the young heroes and heroines face are what really engages the reader's interest, however. The plight of Bonnie and Sylvia in *The Wolves of Willoughby Chase,* Dido and Penitence in *Nightbirds on Nantucket* (1966) at the hands of the evil Mrs. Slighcarp, and the threatened transportation of Tobit in *The Cuckoo Tree* (1971) seem more important than large-scale political machinations – that the dastardly plots of these evil people are also thwarted is frosting on the cake.

Although the pair of heroines introduced in *The Wolves of Willoughby Chase* is absent from the later books, Simon, the orphan boy who befriends them, reappears as the hero in *Black Hearts in Battersea* (1964), which introduces Aiken's most appealing heroine, the tough little cockney Dido Twite. Lost at sea at the novel's end, she is rescued in the next novel, *Nightbirds on Nantucket,* which utilizes an American setting, providing new scope for Aiken's humor. Dido is able to enlist aid from Dr. Mayhew, a laconic New England doctor, not because the English monarchy is threatened but because a side effect of the plot to fire a cannon across the Atlantic Ocean would involve blowing Nantucket into Long Island. When he learns of this eventuality, he asks indignantly, "Why didn't you tell me that before? Push our island over into that crowd of money grabbing roustabouts and frauds in New York?"

Absent from the next novel in the series, *The Whispering Mountain* (1968), which won the Guardian Award in 1969, Dido Twite reappears in the next three, *The Cuckoo Tree, The Stolen Lake* (1981), and *Dido and Pa* (1986), which introduces her sister, Is, later to be the heroine in *Is Underground.* In *Dido and Pa* the Hanoverians receive a major setback when the pretender, George, dies without issue, but by the time of *Is Underground,* the forces of evil have found a new leader in Gold Kingy, another Twite relative who lures children to Blastburn to work in the mines. Fortunately Is in this book seems to be a virtual clone of her sister, Dido, and is equally successful in marshaling the seeming underdogs to employ cleverness, diligence, and unity to defeat sheer power and greed. The exploitation of children in industrial England is a recurring theme in Aiken's work, and she handles it with greater success in the more realistic setting of *Midnight Is a Place.*

The Wolves Chronicles, which span Aiken's entire career, are comprised of distinct works that are nevertheless all of a piece. Variety and vividness of setting provide much of their distinction as the action moves to Wales in *The Whispering Mountain,*

The children face the evil Miss Slighcarp in Aiken's The Wolves of
Willoughby Chase *(1962; illustration by Pat Marriott).*

Nantucket in *Night Birds on Nantucket,* and the Andes in *The Stolen Lake.* Even the English settings differ widely. *The Wolves of Willoughby Chase* begins in the north of England and moves to London, the setting of its sequel, *Black Hearts in Battersea* (1965). *The Cuckoo Tree* returns to the combination of rural England and London as does *Dido and Pa,* while the major setting in *Is Underground* is northern England, more specifically Blastburn.

Aiken is often praised for her ability to evoke the spirit of place not only through concise, evocative descriptive writing, but also through dialect and occasionally through characterization. Somehow the coolheadedness of Sophia and Simon embody the calm self-reliance of rural England, whereas Dido Twite represents the brash, gregarious, and ever resourceful cockney. This sense of place both distinguishes one novel from the next and provides a common link among them. Many of the novels in this series also play against a background of allusions to literary classics, but exactly what role these allusions play depends upon the

reader. Young children probably take Rosy the Whale of *Nightbirds on Nantucket* at face value, but to more-sophisticated readers the obsessive search for the pink whale provides a humorous allusion to Herman Melville's *Moby-Dick* (1851). Others may see a satire of the Gothic novel in *The Wolves of Willoughby Chase* with its house of secret passages, wicked governess, and evil schoolmistress who exploits her half-starved and frozen pupils. In *Children and Books* (1991) Zena Sutherland calls *The Whispering Mountain* "a broad burlesque of the fanciful adventure story."

Differentiated by setting and literary allusion, Aiken's works are linked by recurrent characters and by the ongoing conflict between the Hanoverian plotters and the rightful Stuart monarchy. The moral universe of these novels and all of Aiken's works is one in which courage, energy, resourcefulness, intelligence, artistic talent, and concern for and protection of the weak are valued. Evil usually comes in the forms of cruelty or usurpation of life, property, or talent. Many of the villains in these and other works are people in charge of children, and they have no scruples about exploiting or abusing even their own children. In *A Sense of Story: Essays on Contemporary Writing for Children* (1971), John Rowe Townsend quotes Aiken's comment that "children's books should never minimize the fact that life is tough; virtue ought to triumph in the end because even the best regulated children's lives are so insecure that they need reassurance, but there's no sense in pretending that wickedness and hardship don't exist."

As the Wolves Chronicles developed, Aiken also produced her first novels for adults, which she began publishing between *Black Hearts in Battersea* and *Nightbirds on Nantucket*. These early works were thrillers, shortened versions of which had been published in periodicals. As in her juvenile publications, Aiken's works for adult readers present enterprising heroines confronting the wickedness of the world. Unlike her juveniles, however, these novels guarantee no happy endings. The protagonist may die, as in *The Embroidered Sunset* (1970), or may suffer intense cruelty, as in *The Weeping Ash* (1980). Even children are not guaranteed safety. In *Castle Barebane* (1976) the young girl whose developmental problems have provoked the heroine's sympathy is thrown into the sea, where she drowns. In *Died on a Rainy Sunday* (1970) the heroine leaves her young children in the care of a madwoman who murders their father. In spite of this violence, *Died on a Rainy Sunday* is often listed as a juvenile work, making it one of several of Aiken's books that alternate between juvenile and adult categories. In a lighter vein are Aiken's novels set in the Regency period, *The Five-Minute Marriage* (1977) and *The Smile of the Stranger* (1978), in which struggling heroines eventually wind up safely married. Similarly upbeat are *Mansfield Revisited* and *Jane Fairfax*. In general Aiken's adult novels have won less favorable criticism than her juvenile novels, but they display variety and imagination, and some, such as *The Weeping Ash* and *Voices in an Empty House* (1975), are paced slowly enough for fully rendered characters and situations that linger in the mind after the last page is turned.

Established as a professional writer with good sales, especially from the Wolves Chronicles, Aiken returned to short stories in 1968 with *The Necklace of Raindrops and Other Stories,* a collection of modern fairy tales. Another collection of stories, *Armitage, Armitage, Fly Away Home* (1968), centers on a family that finds the world of magic a pleasant complication that keeps life interesting. Other Aiken stories, such as those in *A Touch of Chill,* reveal the darker side of the supernatural, in which magic can be a source of terror both to those who wield its power and to those who suffer its effects. Aiken also used this shorter form to introduce one of her most popular characters, Mortimer the talking raven, in 1982. Mortimer is blessed not only with speech but also with a kind owner, Arabel; a magnificent digestive system; and what must be the world's most patient and long-suffering family.

In 1976 Aiken married painter Julius Goldstein and continued to write prolifically, producing two particularly impressive works in the 1970s: *Midnight Is a Place* and *Go Saddle the Sea* (1977). The former, like *Died on a Rainy Sunday,* migrates from juvenile to adult classification, but although the novel is not lighthearted, there is a satisfactory resolution, and the focus is on the two young protagonists, not on the adult figures, as in the earlier novel, thus making the book appropriate for a wide readership, from advanced intermediate through adult.

One of Aiken's most distinguished works, *Midnight Is a Place* is set in Blastburn, an industrial town. There are no Hanoverians, pink whales, or trains to Playland, just a grim house called Midnight Court and a grimmer carpet factory. Aiken does not soften the harshness of nineteenth-century child labor. The two protagonists first confront the world at one remove when Lucas Bell, accompanied by Anna-Marie Murgatroyd (who, like Lucas, has come under Sir Randolph Quimby's care), visits the factory he may one day own. Later, after Midnight Court burns and the two young people are unable to establish their identities, they are forced to earn their own living. Anna-Marie has the dangerous job of snatching stray tufts of thread out of the carpet before the heavy machinery descends again, and Lucas must work as a "tosh" boy, assisting a madman in scanning the sewers for salvage. Although Lucas and Anna-Marie escape their experiences with the working world without permanent injury, they encounter maimed children who were not so lucky and a weeping mother who has lost all her children. What makes the grimness bearable for readers of various ages (except very young children) is the toughness and resourcefulness of the two young people. Anna-Marie matures from a baby crying for her cat to an enterprising young woman who braves the dangers of the factory, and Lucas must adapt from his sheltered life to that of the sewers.

As usual, the story's setting is evocative. The book's title comes from a song written by Anna-Marie's father ending "Midnight is no moment / Midnight is a place" and suggests the symbolic association of place, time, and atmosphere. However, like all good symbols, the relationship suggested is complex: Midnight Court is a place of evil, but there Lucas and Anna-Marie meet and first begin a relationship of love and support; and the sewers, foul harbors of refuse patrolled by a madman, nevertheless contain "tosh" of value. Light and dark, good and evil, and love and hate mingle satisfyingly and convincingly in the work. What *Midnight Is a Place* lacks in extravagant flights of imagination is compensated for by the blend of grim realism, humor, and the capacity of the characters for courage and tenderness.

Aiken's work has been likened to that of Charles Dickens, and *Midnight Is a Place* creates a Dickensian cosmos, which, though a grim place on the whole, is brightened by clusters of people who genuinely care for each other. Those who look for literature that promotes family values would do well to ponder how Aiken, like Dickens, often starts with the biological family and expands the concept to include others made kin by recognition of their common humanity.

Go Saddle the Sea introduces the character Felix de Cabezada y Brooke, who narrates his own adventures, which are continued in *Bridle the Wind* (1983) and *The Teeth of the Gale* (1988). Felix, the orphan son of an English aristocrat and the grandson of a Spanish count, decides to run away when his sole ally – his grandfather's cook – dies. Felix's adventures as he finds his way to England, where he finds a title and respect but no love or real family, makes exciting reading. *Bridle the Wind* finds Felix on his way home to Spain and introduces Juan, a comrade in his adventures who reappears in the sequel, *The Teeth of the Gale*. Critics call these novels picaresque, and the label fits their structure, although their adventures are linked not just by the presence of Felix but by some overriding purpose. Felix, however, though a bit mischievous at times, is too much a straight arrow to be a true picaro. He has all of Dido Twite's essential integrity and loyalty, wrapped up in a more polished and grammatical package. He perhaps more resembles Dido's friend Simon, an essentially decent and quiet fellow who rises superbly to the occasion when personal or political situations demand heroics. Interestingly, Aiken regards the Spanish novels as some of her favorites, noting, "Sometimes when you write a book you can feel it take off and lift away from you into unexplored regions – I felt those two did that."

These novels also introduce a new element to Aiken's work: orthodox religion, if present at all, is limited to conventional piety, whereas most power is derived from some magical force or, more frequently, from the characters' own inner strength. Felix, however, maintains a vivid awareness of God as a providential force, as in this passage from *Go Saddle the Sea:* "I felt somewhat awestruck at the working of Providence, which, it seemed playing back and forth like a shuttle on some great loom, had woven this web between England and Spain without my being in the least aware of it." Although Felix's view of God is fairly orthodox, it is not stuffy. In *Bridle the Wind,* he delights in the warmth and humor of God:

> Clear and quiet above the sigh came, inside my head, the voice of God: Felix, if I have preserved you, it is because there are still tasks for you to perform in this world. Be of good courage always, do not forget in danger that love is a powerful weapon and laughter a strong shield. Remember, too, that you and I have had a few jokes together in the past; it may be that in the future we shall have more.

Although this theme of God's loving providence exists in all three novels, it never becomes intrusive, nor does Felix's faith dilute his sense of responsibility for his life and behavior. Another new strain – for Aiken – in these novels is the growing romantic relationship, culminating in the marriage at the conclusion of *The Teeth of the Gale*.

Although best known for her fiction, Aiken also writes poetry and drama. Her plays seem to have been inspired by her children's interest in drama and are similar to her juvenile fiction, full of fantastic situations where intrepid children and young people solve the problems created by their elders. Several of her plays have been professionally produced with music written by Johann Sebastian Brown.

Aiken's earliest published work was poetry, although she learned early (when her first acceptance earned her only a copy of the publication) that poetry does not pay. Her book-length collection of children's verse, *The Skin Spinners* (1976), shows her usual variety, although the comic poem predominates. The collection is subdivided into sections titled "Simple Things," "Mysterious Things," "Legends," "People," and "Ballads." The title poem of "People" compares poets to spiders who "watch with penetrating eyes / and turn the living and the dead / impartially to daily bread." Some of Aiken's best poems, such as "Bridge," present new views of simple, everyday things. The poems show mastery of a variety of styles: the majority in traditional rhyme and meter, with some in free verse and experimental forms. Similarly varied are the subjects:

*Dust jacket for a collected edition of Aiken's stories about a little
girl and her pet raven*

dreams, ordinary household incidents, legends, and myths, including that of alligators in the New York sewers. The tone of the poems ranges from humorous to frightening. Sometimes the fear comes from the supernatural, sometimes simply from the dark side of human nature as in the opening stanza of "I Have":

> Possessions tie him to his grave
> He cannot breathe, he cannot move
> Bound by the terrible I have
> He shuts himself from air and love.

Summing up a career as varied as Aiken's is challenging, especially since it continues to flourish. In addition to continuing the adventures of Felix and Dido, Aiken has also developed new fictional territory during the 1980s and 1990s. *The Shadow Guests* (1980) is a fantasy given a realistic framework. The protago-

nist, Cosmo Curtoys, moves from Australia to England after his mother and older brother Mark are presumed dead. Cosmo's cousin Eunice Doom, a young professor of mathematics at Oxford, enrolls him in a boarding school but takes him home to the family millhouse on weekends. The book in effect tells two tales: the realistic story of Cosmo's efforts to adjust to a school where group roles have already been established, and the story of the millhouse — the source of poltergeists, a phantom coach, and a family curse. Cosmo meets Con and Simon, two young men from the past, and Eunice tells him of the family curse that drove the Curtoys family from England to Australia. She and Cosmo conclude that Mark and his mother's suicidal venture into the desert was a further effort to break the pattern of the curse where for generations since Roman Britain the eldest Curtoys son has died in battle, and his mother has died of grief.

The fantastic story is made credible by the level-headedness of the people who believe it, and further verisimilitude is achieved through Professor Doom's scientific explanation of seemingly supernatural phenomena. Whether the curse is broken or not remains uncertain, but Cosmo clearly has to contend with malevolent as well as kindly forces from the past, and after escaping injuries from a rotten guardrail and a fallen wardrobe, he nearly succumbs to pneumonia. His ability to withstand not only supernatural happenings but also everyday harassment wins the respect of his schoolmates, and the novel ends satisfactorily. The characters in *The Shadow Guests* are more subtly drawn than those in Aiken's previous juvenile fiction. The good are not necessarily heroic, and the evil have their sympathetic moments. Likewise the issues are not clear-cut. Whether Mark and Mrs. Curtoys were brave to sacrifice themselves to break the curse or acted from selfish and cowardly motives is never explicitly resolved.

The Haunting of Lamb House (1991) also represents a new development in Aiken's career. It consists of three interrelated stories linked by their common setting, an old house in Rye. The first and longest story, "The Stranger in the Garden," purports to be the narrative of Toby Lamb, a young crippled boy whose already painful existence threatens to become unbearable when his favorite sister, Alice, leaves to become a surrogate daughter to her childless cousin Honoria and her rakish husband. Later events prove that the parting is more tragic for Alice, who leaves her imperfect but normal family for a life of mockery and sexual abuse. Toby, on the other hand, receives a good education and friendship, thanks to the arrival of a wealthy but physically delicate young man, Hugo Grainger, in need of a companion. When Alice returns years later, a combination of an abused child and a bitter young woman, Toby's friend falls in love with her. Toby, to whom Alice has revealed the full horror of her years away, must then decide whether or not to tell his friend – he fears he must betray either his sister or his friend. Again Aiken displays moral complexities rather than clear-cut choices. Toby's decision to reveal Alice's past leads to her suicide and to somewhat blighted lives for Toby and his friend.

The other two stories, "The Shade in the Alley" and "The Figure in the Chair," involve the authors Henry James and E. F. Benson, who actually lived in Lamb House at separate times. In Aiken's stories James finds Toby's manuscript and desires to tell the young man's tale, but he is unable to rewrite it in a way that will satisfy various friends as well as himself. Finally it remains for Benson to soothe James's troubled spirit which haunts the house years later. Toby's story is interesting in its own right, and the literary associations of the two authors add a satisfying touch. Published when Aiken was in her late sixties, *The Haunting of Lamb House* contains the familiar elements of ghosts, literary allusions, and a strong sense of place. But these familiar elements are put together in a package displaying less fantastic imagination and more classic supernatural elements blended with psychological realism than her previous work.

The sheer number of Aiken's books, many of them admittedly written to formula to entertain the reader and support the writer, has hindered an appreciation of her full stature as a serious writer. Nevertheless, her best work goes beyond mere entertainment to affirm values like courage, resourcefulness, and kindness. Her children's novels especially show that fast-paced entertainment is compatible with serious thematic development, for undergirding the high-spirited adventure of her best fiction is a bedrock of humane values.

Interview:
Cornelia Jones and Oliver R. Way, "Joan Aiken," in their *British Children's Authors: Interviews at Home* (Chicago: American Library Association, 1976), pp. 3–10.

References:
Lesley Aers, "Joan Aiken's Historical Fantasies," *Good Writers for Young Readers: Critical Essays,* edited by Dennis Butts (Frogmore: Hart-Davis Educational, 1977);

Marilyn Apseloff, "Joan Aiken: Literary Dramatist," *Children's Literature Association Quarterly,* 9 (Fall 1984): 116–118, 128;

Mary Cadogan and Patricia Craig, *You're a Brick, Angela! A New Look at Girls' Fiction from 1839 to 1975* (London: Gollancz, 1976), pp. 355–372;

Charles F. Reasoner, *A Teacher's Guide to the Novels of Joan Aiken* (New York: Dell, 1982);

Zena Sutherland and May Hill Arbuthnot, *Children and Books,* eighth edition (New York: Harper-Collins, 1991), pp. 48, 274;

John Rowe Townsend, *A Sense of Story: Essays on Contemporary Writing for Children* (Philadelphia: Lippincott, 1971), pp. 17–27;

Malcolm Usrey, "America's Gift to British Children: The Tall Tales of Joan Aiken," in *Children and Their Literature: A Readings Book,* edited by Jill P. May (West Lafayette, Ind.: Children's Literature Association, 1983), pp. 58–64.

Gillian Avery

(30 September 1926 –)

David L. Russell
Ferris State University

BOOKS: *The Warden's Niece* (London: Collins, 1957; New York: Penguin, 1963); republished as *Maria Escapes* (London: Simon & Schuster, 1992);

Trespassers at Charlcote (London: Collins, 1958);

James Without Thomas (London: Collins, 1959);

The Elephant War (London: Collins, 1960; New York: Holt, 1960);

To Tame a Sister (London: Collins, 1961; New York: Van Nostrand, 1964);

Mrs. Ewing (London: Bodley Head, 1961; New York: Walck, 1964);

The Greatest Gresham (London: Collins, 1962);

The Peacock House (London: Collins, 1963);

The Italian Spring (London: Collins, 1964; New York: Holt, 1972); republished as *Maria's Italian Spring* (London: Simon & Schuster, 1993);

Nineteenth Century Children: Heroes and Heroines in English Children's Stories, by Avery and Angela Bull (London: Hodder & Stoughton, 1965);

Call of the Valley (London: Collins, 1966; New York: Holt, 1968);

Victorian People in Life and Literature (London: Collins, 1970; New York: Holt, Rinehart, 1970);

Authors' Choice, by Avery and others (London: Hamish Hamilton, 1970; New York: Crowell, 1971);

A Likely Lad (London: Collins, 1971; New York: Holt, 1971);

Ellen's Birthday (London: Hamish Hamilton, 1971);

Ellen and the Queen (London: Hamish Hamilton, 1971; Nashville, Tenn.: Nelson, 1974);

Jemima and the Welsh Rabbit (London: Hamish Hamilton, 1972);

The Echoing Green: Memories of Regency and Victorian Youth (London: Collins, 1974);

Childhood's Pattern: A Study of the Heroes and Heroines of Children's Fiction, 1770–1950 (London: Hodder & Stoughton, 1975);

Gillian Avery's Book of the Strange and Odd (London: Kestrel, 1975);

Freddie's Feet (London: Hamilton, 1976);

Huck and Her Time Machine (London: Collins, 1977);

Mouldy's Orphan (London: Collins, 1978);

Sixpence! (London: Collins, 1979);

The Lost Railway (London: Collins, 1980);

Onlookers (London: Collins, 1983);

Child's Eye: A History of Children's Books Through Three Centuries (London: Channel 4 Television & Bodleian Library, Oxford, 1989);

The Best Type of Girl: A History of Girls' Independent Schools (London: Deutsch, 1991);

Behold the Child: American Children and Their Books, 1621–1922 (Baltimore: Johns Hopkins University Press, 1994).

OTHER: Juliana Horatia Ewing, *A Flat Iron for a Farthing,* edited by Avery (London: Faith Press, 1959);

Ewing, *Jan of the Windmill,* edited by Avery (London: Faith Press, 1960);

In the Window-Seat: A Selection of Victorian Stories, edited by Avery (Oxford: Oxford University Press, 1960; New York: Van Norstrand, 1965);

The Sapphire Treasury of Stories for Boys and Girls, edited by Avery (London: Gollancz, 1960);

Annie Keary, *Father Phim,* edited by Avery (London: Faith Press, 1962);

Unforgettable Journeys, edited by Avery (London: Gollancz, 1965; New York: Watts, 1965);

Margaret Roberts, *Banning and Blessing,* edited by Avery (London: Gollancz, 1967);

Ewing, *A Great Emergency and A Very Ill-Tempered Family,* edited by Avery (London: Gollancz, 1967);

Andrew Lang, *The Gold of Fairnilee and Other Stories,* edited by Avery (London: Gollancz, 1967);

School Remembered: An Anthology for Young Adults, edited by Avery (London: Gollancz, 1967; New York: Funk & Wagnalls, 1968);

Charlotte Yonge, *Village Children,* edited by Avery (London: Gollancz, 1967);

"Brenda," (G. Castle Smith) *Froggy's Little Brother,* edited by Avery (London: Gollancz, 1968);

The Hole in the Wall and Other Stories, edited by Avery (Oxford: Oxford University Press, 1968);

Gillian Avery

Mary Louisa Molesworth, *My New Home,* edited by Avery (London: Gollancz, 1968);

"Brenda," and Margaret Scott Gatty, and Frances Hodgson Burnett, *Victoria-Bess and Others,* compiled, with an introduction, by Avery (London: Gollancz, 1968); republished as *Victorian Doll Stories* (New York: Schocken, 1969);

G. E. Farrow, *The Wallypug of Why,* edited by Avery (London: Gollancz, 1968);

Anonymous, *The Life and Adventures of Lady Anne,* edited by Avery (London: Gollancz, 1969);

Margaret Roberts, *Stephanie's Children,* edited by Avery (London: Gollancz, 1969);

E. V. Lucas, *Anne's Terrible Good Nature and Other Stories for Children,* edited by Avery (London: Gollancz, 1970);

Keary, *The Rival Kings,* edited by Avery (London: Gollancz, 1970);

Red Letter Days, compiled by Avery (London: Hamish Hamilton, 1971);

"Fashions in Children's Fiction," in *Signposts to Criticism of Children's Literature,* edited by Robert Bator (Chicago: American Library Association, 1983), pp. 222–231;

Children and Their Books: A Collection of Essays to Celebrate the Work of Iona and Peter Opie, edited by Avery (Oxford: Oxford University Press, 1989);

"George MacDonald and the Victorian Fairy Tale," in *The Gold Thread: Essays on George MacDonald,* edited by William Raeper (Edinburgh: Edinburgh University Press, 1990), pp. 126–139;

"Home and Family: English and American Ideals in the Nineteenth Century," in *Stories and Society: Children's Literature in its Social Context,* edited by Dennis Butts (New York: St. Martin's Press, 1992), pp. 37–49;

The Everyman Anthology of Poetry for Children, compiled by Avery, illustrated by Thomas Bewick (London: Dent, 1994; New York: Knopf, 1994);

Charles Dickens, *Holiday Romance and Other Writings for Children,* edited by Avery (London: Dent, 1995; Rutland, Vt.: Tuttle, 1995);

Russian Fairy Tales, adapted by Avery (New York: Knopf, 1995).

SELECTED PERIODICAL PUBLICATIONS – UNCOLLECTED: "The Quest for Fairyland," *Quarterly Journal of the Library of Congress,* 38 (Fall 1981): 220–227;

"The Cult of Peter Pan," *Word and Image: A Journal of Verbal Visual Inquiry,* 2 (April–June 1986): 173–185;

"Fantasy and Nonsense," in *New History of Literature, VI: The Victorians,* edited by Arthur Pollard (New York: Bedrick, 1987), pp. 287–306;

"The Puritans and Their Heirs," in *Children and Their Books: A Celebration of the Work of Iona and Peter Opie,* edited by Avery and Julia Briggs (Oxford: Clarendon Press, 1989);

"'Remarkable and Winning': A Hundred Years of American Heroines," *The Lion and the Unicorn: A Critical Journal of Children's Literature,* 13 (June 1989): 7–20.

Gillian Avery seems always to have felt more at home with the Victorians than with her twentieth-century contemporaries, and indeed, few modern writers bring the Victorian period to life more vividly than she. Avery was born in Reigate, Surrey, on 30 September 1926, the daughter of an estate agent, Norman Bates Avery, and his wife, the former Grace Elise Dunn. She was educated in Reigate at Dunottar School, and she depicts her childhood as rather intellectually deprived. She was always a voracious reader, but books were a precious commodity. In an unpublished letter she recalls: "There was in effect no public library in the small Surrey town where I grew up (just a dingy reference library, open for a few hours a week, in a room above the public lavatories. We never went there, and wouldn't have been allowed to use it because of 'germs.'" Her interest in things Victorian began when she was a teenager. At about fourteen she read Juliana Horatia Ewing's *A Flat Iron for a Farthing* (1872), and she became enthralled by Anthony Trollope's novels.

Avery began her career in 1944 as a newspaper reporter with the *Surrey Mirror* in Redhill. She worked in London on the staff of the *Chambers Encyclopaedia* from 1947 to 1950 and then served as assistant illustrations editor with the Clarendon Press at Oxford from 1950 to 1954. While at Oxford she met Anthony O. J. Cockshut, a junior fellow of Balliol College, whom she married on 25 August 1952. They have one daughter, Ursula Mary Elise Cockshut. Cockshut shared Avery's deep interest in the Victorian age, and his first book was a critical study of Anthony Trollope, an author whom they both admired. But Avery did not begin to write novels until the family moved from Oxford to Manchester, which seemed to her dreary and desolate in comparison. Out of homesickness she turned to writing a story about a girl who wished to live in Oxford and wanted to become a professor of Greek.

She began writing for children, as many writers have, rather accidentally – she wanted to write about "a child groping to satisfy an ambition," and that theme best fitted into a book for children. Avery claims that she made her heroine a Victorian child because she felt she understood late-nineteenth-century children better than mid-twentieth-century children. She adds, "Besides, in many ways they resembled me and my contemporaries with our meek acceptance of the poor of the adult world more than the post-war generation, with their bounce and assurance." The result of this effort was *The Warden's Niece* (1957), which has remained one of the author's most popular works; it was republished in 1992 as *Maria Escapes.*

The book illustrates Avery's ability to create an interesting array of characters as well as her penchant for the comedic and satiric. The setting is Victorian England in the early 1870s, and the central character is the orphaned Maria Henniker-Hadden, who is sent to live with her elderly uncle, the scholarly warden of Canterbury College at Oxford. Maria's dreams of becoming a famous professor of Greek at Oxford are surprisingly not discouraged by her uncle – he is decidedly un-Victorian in that regard. Although her uncle is kindly, his household is staid and proper, thanks to his overbearing housekeeper, Mrs. Clomper. But Maria soon meets the Smith brothers (Thomas, Joshua, and James) who live in a much livelier house next door. Through her adventures with these rambunctious neighbors, Maria sets out on a quest to uncover the mystery surrounding a seventeenth-century noble family who met disaster during the English Civil War. She researches in the Bodleian Library and pokes about the family's country seat near Oxford. Maria's gradual piecing together of the puzzle gives the novel a unity not often found in Avery's succeeding works.

In this novel Avery also introduces one of her more delightful inventions: the character of the inimitable and exasperating Mr. Copplestone, who has been hired on as a temporary tutor to the Smiths. Copplestone is the only one of Avery's creations consciously based upon a real individual, an unnamed acquaintance of Avery's who was very tall, "wayward, irresponsible, unpredictable." The children and their tutor enjoy a series of adventures in and around Oxford – the book is rich in evocative descriptions of both the countryside and the Oxford colleges. In the end Maria succeeds, with some assistance from her uncle, in solving the seventeenth-century mystery, where scholars before her had failed. Adult readers are likely to see the conclusion as a test of credulity, for it depends upon an extraordinary collection of coincidences. A principal theme is the role of the Victorian woman and the interaction between males and females – and Avery clearly argues for the strong-willed female. She also focuses on the importance of the protagonist's discovery of her own inner strength, persistence, and resilience, and the contrast between the convention-bound adult world and the spirited, imaginative world of youth. Both the themes and the swift denouement become familiar hallmarks in much of Avery's children's fiction.

Avery found that writing about Oxford was a form of therapy, an "escape from the weeping Manchester skies and the raw fogs," and she "would settle down each January to write another [novel]." Her Oxford books all contain similar themes – the folly of adults, the rigidity of Victorian behavioral codes, and the ingenuity of the children as they discover ways of dealing with this rigidity. Two more books about the Smith boys appeared in succession, including *Trespassers at Charlcote* (1958) and *James without Thomas* (1959). They make a final appearance, although in supporting roles, in *The Elephant War* (1960), which takes its title from a historical incident: the sale of the elephant Jumbo by the London Zoo to the American showman P. T. Barnum. The actual event, which created an enormous controversy in Britain, particularly among children and animal activists, took place in 1882, but Avery sets it in 1875, apparently to accommodate the Smith boys.

The book's central character is Harriet Jessop, who is caught up in the elephant fanaticism. The true conflict in this tale, however, is between Harriet and the Smith boys, who both intrigue and infuriate her. She is convinced that they are part of some nefarious plot against her and begins keeping track of "victories" and "defeats" in her ongoing war with the boys as one misunderstanding after another keeps the children at odds. Following many amusing adventures, the cause of Jumbo is lost and the elephant is shipped to America. The unfortunate coincidences that have kept Harriet and the Smiths at bay are revealed one by one, and all turns out well in the end. Through the eyes of the children, much of the folly of adults is revealed, a favorite theme of Avery's. Once again the setting is Oxford, with lovely descriptions of the university town in Victorian times. Although the readers now say farewell to the Smiths, Harriet returns briefly in *The Italian Spring* (1964), the sequel to *The Warden's Niece*. Avery, in allowing her characters to grow up in successive novels, resisted the temptation to recy-

cle her heroes and heroines endlessly in series books. Instead, they mature, leave their nests, and eventually head out on their own.

It is tempting to see Avery as the chronicler of the middle-class Victorian household, for her works show a fascination for the workings of that formidable institution, particularly as viewed from the children's point of view. In *To Tame a Sister* (1961) Avery creates an almost entirely new cast of characters in the Harding children: Charles, Arthur, and their mildly overbearing sister, Margaret. They spend the summer holidays in the country with their well-to-do and exceedingly eccentric, relatives, the Fulkes: Cousin Hester, an effete writer; her husband, Aethelstan, an equally effete scholar; and their fragile daughter, Guenevere. The Fulke household is overrun with visiting artists, writers, and musicians, and the reader experiences a child's view of that great Victorian tradition – the weekend house party.

The book resembles a novel of manners, depicting life among the gentry during mid-Victorian England. As might be expected, Avery depicts the gentry and their sophisticated house guests as foolish and preoccupied with trivial matters. Cousin Hester is writing a study of childish loneliness, which she is calling *Just One*. "The child," she explains, "makes a playmate of his image in the looking-glass, and weaves all manner of fantasies about it. I must show you the little picture that has inspired me. It stands on my writing table as I work, and I drink great draughts of inspiration from it." This satiric jibe is, like much of the humor of the book, likely to be lost on most children.

The book's most interesting character is Mr. Copplestone, fresh from his appearance in *The Warden's Niece*. Margaret and her brothers quickly discover that he is a fraud, although he deceives his employers for some time with his grandiose language, his fabrications (especially regarding his own abilities and experiences), and his hair-brained schemes. He is hired as Guenevere's tutor in Italian and ancient history (although he knows precious little history and less Italian, and is anxiously awaiting for a translation of Dante to arrive by post). He spends little time tutoring the languishing Guenevere, explaining to Margaret that "*Imprimis,* Miss Guenevere is too preoccupied with her piano at the moment to bother her head with ancient history; *secundo,* Mr. Steele's translation of Dante has not yet arrived, therefore I am in darkness so far as Dante is concerned; *tertio,* I confidentially expect her to die before the end of the year, and what good will ancient history be to her then?" The principal theme of the book – to judge from the title – is the correction of Margaret's character flaw, the rather superior attitude she holds toward her brothers. By the end of the story Margaret presumably has come to know her brothers better and to appreciate their freshness, their energy, and their genuineness – so contrary to the lethargic phoniness of the Fulke household. Not all readers will see this transformation as the focal point of the book. The most interesting parts describe the escapades of Margaret and Copplestone among the literary and artistic "greats." Eventually, what begins as a sort of comedy of manners turns out to be an almost farcical comedy of errors, containing some of Avery's most amusing scenes.

Avery moves her setting to the suburbs in her next novel, *The Greatest Gresham* (1962), in which she explores once again the Victorian family and character growth. Set in a Victorian London suburb in the last decade of the nineteenth century, the story focuses on the interactions between the children of two families, the three Greshams (Julia, Henry, and Amy), whose parents lead a painfully proper and therefore dull lifestyle, and the two Holts (Richard and Kate), whose widowed father is a disheveled scholar aided by his easygoing sister in their rather unconventional and much more interesting household. The title refers to the attempt by Julia Gresham to become "great"; although she puzzles over how her goal is to be accomplished. In fact, it is Julia's shy brother, Henry, who becomes the "greatest Gresham," by triumphing over his reticence and embarking on a brave (albeit unnecessary) journey on his own. The more interesting focus is the conflict between the staid social expectations of Victorian children and the children's own rebellious spirits. It is typical of Avery's novels that the parents of her heroes and heroines, when they are not distant, are censorious and even overbearing, and every family has its eccentric.

The title suggests the theme of many of Avery's novels – the ambition of youth. Many of her protagonists, both male and female, have lofty aspirations, childlike both in their naiveté and in their expression of hopeful optimism. Their ambitions are never fully realized, however, in part because they are so lofty (Maria wants to become a professor of Greek; Julia wants to be "great"). Nevertheless, by the story's conclusion the protagonist is able to place his or her ambition in a more realistic perspective. The growth of most of Avery's protagonists is in the direction of a deeper understanding of their roles in the order of things, and, as often happens with protagonists, they emerge a bit deflated but wise beyond their years.

So it is with Kate Holt, the protagonist of *The Peacock House* (1963), set in rural Oxfordshire in 1894. This work focuses on the Greshams' neighbors, the Holts, now transplanted from their London home. Mr. Holt has remarried, and twins are added to the family. Kate is alone and lonely, Richard having gone off to school. The Peacock House is actually the old Fulke residence from *To Tame a Sister,* and *Peacock House* takes place a generation later than the earlier novel. The elder Fulkes are dead and the house now belongs to the reclusive daughter, Guenevere. The house and its owner present an irresistible challenge to Kate, who wants to rescue Guenevere from her apathy. She is aided in this pursuit by Henry Gresham, who happens to be attending school nearby. There is also the usual conflict between the Victorian female, Kate, and the Victorian male, in this case two students her father is tutoring. The reader also encounters (for the last time) Mr. Copplestone, who has been a clergyman for some twenty years at a nearby church and longs to be forgiven by Guenevere for his outrageous behavior as her tutor. The story ends in typical Avery style, resolved swiftly and with the misunderstandings set aright. Peacock House is a symbol of the stifling Victorian sense of propriety, which proves to be unforgiving, and Kate's objective is to bring light and happiness into the house and to help break the social shackles that have bound Guenevere for many years.

A similar contrast between individual freedom and social expectations is at the heart of *The Italian Spring,* the last novel that Avery devoted to these Oxfordshire characters. It resumes Maria's story soon after the conclusion of *The Warden's Niece.* The sudden death of her uncle Hadden upsets Maria's life once more, and she is put in the charge of a distant cousin, Mr. Burghclere, a scholarly recluse. Mr. Burghclere takes Maria to Italy, beginning with Venice, which is depicted as a dank, unhealthy place. Mr. Burghclere relishes taking Maria about to the cultural sites, but she falls desperately ill with a fever. Although she slowly recovers, Maria becomes a virtual recluse when she is taken to Mr. Burghclere's home near Florence. She is gradually aroused from this lethargy by a spunky English neighbor, Cordelia, who brings Maria out of her shell and shows her again the value of human companionship and the delights of childhood.

Maria's growth from a cold, distant child who distrusts people and has difficulty relating to children her own age into a "normal" twelve-year-old delighting in companionship with others her own age is only one of the book's concerns. The nature of art is also explored, as Maria moves from a purely intellectual appreciation to a true love of art as an expression of human emotion. This situation reflects the conflict between the world of intellect (that of the artist and the scholar) and the world of action, a theme suggested as early as *The Warden's Niece,* in which Maria is depicted as an individual of action, discovering secrets that her uncle's bookish colleagues had overlooked. It is most completely developed in *The Italian Spring,* however, in which Maria's attempt to escape human contact (a natural inclination given the fact that she was so frequently abandoned in her childhood) had led her to scholarly pursuits at an early age. Mr. Burghclere (who is a reclusive bachelor with little use for people of any age) takes to her because of her interest in and knowledge of the classical world. With the best of intentions, he introduces her to the finest that Italian culture has to offer, but as he and Maria tramp in solitude through darkly lit churches and damp, remote antiquities, she soon finds Venetian art sterile and without human emotion.

Cordelia, however, who is first and foremost a young girl, restores Maria's love of art when they steal away to view a painting by Piero della Francisca in a little village nearby. There Maria is moved by the deep attachment the villagers have to the painting, the *Madonna della Misericordia,* and she realizes that art is important only as individuals respond to it and only as it adds meaning to their lives — that it is not meant to be a cold, intellectual experience, but a moving, vital interaction between the object and the observer. A similar message is found in *To Tame a Sister,* which humorously satirizes a certain class of pretentious intellectual (including musicians, writers, painters, and scholars), revealing the callowness and insensitivity found in lives devoid of human contact and sympathy. The wan, delicate Guenevere is an effete in the making, and her reappearance in adulthood in *The Peacock House,* where she is a friendless recluse living on a decaying estate, only reaffirms the emptiness of this lifestyle.

A third theme explored in *The Italian Spring* is that of the role of women in Victorian society. When she decides to go with Mr. Burghclere, Maria declines an opportunity to attend a girls' school because she felt confined there and is uncomfortable with others her own age. Cordelia is horrified when she learns of this spurned opportunity. "Do you mean you would like to go to school?," Maria exclaims in disbelief. Cordelia replies: "It would be escape from a gilded cage. . . . Besides, it is the gateway to higher education, to equal opportunities for

The children meet Mr. Cobblestone; illustration by John Verney in Avery's To Tame a Sister *(1961)*

women." Cordelia is espousing rather un-Victorian attitudes and ambitions that "respectable" Victorian girls would hardly express, yet modern readers see the sense in Cordelia's sentiments. Finally, Maria learns a lesson similar to that of Margaret in *To Tame a Sister* — that there is no virtue in growing up too fast and that children should enjoy the pleasurable experiences of youth.

Avery recalls that when she and her husband returned to Oxford in 1964, she discovered that she no longer cared to write about Oxford — "Instead I wrote about Manchester." She admits that she wrote about England's great industrial city with distaste in *Call of the Valley* (1966), which opens in a Welsh valley, where young Sam Williams, his stern, almost fanatically religious mother, and his meek sister live with his savage, drunken uncle on a broken-down farm. Sam, a willful lad, runs away from this grim atmosphere and becomes a servant in the household of a well-to-do Manchester family. He is miserable in the city, however, and Avery vividly portrays the deplorable conditions under which household servants lived at the time. Eventually, Sam's Welsh temper and pride cost him his job, and he finds that he misses the valley. Unwelcome at home – his uncle drives him off the property – Sam sets out to make it on his own in a deserted house a few miles away. Soon he learns that his uncle has been killed in a fall and that his mother has fallen desperately ill, apparently out of remorse for her unfeeling treatment of her son. Sam returns home to assume the burdens of responsibility and repents of his headstrong ways, and all ends satisfactorily.

Call of the Valley markedly illustrates both Avery's strengths and weaknesses. The author effectively captures life backstairs in a large Victorian household, and the entire book bears a decidedly Dickensian quality, sometimes achieving the melodramtic. More important, the character depth and motivation are never fully realized. At the outset Sam's mother is a humorless woman who forbids her daughter to wear a colored ribbon in her hair, but she rather easily reforms into a loving mother figure once her cruel brother is dead. Nor is this the first Avery novel in which a virtual deus ex machina is employed to effect a happy ending.

A Likely Lad (1971), another novel of Manchester, was the last full-length novel Avery wrote for children. It treats England's industrial area with a bit more sympathy, and the reader is informed that the story was drawn from the recollections of Avery's father-in-law, who grew up in Lancashire. The story is set in 1901, the year of Victoria's death, and is full of details of working-class life in Manchester. The novel recounts the coming of age of twelve-year-old Willy Overs, the elder son of a Manchester shopkeeper. Willy's father has great ambitions for his son and is anxious to have him begin working in one of the great Manchester business firms so that he might begin climbing the ladder of success. But Willy is a studious, introspective boy who wants a college education. Further complicating the plot is a family rivalry with the Sowters, Willy's cousins, who are slightly better off financially than the Overs and a great deal snobbier.

A Dickensian touch is introduced with Aunt Maggie Chaffy, who has been kept a secret from Willy all his life. She had raised Willy's mother but disowned her when she married his father. She is one of Avery's eccentrics, a bitter old woman who never leaves her bed and sleeps on her money. She rails at everyone – even passersby on the street – but takes a liking to Willy. He eventually runs away from home to the country, where he learns (in a re-

markably short period of time) assertiveness and self-reliance and earns his father's esteem. Consequently, his father, presumably having learned the value of education, permits Willy to continue his schooling. The haughty Sowters are doomed to disappointment. Aunt Maggie, whose money they fully expected to inherit, dies, but not until after she watches in horror as her two fierce watchdogs get loose and eat all of her bank notes – one of Avery's more comically grotesque scenes. The Sowters and the Overs are thus saddled with paying her funeral expenses, and everyone learns a lesson.

In the Manchester novels Avery clearly depicts working-class values of the late-Victorian period, including the disdain for "too much" education and the desire for material wealth as evidence of success. However, her sentiments are clearly on the side of education, and her heroes discover that there are things far more important than money. The various settings of Avery's novels play enormous roles in her underlying themes. When she sets a novel in Oxford, that ancient seat of learning, her stories caution the reader against dangers of cold intellectualism and scholarly pursuits at the expense of meaningful human interaction. When she sets a novel in Manchester, the birthplace of the industrial age, her stories caution the reader against the dangers of crass materialism and the pursuit of wealth for its own sake.

Following *A Likely Lad,* Avery wrote six short books aimed at a much younger audience. Two will serve as examples of these works. *Ellen and the Queen* (1971) is about a mischievous girl who manages to find her way into an earl's house and into the bedroom used by visiting Queen Victoria. While hiding beneath the queen's bed, Ellen sees a rare sight – the queen's legs – but, of course, she cannot tell a soul her secret lest her transgression be discovered. In a more serious vein, especially given the supposed audience of six- to eight-year olds, is *Mouldy's Orphan* (1978), in which an Oxfordshire girl nicknamed Mouldy brings home an orphan named Benjy and insists her family keep him. Her parents' attempts to take Benjy to the proper authorities are thwarted by the strong-willed Mouldy, who wins out in the end and sees Benjy adopted by her family. Aside from being an adventure story, the book also carries a heavy message about the often deplorable social conditions in Victorian England.

Although her novels provide extraordinarily detailed pictures of Victorian life and society, Avery never deliberately researched her novels. She has read deeply in Victorian literature and has a confident command of the Victorian milieu, and it is easy to see the influence of both Dickens and Trollope in her novels. In fact, after she and her husband moved to Oxford and she had ready access to the Bodleian Library, Avery began seriously researching nineteenth-century Britain, became increasingly absorbed in Victorian social history, and gradually turned to writing more nonfiction.

After *A Likely Lad* and the six novellas, Avery abandoned fictional writing for children. She has noted that, aside from "broadening a child's horizons," little was expected of a child's book in the 1950s, and once she had begun in the field it seemed natural to continue writing children's stories. However, by the early 1980s Avery had become so disillusioned with the "many rules and directives and prohibitions, and earnest puritans who dictate what should be put into the hands of children" that she lost her desire to write more children's books. She has written two novels for adults, *The Lost Railway* (1980) and *Onlookers* (1983), both set in Victorian England and with a flavor similar to her children's books. Like her children's novels, these stories are leisurely paced and likely to appeal to a select audience eager to be fully immersed in the Victorian atmosphere.

Avery has never lost her interest in children, however, and continues to edit and compile works related to the field of children's literature, including essays on the literature as well as collections of primary works — all relating to the Victorian period. Her nonfiction includes the informative *Victorian People in Life and Literature* (1970), a study of nineteenth-century life and mores. Avery draws on her wide reading in the period to illustrate the richness and the variety of Victorian society. She has also written a television history of children's books.

In reviewing Avery's *Call of the Valley,* Elinor S. Cullen sums up both Avery's strengths and weaknesses as a novelist: "Not only is this story de-

scriptive of the social conditions of the late nineteenth century, but its plot and characters seem to be drawn from the stereotypes of Victorian melodrama. . . . The descriptive material is solid; the story is dated and its diversion value to preteens, predictable, forgettable." The shortcomings of her plot and character development notwithstanding, Avery's work conveys the essence of nineteenth-century England. Her books are full of descriptions of chilly rooms, damp weather, parlor bric-a-brac, teatime rituals, English cooking, and day-to-day living in general. The psychology is modern, however, making her child heroes and heroines appealing to twentieth-century readers. Her protagonists — both boys and girls — have ambitions and are frequently rebellious and mischievous; in short, they are much like children of today. Also distinguishing Avery's work from that of her Victorian counterparts, she always tells her stories from the child's point of view." It is regrettable that so many of her children's books have gone out of print. Not only do they provide pleasurable reading, but they convey the flavor of Victorian England as no other modern writer has done. This characteristic may be both her blessing and her curse, explaining why her stories bear so deep a mark of authenticity and why they have appealed to a limited audience. Avery's books are for a specialized audience, whether she is writing for children or adults. But for those who belong to that audience, her writing brings a deep and abiding pleasure.

References:

Elinor S. Cullen, Review of *Call of the Valley, Library Journal,* 93 (July 1968): 2736;

John Rowe Townsend, *Written for Children: An Outline of English-Language Children's Literature* (Boston: Horn Book, 1974), pp. 261–262.

Nina Bawden

(19 January 1925 –)

Louisa Smith
Mankato State University

See also the Bawden entry in *DLB 14: British Novelists Since 1960.*

BOOKS: *Who Calls the Tune* (London: Collins, 1953); republished as *Eyes of Green* (New York: Morrow, 1953);

The Odd Flamingo (London: Collins, 1954);

Change Here for Babylon (London: Collins, 1955);

The Solitary Child (London: Collins, 1956; New York: Lancer, 1966);

Devil by the Sea (New York: Collins, 1957; Philadelphia: Lippincott, 1959; abridged for children, 1976);

Just Like a Lady (London: Longmans, 1960); republished as *Glass Slippers Always Pinch* (Philadelphia: Lippincott, 1960);

In Honour Bound (London: Longmans, 1961);

Tortoise by Candlelight (London: Longmans, 1963; New York: Harper, 1963);

The Secret Passage (London: Gollancz, 1963); republished as *The House of Secrets* (Philadelphia: Lippincott, 1964);

On the Run (London: Gollancz, 1964); republished as *Three on the Run* (Philadelphia: Lippincott, 1965);

Under the Skin (London: Longmans, 1964; New York: Harper, 1964);

A Little Love, a Little Learning (London: Longmans, 1965; New York: Harper, 1966);

The White Horse Gang (London: Gollancz, 1966; Philadelphia: Lippincott, 1966);

The Witch's Daughter (London: Gollancz, 1966; Philadelphia: Lippincott, 1966);

A Handful of Thieves (London: Gollancz, 1967; Philadelphia: Lippincott, 1967);

A Woman of My Age (London: Longmans, 1967; New York: Harper, 1967);

The Grain of Truth (London: Longmans, 1968; New York: Harper, 1968);

The Runaway Summer (London: Gollancz, 1969; Philadelphia: Lippincott, 1969);

Nina Bawden in 1953

The Birds on the Trees (London: Longmans, 1970, New York: Harper, 1970);

Squib (London: Gollancz, 1971; Philadelphia: Lippincott, 1971);

Anna Apparent (London: Longmans, 1972; New York: Harpers, 1972);

Carrie's War (London: Gollancz, 1973; Philadelphia: Lippincott, 1973);

George Beneath a Paper Moon (London: Allen Lane, 1974; New York: Harper, 1974);

The Peppermint Pig (London: Gollancz, 1975; Philadelphia: Lippincott, 1975);

Afternoon of a Good Woman (London: Macmillan, 1976; New York: Harper, 1977);

Rebel on a Rock (London: Gollancz, 1978; Philadelphia: Lippincott, 1978);

Familiar Passions (London: Macmillan, 1979; New York: Morrow, 1979);

The Robbers (London: Gollancz, 1979; New York: Lothrop, 1979);

Walking Naked (London: Macmillan, 1981; New York: St. Martin's Press, 1982);

William Tell (London: Cape, 1981; New York: Lothrop, 1981);

Kept in the Dark (London: Gollancz, 1982; New York: Lothrop, 1982);

The Ice House (London: Macmillan, 1983; New York: St. Martin's Press, 1983);

St. Francis of Assisi (London: Cape, 1983; New York: Lothrop, 1983);

The Finding (London: Gollancz, 1985; New York: Lothrop, 1985);

Princess Alice (London: Deutsch, 1985);

Circles of Deceit (London: Macmillan, 1987; New York: St. Martin's Press, 1987);

Keeping Henry (London: Gollancz, 1988), republished as *Henry* (New York: Lothrop, 1988);

The Outside Child (London: Gollancz, 1989; New York: Lothrop, 1989);

Family Money (London: Gollancz, 1991);

Humbug (Bath: Chivers, 1992; New York: Clarion, 1992);

The Real Plato Jones (New York: Clarion, 1993; London: Hamilton, 1994);

In My Own Time: Almost an Autobiography (London: Virago, 1994).

In Nina Bawden's *The Birds on the Trees* (1970) a young man named Toby, who is trying to cope with life rather unsuccessfully, states, "Families are terrible"— a perception of family life that defines much of Bawden's work for children. Her child protagonists either have families that do not understand them or else live apart from their families because their parents are ill, abroad, or dead. The misperception of parental intentions, or the complete absence of parents, often establishes the action and conflict in Bawden's work.

Born in London on 19 January 1925, Nina Mary Mabey was educated at Ilford County High School and at Somerville College, Oxford. Upon receiving her B.A. in 1946, she married H. W. Bawden, by whom she had two sons, Nicholas and Robert Humphrey Felix. She worked for Town and Country Planning Associates in 1946–1947, becoming a full-time writer in 1952. After the dissolution of her marriage to Bawden, she married a broadcast executive, Austen Steven Kark; they have one daughter, Perdita Emily Helena.

Beginning her publishing career with adult mysteries in the early 1950s, Bawden wrote her first children's book, *The Secret Passage,* in 1963. As she told Edward Blishen in a 1975 interview, writing "for children was a logical development for me. I wanted to write, not as a grown-up looking back, but as a former child, remembering the emotional landscape I had once moved in, how I had felt, what concerned me, what I wanted to know." Child characters in her adult work experience some of the same concerns and adventures, but the perspective is not the limited, focused view presented in the juvenile titles. "When I started to write it never occurred to me to write for children. I wrote about them, for adults, partly because the child's viewpoint is (as Henry James knew) a sly way of commenting on adult society, and partly because I remembered my own childhood so vividly, particularly the frustrations of being a child. Children think and feel deeply, in some ways more deeply than adults."

During the thirty years that Bawden has written children's books, this intensity of feeling has been a fulcrum of her work. As Nicholas Tucker points out in *The Child and the Book* (1981), "the various misapprehensions of her main child characters are always due to the romantic, sometimes superficial perception of things typical of younger children's thinking – just the sort of misunderstanding a slightly older audience should be growing away from. Immediately, therefore, Miss Bawden's stories have elements within them which most children can recognise from their own past or even present."

Mitigating this intensity is the adventure the children become involved in – frequently a mystery. Children must cope with the problem on their own, sometimes hiding out or moving away from home; seldom can they turn to their parents. Often the mother is distracted by her own pursuits, and the father works or is absent. If there is anyone to confide in, it is a grandmother or a maiden aunt. These confidantes, however, tend to have the same problems communicating with authorities as the children do, and the resulting frustrations complicate the danger and add to the excitement. The story resolutions, though satisfactory, seem to occur only when the children are worn out from the events. All other avenues to the solution are closed, but enjoying the one that remains is compromised by the children's exhaustion.

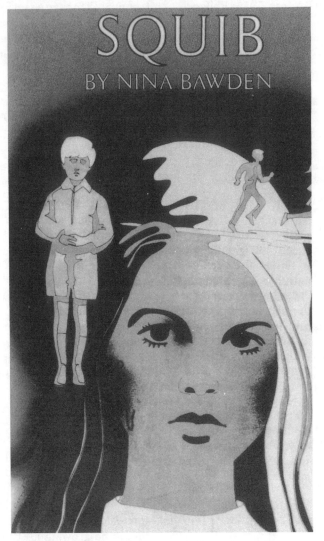

Dust jacket for Bawden's novel about two children who befriend an abused boy

The Secret Passage owes a debt to Frances Hodgson Burnett's *The Secret Garden* (1911), Bawden's "favorite book, in the sense that I read it not once but several times a year, returning to it always with a special kind of pleasure." Although Bawden's impetus for writing a children's book began with her own children's discovery of a "dusty way through from our cellar to the cellar of the house next door" and her husband's encouragement, the tribute to Burnett's book is apparent. The child protagonists, John, Mary, and Ben, come to England from Kenya after their mother's sudden death, just as Burnett's Mary Lennox comes to England from India after the death of her parents. Both the Mallories and Mary end up with unknown relatives in mysterious houses, and both meet a child in need of psychological help, Colin in *The Secret Garden* and Victoria

Clark in *The Secret Passage*. Vickie, an orphan living with an unappreciative foster mother, is a musical prodigy who breaks into the uninhabited house next door to Aunt Mabel's to play the piano. John, Mary, and Ben discover her when they find the connecting secret passage, and she tells them she is the daughter of the owner, Mr. Reynolds. The conclusion finds Mr. Reynolds appreciative of Vickie's talent and willing to sponsor her lessons. Aunt Mabel's elderly lodger, thought to be destitute, generously compensates Aunt Mabel for all the years she has looked after Miss Pin, and the lost father returns to England. In an afterword she wrote for an edition of *The Secret Garden,* Bawden comments, "I think the beauty of this book is that it expresses this natural human need (peace and goodness) in a simple, straightforward, and exciting story. And one with a superb happy ending." One could say exactly the same of Bawden's book.

Besides the child characters, two other character types are introduced in this book. The first is the capable maiden aunt who takes in the children. Once the children adjust to her ideas, they admire her spirit, her devotion to them, and her practical approach to life. A strong, capable older woman will appear frequently in Bawden's work, a refuge for children to turn to. The other character type is the old woman whom most adults write off as slightly batty. Miss Pin could be dismissed as a woman living in her own private world, untouched by reality. But befriended by Ben, who likes her stories, she acts when necessary.

The setting of *The Secret Passage* is Henstable, on the southeast coast of England. Bawden's second children's book, *On the Run* (1964), revisits this setting. Bawden's characters do not usually reappear in sequels, but Ben from *The Secret Passage* returns in *On the Run*. He is visiting his father and his father's fiancée in London, and his return to Henstable is delayed when he learns that Mary and John have measles. In London he meets Thomas Okapi, whose father is the deposed prime minister of Tiga, East Africa. Thomas's uncle is plotting to kidnap his nephew and force the prime minister to return and end the opposition to the dictatorship that has seized power. Ben discovers this plan, and together with Lil, a slum child, accompanies Thomas to Henstable, where the three children hide out in a cave, outwit their pursuers, and effect the reinstatement of the rightful government of Tiga.

According to Bawden, the idea for *On the Run* originated in fact: "Some time ago there was an African boy in England whose father, a Prime Minister in Africa, was in prison. There was a great excitement for fear the boy would be kidnapped. I thought it would be very exciting if one had a chance like this to put the boy down in London and have some other children meet him and rescue him from a terrible political situation. . . ." She talks of contrasting characters, all of whom are running away from something. In contrast to the elegant Thomas, Bawden created Lil, a slum child who has managed to avoid school and welfare workers, hiding out at home and at a bomb site. Tough and resourceful, Lil represents a character type who reappears in Bawden's works: an independent, usually uneducated child who survives by outwitting the establishment's good intentions – for example, Vicki in *The Secret Passage.*

In *The White Horse Gang* (1966) the same character type reappears in the person of Abe Tanner.

Abe lives with his blind grandmother, who is rumored to be a witch. Though impoverished and academically unsuccessful, Abe is good with his hands and sings beautifully. Sam Peach admires Abe, and when his cousin, Rose, comes to stay with Sam's family, the three young people form a gang. Rose, who has been educated in various countries, speaks several languages. Sam lacks a normal family life – his mother is emotionally distant, investing most of her time in the dogs she breeds – and all three children are free from close parental supervision. Abe has an old white horse, which he adores. The three devise a plan to kidnap Percy, a tiresome, rich child with an overprotective mother. Percy, however, is delighted to be free from parental restraint and refuses to go home until disaster strikes, resulting in the death of the white horse.

The resolution of the story finds Abe adopted by Farmer John, who appreciates his talents; Rose's parents coming back for her; and Sam's mother showing more concern for her son. Abe recognizes that the time has come for the gang to disband: "It's jus' that things is always different,' he managed finally. 'I mean t'was fine, bein' a gang an' all, but t'won't be the same next year, t'won't be the same every again.' " Although the ending provides what each child needs, it is touched with pathos. Everyone must give something up. The character of Abe is based on a boy Bawden had met during World War II: "We thought he was wonderful because he could ride a horse, could shoot, and do all the things we couldn't do. . . . I put him into this book really as he was, I think, a rather independent, wild boy." Similar characters appear in *Keeping Henry* (1988) and *The Robbers* (1979).

The Witch's Daughter (1966) is set on the Scottish island of Mull, called Skua in the book. According to Bawden, her family and some friends went on holiday to that island. One of the daughters of the other family was blind, and she asked for a book about a blind girl that did not portray her as sad. "So I said, 'What sort of story would you like?' She said she'd like a story about Mull and about a blind girl who did something, something brave, like catching jewel thieves or robbers." During Bawden's stay on the island, the families went into a cave and their flashlight failed. The turning point in *The Witch's Daughter* comes when the blind child, Janey, leads the others out of a dark cave where they have been abandoned by the diamond robbers.

The title character, Perdita (also the name of Bawden's daughter), lives with Annie MacLaren, her foster mother, who runs a boarding house used by the diamond robber, Mr. Smith, as his headquar-

Bawden in Turkey, 1972

aunt, and her grandfather, but mostly herself: "Mary went into her bedroom and scowled at herself in the looking glass. 'I hate you, too,' she said aloud. 'Pig.' " She steals a candy bar but is observed by Poll and Anna, Simon's twin sisters. By way of explanation, Mary tells Simon a series of lies about her treatment at the hands of her aunt. Simon and Mary rescue Krishna Patel, an immigrant from Kenya who has been dumped on the coast by unscrupulous profiteers, and hide him in a cave. When Krishna becomes gravely ill, the children are forced to turn to Aunt Alice for help. Mary has misread her aunt, who manages both to rescue the boy and preserve Simon and Mary's dignity as she exclaims, "There is no point in sweeping things under the carpet! Pretending Mary and Simon didn't know what they were doing, and it was just a childish prank. It's – well – it's insulting to them both!" When given a choice of joining her mother or staying with Aunt Alice and Grampy, Mary chooses the latter.

Bawden claims that she enjoyed writing about Mary "because she was very cross, and when I was that age I was also very cross and wanted to hit people." Mary is a difficult, unmalleable child, and no one is more aware of these characteristics than the child herself. (Bawden had introduced a similar child named Hilary in *Devil by the Sea,* first published as an adult novel in 1957 and then abridged and published as a children's book in 1976. Even then, the subject of a child murder was considered too strong for young audiences by most critics.)

Thirty years after her experiences in World War II, Bawden wrote *Carrie's War* (1973), which in 1993 won the Phoenix Award, presented by the Children's Literature Association. In her acceptance speech Bawden described a transitional work, *Squib* (1971), based on an incident that came to her attention while she was sitting as a justice of the peace for Surrey from 1968 to 1976. A child had been found locked in a henhouse, chained to the floor. The case caused Bawden to recall a similar one from her own childhood: "I remembered something that had happened in the war, on a farm near where my mother and brothers were staying and where I went in the holidays." Two young boys starved to death in the wartime incident.

Most critics point to *Squib* as a juncture in Bawden's writing. Squib is an abused child who is tied in a laundry basket when his foster parents want him quiet and out of the way. Although two children, Robin and Kate, suspect something is wrong, the discovery of Squib in the caravan horrifies them. Robin "tore open the strap that fastened

ters because it is out of the way. Janey and Tim come to the island with their botanist parents. The three children meet on the beach, and Perdita asks Janey to teach her her letters. While the girls are absorbed in the lesson, Perdita realizes through her "second sight" that Tim is in trouble. "'I've got Powers,' Perdita said. 'Annie says so. She says my mother was a witch.'" By combining their talents, the children defeat the robbers. When Tim is praised for figuring out the identity of the diamond robbers and told he should be a detective, he replies, "I think I'd rather be a botanist, like my father. Not so many people get hurt." The character of Perdita resembles Abe, Lil, and Vickie, wise and unschooled. She is shier than the other three, but like them she lives with a single guardian and is isolated from other children.

A different kind of child appears in *The Runaway Summer* (1969). Mary hates the world, her the lid and saw him, scrouged up at one end, his pale, cottony head drooping forward. He whimpered and screwed up tighter as Robin touched him." For some time Kate fantasizes that Squib is her brother, Rupert, who had been lost in a drowning accident. In the end, her mother explains, "In real life there aren't any right true happy endings. You have to get used to things as they are." Robin's older sister is awarded custody of Squib, however, so Kate can continue seeing him.

Bawden first invoked the lost-child-returned motif in *The Secret Passage,* in which the children mistake a comment of Miss Pin's about Aunt Mabel losing a child and hope that Vickie is that child. Another lost child is discovered in *The Finding* (1985). Jill Paton Walsh comments that "there are brilliant insights" in *Squib,* "especially the pathetic muddle of half-baked fear (of walking in the woods, of witches) which overlie the awful knowledge that Squib has been shackled in a laundry basket, and simply confuse the children about what is real and what is not, so that they hardly know if they are playing or rescuing a real victim."

After *Squib* Bawden wrote an adult book, *Anna Apparent* (1972), in which the title character is sent to a farm during the war and her mother killed. Toward the end of the book, Anna, now a grown woman, reads about the case of a man who kept his eldest son "locked in a hen house for a year. He had other, young children: a girl of three and a small boy. . . . He looked an ordinary man, an affectionate father, but he had chained a seven-year-old child to an iron staple driven into the ground and left him, naked except for a piece of sacking, lying in his own filth."

Carrie's War was originally meant to be an adult novel: "I suppose this is why I began with the grown-up and widowed Carrie coming back with her own children to look at the town, and the railway line." Retaining the framework, Bawden adopted thirteen-year-old Carrie's perspective as she and her brother, Nick, are housed with a brother and sister, Samuel Isaac Evans and Louise Evans. The sister appears cowed by her older brother, and her actions resemble those of Aunt Alice in *The Runaway Summer*. Another sister, Mrs. Gotobed, is estranged because she married a mine owner, the enemy of the miners. She lives at Druid's Bottom, where Albert Sandwich, another child refugee, is also sent, and which becomes a refuge for Nick and Carrie. When Mrs. Gotobed dies, Mr. Evans inherits Druid's Bottom.

Mingled with the lonely setting of Druid's Bottom is a curse. A mysterious skull, supposedly that of an African boy, is believed to protect the house,

but Carrie, in anger, throws the skull into the horse pond. Later, on their way to Glasgow to reunite with their mother, the children see Druid's Bottom burning. As an adult, Carrie continues to feel guilt for the fire, which she believes she caused. Nick represents another character type in Bawden's work, the younger brother who is more easily upset than the older sister, slighter of build, and apt to be delicate and fair. The delicate younger brother, a type introduced in *Devil by the Sea,* appears in other Bawden books, such as *The Peppermint Pig* (1975) and *Keeping Henry. Carrie's War* received a Carnegie commendation in 1973 and in 1993 won the Phoenix Award for a notable book published twenty years earlier.

The Peppermint Pig also portrays strong, older women – two aunts who provide a home for the Greengrass family when it falls on hard times. The story begins when the father, a coach painter, foolishly accepts blame for a theft committed by another and goes to seek his fortune in America, leaving the family temporarily without support. The mother, a dressmaker, takes in work. The central child in this story is Poll, the youngest of four children, beautiful and headstrong. The title of the book refers to a pig the mother brings into the family, names Johnnie, and treats like a pet. Later Johnnie is sent to the butcher, and Poll loses her hope for the future. She is not angry, but she has little hope that her father will come home or that anything good will happen. Her Aunt Sarah understands, and encourages Poll: "Oh you have to be brave to look forward. . . . Things do go right sometimes." Soon, Poll's father does return.

The story is based on events in Bawden's mother's life. "My mother's memory for detail was excellent, and her older siblings, my aunts and my uncle, although in their eighties then were not far behind." Bawden's grandfather had gone to America in the 1870s and her great-grandfather had taken to the road. Bawden includes the latter in *The Peppermint Pig* as the aunts' father; he surfaces as a tramp. The aunts explain that "a settled life didn't suit him, and he took to the road." Poll's reaction is subdued excitement and curiosity: "No one else she knew had a tramp in their family! This was different – and rather exciting!"

The Peppermint Pig, which won the Guardian Award in 1976, employs some familiar Bawden characters and family interactions: the absent father, the coping mother, the independent and scholarly aunts, the various interplay among siblings, and the central character who pushes the limits, asks too many questions, and goes where she is told not to go.

Dust jacket for one of Bawden's best-known works, based on events in the life of her mother

In *Rebel on a Rock* (1978) Bawden returns to the characters of *Carrie's War*. The adult Carrie adopts two children, marries Albert Sandwich, and travels to Ithica, a country recently overtaken by a dictator. The book introduces a new element in Bawden's children's work: a stepparent. Albert, who becomes a stepfather when he marries Carrie, proves an intelligent, understanding, and exciting parent. In *A Little Love, a Little Learning* (1965), written for adults, Bawden had already portrayed a sympathetic stepfather in Arthur Boyd, a physician with three stepdaughters. This adult novel is told in first person by the middle daughter, Kate, who is perceptive, intelligent, and headstrong. Joanna, the older daughter, provides a similar perspective in *Rebel on a Rock*.

Paton Walsh points out that this book returns to Bawden's earlier adventurous style, but certainly the attentive child of *Carrie's War* and *The Peppermint Pig* is also present in Joanna. Hers is a limited perspective that does not foresee consequences, as

when, by not believing that Alexis is the son of the popular deposed president, she scuttles the resolve of the president who chooses to save his son over his country. Among the book's characters are two older American women who consider themselves freelance journalists and who resemble the resourceful and brave aunts of Bawden's other works. Like *Carrie's War* this book has a frame story written in the first person reflecting on Joanna's experience. Albert, the stepfather, cautions her that "writers are powerful people, Jo. That's why you must always try to write the truth. As near as you can get to it, anyway."

In *The Robbers* Bawden draws several familial themes together. Eight-year-old Philip has been living with his grandmother when he is sent to London to live with his father and his new American stepmother. Philip's father is domineering, and he does not know his son well. His grandmother's position is shaky; the rights of a father supersede hers, but in the end Philip is returned to her. In the meantime he has learned about class distinction: his good friend Darcy, a promising singer resembling Abe in *The White Horse Gang,* is placed on probation for breaking into a house and stealing an ivory chesspiece, an act for which Philip is only chastised. When Philip asks, "But it isn't fair, is it? I mean, the *law* isn't fair. Taking Darcy to court and not me," he is reminded that he has a father, whereas Darcy's father is crippled; his brother in jail; and his sister-in-law black and pregnant. The grandmother understands Philip's concern for Darcy, whose talent she hopes to encourage; the father sees in Darcy only an undesirable companion.

Family relationships are further developed in *Kept in the Dark* (1982). Out-of-work actor parents send their three children, Noel, Clara, and Bosie, to live with their maternal grandparents, whom the children have never met. Their military grandfather terrorizes the children until they get to know him; then, after adjustments have been made on both sides and a balanced relationship develops, the action takes an unexpected turn. The children's older half-brother, David, appears; power shifts; and with David in control the residents become prisoners. Noel senses immediately that David is dangerous, but Bosie is slow to catch on. The housekeeper is dismissed and everyone is assigned tasks. The unstable David's tyranny comes to an end through a simple coincidence. When Bosie is brought home by the police after school, David thinks they have come for him and leaves. The grandparents ask the children not to tell their parents about David; they acquiesce, and when the parents arrive they are welcomed as if nothing had happened.

Kept in the Dark, with its combinations of suppressed danger and conspiratorial secrecy, is one of Bawden's grimmer books. The secret of the disturbed half-brother pales, however, before what awaits Jane Tucker in *The Outside Child* (1989): she discovers that her widowed father has remarried and that she has three half-siblings. Jane has always lived with her father's unmarried sisters, who are eccentric, accomplished women – one an artist, the other a drummer. Jane's good friend, Plato Jones, lives with his mother while his divorced father lives in America with Plato's sister. Jane's and Plato's family lives both are unusual, one of the bonds of their friendship, so when Jane discovers the picture of her father's other family, she turns to Plato for help in locating them. After she meets and befriends them, Jane takes them a copy of *The Peppermint Pig* and a music box. The mother then recognizes Jane, who had lived with the family when she was a young girl but had dropped her baby stepsister, re-sulting in the girl's deformed hand. After this incident she was sent to live with her aunts. Bawden's own father had been previously married, a fact she did not discover until she was twenty-six. Her father's older daughter was sent to live with cousins when it was thought that she had shoved Bawden downstairs out of jealousy; this book was dedicated to that half-sister. In 1983 *Kept in the Dark* was nominated for the Edgar Allan Poe Award and received a Parents' Choice citation that same year.

Plato Jones faces his own family situation in *The Real Plato Jones* (1993). This time the problem lies with his grandfathers, one Greek, one Welsh. When the Greek grandfather dies, Plato learns that he had been considered a traitor during World War II because he chose to save the people of his village rather than the Greek resistance fighters. In two separate visits to Greece, the second with Jane, Plato begins to value his Greek heritage. This is not Plato's only change. Physically he has been small, even shorter than his younger sister; between visits he grows. His decision at the end of the book is to become a citizen of the world rather than trying to figure out if he is British, Welsh, or Greek.

An adoptive grandmother plays an important part in *The Finding,* a story of generational conflict and misunderstanding which, like *Kept in the Dark,* was awarded a Parents' Choice citation. Alex is discovered as a baby near Cleopatra's Needle on the Embankment. His adoptive family includes Laura, Bob, and Ellie, and a grandmother who encourages Mrs. Angel, an elderly neighbor, to think of Alex as her missing daughter's child. Whether or not she believes this, Mrs. Angel does leave her estate to Alex and her daughter, rather than to her nephew who has looked after her. When the legacy causes ill feeling, Alex runs away and is taken in by an odd assortment of people. By the time he returns, the grandmother has met a gentleman friend who diverts her attention. Mrs. Angel's nephew explains that the "missing" daughter had left because her mother disapproved of her marriage to an Indian doctor. Both older women had rejected their daughters; Alex's disappearance allows both families to sort out old problems.

Another mismatched daughter and mother appear in *Humbug* (1992), though this time the reader's sympathy is with the mother. Ma Potter is a virtual prisoner of her daughter, Sunday Dearheart, and her granddaughter, Angelica, a spoiled, vicious child who, like several earlier Bawden characters, has eyes of different colors. When Alice, William, and Cora's parents go to Japan for six months, it is arranged for them to stay with their grandparents, next door to Ma Potter. Unbeknown to the parents, however, the grandmother has been hospitalized, and when the children arrive, Cora is sent next door by her grandfather because Angelica is her age. Angelica terrorizes Cora in much the same way she does her grandmother – teasing, ridiculing, and bullying her – and Cora and Ma Potter become allies.

Angelica appears so devoted that Cora's grandfather refuses to listen when Cora tries to tell of her vicious behavior; both Ma Potter and Cora are ignored. Bawden often suggests that people do not listen to youngsters or old people, and this situation heightens the suspense in her books, as the victims must become especially resourceful. In this instance they run away to Ma Potter's old home, much as Alex had done in *The Finding.* The title of the book refers to their only defense, the application of the word *humbug* to the lies constructed by Angelica and her mother. As Peter Hunt points out in the *Times Literary Supplement,* "she does not defeat the evil – it is self-defeating – but she survives, there is a happy ending. But to make the confrontation work, Cora has to be abandoned by almost everyone, and behind the child-sized drama lies a world where every adult is flawed, unreliable, and weak."

The most autobiographical of Bawden's children's book is *Keeping Henry,* the fictionalized story of her family's evacuation to Shropshire, after the evacuation in Wales. There are three children, James, the unnamed female narrator, and Charlie. The mother is distracted, like the mother in *The White Horse Gang;* and the farmer's son, who dreams of training race horses, is kept on the farm by the death of his mother, just as Tom in *The Robbers* and Abe in *The White Horse Gang* are trapped with the care of a relative because there is no money for hired care. Mrs. Jones, the farmer's wife, is the steadying person like the aunts in *The Peppermint Pig.*

The action revolves around a pet squirrel, Henry. The children's attachment to their pet exposes the family's strengths and weaknesses as much as does the displacement caused by the war. Charlie, too young to know his father, attaches himself first to Bill the farmhand and then to an Italian prisoner who comes to help on the farm. The narrator, away at school, feels distanced from her brothers and mother, who remain on the farm as a unit. (The displaced daughter appears in several of Bawden's works, particularly in *Walking Naked* (1981). After her return the narrator is ignorant of changes in Henry's regime and lets him out just as she did before she went to school; he never returns. *Keeping Henry* opens with Kate's statement, "My

brothers, Charlie and James, have always blamed me for what happened to Henry." Like Carrie, the narrator is still carrying guilt, and this story, like *Rebel on a Rock* and *Carrie's War,* is written as a memory piece, reexamining the past. The time lapse, in this instance, does not ease the loss, probably a reflection on the larger loss families felt during the war. Kate's memories include moments of hope, however, such as the mother's assuaging comment of "we were lucky to have had him so long." Change inevitably involves loss in Bawden's works.

Bawden has commented on reviewing the body of her work that it reads like a coded autobiography. Delving into tough subjects is perhaps a reflection of increasingly serious subjects the field of children's literature allows, but, as David Rees points out, Bawden has never shied away from hard topics, even in her early books: "One of Nina Bawden's greatest strengths has been her ability to move into these new areas, taking the children with her, demanding a deeper and more complex response." Rees suggests that her early works for children are weaker than the later ones, but a reader can observe most of the author's characters and themes even in the early work: poverty's effects, misunderstood and neglected children, strong older women, and coping.

Interviews:

Cornelia Jones and Olivia R. Way, "Nina Bawden," in their *British Children's Authors: Interviews at Home* (Chicago: American Library Association, 1976), pp. 41–48;

Peter Hunt, "The Handicaps of Being a Child," *Times Education Supplement,* 15 May 1992, p. 511.

References:

Nina Bawden, "The Imprisoned Child," in *The Thorny Paradise: Writers on Writing for Children,* edited by Edward Blishen (Harmondsworth: Penguin, 1977), pp. 62–64;

Barbara Freedman, "The Writer and the Reader in *Carrie's War,*" *Children's Literature in Education,* 22 (March 1991): 35–43;

Cornelia Jones and Olivia Way, *British Children's Authors: Interviews at Home* (Chicago: American Library Association, 1976), pp. 41–48;

David Rees, "Making the Children Stetch," in his *The Marble in the Water* (Boston: Horn Book, 1980), pp. 128–140;

Nicholas Tucker, *The Child and the Book* (Cambridge: Cambridge University Press, 1981), pp. 147–151.

Michael Bond

(13 January 1926 –   )

Charles E. Matthews
College of Charleston

BOOKS: *A Bear Called Paddington* (London: Collins, 1958; Boston: Houghton Mifflin, 1960);

More about Paddington (London: Collins, 1959; Boston: Houghton Mifflin, 1961);

Paddington Helps Out (London: Collins, 1960; Boston: Houghton Mifflin, 1961);

Paddington Abroad (London: Collins, 1961; Boston: Houghton Mifflin, 1972);

Paddington at Large (London: Collins, 1962; New York: Dell, 1962; Boston: Houghton Mifflin, 1963);

Paddington Marches On (London: Collins, 1964; Boston: Houghton Mifflin, 1965);

Here Comes Thursday (London: Harrap, 1966; New York: Lothrop, 1967);

Paddington at Work (London: Collins, 1966; New York: Dell, 1966; Boston: Houghton Mifflin, 1967);

Paddington Goes to Town (London: Collins, 1968; Boston: Houghton Mifflin, 1968);

Thursday Rides Again (London: Harrap, 1968; New York: Lothrop, 1969);

Parsley's Good Deed (London: BBC, 1969);

The Story of Parsley's Tail (London: BBC, 1969);

Herbs Annual, 2 volumes (London: BBC, 1969, 1970);

Thursday Ahoy! (London: Harrap, 1969; New York: Lothrop, 1970);

Paddington Takes the Air (London: Collins, 1970; New York: Dell, 1970; Boston: Houghton Mifflin, 1971);

Parsley's Last Stand (London: BBC, 1970);

Parsley's Problem Present (London: BBC, 1970);

Thursday in Paris (London: Harrap, 1971);

The Parsley Annuals, 2 volumes (London: BBC, 1971, 1972);

The Tales of Olga da Polga (London: Penguin, 1971; New York: Macmillan, 1973);

Parsley the Lion (London: Collins, 1972);

Parsley Parade (London: Collins, 1972);

Paddington Bear (London: Collins, 1972; New York: Random House, 1973);

Michael Bond

Paddington's Garden (London: Collins, 1972; New York: Random House, 1973);

The Day the Animals Went on Strike (London: Studio Vista, 1972; New York: American Heritage Publishing, 1973);

Olga Meets Her Match (London: Longman, 1973; New York: Hastings House, 1975);

Paddington at the Circus (London: Collins, 1973; New York: Random House, 1974);

Paddington Goes Shopping (London: Collins, 1973; New York & London: HarperCollins, 1992);

revised as *Paddington's Lucky Day* (New York: Random House, 1974);

The Adventures of a Bear Called Paddington, by Bond and Alfred Bradley (London: French, 1974);

Paddington on Stage, by Bond and Bradley (London: Collins, 1974; Boston: Houghton Mifflin, 1977);

Paddington on Top (London: Collins, 1974; Boston: Houghton Mifflin, 1975);

Paddington's Blue Peter Story Book (London: Collins, 1974); revised as *Paddington Takes to T.V.* (Boston: Houghton Mifflin, 1974);

How to Make Flying Things (London: Studio Vista, 1975);

Mr. Cram's Magic Bubbles (London: Penguin, 1975);

Windmill (London: Studio Vista, 1975);

Paddington at the Seaside (London: Collins, 1975; New York: Random House, 1978);

Paddington at the Tower (London: Collins, 1975; New York: Random House, 1978);

Olga Carries On (London: Kestrel, 1976; New York: Hastings House, 1977);

Paddington at the Station (London: Collins, 1976; New York: Carnival, 1992);

Paddington's Loose-End Book: An ABC of Things to Do (London: Collins, 1976);

Paddington's Party Book (London: Collins, 1976);

Paddington Takes a Bath (London: Collins, 1976; New York & London: HarperCollins, 1992; New York: Carnival, 1992);

Paddington Goes to the Sales (London: Collins, 1976; New York: Carnival, 1992);

Paddington's New Room (London: Collins, 1976; New York: Carnival, 1992);

The Great Big Paddington Book (London: Collins, 1976; Cleveland: Collins World, 1977);

Fun and Games with Paddington (London: Collins, 1977; Cleveland: Collins World, 1978);

Paddington Does It Himself (London: Collins, 1977; New York: Carnival, 1989);

Paddington Hits Out (London: Collins, 1977; New York: Carnival, 1989);

Paddington in the Kitchen (London: Collins, 1977, 1988; New York: Carnival, 1989);

Paddington's Birthday Party (London: Collins, 1977, 1988; New York: Carnival, 1989);

Paddington's Pastime, 4 volumes (London: Collins, 1977);

Paddington's Pop-Up Book (London: Collins, 1977);

Paddington's Picture Book (London: Collins, 1978);

Paddington Takes the Test (London: Collins, 1979; Boston: Houghton Mifflin, 1980);

J. D. Polson and the Liberty Head Dime (London: Octopus, 1980; New York: Mayflower, 1980);

Paddington in Touch (London: Collins, 1980; New York: Carnival, 1989);

Paddington and Aunt Lucy (London: Collins, 1980; New York: Carnival, 1989);

Paddington Weighs In (London: Collins, 1980; New York: Carnival, 1989);

Paddington at Home (London: Collins, 1980);

Paddington Goes Out (London: Collins, 1980);

J. D. Polson and the Dillgate Affair (London: Hodder & Stoughton, 1981);

Paddington on Screen: A Second Blue Peter Storybook (London: Collins, 1981; Boston: Houghton Mifflin, 1982);

J. D. Polson and the Great Unveiling (London: Hodder & Stoughton, 1982);

Olga Takes Charge (London: Kestrel, 1983; New York: Dell, 1983);

Paddington's Suitcase (London: Collins, 1983);

The Caravan Puppets (London: Collins, 1983);

Paddington's Storybook (London: Collins, 1983; Boston: Houghton Mifflin, 1984);

Paddington on the River (London: Collins, 1983; New York: Carnival, 1989);

Monsieur Pamplemousse (London: Hodder & Stoughton, 1983; New York: Beaufort, 1985);

Monsieur Pamplemousse and the Secret Mission (London: Hodder & Stoughton, 1984; New York: Beaufort, 1986);

Paddington and the Knickerbocker Rainbow (London: Collins, 1984; New York: Putnam, 1985);

Paddington at the Zoo (London: Collins, 1984; New York: Putnam, 1985);

Paddington at the Fair (London: Collins, 1985; New York: Putnam, 1986);

Paddington's Painting Exhibition (London: Collins, 1985); revised as *Paddington's Art Exhibition* (New York: Putnam, 1986);

Monsieur Pamplemousse on the Spot (London: Hodder & Stoughton, 1986; New York: Beaufort, 1986);

Paddington at the Palace (London: Collins, 1986; New York: Putnam, 1986);

Paddington Minds the House (London: Collins, 1986; revised as *Paddington Cleans Up* (New York: Putnam, 1986);

Paddington Posts a Letter, by Bond and Karen Bond (London: Hutchinson, 1986); revised as *Paddington Mails a Letter* (New York: Macmillan, 1986);

Paddington's Clock Book, by Bond and Karen Bond (London: Hutchinson, 1986; New York: Macmillan, 1986);

Paddington at the Airport, by Bond and Karen Bond (London: Hutchinson, 1986; New York: Macmillan, 1986);

One of Peggy Fortnum's illustrations for Paddington at Large *(1962), in which Bond's best-known character travels to France*

On Four Wheels: Paddington's London, by Bond and Karen Bond (London: Hutchinson, 1986); revised as *Paddington's Wheel Book* (New York: Macmillan, 1986);

Oliver the Greedy Elephant, by Bond and Paul Parnes (London: Golden Books, 1986);

Trouble at the Airport (New York: Caedmon, 1986);

Paddington and the Marmalade Maze (London: Collins, 1987);

Paddington's Busy Day (London: Collins, 1987);

Monsieur Pamplemousse Takes the Cure (London: Hodder & Stoughton, 1987; New York: Random House, 1988);

The Pleasure of Paris (London: Pavilion, 1987; New York: Potter, 1988);

The Life and Times of Paddington Bear, by Bond and Russell Ash (London: Pavilion, 1988);

Paddington's Magical Christmas (London: Collins, 1988; New York: Picture Lions, 1988);

A Mouse Called Thursday (London: Chancellor, 1988);

Monsieur Pamplemousse Aloft (London: Hodder & Stoughton, 1989; New York: Fawcett Columbine, 1989);

The Giant Paddington Storybook (New York: Gallery Books, 1989);

Monsieur Pamplemousse Investigates (London: Hodder & Stoughton, 1990; New York: Fawcett Columbine, 1990);

Paddington's ABC (London: Collins, 1990; New York: Viking, 1991);

Paddington's 123 (London: Collins, 1990; New York: Viking, 1991);

Paddington Meets the Queen (London: Collins, 1991; New York: Harper, 1993);

Paddington Rides On (New York: Carnival, 1991);

Paddington's Colors (New York: Viking, 1991);

Monsieur Pamplemousse Rests His Case (London: Headline, 1991; New York: Fawcett Columbine, 1991);

Paddington's Opposites (New York: Viking, 1991; London: Picture Lions, 1992);

Paddington's Colours (New York: Picture Lions, 1992);

Paddington Has a Bath (New York & London: Harper-
Collins, 1992);

Paddington Breaks the Peace (London: Young Lions,
1992);

A Day by the Sea (London: Young Lions, 1992);

Jar of Jokes (New York: Carnival, 1992);

Michael Bond's Book of Bears (New York: Aladdin
Books, 1992);

Something Nasty in the Kitchen (London: Young Lions,
1992);

Paddington's Things I Do (New York: Harper Festival,
1994);

Paddington's Things I Feel (New York: Harper Festival,
1994).

OTHER: *Michael Bond's Book of Bears,* edited by
Bond (London: Purnell, 1971);

Michael Bond's Book of Mice, edited by Bond (London:
Purcell, 1972);

H. G. Fischer-Tschop and Barbara von Johnson,
The Motormalgamation, translated by Bond and
Eve Barwell (London: Studio Vista, 1973).

Thomas Michael Bond, creator of one of the
world's most recognizable fictional characters, Paddington Bear, continues to delight his fans in Great
Britain, the United States, Canada, Denmark, Swe-
den, Holland, Germany, Italy, Israel, and Japan with
the adventures of the inimitable Paddington Bear. His
books about an orphan mouse named Thursday,
Parsley the Lion and other animals with herb names,
a precocious guinea pig Olga da Polga, and J. D. Polson, an armadillo from the United States, further cement this author's hold on the imaginations of children throughout the world. In addition, Bond has
written television and radio plays produced in Great
Britain, the United States, Canada, South Africa, Holland, Hong Kong, Italy, and Ceylon. But by far the
most successful and recognizable of his stories are
those about the bear from "darkest Peru," the bear
discovered by the Brown family at Paddington Station, the bear that can get himself into and out of the
most trouble imaginable: Paddington Bear.

Michael Bond was born on 13 January 1926,
in Newbury, Berkshire, England. He is the son of
Norman Robert Bond, a civil servant, and Frances
Mary (Offer) Bond. He married Brenda Mary Johnson on 29 June 1950; the couple divorced in 1981,
and Bond married Susan Marfrey Rogers in 1982.
There are two children, Karen Mary (Jankel) and
Anthony Thomas. Bond was educated at Presentation College, Reading. He served as a navigator in
the Royal Air Force in 1943 and 1944 but, because
of extreme air sickness, was allowed to transfer to

the army, where he served with the Middlesex Regiment from 1944 to 1947. Bond worked for the British Broadcasting Corporation (BBC) as an engineer's assistant (1941–1943), worked after the war
with a monitoring service (1947–1950), and served
as a television cameraman with the BBC from 1950
to 1965. Since 1966 he has been a full-time writer
and serves as director of Paddington Productions,
Limited.

According to the author, *A Bear Called Paddington* (1958), the first of the Paddington stories, was
written in a ten-day period after the purchase of a
stuffed toy bear on Christmas Eve as a gift for his
wife. The story introduces the Brown family –
Mother, Father, Jonathan, and Judy – as well as the
bear, named Paddington after the station in which
the Browns find him. Later at the Browns' home,
Paddington is introduced to Mrs. Bird, the housekeeper who is not quite as fond of the bear as the
Browns; Mr. Gruber, the keeper of the antique
shop, who, like Paddington, is originally from a distant land; and Mr. Curry, the next-door neighbor
who serves as a foil for Paddington. The duffle coat
that Paddington wears was in fashion at the time of
his creation, and his hat is similar to one the author
wore. The addition of boots to Paddington's wardrobe came later. Peggy Fortnum's illustrations capture the spirit of Paddington even in the initial
drafts, and her work provides the definitive image
of Paddington for many readers.

Bond had originally intended the bear to be
from "darkest Africa" until he discovered that there
were no bears there; research revealed that Peru
was an exotic locale with native bears, so that became Paddington's birth place. Paddington's Aunt
Lucy from "darkest Peru" had prepared the young
bear well for his travels across the ocean and future
relationships with those whom he meets, and he regularly sends post cards, presents, and letters to the
home for retired bears in Lima, Peru, where his
Aunt Lucy resides. Although Paddington does not
actively seek trouble in his new home, trouble
seems to attach itself to whatever project he pursues. His near disasters usually turn out positively
in the end, however, as evidenced by his painting
and wallpapering project in *More About Paddington*
(1959). Even though the paint is spilled all over the
floor and smeared over the window and wallpaper
covers the door blocking any escape, Mr. Brown
and the rest of the family are relieved since a professional will have to be brought in, freeing Mr. Brown
from having to do the job himself.

After the success of the first book, Bond wrote
a book a year for six years, then for a time he

Olga da Polga, the guinea-pig protagonist of Bond's Olga Carries On *(1976); illustration by Hans Helweg*

slowed down to one book every two years. *More About Paddington* further reveals the nature of Paddington and his relationships with his friends. The bear purchases an antique camera for three and sixpence at a sale at the market, makes a family portrait that is somewhat blurred, but gets free pictures of the entire Brown family at the camera shop by agreeing to let the proprietors borrow his camera and photograph for display in their historical exhibit. In another episode Paddington plays detective and tries to catch the thief who has stolen Mr. Brown's best marrow from the garden, but all he succeeds in catching is a policeman. It is revealed, however, that Mrs. Brown had cut the prize marrow by mistake and served it for dinner the previous night. Finally, when Paddington becomes ill after playing in the snow, his friends all come to visit. Mrs. Bird, who has become one of the bear's staunchest defenders, moves into his room in case he needs anything during the night, and even Mr. Curry, who often takes advantage of the friendly and accommodating young bear, brings Paddington an apple and a jar of calves' foot jelly.

The success of the first few Paddington books enabled Bond, beginning in 1966, to devote his full time and energies to writing, and in *Paddington Goes to Town* (1968) the bear's misadventures continue. A bride and groom invite Paddington to be an usher in their wedding. He is not supposed to have anything to do with the wedding ring, but hearing the groom promise to give a "ring" (telephone call) to Mrs. Brown, Paddington slips it on his finger to save the groom the trouble of delivering it. Part of the Paddington books' appeal to young readers is in the humor derived from such misunderstood messages and confused vocabulary. Several golf-related examples in another episode of *Paddington Goes to Town* include Paddington's confusion over the phrase "address the ball" and the word *stance,* which he mishears as *stamps,* as well as the homonyms *tea* and *tee.*

In *Paddington Takes the Air* (1970), after an encounter with a particularly sticky batch of Paddington's homemade toffee, it becomes necessary for the bear to visit a dentist. The author is careful to point out that Paddington gets treatment as a pri-

Paddington Bear as he appeared in the 1981 television adaptation of Bond's work

vate patient, since he is not on the National Health Plan. The book is partly intended to lessen young readers' anxieties about visits to a dentist. The bear's assumption that the dentist will be joining him in receiving an injection, since the dentist uses the pronoun *we* in announcing the procedure, is hilarious for some younger readers. Additional broad humor is added when the dentist places a cardboard wedge between Paddington's teeth and tells him to bite hard. Paddington obeys – while the dentist's hand is still in his mouth. In the end the new gold tooth that Paddington is to receive more than compensates for the trouble that he has undergone in this adventure. Humor for the more experienced reader is provided by Carlton Dale, Paddington's favorite detective, a parodic version of Sherlock Holmes; Duncan Hyde, a food critic who awards different shaped hats to restaurants after sampling their offerings; and Alf Weidersein, an orchestra leader who plays for the dance contest in which Paddington is entered.

Assigning Paddington responsibility for reading the maps and planning the itinerary for the Browns' trip to France would seem to be a recipe

for disaster in *Paddington Abroad* (1961). The family does in fact become hopelessly lost on their first day in France, but, while searching for firewood, Paddington finds a remote seaside village with people who welcome the vacationing English folk with open arms and help to create the perfect holiday. The members of the Brown family get to participate in the local festivities and are practically adopted by the citizens of the isolated French village in which they have landed. In *Paddington on Top* (1974), *Paddington Takes the Test* (1979), and *Paddington on the River* (1983) the bumbling efforts of the hero to learn, to help, to earn, and to live continue to get him into trouble. Well-meaning intentions go hilariously wrong, but beguiling innocence and dauntless enthusiasm always save the day.

More than thirty years after the bear's first introduction, Paddington books continue to appear in bookstores and libraries throughout the world and have been translated into more than twenty different languages. The concept books *Paddington's Things I Do* (1994) and *Paddington's Things I Feel* (1994) present colorful pictures in connection with simplified vocabulary to teach and entertain young children.

While the Paddington books were becoming more and more successful, Bond began a separate series abut Olga da Polga, a vain but loquacious guinea pig. These books have not attained the popularity of the Paddington books. It has been suggested by some critics that none of Bond's other animal characters exhibit the universal appeal of Paddington because they retain too many of the natural characteristics of the animals on which the stories were based. Nevertheless, Olga da Polga is a fascinating character and the plot structures of the stories are appealing. Pet owners everywhere recognize elements of themselves in the relationships between Olga and her "sawdust people," as she calls her owners. The irrepressible Olga compensates for her limited contacts with the outside world by making up fantastic tales about how guinea pigs lost their tails and why they have such beautiful eyes. Her tales are immensely entertaining for the other animals in her world such as Noel, the cat; Fangio, a hedgehog; and Graham, the tortoise. Olga has limited reading and writing skills. She succeeds in writing her name in the sawdust at the bottom of her hutch when the family is discussing giving her another name, but in her excitement she tramples the writing before anyone but the child, Karen, can see it. Olga had bragged that she would go places when she was in the pet shop, but she is not very adventurous when she gets out in the world. Her one venture into the outside world – to visit the Elysian

Fields that Fangio has told her about – ends in near disaster when thorns and brambles tangle her beautiful fur and a sudden rainstorm splashes cold water on the outing. Afterward both Olga and the the sawdust people make sure that her wire cage has no gaps underneath it when it is placed in the yard.

In 1966 *Here Comes Thursday,* the story of a mouse from a big family, was published. It was followed by three more Thursday books, *Thursday Rides Again* (1968), *Thursday Ahoy!* (1969), and *Thursday in Paris* (1971). Bond visited Paris and examined the pneumatic system of the post office there in preparation for the story of the mice preparing to send high explosives through a similar system designed for sending messages. This attention to detail is characteristic of the author, and the plots of some of these stories anticipate the action in Bond's adult mysteries featuring Monseiur Pamplemousse. Bond has suggested that the plots of the Thursday books may have been too complex and that the appeal of mice may not be quite as universal as that of bears as possible explanations for the limited popularity of the series.

The Parsley series (*Parsley's Parade* and *Parsley the Lion,* 1972) resulted from the author's daydreaming about the resemblance of Parsley to a lion's mane. A representative from the BBC happened to call at that moment to ask for ideas for a television series. It was decided to do the film version in "stop/start animation," and the series *The Herbs,* about the lion, Parsley, was created. Shortly afterwards the idea of doing a Paddington series was suggested; a pilot was done; thirty-two five-minute films were done with Paddington as the hero, and Parsley was largely forgotten.

Bond also wrote three J. D. Polson books. The author chose an armadillo as the leading character for this series and, since the armadillo is an American animal, the stories were set in America. It was the author's intention to do a picture book for young children with something different on every page, but apparently the stories were a bit too sophisticated for the audience and the series was dropped. According to the author, he has no intention of doing more books in this series.

Monseiur Pamplemousse, the first of Bond's series of books written for adults about a French detective formerly with the Surete, was published in 1983. The series continues to be extremely popular, especially in the United States. The author obviously likes the wider range of language and subject matter allowed in the adult books. Bond's output of both

adult and children's books shows no signs of slackening. The Paddington series and its many commercial spinoffs continue to please children who are just discovering the pleasures of being able to read longer books.

Some of the adaptations, spinoffs, and modifications of the original Paddington stories have been criticized as oversimplifications, however. Many critics would have readers wait until they are old enough to enjoy the full, original versions. Katherine Heylman has suggested that Paddington is poorly served and actually misrepresented by short retellings of his arrival at Paddington Station and subsequent adoption by the Brown family. She concludes that the simplified vocabulary loses too much of the flavor of the original stories, while the retellings are still too difficult to be classified as easy reading. On the other hand, Barbara Dill concludes that the simplified texts aimed at the kindergarten to second-grade audience are similar to the originals intended for older audiences.

Most critics agree, however, that to think of Michael Bond is to think of Paddington Bear. Many hypotheses have been offered to explain the immense popularity of the character. Some have suggested that the serendipitous selection of a small bear to be the main character in the stories is responsible for their success, since most children love bears, whether they be teddies or live bears. Paddington behaves more like a child than a bear, however, and is viewed by the Browns and most of their friends as a regular member of the family. By contrast, Olga da Polga, Parsley, Thursday, and J. D. Polson can never match the general appeal of Paddington Bear. Only Paddington transcends the animal realm to become a functioning, loving member of the family.

Interview:

Cornelia Jones and Olivia R. Way, "Michael Bond," in their *British Children's Authors: Interviews at Home* (Chicago: American Literary Association, 1976), pp. 49–54.

References:

Barbara Dill, "Picturely Books for Children," *Wilson Library Bulletin,* 48 (January 1974): 380–381;

Pico Iyer, "A Rare Bear," *Village Voice,* 16 July 1985;

Anne Royall Newman, "Images of the Bear in Children's Literature," *Children's Literature in Education,* 18, no. 3 (1987): 131–138.

Lucy M. Boston

(10 December 1892 – 30 July 1990)

Jon C. Stott
University of Alberta

BOOKS: *Yew Hall* (London: Faber & Faber, 1954);

The Children of Green Knowe, illustrated by Peter Boston (London: Faber & Faber, 1954; New York: Harcourt, Brace, 1955);

The Chimneys of Green Knowe, illustrated by Peter Boston (London: Faber & Faber, 1958); republished as *Treasure of Green Knowe* (New York: Harcourt, Brace, 1958);

The River at Green Knowe, illustrated by Peter Boston (London: Faber & Faber, 1959; New York: Harcourt, Brace, 1959);

A Stranger at Green Knowe, illustrated by Peter Boston (London: Faber & Faber, 1961; New York: Harcourt, Brace, 1961);

An Enemy at Green Knowe, illustrated by Peter Boston (London: Faber & Faber, 1964; New York: Harcourt, Brace, 1964);

The Castle of Yew, illustrated by Marjery Gill (London: Bodley Head, 1965; New York: Harcourt, Brace, 1965);

The Sea Egg, illustrated by Peter Boston (London: Faber & Faber, 1967; New York: Harcourt, Brace, 1967);

The House that Grew, illustrated by Caroline Hemming (London: Faber & Faber, 1969);

Persephone (London: Collins, 1969); republished as *Strongholds* (New York: Harcourt, Brace, 1969);

The Horned Man; or, Whom Will You Send to Fetch Her Away? (London: Faber & Faber, 1970);

Nothing Said, illustrated by Peter Boston (London: Faber & Faber, 1971; New York: Harcourt, Brace, 1971);

Memory in a House (London: Bodley Head, 1973; New York: Macmillan, 1974);

The Fossil Snake, illustrated by Peter Boston (London: Bodley Head, 1973; New York: Atheneum, 1976);

The Guardians of the House, illustrated by Peter Boston (London: Faber & Faber, 1974; New York: Atheneum, 1975);

Lucy M. Boston

The Stones of Green Knowe, illustrated by Peter Boston (London: Bodley Head, 1976; New York: Atheneum, 1976);

Perverse and Foolish: a Memoir of Childhood and Youth (London: Bodley Head, 1979; New York: Atheneum, 1979).

Edition: *Memories: Incorporating* Perverse and Foolish *and* Memory in a House (Hemingford Grey: Colt, 1992).

PERIODICAL PUBLICATIONS: "Christmas at 'Green Knowe,' " *Horn Book,* 31 (December 1955): 471–473;

"A Message from Green Knowe," *Horn Book,* 39 (June 1963): 259–264.

Lucy M. Boston is one of the most remarkable children's writers of the twentieth century. In 1954, when she was sixty-two, she published *Yew Hall,* a realistic novel for adults, and *The Children of Green Knowe,* a fantasy for children. Unlike such well-known British children's writers as Kenneth Grahame or her contemporary Mary Norton, she did not draw on memories of the people, places, or events of her childhood for her children's books. Instead, she used the Manor at Hemingford Grey, a place she had purchased as a middle-aged divorcée with a grown son, as her principal setting, and cast herself, fictionally altered, as the central adult character of the book, Great-grandmother Oldknow. When Boston wrote *The Children of Green Knowe,* she had no intention of creating more stories about the house. However, during the next twenty-two years she wrote five other novels about Green Knowe, establishing a reputation as one of the major twentieth-century authors of children's literature.

Born on 10 December 1892 at Southport, Lancashire, England, the fifth of six children of James and Mary Wood, Lucy Maria Wood was raised in what she later called a "rigidly, rabidly puritanical" Wesleyan home. After her father's death when she was six, Wood discovered that "landscape was what moved me most. A few years later I knew it as both my anchorage and my motive force." At a boarding school in Sussex she and her sister were often ridiculed for their northern accents and felt isolated and different. After attending finishing school in Paris and studying at Somerville College, Oxford, she worked as a nurse's aide in Paris during World War I. In 1917 she married Harold Boston, a cousin who was frowned on by members of her family.

Lucy Boston's admitted fondness for her father, the marked distance between the children and the parents in her family, and the sense of loneliness she and her sister felt at boarding school must certainly have gone into her portrayal of many of her fictional characters. Certainly the characters' love of the landscape and river at Green Knowe, as well as the importance of flowers to Mrs. Oldknow, have their genesis in the author's childhood responses to her environment. The encroachments of the modern world into the idyllic landscape of Green Knowe in the author's later novels may in part find their source in Boston's memories of the urban dullness of Southport.

Boston publicly said little about her marriage, which lasted from 1917 to 1935. The couple had one son, Peter, who was to become the illustrator of all but two of her children's books and a model for Tolly, a character in the Green Knowe series. The family lived in the industrial north, where the increasing air pollution appalled Boston. In the darkening years before World War II, she traveled to Europe hoping to become a painter, but she returned to England, settling in a flat in Cambridge.

In 1939 Boston purchased the Manor, a twelfth-century Norman house in Hemingford Grey, Huntingdonshire, west of Cambridge, where she was to spend the rest of her life and where she died on 30 July 1990. Her life there can be divided into three periods: from 1939 to 1954, during which time she restored the house and offered it as a kind of sanctuary to soldiers during World War II and afterward to other displaced persons; from 1954 to 1976, when she created an imaginative history for the house in an autobiography, two adult novels, and ten children's novels; and from 1977 to 1990, when she spent much of the time in a pessimistic and embattled defense against the encroachments of the industrial, urban world. Boston wrote that moving to the Manor "was like falling in love" and that "I have never wanted to be anywhere else. I hardly leave it for a day." She asserted that "one place closely examined will yield more than continents passed through."

Boston's activities during the early years at the Manor found their way into her novels. "As I dug into the house, finding signs of its great antiquity, I was so full of it that I wanted badly to tell its story." Fear that it might be in danger from the advances of the modern world contributed to her desire to write about it: "My passionate desire that it should have a future made me provide it in the books with such a firm lineage." And, when she found herself living in it alone, "To fill it for myself, I invented Tolly and his friends." The Manor's original appearance is described in *The Stones of Green Knowe* (1976), and its seventeenth- and early-nineteenth-century forms are depicted in *The Children of Green Knowe* and *The Chimneys of Green Knowe* (1958), respectively. The author's own roses and topiary figures are found in many of the books; Tolly's dog, Orlando, is Boston's terrier; and many of the ornaments of Green Knowe are based on those she bought for her own home. Her gardener, Bloomfield, was the model for Mrs. Oldknow's gardener, Boggis.

With the 1954 publication of *Yew Hall* and *The Children of Green Knowe,* Boston began transforming her life at Hemingford Grey into art. The former

Boston at age two

had been written much earlier and, Boston claimed, was kept hidden. The latter, written while the author searched for a publisher for *Yew Hall,* was classified as a children's book because it contains illustrations. Both are set in the fictionalized versions of the Manor, and both involve displaced people coming to live with the aging owner of the house. In tone and subject matter, however, they are very different.

The Children of Green Knowe is the story of seven-year-old Toseland or Tolly, who, traveling by train to spend Christmas with a great-grandmother he has never met, "wished he had a family like other people — brothers and sisters, even if his father were away." Like Mary Lennox in Frances Hodgson Burnett's *The Secret Garden* (1911), Tolly finds a home early in the novel and, during the rest of the story, proves himself worthy of it. At the conclusion he has found siblings. However, *The Children of Green Knowe* is no mere mid-century repetition of a

stock theme of Edwardian children's literature. How a lonely little boy becomes one of the home's children is told with great originality, challenging complexity, and technical dexterity.

The novel takes place during twelve days, concluding with Christmas, on which Tolly finally sees Feste, the black stallion that belonged to Toby, his much-admired seventeenth-century ancestor. This sighting completes Tolly's initiation into the world of Green Knowe, a process that begins almost at the moment he arrives, when his great-grandmother Oldknow says to him: "So you've come back!" The resemblance to his grandfather, whose nickname, "Tolly," she bestows on the boy, suggests that he is beginning to assume his place within the continuity of generations that characterizes the house. Before falling asleep he asks if other children are sometimes there, and the next day he sees a portrait of his seventeenth-century ancestors, Toby, Alexander, and Linnet, as well as their mother and their grandmother. Tolly moves from pretend to actual contact with his ancestors, thus becoming part of their family and a member of the eternal community of the house. During the narrative he finds the physical objects they were holding in the painting; learns about the three children through four stories told by his great-grandmother; hears, glimpses, and then meets them; and finally becomes a member of their circle.

Before revealing themselves to him, Tolly's ancestors both tease and test him. He hears their laughter, whistles, and whispers; feels their hands covering his eyes; and sees a marble roll across the floor. Because he has been kind to a chaffinch that lives in Linnet's wicker cage, the bird (in a scene reminiscent of *The Secret Garden*) leads him to the key for a wooden chest, which contains the objects in the portrait. He first glimpses Alexander and Linnet on the fourth day but does not meet them until the sixth, after he has opened the chest and learned from Mrs. Oldknow that the three children had died in the plague. He is devastated by the information, until the old lady states that they had merely passed from one state of being in the house to another. Tolly thus learns not only about the reality of death, but also about the existence of the timeless, eternal realm of Green Knowe.

Tolly meets Toby, Alexander, and Linnet after the first heavy snowfall of the season when "the world was almost magical" and when, "with everything unrecognizable, it was quite hard to know where he was." He sees them sitting beneath a yew tree surrounded by wild animals, all listening to Alexander playing the flute (in another scene similar to *The Secret Garden*). They look at but do not address him. After a screeching peacock causes them to disappear, Tolly feels bewildered, wondering if he has been dreaming, and makes his uncertain way back to the house and the comfortable reality of his great-grandmother. Later, as she gives Tolly a lesson on the old flute they had discovered, she tells him: "I think Alexander has given you his flute." Although they have yet to speak to Tolly, they have accepted him.

They do talk to him the next morning, telling him about the insignificance of their deaths by the plague, confirming Alexander's gift of the flute, and, most significant, warning him about the dangers of Green Noah, an overgrown topiary figure in the garden said to bear an evil curse. Toby and Alexander explain that, although they are safe from the figure, Tolly is not. His future development will depend partly on how he responds to the figure and the warning. He is disconsolate when the children

again disappear: immature and lonely, he wants them around all the time and does not understand that they have their own lives and that he must develop his inner resources. However, he does find some consolation when he discovers another object from the painting, Linnet's bracelet, which he gives to Mrs. Oldknow. Another link between past and present has been forged.

Looking at the topiary figure the next day, Tolly is terrified and runs in panic; during the afternoon he reads an article about its curse. However, the following day, ignoring warnings, he dances around the figure, taunting it with a saucy rhyme he learned from Linnet. That night, outside alone during an electrical storm, Tolly becomes lost in the garden and, as the lightning flashes, sees Green Noah lurching toward him. The voices of Alexander, Toby, and Linnet call out, imploring the aid of Saint Christopher, and a bolt of lightning destroys the tree. The first of many evil forces to threaten the house has been defeated.

In the following days Tolly acts unselfishly, searching for the ideal gift for Mrs. Oldknow and acquiring gifts for his ancestors and the many animals — past and present — that live at Green Knowe. As he dozes during Christmas Mass, he sees the past and present coalesce as the seventeenth-century Oldknow family enters the church. On Christmas morning he discovers Toby's jacket in his bedroom and, putting it on, rushes to the old stables where he sees the ghost of the horse Feste. Tolly has "gained a new confidence, perhaps because he was wearing Toby's coat," and he no longer needs his ancestors' constant presence.

Although most of Tolly's major experiences take place in her absence, Mrs. Oldknow plays an important role in the boy's growth. As a young orphan she had gone through similar experiences and is aware that others before her had too. She uses this knowledge to help Tolly help himself. On his arrival she had seen in him the potential ability to respond to and become a part of the house. Early in the novel she tells the old gardener, Boggis, "Yes, he seems to belong here. . . . He has it all hidden in him somewhere. I like to see him finding his way about." In many ways she is like the fairy godmother of folktales or the archetypal crone — the wise old woman — found in many societies, carefully and gently using her experience and wisdom to assist a young person in discovering for himself his own identity and place of belonging.

Mrs. Oldknow plays a direct role, however, in one aspect of Tolly's development, telling him stories about a past that he did not know existed. From a vast knowledge of the Oldknow history, she picks those stories that will be most valuable to the boy and tells them at just the right time. Her story of Toby's nighttime ride to seek medical help for his sister introduces Tolly to a strong, courageous, and caring older-brother figure and stresses the importance of consideration and respect for animals. Linnet's Christmas Eve vision of Saint Christopher prepares him for the powers of goodness that will oppose the evil forces seeking to hurt the family. The tale Mrs. Oldknow tells of an encounter between the horse thief Black Ferdie and the ghost of Feste emphasizes the dangers of approaching the past with the wrong attitudes. Finally, her account of Alexander's successful musical performance before Charles II alerts Tolly to the potentials each person has within. Like all good teachers and guiders of the young, Mrs. Oldknow does not impose her beliefs on Tolly; instead, she lets him arrive at his own conclusions.

Yew Hall, intended for adult readers, also deals with relationships between people without permanent homes and the old woman owner of the home at which they arrive. Their characters, as was the case with Tolly, are revealed partly by their responses to the new environment in which they find themselves. Mark and Arabella have come to Yew Hall during the housing shortage following World War II. He develops a fondness for the ancient hall and the gardens; she is bored and at times contemptuous. They are visited by Roger, an actor and Mark's twin, toward whom Arabella reveals a love-hate attitude. She is murdered by Roger, who then commits suicide. The story is narrated by the unnamed owner of the house, who, after the violent events, finds consolation in the enduring and restorative powers of her home.

In addition to what might be called its adult subject matter, *Yew Hall* differs from *The Children of Green Knowe* in its narrative point of view. While the latter uses a third-person narrator whose major focus is on Tolly, the former is as much about the narrator's responses to her tenants, their actions, and their attitudes to her home. In addition, *Yew Hall* includes many passages, often several pages in length, describing the house and garden and the owner's activities in them. The result is a meditation about what Boston seems to consider universal human passions – she remarks, "It seems reasonable to suppose that in such a length of time some version of every possible passion good and bad will have played itself out here" – and a celebration of the goodness of the narrator's home. By contrast, character, not theme and panegyric, is the focus of

The Children of Green Knowe. Boston seems to be more successful in depicting a child's affirmative response to the fictionalized version of the Manor than adults' mixed and sometimes negative ones.

The second book of the Green Knowe series appeared in 1958, four years after the first, and was followed by three more by 1964. *The Chimneys of Green Knowe,* published in the United States as *Treasure of Green Knowe* (1958), takes place a few months after Tolly's first visit (although, inexplicably, he is portrayed as being nine years old). It also opens with a description of the boy's train ride to his grandmother's home. However, the differences between his present and earlier situations and attitudes foreshadow the different role he will play in the events that follow. The once-lonely boy is excited by the familiar landmarks and thinks of his destination as a "miraculous house." As he crosses the threshold, however, his sense of joy and security is shaken: the seventeenth-century family portrait no longer hangs on the wall and may have to be sold to finance urgently needed repairs to the house. In its place is a piece of needlepoint that, as he realizes on the last day of his vacation, may provide the clue to discovering long-lost family jewels needed to save the house. The portrait is finally restored to the wall, and Tolly prepares to return to school.

During his vacation he meets more of his ancestors, early-nineteenth-century Oldknows who lived at Green Knowe when the jewels disappeared, and learns more about the house itself as he explores inside and through the gardens for the jewels. In *The Chimneys of Green Knowe* the process of Tolly's integration with the house is completed. Through an act of his own will he enters into the early nineteenth century and plays a role in the family history. He undergoes a learning, developing process before he earns the right to find the lost jewels. He learns that the house did not always look as it now does, that additions had been destroyed by fire at the start of the nineteenth century, and that jewels from that time had been lost.

A patchwork quilt (made by Tolly's grandmother from the clothes of people who lived in the nineteenth century) is used as a unifying device and symbol. As had been the case for Mrs. May in Mary Norton's *The Borrowers* (1952), the act of sorting out pieces of cloth and sewing the quilt becomes a metaphor for the restoration and re-creation of the past. Many feminist critics have used the quilting metaphor to discuss the female role as re-creator, conservator, and storyteller; the importance of storytelling as an element in the creating and defining of personal and group identity; and the function of the wise old woman, the crone, in this process. Mrs. Oldknow, as her name implies, is this kind of person. She makes Tolly an active, independent discoverer of his own identity and past, refusing to name the original wearer of a green and scarlet patch. This person is Jacob, a black slave whom Tolly desires to meet and know as he had Toby.

Although the boy's search for the treasure proves unsuccessful the next day, he makes many discoveries that prepare him for eventual success and for an encounter with the blind girl Susan. That night he hears how Susan became blind and learns of her intelligence and curiosity, as well as the adults' attempts to repress and confine her. The narrative emphasizes the importance of allowing children to learn in an atmosphere of freedom and to develop a sense of independence. Interestingly, Tolly must play one of the girl's favorite games, hide-and-seek, in his detective work, using his imaginative powers to gain insight into the mysteries of the lives of people long gone and the long-missing jewelry. Appropriately, his discoveries often take place in dark locations, places where he cannot see.

The effect of Susan's story on Tolly becomes apparent the next day, as he plays at being blind and learns of the difficulties a sightless person experiences. He has developed an empathy for another person, and he reveals qualities of character that, it will turn out, Jacob had exhibited in his relationship with Susan. Mrs. Oldknow, recognizing that he is getting closer to meeting the slave boy, tells him that he has "deserved another chapter" and tells the story of Captain Oldknow's meeting with Jacob, a displaced nine-year-old. During the next two days Tolly moves closer to the meeting. Engaging in unproductive detective work, he examines the alcove that was Jacob's room, sees a black hand emerging from the bush during his first early-morning exploration of a bamboo thicket, notices the dog carrying a strange arrow in his mouth, finds an old jackknife, and leaves a gift for Susan. In Mrs. Oldknow's stories Tolly subsequently learns about Jacob's seeing a curly-haired dog, finding the gifts he himself had left, and leaving gifts for a drowned sailor boy (who is Tolly and whom Jacob cannot see just as Tolly cannot see him). One of the stories is about Jacob's climbing up and exploring the house's many chimneys, something Tolly will finally do in his hunt for the jewels.

The meeting between the two boys occurs a few days later when, with his great-grandmother away for the day, Tolly decides to search the garden for Jacob. The situation is described in lan-

One of Peter Boston's illustrations for Lucy Boston's The River at Green Knowe *(1959), the third novel in the acclaimed Green Knowe series*

guage similar to that used in recounting Tolly's first encounter with his seventeenth-century ancestors. He seems to be leaving the ordinary world, and as he enters a dark tunnel he realizes that he has "lost his sense of time." Emerging above ground, where "everything seemed fixed in a trance of eternal sameness," he anxiously proceeds to the house, which seems to be transformed, and discovers that he is in an earlier era. There he meets Jacob, "a companion in a million," and learns from him and Susan that Fred Boggis, an ancestor of the present gardener, has been accused of poaching and is hiding in the tunnel. Selflessly, Tolly aids Boggis and, in so doing, ensures the continuity of that family into the twentieth century. That night, while listening to the next chapter of the story, Tolly excitedly interrupts his great-grandmother's narration with the statement that he was the unknown person involved in Fred's rescue. He has become a part of the story, and the story a part of him.

In the account of the final day of the vacation, all the narrative threads are tied together, and Mrs. Oldknow completes the restoration of the patchwork quilt. Realizing that the chimneys hold a clue to the lost treasure, Tolly enters the attic through

Jacob's room and engages in his most successful detective work to date, using his acquired knowledge of the house's earlier architecture to find the flue in which the jewels are hidden. As Jacob had used his awareness of the chimneys to rescue Susan from the fire, Tolly uses it to save the seventeenth-century portrait and, by extension, the house for himself, his great-grandmother, and his ancestors, who exist as what the old lady calls "others" in the house's timeless dimensions.

In addition to tracing Tolly's development as he actively learns more about the house, its environs, and its past, *The Chimneys of Green Knowe* introduces two important themes — earning the right to become a part of the home partly by protecting it from enemies, and the importance of providing children with the freedom to learn and grow — both of which are examined more fully in Boston's later books. Although many individuals enter into the world of Green Knowe, not all can achieve the sense of contentment that entry should provide. Adults do not generally respond as fully as children, and not all children respond with equal success. Mrs. Oldknow, like Boston at the Manor, understands the need for constant vigilance; she also recognizes the value of providing encouragement and support while allowing Tolly, as he had allowed Susan, to discover Green Knowe and himself freely, at his own pace and in his own way.

Critics have praised *The Chimneys of Green Knowe,* deeming it a worthy successor to and even better novel than the first book. The narration of Tolly's experiences is more closely linked to the stories the old lady tells. The historical characters, particularly Susan and Jacob, are more fully developed and concretely realized than were Toby, Alexander, and Linnet. As American fantasist Eleanor Cameron noted, Boston's handling of a fairly conventional plot — the search for lost treasure — "is shining proof that almost any idea . . . can be made the heart of an original creation in the hands of an artist."

The third novel of the series, *The River at Green Knowe* (1959), was less enthusiastically received. Neither Mrs. Oldknow nor Tolly is present, the old lady having let the house for the summer to an archaeologist, Dr. Maud Biggin, who invites three children to Green Knowe: her great-niece Ida and two displaced boys, Oskar, the orphaned son of a murdered Polish intellectual, and Ping, a Burmese refugee whose father is presumed dead. Dr. Biggin believes that the children's experiences are "too foolish to interest grown-ups," an attitude in sharp contrast to Mrs. Oldknow's view.

The trio, under Ida's direction, decides to explore the river's many islands at dawn and at night, when it possesses an aura of mystery and magic. In the early mornings they discover a derelict house, the aging, dilapidated condition of which contrasts the lovingly preserved antiquity of Green Knowe; meet a hermit who had quit his job as a London bus driver and has had a mysterious vision of prehistoric hunters; watch Oskar briefly shrink to the size of a field mouse; and befriend Terak, a giant who lives undetected in an abandoned windmill. At night they canoe to an island of winged horses who come to the children when signaled by Ping, and, in the penultimate episode, the three are transported into the distant past where people perform a ritual dance before a wattle dwelling occupying the same space as Green Knowe.

While some critics have called the novel loosely episodic, it is, in fact, tightly organized and relates to a theme explored in the first two books: the ability of children to enter into the timeless world of Green Knowe. Displaced visitors though they are, Ida, Oskar, and Ping can respond fully to the physical and magical environment. Although not portrayed in the depth that Tolly is, each is a fully realized character. Ida is in charge, organizing expeditions and directing the making of a large map depicting the islands they explore. Oskar, proud and independent, remembering the assassination of his father, sympathizes with the displaced bus driver and the giant. Ping possesses an oriental grace and charm and a mystic sensibility that seems to make him the most responsive to the nighttime enchantments. During the time they are enjoying such wonderful adventures, Dr. Biggin works on a book about the prehistoric existence of a race of giants, unable to experience the presence of the past in the contemporary environment of Green Knowe and, because of their secrecy, totally unaware that the children have been able to. Wanting Dr. Biggin to see Terak the giant, who has joined the circus as a clown after the children have helped him to experience the joy of laughter, they invite her to see him perform. However, in the face of living proof of the accuracy of her hypotheses, she pronounces him an ingenious mechanical contrivance, a fake. Oskar observes: "They don't like *now*. If it's really interesting it has to be then."

The novel presents a new dimension in Boston's ongoing fictional exploration and celebration of her home, expanding the scope, looking at the river, giving as much significance to setting as to the characters' responses to it, and extending the time frame back to prehistoric and even mythological

The Manor at Hemingford Grey, Huntingtonshire, the model for Boston's fictional Green Knowe

ages. The river is described with a lyrical clarity and preciseness reminiscent of Kenneth Grahame's depiction of the river in *The Wind in the Willows* (1908), a book Boston admired. Whereas many of the characters consider it only as a site for recreation or a place of retreat or escape, the children, exploring by day and night, discover wonders unknown to others.

A Stranger at Green Knowe (1961), the fourth book of the series, received the Carnegie Medal. The story emerged after the author had visited the London Zoo, where she felt it wicked that Guy, the mountain gorilla, was confined in so small a cage. It is also an outgrowth of Boston's alarm at the spread of industrialization and urbanization closer to her own home. The book describes the friendship of two displaced individuals: Ping, who has been invited by Mrs. Oldknow to spend a summer vacation at Green Knowe; and Hanno, the gorilla who seeks refuge there after escaping from the zoo. As in the earlier novels, its plot is constructed around two narrative lines: Ping and Hanno's stories, which converge during the final days. However, it contains neither magic nor time shifting.

Part 1 includes a description of the habitat and habits of mountain gorillas and an account of the capture of the baby Hanno. The opening sentence,

inviting the reader to "Imagine a tropical rain forest so vast you could roam in it all your life without ever finding out there was anything else," offers an implicit contrast to the diminishing wilderness around Green Knowe and provides a magnificent starting point for a journey that ends so violently for the adult Hanno on the cultivated grounds before Mrs. Oldknow's house. The young Hanno goes from an elemental, seemingly timeless environment to a sanctuary where time runs out for him and, the author implies, may be running out for Green Knowe itself. The hunt for a baby gorilla, with the relentless advance of sounds, machines, and men through the heretofore impenetrable jungle, anticipates the account of Ping's memories of the jungle wars in southeast Asia that left him as displaced as the captive gorilla. Finally, the leisurely diurnal and seasonal rhythms that govern the life of the wild gorillas contrast both the starkness of Hanno's monotonous captive life and the almost frenetic pace of the hunt at Green Knowe.

Part 2 depicts Ping's first encounter with Hanno and the tremendous impact it has on his sensitive, imaginative nature. On first seeing Hanno, Ping quickly senses the similarities in their situations and feels empathy toward the primate captive. Ping is not a captive, however; he has friends, even though they do not always understand him, and, with his quiet self-effacing manner, is not conspicuous to the human beings around him, as Hanno is. These differences are important, for they emphasize the poignancy of the relationship that develops between this modern-day Androcles and his "lion," and they help to influence the different fates for each of the characters. Hanno, who because of his size and species cannot find lasting refuge in the shrinking natural world around Green Knowe, chooses death rather than confinement in the zoo. Ping, who has contributed to the animal's "three real days" at Green Knowe, is offered a home there, a future with the promise of happiness and companionship.

In part 3 Ping goes to Green Knowe for the summer; Hanno, escaped from the zoo, travels north and hides in the thicket bounding Green Knowe; and the two other most important human beings in the animal's life, his captor and his zookeeper, converge on the area to recapture him. On the train ride to Green Knowe, one not unlike Tolly's return to his great-grandmother's, Ping, seeing a newspaper account of Hanno's escape, begins to imagine the passing scenery from the point of view of a gorilla seeking places to hide. When he first explores the thicket and hears noises in it, he again thinks imaginatively, wondering if the junglelike enclosure could possibly contain the escapee, as it does. His imaginative speculations confirm Mrs. Oldknow's belief that "events follow ideas" and that the ideas of children are more likely to be actualized than those of adults. She recognizes that Ping, like Tolly, has the qualities needed to become a part of the world of Green Knowe. Ping faces a dilemma: should he share his suspicions with Mrs. Oldknow, as his respect for her and sense of moral rightness toward his host dictates, or should he keep silent, allowing his loyalty and concern for the safety of the creature he so admires to dominate?

When, awakening from a nap in the thicket, he encounters Hanno for the second time, Ping responds with both awe and humility. Ping's inner tensions mount. How can he ensure that the gorilla will not wander from the thicket and be discovered, recaptured, or shot? Will Hanno, who seems to consider Ping a young gorilla under his protection, refuse to let him leave the thicket? To feed him, Ping must continue to keep his secret from Mrs. Oldknow; more reprehensible, he must steal food and lie to her. Although deeply troubled, Ping accepts his responsibilities and the possible consequences for him. As both his inner turmoil and the outward

heat wave increase, the danger to Hanno becomes greater. A policeman and Hanno's captor inform an outraged Mrs. Oldknow that the next morning they will enter the thicket that she calls a sanctuary to look for the fugitive. When a storm breaks with a fury like the storms of equatorial Africa, Ping's inner storm rages as he wrestles with his secret knowledge and his fear of what might happen the next day.

As he has become a little gorilla in the animal's eyes, Ping enables Hanno to become an adult leader like the father the animal had admired in the Congo. As the boy entices the gorilla to cross the moat on a fallen log bridging the thicket and the garden, he realizes that Hanno is attempting to take his "troop" to safety. The gorilla's awesome appearance at the door of Mrs. Oldknow's dining room indicates that he will not leave the dangerous environment while the safety of one of his young is in question. As his father had done to threatening animals in the jungle, Hanno kills a maddened cow as it is about to gore Ping. Moments before he is shot by his original captor, Hanno's "heart swelled with a fury that was like a great joy." Ping, exhibiting his characteristic imaginative empathy, recognizes the fulfillment Hanno briefly experienced.

As Hanno has resolved the frustrated rage and the "patient impatience" experienced during his eleven years in captivity, so Ping resolves his inner turmoil. When she sees Hanno at the door, Mrs. Oldknow now perceives the nature of the secret she has long thought he possessed, and she understands and accepts Ping's deeds and motives. The keeper tells Ping, "If you had told at the beginning, this would never have happened," but Ping's reply is that his silence had made possible Hanno's fulfillment. He knows that Hanno had chosen death over recapture.

Hanno finds fulfillment in death; Ping finds it in a new life at Green Knowe, where he is offered a permanent home. Unlike Tolly, for whom Green Knowe had been a completely new, unique landscape, Ping sees in the area many similarities to his home in Burma. His pagoda, also shaped like a boat, had a forest, much of it bamboo, close by and a river adjacent. In the house he is served tea in Chinese cups like those of his dead mother. Green Knowe is a place to which he can respond with an imaginative spirit.

The house itself assumes larger thematic importance than it had in the earlier novels. Early in part 3 Ping notices that it emanates a "feeling of love and enchantment." He believes that it is "a guardian of happiness and strange thoughts, a keeper of secrets" and confides his own secret about Hanno to its walls. Whereas Hanno had been monstrously out of place during his brief entry into the house, Ping fits in, as Mrs. Oldknow intuitively understands.

A Stranger at Green Knowe also contrasts adults' and children's attitudes to the marvelous aspects of the world in which they live. In earlier books attitudes to the house had been contrasted; in this book it is attitudes to Hanno. Ping, of course, achieves the fullest understanding of the gorilla. The zookeeper, who loves him, does not realize as much as Ping does; he has never seen Hanno away from his cage and treats him as a child. In contrast, the underkeeper views him as a dangerous, untrustworthy beast. Visitors to the zoo consider him ugly and prefer the chimpanzees. The villagers think of him as a "kind of chimp, a cannibal" or "a kind of a man." Mrs. Oldknow's visitors, whose very presence in her garden suggests that they have some sensitivity, fail to comprehend fully. Even she does not have the depth of understanding that Ping has, and in the end she learns from him. In her willingness and ability to learn from a child, she possesses something most of the other adults of the novels do not.

The threats to Green Knowe from the outside world increase in this novel. Trucks rumble across the grounds, the old lady's beloved hedge is cut away, and curious onlookers trample the lawns and flower beds. Perhaps for the first time in the history of Green Knowe, a gun is fired on the grounds, and Hanno becomes a victim of the modern world that had taken him from his rightful home. Although peace is restored, the conclusion of the book does not offer the sense of security found in the earlier volumes.

Although Boston did not respond favorably to the novel's winning the Carnegie Medal, stating that the many conditions attached to the award, such as previous winners not being eligible, diminished its significance, *A Stranger at Green Knowe* is worthy of the critical acclaim it has received. The characterization of Ping exceeds that of Boston's other characters, as the author reveals with great delicacy the full extent of his gracious, sensitive, imaginative, and courageous nature. Boston also exhibits in this book the greatest control of language found in any of her fictions. Settings are fully realized and are an integral part of plot and theme. The cement world of the London Zoo and Ping's various refugee dwellings are contrasted to the African and Burmese jungles, and the similarities and differences among all of these settings are subtly pre-

sented. In addition, Boston juxtaposes the style of direct narration and description of Hanno and his period of escape with the journalistic style of newspaper and television reports, enhancing the difference between those who know and love Hanno intimately and those who have only impersonal and distant information about him. Jasper Rose compared Boston's portrayal of Hanno to the best of D. H. Lawrence's animal poems; Peter Hollindale considered it "a work of reverence for the wonder and uniqueness of the animal creation;" and John Rowe Townsend grudgingly admitted that the book was "both audacious and successful."

The dangers to Green Knowe assume their most threatening and evil form in the fifth book of the series, *An Enemy at Green Knowe* (1964). Melanie D. Powers, a servant of the devil, launches a series of attacks against the house, seeking first to control and later to destroy it in order to gain possession of an ancient book about magical power that she believes is hidden in its walls. Tolly and Ping return to Green Knowe from a seaside vacation just in time to combat forces against which Mrs. Oldknow seems powerless.

On their first evening home, Tolly tells Ping, "The queer thing about Granny's stories . . . is that bits of them keep coming true now, although they are all so old," and, in fact, details of the story she tells that night appear in the adventures that follow. A seventeenth-century sorcerer possesses a box of snakes that may be the ancestors of those that later infest Mrs. Oldknow's house and garden; he has a great nighttime bonfire not unlike that lit by Melanie D. Powers; each of his eyes seems to move independently of the other, as do her feet; and when his evil turns upon him, his appearance alters drastically as does Powers's after her plans are thwarted. The presence of these elements implicitly emphasizes a theme seen throughout the series: that within the house and grounds basic human passions and emotions constantly recur.

One element that recurs is evil; Mrs. Oldknow explains that her home "has enemies and it needs guarding all the time," and she tells her great-grandson that she is counting on him "to be one of the stalwart guardians of the place." Set in the autumn, with a large number of scenes occurring in the evening, the novel makes it implicit that Mrs. Oldknow is conscious of her mortality. She needs Ping's assistance to resist the witch's first two direct attacks on her, and she depends on the birds and then Ping and Tolly to repulse the last four. Until alerted by the boys, she is unaware of her visitor's evil, something they had quickly perceived. In

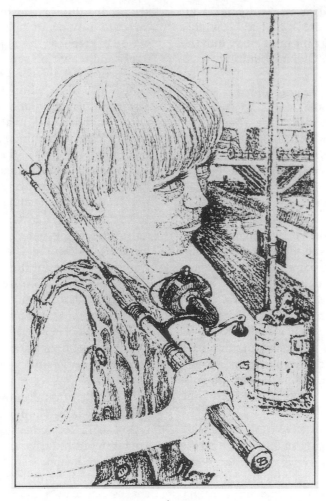

Peter Boston's illustration depicting Tom Morgan, for Lucy Boston's The Guardians of the House *(1974)*

youth lies the safety and hope for the future of Green Knowe.

It seems possible that Boston intended *An Enemy at Green Knowe* to be the last of the series. Just as she said she wrote the novels to provide her own often embattled home with a solid lineage, so Mrs. Oldknow gives Tolly a sense of his own lineage so that he can provide Green Knowe with a future. That it may have been intended as the last in the series is further suggested by the fact that the book contains more references to and parallels with actions and characters from earlier books than had any of the preceding novels. It is almost as if Boston, like the classical composers for whose works she often professed admiration, is gathering together themes and motifs as she moves toward the coda at the conclusion of the final movement of her great composition. She reexamines areas of the house, the garden, and the river that had been so important in earlier works. In order to end the cats'

attack on the birds of the garden, Ping evokes the spirit of Hanno, kneeling before the place in the garden where the gorilla had been shot. The stone statue of Saint Christopher that had protected Tolly and the house against the attack of Green Noah is, Boston implies, one of the guardians protecting house and occupants against Powers's onslaughts. Powers's letter to Mrs. Oldknow virtually inviting herself to Green Knowe is in contrast to Ida's written request that Ping be allowed to return to Green Knowe.

Critical response to *An Enemy at Green Knowe* has been divided. *The New York Times Book Review* called the plot "scrappy" and the style "precious"; and Townsend judged that the book lacked "credibility even in its own terms." However, David Rees considered the novel the best of the series, and the *Junior Bookshelf* called it the creation of "a very good writer at the height of her powers." In its presentation of the conflict between the powers of good and evil frequently found in high fantasy, *An Enemy at Green Knowe* achieves limited success, partly because the small area around the house lacks the geographical vastness and sublimity usually found in the settings of the genre and partly because Melanie D. Powers seems impertinently aggressive, devious, and mean-spirited rather than overwhelmingly evil. More successful are the loving and lyrical descriptions of the setting that evoke readers' desire for its safety. The depictions of the fragility of Mrs. Oldknow and the cleverness and pluck of Tolly and Ping are also convincing. Finally, the appearance on the last page of the fathers of Tolly and Ping creates an emotionally satisfying closure.

"Stories never really end. They can go on and on – and on: it's just that at some point or another the teller may cease to tell them." These words from the epilogue to Mary Norton's *The Borrowers Aloft* (1961) could be applied to *An Enemy at Green Knowe*. In 1964 it appeared that Boston had finished the story, but, like Norton, she had not; both authors were to return to their respective series after many years, achieving more definite closure. Between 1964 and 1976, when *The Stones of Green Knowe* appeared, Boston wrote six shorter books for children; an adult novel, *Persephone* (1969; published in the United States as *Strongholds*); and a memoir of her years at the Manor, *Memory in a House* (1973).

Readers of the *Green Knowe* series would have found neither the plots nor the characters of Boston's shorter children's stories surprising, for they echo elements from the novels. In *The Castle of Yew* (1965) a young boy is given permission by an old lady to explore her garden. Shrinking like Oskar in *The River at Green Knowe,* he enters into a topiary castle in the garden and, like Tolly with Toby, develops a friendship with an older, more assured boy. *The Sea Egg* (1967), one of Boston's favorites and in the opinion of some critics her best story, is about two brothers who, during a seaside vacation, discover a sea egg that hatches a triton; like the children at Green Knowe, they keep their discovery a secret from adults. *The House that Grew* (1969) recounts a girl's observation of a tiny dwelling's growth into a house the size and resemblance of the Manor. *Nothing Said* (1971), which portrays the friendship between a girl and a middle-aged woman (as does *Persephone*), reconsiders the theme of unstated, shared understandings between a young person and a grown-up. The heroine, like Ping, provides temporary refuge for a displaced being, in this case a dryad whose tree home is destroyed in a storm. In *The Guardians of the House* (1974) a boy enters an old lady's property, this time

without her permission and while she is absent. Like those who approached Green Knowe without the proper attitude, he discovers that it has protectors. Tom Morgan, the central figure of *The Fossil Snake* (1973), feels alienated in the factory town to which his family has moved. A strange egg he finds hatches into a prehistoric snake that he hides for its protection; it, like Hanno, helps its benefactor in a time of great need.

If these books are grace notes to the Green Knowe series, they are, with one exception, minor ones, pleasant but relatively inconsequential variations on Boston's major themes. *The Sea Egg,* different in scope and tone from the novels, reveals new areas of Boston's talents. Townsend praised the author's celebration of the sea: "In this book, the power and beauty of Mrs. Boston's style are fully matched by the power and beauty of what she is describing." *The Sea Egg* is a mythic story, describing the sea change of those who have been enveloped by the ocean. Toby and Jo seem to their mother to have grown up at the end of the two-week holiday.

Boston's last two works, *The Stones of Green Knowe* and *Perverse and Foolish: a Memoir of Childhood and Youth* (1979), bring her literary career full circle, back to its fictional and biographical beginnings. The former is the story of a boy who is a member of the first family of Green Knowe and who has witnessed its construction; the latter is an account of the events, people, and personal responses that helped to shape the character of the mature writer.

The Stones of Green Knowe expands on an idea advanced by Mrs. Oldknow in *The Chimneys of Green Knowe,* one that echoes a line in T. S. Eliot's "East Coker" (1940): "The beginning and the end so near together like a telescope when you shut it up." Roger, the central character of the last novel of the series, visits children from the different time periods and sees the house survive various threats. Although he is watching a new house, Green Knowe, being built, Roger, an Anglo-Saxon, has a reverence for old things: "He did not need to fear things for being old. It was rather a reason for loving them." Thus, when he first sees two magic stone seats hidden in dense woods, he relates them to his wish for the new house to have a future, to become, as it were, old: "He supposed all stone was the same age, all dating back to the day of the creation when God made the earth so that really the windows of his house, though newly tooled, were as old as the Stones. They could last as long into the future as those went back into the past. He passionately wanted the new house to be there forever." Each of Roger's travels into the future is motivated by his wish to see if the house has survived, and in his trips he comprehends more fully its timeless essence. He confidently announces to his mother: "I'll always come home, always. . . . And this will always be here."

Roger's trip to the twentieth century fills him with the greatest misgivings. We are told that, "Far as he had gone into the future, except that each time more land was cultivated and new ways of building and dressing had come in, there had been nothing totally strange to him, nothing totally beyond his comprehension." In the twentieth century, however, he is appalled by "the stale dead air," misses the sounds of animals and birds, and is terrified by automobiles and airplanes. Only in the garden at Green Knowe does he feel relief: "he now felt confident again. This was his house, his land where surely he had a right to be, where he was coming to meet others who also were there by right loving it as he did. He forgot the nightmares he had on the way there. This was Green Knowe."

He meets the children and Mrs. Oldknow as a girl, who pledges: "I'll keep this house for you, Roger the First, and Tolly will do so after me." She gives him a ring that she knows will return through the ages to her. In so doing, she creates an inviolable, endless circle of time. From her present, she gives a gift to the past; Roger in his present will pass the gift on to the future. Although, at the conclusion of the novel, the stones are moved to a museum, the final note is one of confidence. The love and reverence of the children, their services to the house, and their eventual translation into "others" suggest that Green Knowe has guardians who will ensure its survival.

Although *The Stones of Green Knowe* lacks the urgency of conflict and intensity of emotion of its predecessors, it is a sensitive and thought-provoking conclusion to one of the most significant British children's fantasy series and to the author's career as a children's novelist. One reviewer dismissed it as "a fill-up in the chronicles of her house rather than a compelling novel." It is nonetheless a remarkable and remarkably wise achievement for a writer who was eighty-four at the time of its publication.

During a writing career that extended from age sixty-two to eighty-seven, Boston wrote seventeen books, including two adult novels, two autobiographies, and one play, but it is for the six volumes of the Green Knowe series — particularly *The Children of Green Knowe, The Chimneys of Green Knowe,* and *A Stranger at Green Knowe* — and to a lesser extent *The Sea Egg* that she is chiefly remembered. Her works are a part of the British tradition of children's litera-

ture and reflect genres and specific works that were popular during the "Golden Age of Children's Literature," as the period from the 1870s to the outbreak of World War I in 1914 has frequently been called. Boston does far more, however, than echo specific works or use the patterns of genres from the late Victorian and the Edwardian eras. Writing after midcentury and keenly aware of the rapid social changes and unsettling political conditions in England and abroad, her child characters use their vacations to discover their identities and to find locations where they belong. Victims of political forces or fragmented families, they find in Green Knowe escapes from modern, industrialized, urbanized England and chances to reintegrate their shattered, fragmented lives. While the term *problem novel* had not been coined when Boston began to write her children's books, they could be considered a fusion between this recent genre and the more traditional ones.

Green Knowe, the place to which the children travel and in which they thrive, has become one of the best-known and best-loved houses in children's fiction. It may be one of the most fully realized settings in children's fiction. As critics have often noted, it is more than just a locale for the events; it is almost a character in the novels: friend, confidant, protector, and teacher, accepting freely within its ancient stone walls those who come with the right spirit and who are willing to defend it against those who lack respect for or who wish to destroy it. Surrounded by a world torn apart by political, social, and religious forces, it exists in a timeless now, in which occupants from the past, the "others" as Mrs. Oldknow calls them, can interact with individuals from other past eras and the present.

The thematic aspects of the Green Knowe books will probably be of most interest to older or more sophisticated readers, but the characterizations of the children, especially Tolly, Susan, Toby, and Ping, and the relationships — between Tolly, Ping, and Mrs. Oldknow and between Ping and the gorilla, Hanno — will appeal to readers of ages eight to twelve. Like Boston, Mrs. Oldknow understands children, both their love of secrets and independent explorations and their need for secure homes and loving adults. In fact, it is probably not an exaggeration to suggest that the relationships between child and great-grandmother portrayed in the Green Knowe series are among the best to be found in twentieth-century children's literature.

Finally, it should be stated that Boston is a demanding writer, expecting of her readers an ability to engage actively with her advanced vocabulary, intricate metaphors, involved sentence structures, complex narrative patterns, and subtle themes. Her works do not fall into a formulaic pattern as do, for example, the later books of Mary Norton's Borrowers series, which appeared at roughly the same time. Readers who approached each volume of the Green Knowe series expecting a comfortable read would have been disappointed. Like the baroque and classical composers for whose music she professed admiration, Boston was a master at producing complex variations on themes. Familiar though Green Knowe becomes, each entry into a new novel about it is an adventure of creative discovery. Traveling to Green Knowe to spend a summer with Mrs. Oldknow, Ping joyously thinks, "The world was full of surprises and possibilities," and he is delighted to find that Green Knowe seems different from the year before. For the attentive, responsive, imaginative reader the same is also true of each newly encountered work of Lucy M. Boston.

Interviews:

Justin Wintle and Emma Fisher, "Lucy Boston," in their *The Pied Pipers: Interviews with the Influential Creators of Children's Literature* (New York: Two Continents, 1975), pp. 277–284;

Cornelia Jones and Olivia R. Way, "Lucy Boston," in their *British Children's Authors: Interviews at Home* (Chicago: American Library Association, 1976), pp. 55–63.

References:

Gloria Blatt, "Profile: Lucy M. Boston," *Language Arts,* 60 (February 1983): 220–225;

Diana Boston, ed., *Lucy Boston Remembered: Reminiscences Collected by Diana Boston* (Hemingford Grey: Oldknow, 1994);

Eleanor Cameron, *The Green and Burning Tree: On the Writing and Enjoyment of Children's Books* (Boston: Atlantic Monthly Press, 1969), pp. 107–118;

Peter Hollindale, "The Novels of L. M. Boston," in *Good Writers for Young Readers,* edited by Dennis Butts (Saint Albans: Hart-Davis Educational, 1977), pp. 25–33;

Hollindale, "Timescape at Hemingford Grey: Lucy Boston's Centenary," *Children's Literature,* 22 (1994): 139–148;

David Rees, "Green Thought in a Green Shade – L. M. Boston," in his *Painted Desert, Green Shade: Essays on Contemporary Writers of Fiction for Children and Young Adults* (Boston: Horn Book, 1984), pp. 1–16;

Jasper Rose, *Lucy Boston* (New York: Henry Z. Walck, 1965);

Lynne Rosenthal, "The Development of Consciousness in Lucy Boston's *The Children of Green Knowe,*" *Children's Literature,* 8 (1980): 53–67;

Jon C. Stott, "From Here to Eternity: Aspects of Pastoral in the Green Knowe Series," *Children's Literature,* 11 (1983): 145–155;

Judy Taylor, "*Memories,* by Lucy Boston," *Spectator,* 25 July 1992, p. 32;

John Rowe Townsend, "L. M. Boston," in his *A Sense of Story: Essays on Contemporary Writers for Children* (Philadelphia: Lippincott, 1971), pp. 28–38.

Hester Burton

(6 December 1913 –   )

Virginia A. Walter
University of California, Los Angeles

BOOKS: *Barbara Bodichon, 1827–1891* (London: John Murray, 1949);

The Great Gale, illustrated by Joan Kiddell-Monroe (London: Oxford University Press, 1960); republished as *The Flood at Reedsmere,* illustrated by Robin Jacques (Cleveland: World, 1968);

Castors Away!, illustrated by Victor Ambrus (London: Oxford University Press, 1962; Cleveland: World, 1963);

A Seaman at the Time of Trafalgar, illustrated by Ambrus (London: Oxford University Press, 1963);

Time of Trial, illustrated by Ambrus (London: Oxford University Press, 1963; Cleveland: World, 1964);

No Beat of Drum, illustrated by Ambrus (London: Oxford University Press, 1966; Cleveland: World, 1967);

Otmoor For Ever, illustrated by Gareth Floyd (London: Hamish Hamilton, 1968);

In Spite of All Terror, illustrated by Ambrus (London: Oxford University Press, 1968; Cleveland: World, 1969);

Through the Fire, illustrated by Floyd (London: Hamilton, 1969);

Thomas, illustrated by Ambrus (London: Oxford University Press, 1969); republished as *Beyond the Weir Bridge* (New York: Crowell, 1970);

The Henchmans at Home, illustrated by Ambrus (London: Oxford University Press, 1970; New York: Crowell, 1972); republished as *The Day That Went Terribly Wrong and Other Stories* (New York: Scholastic, 1970);

The Rebel, illustrated by Ambrus (London: Oxford University Press, 1971; New York: Crowell, 1972);

Riders of the Storm, illustrated by Ambrus (London: Oxford University Press, 1972; New York: Crowell, 1973);

Kate Rider, illustrated by Ambrus (London: Oxford University Press, 1974); republished as *Kate Ryder* (New York: Crowell, 1975);

Hester Burton

Through the Fire (Feltham: Beaver, 1976);

To Ravensrigg, illustrated by Ambrus (London: Oxford University Press, 1976; New York: Crowell, 1977);

A Grenville Goes to Sea, illustrated by Colin McNaughton (London: Heinemann, 1977);

Tim at the Fur Fort, illustrated by Ambrus (London: Hamilton, 1977);

When the Beacons Blazed, illustrated by Ambrus (London: Hamilton, 1978);

Five August Days, illustrated by Trevor Ridley (London: Oxford University Press, 1981).

OTHER: *Coleridge and the Wordsworths,* edited by Burton (London: Oxford University Press, 1953);

Tennyson, edited by Burton (London: Oxford University Press, 1954);

A Book of Modern Stories, edited by Burton (London: Oxford University Press, 1959; New York: Oxford University Press, 1972);

Her First Ball: Short Stories, edited by Burton, illustrated by Susan Einzig (London: Oxford University Press, 1959).

SELECTED PERIODICAL PUBLICATION – UNCOLLECTED: "The Writing of Historical Novels," *Horn Book,* 45 (June 1969): 271–277.

Hester Burton is known primarily for her historical novels for young people, novels that focus on the lives of everyday people involved in extraordinary events in English history. They tend to deal with themes of social justice, encouraging the reader to make connections between past and present events. All of her writing is infused with a love of England – its people, its countryside, and its values. Burton's work has been generally well received by reviewers, and she was awarded the prestigious Carnegie Medal in 1964 for *Time of Trial* (1963).

Hester Wood-Hill was born 6 December 1913 in Beccles, on the Suffolk coast of England. Her parents were Henry G. and Amy Crowfoot Wood-Hill. Her father was a family doctor who served as the model for some of the most memorable characters in Burton's novels, including the idealistic old bookseller in *Time of Trial.* She was educated at Oxford, receiving an honors degree in English literature in 1936. In 1937 she married Reginald W. B. Burton, a tutor and lecturer in classics at Oxford. The Burtons lived at Mill House, Kidlington, Oxford, where they raised three daughters – Catharine, Elizabeth, and Janet. Early in her career Burton worked as a part-time grammar-school teacher and as an examiner in public education. She also edited the works of Samuel Taylor Coleridge, William and Dorothy Wordsworth, and Alfred Tennyson for Oxford University Press and served as an assistant editor for the *Oxford Junior Encyclopedia* in the late 1950s. She adapted two of her children's books into other media, creating a radio play from *The Great Gale* and a television play from *Castors Away!*

In 1960 Oxford University Press published Hester Burton's first novel for young people, *The Great Gale,* republished in the United States eight years later as *The Flood at Reedsmere.* A historical note explains that the novel is based on a real event,

the great storm of 1953. While the twentieth-century setting is somewhat atypical for Burton, building a story on an actual event in British history is a device she often uses in her novels. This first novel also shows the author's admiration for some traditional British values – concern for one's neighbors, practical response to emergency situations, and a sense of personal responsibility – as well as her sense of the British landscape, in this case, that of the wild Norfolk coast.

The story is told from the point of view of Mark and Mary Vaughan, upper-middle-class children who are home alone when a great storm causes the sea to break through the seawall and flood the coast. They find a boat and help their elderly neighbors escape to safety, first in the church and then at Reedsmere Hall, the highest spot in the village. The first half of the story, focusing on the flood and various rescues, is exciting, but the plot loses momentum during the last section, which deals with the recovery effort in the village. Burton carefully delineates British class structure in this story, setting up the aristocratic residents of Reedsmere Hall, the solid, upper-middle-class professional families such as the Vaughans, and the working-class villagers. *The Great Gale* was praised more for its authenticity than for its distinction in either plot or characterization and was not published in the United States until Burton had established her reputation through several other historical novels.

Castors Away! (1962), Burton's second novel for young people, introduces the Henchman family. The book tells a piece of Burton's own family history from the time of the Battle of Trafalgar in 1805. William Henchman, a widowed surgeon in the small town of Rushby, is raising four children with the help of the strict Aunt Julia. During a terrible storm a British battleship is wrecked off the coast, and one sailor is left for dead. Mr. Henchman and the children work for thirteen hours to revive him, only to have the authorities arrest the man and sentence him to 250 lashes for having been drunk when the storm hit. The children know that he will die if he receives this punishment, so they decide to rescue him from jail. When young Tom goes off to join the Navy, he brings the sailor with him, claiming that he is the village carpenter the ship's captain had sent for. The children eventually tell their father about their deception, fully expecting to be punished, but he is proud of their actions. Tom finds battle less glamorous than he had expected; Edmund becomes a surgeon like his father; Nell marries one of Edmund's fellow medical apprentices, a young man with progressive ideas about

*Cover for Burton's novel set during the British retreat
from Dunkirk in 1940*

women's rights; and little Martin grows up to be a scholar. In this novel Burton repeats earlier themes of personal and social responsibility and introduces the concept of rights for women. The sense of period and place are strong, and the young people are convincing, attractive characters. While the plot is still secondary to the background, Burton's storytelling skills have evolved considerably.

Time of Trial shows Burton at the peak of her powers. Set in England in 1801, this complex historical romance is told from the point of view of seventeen-year-old Margaret Pargeter, the daughter of an impoverished London bookseller who holds strong and unpopular political views. The focus of the novel is Mr. Pargeter's arrest for sedition after publishing a manifesto denouncing the landlords who were renting unsafe tenements to poor people. He is brought to trial and ultimately sentenced to six

months in prison. An angry mob burns his bookstore to protest his criticism of child labor.

In the meantime, Margaret has fallen in love with Robert Kerridge, a young medical student who has been boarding with the Pargeters. Robert's wealthy father arranges for Margaret, their housekeeper, and an orphaned tenement boy they have informally adopted to live in his Suffolk coast town of Herringsby while her father serves his term. It is soon apparent that a wide gap exists between the comfortable, affluent world of the Kerridges high on the sandstone cliffs and the humble world of the Pargeters in a small cottage on the shore. Robert's parents make no secret of their disapproval of Margaret as a match for their son, but as soon as Robert achieves financial independence, he marries her. While Robert's parents remain estranged from the young couple, old Mr. Pargeter, still in prison, is delighted for them. Mr. Pargeter's spirits are irrepressible. As the novel ends, he is planning to start a new bookshop and take up the cause of literacy when he is released from prison.

In *Time of Trial* Burton shows her interest in people's lives during times of turbulent social change. She also creates an appealing heroine who has a strong sense of self. Maggie voices no anachronistic feminist slogans; she simply knows who she is and what she is entitled to expect from her life. John Rowe Townsend refers to her in *Written for Children: An Outline of English Language Children's Literature* (1974) as "a girl of flesh and blood" and cites her words to Robert: "I wonder what on earth we did with ourselves before we loved." He points out that this is a near quotation of a poem by John Donne that celebrates the physical act of love, a reference almost certainly over the heads of most contemporary young readers.

Time of Trial received high critical praise at the time of its publication for its strong writing, subtle social message, and historical authenticity. In the June 1969 issue of *Horn Book,* Burton tells how she approached her research for the novel by searching for contemporary materials that would give her the feeling of London in 1801. In *A Guide to Visitors to London Newly Come Up from the Country,* published at the turn of the century, she learned about coffeehouses, tea gardens, and the Poultry Compter Prison, where Mr. Pargeter is incarcerated in the novel; in another book from the same era, this one intended for children, Burton found color plates of street vendors indicating their particular street cries. Details helped to bring the period alive for her and ultimately for the reader.

If *Time of Trial* were only an example of meticulous historical research, however, it would not have been so well received. In the 10 May 1964 *New York Times Book Review* Mary Stolz comments on Burton's seamless integration of research and romantic plot. "At the same time," Stolz adds, "she makes it painfully clear that human problems simply do not change." *Time of Trial* received the Carnegie Medal, the highest honor that is awarded to children's literature in England.

Themes of social injustice and social change also dominate Burton's next novel, *No Beat of Drum* (1966). The novel opens in rural England in 1830, when the introduction of new machinery and rising food prices have created extreme economic deprivation for villagers and farm laborers accustomed to earning their living by threshing the crops for land owners. Sixteen-year-old Joe Hinton and his older brother, Dick, who are the sole support of their mother and their little sister, Phoebe, are having trouble surviving, even with the poaching that the boys risk from time to time. Joe is in love with Mary, his foster sister, who has been raised by their parents since she was orphaned as a child. Through a variety of misadventures, first Mary and then the two boys are arrested and sentenced to be transported to Van Diemen's Land. Joe and Mary eventually reunite there, earn their freedom, and marry, sending for Joe's mother and Phoebe to join them. Dick, in the meantime, escapes from the chain gang to which he has been sentenced and becomes a notorious outlaw, dying at last in a violent encounter with the militia.

Despite the obvious plot contrivances, *No Beat of Drum* is an evocative piece of historical writing. Burton portrays the fascinating topic of transporting British convicts to Australia with considerable objectivity. Dick and Joe make an interesting pair of contrasting heroes, and Mary is another of Burton's multidimensional female characters. Though critics noted weaknesses in the plot, they praised *No Beat of Drum* for its skillful characterizations and unstinting recreation of a sordid period in history.

In Spite of All Terror (1968) is set in the twentieth century, focusing on the British retreat from Dunkirk during World War II. An author's note explains that the book is based on her own recollections of 1940. Fifteen-year-old Liz Hawtin is the orphaned daughter of an eccentric Communist printer and has lived for three years with her maternal uncle's working-class family. Her father had passed on to Liz his passion for education, and she has won a scholarship to the local Grammar School. It is now 1939, and her entire school has been evacuated to the Norfolk village of Chiddingford. Liz is housed with the aristocratic Breretons, a family with three sons. Old Sir Rollo and Ben, the middle son, secretly leave to participate in the evacuation of five hundred thousand British soldiers from Dunkirk. Liz figures out where they are going and runs off to join them. They refuse to allow her into the boat because she is a girl, but she stays on shore in Ramsgate, helping the Women's Voluntary Service serve tea to the returning British Expeditionary Forces and sending telegrams to the soldiers' families letting them know they are safe. Sir Rollo is killed when a nearby ship is blown up, but Ben carries on.

After Dunkirk, Liz returns to her neighborhood in London, where she finds that her street has been nearly leveled by bombs and that her cousin Rose has been turned out of the house because she is pregnant. The Breretons agree to take Rose in as

Dust jacket for Burton's 1970 novel, her second book based on her family's history

early days of the Quaker movement in England and also gives a brief but graphic glimpse at the Great Plague of London in 1665. Richard Holder, Richenda Bemmerton, and Thomas Egerton are childhood companions because of their mothers' friendship. The story opens in 1651 with the three seven-year-old children playing near a narrow plank bridge that spans a weir on the estate that belongs to Thomas's father. Richard, jealous of Thomas's wealth, impulsively crosses the bridge over the racing water and dares Thomas to follow him. Oblivious to Richard's malice, Thomas crosses, and Richenda follows after him. This opening scene sets up the dynamics that propel the action. Both young men grow up loving Richenda, but she marries Thomas, after they have both converted to the Quaker religion. Charles II has been returned to the throne, and the Quakers are persecuted as traitors because they refuse to swear loyalty to the king.

In the meantime, Richard works as an apprentice to a physician in London when the plague strikes. Over Richenda's protest Thomas goes to join Richard in the work of caring for Quaker patients. He contracts the disease himself and dies, while Richenda gives birth to a son, whom she names Thomas. The book ends with Richard, Richenda, and the toddler Thomas down by the weir bridge. Little Thomas strays onto the bridge and is standing two feet above the falling water. Richard rescues the boy and brings him back to Richenda, presenting him as "our son – Thomas's, yours, and . . . mine."

While Thomas is clearly meant to be the book's hero, Richard is a more interesting character. He grows and develops, while Thomas seems to have been good from birth. Both love stories are convincing. The historical background is particularly interesting in this novel. Some critics found the characters overshadowed by the magnitude of the historical events in this novel, although the love story won most reviewers' hearts. All agreed, however, that events are powerfully portrayed here, possibly motivating young readers to greater curiosity about English history.

The Henchmans at Home (1970) is Burton's second treatment of her own family history. Six related stories feature the children of the Henchmans, the family in Victorian England introduced in *Castors Away!* Each story focuses on one of the three children during a ten-year period, from the youngest child Rob's seventh birthday to Ellen's falling in love at about eighteen. While the children are at the center of these stories, the parents, a dedicated

well. As the story ends, Ben has gone for six months of flight training in Canada. Liz is still with the Breretons, who have come to feel like family.

In Spite of All Terror offers Burton many opportunities for commentary on class differences in England. Left unresolved is the relationship between Liz and Ben; they show more than ordinary platonic affection for each other. This is one of Burton's more accessible novels, perhaps because the events are more familiar to an American reader. Liz is a captivating character – awkward, earnest, aware of her lower-class background but not ashamed of it – and her reactions to the upper-class Breretons are convincing. Critics focused their attention on the wartime setting. Most found the book to be a successful eyewitness account of the time and place, personalizing the big events effectively for contemporary young people.

Thomas (1969) is a complex novel set just after the English Civil War. It focuses on the country doctor and his conventional Victorian wife, are also well drawn. It is likely that Burton's father served as the model for the Henchman father as well as for Mr. Pargeter in *Time of Trial* and William Henchman in *Castors Away!* Critics noted that these stories present solid slices of social history in a small Suffolk town during a period of changing values and mores. Some reviewers were disappointed, however, in what appeared to be a somewhat superficial, even sentimental, look at comfortable, middle-class, Victorian England, especially coming after the grittier realism of *Thomas*.

In *The Rebel* (1971) historical events – encompassing the centenary of the British constitutional revolution, the beginning of the French Revolution, and the subsequent war between France and England – overwhelm the hero and threaten to swamp the reader as well. It is set in 1788, and Stephen Parkin, an orphaned country boy, is disgusted by the preparations for the celebration of the constitutional centenary. He feels that the past hundred years have brought no freedom from hunger, disease, or injustice for poor English people. Later, at Oxford, he becomes disillusioned with pomp, ritual, and irrelevant texts.

During a break he and his friend John Taverner leave for France, where the Revolution has begun. There Stephen is involved in the liberation of an aristocrat's estate at St. Gilles and is hailed as a hero by the common people. Later, in a second trip to France he is nearly killed by a mob who fails to see him as a supporter of the Revolution. When he finally returns to England, he is disoriented, half-crazed, and filled with self-loathing. He feels that he has followed a vain dream of freedom and turned out to be a curse to everybody he loved. Stephen's uncle sends him to a headmaster who had been kind to him as a boy. Stephen slowly recovers his health and discovers that he loves teaching. At the close of the novel he rediscovers a sense of purpose when he agrees to work in a slum school in Manchester.

Although Stephen is an interesting character – idealistic, arrogant, impractical, impetuous, and dedicated – there are flaws in the book's plot. Much is made of Stephen's lack of French, for example, yet at times he is able to communicate quite well. His madness is not convincing, nor is his recovery. The frequent subplots add nothing to the overall story or theme. Critics found *The Rebel* to be vivid and dramatic, with a compelling hero. Most agreed, however, that Burton tried to do too much here and allowed the events of the plot to get away from her. Some of the problems raised in this work are resolved in its sequel, *Riders of the Storm* (1972).

Riders of the Storm continues the story of Stephen Parkin, who has become a teacher in a school for poor slum children. The school is sponsored by Mr. Winter, a progressive manufacturer of fustian, a rough fabric made of cotton and flax. The schoolmaster also has progressive ideas, and both he and Mr. Winter belong to the "Friday Club," which meets to discuss politics and current affairs. When Stephen helps Winter write an article about the unfair trials of reformers charged with treason, the local Tory establishment stirs up the common townspeople. A mob attacks the printer who had published the article, burning his shop and killing his cat, and then turns to Mr. Winter's home and business. Stephen helps to defend the place, firing off a rifle loaded only with powder.

Later, a spy in Winter's employment charges that he has organized a private army, and Mr. Winter is arrested. Stephen is also arrested on trumped-up charges of treason resulting from some drunken rantings in a pub. Eventually, the two men are acquitted, but the manufacturer, discouraged by all of these events, moves out of Manchester to his country home where he starts another business and another school. In a somewhat underdeveloped subplot, Stephen falls in love with Lucy, Mr. Winter's niece. At the novel's close, they are engaged to be married and plan to continue working at the school in the country. Ideas take precedence over characters in *Riders of the Storm*. Readers learn more about the importance of literacy in producing social change and the plight of the underclass in Manchester at the end of the eighteenth century than they do about Stephen and Lucy. Stephen seems immature and impulsive, perhaps in need of another sequel to establish that he has learned to combine individual responsibility with his sense of social responsibility.

In *Kate Rider* (1974) Burton returns to the formula for which she is most noted. Here she depicts the English Civil War of 1646 from the perspective of a young English country girl, a yeoman farmer's daughter. Kate's father has been gone for four years, fighting on Parliament's side in the civil war. In the meantime, her brother Adam has become a Royalist and has fallen in love with Tamsin, who also supports the king. Mr. Rider reluctantly consents to the marriage, but Tamsin's family forbids the match. The young couple elopes, and Adam finds work in nearby Colchester.

When the war heats up, Adam joins the Royalists, and father and son find themselves on opposing sides at the battle and siege of Colchester. Kate has gone to Colchester to help Tamsin, who is expecting a child; the women are trapped in the town dur-

*Dust jacket for the American edition of Burton's novel about a
farmer's daughter during the English Civil War*

ing the siege, a time of terrible hardship. The baby
is born, and they all nearly starve. Adam is killed.
After the war Tamsin and the baby, Abel, move in
with the Riders at the farm, and the family tries to
put its life in order again. Kate is sustained by her
love of the land and her hope that her father will
find a good man for her to marry who lives nearby.

There is some good characterization in the
novel, as well as a chilling description of the effects of
war on noncombatants. However, there is little story
outside of the historical events. Kate, in particular,
seems to be a passive onlooker rather than a partici-
pant in her own life. Jill Paton Walsh, in her review in
the 4 April 1975 *Times Literary Supplement,* notes that
"Few people read novels for the history, and so these
lapses would hardly matter if the fate of the Rider
family were story enough on its own; but what happens to them all, though plausible enough and sometimes touching, lacks a coherent shape."

The setting of *To Ravensrigg* (1976) is England
in the 1780s, when abolitionists were working to

end the illegal slave trade in England. The story
opens with the heroine, fifteen-year-old Emmie
Hesket, in her bedroom, looking out on her world.
That world is a calm, middle-class corner of Green-
ford, a seacoast town. She lives with her Aunt
Fanny and cousin Hannah because her mother is
dead, and her father is a sea captain. She knows little about her past, except that her parents had been
very much in love. She is discontented. The complex plot is set in motion when she helps a young
runaway slave escape from his Jamaican master.
Aunt Fanny, distressed by Emmie's wayward behavior, threatens to send her away to school, but
Emmie begs her father to take her on his next sea
voyage instead. The ship is wrecked before it leaves
British waters; Emmie is washed ashore; and her father dies. His last words to his daughter advise her
to go to Ravensrigg – to her mother's people – if
anything should happen to him.

Emmie soon discovers that there is a mystery
about her birth and that nobody knows where

Ravensrigg is. A young Quaker named James Kendall, who is working with the vicar in the abolitionist movement, agrees to ask about Ravensrigg as he travels about England working for the cause. Eventually, Emmie travels with James to the estate in Cumberland that belongs to her mother's family. The mystery of her birth is revealed, and she and James agree to be married the following month, when she turns sixteen.

If *Kate Rider* has not enough plot, *To Ravensrigg* has too much. The twists and turns of Emmie's quest for her identity seem both melodramatic and contrived. There are interesting details about the dangerous work of the abolitionists, but they are lost in the background of the heroine's melodramatic existence.

Burton has made an important contribution to the genre of historical fiction for young people. She is somewhat defensive about the genre, noting in a June 1969 *Horn Book* article that the literary establishment frowns on historical fiction for being a misuse of writers' talents, while historians worry about the distortion of the record. Her solution to these problems is to be wary of where history ends and where fiction begins. She immerses herself in research but never makes an actual historical figure the focus of a novel, and she is careful to avoid putting a real person into a fictional adventure. She also tries to limit the point of view to a single character or small group of characters, finding that this makes for both better history and better literature.

Burton claims to be fascinated by the situation of a young person thrown into a terrible predicament or danger, and she finds contemporary life to be either lacking in those situations or too bewildering to write about. In her *Horn Book* article she claims that she fails to understand the complex minutiae of the present age: "If I look back at a past age, however, the fog clears; the facts and figures fall into place. Not only have the accidents of time selected the evidence but historians have interpreted that evidence for us and taught us to see the past in perspective."

While Burton is interested in the experiences of ordinary people who lived through great events of the past, she is aware that she brings a modern consciousness to her understanding of those events. She explains in the *Horn Book* article that she found connections between the battle of Trafalgar as depicted in *Castors Away!* and the summer of 1940, when England was again threatened with invasion. She acknowledges that *Time of Trial* and *Thomas* present contemporary themes of endangered individual rights, while *No Beat of Drum* focuses on the plight of the poor in a world of the wealthy.

It is ironic, then, that so few young people read Burton's novels today. They might find their own times illuminated in useful ways by her sense of history. They might find it helpful in their own quest for meaning to share Stephen Parkin's confusion about his loss of revolutionary ideals or Maggie Pargeter's outrage at her fiancé's parents' snobbery. All of Burton's books are out of print in the United States, although they are still available in many public and school libraries. Young people have complained that they were intimidated by the books' daunting "British" format, with its small print. The novels are quite long by contemporary standards, and the historical events are unfamiliar to most American children. It is tempting to speculate, however, that new paperback editions might succeed in introducing Hester Burton's historical novels to a generation of young readers in need of some perspective on their own troubling times.

References:
Frank Eyre, *British Children's Books in the Twentieth Century* (New York: Dutton, 1973), pp. 110–111;

Zena Sutherland and May Hill Arbuthnot, *Children and Books,* eighth edition (New York: HarperCollins, 1991), pp. 429–430;

John Rowe Townsend, *Written for Children: An Outline of English Language Children's Literature* (Harmondsworth: Kestrel, 1974), pp. 222–223;

Pauline Clarke

(19 May 1921–   )

Joel D. Chaston
Southwest Missouri State University

BOOKS: *The Pekinese Princess,* illustrated by Cecil Leslie (London: Cape, 1948);

The Great Can, illustrated by Leslie (London: Faber & Faber, 1952);

The White Elephant, illustrated by Richard Kennedy (London: Faber & Faber, 1952; New York: Abelard Schuman, 1957);

Merlin's Magic, as Helen Clare, illustrated by Leslie (London: John Lane, 1953);

Five Dolls in a House, as Helen Clare, illustrated by Leslie (London: John Lane, 1953); illustrated by Aliki (Englewood Cliffs, N.J.: Prentice-Hall, 1965);

Smith's Hoard, illustrated by Leslie (London: Faber & Faber, 1955); republished as *Hidden Gold* (New York: Abelard Schuman, 1957); republished as *The Golden Collar* (London: Faber & Faber, 1967);

Sandy the Sailor, illustrated by Leslie (London: Hamish Hamilton, 1956);

The Boy with the Erpingham Hood, illustrated by Leslie (London: Faber & Faber, 1956);

Bel the Giant and Other Stories, as Helen Clare, illustrated by Peggy Fortnum (London: John Lane, 1956); republished as *The Cat and the Fiddle, and Other Stories,* illustrated by Ida Pellei (Englewood Cliffs, N.J.: Prentice-Hall, 1968);

Five Dolls and the Monkey, as Helen Clare, illustrated by Leslie (London: John Lane, 1956); illustrated by Aliki (Englewood Cliffs, N.J.: Prentice-Hall, 1967);

Five Dolls in the Snow, as Helen Clare, illustrated by Leslie (London: Bodley Head, 1957); illustrated by Aliki (Englewood Cliffs, N.J.: Prentice-Hall, 1967);

James the Policeman, illustrated by Leslie (London: Hamish Hamilton, 1957);

James and the Robbers, illustrated by Leslie (London: Hamish Hamilton, 1959);

Torolv the Fatherless, illustrated by Leslie (London: Faber & Faber, 1959);

Pauline Clarke

Five Dolls and Their Friends, as Helen Clare, illustrated by Leslie (London: Bodley Head, 1959); illustrated by Aliki (Englewood Cliffs, N.J.: Prentice-Hall, 1968);

Seven White Pebbles, as Helen Clare, illustrated by Cynthia Abbott (London: Bodley Head, 1960);

The Lord of the Castle, illustrated by Leslie (London: Hamish Hamilton, 1960);

The Robin Hooders, illustrated by Leslie (London: Faber & Faber, 1960);

James and the Smugglers (London: Hamish Hamilton, 1961);

Keep the Pot Boiling, illustrated by Leslie (London: Faber & Faber, 1961);

Silver Bells and Cockle Shells, illustrated by Sally Ducksbury (London & New York: Abelard Schuman, 1962);

The Twelve and the Genii, illustrated by Leslie (London: Faber & Faber, 1962); republished as *The Return of the Twelves* (New York: Coward-McCann, 1964);

James and the Black Van, illustrated by Leslie (London: Hamish Hamilton, 1963);

Five Dolls and the Duke, as Helen Clare, illustrated by Leslie (London: Bodley Head, 1963); illustrated by Aliki (Englewood Cliffs, N.J.: Prentice-Hall, 1968);

Crowds of Creatures, illustrated by Leslie (London: Faber & Faber, 1964);

The Bonfire Party, illustrated by Leslie (London: Hamish Hamilton, 1966);

The Two Faces of Silenus (London: Faber & Faber, 1972; New York: Coward-McCann, 1972).

OTHER: "Henry Treece. Lament for a Maker," in *TLS 5. Essays and Reviews from the Times Literary Supplement. 1966* (London: Oxford University Press, 1967), pp. 128–135;

"The Rolling, Windy Acres and the Powerful, Timeless Sea," in *My England: Impressions for Young Readers,* by Richard Church, Pauline Clarke, Helen Cresswell, Leon Garfield, Jacynth Hope-Simpson, Penelope Lively, and Elfrida Vipont, illustrated by Anthony Colbert (London: Heinemann, 1973), pp. 45–67;

Peter Hunter Blair, *Anglo-Saxon Northumbria,* edited by Michael Lapidge and Pauline Hunter Blair [Clarke], with biographical article on Peter Hunter Blair by Clarke (London: Variorum, 1984).

SELECTED PERIODICAL PUBLICATIONS – UNCOLLECTED: "The Chief Genii Branwell," *Junior Bookshelf,* 27 (July 1963): 119–123;

"The Values that Endure," *Times Literary Supplement,* 2 April 1971, p. C379.

While Pauline Clarke Hunter Blair is best known for her award-winning novel *The Twelve and the Genii* (1962), her distinguished career includes writing fantasy, historical fiction, adventure stories, domestic tales, and poetry. Critics have praised her historical books for their accuracy and her later fantasies for their believability. Although her work encompasses several genres, it focuses on a few main themes – particularly the power of the imagination, the value of the past (sometimes represented by historical or literary artifacts), and the difficulty of de-

veloping trust and maintaining loyalty. Her books evoke a strong sense of place, whether they are set in London, Norfolk, Yorkshire, Italy, or inside a doll's house.

Clarke, the youngest of three daughters, was born on 19 May 1921 in Kirkby-in-Ashfield to Charles Leopold Clarke, a minister, and Dorothy Kathleen Milum. Their house was filled with books. In fact, her father wrote theology and her mother stories for women's magazines. Clarke was educated in girls' grammar schools, first in London and then in Essex. She went on to Somerville College, Oxford, and took a degree in English language and literature, a background evident in her many literary allusions. She chose to study English because, even as a young adult, she knew that she wanted to be a writer. After college Clarke worked as a freelance writer, first as a journalist and then on a children's magazine. She became friends with painter and illustrator Cecil Leslie, and the two women began a partnership that lasted through twenty years and twenty books, while they shared an ancient house in Norfolk.

While living with Leslie, Clarke, who had not originally planned on writing for children, decided to create a story for her friend to illustrate; the result was her first book, *The Pekinese Princess* (1948), the first of three fantasy adventure stories. These early humorous fantasies, which include *The Great Can* (1952) and *Merlin's Magic* (1953), contain the kinds of nonsense humor and poems found in works like Lewis Carroll's *Alice's Adventures in Wonderland* (1865), a book that plays an important role in one of Clarke's later realistic novels, *Keep the Pot Boiling* (1961).

Long out of print, *The Pekinese Princess* is notable because, as in later works, Clarke draws from her immediate surroundings to create a fantasy; in this case, the models for some of the characters were Leslie's dogs. *The Pekinese Princess* is a fairy tale–like story about a kingdom of Pekinese dogs located "beyond Samarkand, beyond Mongolia and beyond the great mountains and plateaux which separate these from China." The Pekinese have fought a fierce battle against their archenemies, the Monkeys, and as a reward for his success, the mandarin dog Amber Face is to marry the Emperor's daughter, Princess Stars in a Dark Pool. On her wedding day the Princess and her companion, Golden Bells, are kidnapped by a revengeful monkey, Wang the Wise. The story details how Amber Face, his friend Chu-i, and ten Pekinese soldiers search for the Princess and Golden Bells. As in many oral folktales, they are helped by other creatures such as a cormorant, an ancient turtle, a herd of mountain goats, a mother dragon and her son, and a sacred leopard. The story ultimately becomes a sort of *pourquoi* tale – the Lord of Heaven transports the whole Pekinese kingdom to the mountain where the immortals live, although a few Pekinese slip back to earth and still live there today. Like many of Clarke's fantasies, *The Pekinese Princess* is a fairly simple quest tale. It also contains several songs – including a ballad, "The Song of the Journey," and a battle song – which look forward to the rhymes in *Silver Bells and Cockle Shells* (1962), Clarke's later book of poetry for children.

Clarke's next fantasy, *The Great Can,* focuses on two children, Henry and Teresa, who inexplicably find themselves in the country of the Great Can, a magical ruler who can do practically anything he likes. The Great Can enlists the help of Henry and Teresa to seek his magical Golden Recipe Book. Among their helpers is the pessimistic "Great Cant," a contrast to the life-affirming "Great Can." Their adventures carry them to many fantastic places such as Cuckoo-Land, where the moon is blue and the grass is pink, and the Milky Way, where the constellations put on a "Celestial Circus," after which the children slide down the pole star to the home of the Four Winds. The North Wind accompanies them to Cloudland, where they find the Great Recipe Book and use a rainbow to return to Earth; the Recipe Book returns of its own accord. Ultimately the trip serves as a backdrop for the characters' humorous interactions.

Of her three early fantasies, Clarke feels that *Merlin's Magic* is the most important. It was the first of several books written under her pseudonym "Helen Clare." (Clarke's secondary publisher, Bodley Head, had wanted her to be someone different from the Pauline Clarke who was being promoted by Faber and Faber.) The book involves six children who set out on a treasure hunt during which, as an early review summarizes, "each child has to follow a clue which leads to the intangible treasures of his own heart and mind" and to fight off "robot-like monsters, who, lacking imagination themselves, want to seize it from those so gifted." As in many of her later books, Clarke mines English legend for characters and plot devices. With the help of the magician Merlin and a mythological hippogriff who speaks with a Cockney accent, the children journey to the days of King Arthur, Elizabeth I, and Kubla Khan, as well as to a faraway planet.

Clarke writes that *Merlin's Magic* is her first statement of a lifelong belief "in the power of the human imagination, and its close and intimate con-

nection to our creativity and therefore to our spirituality." It is a theme, she maintains, that she is still exploring in her final book, *The Two Faces of Silenus* (1972), which also draws on classical literature. Although Clarke feels that the book is now somewhat dated, *Merlin's Magic* looks forward to her later, more mature works of fantasy.

In 1952 Clarke had just written her first non-fantasy, *The White Elephant,* in which she had infused a potentially unbelievable plot with credibility. *The White Elephant* takes place during a single day in which its narrator, Georgina "Georgie" Murray, and her brother Alister go to London with their older cousin Nona, who has decided to sell an heirloom casket that she feels is a "white elephant." At a seedy shop where Nona buys a fur coat with some of the money from the casket, two jewels are put into her pocket, and a band of thieves determines to retrieve them. The thieves follow Nona, Alister, Georgie, and even their great-aunt Edith Ferguson through various locations in London, including the British Museum and the Adelphi Theatre, before being defeated with the help of the police. While the book relies heavily on coincidence, it is strengthened by Georgie's narration as well as Clarke's attention to detail. The book, which includes a map of London, carefully describes each place the characters visit during the day, allowing readers to enjoy vicariously a rather extravagant outing.

A sequel, originally published as *Smith's Hoard* (1955), again involves Alister and Georgie in a mystery. This book, however, is less frenetic than *The White Elephant* and demonstrates Clarke's interest in history. It begins when Alister and Georgie visit Aunt Edith in Norfolk, where she has recently bought a cottage. On the train ride there, the children meet a man who has in his possession half of a "torc," a chieftain's collar from the Iron Age. After arriving in Norfolk, they discover that a local man, Mr. Jobson, has unearthed artifacts from the Iron Age and that the man they encountered on the train, Pooley, is intent on selling them. With the help of two other children, Jill and Julian Irving, the Murrays help recover the treasure for the crown. The strength of the story, which was based on a real "hoard" found in a Norfolk farmer's field in the 1950s, is Clarke's skillful interweaving of historical fiction, in the form of Alistair's stories, with the children's present-day search for treasure. *Smith's Hoard* looks forward to other books by Clarke, such as *The Lord of the Castle* (1960) and *The Twelve and the Genii,* in which contemporary children try to preserve historical objects or places from adults who do not respect them. As in these other books, *Smith's*

Hoard educates the reader about past events, and its protagonists come to appreciate the value of history. When first published, this book was praised for its setting and narrative style.

In 1953, as Helen Clare, Clarke published *Five Dolls in a House*, the first of several books about dolls that come to life, books that show the same interest in toys that later produced *The Twelve and the Genii*. Clarke continued the adventures of these dolls in *Five Dolls and the Monkey* (1956), *Five Dolls in the Snow* (1957), *Five Dolls and Their Friends* (1959), and *Five Dolls and the Duke* (1963) — light, humorous stories full of verbal comedy that captures the imaginative play that children often create with dolls. In the first book Elizabeth, the human protagonist, discovers that the ginger-colored monkey she has received for her birthday can talk. He tells her that she can make herself small and visit her dolls' house, something she has always desired, but he also warns her that dolls are as bad as humans and often quarrel. Thus begins a series of visits to her dolls, visits in which Elizabeth experiences events any child playing with dolls might imagine as "real." In fact, Clarke based some parts of the books on conversations she overheard between a real-life "Elizabeth" and a friend.

Elizabeth soon discovers that her five dolls have very distinct personalities. The leader of the dolls is bossy Vanessa, who pretends that she knows royalty and calls anything nice "genteel." She also takes it upon herself to educate the other dolls, although she cannot even spell. Jacqueline, the prettiest doll, knows little English and is called the "Paying Guest." Lupin, who is made of "cotton waste," is not very bright. Amanda, smallest of the dolls, likes the toy monkey; helpful Jane becomes a poet. The humor in the books often involves the dolls' interactions with a toy monkey who lives on their roof and spies on their adventures through the chimney.

Throughout the five books Elizabeth uses her ingenuity to make objects from the human world useful for the dolls. She uses a mirror for a skating rink, tissue paper for dress patterns, an iced bun as a birthday cake, knitting needles for the monkey's television aerial, a matchbox for a pram, and a fur glove for muffs and boots.

While all five books about these dolls are episodic, some center on holidays or major events such as Christmas Eve, Guy Fawkes Day, Easter, April Fools' Day, a birthday, a wedding, a funeral, and a christening — or outings, such as visits to a sweet shop, a farm, the zoo, or a toy castle. In *Five Dolls in a House* Clarke is especially interested in developing the relationships among the five dolls. In the book's most

Dust jacket for the novel that Clarke calls her favorite of her works, the story of a nine-year-old orphan who is befriended by a Viking leader

humorous scene the Monkey, disguised as a duchess, comes to tea. The book ends with the Monkey's "marriage" to Amanda and the advent of the summer holidays, which Elizabeth is to spend on the Isle of Wight, while the dolls are to visit Vanessa's uncle, the Duke of Cranberry, in Cranberry Castle.

Five Dolls and the Monkey is similar to *Five Dolls in a House* but introduces new characters, such as the figures from Elizabeth's toy farm and a new pet for the dolls, a parrot. The dolls go on an outing to the farm, teach the parrot to talk, and have a joint birthday party. In *Five Dolls in the Snow* Elizabeth brings the other dolls a tiny baby doll which they christen "Robin." The dolls give a garden party, have dancing lessons, and travel to a toy castle. Elizabeth also tells her toys about Guy Fawkes Day by creating a "bonfire" from a night-light and putting sparklers in their garden. *Five Dolls and Their Friends* features Elizabeth playing surgeon, a trip to the zoo, Jane's attempts at becoming a poet, and an Easter celebration. *Five Dolls and the Duke* focuses on a new addition to the group of dolls – Vanessa's father, a duke. The dolls have a series of athletic contests, write letters, celebrate April Fools' Day, go to the theater, and experience an earthquake caused when Elizabeth's brother moves the house.

All of the "Five Dolls" books were published in the United States and were well reviewed, although the illustrations of the American editions, by Aliki, are cartoonish and undercut the reality created by Clarke's text, unlike Cecil Leslie's more lifelike drawings for the original British editions. All five books effectively depict the joy of small moments and celebrate childhood play and imagination. Clarke has written that in creating the Five Dolls books, she employed some specific rules. For example, no grown-ups appear in the books, which are set only in the dolls' world. "The real world," Clarke explains, is talked about, but it does not really come into the stories, "although all the things the dolls do are simply what children do in real life." Clarke adds that the books just present life from "a doll's-eye view." At the same time she meant the stories "for a lark" and "to be funny." They simply "bubbled up, and if they ceased to bubble," Clarke explains, "I had to stop and wait."

In Clarke's own bibliography of her work, she classifies *The White Elephant* and *Smith's Hoard* as "adventure stories." In 1956 she published *Sandy the Sailor,* the first of six books which she describes as adventure stories for younger children. These books were published as Reindeer Books and Antelope Books, two series from Hamish Hamilton for very young readers. *Sandy the Sailor* recounts the adventures of Sandy and his parents, who travel to and from New Zealand on a clipper ship. Many events and details in this book are based on stories related by Cecil Leslie's father, who had made a similar ocean voyage at the age of eight, and books such as Basil Lubbock's *The Last of the Windjammers* (1927).

Sandy the Sailor was followed by four books set in Norfolk that recount events in the lives of a boy named James and his friends. In *James the Policeman* (1957) three young boys – James, Andy, and Tim – play at being policemen. In this series, which includes *James and the Robbers* (1959), *James and the Smugglers* (1961), and *James and the Black Van* (1963), the boys encounter thieves and smugglers and, mostly through luck, help solve mysteries. Clarke explains that "The boys, the setting, their headquarters, which they made, and many of the local characters are all based on actual people." When first

published, these stories were quite popular in the United Kingdom and went into school editions to be used as readers. While critics have recognized something mechanical about many of the Antelope Books, Clarke's additions to this series have been commended for their engaging characters and their evocation of the Norfolk countryside, as well as for Leslie's illustrations, which, Clarke states, were drawn from life. As in the books about Georgie and Ali Murray, Clarke suggests that children can contribute to the adult world and that, at times, their world may be a better one than that of adults.

Clarke's final adventure book for Hamish Hamilton, *The Lord of the Castle,* was published in 1960. Like *Smith's Hoard, The Lord of the Castle* suggests that an object from the past, in this case a castle in Norfolk, ought to belong to someone who will appreciate it and its history. A boy named Roderic has a grandfather who is caretaker to Castle Harling, which was built by a Norman baron. Both Roderic and his grandfather love the old stories about the castle. The current lord of the castle has recently died and left it to a distant relative instead of to his estranged son. Roderic and his grandfather befriend Henry de la Haye, son of the true heir and also a history student at Cambridge. Henry clearly appreciates the castle's true worth, and Roderic helps him convince his relative, Geoffrey Owen, that the castle is haunted and that Henry's father should have what is rightfully his. The book ends with a Guy Fawkes celebration and Henry's reunion with his father. The book, though simple, is pleasantly humorous and effectively presents Roderic's awe as he discovers the castle's secrets.

In 1956, the same year that *Sandy the Sailor* appeared, Clarke published a more complex historical work, *The Boy with the Erpingham Hood.* One of Clarke's best novels, it is the story of Simon Forester, a boy who becomes an archer and is present at the Battle of Agincourt, and his second cousin, Julian Pennyng, whom he eventually marries. While the plot is familiar, Clarke creates believable scenes and characters and effectively depicts life in the fifteenth century. The book, which begins in 1413 shortly after the coronation of King Henry V and ends in 1423, the year of his death, chronicles ordinary events in Simon's and Julian's lives as well as their participation in historical events and their interactions with historical figures such as Sir Thomas Erpingham, Dick Whittington, and King Harry. According to Clarke's "Author's Note," most of its events actually took place. Along the way the reader is introduced to a variety of historical customs and events, including those of the reign of Henry V, the Guild of Saint George, Julian's education in an abbey, and celebrations of Saint Valentine's Day and the feast of Saint George. Besides bringing the past to life, the novel treats the reality of war. While most of the characters are intensely loyal to their king and the novel features many battle scenes, Clarke does not glorify violence, as evidenced by the death of Simon's friend Stephen. At the same time, *The Boy with the Erpingham Hood* stresses the importance of both determination and loyalty, two qualities that help Simon and Julian face their particular struggles. In the end they are married, and, as a result of his loyalty to Sir Thomas, Simon obtains his goal of becoming a stonemason and sculptor.

The Boy with the Erpingham Hood was published the same year as many other children's books set in medieval times, including Marchette Chute's *The Innocent Wayfaring*, John Hampden's *The Crusader King*, E. K. Seth-Smith's *At the Sign of the Gilded Shoe*, and Barbara Leonie Picard's *Ransom for a Knight. The Boy with the Erpingham Hood* received some of the best reviews of these books; one writer suggested that Clarke "has been casting about for some time to find a theme and manner appropriate to her talent" and that "she seems to have found her medium here." The book has also been praised because it does not romanticize the historical period it presents. In writing the book Clarke used contemporary accounts of the Agincourt campaign, including the battle.

Yet another of Clarke's books, a collection of short stories titled *Bel the Giant and Other Stories,* appeared in 1956 under her pseudonym, Helen Clare. Most of the stories in this volume have the qualities of folktales. In the title tale a giant is defeated by Farmer Hook, who tricks him by playing on his pride, much as in "Puss in Boots." "The Selkie Boy" uses the traditional motif of a "selkie," or seal, who has taken human form and wants to return to the sea. The main character of the cumulative tale "The Boy Who Ran Away" escapes from home by taking a scooter, a tricycle, a bicycle, a motorcar, an omnibus, an engine, a steamer, and an airplane, finally coming back in a postman's bag. Other tales involve a black kitten who wants to become white, a cat who learns to play the fiddle, a princess's musical box, a Christmas celebration at a zoo, a magical walking stick, a family of rabbits, a donkey in search of a master, and a realistic story about a family that finds a mouse at a picnic. In this book Clarke again demonstrates her ability to write focused and believable fantasy by creating magic out of seemingly ordinary events. Several of the stories

were republished in an American edition called *The Cat and the Fiddle, and Other Stories* (1968).

In 1959 Clarke published *Torolv the Fatherless,* which she claims is her favorite of all of her books. The book centers on Torolv, a nine-year-old orphan from the island of Jomsborg who drifts out to sea in a small boat and is picked up by a Viking ship. There Torolv is befriended by the Viking leader Ali, who wins his loyalty. Eventually the ship sails to England where Torolv tries to capture a pig for Ali and is accidentally left behind. Torolv soon presents himself to the Earl Brihtnoth and Lady Alfled, who treat him as part of their family. He is educated by the chaplain, Edgwine, and befriended by a hostage, Ashferth, who can speak Norse. A year later Torolv pledges loyalty to the earl and is then tested when his old friend Ali and a horde of Vikings attack the English coast of Maldon, the climax of the book being this famous Battle of Maldon. In the end Torolv remains loyal to his new friends, many of whom are killed – including the earl. Torolv is also present when Edgwine (as the story suggests) composes the anonymous Old English poem "The Battle of Maldon." This poem provides the main plot for the story, and Clarke includes her own translation of it at the end of her narrative.

As in *The Boy with the Erpingham Hood,* Clarke effectively mingles historical fact with fiction to create a child's view of a historical period. Torolv's struggle with his own loyalties heightens the tension in the final scenes and gives the work a seriousness not present in some of Clarke's earlier works. The book has been compared to the work of Rosemary Sutcliff and lauded for its use of minute detail. In *The Nesbit Tradition* (1972) Marcus Crouch calls the book a "clever story . . . deeply pondered and written with clarity and, in the battle-scene, with passion." He suggests that much of the spirit of Clarke's novel is in the famous poem of the Battle of Maldon and "its insistence on courage and integrity . . . and its constant reminder that Fate, which haunted the lives of these brave and industrious Anglo-Saxons, would inevitably change and blow away happiness like 'fleet clouds.'" In 1991 Clarke reprinted this book in conjunction with the millennium of the Battle of Maldon.

In the 1960s Clarke wrote four books which she describes as domestic stories. In the first, *The Robin Hooders* (1960), four children (Robert, Serena, Tom, and their baby sister, Mary Jane) invent a game in which they imitate Robin Hood and his band of merry men in order to help the poor. In some ways the plot and tone of the book are reminiscent of E. Nesbit's *The Story of the Treasure Seekers*

(1899), which recounts how the Bastable children try to help their family. In seven short chapters Clarke describes how the children try to gather sticks for Mrs. Gipsy; collect mushrooms for the poor; buy food for the Salters; provide a cabbage for their daily help, Mrs. Jarvis; and find goose eggs for their friend, Miss Laurel.

Like many of Clarke's other books, this one is filled with literary allusions, including references to Robin Hood, *The Tailor of Gloucester* (1903), and *Alice's Adventures in Wonderland*. As in *The Twelve and the Genii*, a set of literary objects becomes important in the plot: a packet of old letters written by novelist George Eliot are the focus of the Robin Hooders' final good deed; the children's discovery of these letters allows Miss Laurel to live comfortably in her old age. The book manages to avoid becoming either sentimental or saccharine, in part because of Robert's narration and the lively, realistic interactions between the children.

Seven White Pebbles (1960), a book for young children, deals with similarly ordinary events. Polly, the youngest in her family, is going to the seashore and counts off the days with seven white pebbles which she keeps on her windowsill. According to Clarke, the scene in which Polly falls asleep in a tea chest and was thought to be lost actually happened.

In the following year Clarke published *Keep the Pot Boiling*, perhaps the best of her domestic novels. While this book is not strictly autobiographical, many of its episodes (including the incidents with the sledge, finding a plaster leg in the cellar, dressing up to take people in, and tracking an adult on a journey) were inspired by real-life events from Clarke's childhood. According to Clarke, the character Randolph was "sparked off" from a boy cousin who also drew a picture of the Good Samaritan and organized things like shadow shows. This book presents the adventures of Randolph, Kate, Emma, and Claire Carlisle – whose father is a minister, as was Clark's own father.

An important theme in *Keep the Pot Boiling* concerns the value of literature. The Carlisle children's reading often inspires their activities, as when they put on "shadow-show" versions of the ballads "Lord Randall" and "Binnorie." Once again Clarke's characters often quote other works of literature, in this case William Shakespeare's *The Merchant of Venice* (1600), Kenneth Grahame's *The Wind in the Willows* (1908), T. S. Eliot's *The Wasteland* (1922), and E. Nesbit's *The Enchanted Castle* (1907), whose setting resembles a house they visit. One of the novel's best episodes, "Curiouser and Curiouser," involves a copy of *Alice's Adventures in Wonderland* from a church bazaar. Emma does not want to part with the volume when she discovers it is a valuable first edition; like the children in *Smith's Hoard,* Emma discovers that objects are sometimes worth more than money. As her mother tells the other children, "She values the story itself, which is the right value, the real value."

The book also celebrates the excitement of being a child and validates the Carlisles' continual attempts to "keep the pot boiling," a phrase referring to a game that involves jumping on a bed. Clarke makes this clear when, in the novel's second chapter, she contrasts the Carlisles, who use their imaginations to compensate for a lack of money, with their well-to-do cousins Lance and Fanny, who have "a shortage of ideas." Like E. Nesbit's Bastables, the Carlisles are imaginative, often playing games which precipitate real-life adventures. These include pretending that Randolph is Chinese when they go Christmas caroling so that they can help raise money for World Refugees, making a bet in which Kate impersonates a grown-up in front of her mother's sewing group, and secretly following their mother when she makes a mysterious trip to London.

The year after *Keep the Pot Boiling* was published, Clarke produced another novel about a group of imaginative children, a fantasy that also stresses the value of literary objects. Critics generally agree that *The Twelve and the Genii* is Clarke's greatest achievement. Clarke had originally titled the book *The Return of the Twelves* (the title of the 1964 American edition), but the publishing house of Faber and Faber asked her to change it because it sounded like a sequel. The book received several important awards, most notably the 1962 Carnegie Medal, and the American edition was named an honor book in the *New York Herald Tribune* Children's Spring Book Festival in 1964 and went on to win the Lewis Carroll Shelf Award in 1965. It won further international awards, including being named to the Hans Christian Andersen Honor List in 1964 and receiving the German Jugend Buchpreis for 1968.

Many writers have noted that *The Twelve and the Genii* shares similarities with other stories about little people or toys that come to life, in particular T. H. White's *Mistress Masham's Repose* (1946), which Clarke knew and loved, and Mary Norton's *The Borrowers* (1953), which Clarke maintains she has never read. Lois Rostow Kuznets discusses *The Return of the Twelves* at length. As in earlier books, Clarke once again treats the intrinsic value of his-

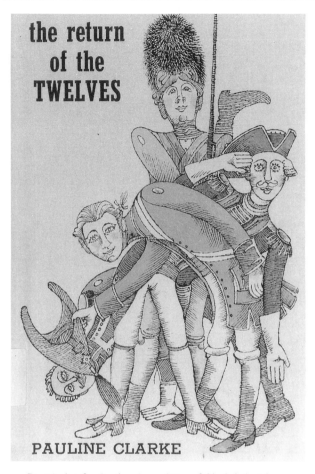

*Dust jacket for the American edition of Clarke's best-known
novel, a fantasy about a boy who brings twelve toy
soldiers to life*

torical objects and the magic created by children's imaginations. Initially the book focuses on eight-year-old Max Morley, who has discovered twelve toy soldiers under a loose board in the attic of his new house in Yorkshire. He inadvertently brings the soldiers to life by beating on an old Ashanti drum. Max, his sister Jane, and eventually their brother Philip win the Twelves' confidence, becoming the "Genii," the guardian spirits who protect the soldiers. The children come to respect the Twelves and recognize that they must not do everything for these soldiers.

From neighborhood parson, Mr. Howson, the children learn about twelve soldiers who once belonged to the Brontës, who grew up at nearby Haworth. As children, these Brontës had created many adventures for the toys, some of which were recorded by Branwell Brontë. The Morley children soon realize that their Twelves are indeed the Brontës' soldiers. Meanwhile Philip has written about them to an American professor who has of-

fered a £5,000 reward for information about them. Afraid of being taken to America, the Twelves flee across the countryside by using one of Max's roller skates as a carriage. With the help of Mr. Howson and the children, the Twelves ultimately find their way to Haworth, which is now a Brontë museum. There they are safe, coming back to life only at night or when Max comes to visit.

Early reviewers of the novel noted something mystical about the book. More recently, children's novelist Katherine Paterson has suggested that the book is filled with allusions to the Old Testament and at times seems almost allegorical. Certainly *The Twelve and the Genii* does use religious allusions: throughout their journey the Twelves are compared to the children of Israel after they fled from Egypt, and the children develop a godlike relationship with the Twelves, who need their protection but also desire independence. The biblical allusions, Clarke explains, were present in Branwell's original stories, which is not surprising since he and his sisters were rectory children. The spiritual elements in the novel also seem connected to Clarke's treatment of the boundless power of the imagination, which brings the soldiers to life and then helps Max discover where they are after they have escaped. As Mr. Howson notes, the "creative genius" of the Brontë children (and also the Morleys') echoes that of the Creator.

Clarke uses the Twelves' adventures to explore many ethical concerns, including the value of the individual, the responsibility that comes with power, and the importance of free will. After observing the Twelves, the Morley children come to value their individuality. Each of the Twelves has his distinct personality and makes important contributions to the group. The children also develop a feeling of responsibility for the toys, which leads them to eschew the fame and money they would receive if they give them up. At the same time, Max discovers that part of the Twelves' lives depends on their independence. For this reason, the soldiers must make the journey to Haworth on their own, with only occasional help from the Genii.

As with Clarke's historical novels, this book was carefully researched. The inspiration came from Clarke's reading of Branwell Brontë's "The History of the Young Men" in *The Miscellaneous and Unpublished Writings of Charlotte and Patrick Branwell Brontë* (1931) that he based on the games he and his sisters made up about his toy soldiers. While Branwell's sister Charlotte also wrote stories about the soldiers, Clarke has relied primarily on his description of the soldiers' personalities. The Ashanti drum, canoe, and stool in Clarke's story were inspired by real objects that her missionary grandfather had brought back from West Africa. These naturally connected with the voyage of the Twelves, who, according to Branwell's stories, had gone off to Africa and actually arrived in Ashanti. The soldiers' march back to Haworth was based on a visit to the museum Clarke made in 1953, as well as on maps and photos. In addition, Cecil Leslie, who did the original illustrations, actually walked the route which the Twelves took and suggested revisions to Clarke. Another of Clarke's concerns was that of maintaining her readers' willing suspension of disbelief. This she tried to accomplish by developing both her characters and the setting and by keeping the size of the soldiers in mind, particularly when she described their adventures.

The novel has been praised for many reasons, including its plot (called brilliant and original), its characterization of the Twelves and the Morley children, its detailed setting, and its thematic con-

cern with the power of the imagination. Roger Lancelyn Green argued that the book is "not easy to forget," while author and critic Eleanor Cameron in *The Green and Burning Tree* (1962) has described it as a work of "superlative fantasy" that succeeds because it elicits the reader's trust. While Kuznets recognized the potentially allegorical nature of Clarke's book, she also argued that it is a complex story, one that works against a single pat interpretation and is enriched by language play, such as that in Max's use of the term "Brontyfan," and its intertextuality. *The Twelves and the Genii* is the one book of Clarke's that is currently in print in the United States, and it is still frequently mentioned in scholarly discussions of books about toys.

The same year that she published *The Twelve and the Genii*, Clarke also produced *Silver Bells and Cockle Shells*. That Clarke would write a collection of children's poetry should not be surprising to anyone who has read *The Great Can*, which features nonsense and humorous verses. *Silver Bells and Cockle Shells* was generally well received by critics, who praised its variety and its imaginative quality, although a few reviewers felt the poems were derivative and above children's heads. The book is divided into three sections: "Rhymes and Sayings," "Summer and Winter," and "Birds and Beasts." Most of the eleven poems in the first section are reminiscent of traditional nursery rhymes. Many — such as "Sluggery-wuggery" (a speaker with many humorous names) and others about children who ponder the "ill wind" and a literal rain of cats and dogs — are narratives spoken by a child or a child-like character. Some of these poems are reminiscent of verses by Lewis Carroll and Edward Lear. The second section, a series of twenty-two poems depicting holidays and months, is the most effective. "New Moon in January" and "The Song of December," which begin and end this section, are lyrical poems that personify nature and the months of January and December. The final section features six short animal poems that seem tacked on to the collection.

In 1963 Clarke was asked to run a seminar for the British Council in Accra, the purpose of which was to teach Ghanaians how to write children's stories in English. At this time she scripted a series of short plays about an African family for the BBC Overseas Educational Department, a series to be used in teaching African children. The following year she published her only picture book, *Crowds of Creatures*. This alphabet book, once again illustrated by Leslie, begins by suggesting that sometimes creatures like to be alone and sometimes in the company of other animals. Clarke then goes on to list various nouns of multitude, such as a "pace of asses," a "sloth of bears," and a "clowder of cats."

Another book for the very young, *The Bonfire Party*, appeared in 1966. Based on a true incident, the book centers on six-year-old Alison and four-year-old Jennett, who are excited about the prospect of a bonfire party. Their mother makes them a "Guy" (an effigy which is to be burnt on Guy Fawkes Day), which they nickname "Salty" because he looks like a sailor. Coming to the realization that Salty is to be burnt, Alison hides him under her bed. Clarke writes that her story concerns "how much we love what we have created, whether a guy or a poem" and "how much love has to do with creation." Early reviewers focused on the book's engaging humor and simple but expressive style.

In 1966 Clarke met Peter Hunter Blair, a fellow of Emmanuel College, Cambridge, who specialized in Anglo-Saxon history and was author of many historical books, including *An Introduction to Anglo-Saxon England* (1956) and *The World of Bede* (1970). Clarke had been familiar with Hunter Blair's scholarly work, which she had used for background when writing *Torolv the Fatherless*. When Hunter Blair wrote and published a children's story, *The Coming of Pout* (1966), Clarke was asked to review it for her local paper. In order to question him for the review, Clarke met Hunter Blair, and in 1969 they were married. According to Clarke, Hunter Blair taught her how to do historical research properly. In 1982 Hunter Blair died, and shortly after that Clarke helped edit a collection of his essays, *Anglo-Saxon Northumbria* (1984).

Clarke writes that her career as a children's writer ended with the publication of *The Two Faces of Silenus* in 1972. After *The Twelve and the Genii*, this is Clarke's best fantasy novel. Like *The Twelve and the Genii*, the book involves the magical animation of lifeless objects and draws on other literary works, in this case classical tales about Silenus and Medusa. The book grew out of a visit that Clarke and her husband had made to the Italian town of Spoleto the year they were married. Clarke had often wandered alone while her husband attended a history conference; she had found a carved stone face of the satyr Silenus, from which water poured into a basin, and immediately knew that Silenus would be part of her next story.

At its beginning Rufus and Drusilla Greenwood have come to a small Italian town with their parents. Their father, a historian like Clarke's husband, is attending a conference there. The children throw coins into a water basin, wishing for the stone face of Silenus, carved above the basin, to come to life. It does, and, one by one, the three children and their parents have mystical encounters with Silenus that change their perspectives. However, Silenus's enemy, the ancient Gorgon Medusa, is out to destroy him. Eventually the children help save Silenus, who returns to his place in the wall.

One of the major themes of the book is expressed in the title of chapter 19, "New Ways of Seeing Things." After spending time with Silenus, all of the major characters become different. The children become more mature; their parents feel young again. The final chapters are suspenseful, especially when Silenus is attacked by Medusa's cohorts and the children are transformed into animals. The most effective parts of the book, however, are the pastoral sequences, the best of which rival Kenneth Grahame's description of Pan in *The Wind in the Willows*. Much of the book's power grows out of Clarke's evocation of setting: the Roman theater, the woods where Luigi and Drusilla meet Silenus, and the church and cemetery where the older Greenwoods encounter him. The book is filled with classical allusions, tempting readers to take James Greenwood's advice to Rufus to reread Virgil. Virginia Haviland praised the book as "ingenious, well-based, and dramatic," with "a tremendous climax."

Largely because of *The Twelve and the Genii*, Pauline Clarke has assured her position as an important twentieth-century children's writer. Indeed, this book may have helped inspire more recent books about toy figures, books such as Lynne Reid Banks's *The Indian in the Cupboard* (1981) and its sequels and Elizabeth Winthrop's *The Castle in the Attic* (1985). Many of Clarke's other books, however — particularly *The Boy with the Erpingham Hood, Torolv the Fatherless*, and *The Two Faces of Silenus* — deserve further critical attention. Creating a willing suspension of disbelief, all three of these works realistically present myth or history. Pauline Clarke is notable as a children's writer who has been successful in a variety of genres and whose books, through their interest in earlier literature, have encouraged readers to study the past and become reacquainted with other serious writers.

Interview:

"Pauline Clarke," in *British Children's Authors: Interviews at Home*, edited by Cornelia Jones and Olivia R. Way (Chicago: American Library Association, 1976), pp. 65–75.

References:

Eleanor Cameron, "The Inmost Secret," *Horn Book,* 59 (February 1983): 17–24;

Cameron, "The Unforgettable Glimpse," in her *The Green and Burning Tree: On the Writing and Enjoyment of Children's Books* (Boston: Little, Brown, 1962), pp. 3–47;

Marcus Crouch, *The Nesbit Tradition: The Children's Novel in England, 1945–1970* (Totowa, N.J.: Rowman, 1972);

Crouch, "1962: 'The Twelve and the Genii,' by Pauline Clarke," in *Chosen for Children: An Account of the Books Which Have Been Awarded the Library Association Carnegie Medal, 1936–1975,* edited by Crouch and Alec Ellis, third edition (London: Library Association, 1977), pp. 117–123;

Frank Eyre, "Fiction for Children 'The Twelve and the Genii,' " in his *British Children's Books in the Twentieth Century,* revised edition (London: Longman, 1971), pp. 125–126;

Margery Fisher, *Intent upon Reading: A Critical Appraisal of Modern Fiction for Children* (Leicester: Brockhampton Press, 1961);

Virginia Haviland, "Review of *The Two Faces of Silenus,*" *Horn Book,* 48 (December 1972): 594–595;

Ravenna Helson, "Fantasy and Self-Discovery," *Horn Book,* 46 (April 1970): 121–133;

Lois Rostow Kuznets, "Good News from the Land of the Brontyfans, Intertextuality in Clarke's *The Return of the Twelves,*" in *Where the Rivers Meet: Confluence and Concurrence. Selected Papers from the 1989 International Conference of the Children's Literature Association,* edited by Susan R. Gannon and Ruth Thompson (Pleasantville, N.Y.: Pace University, 1991), pp. 67–74;

Kuznets, *When Toys Come Alive: Narratives of Animation, Metamorphosis, and Development* (New Haven: Yale University Press, 1994);

"Medieval People," *Times Literary Supplement,* 11 May 1956, p. xiii;

"Merlin's Magic," *The Junior Bookshelf,* 17 (July 1953): 111–112;

Katherine Paterson, "Afterword," in Clarke's *The Return of the Twelves* (New York: Dell, 1986), pp. 182–184;

Ann Swinfen, "Experience Liberated: 'The Twelve and the Genii,' " in her *Defence of Fantasy: A Study of the Genre in English and American Literature Since 1946* (London: Routledge & Kegan Paul, 1984), pp. 127–128.

Susan Cooper
(23 May 1935 –)

Joel D. Chaston
Southwest Missouri State University

BOOKS: *Mandrake* (London: Hodder & Stoughton, 1964);

Over Sea, Under Stone, illustrated by Margery Gill (London: Cape, 1965; New York: Harcourt, Brace & Ward, 1966);

Behind the Golden Curtain: A View of the U.S.A. (London: Hodder & Stoughton, 1965; New York: Scribners, 1966);

J. B. Priestley: Portrait of an Author (New York: Harper & Row, 1970; London: Heinemann, 1970);

Dawn of Fear, illustrated by Gill (New York: Harcourt, Brace & Ward, 1970; London: Chatto & Windus, 1972);

The Dark is Rising, illustrated by Alan E. Cober (New York: Atheneum, 1973; London: Chatto & Windus, 1973);

Greenwitch (New York: Atheneum, 1974; London: Chatto & Windus, 1974);

The Grey King, illustrated by Michael Heslop (New York: Atheneum, 1975; London: Chatto & Windus, 1975);

Silver on the Tree (London: Chatto & Windus, 1975; New York: Atheneum, 1977);

Jethro and the Jumbie, illustrated by Ashley Bryan (New York: Atheneum, 1979; London: Chatto & Windus, 1980);

Seaward (New York: Atheneum, 1983; London: Bodley Head, 1983);

The Silver Cow: A Welsh Tale, illustrated by Warwick Hutton (New York: Atheneum, 1983; London: Chatto & Windus, 1983);

Foxfire, by Cooper and Hume Cronyn (New York & London: French, 1983);

The Selkie Girl, illustrated by Hutton (New York: Margaret McElderry/Macmillan, 1986);

Tam Lin, illustrated by Hutton (New York: Margaret McElderry/Macmillan, 1991);

Matthew's Dragon, illustrated by Jos[eph] A. Smith (New York: Margaret McElderry/Macmillan, 1991);

Susan Cooper (photograph by Zoë Dominic F.R.P.S.)

The Boggart (New York: Margaret McElderry/Macmillan, 1993);

Danny and the Kings, illustrated by Smith (New York: Margaret McElderry/Macmillan, 1993).

PLAY PRODUCTIONS: *Foxfire,* by Cooper and Hume Cronyn, Stratford, Ontario, 1980; revised, Minneapolis Guthrie Theatre, 1981; revised again, New York City, Ethel Barrymore Theatre, 11 November 1982.

MOTION PICTURE: *George Balanchine's Nutcracker,* narration by Cooper, Warner Brothers, 1993.

TELEVISION: *The Dollmaker,* teleplay by Cooper and Hume Cronyn, ABC, 13 May 1984;

Foxfire, teleplay by Cooper, CBS Hallmark Hall of Fame, 13 December 1987;

To Dance with the White Dog, teleplay by Cooper, CBS Hallmark Hall of Fame, 5 December 1993.

OTHER: "Snoek Piquante," in *The Age of Austerity: 1945–51,* edited by Michael Sissons and Philip French (London: Hodder & Stoughton, 1963), pp. 35–54;

J. B. Priestley, *Essays of Five Decades,* edited, with a preface, by Cooper (Boston: Little, Brown, 1968; London: Heinemann, 1968);

"In Defense of the Artist," in *Proceedings of the Fifth Annual Conference of the Children's Literature Association,* edited by Margaret P. Esmonde and Priscilla A. Ord (Villanova: Children's Literature Association, 1979), pp. 20–28; republished in *Signposts to Criticism of Children's Literature,* edited by Robert Bator (Chicago: American Library Association, 1983), pp. 98–108;

"Escaping into Ourselves," in *Celebrating Children's Books: Essays on Children's Literature in Honor of Zena Sutherland,* edited by Betsy Hearne and Marilyn Kaye (New York: Lothrop, Lee & Shepard, 1981), pp. 14–23; republished in *Fantasists on Fantasy: A Collection of Critical Reflections by Masters of the Art,* edited by Robert H. Boyer and Kenneth J. Zahorski (New York: Avon, 1984), pp. 280–287;

"My Links with Wales," in *Loughborough '83: Proceedings of the 16th Lougborough International Seminar on Children's Literature* (Aberystwyth, Wales: Welsh National Centre for Children's Literature, 1984);

Nancy and John Langstaff, *The Christmas Revels Songbook in Celebration of the Winter Solstice: Carols, Professionals, Rounds, Ritual and Children's Songs,* preface by Cooper (Boston: Godine, 1985), p. vii;

"Nahum Tarune's Book," in *Innocence and Experience: Essays and Conversations on Children's Literature,* edited by Barbara Harrison and Gregory Maguire (New York: Lothrop, Lee & Shepard, 1987), pp. 195–209;

E. Nesbit, *The Phoenix and the Carpet,* concluding essay by Cooper (New York: Dell, 1987), pp. 236–239;

"Long Ago and Far Away," in *Travellers in Time: Past, Present, and to Come: Proceedings of the Summer Institute at Newham College, Cambridge University, England* (Green Bay, Wis.: Children's Lit-

erature Institute of New England, 1990), pp. 95–102;

"Susan Cooper," in *Something About the Author: Autobiographical Series,* volume 6, edited by Adele Sarkissian (Detroit: Gale Research, 1990), pp. 67–85;

"Susan Cooper," in *Speaking for Ourselves: Autobiographical Sketches by Notable Authors of Books for Young Adults,* edited by Donald R. Gallo (Urbana: NCTE, 1990), pp. 54–56.

SELECTED PERIODICAL PUBLICATIONS – UNCOLLECTED: "When Term Is Over," *Times* (London), 31 August 1956, p. 10;

"Strains of Mark Twain," *Christian Science Monitor,* 1 May 1974, p. F5;

"A Love Letter to the *Horn Book,*" *Horn Book,* 50 (October 1974): 182–183;

"Address Delivered at the Children's Round Table Breakfast: Is There Really Such a Thing as a Species Called Children's Books?," *Texas Library Journal,* 52 (May 1976): 52–54;

"Newbery Acceptance," *Horn Book,* 52 (August 1976): 361–366;

"A Dream of Revels," *Horn Book,* 55 (December 1979): 633–640;

"A Second Look: 'The Nargun and the Stars,' " *Horn Book,* 62 (September/October 1986): 572–574;

" 'Many Waters' by Madeleine L'Engle," *New York Times Book Review,* 91 (30 November 1986): 40;

"Preserving the Light," *Magpies,* 3 (May 1988): 5–6;

"Fantasy in the Real World," *Horn Book,* 66 (May/June 1990): 304–315;

"How I Began . . . ," *New Welsh Review,* 2 (May–June 1990): 19–21;

"Creating the Tools," *Youth Librarian Review,* 11 (1991): 6–8, 10–14.

Well known largely for her award-winning fantasy series "The Dark is Rising," Susan Mary Cooper has enjoyed great critical success in a variety of genres – newspaper articles, essays, biography, science fiction, drama, screenplays, and children's fiction. Cooper's novels and picture books for young readers are mostly fantasies that draw on British and Celtic myths and legends – exploring the struggle between good and evil, the "Light" and the "Dark," tradition and technology. Her work has elicited much critical discussion and has won virtually every major British and American award for children's writing.

Cooper was born in Burnham, Buckinghamshire, England, on 23 May 1935 to John Richard Cooper and Ethel May Field. Her father had worked in the reading room of the natural history museum until going off to fight in World War I, from which he returned with a wounded leg. He then pursued a career in the offices of the Great Western Railway. Because he held this job, the family was able to take yearly trips to places such as Wales, Cornwall, and Devon, some of which were to become the settings of Cooper's stories and novels. Sharing music and poetry with her own children, her mother was a teacher of ten-year-olds and eventually became deputy head of a large junior high school. Like Cooper, her younger brother Roderick also grew up to become a writer, producing what she describes as "thrillers." According to Cooper, her writing talent probably came from her mother's parents: her grandfather, Frederick Benjamin Field, a stagestruck draper's assistant who encouraged her to read, and her grandmother, Mary Ellen Davies, who came from Aberdovey, Wales.

When Cooper was four years old, World War II began, an event which still affects her. "I am haunted by the sounds of war," she wrote, recalling the air raids and bombs she experienced until the war ended when she was ten. Her experiences growing up in the war became the basis for *Dawn of Fear* (1970), which she calls thinly disguised autobiography, and she admits that World War II probably influenced her portrayal of evil in the Dark is Rising series.

Cooper took an interest in writing as a child — creating puppet plays, newspapers, and a small illustrated book. She enjoyed listening to the radio, especially the BBC's "Children's Hour," which dramatized novels like John Masefield's *The Box of Delights* (1935). She read a variety of poetry, as well as the works of Rudyard Kipling, John Masefield, E. Nesbit, Arthur Ransome, Jack London, and Charles Dickens. Like her grandfather she was entranced by the theater and remembers the awe she felt when she attended a Christmas pantomime for the first time at about the age of three.

Cooper attended Slough High School for girls and subsequently won a scholarship to Somerville College, Oxford, where she read English and eventually became the first woman editor of the newspaper, *Cherwell*. During her college years she attended lectures by C. S. Lewis and J. R. R. Tolkien, themselves writers of fantasies. In 1956 Cooper graduated with a degree in language and literature and made her first professional sale as a writer, publishing an anonymous essay about leaving Oxford on 31 August 1956 in the London *Times*.

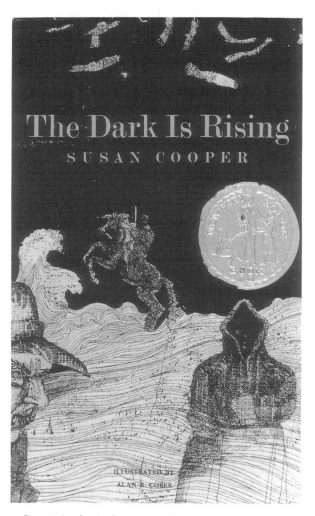

Dust jacket for the fantasy novel that Cooper was inspired to write while cross-country skiing in Massachusetts

After college Cooper worked as a temporary reporter at the *Sunday Express,* then was hired by the *Sunday Times,* where she worked as a reporter and feature writer for seven years. Occasionally Cooper furnished articles for one of the paper's regular columns, "Mainly for Children," writing about subjects like King Arthur, medieval castles, and brass rubbings — topics which would later find their way into her books.

While at the *Sunday Times*, Cooper tried her hand at writing novels. "The first of these," Cooper explains, "was an autobiographical novel about a love affair, a piece of apprenticeship writing which was never published. . . ." Cooper's next attempt was a science-fiction novel, *Mandrake,* which was accepted by Hodder and Stoughton and eventually published in 1964.

Although written for adults, *Mandrake,* which has long been out of print, would be likely to interest young adults who are reading dystopian novels such as George Orwell's *1984* (1940), Aldous Huxley's *Brave New World* (1932), or Lois Lowry's *The Giver* (1993). *Mandrake,* set in what was then the future (the 1980s), describes an England which has come under the control of the Ministry of Town and Country Planning, headed by the enigmatic Mandrake. A major result of the ministry's actions is that people are permitted to live only in the town or community where they have been born. The novel's protagonist David Queston, an anthropologist and writer, is a potential threat to the ministry and is continually pressured to work for Mandrake. During the last half of the book Queston becomes a homeless fugitive who rescues other outcasts, including twenty-three-year-old actress Beth Summers; a "sensitive," or medium, Neville Warren; and journalist Christopher Oakley. In pursuing Queston, Mandrake is destroyed by a laser, part of the technology that his administration has helped encourage.

The novel explores many philosophical questions, such as the danger of becoming too rooted to one place – an idea reinforced by the minister's name, Mandrake. The notion of evil hidden within seemingly ordinary people is in this novel an important theme, one which Cooper treats in her later work.

After completing *Mandrake* Cooper began writing a children's novel to enter a contest offered by E. Nesbit's publisher, Ernest Benn, for family-adventure stories like those written by Nesbit. Cooper did not enter the contest but eventually completed the manuscript. After it was turned down by twenty or more publishers, she sent it to a friend of a friend who was reading manuscripts for Jonathan Cape – and who decided to publish it as *Over Sea, Under Stone* in 1965.

Over Sea, Under Stone begins when three Nesbit-like characters (Simon, Jane, and Barney Drew) travel to the Cornish town of Trewissick to spend a few weeks during the summer. The children are soon plunged into a struggle between good and evil (described in later books of the series as "The Light" and "The Dark"). With the help of their scholarly "Great-Uncle" Merriman "Merry" Lyon, they use an ancient map to recover what is apparently the Holy Grail. As in Cooper's other novels, the children discover that it is not always possible to tell good from evil. Indeed, they are temporarily misled by members of The Dark posing as two tourists, Norman and Polly Withers; as a housekeeper, Mrs. Palk; and as the local vicar, Mr. Hastings. Although less complex than other books in the series, Cooper's descriptions of the Drews' moonlight jour-

ney to the standing stones on Kenmare Head and Barney's kidnapping during the annual Trewissick carnival are masterful. While Cooper had no plans to write a series when she began this book, Barney's suggestion, at the end of the novel, that the children will someday know the truth about King Arthur and the manuscript they have found leaves the door open for their adventures to continue.

Over Sea, Under Stone was well received. Reviewers noted that the book begins as a mystery-adventure story and becomes a sort of morality tale full of mysticism and elements of Arthurian legend. Because it later became a part of a series, *Over Sea, Under Stone* has continued to gain new readers. In a *Horn Book* essay, "A Second Look: *Over Sea, Under Stone,*" written eleven years after the novel's publication, Dwight Dudley Carlson argues that Cooper's superb abilities as a storyteller, the novel's clear delineation of good and evil, and the believability of the Drew children have contributed to its lasting success with young readers.

On 3 August 1963, at the age of twenty-eight, Cooper married Nicholas J. Grant, a forty-six-year-old scientist and widower with three teenage children. Despite various job offers, Cooper moved to Winchester, Massachusetts, about ten miles north of Boston, with her new family. For some time Cooper continued to cover American stories for the *Sunday Times* and wrote a weekly column, "Susan Cooper in America," for the national morning paper of Wales.

Perhaps as an outgrowth of this column, Cooper wrote a nonfiction book, *Behind the Golden Curtain: A View of the U.S.A.* (1965), reflecting on differences between British and American cultures. Selected as a Book Society Choice in England, *Behind the Golden Curtain* presents Cooper's view that the differences between British and American culture are greater than are generally recognized: the barrier "of incomprehension on the one side and misunderstanding on the other" she calls "the Golden Curtain." Among other topics, Cooper explores how religion, sports, education, politics, and television have contributed to the creation of this barrier.

The same year that *Behind the Golden Curtain* was published, Cooper gave birth to her son, Jonathan Roderick Howard, and the following year her daughter, Katharine Mary, was born. In 1968 Cooper edited a collection of essays by longtime British friend, novelist, dramatist, and essayist J. B. Priestley. In her preface to the volume Cooper praises the essay as the most personal form of writing, one which most expresses a "distinct personality." Cooper continued to correspond with Priestley and visited him on trips to England as she gathered material for a biography that was published in 1970.

Around this time Cooper began working on an autobiographical manuscript, "The Camp," which drew from her experiences growing up in World War II England. Cooper credits editor Margaret McElderry for helping her to realize that "The Camp" might become a children's book. After Cooper made some suggested revisions, she published it with a new title, *Dawn of Fear,* in 1970.

Dawn of Fear explores a young boy's gradual education into the horrors of World War II. Derek "Derry" Brand lives with his parents about twenty miles outside London and enjoys playing with his two young friends, Geoff Young and Peter Hutchins. The three are involved in building a "camp" or secret hideout in a ditch near their homes. When Derry, Geoff, and Peter prevent a gang from hanging a cat, the other boys retaliate by destroying the camp, stealing Peter's gun, and killing the cat anyway. Derry and his friends, helped by an older boy named Tommy Hicks, try to get revenge through pelting their rivals with mud balls and provoking a fight between Tommy and his lifelong enemy Johnny Wiggs, a fight which is interrupted by an air raid. The growing enmity between the groups of boys is reinforced by the impact of the war itself. Airraids become more frequent, and Derry and his family spend nights in a shelter. A bomb kills a woman who has lived near Derry's school, and at the end of the novel another one destroys Peter's home and kills Peter and his family. When Johnny Wiggs's younger brother David returns Peter's stolen gun, Derry symbolically throws it away, sobbing at the loss of his friend.

Dawn of Fear, like *Over Sea, Under Stone,* continues to attract young readers. Initially critics found the book powerful, citing its evocation of the horrors of World War II and its moving treatment of the death of a child. *Dawn of Fear* was also the subject of a special *Horn Book* column in which Sarah Ellis rightly praised the book and noted its powerful treatment of "endings and beginnings: the end of the isolated, free, subtle, and cruel world of childhood and the dawn of an adult sense of morality and compassion." *Dawn of Fear* was named to the *Horn Book* Honor List and cited as a Notable Book by the American Library Association.

In 1973 Cooper published *The Dark is Rising,* the first of four books continuing the story begun in *Over Sea, Under Stone.* This book, in which the conflict between good and evil is more intensely presented, was a greater critical success than *Over Sea,*

Dust jacket for the most critically acclaimed book in the Dark Is Rising series, the story of a boy who must recover a golden harp and awaken ancient "Sleepers"

Under Stone and received a variety of awards, including the *Boston-Globe Horn Book* Award for fiction. It was a runner-up for both the Newbery and Carnegie Medals and was also named an American Library Association Notable Book. The idea for *The Dark is Rising* came while Cooper and her husband were cross-country skiing in Massachusetts. A snowy landscape made her think of a novel with a similar wintry setting in which a boy wakes up on his birthday to discover that he can work magic. Cooper began writing the novel and, after rereading *Over Sea, Under Stone,* created outlines, characters, and plots for a series of books. She also completed the last page of the last book in the series, which she used, largely unchanged, at the end of *Silver on the Tree* (1975).

Cooper originally planned to give *The Dark is Rising* a title that her publisher felt was confusing, "The Gift of Grammayre." The novel's protagonist, Will Stanton, a young boy living in rural England, Cooper writes, was named "after the most remarkable Englishman of all," William Shakespeare. On the morning of his eleventh birthday (Midwinter Day) Will, the seventh son of a seventh son, is transported back in time to a wintry setting where he is approached by the "Black Rider," a lord of The Dark who tries to get Will into his power. Will resists the rider and makes his way through wooden doors on a hilltop and into a great hall, where he meets Merriman Lyon of *Over Sea, Under Stone* and a woman called "the Lady." They tell him that he is the last of the "Old Ones," ancient magical beings of great power. It is Will's task to collect the six signs of The Light as part of a final cosmic battle against the forces of The Dark.

During the twelve days of Christmas Will battles various agents of The Dark as he moves back and forth through time, searching for the signs and obtaining them from various individuals (a local farmer and a vagrant called "the Walker") and places (a secret panel in Miss Greythorne's manor, a wall of the local church, and a ship bearing the body of a king). The growing powers of The Dark are a constant threat, creating a terrible blizzard and kidnapping one of Will's sisters.

A powerful book, *The Dark is Rising* contains some of the most suspenseful moments in the series. From the moment a flock of rooks throws itself at the skylight in Will's attic bedroom to the nightmarish "Wild Hunt" in which an antlered mask (a Christmas present sent from Will's eldest brother) transforms a man into an ancient mythical being, the reader is drawn into an intense struggle between good and evil that never lets up. Early reviewers compared the novel to Tolkien's *Lord of the Rings* (1955) and Ursula K. Le Guin's *A Wizard of Earthsea* (1968) and noted the rich quality of Cooper's style. Virginia Haviland praised Cooper's "superb storytelling," which propels the reader to a "clear, convincing and satisfying conclusion."

In *Greenwitch* (1974) the three Drew children return to Trewissick, along with their Great-Uncle Merry and Will Stanton, to recover the ancient Grail, which has been stolen from the British museum, where it had been placed at the end of *Over Sea, Under Stone*. Their primary antagonist is a painter who is trying to become a lord of The Dark and locate the manuscript that can interpret the writing on the Grail he has stolen. The strongest and most lyrical sections of the book involve Jane

Drew, who plays a more important role than in the earlier works. Jane participates in the annual creation of the "Greenwitch," an image created from Hawthorne branches at the Lammas carnival, which comes to life as part of the neutral "Wild Magic." Through her compassion Jane obtains the coveted manuscript from the Greenwitch and thus allows the Old Ones to discover the next part of their quest to keep The Dark from rising.

Not surprising, reviewers frequently have compared *Greenwitch* to *The Dark is Rising* and found it tighter and simpler, along the lines of *Over Sea, Under Stone*. The creation of the Greenwitch, a creature who is from neither The Light nor The Dark, has also been praised. *Greenwitch* received a Notable Book Citation from the American Library Association.

The next book in the series, *The Grey King* (1975), received the Newbery Prize. In addition, it was given the Tir na N'og Award (Wales) for being the best book of the year written in English and set in Wales, as well as a commendation for the Carnegie Medal. Like other books in this series, *The Grey King* concerns a specific holiday and season – in this case, All Hallow's Eve and autumn. Will Stanton, who has become ill, is sent to stay with David Evans, an honorary uncle, in Tywyn, Wales. While he is there Will must accomplish two important quests. By answering riddles posed by three hooded Lords of High Magic (Merriman, King Arthur, and The Grey King), he must first recover a golden harp that is hidden in the nearby hills. Then he must awaken the ancient "Sleepers."

Will is helped by an important new character in the series, a Welsh boy named Bran Davies, who has white hair and no pigment. It eventually is revealed that Bran, who had been taken in during his infancy by a local farmer, is the son of King Arthur and Guinivere and has been hidden in the future for protection. In this book The Dark takes the form of a mysterious being called The Grey King, who uses gray foxes and a vindictive human named Caradog Prichard to carry out his wishes. Caradog is driven mad as a result of his unwitting manipulation by The Grey King, but not before he kills Bran's companion, a white Welsh sheepdog named Cafall.

The Grey King has been the most lauded book of the series. Children's novelists Natalie Babbitt and Jill Paton Walsh, despite their few criticisms of the series' unevenness, praise Cooper's ability to create a powerful, suspenseful story. One new idea in this novel is the suggestion that The Light itself is sometimes cold and unfeeling in using individuals to accomplish its purposes.

Cooper completed the series in 1975 with *Silver on the Tree,* also a recipient of the Tir na N'og Award. In this book Will Stanton uses the horn he had been given in *The Dark is Rising* to summon the Old Ones to battle against The Dark and to bring together the circle of friends (the Drew children, Bran Davies, and Merriman), who are slated to push The Dark back for a final time. Gathered together in the same part of Wales described in the previous book, the group attempts to make the mountains "sing," as described in an ancient rhyme. Jane meets the powerful "Lady" from *The Dark is Rising,* a figure who tells her about a crystal sword to be found in the lost lake. Bran and Will travel to a city in the past where they face the Black Rider and another evil being, The White Rider, while the Drew children find themselves in the nineteenth century. Later they all reunite on a mystical train. Eventually they find the fabled Midsummer Tree, where the Sleepers finally vanquish the Dark lords.

Cooper has acknowledged that this book is the weakest of the series, although she takes pride in certain vivid scenes. Some reviewers, such as Ann A. Flowers, however, have pronounced the book "a tour de force" that masterfully weaves together strands from the previous books. Cooper's strength as a storyteller again has received high marks, although some critics feel the book is "weighty," trying to do too much. Nearly every reviewer has commented on the high quality of Cooper's writing in describing specific settings and supernatural occurrences.

The Dark is Rising series has continued to interest scholars and critics and inspire much criticism – something Cooper does not particularly care for, as she explained in a keynote speech at the 1978 Annual International Conference of the Children's Literature Association. In this speech, later published in the conference's proceedings, Cooper argued that much literary analysis of children's books is appalling and artificial. She pleaded that critics not forget that children's writers are, after all, telling stories.

Despite Cooper's feelings about criticism, a continued interest in Arthurian literature has led to many studies of the mythical and legendary sources in the series by critics such as Emrys Evans, Gwyneth Evans, and Peter Goodrich. Both Raymond L. Plante and Gary D. Schmidt have focused on the development of characters in the series, while Stephen Canham, Lois R. Kuznets, and Charlotte Spivak have discussed the series as part of the genre of "High Fantasy." Recently Mary Harris Veeder has questioned Cooper's treatment of female characters and argued that they are marginalized in the series.

Among Cooper's books for children, the Dark is Rising series is her masterwork. The five novels in it are rich with symbolism and poetic passages. *The Dark is Rising,* perhaps the best single book of the series, certainly rivals and sometimes surpasses the work of the major fantasy writers – with whose work it is frequently compared.

Two years after completing the Dark is Rising series, Cooper published the first of six picture books. *Jethro and the Jumbie* (1979), Cooper explains, was written for children of the British Virgin Islands, where she had written much of the Dark is Rising series. Illustrated by her friend Ashley Bryan, the book tries to imitate the "lilting Caribbean speech." Cooper would have liked to have continued the adventures of her tough little hero, but since the book did not sell well she decided not to write a sequel. Critics, however, liked the book – especially its polished writing, its melodic use of dialect, and its young protagonist.

The main character of the book, Jethro Penn, a nearly eight-year-old black boy living in the British Virgin Islands, wants to go fishing with his older cabdriver brother, Thomas. Angered because his brother feels he is too small, Jethro goes off down the "jumbie trail," where he meets a "jumbie," a spirit that looks like a glowing ball. Jethro refuses to believe in the jumbie, even when it transforms itself, one at a time, into a giant mosquito, a scorpion, and a crab. Jethro finally admits that he believes in the jumbie in order to keep it from disappearing, as when Peter Pan tries to save Tinker Bell in J. M. Barrie's play *Peter Pan* (1904). The jumbie, in turn, tries to solve Jethro's problem first by making him big, then by giving him giant muscles. Finally he makes Thomas have a bad dream that convinces him to take Jethro along when he goes fishing. This simple tale is well crafted, and young Jethro is believable. The way in which a supernatural entity from the past is introduced into a more modern world, albeit a pastoral one, looks forward to the plot of Cooper's later novel *The Boggart* (1993).

During the time she wrote and published *Jethro and the Jumbie,* Cooper found herself increasingly drawn to the theater. Cooper, who admits that she has always been stagestruck, wrote a couple of plays for a local children's theater and then met John Langstaff, whose annual production, "The Christmas Revels," is performed in Harvard University's Sanders Theatre as well as in locations across the country. Hearing that Cooper was a children's writer, Langstaff asked her to contribute

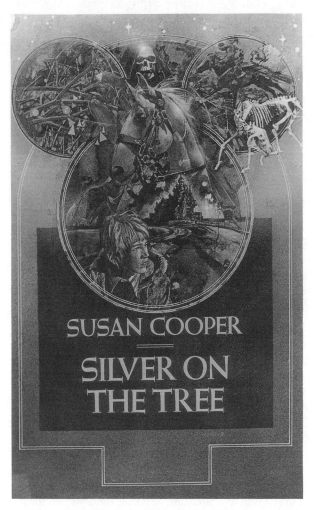

Dust jacket for the final novel in the Dark is Rising series in which the Dark lords are finally vanquished

in his introduction to his autobiography *A Terrible Liar: A Memoir* (1991) – which, he claims, he wrote at Cooper's insistence.

In 1978 Cooper introduced Cronyn to the *Foxfire* anthologies of articles about rural life. These books were begun as a project for high-school students in Rabun Gap, Georgia, by Eliot Wigginton. Initially Cooper and Cronyn talked about adapting material from these books into a reading that Cronyn and Tandy would perform. Instead, Cooper and Cronyn began incorporating a fictional mountain family into a play, in which Cronyn and Tandy eventually starred. Much of the writing and rewriting of this play took place on the road, as Cronyn and Tandy toured the United States, Britain, and the Soviet Union in D. L. Coburn's play *The Gin Game* (1977). The first production of *Foxfire* was at the Shakespearean Festival in Stratford, Ontario, in 1980, followed by revised versions performed in Minneapolis, Boston, Baltimore, and finally in New York, where it premiered on Broadway at the Ethel Barrymore Theatre on 11 November 1982 and played for seven months.

In *Foxfire* aging Annie Nations lives alone in a cabin high in the Blue Ridge Mountains. She has long conversations with her dead husband, an important character in the play, and flashbacks to important moments in her life – her courtship, the birth of a child, and the death of her husband. At the same time Dillard, her country-singer son, tries to persuade her to come and live with his family in Florida. In hanging on to her past, Annie is like "foxfire," a lichen which lives on dead trees and glows in the dark. In the end she chooses the present over the past, leaving behind her husband's ghost in order to care for Dillard and his children.

In general *Foxfire* was a success with New York theater critics, who focused on the brilliance of Tandy's performance as Annie Nations. Edwin Wilson argued that *Foxfire* is "not so much an evocation of a place as an evocation of a time and a set of values," as well as "a superb rendition of the hardship, the losses and most of all the love shared by the protagonists." Some critics found the mechanics of the plot contrived and suggested that it did not come to a great climax. As T. E. Kalem explained in a *Time* magazine review, however, the play "speaks for things too long mute: love of the land . . . , the inviolability of the family, the rigorous ethic of hard work. . . . *Foxfire* has already been called a 'hillbilly *Our Town*,' which is close to the mark."

Cooper and Cronyn collaborated again, co-writing the script for the television motion picture *The Dollmaker,* based on the novel by Harriet

miniature plays, verse, and songs to his "Revels," a task that delighted her. In 1979 Cooper wrote an essay describing the "Revels" for the *Horn Book,* and in 1985 she wrote a brief introduction to Langstaff's *The Christmas Revels Songbook: Carols, Processionals, Rounds, Ritual and Children's Songs in Celebration of the Winter Solstice.*

Within a year of meeting Langstaff, Cooper was collaborating on a full-length play with actor Hume Cronyn. A few days after *The Dark is Rising* was named a Newbery Honor Book, Cooper and her husband, who had been staying at their holiday home in the British Virgin Islands, met Cronyn and his actress wife, Jessica Tandy. Tandy had already read and admired *The Dark is Rising,* and they all became close friends. Indeed, Cooper's professional collaboration with both Cronyn and Tandy continued over the years. The importance of Cooper's professional relationship with Cronyn is hinted at

Arnow. This motion picture was first shown on ABC on 13 May 1984 and starred Jane Fonda as Gertie Nevels, mother of five from rural Kentucky, a role that earned her an Emmy Award. In addition Cooper and Cronyn received the Christopher Award, the Writers Guild of America Award, the Humanitas Prize, and an Emmy Award nomination from the Academy of Television Arts and Sciences for their script. Discussing her move from writing plays to screenplays, Cooper explains that writing for the screen is "something which comes more easily to a novelist, even a stagestruck novelist, than play writing."

The Dollmaker, like *Foxfire*, features a protagonist loath to leave her rural community and way of life. Forced to move her family to Detroit when her husband takes a job in a factory, Gertie Nevels reluctantly confronts the problems of an urban world – unions, public schools, and bigotry. In the end Gertie uses her talent for carving dolls and figurines to earn money so that her family can move back home. Along the way she weathers the death of her youngest daughter, who is killed by a train. Cooper and Cronyn's teleplay highlights many of the same themes as *Foxfire*, especially a yearning for the simple life and a validation of folk art and customs.

In 1987 *Foxfire* was made into a television movie and was presented on 13 December as a Hallmark Hall of Fame production. Its script by Cooper, the production starred Jessica Tandy, Hume Cronyn, and John Denver. For this production Cooper received an Emmy Award nomination and a Writers Guild of America Award. For the most part the film follows the play, although it fleshes out the role of Dillard and benefits from the use of "authentic" scenery.

Tandy and Cronyn again starred in a television play written by Cooper, a Hallmark Hall of Fame production broadcast on 5 December 1993. This time Cooper adapted the novel *To Dance with the White Dog* (1990) by Terry Kay. The plot of this movie is a little like a reverse-gender *Foxfire*. Robert Samuel Peek, an elderly man living in Georgia, misses his dead wife, Cora, and occasionally talks to her spirit and has flashbacks to their past together. His children are worried about him, because he claims to have taken in a white dog that, for most of the film, his family cannot see. Like *Foxfire*, the film validates the love of two elderly people and the value of small-town life. In 1995 ABC bought another Cooper and Cronyn teleplay, an adaptation of Ann Tyler's *Dinner at the Homesick Restaurant* (1982), which was originally scripted ten years earlier.

Cooper's first novel after completing the Dark is Rising series was *Seaward* (1983), written during the years that she had worked on *Foxfire*. This was a difficult period; the death of Cooper's father was followed by that of her mother six weeks later. During this time Cooper's own marriage had broken up, and she explains that working on this book helped her through this time. She writes, "It's a book about loving, and death, and life, and there are probably elements in it that I did not put there with conscious intent."

The two protagonists of *Seaward*, Westerly (West) and Cally, have recently experienced the death or disappearance of family members. Each of them has separately found a way into a fantastic world, Westerly through a door and Cally through a mirror. Unclear as to their purpose in this new world, the two instinctively travel toward the sea. Along the way they are threatened by this world's ruler, the mysterious Lady Taranis, and helped by the equally powerful Lugan. Cally and West eventually join forces to accomplish their quest and slowly develop love and respect for each other. They are nearly trapped by their dreams but are saved by the mysterious Snake and the monsterlike Peth. In the end Cally and West arrive at the sea, where they discover that they are in the country of life and death, that Taranis is herself Death and Lugan Life. They also learn that their parents are indeed dead and that Cally is a descendant of a "selkie," a seal who can take human form. Both Cally and West choose to return to their own world instead of crossing to the land of the dead or, in Cally's case, becoming a selkie. As a result they are promised that, although they live in different countries, they will meet again and spend their lives together.

Seaward, although not as popular as the Dark is Rising series, has been praised by critics who describe it as dreamlike, allegorical, and poignant. Paul Heins compared it to the works of nineteenth-century British fantasy writer George MacDonald and argued that, like MacDonald, Cooper "has endowed the concept of human responsibility – of human choice – with the face of fantasy." In 1989 *Seaward* received the B'nai B'rith Janusz Korczak Award.

The same year that *Seaward* appeared, Cooper published the first of three retellings of folktales, all illustrated by English watercolorist Warwick Hutton. *The Silver Cow: A Welsh Tale* (1983), based on a story Cooper had heard as a child, is set in Aberdovey, Wales, where her family has lived for over two hundred years. The story's protagonist,

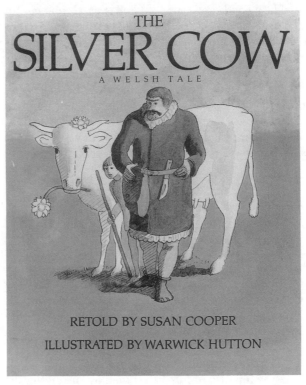

THE
SILVER COW
A WELSH TALE

RETOLD BY SUSAN COOPER

ILLUSTRATED BY WARWICK HUTTON

Dust jacket for Cooper's 1983 book based on a story she had heard as a child

Gwilym Hughes, lives in the "green hills of Wales" near a mountain lake that is now called "Llyn Barfog," the bearded lake. Small-hearted Gwilym forces his son, Huw, to look after the cattle rather than go to school. Occasionally Huw takes his harp with him, playing for the animals and eventually attracting a mysterious, shining silver cow who gives three times more milk than normal. Huw instinctively knows that the cow has been sent by the Tylwth Teg, "the magic people," although his father scoffs at his answer.

The cow and her progeny bring Gwilym riches, but when the cow grows old he plans to have it butchered. As the cow is about to be killed, a voice from the lake calls the cow and all of her children – who plunge into the water and disappear. At the same time all of the money that Gwilym has stored in his chest flies away. At this point Huw also leaves home, but he notes that white water lilies have appeared on the lake, one for every cow that has vanished.

The Silver Cow caught the attention of reviewers, who praised both its text and illustrations. Patricia Dooley felt that Cooper's retelling of this story was "sensitive and lyrical," a description echoed in other reviews. Several reviewers praised

Cooper's addition of the character Huw to the traditional tale. The language in this book is indeed poetic and suggests the power of the oral tradition, which has clearly influenced most of Cooper's writing.

Cooper's second book with Hutton, *The Selkie Girl* (1986), draws on the ancient legends of selkies, as did *Seaward*. In recent years many children's writers have created stories and novels about selkies, including Pauline Clarke ("The Selkie Boy" in her *Bel the Giant and Other Stories,* 1956), Mollie Hunter (*A Stranger Came Ashore,* 1975), Jane Yolen ("Greyling" and "Ballad of the White Seal Maid" in her *Neptune Rising,* 1982), Mordicai Gerstein (*The Seal Mother,* 1986), and Sylvia Peck (*Seal Child,* 1989).

In Cooper's tale a man named Donallan falls in love with a selkie maid, the daughter of the king of Lochlann. With the help of a wise seaman, Old Thomas, Donallan steals the selkie's sealskin, forcing her to stay on land and marry him. His selkie wife, whom he calls Mairi, bears him five children, one of whom inadvertently tells his mother where her skin is hidden. Mairi explains to her human children that she must return to the sea – she has five seal children in the water as well – but she continues to look out for Donallan and his children, as she blesses them with fine catches when they go fishing and sings to them in the wind.

Again reviewers praised Cooper's retelling for its rhythmic, direct style, although both the *Bulletin for the Center of Children's Books* and *School Library Journal* preferred Gerstein's *The Seal Mother*, which was published the same year. Although the story is a retelling of a folktale, Cooper puts her own stamp on the tale by personalizing characters, providing them with names and putting them in a specific location.

Tam Lin (1991), Cooper's most recent book with Hutton, is a retelling of an old Scottish ballad. Margaret, the king's daughter, longs for adventure and does not feel like waiting for a man to pick her for a wife as he would pick a flower. She runs off to the wood of Carterhays to pick roses and meets a handsome young man who spends the day with her. When she returns to the castle, she is accused of having been enchanted by the Elfin knight Tam Lin. Learning that the man she met is indeed Tam Lin, Margaret attempts to save him from the Elfin Queen, who intends to send him to hell on Midsummer's Eve. Like the jumbie who transforms himself into several monstrous shapes in Cooper's *Jethro and the Jumbie,* Tam Lin is turned into various things – a wolf, a snake, a wild deer, and a red-hot bar of iron. Margaret breaks his enchantment by keeping hold of him, regardless of his terrifying metamorphoses.

Cooper's version of the story provides Margaret with a modern, independent personality and describes the setting and supernatural events with some of the same style as that of her fantasy novels. Cooper and Hutton's *Tam Lin* was published the same year as another version of the tale, one retold by Jane Yolen and illustrated by Charles Mikolaycak. Both books received favorable reviews. Denise Wilms in *Booklist* suggested that Hutton's illustrations seem consciously created to avoid romantic clichés, while Helen Gregory wrote that Cooper's version is "alive with dialogue" but gives little background information.

In 1991 Cooper also published the first of two picture books illustrated by Jos[eph] A. Smith. Unlike her books illustrated by Warwick Hutton, *Matthew's Dragon* is a contemporary fantasy tale, not merely a retelling of a traditional folktale or ballad. According to the book jacket, *Matthew's Dragon* was originally written as a bedtime story for Cooper's step-grandson, who loved dragons, and among the names on the dedication page is that of a real-life Matthew. The story begins with a mother reading Matthew a bedtime story from a book which, in Smith's illustration, is titled *Dragons*. After the book

has been placed on a bedside table and Matthew has tried to sleep, a tiny dragon emerges from the book. The dragon miniaturizes Matthew, and the two fly out of a partly opened window into the garden, where they are threatened by a cat and forced to take refuge in a greenhouse. The dragon rescues Matthew, and the two fly off into the sky, where they meet every "dragon ever imagined," all singing and swirling around. At this point both the dragon and Matthew agree that they are ready to go to sleep, and they return home. *Matthew's Dragon* is a simple but pleasing bedtime story recalling the nocturnal flight in Raymond Briggs's *The Snowman* (1978), as well as Peter's daylight adventures in the toolshed in Beatrix Potter's *The Tale of Peter Rabbit* (1902).

Smith also illustrated Cooper's latest picture book, *Danny and the Kings* (1993), which draws on the biblical story of the wise men who visited the baby Jesus. A departure from Cooper's pure fantasies, this book has a mystical feeling appropriate for a Christmas story. Ann A. Flowers, writing in the *Horn Book,* found Cooper's use of the three kings clever and contributing to a "warm-hearted story with warm and glowing Christmas illustrations."

The protagonist of the story is Danny, a young boy who lives in a trailer and is excited about Christmas but whose family has no money for a tree. When Danny tries to bring home a small tree given him by a friend, it falls underneath the wheels of a truck while Danny is crossing the highway and is crushed to bits. Jake, the driver of the truck, is worried about Danny and takes him inside a truck-stop café, where he meets two other truckers, Bud and Richard – one black and the other Native American. All three drivers have trucks bearing the name "King of the Road." The drivers return Danny to his school, where he plays the part of one of the three kings in a Christmas play. When he and his family return home, they find a beautiful tree and, lying in the snow, a single light bulb like the ones that had decorated the trucks belonging to the three "Kings of the Road."

The Boggart, Cooper's first children's novel in ten years, was also published in 1993. The novel, like some of her picture books, draws heavily on Welsh and Scottish folktales and is more humorous and pleasant than the Dark is Rising books. In *The Boggart* Cooper expands on the traditional tales of "boggarts" – invisible, playful spirits who are said to haunt some families. The first part of the novel resembles Mollie Hunter's *The Wicked One* (1977), for in both novels an ancient, invisible creature plagues a Scottish family and then immigrates with them to North America.

Dust jacket for Cooper's 1993 Christmas story, based on the account of the Three Wise Men

In Cooper's novel the playful, childlike boggart accompanies the Volnik family back to their home in Toronto, Canada, after their visit to a castle they have inherited on the Scottish island of Appin. The Volnik children, twelve-year-old Emily and nine-year-old Jessup, gradually come to realize that a boggart is living in their house and making their lives miserable: it follows Jessup to school (where it causes problems at lunch and at a hockey practice), attacks Emily and Jessup's costumed mother on Halloween because it thinks she is a supernatural creature, and levitates antiques in their mother's shop. In the novel's best scene Cooper draws on her theater experience to describe how the boggart disrupts a production of Shakespeare's *Cymbeline* (1623) by Mr. Volnik's theater company. Although the boggart seems willfully mischievous, it is actually perplexed by a modern, technological society and longs to return to its ancestral home in Scotland. In the end this is accomplished when Emily, Jessup, and a group of teenage computer enthusiasts manage to trap the boggart on a floppy disk. Thus using modern technology to everyone's advantage, they then mail this disk to Tommy, a Scottish boy who lives near the Boggart's old castle.

The Boggart was published to rave reviews in the *Horn Book,* the *Times Literary Supplement,* and *The New York Times Book Review.* In a *Horn Book* review Ann Flowers praised the novel's "seamless fusion of the newest technology and one of the oldest forms of wild magic." Lindsay Duguid felt that Cooper's screenwriting influenced *The Boggart* by making the novel "markedly tighter than the diffuse earlier work." Duguid also noted that the evil in the book comes from contemporary technology, not old magic. The children in the novel are at risk from "20th-century things: cars, tabloid newspapers, flying objects," and the villain is a child psychiatrist. While Rafael Yglesias recognized that the novel uses a familiar plot – "a mysterious and possibly ancient being befriending modern kids and making trouble in their world" – he praised Cooper's ability to make the plot seem fresh and the boggart's magic credible.

Susan Cooper currently lives in Cambridge, Massachusetts, and, according to Duguid, plans on writing another book about the boggart as well as another with a Shakespearean theme. Cooper also talks of a motion-picture version of the Dark is Rising books. According to Duguid, Cooper "sees her life in ten-year cycles: ten years of journalism; ten years of writing novels; ten years of film and theatre work" – and it appears that "her new cycle is starting to combine all these elements."

Cooper's novels, particularly the Dark is Rising books, are as popular as when they were first published. The series is available in boxed sets, still in print both in paperback and hardback editions in the United States. Cooper's more recent literary works, as well as her television movies, have continued to broaden her audience and help secure her reputation as one of the most versatile, popular, and critically acclaimed children's writers of the twentieth century.

Cooper has written that the value of fantasy is that it allows readers to escape inward into "the dreamlike world which has in it all the images and emotions accumulated since the human race began." It is "the metaphor through which we discover ourselves." In her best moments Cooper enables her readers to make this metaphorical journey.

Interview:

Jon Stott, "Nature of Fantasy: A Conversation with Ruth Nichols, Susan Cooper, and Maurice Sendak," *World of Children's Books* (Fall 1978).

References:

Gillian Avery, "Fashions in Children's Fiction," *Children's Literature in Education,* 12 (September 1973): 10–19;

Natalie Babbitt, "For Young Readers: 'The Grey King,' " *New York Times Book Review,* 28 September 1975, pp. 10, 12;

Dainis Bisenieks, "Children, Magic, and Choices," *Mythlore: A Journal of J. R. R. Tolkien, C. S. Lewis, Charles Williams, and the Genres of Myth and Fantasy,* 61 (Fall 1979): 13–16;

Stephen Canham, "Evil and the High Ethical Fantasy of Susan Cooper's *The Dark is Rising,*" in *Literature and Hawaii's Children. Imagination: A Bridge to Magic Realms in the Humanities* (Honolulu: Literature and Hawaii's Children, 1990), pp. 107–111;

Dwight Dudley Carlson, "A Second Look: 'Over Sea, Under Stone,' " *Horn Book,* 52 (February 1976): 522–523;

Patricia Dooley, "*The Silver Cow,*" *School Library Journal,* 29 (April 1988): 99;

Lindsay Duguid, "A Permanent Resident Alien," *Times Educational Supplement,* 4 June 1993, p. A11;

Sarah Ellis, "A Second Look: *Dawn of Fear,*" *Horn Book,* 58 (February 1982): 436–439;

Emrys Evans, "Children's Novels and Welsh Mythology: Multiple Voices in Susan Cooper and Alan Garner," in *The Voice of the Narrator in Children's Literature: Insights from Writers and Critics* (New York: Greenwood Press, 1989), pp. 92–100;

Gwyneth Evans, "Three Modern Views of Merlin," *Mythlore: A Journal of J. R. R. Tolkien, C. S. Lewis, Charles Williams, and the Genres of Myth and Fantasy,* 16 (Summer 1990): 17–22;

Katherina Filips-Juswigg, "Echoes of Chekov's *The Cherry Orchard* in *Foxfire,*" *Zapiski Russkoi Akademicheskoi Gruppy, Transactions of the Association of Russian American,* 28 (1985): 303–306;

Ann A. Flowers, "For Intermediate Readers: 'The Bogart,'" *Horn Book,* 69 (February 1993): 330–332;

Flowers, "Stories for Intermediate Readers: 'Silver on the Tree,' " *Horn Book,* 53 (December 1977): 660–661;

Betty Gilderdale, "Susan Cooper: *The Dark is Rising* and the Legends," *Children's Literature Association Yearbook* [New Zealand] (1978): 11–23;

Peter Goodrich, "Magical Medievalism and the Fairy Tale in Susan Cooper's *The Dark is Rising* Sequence," *The Lion and the Unicorn: A Critical Journal of Children's Literature,* 12 (December 1988): 165–177;

Helen Gregory, "Review of *Tam Lin,*" *School Library Journal,* 37 (May 1991): 88;

Dust jacket for Cooper's 1993 children's novel, based on traditional tales of playful spirits who haunt families

Virginia Haviland, "A Child's Garden of Ghosts, Poltergeists and Werewolves," *Bookworld–The Washington Post,* 8 July 1973, p. 13;

Paul Heins, "Seaward," *Horn Book,* 60 (February 1984): 59;

T. E. Kalem, "Ghosts Walk in Appalachia," *Time,* 120 (22 November 1982): 176;

Barbara Z. Kiefer, "Wales as a Setting for Children's Fantasy," *Children's Literature in Education,* 13 (Spring 1982): 95–102;

Lois R. Kuznets, " 'High Fantasy' in America: A Study of Lloyd Alexander, Ursula Le Guin, and Susan Cooper," *The Lion and the Unicorn: A Critical Journal of Children's Literature,* 9 (1985): 19–35;

Kuznets, "Letters to the Editor: Susan Cooper," *Children's Literature Association Newsletter,* 3–2 (Spring 1978): 14–16; republished as "Susan Cooper: A Reply" in *Signposts to Criticism of Children's Literature,* edited by Robert Bator (Chicago: American Library Association, 1983), pp. 109–113;

Betty Levin, "A Journey through Mountain and Mist: *The Grey King*," *Horn Book,* 52 (February 1976): 443–445;

Margaret K. McElderry, "Susan Cooper," *Horn Book,* 52 (February 1976): 367–372;

Meet the Newbery Author: Susan Cooper (Westminister, Md.: Miller-Brody, 1977), audiocassette;

Neil Philip, "Fantasy: Double Cream or Instant Whip?," *Signal,* 35 (May 1981): 82–90;

Raymond L. Plante, "Object and Character in *The Dark is Rising*," *Children's Literature Association Quarterly,* 11 (Spring 1986): 37–41;

David Rees, "Children's Writers: Susan Cooper," *School Librarian,* 32 (September 1984): 197–205; republished as "The Dark is Risable," in Rees's *What Do Draculas Do?: Essays on Contemporary Writers of Fiction for Children and Young Adults* (Metuchen, N.J.: Scarecrow Press, 1990), pp. 175–189;

Gary D. Schmidt, "See How They Grow: Character Development in Children's Series Books," *Children's Literature in Education,* 18 (March 1987): 34–44;

Gillian Spraggs, "A Lawless World: The Fantasy Novels of Susan Cooper," *Use of English,* 33 (Spring 1982): 23–31;

C. W. Sullivan III, "Traditional Welsh Materials in Modern Fantasy," *Extrapolation,* 28 (Spring 1987): 87–97;

Mary Harris Veeder, "Gender and Empowerment in Susan Cooper's 'The Dark is Rising' Sequence," *Children's Literature Association Quarterly,* 16 (Spring 1991): 11–16;

Denise Wilms, "Review of *Tam Lin*," *Booklist,* 87 (15 February 1991): 1191;

Edwin Wilson, "Tandy and Cronyn Give a Lesson in Great Acting," *Wall Street Journal,* 16 November 1982, p. 32;

Rafael Yglesias, "The Gremlin on the Floppy Disk," *New York Times Book Review,* 16 May 1993, p. 23.

Papers:
Cooper's manuscripts are held in the Lillian H. Smith collection, Toronto Public Library, Toronto, Ontario, Canada.

Helen Cresswell

(11 July 1934 –   )

Catherine L. Elick
Bridgewater College

BOOKS: *Sonya-by-the-Shore,* illustrated by Robin Jane Wells (London: Dent, 1960);

Jumbo Spencer, illustrated by Clixby Watson (Leicester: Brockhampton, 1963); illustrated by Victoria de Lorrea (Philadelphia: Lippincott, 1966);

The White Sea Horse, illustrated by Robin Jacques (Edinburgh: Oliver & Boyd, 1964; Philadelphia: Lippincott, 1965);

Jumbo Back to Nature, illustrated by Leslie Wood (Leicester: Brockhampton, 1965);

Pietro and the Mule, illustrated by Maureen Eckersley (Edinburgh: Oliver & Boyd, 1965; Indianapolis: Bobbs-Merrill, 1965);

Jumbo Afloat, illustrated by Wood (Leicester: Brockhampton, 1966);

Where the Wind Blows, illustrated by Peggy Fortnum (London: Faber & Faber, 1966; New York: Funk & Wagnalls, 1968);

The Piemakers, illustrated by V. H. Drummond (London: Faber & Faber, 1967; Philadelphia: Lippincott, 1968);

A Day on Big O, illustrated by Shirley Hughes (London: Benn, 1967; Chicago: Follett, 1968);

A Tide for the Captain, illustrated by Jacques (Edinburgh: Oliver & Boyd, 1967);

The Signposters, illustrated by Gareth Floyd (London: Faber & Faber, 1968);

Jumbo and the Big Dig, illustrated by Wood (Leicester: Brockhampton, 1968);

The Sea Piper, illustrated by Jacques (Edinburgh: Oliver & Boyd, 1968);

Rug Is a Bear, illustrated by Susanna Gretz (London: Benn, 1968);

Rug Plays Tricks, illustrated by Gretz (London: Benn, 1968);

The Barge Children, illustrated by Lynette Hemmant (Leicester: Brockhampton, 1968);

The Night-Watchmen, illustrated by Floyd (London: Faber & Faber, 1969; New York: Macmillan, 1969);

Helen Cresswell

A Gift from Winklesea, illustrated by Janina Ede (Leicester: Brockhampton, 1969);

A Game of Catch, illustrated by Floyd (London: Oliver & Boyd, 1969); illustrated by Ati Forberg (New York: Macmillan, 1977);

A House for Jones, illustrated by Margaret Gordon (London: Benn, 1969);

Rug Plays Ball, illustrated by Gretz (London: Benn, 1969);

Rug and a Picnic, illustrated by Gretz (London: Benn, 1969);

The Outlanders, illustrated by Doreen Roberts (London: Faber & Faber, 1970);

Rainbow Pavement, illustrated by Hughes (London: Benn, 1970);

The Wilkses, illustrated by Floyd (London: BBC Publications, 1970); republished as *Time Out,* illustrated by Tessa Hamilton (Cambridge: Lutterworth, 1987); illustrated by Peter Elwell (New York: Macmillan, 1990);

John's First Fish, illustrated by Prudence Seward (London: Macmillan, 1970);

At the Stroke of Midnight: Traditional Fairy Tales Retold, illustrated by Carolyn Dinan (London: Collins, 1971); republished as *The Second Armada Lion Book of Fairy Tales* (London: Collins, 1973); republished as *A Kingdom of Riches: Traditional Fairy Tales Retold by Helen Cresswell* (London: Fontana, 1981); republished as *Classic Fairy Tales,* illustrated by Carol Lawson (New York: Artists & Writers Guild, 1993);

The Bird Fancier, illustrated by Renate Meyer (London: Benn, 1971);

Up the Pier, illustrated by Floyd (London: Faber & Faber, 1971; New York: Macmillan, 1972);

The Weather Cat, illustrated by Margery Gill (London: Benn, 1971); illustrated by Barbara Walker (New York: Gallery, 1989);

The Beachcombers, illustrated by Errol Le Cain (London: Faber & Faber, 1972; New York: Macmillan, 1972);

Bluebirds over Pit Row, illustrated by Richard Kennedy (London: Benn, 1972);

Jane's Policeman, illustrated by Gill (London: Benn, 1972);

The Long Day, illustrated by Gill (London: Benn, 1972);

Roof Fall!, illustrated by Kennedy (London: Benn, 1972);

Short Back and Sides, illustrated by Kennedy (London: Benn, 1972);

The Beetle Hunt, illustrated by Anne Knight (London: Longman, 1973);

The Bongleweed, illustrated by Ann Strugnell (London: Faber & Faber, 1973; New York: Macmillan, 1973);

The Bower Birds, illustrated by Gill (London: Benn, 1973);

The Key, illustrated by Kennedy (London: Benn, 1973);

Lizzie Dripping, illustrated by Jenny Thorne (London: BBC, 1973);

Cheap Day Return, illustrated by Kennedy (London: Benn, 1974);

The Trap, illustrated by Kennedy (London: Benn, 1974);

Shady Deal, illustrated by Kennedy (London: Benn, 1974);

Lizzie Dripping by the Sea, illustrated by Faith Jaques (London: BBC, 1974);

Lizzie Dripping and the Little Angel, illustrated by Jaques (London: BBC, 1974);

Lizzie Dripping Again, illustrated by Jaques (London: BBC, 1974);

Two Hoots, illustrated by Martine Blanc (London: Benn, 1974; New York: Crown, 1978);

Two Hoots Go to Sea, illustrated by Blanc (London: Benn, 1974; New York: Crown, 1978);

More Lizzie Dripping, illustrated by Jaques (London: BBC, 1974);

Butterfly Chase, illustrated by Gill (Harmondsworth: Kestrel, 1975);

The Winter of the Birds (London: Faber & Faber, 1975; New York: Macmillan, 1975);

Two Hoots in the Snow, illustrated by Blanc (London: Benn, 1975; New York: Crown, 1978);

Two Hoots and the Big Bad Bird, illustrated by Blanc (London: Benn, 1975; New York: Crown, 1978);

Awful Jack, illustrated by Joanna Stubbs (London: Hodder & Stoughton, 1977);

Two Hoots and the King, illustrated by Blanc (London: Benn, 1977; New York: Crown, 1978);

Two Hoots Play Hide and Seek, illustrated by Blanc (London: Benn, 1977; New York: Crown, 1978);

Ordinary Jack: Being the First Part of the Bagthorpe Saga, illustrated by Jill Bennett (London: Faber & Faber, 1977; New York: Macmillan, 1977);

Donkey Days, illustrated by Hughes (London: Benn, 1977);

Absolute Zero: Being the Second Part of the Bagthorpe Saga, illustrated by Bennett (London: Faber & Faber, 1978; New York: Macmillan, 1978);

Bagthorpes Unlimited: Being the Third Part of the Bagthorpe Saga, illustrated by Bennett (London: Faber & Faber, 1978; New York: Macmillan, 1978);

The Flyaway Kite, illustrated by Bridget Clarke (Harmondsworth: Kestrel, 1979);

Bagthorpes Versus the World: Being the Fourth Part of the Bagthorpe Saga, illustrated by Bennett (London: Faber & Faber, 1979; New York: Macmillan, 1979);

My Aunt Polly by the Sea, illustrated by Gordon (Exeter: Wheaton, 1979);

Nearly Goodbye, illustrated by Tony Morris (London: Macmillan, 1980);

Penny for the Guy, illustrated by Nicole Goodwin (London: Macmillan, 1980);

Henry and a tramp; illustration by Gareth Floyd for Cresswell's The Night-Watchmen *(1969)*

Dear Shrink (London: Faber & Faber, 1982; New York: Macmillan, 1982);

The Secret World of Polly Flint, illustrated by Shirley Felts (London: Faber & Faber, 1982; New York: Macmillan, 1984);

Ellie and the Hagwitch, illustrated by Jonathan Heap (London: Hardy, 1984);

Bagthorpes Abroad: Being the Fifth Part of the Bagthorpe Saga (London: Faber & Faber, 1984; New York: Macmillan, 1984);

Bagthorpes Haunted: Being the Sixth Part of the Bagthorpe Saga (London: Faber & Faber, 1985; New York: Macmillan, 1985);

Petticoat Smuggler, illustrated by Shirley Bellwood (London: Macmillan, 1985);

Whodunnit?, illustrated by Caroline Browne (London: Cape, 1986);

Greedy Alice, illustrated by Martin Honeysett (London: Deutsch, 1986);

Moondial (London: Faber & Faber, 1987; New York: Macmillan, 1987);

Trouble, illustrated by Margaret Chamberlain (London: Gollancz, 1987);

Dragon Ride, illustrated by Liz Roberts (Harmondsworth: Viking Kestrel, 1987; New York: Viking, 1987);

Fox in a Maze, illustrated by Browne (London: Cape, 1988);

The Story of Grace Darling, illustrated by Paul Wright (Harmondsworth: Viking Kestrel, 1988);

Bagthorpes Liberated: Being the Seventh Part of the Bagthorpe Saga (London: Faber & Faber, 1989; New York: Macmillan, 1989);

Rosie and the Boredom Eater (London: Heinemann, 1989);

Whatever Happened in Winklesea?, illustrated by Shoo Rayner (Cambridge: Lutterworth, 1989);

Almost Goodbye Guzzler, illustrated by Judy Brown (London: Black, 1990); republished as *Almost Good-Bye* (New York: Dutton, 1992);

Hokey Pokey Did It!, illustrated by Frank James (Loughborough: Ladybird, 1990);

Meet Posy Bates, illustrated by Kate Aldous (London: Bodley Head, 1990; New York: Macmillan, 1992);

Posy Bates, Again!, illustrated by Aldous (London: Bodley Head, 1991; New York: Macmillan, 1994);

Lizzie Dripping and the Witch, illustrated by Chris Riddell (London: BBC, 1991);

The Bagthorpe Triangle, illustrated by Bennett (London: Faber & Faber, 1992);

The Return of the Psammead, illustrated by John Holder (London: BBC, 1992);

The Puffin Book of Funny Stories, illustrated by Ainslie Macleod (New York: Viking, 1992; London: Puffin, 1993);

Posy Bates and the Bag Lady, illustrated by Aldous (London: Bodley Head, 1993; Hampton, N.H.: Chivers, 1993);

The Watchers: A Mystery at Alton Towers (London: Puffin, 1993; New York: Macmillan, 1994);

Birdspell, illustrated by Aafke Brouwer (London: Heinemann, 1995).

OTHER: "Ancient and Modern and Incorrigibly Plural," in *The Thorny Paradise: Writers on Writing for Children,* edited by Edward Blishen (Harmondsworth: Kestrel, 1975), pp. 108–116.

TELEVISION: *Lizzie Dripping,* BBC, six episodes, 1973; five episodes, 1975;

Dick Whittington, BBC, 1974;

Jumbo Spencer, BBC, five episodes, 1976;

For Bethlehem Read Little Thraves, BBC, 1976;

Lizzie Dripping and the Witch, BBC, 1977;

The Day Posy Bates Made History, BBC, 1977;

The Secret World of Polly Flint, ITV Central Television, seven episodes, 1983;

The Haunted School, Revcom (France) and Australian Broadcasting, eight-part miniseries, 1986.

Rarely does a writer achieve productivity and variety such as Helen Cresswell's – without sacrificing either excellence or distinctiveness in her prose. Not only has Cresswell produced over ninety works since her first book appeared in 1960, but she has excelled in nearly every form of children's fiction: novels for intermediate readers, picture books, easy-to-read stories for reluctant as well as beginning readers, fairy-tale retellings, and television screenplays. Her novels of fantasy and high comedy especially have won favor with readers and earned her four Carnegie Medal nominations. Critics consistently praise her masterful style. Whether it be in

timeless tall tales like *The Piemakers* (1967) and *The Signposters* (1968), madcap family adventures like the multivolume Bagthorpe Saga (1977–1992), or lyrical mysteries like *The Night-Watchmen* (1969) and *Moondial* (1987), her prose runs pure and sparkles with wit.

Cresswell's novels frequently circle to reencounter themes engaged in her earlier work. For example, the occasional exasperations and more-frequent comforts of family life are explored in diverse ways. Often in close-knit family threesomes, a child and two parents unite to attain a common goal. *The Signposters,* in which Dyke organizes a reunion of the entire Flockshire Smith clan, celebrates the joys of the extended family. *Dear Shrink* (1982) pits sibling love against an impersonal foster-care system. In a breezier vein are the books of the Bagthorpe Saga, which irreverently exploit sibling rivalry and parental frustrations for all the humor they are worth. Other favorite Cresswell themes are the pride of craftsmanship and the power of the artist's imagination. Always in her books attempts are made to squelch creative forces, and always those attempts are foiled or at least temporarily checked. Complementing this love for artistry is a love for the English countryside and for nature in general. Finally, Cresswell's child protagonists frequently encounter new worlds and rectify old wrongs through time travel.

Although the time settings of her novels may not always be specified, their geographical settings are often recognizable as Nottinghamshire, England's heartland and the county where Cresswell has resided most of her life. She was born in Nottingham in 1934, the second of three children, to J. E. Cresswell, an electrical engineer, and A. E. (Clarke) Cresswell. She began writing poetry at the age of six or seven and continued to do so through her early twenties, sometimes imitating the styles of favorite poets such as John Keats and Edmund Spenser. While still a teenager Cresswell won her first literary award – a prize for best poem submitted to the Nottingham Poetry Society in 1950. She views this early poetry as an apprenticeship for the fantasy she now writes.

After her education at Nottingham Girls' High School and King's College, London, where she received a B.A. with honors in English in 1955, her career was remarkably varied. She worked as a literary assistant to a Dutch shipowner, a fashion buyer, a teacher, and an employee of BBC television. Her avocational interests range as widely as these early job experiences; they also connect her with some of her fictional characters. For instance, she claims to enjoy gardening, like Becky in *The Bongleweed* (1973); "ticking," or exploring new places, like Josh in the 1969 novel *The Night-Watchmen;* and "collecting coincidences," like Oliver in *Dear Shrink.* By the time she married Brian Rowe on 14 April 1962, she had begun to publish children's books. Within the next few years Cresswell and her husband had two daughters, Caroline Jane and Candida Lucy.

The first novel to capture a sizable readership and demonstrate Cresswell's flair for comedy was *Jumbo Spencer* (1963). Eleven-year-old Jumbo is casting about for an exciting way to spend the school holidays when he hears a television news announcer say that someone is a great reformer and a leader of men. Thinking that he would like that said of himself someday, he founds the Jumbo Spencer Reform Club. The beneficiary of the club's reforming zeal is its own rural village of Shoredale. The club members start in small ways, first painting an unauthorized crosswalk on the pavement so that little Miss Mogg can make her daily trip to the post office in safety, and they then move on to bigger projects. Eventually Jumbo wins the support of Mr. Bennet, a local writer and philanthropist who agrees to fund a town hall, playing fields, and a pavilion for the village.

Some readers have claimed to find Jumbo's grand schemes more irritating than entertaining. Certainly Cresswell's humor and characterization are less subtle here than in later creations. However, most critics recognize that the central appeal of a character like Jumbo Spencer is in his unshakable self-assurance, his exaggerated self-importance. *Jumbo Spencer* was the first of Helen Cresswell's books to spawn a series: *Jumbo Back to Nature* (1965), *Jumbo Afloat* (1966), and *Jumbo and the Big Dig* (1968). Cresswell also adapted these stories for BBC television in 1976.

With her next work Cresswell directed her attention from Jumbo's real – though humorously hyperbolic – contemporary English life to a fantastic English past. In *The White Sea Horse* (1964) Molly Flower and her fisherman father live on a houseboat anchored along the seacoast outside the village of Piskerton. One evening Mr. Flower brings aboard a tiny sea horse with an icy white coat and golden hooves, a creature that he has accidentally caught in his nets. Respecting the little sea horse's freedom, the Flowers plan to release him after he has eaten and rested. However, the villagers of Piskerton, egged on by their mayor, Mr. Winkle, decide to cage the little creature instead – first to bring them luck and then to give as a gift to the king and queen. But when the six donkeys belonging to

Peter, Molly's friend, run amok through the marketplace and disappear into the sea, the villagers are finally convinced that Peter's donkeys and Piskerton's good luck can only be restored by setting the little sea horse free. Their act of kindness is rewarded when the sea horse returns briefly to lead the bewitched donkeys back to land. Each donkey carries in its mouth an oyster containing a huge pearl to drop at the feet of their majesties.

Readers found enchanting the style of *The White Sea Horse,* with its dreamy sea imagery; but some considered the plot too slender to sustain an entire book. In *A Sense of Story: Essays on Contemporary Writers for Children* (1971) John Rowe Townsend points to the stereotyped characters such as the mayor and the slapstick humor in many scenes, and he rightly argues that the author had not yet learned to match the quality of her humor to that of her fantasy. Even though *The White Sea Horse* must be viewed as apprentice work, it does broach themes important to much of Cresswell's writing: the right of all creatures to live free, untrammeled lives and the threat posed to their existence by human greed and ignorance.

The Piemakers was Helen Cresswell's first big success and, though an early work, one of her greatest achievements. Cresswell's two creative springs had remained largely separate and unequal up to this point. Now the straight-faced hilarity of the Jumbo books and the delicate fantasy of *The White Sea Horse* flowed together.

The Piemakers is a fantasy wrought without magic. Fantasy and comedy are achieved simultaneously by telling with great solemnity what is obviously a tall tale. Arthy, Jem, and their daughter Gravella Roller belong to a generations-old family of pie makers in Danby Dale. When Arthy is first commissioned to make a pie that will serve two hundred, one of whom will be the king, he unwisely involves his brother Crispin, head of the rival Gorby Dale pie makers. The pie made by Uncle Crispin's recipe is so heavily peppered as to be inedible, and Arthy takes the drastic measure of burning his own bakehouse, with the pie in it, rather than risk his family's reputation. Things look bleak for Arthy, Jem, and Gravella until their neighbors persuade them to represent Danby Dale in a Grand Contest announced by the king's herald. The blacksmith's brother forges a pie dish so large that they disguise it as a boat and float it down the river to Farmer Leary's barn, where a special oven has been built large enough to accommodate a pie for two thousand. With all the Dalesmen working together in secrecy, Arthy is able to produce a historic pie that

Dust jacket for one of Cresswell's domestic-comedy novels

wins the king's praise and even the grudging congratulations of Uncle Crispin.

Readers and reviewers of *The Piemakers* have been as lavish in their praise as the proportions of Arthy's pie. It was the first of Cresswell's works to be runner-up for the prestigious Carnegie Medal in 1967; it also received the Guardian Award for children's fiction in that year. Some reviews cited similarities between Cresswell's pie makers and the title characters of Mary Norton's *The Borrowers* (1952). Although Norton's borrowers are small in scale and the Danby Rollers' efforts are grandiose, both works do indeed focus on the warm, supportive family life of two parents and their daughter. The daughters at the beginning of each novel feel somewhat aloof from their families' professions, but they become fascinated in spite of themselves. Pie making, even more than borrowing, is presented as work to be done with skill and pride; the dedication of the craftsman is a theme Cresswell returns to again and again. Both novels have frameworks to explain how the tales came to be told, and Cresswell

jestingly produces both archival and archaeological evidence. Not only does the narrator claim to have found in her great-grandmother's attic a sheaf of yellowing manuscript pages titled "The Danby Chronicles," but in an epilogue she asks the observant reader to pay close attention to the duck pond in Danby Dale's village green – it is the pie dish! Finally, both books are marked by the authenticity of their domestic details and the quiet perfection of their styles.

Fast upon the heels of *The Piemakers* followed *The Signposters,* another book about family loyalty, artistry, and threats to creativity. Like *The Piemakers,* it is set in an idealized England of times past. Dyke Signposter, like Arthy Roller, is an artist whose creativity is expressed in the splendid signs he carves for country crossroads. Yet unlike Arthy, Dyke is a wanderer. The law prescribes that every twenty years each road in the County of Flockshire must have its length repaced and its signs refurbished. Consequently Dyke, Hetty, and daughter Barley live in a tent during the spring and summer months, and the joys of a wayfaring life are celebrated. As Dyke paces the country roads, he dreams of bringing together the entire clan of the Flockshire Smiths in a great family reunion, a goal he is able to accomplish with the help of his immediate family.

Threats to creativity can come in many forms. Uncle Crispin in *The Piemakers* is motivated by envy to sabotage Arthy's pie. The creativity of Uncle Wick, one of the candle-making Smiths, is perverted by an urge to conformity. His handmade candles look mass-produced – each one the same size, shape, and dull color. But like Crispin, Uncle Wick is not villainous, merely misguided. Ultimately creativity wells to the surface even in a man like Uncle Wick, and he begins to express it in candles of eccentric design and color.

Dangers faced by the artist are far more frightening in Cresswell's next major novel, and the likelihood of the artist's escaping those dangers is far from certain. *The Night-Watchmen* signaled a departure for Cresswell. The setting is neither timeless nor pastoral but a contemporary provincial town called Mandover. The trio of main characters is not a family but a boy and two mysterious tramps he meets in the park. There is an element of the supernatural in this fantasy, as well as a much darker atmosphere. The threats to creativity and spontaneity no longer lie within the artist but are embodied in menacing and enigmatic figures called the Greeneyes.

Josh and Caleb are self-appointed night watchmen; they dig a hole under a railway bridge, erect their tent home, and place a "Danger – Men at Work" sign nearby to divert the attention of the authorities. The boy Henry is drawn to the "do-as-you-please" lifestyle of the two tramps. He comes to realize, however, that they are more than tramps: they are also artists. The prickly Caleb expresses himself in herb-flavored chicken and lemon meringue pie, all miraculously prepared on a camp stove. The more affable Josh spends his time "ticking" – that is, observing the inner workings of all the places they visit – and writing a never-ending book on the subject. Ultimately they reveal to Henry that they are from There, not Here; their nemeses, the Greeneyes, whose home is neither Here nor There, hound them from place to place, jealous of the night watchmen's freedom and imagination. Their only hope for escape is to whistle up the Night Train; the delicate timing of this operation requires Henry's help. In gratitude they allow Henry a brief ride on the magical train.

When Henry returns, he is left with a fresh appreciation of Here, of the potentialities of his own world. His experience has also convinced him of the existence of another world, a There secretly bordering his own Here. The fate of Josh and Caleb is more ambiguous; their escape, though successful, is narrow. The reader is left to wonder: Will they continue to elude the relentless Greeneyes? Will artists always be pursued by those envious of their powers?

The mature characterizations, the mixing of comedy with darker fantasy, the deliberately unresolved ending – all these things revealed surprising new depths in Helen Cresswell's work. For the second time one of her books was named runner-up for the Carnegie Medal, and in 1989 the Children's Literature Association further honored *The Night-Watchmen* with its Phoenix Award.

In *The Outlanders* (1970) the unspecified rural English past and the family threesomes of *The Piemakers* and *The Signposters* are combined with the mystery and magic of *The Night-Watchmen*. Tam Rhymer, who lives in the town of Bray with his wife Sary and son Piers, has a problem: despite his name and family heritage, he cannot rhyme. One day a fairy named Boy, who is from the outlands, an unknown and frightening region beyond the mountains, comes to stay with them, and Tam utters his first spontaneous verse. The townspeople of Bray – who, critics note, maintain a provincial and timid approach to life – appear as a mob outside the Rhymers' house. They claim that Boy has brought wolves from the outlands into the town and threaten to burn the house down. During the night Boy runs away.

The rest of the novel takes the form of a quest. Tam knows that he must leave the security of Bray and follow Boy into the fearsome outlands if he is ever to release his creative powers as a poet. The Rhymer family is accompanied on this journey by Emily, a young girl who, along with her laundress mother, wishes to escape the drudgery of life among the washtubs, and also by Emily's grandmother Olemary, who believes she is a witch but is too afraid of societal retaliation to test her powers. At the edge of the sea and at the end of their quest, the travelers find the radiant fairy boy. With a whispered word to each member of the group, he grants their dearest wishes. Young Piers, whose wish is to overcome his great fear of wolves, learns that he must look inward and confront his own cowardice. As critics recognized, the journey into the outlands is a journey from the known and comfortable into the unknown and potential, a journey all must take.

Up the Pier (1971) makes full use of the device of time travel, with which Cresswell had experimented in the briefer works *A Game of Catch* (1969) and *The Wilkses* (1970). While the father of ten-year-old Carrie finds a new home for her and her mother, she and her mother wait at a Welsh seacoast resort during the off-season. Feeling at loose ends, Carrie wanders the deserted pier and meets the Pontifex family, who have been torn from their home – and their decade. They have been magically transported fifty years into the future by a selfish relative who, as the last of the Pontifexes, wishes no longer to be alone. First Carrie helps the little family set up a provisional home in one of the empty kiosks along the pier. Then she unselfishly channels her powers to send them, her only companions, back to their real home in 1921. Her father arrives, and Carrie's own home life is restored. *Up the Pier* garnered for Cresswell her third Carnegie Medal nomination.

The Beachcombers (1972) focuses on another lonely child cast temporarily adrift in an off-season seaside town. This time the protagonist, Ned Kerne, encounters two unusual families – the Dallakers and the Pickerings. The Dallakers are true Beachcombers. They live aboard a skeletal but elegant old three-master named the *Sea Queen;* they eke out a living by harvesting driftwood as they wait for the tide to yield up a brass-bound trunk bearing their family fortune. The Pickerings, with whom Ned lodges, are scavengers – former beachcombers whose acquisitive natures have brought them to land, where they pick through the broken-down junk they collect and try to cheat their beachcomber cousins of their treasure.

Ned is drawn to the Dallakers because of their generosity and freewheeling existence, but, being a creature of dry land, he cannot completely disown connection with the unpleasant Pickerings. Does Ned sail away into the enticing unknown with the Dallakers or return to the cramped but familiar world of the Pickerings and ultimately to his own home and mother? Most critics recognize that the novel's ambiguous ending is essential to its artistic integrity. The choice must be left to Ned and the reader.

Although set in contemporary times, *The Bongleweed* returns to features that made *The Piemakers* successful. Becky and her parents, Else and Finch, comprise another of Helen Cresswell's close-knit family threesomes. Once again the fantasy and humor derive largely from violating normal expectations about the proportions of things: instead of a pie for two thousand, a weed invades an entire garden overnight.

Authority figures such as Mrs. Harper, owner of Pew Gardens, react to the inexplicable and powerful Bongleweed with fear: it must be chopped down, they say. The children, Becky and Jason Harper, and the Finches, who are natural gardeners, feel awe and love for the mysterious weed. Finch goes so far as to give notice to leave his post as head gardener at Pew rather than be forced to destroy it. But nature takes its own course, and a killing frost strikes overnight, leaving the Bongleweed blackened and shriveled. Becky, who ought to feel relieved that she will not be forced to leave her lifelong home and beloved gardens, brokenheartedly sobs.

"Oh, sweet mystery of life!," Becky is frequently provoked to exclaim when she sees this unusual plant. Yet even after the Bongleweed has passed the way of all natural things, Becky is still left with a sense that, in a world where such rampant and reckless beauty has sprung, anything is possible. The Bongleweed symbolizes those infinite possibilities usually left to slumber dormant just below the surface of things but which can be called miraculously to life by the power of the creative imagination. The evocative prose style and life-affirming theme of *The Bongleweed* won for Helen Cresswell her fourth Carnegie Medal nomination.

When *Lizzie Dripping* (1973) appeared in print, readers welcomed its heroine as an old friend – not only because of their familiarity with her through the scripts Cresswell had written for BBC television but also because, as her creator notes, every community seems to have someone like her. She is the child, both dreamy and daring, who unwittingly turns things topsy-turvy.

Perhaps because Cresswell was creating for two media simultaneously, each of the installments in the Lizzie Dripping series is episodic, and this makes them more like short-story collections than novels. Readers and viewers alike have been fascinated by Lizzie's relationship with a rather surly witch who lives in the churchyard and who may or may not be a figment of Lizzie's imagination. One book in the series, *Lizzie Dripping and the Witch* (1991), focuses on their encounters. Critics disagree over which media they prefer, some saying that television's visual impact helps audiences realize the individualities of the characters, but others arguing that the written word rightfully allows supernatural elements such as the witch's existence to remain equivocal.

With *Ordinary Jack: Being the First Part of the Bagthorpe Saga* (1977), and the subsequent entries in the Bagthorpe series, Cresswell took temporary leave of the realms of fantasy in order to combine humor and realism, as she had done in the earlier

Jumbo Spencer books. In this saga she forges a brand of domestic comedy seldom encountered in children's literature. There is no sentiment, no softened portraiture – only acid-etched eccentrics in outrageous situations.

Jack is the only ordinary member of this family. He and his pudding-footed, mutton-headed mongrel Zero, featured in the second book of the series, have no strings to their bows, unlike the rest of his multitalented but immodest family. For instance, thirteen-year-old Tess reads Voltaire in the original, sports a black belt in judo, and plays the oboe and piano. Siblings William and Rosie are equally accomplished in diverse ways. Jack's mother writes an advice column for a newspaper and serves as magistrate for a juvenile court but has little luck managing her own children. Mr. Bagthorpe, self-proclaimed literary genius and actual television scriptwriter, is always keen for one of their spirited family rows but disappears into his study at the first whiff of housework. His mother, affectionately known as Grandma Bag, defies all matronly stereotypes. She is so competitive – a true Bagthorpian trait – that she cheats shamelessly at family games and even starts a riot at a local bingo parlor rather than lose. The family member with whom Grandma Bag has the most rapport is four-year-old cousin Daisy, a recovering pyromaniac who now channels her creativity into smashing police cars and staging funerals.

Helen Cresswell's mastery of language is never more evident than in the Bagthorpe saga. Here is comedy of the highest order, deriving not just from fast-paced, preposterous plots but from character taken to the brink of caricature and from a style wisely restrained in the face of so much inanity. Occasionally the values one expects to find reinforced in domestic realism surface fleetingly. For example, family solidarity emerges in *Bagthorpes Unlimited: Being the Third Part of the Bagthorpe Saga* (1978) when the Bagthorpe children unite against a priggish cousin who threatens to become Young Brain of Britain on a radio quiz program. But readers are mostly content to be entertained by comedy that is at once intellectually stimulating and side-splitting, a rare combination for children's literature in the age of new realism.

The Bagthorpe books have become British cult favorites and will likely prove to be Cresswell's greatest claim to fame. Although the books are much less well known to American than to British children, Bagthorpe humor does translate; however, mainly the older and more gifted readers on both sides of the Atlantic best appreciate the some-

Dust jacket for Cresswell's popular novel about a girl who travels in time to help children living in the past

times sophisticated wit. Some critics claim to have grown weary of the antics of this irrepressible clan; others think Cresswell has overworked this vein and resent the time she has spent away from fantasy writing. Most readers and critics, however, greet each new volume in the continuing saga with shouts of joy.

For younger readers who might also enjoy comic family adventures, Cresswell has created several books about eight-year-old Posy Bates. Rivaling the Bagthorpe Saga for breakneck humor, books such as *Meet Posy Bates* (1990) and *Posy Bates, Again!* (1991) also share the episodic structure that makes the Lizzie Dripping series so enjoyable to read aloud.

After experiencing success with several realistic comedies, Cresswell made a brilliant return to fantasy with *The Secret World of Polly Flint* (1982) and *Moondial* (1987), novels that share many similarities. Both inspired popular television adaptations. Both have protagonists forced to leave their homes and disrupt their lives because a parent is recuperating from a serious accident. Both heroines learn to manipulate time travel in order to aid some unfortunate children from an earlier era. Finally, the settings in both novels are real places near Helen Cresswell's home. *Moondial* is set at historic Belton House near Newark, and *The Secret World of Polly Flint* takes place in Rufford Park and the village of Wellow. Informal Polly Flint pilgrimages are made there by local schoolchildren, and Cresswell occasionally appears to greet them.

The similarities end there. Polly Flint's world is simpler, brighter than that of *Moondial*. She first encounters the Time Gypsies while she is dancing around the famous Wellow maypole. Polly discovers that they are the inhabitants of the lost village of Grimstone, a kind of Brigadoon which has slipped the net of time. She helps them find their way back through a time tunnel, as she returns with them for a brief visit. Even Old Mazy, who seems at first to be an antagonist maliciously stalking the Time Gypsies, turns out merely to need Polly's help in returning home.

The world of *Moondial* is darker, with real evils to be fought. In *The Secret World of Polly Flint* the young protagonist detects the children of Grimstone through pleasant means, by glimpsing them May-dancing and by hearing the faint sound of church bells ringing underground. In *Moondial* Minty Kane is made aware of the children she helps when she feels pockets of icy air and hears the sound of crying, which has haunted the Belton House estate for over sixty years. She learns to use the garden sundial, which really measures "moontime," to help a trio of Dickensian waifs: Tom, a mistreated Victorian servant boy; Dorrie, his consumptive younger sister who works as a London gutter-picker; and Sarah, a lonely little rich girl who is psychologically abused because of a facial birthmark. To rescue them Minty must battle the sinister Miss Raven, who alarmingly also lives in the nineteenth century as Miss Vole, Sarah's cruel governess. There is no happy home to which these children can be restored; the most Minty can do is to release them into the dateless mists of moontime.

Helen Cresswell might justly be considered a late-century E. Nesbit. Cresswell is as prolific as the earlier writer and as versatile, excelling equally at humorous family adventures and fantasies. Her Bagthorpes can be viewed as rather cynical successors to Nesbit's Bastables, and her fantasies are often as fanciful and funny as Nesbit's *Five Children*

and It (1902) and its sequels. That Cresswell feels comfortable donning Nesbit's mantle was confirmed by *The Return of the Psammead* (1992), which continues the adventures of the sand fairy who vexed Nesbit's five children.

Originality of character and plot is not of paramount importance in Cresswell's novels. Observant readers will no doubt find that the family in *The Piemakers* is like those in *The Signposters, The Outlanders,* and *The Bongleweed;* and the dilemmas faced by the protagonists in *Up the Pier, The Beachcombers,* and *The Secret World of Polly Flint* are similar in nature and resolution. The many readers who devotedly follow Helen Cresswell's career do so because they are consistently rewarded by her polished prose style and enlivening humor.

References:

Barbara H. Baskin and Karen H. Harris, "Ordinary Jack," in their *Books for the Gifted Child* (New York: R. R. Bowker, 1980), pp. 117–118;

David Bennett, "Authorgraph No. 42: Helen Cresswell," *Books for Keeps,* 42 (January 1987): 12–13;

Marcus Crouch, "Helen Cresswell – Craftsman," *Junior Bookshelf,* 34 (June 1970): 135–139;

Margaret Greaves, "Warm Sun, Cold Wind: The Novels of Helen Cresswell," *Children's Literature in Education,* 5 (July 1971): 51–59;

Michele Landsberg, "Fantasy," in her *Reading for the Love of It: Best Books for Young Readers* (New York: Prentice-Hall, 1987), pp. 157–182;

Anne Merrick, "*The Nightwatchmen* and *Charlie and the Chocolate Factory* as Books to Be Read to Children," *Children's Literature in Education,* 16 (Spring 1975): 21–30;

"The 1989 Phoenix Award Winner: *The Night Watchmen* by Helen Cresswell," in *The Phoenix Award of the Children's Literature Association, 1985–1989,* edited by Alethea Helbig and Agnes Perkins (Metuchen, N.J.: Scarecrow Press, 1993), pp. 119–144;

Ann Swinfen, "Worlds in Parallel," in her *In Defence of Fantasy: A Study of the Genre in English and American Literature Since 1945* (London: Routledge & Kegan Paul, 1984), pp. 44–74;

John Rowe Townsend, "Helen Cresswell," in his *A Sense of Story: Essays on Contemporary Writers for Children* (Philadelphia: Lippincott, 1971), pp. 57–67.

Gillian Cross

(24 December 1945 –   )

Kathy Piehl
Mankato State University

BOOKS: *The Iron Way,* illustrated by Tony Morris (Oxford & New York: Oxford University Press, 1979);

The Runaway, illustrated by Reginald Gray (London: Methuen, 1979);

Revolt at Ratcliffe's Rags, illustrated by Morris (Oxford & New York: Oxford University Press, 1980); republished as *Strike at Ratcliffe's Rags* (London: Magnet, 1987);

Save Our School, illustrated by Gareth Floyd (London: Methuen, 1981);

A Whisper of Lace (Oxford & New York: Oxford University Press, 1981);

The Dark Behind the Curtain, illustrated by David Parkins (Oxford: Oxford University Press, 1982; New York: Oxford University Press, 1984);

The Demon Headmaster, illustrated by Gary Rees (Oxford: Oxford University Press, 1982; New York: Oxford University Press, 1987);

The Mintyglo Kid, illustrated by Floyd (London: Methuen, 1983);

Born of the Sun (Oxford: Oxford University Press, 1983; New York: Holiday House, 1984);

On the Edge (Oxford: Oxford University Press, 1984; New York: Holiday House, 1985);

The Prime Minister's Brain, illustrated by Sally Burgess (Oxford: Oxford University Press, 1985; New York: Oxford University Press, 1987);

Swimathon!, illustrated by Floyd (London: Methuen, 1986);

Chartbreak (Oxford: Oxford University Press, 1986); republished as *Chartbreaker* (New York: Holiday House, 1987);

Roscoe's Leap (Oxford: Oxford University Press, 1987; New York: Holiday House, 1987);

A Map of Nowhere (Oxford: Oxford University Press, 1988; New York: Holiday House, 1989);

Rescuing Gloria, illustrated by Floyd (London: Methuen, 1989);

Gillian Cross (photograph by Lark Gilmer)

Wolf (Oxford: Oxford University Press, 1990; New York: Holiday House, 1991);

Twin and Super-Twin, illustrated by Maureen Bradley (Oxford: Oxford University Press, 1990; New York: Holiday House, 1990);

Monster from Underground, illustrated by Peter Firmin (London: Heinemann, 1990);

Gobbo the Great, illustrated by Philippe Dupasquier (London: Methuen, 1991);

Rent-a-Genius, illustrated by Glenys Ambrus (London: Hamish Hamilton, 1991);

The Great Elephant Chase (Oxford: Oxford University Press, 1992); republished as *The Great*

American Elephant Chase (New York: Holiday House, 1993);

Beware Olga!, illustrated by Arthur Robins (London: Walker, 1993);

The Furry Maccaloo, illustrated by Madeleine Baker (London: Heinemann, 1993);

The Tree House, illustrated by Paul Howard (London: Methuen, 1993);

What Will Emily Do?, illustrated by Howard (London: Methuen, 1994);

Hunky Parker Is Watching You, illustrated by Bradley (Oxford: Oxford University Press, 1994); republished as *The Revenge of the Demon Headmaster* (London: Puffin, 1995);

New World (Oxford: Oxford University Press, 1994; New York: Holiday House, 1995);

The Crazy School Shuffle (London: Methuen, 1995);

Posh Watson (London: Walker, 1995).

Collection: *Save Our School!,* compilation of *Save Our School, The Mintyglo Kid, Swimathon!,* and *Gobbo the Great* (London: Dean, 1992).

SELECTED PERIODICAL PUBLICATIONS – UNCOLLECTED: "How I Started Writing for Children," *Books for Your Children,* 19 (Summer 1984): 15–16;

"Twenty Things I Don't Believe about Children's Books," *School Librarian,* 39 (May 1991): 44–46;

"Carnegie Medal Acceptance Speech," *Youth Library Review,* 12 (Autumn 1991): 7–8.

For more than a decade Gillian Cross has demonstrated her versatility as a writer in novels ranging from historical fiction to school stories and suspense. In recent years her books for children and young adults have earned a succession of literary awards, including the Carnegie Medal and the Whitbread Children's Novel Award. Yet above all she tries to keep in mind the demands of the reluctant reader, whom she identifies as "the practical, unliterary one who doesn't usually read, but who might – just might – pick up one of my books."

Gillian Clare Arnold was born in London on 24 December 1945. Her father, James Eric Arnold, had a Ph.D. in chemistry and was managing director of a paint company. In addition he served as organist and choirmaster at All Saints', Margaret Street, noted for its music. Her mother, Joan (Manton) Arnold, was an English teacher. Cross grew up in the northern suburbs of London, first in Wembley and later near Harrow. In an autobiographical sketch in the *Sixth Book of Junior Authors and Illustrators,* Cross remembered her home as "full

of books and stories. Books filled the shelves and cupboards. They were stacked in cardboard boxes and piled in heaps on the floor. Before we could read our mother made up stories to tell us and our father read stories onto tape on his big reel-to-reel taperecorder–long before commercial story cassettes were dreamt of."

Cross continued the storytelling tradition by making up her own tales, not only for her younger brother and sister but also for classmates. She began her education at a local state primary school and then attended North London Collegiate School for Girls, a well-known academic day school. On the train journey to and from school she made up stories to entertain friends, whom she included as heroines. Although Cross was a good student who enjoyed school, she made a distinction between the formal writing she did for her teachers and the writing she did for herself. The private work usually remained unfinished but revealed to Cross her intense desire to fill "clean, blank sheets of paper."

Before she began attending Somerville College at Oxford, Cross worked as a volunteer teacher for teenagers in a poor part of London quite different from the suburbs in which she had grown up. In *Contemporary Authors* she notes that because of this experience, "I began to see that life was more varied and more demanding than I had realized." At Somerville she pursued a degree in English literature. While still a student she married John Martin Cross on 10 May 1967. She left her studies for a year to have their first child, Jonathan George, and worked as a baker's assistant in Garsington, near Oxford. The experience of working with the village baker, who still used an old-style brick oven, later provided her with information for her description of a village bakery in her novel *The Iron Way* (1979), set in the Victorian era.

After graduating in 1969 from Somerville with first-class honors, Cross enrolled at the University of Sussex. In 1974 she completed her Doctor of Philosophy degree in English literature after writing her thesis on G. K. Chesterton. Although she had intended to teach at a university, she eventually changed her mind. She notes that "by the time I'd finished the degree, and done a bit of free-lance university teaching, I knew that I would not take enough trouble to do it properly, so I abandoned the idea."

With her formal education complete, she found she had time to write. Her son had been joined by a sister, Elizabeth Jane, and Cross had continued her storytelling with her children. The family lived in Lewes, a small town in Sussex where

Dust jacket for Cross's 1981 historical novel about a family's involvement in a smuggling operation

Cross helped start a children's book group. In 1976 the family moved to Gravesend, Kent, and Cross decided that she was ready to write her first book.

In an afterword to *The Iron Way* Cross describes her efforts with the manuscript of what was to be her first novel, "Such a Nice Girl," which she spent six or seven months writing: "I tried very hard and worked it all out carefully. . . . I made sure there were good psychological explanations for everyone's behavior. Into that first book of mine, I put everything that I thought a book should have." Nonetheless, she continues, "It was terrible. A leaden pudding of a book, with all sorts of bits tacked on to it here and there, to make it more like a Real Book. I'm incredibly relieved, now, that it has never been published."

While she waited to hear from publishers about this manuscript, she began her next novel, and this time the process of writing was much different. *The Iron Way,* which centers on the building of the railway in the South Downs of England, began with a picture of a country boy watching the railway construction men, or navvies, as they labored

to set down the rail lines that would alter rural society. Cross remembers that "there were not words with the picture. No dramatic, extraordinary actions. No psychological complexities. But in my mind it was charged with a precise and particular excitement." The boy in Cross's novel, twelve-year-old Jem Penfold, is fascinated by the railroad and the navvies – who, as Irishmen, are despised by most of the villagers. Jem's father has been transported for poaching, and his sixteen-year-old sister, Kate, struggles to care for Jem and baby Martha. Their mother had died in childbirth, and the shadow of the workhouse stands over the impoverished family, which has subsisted through the summer on Jem's wages from farm labor and on Kate's earnings from sewing.

When a navvy, Conor O'Flynn, asks to rent a room, Kate reluctantly agrees for the sake of the income. But her decision turns the navvy-hating villagers against the Penfolds and reveals to Jem the destructiveness of prejudice. Conor and Kate gradually fall in love, but her duty to her siblings leads her to reject his marriage proposal. Tension between villagers and navvies escalates into violent encounters. While Conor takes Kate, Jem, and Martha on a train ride, their neighbors vandalize the Penfolds' home. Only the rector's daughter finds the courage to stand by the family, but the violence continues until Conor is beaten to death by fellow navvies angry at him for trying to save the townspeople who had plotted to blow up the railway tunnel.

Although the novel is set in the Victorian era, its depictions of a society's fear of change and outsiders and of mounting violence that feeds on itself resonates with modern parallels. Cross says that as she wrote *The Iron Way* she checked historical details and walked the Downs to look at railway tunnels, but such activities were not merely in search of material to tack onto a plot. The story grew from her first vision of a boy watching the navvies. "The whole thing was inevitable. Once Conor came strolling in, the plot was fixed, with him set firmly in the centre. I could not choose to let him live and set up home with Kate and Jem and Martha. I knew he would have to die," Cross comments.

The Iron Way appeared almost simultaneously with *The Runaway* in 1979. Although the books share a broad theme of the need for trust between people of varying backgrounds, the settings are quite different. *The Runaway,* with its contemporary urban locale, explores the complexity of a multiracial society. When Denny's grandmother is hospitalized after an accident, he runs away rather than go to the Children's Home, where school bully Bouncer Bradley lives. Denny encounters Nachtar, an Indian boy, and together they hide in an empty house where they are joined by Tracy, a girl from the fish-and-chips shop. With Nachtar's help Denny survives until his grandmother recovers and returns home. *Junior Bookshelf* predicted that readers aged nine or ten would "enjoy the action and interest which two young children from radically different racial backgrounds can bring to an exciting contemporary story."

Readers in that age group could also appreciate the humor in Cross's *Save Our School* (1981). The brief novel establishes the setting and main characters for what Cross would develop into a series of school stories. Three friends – Clipper (Caroline Young), Spag (James Barlow), and Barny (Gobbo) – find themselves in a string of humorous adventures, often to save their own honor or that of their school, Bennett Junior High. In this first novel the old building is threatened with closure, and the three develop schemes to draw attention to Bennett's plight – schemes such as attempts to win

art competitions or to stage a parade. Despite the failure of one plan after another, the school eventually survives. When the three return in a second novel, *The Mintyglo Kid* (1983), the emphasis is on their own survival. Spag must keep his eight-year-old cousin, Dreadful Denzil, out of mischief for six weeks while his aunt and uncle enjoy the cruise they have won in a Mintyglo toothpaste contest. Unfortunately Denzil is accompanied by a five-year supply of toothpaste, a perfect medium for creating havoc at school and in the neighborhood. Clipper and Barny try to help Spag control Denzil while they concentrate on preparing for an important cricket match. Although Denzil is temporarily brought under control when he is allowed to use his batting skills, the three protagonists find few truces with their rival Thrasher Dyson.

Because Thrasher attends Kings' Road School, a more modern building than Bennett, he scorns the three friends. *Swimathon!* (1986) pits Dyson and his companions against the trio in a swimming competition that Barny and Spag arrange to help raise money to replace their school's vandalized minibus. Unfortunately the boys mistakenly assume that the athletic Clipper can swim. When they discover their mistake, they devise hilarious but drastic methods to teach her before the contest. In their appearances in a fourth novel, *Gobbo the Great* (1991), the headmaster organizes a competition on the question "What about the next 100 years?" in honor of Bennett's centenary. As usual, Thrasher is on hand to sabotage the proceedings – this time Gobbo's Futurescope visions of developments in such areas as food and energy.

This series of comic novels is notable for the camaraderie it depicts across ethnic and gender lines. Clipper, a West Indian girl, easily holds her own with the boys who are her friends. Much of the humor is slapstick, and the triumph of Barny, Spag, and Clipper over Thrasher is predictable. However, those very features plus the familiar setting and school slang help carry even less-than-eager readers through the novels. The continuing popularity of the series was demonstrated by the 1992 publication of a single volume that collects all four of the books under the title *Save Our School!*

According to Cross, her most popular books are her companion school stories mixed with fantasy, *The Demon Headmaster* (1982) and *The Prime Minister's Brain* (1985). In an article in *The School Librarian* she notes that the vast majority of letters she has received from children are about those two works. "They sell more copies and they're borrowed much more often from libraries," she writes.

Cross remembers that *The Demon Headmaster* began as an imagined story written by Clipper for an essay competition at school. The wicked headmaster in Clipper's story so intrigued Cross's eight-year-old daughter, Elizabeth, that she urged her mother to expand the story into a book. As Cross worked on the plot, she discovered the problem of introducing one element of fantasy—the headmaster's talent for hypnosis—into a story based largely in the quotidian world of school. In the course of completely rewriting the novel, she promised herself never to write a similar book.

However, she had not counted on the book's popularity. For a while she rejected the idea of a sequel until the proliferation of computers "caught me off guard," as she explains in an afterword to a new edition of *The Prime Minister's Brain*. "One day, quite without warning, I thought: *The Demon Headmaster must like computers.*" Through many digressions and comic events, Cross ultimately edited her sequel into a manageable plot. Probably part of the attraction that the book holds for young readers lies in the central plot conflict between clever kids and an evil school authority – the stuff of which fantasy is made. The stakes are high because the headmaster's goal is to control not merely his school, but the entire country.

In the first book Dinah Glass enters foster care at the home of the Hunters, who have two sons, Harvey and Lloyd. Dinah's brilliance cannot save her from joining the other pupils at the school, nearly all of whom succumb to the headmaster's hypnosis. The students learn by rote and act like docile robots. Only five pupils, including Hugh and Lloyd, fail to be influenced by the headmaster's peculiar sea-green eyes. The nonconformists create their own group, SPLAT – Society for the Protection of Our Lives Against Them. Eventually they and Dinah figure out that the headmaster plans to have the brightest pupils win the weekly television Great School Quiz, which offers the headmaster of the winning school one minute to speak to the entire nation. Then he will hypnotize everyone into following his lead to create "the first properly-organized, truly efficient country in the world." At the end of the book the headmaster warns Dinah, "You have defeated me this time, but I know I was meant for greatness. I shall succeed in the end!"

True to his word, the headmaster devises another nefarious scheme in *The Prime Minister's Brain*. Setting up a competition for Junior Computer Brain of the year, the headmaster invites the most clever computer students to London, where they are secluded in an impenetrable tower. The competitors, all of whom have beaten the "Octopus Dare" game, include Dinah, who has become obsessed with this computer game. Using combinations of threats and mind control, the headmaster pushes the Brains to follow his commands. Yet SPLAT members manage to infiltrate the fortress and foil the headmaster's attempt to break into the prime minister's computer, become his adviser, and hypnotize world leaders. The frequent references to George Orwell's novel *Nineteen Eighty-Four* (1949) drive home the rather heavy-handed warnings about the necessity for free speech and thought. But the emphasis on the quick-witted children versus the evil headmaster probably subordinates the political message in the minds of most child readers.

In 1994 SPLAT and the headmaster reappeared in *Hunky Parker is Watching You,* retitled *The Revenge of the Demon Headmaster* when the book was issued in paperback. Once again the headmaster employs technology in pursuit of his ultimate goals of thought control and political order. He uses subliminal messages during the phenomenally popular Hunky Parker television show to stimulate mindless devotion to Hunky, a huge, slobbering pig. As Hunkymania sweeps the country, SPLAT members are transported to the Sty, where unwitting tourists are hypnotized and turned into mindless industrial workers producing Hunky, products. SPLAT members manage to alter the headmaster's final Hunky video designed to create political and social chaos. Undoubtedly this third installment will please readers devoted to the earlier books about SPLAT. The headmaster's escape leaves open the possibility of additional sequels.

Cross's exploration of political and social themes has been a staple of many of her novels, although in real life the struggle between good and evil usually lacks the clear definition it can have in fiction with "villains" such as Thrasher Dyson or the Demon Headmaster. In her 1980 novel, *Revolt at Ratcliffe's Rags,* Christopher Benton, Susan Grantley, and Abigail Proctor are assigned to work on a group project to study local industry. Selecting Ratcliffe's Clothing, where Chris's mother works, they investigate factory conditions. Abby, in part to please her intellectual, liberal parents, urges the women to strike for better conditions after one of them has been fired unjustly. Chris is torn between his resolutely prounion father and his ambitious mother, who sees the strike as an opportunity to advance her position in the factory. Susan, whose wealthy parents socialize with Mr. Ratcliffe, defies them to march in support of the workers. Ultimately there are no clear-cut winners in the labor

PERSONAL FILE

FINCH (KELP)

NAME: Janis Mary Finch
BORN: Of course I was. Seventeen years ago, in Birmingham.
NICKNAME AT SCHOOL: Oh, they probably called me all sorts of things, but I wouldn't know what. Never spoke to any of them if I could help it.
HAVE YOU EVER BEEN ON A DIET? Look, my only problem with food is getting enough. I'm five foot eleven and it's twelve stone of bone and muscle, not flab. Want me to come round and demonstrate?
OTHER BANDS YOU'VE SUNG WITH? There isn't any band worth joining except Kelp.
DO YOU PLAY ANY GAMES OR SPORTS? I used to put the shot at school, but now I'm into martial arts. Karate mostly, but I'm very interested in ninjitsu and everything about the ninjas. That's why I wear a ninja suit on stage—and off as well, quite often.
FAVOURITE DRINK: Water.
IS 'FACE IT' REALLY A TRUE ACCOUNT OF HOW YOU MET UP WITH THE BAND? Yes. Job wrote the words as well as the tune, but he was drawing on things I'd told him.
HAVE YOU GOT ANY PETS? Not yet. But I'm going to buy an ocelot. That's a small wild cat from South America. Fantastically fierce and beautiful.

WHAT WAS THE FIRST RECORD YOU BOUGHT? Don't remember.
DOES DAVE REALLY PLAY ALL THOSE DIFFERENT INSTRUMENTS? Yes. *And* he cleans his own teeth and cuts his own toe-nails. He's unbelievably talented.
WHOSE MUSIC HAS INFLUENCED YOU MOST? Christie Joyce's. And if you want to know who influenced *him*, you'll have to ask him.
WHAT HAVE YOU GOT IN YOUR POCKETS? My ninja suit doesn't have pockets. Rollo always carries my money for me.
MOST IMPORTANT CONCERT: The concert in Nottingham on our first tour, when we supported Nitrogen Cycle. That's when everything came 100% right for the first time. An amazing feeling.
WHAT'S YOUR BEDROOM LIKE? A prison cell. Well, no, it's a bit more comfortable than that. I don't share it, for a start. But it's just a room with a wardrobe for clothes and a bed for sleeping. I'm not into interior decoration.
HAVE YOU GOT A BOY-FRIEND? I eat boy-friends for breakfast.
O.K. WHAT DID YOU HAVE FOR BREAKFAST THIS MORNING? Oh, this morning I only had sausages and eggs and chips. I wasn't really hungry.
NOW, CAN WE ASK YOU ABOUT THE BAND'S FIRST-EVER *TOP OF THE POPS* APPEARANCE? Groan. I knew that would be bound to come up.
WELL, EVERYONE'S ALWAYS WANTED TO KNOW. WHAT *WAS* GOING ON? Look, there's no way I can tell you in a couple of words for an interview like this. I couldn't begin to explain it properly without going way back. Right back to the very beginning, in fact.

Smash Hits

An interview segment from Chartbreak *(1986), one of Cross's
experiments with narrative presentation*

dispute, although the workers' plans to establish a cooperative hold some promise for improved conditions. But the strike has torn apart families as well as a community, as Chris's mother tells her husband and son that she "shan't forget . . . that I couldn't rely on my own family either. That you both stabbed me in the back."

Intrigue within a family is more complex in *A Whisper of Lace* (1981), a historical novel of suspense. Francis Merrowby is blackmailed into participating in a smuggling operation that brings French lace into England, a lucrative gamble that turns huge profits for the smugglers at the expense of local lace makers. Playing on his sister's devotion to him and her desire for adventure, Francis draws her into the plot, which is observed and ultimately unraveled by their younger brother, Daniel. Layer after layer of observation and manipulation add to the plot's suspense. Cross carefully establishes relationships among the characters that lead to logical outcomes, as the actions of the central characters are played out. Daniel's realization that the initiator of the smuggling operation is their older brother, the long-absent family heir, leads to a resolution but not a conventional happy ending.

Suspense also drives *The Dark Behind the Curtain* (1982), in which past evil threatens to control a contemporary theater production. The headmaster assigns Colin Jackus to participate in the school play, "Sweeney Todd," as punishment for a theft of which he is accused. His onetime friend Marshall plays the title role of the evil barber who murders without regret and subordinates the poor to do his bidding. Miss Lampeter, the teacher in charge, designs cast exercises intended to create a sense of evil and powerlessness that Todd's victims feel. However, her efforts soon get out of control, as when Marshall systematically insults and berates other students while they paint scenery: "It was not quite the joke it had started as. All over the room, people were growing angry and resentful. . . . Marshall went on sauntering about, with an expression of evil relish on his face." Odd incidents soon suggest to Jackus and his classmate Ann Ridley that the play summons Victorian ghosts who had suffered at the hands of the real Sweeney Todd and who consider the play a chance for revenge. The vandalism and theft blamed on Jackus, a ready suspect, have these spirits as their instigators. Only when Jackus manages to prevent Ann from taking real revenge on Marshall on behalf of past victims can he and the ghosts find freedom from bullying.

For the first time Cross experiments with shifts in narrative point of view, including excerpts from Ann's diary that reveal the girl's growing obsession with righting past injustices. One of the book's intriguing themes is in the exploration of "reality," in relation to the supernatural or through the creation of an alternate world on stage. Despite his initial reluctance to act, Jackus discovers "where the interest of this play business lay. There was something intriguing about being able to put yourself inside somebody else's head." *The Dark Behind the Curtain* was a book highly commended for the Carnegie Award and a runner-up for the Guardian Award.

In her next young-adult novel, *Born of the Sun* (1983), Cross chose a setting far from England, an unusual departure in her writing. Unexpectedly summoned from boarding school, Paula Staszic is to accompany her parents to South America in search of an Incan city that has preoccupied her explorer father, Karel, for years. His recent discovery of directions to the lost city in the land of the Kallawayas spurs the expedition. However, Paula grows increasingly uneasy about the hasty preparations, the refusal of the usual photographer to accompany the expedition, and the unremitting drive to reach the site. Despite her mother's attempts to excuse Karel's actions, his physical and mental deterioration become more apparent as the jungle journey progresses. Only the ministrations of the Kallawaya save him from death. Paula completes both the journey to the city and to acceptance – of herself and of her parents' own strengths and weaknesses. Although Cross did not travel to South America for background, her author's note at the end explains her search for sources describing the cures of the Kallawaya. She credits Ross Slamon's book *My Quest for El Dorado* with generating the excitement that launched the adventure novel.

With the publication of *On the Edge* in 1984, Cross's young-adult novels show a new complexity in theme and style. Cross concentrates alternately on two intertwined stories. One concerns Tug, the son of television reporter Harriet Shakespeare, who has investigated extreme left-wing groups and terrorist organizations. To gain attention for their cause, members of Free People kidnap him and hold him prisoner in a cottage in Derbyshire. The second plot line follows Jinny Slattery, a local girl who grows suspicious about the cottage and tries to persuade authorities to intervene. Her father controls the activities of his children almost as completely as Tug is manipulated by his captors.

In fact, Cross addresses several important questions about the nature of families and the extent to which children are subject to adults. The systematic brainwashing Tug undergoes causes him to question his certainty about the identity of his real mother. Is she the woman on television who has often commented on his cowardice, or is she the woman he is forced to call "Ma," who hits and comforts him and has a photograph that might be of him as a baby? In despair he realizes that he can no longer remember Harriet Shakespeare's face, "which had vanished, as completely as though the memory had been cut out of his brain." Jinny, too, is under orders, receiving assigned work each day to contribute to the family's welfare: "She wondered what it was like to wake in the morning and plan things for yourself. To choose." The Free People's goal of breaking down the conventions of the traditional family holds a certain attraction as the plot reveals that institution's limitations, particularly in the control it exercises over children. The terrorist "father," Doyle, explains that family members make the best torturers of husbands, wives, grandparents, and especially children: "They have you when you're young and weak and they've got you for ever," he tells Tug. The electrifying ending, in which Jinny witnesses Tug's desperate run for freedom, forces both of Tug's "mothers" to make difficult choices.

Cross has written that she began *On the Edge* with two pictures in her mind – one of a boy running free in the sunshine, the other of a hare running into a trap. She writes, "Looking back now, I can see that what appealed to me was some kind of contrast, to do with freedom and individuality. The 'family' theme is simply the other side of that idea. Freedom and limitation, self-expression and dealing with other people, feeling at home and being trapped – all those ideas were somehow tangled together in the feelings I had about the running hare and the running boy." The gripping novel received critical accolades, including a spot on the American Library Association's list of Best Books for Young Adults and runner-up honors for both the Whitbread and Edgar awards.

In her next young-adult novel, *Chartbreak* (1986), Cross explores the world of rock music through the life of Janis May Finch, a seventeen-year-old who runs away from conflict with her mother and joins a band, Kelp. Cross speculates that she may have been able to write *Chartbreak* because her "children were teenagers at the time (although not particularly keen on rock music)." Cross was pregnant when she began writing the novel, a time she describes in an afterword to a new edition. Hearing Finch's insistent voice in her head, Cross hastily wrote the first two chapters of the novel and began reading song lyrics and concert reviews. But the writing had to be delayed until her new baby was three months old, and then Cross discovered that in cleaning she had thrown out her first two chapters.

Her second writing was "painfully slow. Every time I picked up my pen, the baby started to cry," she recalls. *Chartbreak* was the first novel Cross had written largely with first-person narration, a perspective that presented some authorial problems. But the hardest section to write in the book were the song lyrics. Cross used some words from a song written by her daughter and then rewrote the lyrics nine or ten times before they satisfied her. Her work on the novel was recognized when it was named a Carnegie-commended book and again included on the American Library Association's list of Best Books for Young Adults. In *Chartbreak* Cross intersperses Finch's first-person narrative with news articles to contrast the glamorous public presentation with the private reality of character. Fame, money, and stardom cannot prevent Finch and her mother from hurting one another, and the pain continues after the older woman's death from cancer. As Finch gains confidence in herself, she finds the power to confront the band's leader, Christie, who has dominated Finch and turned her life into a spectacle in order to further the group's success. *Chartbreak* presents the uneasy coming-of-age story of an adolescent who works out problems and pain on a stage visible to the world.

The process of healing is more private in *Roscoe's Leap* (1987). The Roscoe family is literally divided, living in separate sections of a huge house built in 1879 by an ancestor, an eccentric millionaire. The house is built on both sides of a river below a waterfall, and the sections are connected by a gallery. On one side Hannah and Stephen live with their mother while their father cares for great-uncle Ernest Roscoe in the other section of the house. The arrival of Nick Honeyball, a researcher interested in the architecture, leads to revelations about more than the house's structure. As they explore the house Nick and the children grow increasingly fascinated with Samuel Roscoe's toy collection, including the automatons. Nick's research leads him to the French Terror, a working model of a guillotine. The sinister air of this huge machine reinforces the brooding quality of the family secrets. Stephen experiences repeated flashbacks to the time before the family's separation, and his fear of the

French Terror grows. Only a re-creation of events that had years ago terrified the four-year-old Stephen, as they had terrified Ernest before him, can initiate a healing process.

For *A Map of Nowhere* (1988) Cross arranged to visit the adventure-game club of the school from which her son had graduated. By the mid 1980s her older children had been joined by a younger brother, Anthony, and a sister, Katherine. While the children were young, Cross paid someone to look after them twelve hours a week while she wrote. Although she never consciously takes ideas from her children's lives, her awareness of teenage interest in topics such as adventure games may have been enhanced by their presence in the household. In *A Map of Nowhere* the adventure games that Nick Miller enjoys turn serious when he realizes that he has been manipulated, by gang members of his older brother, Terry, into establishing a friendship with Joseph Fisher. The motorcycle gang has robbed and vandalized out-of-the-way shops such as the one the Fishers own. Isolated not only by their distance from town but by their rigid moral standards, the Fishers refuse to deceive potential buyers by concealing cracks in the store's foundations. Nick joins Joseph in a series of adventure games controlled by Joseph's sister, Ruth. In order to win they must construct maps and follow complex rules based on the attributes of their assumed characters.

But the real moral choices faced by Nick and Joseph grow more difficult. In the hope of earning a place in the gang, Nick spies on the Fishers and betrays them by revealing where they keep receipts and keys and when they will be gone. The robbery and subsequent fire lead to arrests and seem to promise the Fishers a brighter future bought with insurance money. Only Joseph and Nick know that the gang members did not light the matches that started the blaze. In torment Joseph tells Nick, "Right and wrong don't change, you know. They're like a map, to stop people making mistakes."

The intensity of *A Map of Nowhere* contrasts sharply with the humor of books such as *Rescuing Gloria* (1989), *Twin and Super-Twin* (1990), and *Rent-a-Genius* (1991) — all published for younger readers. As in Cross's Clipper, Spag, and Barny series, these books have contemporary urban settings. In *Rescuing Gloria,* Leo, a new boy in the neighborhood, finds himself taking care of Gloria the goat, whose owner can no longer keep her because his land has been purchased to build a motorway. Leo eventually needs help with his scheme to raise Gloria in an empty lot. Two girls help him in his enterprise, which eventually includes tending ducks and bees as well. The children's sale of milk, vegetables, and other farm products unites neighbors, and the cooperation results in the Mercy Street Community Farm Project when the house on the abandoned lot is demolished.

Twin and Super-Twin combines reality and fantasy in a tale of two rival gangs, each headed by a girl. Twins Ben and David are members of the Nelson Square gang, which lights the wood that the Wellington Street gang had been collecting for the Guy Fawkes bonfire. Caught by exploding fireworks, David's arm mysteriously turns into a Roman candle, the first of several transformations it undergoes. Ben "thinks" David's arm into becoming various items such as sausages, a snake, scissors, a printing block, and helium balloons. The conflict is resolved when the Nelson Square gang convinces people from the entire neighborhood to bring wood and fireworks for a community celebration of Guy Fawkes Day. Sophie Simpson in *Rent-a-Genius* bases a moneymaking plan on her ability to solve other people's problems, but her brashness creates one comic situation after another as she comes to realize that certain problems lie beyond her capacity to change them.

While such novels evoke amusement, *Wolf*, winner of the 1990 Carnegie Medal, calls forth darker emotions. Hastily awakened and bundled off by her grandmother, Nan, thirteen-year-old Cassy Phelan sets off "pulling up the hood of her school mac." She navigates alone through London to join her mother, Goldie, in an abandoned house Goldie shares with West Indian artist Lyall Cornelius and his son, Robert. Lyall's allusive greeting, "Hallo, Little Red Riding Hood," establishes the metaphor implicit in the title of the novel. But only gradually do Cassy and the reader come to realize that in the bag of goodies she has carried from her grandmother lie plastic explosives which Nan is trying to keep from her son. Cassy's father, Michael, an IRA terrorist, is the wolf who stalks her and is willing to kill women, children, and even his own family to advance his political cause.

Cassy is drawn into the research about real wolves that Lyall and Robert pursue as they prepare school presentations. Statistics about and photographs of real wolves alternate with myths and folktales about the animals. The explosive is fashioned inside a horrifying wolf mask, but nothing is as terrifying as the unremitting suspense about Cassy's fate. Snatches of the fairy tale about Red Riding Hood end the chapters and propel readers toward the inevitable confrontation with the wolf. When her father tracks Cassy down, he threatens to

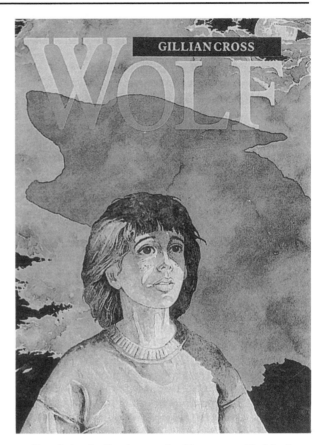

Dust jacket for Cross's story of a thirteen-year-old girl who discovers that her father is an IRA terrorist

kill her grandmother if Cassy doesn't return the explosives within twenty-four hours. Nightmare turns to reality, and Cassy realizes that "*Nothing is too bad to be true! You can't shut out the night! The world is full of bombs and blood and murder and death and violence —*"

Cross believes that *Wolf* may be less frightening for children than for adults. She started the novel by exploring humans' dealings with wolves, in an attempt to unravel the complex emotions people hold toward the animals. She contacted the Ministry of Defence to "find out about the smell and colour and feel of Semtex," the explosive. To discover more about the kind of place where Goldie and Lyall live, Cross read materials intended for squatters. Like Cassy, Robert, and Lyall, she visited the wolf enclosure at the London zoo. She says that the description of that visit included in the novel is the only piece of direct experience in any of her books, and the wolves behaved exactly as she describes them. In her 1991 article in *School Librarian*, Cross claims that violence in children's books is "crucial to the nature of children's fiction. Death and danger and injury are hard, definite, dramatic things. . . .

The events of our lives are – sooner or later – violent and dramatic. Human passions and emotions, of all kinds, are violent and dramatic." In *Wolf* she clearly incorporates this belief.

Cross's return to historical fiction with *The Great Elephant Chase* (1992) garnered both the Smarties Book Prize and the Whitbread Children's Novel Award. The novel takes place in the United States in 1881. After her father is killed in a railway accident, Cissie Keenan is determined to take his elephant from Pennsylvania to Nebraska, where she can join her friend Ketty Svensson. On the journey west she is aided by orphaned Tad Hawkins, and together they keep the elephant safe while they elude two crooks who claim to have bought the elephant before her father's death. Repeatedly the villain, aptly named Hannibal Jackson, almost succeeds in wresting Khush the elephant from Tad and Cissie. However, through coincidences and kindness they beat him to Ketty's farm. Along the way Tad grows in self-confidence through his ability to care for Khush, and boy and animal forge bonds of affection.

Cross says that although she has collected model elephants since childhood, she never intended to write an animal story. Nor did she plan to set a novel in the United States, for "my most successful books had been set in England, in the present," she notes. "They had involved very few characters and taken place over very short periods of time." Yet with her editor's encouragement, Cross began research into United States history and geography and amassed maps and information from state historical societies. She returned to the London Zoo – this time to look at elephants, feel their skins, and talk to their keepers. Cross admits that the details she had accumulated weighed down the book until she concentrated on Cissie, Tad, and Khush. "Suddenly I realised that I wasn't writing a geography book, or a history of the United States. I was writing a story about two people and an elephant, and what happened to them."

Cross's recent books return to familiar themes and settings. She has completed several works for beginning readers, including *The Tree House* (1993), an insightful look at family dynamics and cooperation. Two young brothers grow impatient at their father's lack of progress in building a promised tree house. His extended business trip abroad threatens to delay the project indefinitely. However, construction help from their mother and a series of gifts mailed by their father lead to a happy resolution of the boys' problem.

Cross's novel for young adults, *New World* (1994), evokes a much darker tone. Two teenagers, Stuart and Miriam, are recruited to test a virtual re-ality game. What ostensibly begins as a cooperative exploration quickly turns to competition as they don game gear in separate locations before they meet in playing fields of cyberspace. What they eventually realize is that the game's creators are exploiting knowledge of Stuart's and Miriam's hidden fears to help produce an addiction to the game. When one of the game's developers entices his teenage son Will into exploring the limits of the video game by altering the virtual reality experience for Stuart and Miriam, the level of suspense increases. Ultimately the three teenagers meet in person and recognize the dangers inherent in the game. Internal company memos inserted between narrative chapters reveal the underlying theme of adults' manipulation of teenagers to achieve profit no matter what the human cost. Subplots involving Miriam's family and friends suggest that the strains of human encounters are sometimes more difficult to face than artificially produced dangers of virtual reality. Although not as compelling or richly textured as *Wolf, New World* should sustain Cross's reputation as a fine suspense writer, especially because of the novel's skillful incorporation of new technology popular with its readers.

Cross coordinates her writing schedule with the demands of family life. She writes while her children are in school, not during weekends or school holidays. She says that her husband, the chief executive of an examinations board, "has always encouraged my writing by reading my books, by inventing titles and by urging me to take my work seriously and professionally." Since 1989 the family has lived in Wolston, a village outside Coventry. Cross enjoys gardening, playing the piano, and reading. With her family she goes orienteering regularly.

Cross's ability to hold readers' attention with humor, suspense, or adventure has grown steadily through the years since her first novels were published. As she creates new fictional worlds, she demonstrates her belief that "imagination demands involvement and daring and sheer effrontery."

Interview:
David Self, "First, Catch Your Reader," *Times Educational Supplement Review: Children's Books,* 19 February 1993, p. i.

References:
Keith Barker, *Gillian Cross* (Swindon: School Library Association, 1992);
Winifred Whitehead, "The Novels of Gillian Cross," *Use of English,* 43, no. 1 (1992): 57–66.

Kevin Crossley-Holland

(7 February 1941 –)

Donna R. White
Clemson University

See also the Crossley-Holland entry in *DLB 40: Poets of Great Britain and Ireland Since 1960.*

BOOKS: *On Approval* (London: Outposts, 1961);
Havelok the Dane (London: Macmillan, 1964; New York, Dutton, 1965);
King Horn (London: Macmillan, 1965; New York: Dutton, 1966);
My Son (London: Turret, 1966);
The Green Children (London: Macmillan, 1966; New York: Seabury Press, 1968; revised edition London: Oxford University Press, 1994);
Alderney: The Nunnery (London: Turret, 1968);
The Callow Pit Coffer (London: Macmillan, 1968; New York: Seabury Press, 1969);
Confessional (Frensham, Surrey: Sceptre Press, 1969);
Wordhoard: Anglo-Saxon Stories, by Crossley-Holland and Jill Paton Walsh (London: Macmillan, 1969; New York: Farrar, Straus, 1969);
Norfolk Poems (London: Academy, 1970);
A Dream of a Meeting (Frensham, Surrey: Sceptre Press, 1970);
More Than I Am (London: Steam Press, 1971);
The Pedlar of Swaffham (London: Macmillan, 1971; New York: Seabury Press, 1972);
The Wake (Richmond, Surrey: Keepsake Press, 1972);
The Rain-Giver (London: Deutsch, 1972);
Pieces of Land: Journeys to Eight Islands (London: Gollancz, 1972);
The Sea-Stranger (London: Heinemann, 1973; New York: Seabury Press, 1974);
The Fire-Brother (London: Heinemann, 1975; New York: Seabury Press, 1975);
Petal and Stone (Knotting, Bedfordshire: Sceptre Press, 1975);
Green Blades Rising: The Anglo-Saxons (London: Deutsch, 1975; New York: Seabury Press, 1976);
The Dream-House (London: Deutsch, 1976);
The Earth-Father (London: Heinemann, 1976);
The Wildman (London: Deutsch, 1976);

Kevin Crossley-Holland

The Norse Myths: A Retelling (London: Deutsch, 1980; New York: Pantheon, 1980);
Between My Father and My Son (Minneapolis: Black Willow Press, 1982);
The Dead Moon and Other Tales from East Anglia and the Fen Country (London: Deutsch, 1982);
Time's Oriel (London: Hutchinson, 1983);
Tales from the Mabinogion, by Crossley-Holland and Gwyn Thomas (London: Gollancz, 1984; Woodstock, N.Y.: Overlook Press, 1985);
Axe-Age, Wolf-Age: A Selection from the Norse Myths (London: Deutsch, 1985);
The Fox and the Cat: Animal Tales from Grimm, by Crossley-Holland and Susanne Lugert (Lon-

don: Andersen Press, 1985; New York: Lothrop, 1986);

Storm (London: Heinemann, 1985);

Waterslain and Other Poems (London: Hutchinson, 1986);

British Folk Tales: New Versions (London: Orchard, 1987; New York: Orchard, 1987); selections republished in four volumes as *Boo!, Dathera Dad, Piper and Pooka,* and *Small-Tooth Dog* (London: Orchard, 1988);

The Painting-Room and Other Poems (London: Hutchinson, 1988);

East Anglian Poems (Colchester: Jardine, 1988);

Oenone in January (Llandogo: Old Stile Press, 1988);

The Quest for Olwen, by Crossley-Holland and Thomas (Cambridge: Lutterworth, 1988);

Wulf (London: Faber & Faber, 1988);

The Stones Remain: Megalithic Sites of Britain (London: Rider, 1989);

Under the Sun and Over the Moon (London: Orchard, 1989; New York: Putnam, 1989);

Sleeping Nana (London: Orchard, 1989; Nashville: Ideals Children's Books, 1989);

Sea Tongue (London: BBC/Longman, 1991);

Tales from Europe (London: BBC, 1991);

New and Selected Poems: 1965-1990 (London: Hutchinson, 1991);

Eleanor's Advent (Llandogo: Old Stile Press, 1992);

The Tale of Taliesin, by Crossley-Holland and Thomas (London: Gollancz, 1992; North Pomfret, Vt.: Trafalgar Square, 1995);

Long Tom and the Dead Hand (London: Deutsch, 1992);

The Labours of Herekles (London: Orion, 1993).

OTHER: *The Battle of Maldon and Other Old English Poems,* translated by Crossley-Holland (London: Macmillan, 1965; New York: St. Martin's Press, 1965);

Running to Paradise: An Introductory Selection of the Poems of W. B. Yeats, edited by Crossley-Holland (London: Macmillan, 1967; New York: Macmillan, 1968);

Winter's Tales for Children 3, edited by Crossley-Holland (London: Macmillan, 1967; New York: St. Martin's Press, 1968);

Beowulf, translated by Crossley-Holland (London: Macmillan, 1968; New York: Farrar, Straus, 1968);

Winter's Tales 14, edited by Crossley-Holland (London: Macmillan, 1968);

Storm and Other Old English Riddles, translated by Crossley-Holland (London: Macmillan, 1970; New York: Farrar, Straus, 1970);

New Poetry 2, edited by Crossley-Holland and Patricia Beer (London: Arts Council, 1976);

The Faber Book of Northern Legends, edited by Crossley-Holland (London: Faber & Faber, 1977);

The Exeter Riddle Book, translated by Crossley-Holland (London: Folio Society, 1978); republished as *The Exeter Book of Riddles* (London: Penguin, 1979);

"Kevin Crossley-Holland," in *Fourth Book of Junior Authors and Illustrators,* edited by Doris De Montreville and Elizabeth D. Crawford (New York: Wilson, 1978), pp. 108–109;

The Faber Book of Northern Folk-Tales, edited by Crossley-Holland (London: Faber & Faber, 1980);

The Anglo-Saxon World, translated by Crossley-Holland (Woodbridge, Suffolk: Boydell Press, 1982; New York: Barnes & Noble, 1983);

Beowulf, translated and adapted by Crossley-Holland, illustrated by Charles Keeping (London: Oxford University Press, 1982);

The Riddle Book, edited by Crossley-Holland (London: Macmillan, 1982);

Folk-Tales of the British Isles, edited by Crossley-Holland (London: Folio Society, 1985; New York: Pantheon, 1988);

The Oxford Book of Travel Verse, edited by Crossley-Holland (Oxford: Oxford University Press, 1986; New York: Oxford University Press, 1986);

The Wanderer, translated by Crossley-Holland (Colchester: Jardine, 1986);

Northern Lights: Legends, Sagas and Folk-Tales, edited by Crossley-Holland (London: Faber & Faber, 1987);

Medieval Lovers: A Book of Days, edited by Crossley-Holland (London: Hutchinson, 1988; New York: Weidenfeld & Nicolson, 1988);

The Old English Elegies, translated by Crossley-Holland (London: Folio Society, 1988);

Medieval Gardens: A Book of Days, edited by Crossley-Holland (New York: Rizzoli, 1990);

Peter Grimes: The Poor of the Borough, edited by Crossley-Holland (London: Folio Society, 1990).

In the field of children's literature, Kevin Crossley-Holland is best known for his adaptations of myths, legends, and folktales, although he also writes original fiction for children and young adults. In Minnesota (his home in the early 1990s) and in his native Britain, Crossley-Holland has another identity: he is a highly respected poet who writes mainly for an adult audience. His best children's books combine his love of traditional literature and his poetic sensitivity to language to create moody, musical versions of nearly forgotten old tales, particularly stories from Norse legend, Anglo-Saxon poetry, and East Anglian folklore.

Kevin John William Crossley-Holland was born in Mursley, Buckinghamshire, on 7 February 1941. His father, Peter Crossley-Holland, was a noted ethnomusicologist, and his mother, Joan Mary Cowper, received royal recognition for her services to the arts. The overriding theme of Crossley-Holland's childhood was music: international folksongs performed by his father (or on the gramophone), concerts, visiting musicians, and his own lamented viola lessons. This early musical training underscores Crossley-Holland's poetry and certain passages in his fiction.

Crossley-Holland's more formal education took place at Oxford University, where he earned honors in literature, graduating with a B.A. in 1962. Old English literature in particular sparked his imagination – he was drawn to ancient Anglo-Saxon epics such as *Beowulf* (circa 900–1000 or 790–825) and *The Battle of Maldon* (circa 1000). The fatalistic yet heroic mindset of the Anglo-Saxon warriors attracted him, and the poetic elements of the old verses were a major influence on both his poetry and his prose.

After college Crossley-Holland entered the publishing world as an editor. Although he was already a published poet on the basis of his short pamphlet *On Approval* (1961), he was not yet able to pursue a full-time writing career. Working for Macmillan from 1962 to 1971, he oversaw the publication of works by other young writers and made many useful contacts in the publishing world. In 1963 he married Caroline Fendall Thompson. The couple had two sons, Kieran and Dominic, to whom Crossley-Holland was to dedicate several of his children's books.

Crossley-Holland continued to write while at Macmillan, and the company willingly published his early efforts as a translator and as a children's writer. His first published books for young readers were *Havelok the Dane* (1964) and *King Horn* (1965), two retellings of popular medieval romances. Both books are about disguised princes in exile. In *Havelok the Dane* the young title character loses Denmark to a usurper, but his own life is saved by loyal subjects who hide him in England for many years. As an adult, Havelok rescues an English princess from another usurper and restores both thrones to their rightful rulers. *King Horn* tells a similar story about a prince of Suddenne, whose country is overrun by Saracens. With two initially faithful compan-

ions, Prince Horn conceals himself first in Westernesse, then in Ireland, until he is old enough to rescue his own princess and reclaim his throne.

Neither book is particularly memorable. The tone of these early works is slightly patronizing, and the vocabulary is oversimplified for the intended audience of young adults. However, both books show promise of things to come: an occasional poetic passage, a tighter dramatic structure than in the original romances, and added emotional depth and motivation for the characters. *Havelok the Dane* and *King Horn* are important because these medieval adventure stories are rarely retold and because they give evidence of the strong hold the ancient past had taken on Crossley-Holland's imagination.

Crossley-Holland's next work for a young audience was *The Green Children* (1966), a retelling of several short medieval tales. The title story originated in East Anglia, the region of England where he spent much of his adult life. The folktales and legends of East Anglia would become an important source of material for his writing. In an autobiographical essay for the *Fourth Book of Junior Authors and Illustrators* (1978) Crossley-Holland refers to these stories and the poetry of the Anglo-Saxons as the two mainsprings of his work.

Like many local legends, the story of the green children lacks a defined narrative structure, but the strangeness of the tale makes it memorable. Two green children who speak an unknown tongue wander out of their own country into medieval England, where the boy dies of homesickness and the girl grows up and eventually learns enough English to tell her story. There is little plot, but the cool green country that is forever out of reach provides an attractive mystery. The author's tone also contributes to the sense of wonder. The book proved popular in Britain. In 1968 it won an Arts Council award for the best book for children, and in 1994 it was republished by Oxford University Press with new illustrations. In 1990 Crossley-Holland collaborated with Nicola Le Fanu on a children's opera based on *The Green Children*.

Because of the success of *The Green Children,* Crossley-Holland continued to mine his newfound vein of English folktales and legends in two other children's books, *The Callow Pit Coffer* (1968) and *The Pedlar of Swaffham* (1971). Neither volume was lauded as highly as *The Green Children,* although both were well received. Another children's book of this period proved more popular – *Wordhoard: Anglo-Saxon Stories* (1969), which Crossley-Holland wrote with Jill Paton Walsh. *Wordhoard* is a collection of original short stories set in Anglo-Saxon times. Taking several Old English poems and histories as the basis of the tales, Crossley-Holland and Walsh draw a sympathetic picture of Anglo-Saxon life, ending with the death of Harold, the last Saxon king. Each story is independent, yet the consistent tone of the tales creates a unified volume. The authors' main accomplishment is to re-create successfully an era and a culture so ancient as to be almost inaccessible to modern readers.

At the beginning of the 1970s Crossley-Holland's personal and professional lives underwent major changes. In 1972 he married for the second time, to Ruth Marris, and left Macmillan to become editorial director at Gollancz. This career move effectively severed his publishing relationship with Macmillan, and thereafter his children's books were published by other well-respected publishers. One of the first was Heinemann, which brought out a trilogy of short novels set in seventh-century England: *The Sea-Stranger* (1973), *The Fire-Brother* (1975), and *The Earth-Father* (1976). Each book tells a chapter in the life of an Anglo-Saxon boy named Wulf, who is converted to Christianity by a charismatic monk. After Wulf joins the newly built monastery near his village, he faces a serious conflict of loyalty between his family and his newfound Christian brothers. The books capture the clash between early Christianity and the long-held pagan beliefs of the Anglo-Saxons, dramatizing the conflict by showing its effect on Wulf's relationships with the monks and with his family.

In 1988 these three stories were revised and published by Faber and Faber in one volume under the title *Wulf*. The revisions demonstrate Crossley-Holland's development as a writer. In comparison to *Wulf*, the earlier versions seem wordy and unnecessarily explanatory, and they contain descriptive passages that occasionally strain too hard for poetic effect. For example, an episode in *The Sea-Stranger* — "He hurried across the fort around which the wind whined, hoping to find a crab in the shallow water that slopped and sang against the outside of the massive northeastern wall" — is described more concisely in *Wulf*: "He hurried across the fort, hoping to find a crab in the shallow water chopping and slopping against the outside of the massive north-eastern wall." The revised version is less wordy and has traded two alliterative phrases for one pair of rhymed participles. A careful comparison of the two versions of Wulf's story demonstrates Crossley-Holland's constant movement toward precision and efficiency in his use of language — an outgrowth of his development as a poet. He had by this time

published nine poetic pamphlets and four larger volumes of poetry.

In 1975 Andre Deutsch published *Green Blades Rising: The Anglo-Saxons,* a nonfiction book that introduces the Anglo-Saxon culture in a direct style, easily accessible to older children, using illustrations and quotations from Old English literature. Deutsch followed this the next year with *The Wildman,* a local legend Crossley-Holland drew from the same medieval source in which he had found *The Green Children. The Wildman* represents the best of Crossley-Holland's work; it combines his poetic grasp of language and his storytelling abilities to create a prose poem about a merman who is captured and tortured but eventually escapes to the sea. Told in first person by the merman, *The Wildman* is a moody, evocative piece, both haunting and sad.

Crossley-Holland next turned his attention to Norse materials. He edited two volumes of Norse tales for Faber and Faber — *The Faber Book of Northern Legends* (1977) and *The Faber Book of Northern Folk-Tales* (1980) — and Deutsch published Crossley-Holland's own version of the Norse mythic cycle in *The Norse Myths: A Retelling* (1980). The Faber collections were intended for young adults, while the Deutsch volume was a more scholarly enterprise resulting from the former. As with the Anglo-Saxon poetry that influenced his earlier works, the fatalistic Norse stories struck a chord in Crossley-Holland. His retellings retain the direct simplicity and the grimly humorous understatement of the original sources. All three books were successful and resulted in new editions: in 1985 Deutsch published a selection from *The Norse Myths* in a volume for children entitled *Axe-Age, Wolf-Age,* and in 1987 Faber and Faber republished their two volumes of tales as *Northern Lights: Legends, Sagas and Folk-Tales,* edited by Crossley-Holland.

Crossley-Holland married for the third time in 1982. His third wife, the former Gillian Cook, bore him two daughters, Oenone and Eleanor, who provided new inspiration for his poetry and his children's books. He had given up his position as editorial director at Gollancz in 1977, but he continued to accept editorial commissions and visiting lectureships while he worked full-time as a writer.

The 1980s were a prolific decade for Crossley-Holland, and 1982 was a particularly good year: *The Dead Moon and Other Tales from East Anglia and the Fen Country,* one of Crossley-Holland's best books, was published. Crossley-Holland was still living in East Anglia, and he had been studying the local ghost stories and legends since the 1960s. He col-

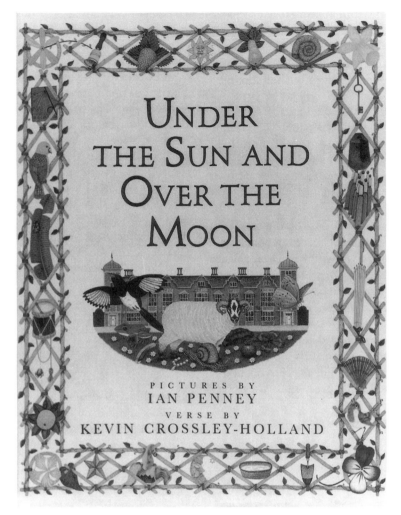

Dust jacket for one of Crossley-Holland's 1989 picture books, a counting book in verse form

lected stories from many sources, including several medieval manuscripts, in *The Dead Moon and Other Tales from East Anglia and the Fen Country*. This volume represents the author at his best. He maintains a unified tone in this collection, attributable to his choice of material, the placement of the stories, his careful use of dialect, and a poetic cadence that runs throughout the book. In this, as in his other best work, Crossley-Holland succeeds in writing what he refers to as "lapidary English," as smooth and polished as a gemstone.

Another of Crossley-Holland's best works also appeared in 1982. He had produced a scholarly verse translation of the Anglo-Saxon epic *Beowulf* in 1968; now Oxford University Press published a prose translation he had done particularly for children, with illustrations by Charles Keeping, the foremost British illustrator of the decade. Crossley-Holland's *Beowulf* is a graphic retelling of the grisly

story of the Anglo-Saxon hero's battles with various monsters. In retrospect the author admits that for a children's story it is "more blood-thirsty than I would want it to be now," but at the time he considered the gore a necessary part of the tale. Told in a direct and powerful voice, this prose version recreates the tone and mood of the original epic.

In 1983 Crossley-Holland was approached by the Welsh Arts Council to collaborate with Gwyn Thomas, a professor of Welsh, on an English version of Thomas's *Y Mabinogi* (1984), a children's version of four medieval Welsh legends. *Tales from the Mabinogion* (1984) was such a successful collaboration that Thomas and Crossley-Holland produced two sequels, *The Quest for Olwen* (1988) and *The Tale of Taliesin* (1992) — both based on Thomas's Welsh versions of these ancient tales. Despite their picture-book format, these collaborations are robust and earthy renditions, true to their originals in tone and plot. Crossley-Holland's contribution to the collaborative effort was editorial and poetic; he smoothed the rough edges of Thomas's English translation.

Collaboration seemed to suit Crossley-Holland. In 1985 he and Susanne Lugert published *The Fox and the Cat: Animal Tales from Grimm,* an illustrated collection of German fables chosen from the Grimms' tales. Because of the selection criteria, the volume is more unified than several of the other folktale collections Crossley-Holland has compiled. The few humans who appear in these stories are unattractive figures, but the animal protagonists act out their parts admirably.

Storm (1985), Crossley-Holland's award-winning ghost story, is almost a prose poem. It is about young Annie, who lives with her parents near a marsh haunted by the ghost of a horseman. When Annie's older sister goes into labor during a storm, Annie is sent out to find a doctor, and she gets a lift from the ghostly rider. The poetic cadence of the language lifts *Storm* above most tales of this sort. In fact, the British Library Association decided that this book was the most outstanding children's book of its year and awarded it the prestigious Carnegie Medal in 1986.

Crossley-Holland next turned his attention to British folktales. After editing a collection for adults in 1985, he retold a number of these stories for children in *British Folk Tales: New Versions* (1987). Four of the tales in this collection were republished in picture-book format in 1988: *Boo!, Dathera Dad, Piper and Pooka,* and *Small-Tooth Dog.* Although there are excellent stories in *British Folk Tales,* the collection as a whole is inconsistent. To borrow from a popular nursery rhyme, when they are good, they are very, very good; but when they are bad, they are mediocre. Some of the stories resonate with Crossley-Holland's poetic feel for language, but the book contains too many abrupt changes in tone and point of view. The modern selections strike a peculiarly jarring note amid the ancient remnants of British legend. The best tales are the older ones of English origin (Crossley-Holland does not exhibit as good a feel for the Irish selections).

In 1989 Crossley-Holland produced two picture books, *Under the Sun and Over the Moon* and *Sleeping Nana.* The former is a counting book in verse form, while the latter is a dream journey in which a little girl travels to many islands, where she explores the senses of sight, taste, smell, and sound. While neither book is particularly outstanding, they are both competent examples of the picture-book genre.

Kevin Crossley-Holland continues to write, translate, and edit books both for adults and for children. Since 1991 he has been a professor of English at the University of Saint Thomas in Saint Paul, Minnesota. Naturally enough, this full-time occupation has reduced his authorial output, but he has not retired from the writing profession. Recent works for children include yet more folktales and a new version of the adventures of Hercules.

Papers:

Most of Kevin Crossley-Holland's children's manuscripts are in the Osborne Collection at the Toronto Public Library. The Kerlan Collection of the University of Minnesota contains material on *Under the Sun and Over the Moon.* Crossley-Holland's poetry notebooks are part of the Brotherton Collection of the University of Leeds.

Peter Dickinson

(16 December 1927 –   )

Raymond E. Jones
University of Alberta

See also the Dickinson entry in *DLB 87: British Mystery and Thriller Writers Since 1940, First Series.*

BOOKS: *Skin Deep* (London: Hodder & Stoughton, 1968); republished as *The Glass-Sided Ants' Nest* (New York: Harper & Row, 1968);

The Weathermonger (London: Gollancz, 1968; Boston: Little, Brown, 1969);

Heartsease (London: Gollancz, 1969; Boston: Little, Brown, 1969);

A Pride of Heroes (London: Hodder & Stoughton, 1969); republished as *The Old English Peep Show* (New York: Harper & Row, 1969);

The Devil's Children (London: Gollancz, 1970; Boston: Little, Brown, 1970);

The Seals (London: Hodder & Stoughton, 1970); republished as *The Sinful Stones* (New York: Harper & Row, 1970);

Emma Tupper's Diary (London: Gollancz, 1971; Boston: Little, Brown, 1971);

Sleep and His Brother (London: Hodder & Stoughton, 1971; New York: Harper & Row, 1971);

The Dancing Bear (London: Gollancz, 1972; Boston: Little, Brown, 1973);

The Iron Lion (Boston: Little, Brown, 1972; London: Allen & Unwin, 1973);

The Lizard in the Cup (London: Hodder & Stoughton, 1972: New York: Harper & Row, 1972);

The Gift (London: Gollancz, 1973; Boston: Little, Brown, 1974);

The Green Gene (London: Hodder & Stoughton, 1973; New York: Pantheon, 1973);

The Poison Oracle (London: Hodder & Stoughton, 1974; New York: Pantheon, 1974);

The Changes: A Trilogy (London: Gollancz, 1974); retitled collection of *The Weathermonger, Heartsease,* and *The Devil's Children;*

Chance, Luck, and Destiny (London: Gollancz, 1975; Boston: Little, Brown, 1976);

The Lively Dead (London: Hodder & Stoughton, 1975; New York: Pantheon, 1975);

Peter Dickinson

The Blue Hawk (London: Gollancz, 1976; Boston: Little, Brown, 1976);

King and Joker (London: Hodder & Stoughton, 1976; New York: Pantheon, 1976);

Annerton Pit (London: Gollancz, 1977; Boston: Little, Brown, 1977);

Walking Dead (London: Hodder & Stoughton, 1977; New York: Pantheon, 1977);

Hepzibah (Twickenham: Eel Pie, 1978; Boston: Godine 1980);

The Flight of Dragons (London: Pierrot, 1979; New York: Harper & Row, 1979);

One Foot in the Grave (London: Hodder & Stoughton, 1979; New York: Pantheon, 1980);

Tulku (London: Gollancz, 1979; New York: Dutton, 1979);

City of Gold and Other Stories from the Old Testament (London: Gollancz, 1980; New York: Pantheon, 1980);

The Seventh Raven (London: Gollancz, 1981; New York: Dutton, 1981);

A Summer in the Twenties (London: Hodder & Stoughton, 1981; New York: Pantheon, 1981);

The Last House-Party (London: Bodley Head, 1982; New York: Pantheon, 1982);

Healer (London: Gollancz, 1983; New York: Delacorte, 1983);

Hindsight (London: Bodley Head, 1983; New York: Pantheon, 1983);

Death of a Unicorn (London: Bodley Head, 1984; New York: Pantheon, 1984);

Giant Cold (London: Gollancz, 1984; New York: Dutton, 1984);

A Box of Nothing (London: Gollancz, 1985; New York: Delacorte, 1988);

Tefuga (London: Bodley Head, 1986; New York: Pantheon, 1986);

Mole Hole (London: Blackie, 1987; New York: Bedrick, 1987);

Merlin Dreams (London: Gollancz, 1988; New York: Delacorte, 1988);

Perfect Gallows (London: Bodley Head, 1988; New York: Pantheon, 1988);

Eva (London: Gollancz, 1988; New York: Delacorte, 1989);

Skeleton-in-Waiting (London: Bodley Head, 1989; New York: Pantheon, 1989);

AK (London: Gollancz, 1990);

Play Dead (London: Bodley Head, 1991; New York: Mysterious Press, 1993);

Bone from a Dry Sea (London: Gollancz, 1992; New York: Delacorte, 1993);

Time and the Clockmice, Etcetera (London: Doubleday, 1993; New York: Delacorte, 1994);

Shadow of a Hero (London: Gollancz, 1994; New York: Delacorte, 1994);

The Yellow Room Conspiracy (New York: Mysterious Press, 1994; London: Warner Futura, 1995).

TELEVISION: *Mandog,* screenplay by Dickinson, BBC, 1972.

OTHER: "A Defense of Rubbish," in *Children and Literature: Views and Reviews,* edited by Virginia Haviland (Glenview, Ill.: Scott, Foresman, 1973), pp. 101–103;

Presto! Humorous Bits and Pieces, edited by Dickinson (London: Hutchinson, 1975);

"Superintendent Pibble," in *The Great Detectives,* edited by Otto Penzler (Boston: Little, Brown, 1978), pp. 175–182;

Hundreds and Hundreds, edited by Dickinson (Harmondsworth: Penguin, 1984);

"Flight," in *Imaginary Lands,* edited by Robin McKinley (New York: Greenwillow, 1986), pp. 63–96;

"The Burden of the Past," in *Innocence & Experience: Essays & Conversations on Children's Literature,* edited by Barbara Harrison and Gregory Maguire (New York: Lothrop, Lee & Shepard, 1987), pp. 91–101;

"The Oral Voices of City of Gold," in *The Voice of the Narrator in Children's Literature: Insights from Writers and Critics,* edited by Charlotte F. Otten and Gary D. Schmidt (New York: Greenwood, 1989), pp. 78–80;

"Time and Times and Half a Time," in *Travellers in Time: Past, Present, and to Come* (Cambridge: Children's Literature New England, 1990), pp. 58–64.

SELECTED PERIODICAL PUBLICATIONS –
UNCOLLECTED: "The Day of the Tennis Rabbit," *Quarterly Journal of the Library of Congress,* 38 (Fall 1981): 203–219;

"Fantasy: The Need for Realism," *Children's Literature in Education,* 17, no. 1 (1986): 39–51;

"Emily Dickinson and Music," *Music and Letters,* 75 (May 1994): 241–245.

"I have a function, like the village cobbler, and that is to tell stories. Everything else is subservient to that." Although he makes no lofty claims for himself in the note he writes for John Rowe Townsend's *A Sounding of Storytellers* (1979), Peter Dickinson has achieved a significant reputation, garnering critical praise and literary awards as a writer for both adults and children. The only writer to win the Carnegie Medal in two consecutive years, he has also won the Whitbread Award twice, the Guardian Award, and the Boston Globe–Horn Book Award for nonfiction. In addition he has received an American Library Association Notable Book Award in 1971 and a Boston Globe–Horn Book Honor Book citation in 1989. Extending his simile for himself as a cobbler, Dickinson has said, "Given good leather I can make a comfortable shoe." Clearly awards committees, literary critics, and ordinary readers, both children and adults, have found that Dickinson often uses the best leather, producing shoes comfortable enough to lure them into numerous exciting and imaginative journeys.

Dust jacket for Dickinson's first book for children, a fantasy in which a brother and sister undertake a quest to save England from madness

Peter Dickinson was born 16 December 1927 in Livingstone, Northern Rhodesia (now Zambia), but he has said that he has little memory of his exotic African roots. When Dickinson was seven his father, Richard Sebastian Willoughby Dickinson, a colonial administrator, moved the family to England in 1935 and died shortly afterward. In 1941 Dickinson won a scholarship to Eton College. Upon graduation in 1946, he was conscripted and served as a district signals officer in the British army. At the end of his military service in 1948, Dickinson enrolled at King's College, Cambridge, and completed his B.A. in English literature in 1951. The next year he began working as an editor and reviewer with *Punch.* Although his career there did not get off to an auspicious start – he was hit by a tram and had to attend the interview covered in blood – he stayed for seventeen years before resigning in 1969 to devote himself full time to writing. On 20 April 1953 Dickinson married Mary

Rose Barnard, with whom he had four children. She died in 1988, and on 3 January 1992 he married the American fantasy writer Robin McKinley.

From 1968, the year he began his career with an adult mystery, *Skin Deep* (published in the United States as *The Glass-Sided Ants' Nest*), and a children's fantasy, *The Weathermonger,* Dickinson has defied easy categorizing and continued to alternate between writing books for adults and for children. Especially in his children's books he resists labeling as a writer of work in a particular genre. As he has written, "I like my stories exciting and as different as possible from the one I wrote last time." Thus, his children's books include fantasies, historical fiction, contemporary thrillers, science fiction, and picture books. In *Painted Desert, Green Shade* (1984) David Rees says that "each new book of his invariably strikes the reader as unpredictable, a pleasant surprise."

Although varied, his books do bear a certain family resemblance. Reviewers and critics have praised his books for fast-paced action in densely rendered settings, and, as if in response to his comment that setting and its "feel" are less important to him than "nuances of character," critics have complained that his characters are the weakest elements of his art. Dickinson has also said that "Most of my books have an element of fantasy in them." In "Fantasy: The Need for Realism" (1986), he declared that mainstream fiction produces "maps of landscapes" that enable us to explore such things as "the hidden country of fear behind a smiling face." In contrast, he says, "Fantasy is the poetry of ideas" that begin with speculation and discover new worlds. Believing that the imagination "is the core of our humanity," Dickinson stimulates it by producing "maps of coherence, which we may imaginatively follow." Whether or not a given book formally qualifies as fantasy, Dickinson manifests the poetry of its ideas through a concern for intellectual and moral problems, many of which are left to the reader to resolve.

Dickinson's first three children's books introduce what he has indicated in "Time and Times and Half a Time" (1990) forms "a side issue" in many of them: "the strangeness of time." In *The Weathermonger, Heartsease* (1969), and *The Devil's Children* (1970) that strangeness is prominent as a plot device to investigate the effects of social myths. Set in a period described as "now, or soon," these three novels form a trilogy linked by description of events during the Changes, a time when people in England suddenly revert to the mentality of the Dark Ages and live by a myth that identifies machinery as wicked. When these novels were republished in an omnibus edition as *The Changes: A Trilogy* (1974), Dickinson arranged them in reverse order of their publication to reflect the chronology of events: *The Weathermonger* describes the end of the Changes; *Heartsease,* a period about a year earlier; and *The Devil's Children,* a period near the beginning of these social changes. Although this rearrangement preserves suspense and the linking prefaces of the omnibus edition provide coherence, Dickinson's own development is better seen by examining the novels in their original order.

The Weathermonger, unlike the other novels, is a fantasy and is the least philosophic of the three. Essentially an old-fashioned adventure novel in which orphaned children display extraordinary courage and perform prodigious deeds, it describes the efforts of a brother and sister, Geoffrey and Sally, who are recruited to locate the cause of the madness that has affected England. Inexplicably free from the madness themselves, they undertake their jour-

ney at first in a lovingly described 1909 Rolls Royce Silver Shadow and then by horse and foot. The novel moves at a breathless pace as Geoffrey uses his skill at controlling the weather to aid their narrow escapes. When they arrive at a mysterious Welsh castle, the pace slackens. There they learn the cause of the Changes: the Arthurian magician Merlin, addicted to morphine by a chemist who had sought to control him, has expressed his hatred for machines through drug-induced dreams that have changed the physical world.

Critics have repeatedly criticized this unsatisfying explanation, with Rees calling it "at best unlikely, at worst trivial or childish," and Townsend declaring it "outrageous" and "an abuse of major legend, as well as being totally unconvincing." Dickinson compounds this weakness by having Merlin end his addiction instantly: when Sally tells him that the drug is evil, he stops taking it. Although the novel presents interesting contrasts between those who have a contemporary love for machines and the viciously intolerant villagers, the wooden characterization, the inconsistency in Geoffrey, a weathermonger who loves machinery, and the undramatic resolution make this a novel more interesting in conception than execution.

The other novels of the trilogy are far more effective because they mention neither the magic of weathermongering nor the cause of the Changes. As a consequence they foreground the contrast between ideas. The central conflict is not really between those who love machines and those who accept the myth of the wickedness of machinery, although this creates surface oppositions. The true conflict is between those who think for themselves and those who merely dream society's dreams. In *Heartsease* Dickinson brings this out through a highly developed presentation of place as both a physical locale and a social atmosphere of shared ideas. Set on a Cotswold farm, *Heartsease* describes the efforts of two fourteen-year-olds, Margaret and her cousin Jonathan, to aid an American spy and a farm servant with a simpleton brother to escape. The spy and the brother are sought as witches.

The five make a perilous journey on an old tug from Gloucester to the sea, following an abandoned canal. The description of their preparations is too prolonged and that of the escape too repetitive, so that the adventure loses tension; still, *Heartsease* forcefully advances ideas about the conflict between individuals and social beliefs. The book is one-sided, however, in its support of machine-age technology, as it makes all those who oppose it seem ignorant and vicious. Mr. Gordon, the sym-

*Dust jacket for Dickinson's fantasy that explores themes of racial
prejudice and the social needs of children*

bolically crippled sexton who devotes his life to discovering evil in others, is a stereotypical bigot who lacks any redeeming qualities. Nevertheless, Dickinson's portraits of farm and village life effectively convey the oppressive atmosphere of an intolerant and superstitious society that cannot examine its own cruelty because to do so would call into question the beliefs that underlie that cruelty. *Heartsease* is in no way allegorical, but it suggests universal problems individuals have always faced in societies dependent on scapegoats – whether that of the Salem witch trials, Germany during the Nazi era, or Washington during Sen. Joseph McCarthy's anticommunist crusade. In this sense it is Dickinson's first success in creating a "poetry of ideas."

For most critics *The Devil's Children* is the most successful novel in the *Changes* trilogy because its characterization contributes far more to the development of plot and theme. Set in the initial period of the Changes, it expands the theme of superstition to include racial prejudice while it simultaneously explores the child's need to belong. Twelve-year-

old Nicola, separated from her parents, attaches herself to a group of wandering Sikhs who, unaffected by the Changes, use her as a "canary" to alert them to dangers they would not otherwise sense. After the group settles on a farm, the novel becomes an effective study of manners, contrasting the chaotically democratic life of the Sikhs to the feudal subservience of the villagers with whom they have an uneasy commercial relationship. Ironically, Nicky becomes central to their survival by conducting trade with the villagers, whose xenophobia makes them avoid the Sikhs – whom they call the devil's children.

The novel builds to a double climax. The divisive social problems are resolved when the Sikhs, in a stirringly described battle, save the village from marauders. The formerly hostile villagers gratefully join them in a celebratory festival that symbolizes the possibility of racial harmony. The personal issues are resolved when the Sikhs, realizing that Nicky has armored her heart and isolated herself, send her to France to join her parents so that she can grow whole. In "The Day of the Tennis Rabbit" (1981) Dickinson says that an overt social aim affected his portrayal of the Sikhs: "I made them goodies. . . . They are slightly unreal, and the whole book is the worse for that." In spite of its didactic intentions and idealized characters, however, the novel avoids preachiness and is, according to Rees, "one of the most thoughtful discussions of racial intolerance in contemporary children's literature." By combining a story of social development with one of personal growth, it achieves both intellectual substance and emotional power.

Didactic intentions, a concern for the intricacies of machinery, the contrast of manners, and a need to belong also shape a much slighter narrative, *Emma Tupper's Diary* (1971). While visiting her cousins in Scotland, fourteen-year-old Emma Tupper joins in their attempt to use a Victorian-era submarine to fool a television station into believing that a monster inhabits their loch. Their discovery of actual plesiosaurs living in a cave in the loch forces a family meeting in which the characters debate the ethical dimensions of their find: whether it is best to open the cave to tourists, to inform only selected scientists, or to hide their discovery. Although some critics have praised it, *Emma Tupper's Diary* lacks a firm center. As an adventure story arguing that man has destroyed too many creatures, it has some success. The banter is sporadically amusing, but the book depends too much on eccentric characters like the beautiful kleptomaniac Poop Newcombe and the domineering and mysterious Major McAndrew. *Emma Tupper's Diary* contains a few good moments, but because of its cluttered variety it never coheres.

In contrast *The Dancing Bear* (1972) is entirely successful, a major work with a grand sweep. Although set in the sixth century, the book is not a historical novel. Dickinson, in an interview by Jay Williams, called it "history science-fiction" because "I know a bit of history and extrapolate the rest." The result is a quest adventure in which the slave Silvester sets out to rescue Lady Ariadne, abducted by the Huns. He crosses vast territories, and the dramatic changes in physical and social settings ensure that episodes differ markedly from each other. Political intrigue also adds tension to the first part of his journey. Unfairly placed on the Lists, the official roll of enemies of the state, Silvester must escape from the Empire's territory before he can rescue Ariadne. These exciting adventures support a theme examining personal identity, as even after he becomes technically free, Silvester continues to think of himself as a slave. He knows his exact value in monetary terms but does not realize that he has another value. His deeds of

compassion, as when he saves the life of a wounded Hun, and his dogged determination to find Ariadne show that he possesses nobility of soul. Only after the rescued Ariadne returns the favor by giving him his manumission does he understand that freedom is something within. As befits an historical romance, *The Dancing Bear* concludes with a poetically appropriate sign of achievement and identity, his marriage to Ariadne. Silvester thus learns that it is the private myth of identity, not the external social scheme, that matters.

In addition to being a superb adventure, *The Dancing Bear* is also a colorful portrait of manners, showing life on the docks of Byzantium, in the elegant houses, among the superstitious frontier peasants who demand that the bear walk on them to cure illness, and in the camps of the Huns. Many of these scenes establish clearly that identity is more a product of personal choices and character than of legal description. Silvester at first thinks of the City, with its elaborate code of laws and its intricate religious debates, as the epitome of civilization, the arbiter of his identity and destiny. By contrasting the manners and mores of various groups with those of Byzantium, however, the novel shows through Silvester's adventures what he does not realize: that the corrupt City can be more barbaric than the Huns. The Hun leader manipulates a trial to enable Silvester to avoid a compulsory death sentence, whereas the relatives of his slain master in Byzantium falsely accuse Silvester and thereby ensure his execution should he ever return.

Both the adventure and the study of manners are effective because of memorable characterization. Silvester's companion Holy John, the argumentative ascetic with a desire to convert the barbarians, displays a religious zeal that complements Silvester's dedication to earthly masters. Furthermore, his complex theological debates throw Silvester's practical Christian compassion into sharp relief. The Khan Zabergan, the Hun leader, shows that wisdom and compassion can coexist with cruelty, just as they do in Byzantium. The Slav Antoninus, who considers himself a civilized Roman among barbarians, adds a somber touch to the novel when he wills his position to Silvester. Silvester accepts the necessity of developing his own identity, but he looks back on his exile from Byzantium almost as if the city were a lost Eden. Together Ariadne and Antoninus lead him from the innocence of slavery to the experience of freedom. Finally Bubba, Silvester's trained bear and a memorable character in her own right, makes the novel an excellent animal story. In addition to revealing Silvester's unacknowledged humanity, she injects humor into many episodes. Never cloyingly cute nor excessively anthropomorphic, she makes notable contributions to the adventure and adds lightness to a novel filled with speculation on serious subjects.

After this major achievement Dickinson produced three lesser books, each in a different genre. To a certain extent *The Iron Lion* (1972), his first picture book, is a parody of folk tales that uses conventional plot materials but modifies them with incongruous, absurd events. Mustapha, the poor prince of Goat Mountain, wins the hand of a Persian princess by performing a seemingly impossible quest: he brings the ferocious Iron Lion of Ferdustan to the court and, unwittingly, saves the kingdom. He succeeds where others have failed because he amuses the beast by using the talent he has developed by working as a circus clown. Furthermore, he oils the Iron Lion to prevent it from rusting and thereby allows it to achieve its wish, to see the world. A drably uninviting book in its first edition, it has been republished with colorful pictures more in keeping with its vivacious spirit. Unusual characters and a wry humor that may be above the heads of many young readers make it an amusing, though not memorable, book.

The Gift (1973), Dickinson's first novel to use the paranormal, combines a thriller with an unsuccessful family-problem story. Possessing the gift of reading others' thoughts, Davy Price saves his father from getting involved in a robbery and prevents a gang member, a psychotic he calls Wolf, from slaughtering his family. *The Gift* is a taut thriller until the final confrontation with Wolf, when Davy, as David Rees notes, acts "as if he were an experienced adult psychiatrist, not a child." In the family story, the grief caused by the legendary gift is evident in the hostility between Davy's grandmother and his father. Davy's gift is contrasted to his sister's humane sensitivity, a contrast suggesting that the latter is a better guide to understanding others. Personal relationships, however, do not receive enough attention to make the rapid reformation of Davy's dysfunctional family seem plausible. The final book of these three, *Chance, Luck, and Destiny* (1975), won the Boston Globe–Horn Book Award for nonfiction. Organized around accounts of three stages in the life of Oedipus, each illustrating one of the title's concepts, this miscellany of tales, statistics, and reflections is a fascinating book for leisurely reading.

With his next children's book – *The Blue Hawk* (1976), winner of the *Guardian* Award – Dickinson produced what both Townsend and Rees have

called his most impressive novel. Set in a fictional land resembling ancient Egypt, it is an adventure that explores ideas about power, change, religion, and personal identity. The central character is Tron, a boy trained from infancy in the exacting rituals and traditional wisdom that the priests use to maintain their tight control of the kingdom. Ironically, Tron, whose training makes him afraid of change, causes a calamitous upheaval. Following the prompting of his heart, he interferes with an important ritual by saving a hawk from sacrifice. As a consequence the priests murder the king and try to consolidate their grip on power. The changes within Tron are just as dramatic. Used to being part of a group, he learns to be alone; conditioned to obey, he learns friendship and trust from the king's son; taught that the priests are beyond questioning, he sees their duplicity and even begins to question his own belief in the gods.

The next stages of Tron's adventure involve a symbolic journey like those of mythic heroes outlined by Joseph Campbell in *The Hero with a Thousand Faces* (1949) and *The Power of Myth* (1988). Agreeing to help the king's son, Tron hides in the coffin of the dead king, floating on a barge toward the afterlife. In the coffin, described as a mouth waiting to swallow him, Tron dies from his former life as servant and begins a journey toward rebirth. He escapes destruction at a waterfall, the entrance to his mythological underworld, only to spend three nights of illness in a cave – a symbolic tomb from which he arises after a dream. His journey now takes him back to the City. Upon his return, however, he feels the gods desert him. Knowing that he has no divine aid and must act alone, Tron heroically performs a ceremony that undoes the curse of the priests and opens up the kingdom. Afterward he is shot by an archer and begins a second symbolic death and rebirth. This time he is reborn completely free of the traditional gods, as a whole person cherishing his freedom and individuality.

The Blue Hawk is an artistic triumph. The skillful integration of custom, history, and myth makes its world absolutely convincing. Its adventures are gripping, and, although it depends on the device of the unlikely child hero, neither Tron nor any of the other characters violates inner logic. *The Blue Hawk* is Dickinson's finest example of the "poetry of ideas." In particular, it powerfully presents the need for change and renewal in every phase of life. At a basic level, change is necessary because the very land, tilled unvaryingly according to ritual prescription, has become exhausted. The political situation parallels this. Closed borders and a refusal to listen

Dust jacket for Dickinson's 1976 novel for children, set in a fictional land resembling ancient Egypt

to new ideas have made the kingdom vulnerable to aggression, so the new king decides to open his land and to seek new territory. The novel also shows the exhaustion of religion. The cynical priests, who use tradition to stave off threats to their power and maintain their oppression, are spiritually empty. Dickinson's portraits of them reveal the dangers of institutionalized religion, but he leaves open the question of whether the gods really exist. Tron himself feels the gods speaking to him, and he suggests at the end that the institutional gods have for too long made such a din that people have been unable to hear the gods within. In any case Tron represents the most compelling case for change by moving from being a blindly obedient servant to a free individual. Through him Dickinson celebrates choice, something the priests did not allow, as the foundation of meaningful human identity.

After this triumph Dickinson returned to ground he had covered earlier. Like *Emma Tupper's Diary,* the disappointing *Annerton Pit* (1977) deals with the proper response to ecological issues, and like *The Gift* it is a contemporary thriller containing suggestions of the paranormal. Thirteen-year-old Jake, blind from birth, encounters with his older brother and their grandfather a group of radical environmentalists plotting to capture a North Sea oil

rig. Imprisoned in a coal mine, the site of a nineteenth-century disaster, Jake turns his disability to advantage and leads his relatives to safety. Jake is a well-realized character, but his brother and grandfather are pallid creations and the environmental terrorists merely tired plot devices. Although most ideas receive only sketchy treatment, the novel introduces some interesting themes — such as the paradox of people supposedly concerned about the planet but who are willing to kill for their cause. Even the teasing introduction of the paranormal is problematic. Jake feels that he is communicating with a presence that guards the mine, but the novel suggests that this presence may be only in Jake's mind. This insinuates that Jake's adventures in the mine are symbolically explorations of his psyche, but the story fails to examine the implications of the fact that both the presence in the mine and the environmentalists resort to terror to protect what they love. In spite of its thematic weaknesses and its deficiencies in characterization, however, *Annerton Pit* has just enough tense moments to make it a readable adventure.

Before publishing his next children's novel, Dickinson again exercised his penchant for variety in two minor books, each of which tries to be humorous. *Hepzibah* (1978), a cheaply produced picture book with an accompanying record, exhibits a prominent feature of many of Dickinson's adult books – a fondness for grotesques and eccentrics. Hepzibah is described as an "awful" girl because she eats soap until bubbles come out her ears, sleeps upside down, keeps a cow in the bath, and creates trouble when she cannot find any. Footnotes offer occasionally humorous comments about the illustrations, but otherwise *Hepzibah* is too strained in its efforts to be funny. *The Flight of Dragons* (1979) is a lavishly illustrated, extended jeu d'esprit. Using descriptions from many literary sources Dickinson, who claims to believe in the existence of dragons, develops a pseudoscientific explanation of all their traits. According to him, dragons flew because, like dirigibles, they were gas-filled, and they breathed fire as a necessary way of venting the gas within. His descriptions of the dragon's system are as detailed and exhaustive as technical descriptions in such novels as *Emma Tupper's Diary*. Although he carries the joke on too long, *The Flight of Dragons* is an entertaining introduction to many features of dragon lore.

Dickinson's next children's novel – *Tulku* (1979), winner of both the Whitbread Award and the Carnegie Medal – reasserted his position as one of the most important children's writers in England. Set in China during the Boxer Rebellion, *Tulku* is an adventure that Rees has praised as an excellent "first-rate yarn." It includes both the heroic exploits of the standard historical romance and the intensely suspenseful action of a thriller. Thirteen-year-old Theodore Tewker, son of an American missionary and the only survivor when rebels destroy his father's mission, joins up by chance with Mrs. Daisy Jones, an amateur botanist, and her Chinese servant, Lung. Together they undertake a perilous journey across China toward Tibet. Pursued by bandits they rely on Mrs. Jones's skill with a gun. Later they are saved by the Lama Amchi, a monk seeking the Tulku, the reincarnation of a great lama. Guided to the monastery at Dong Pe, they learn that the monks believe that Mrs. Jones, who has become pregnant after taking Lung as her lover during the journey, is carrying the new Tulku. The monastery, however, is not simply a place of spiritual contemplation: like the priests in *The Blue Hawk,* the monks are involved in political intrigues, with separate factions vying for control, and, like Tron, Theodore is instrumental in foiling a plot.

Although he set *Tulku* around 1900, Dickinson has said that he wrote it "partly as a way of looking at some far-from-out-of-date worries, such as the nature of religious faith." Theodore's perilous journey is symbolically a spiritual one: he moves from the rigidity of his father's religion to a more generous acceptance of the world. At first he is intolerant, condemning Mrs. Jones for her habitual swearing and her affair with Lung. Gradually he recognizes that her profanity and sexuality do not necessarily make her evil. Theodore's lost faith, suggested through the repeated image of a shut and dusty chapel within him, is restored at the monastery when a monk, in the voice of Theodore's father, orders him to his room. Theodore, who had begun his journey in a violation of his father's last order, obeys, and his frustration and anger dissipate. In a conventional metaphor of Christian faith, Theodore declares himself reborn. Like Tron in *The Blue Hawk,* Theodore has died as a child and is reborn as a hero: he saves the life of the lama and preserves order in the monastery. But Theodore has come to an understanding different from that of the monks: for them, the life of the body is a burden; for Theodore, no longer numbed by the murder of his father, it is a joyous affirmation of identity and purpose. Knowing both who he is and where he belongs, he can return to America to rededicate himself in a mature way to his religion.

In fact, each major character in *Tulku* embodies a philosophical or spiritual attitude that contributes to the exploration of the meaning of religious experience. The palest character among Dickinson's personae, Lung represents the failure of conventional Romanticism. A poet for whom fine feelings seem the only religion, he is unable, because of Mrs. Jones, to accept her choice of a life that excludes him. He is caught up in his own emotions and violent attempts to express them. In contrast, Dickinson characterizes Mrs. Jones in terms of four different sexual stereotypes: "the traditional tomboy adventuress," "the lovable cockney waif," "the chorusgirl-cum-prostitute with a heart of gold," and "the Great Earth Mother." Both practical and spiritual, she tries all approaches to fulfillment. At first, declaring with a laugh that she will never be a holy body, she seeks fame by searching for a flower to bear her name; later, she dedicates herself to a study of Buddhism and to the child she has conceived. The figures of Lama Amchi, Major Price-Evans, and the other monks suggest the variety that even an apparently monolithic institution contains. Dickinson has admitted that, since little is known about practices in eastern Tibet, "I felt free to make the whole thing up." Nevertheless, these characters are alive, and their ceremonies are convincing challenges to Theodore's spiritual provincialism.

Tulku does have weaknesses, especially the unconvincing Cockney accent into which Mrs. Jones implausibly slides at various times. Yet Dickinson's powers of description surpass those of his earlier work, as everything develops character or theme. *Tulku* focuses clearly on religious experience, but it also explores other issues such as chauvinism and provincialism, art as both personal and religious expression, and belief, illusion, and deception. Ultimately the characteristic strength of Dickinson's *Tulku* is that its artistic sophistication in no way blunts the book as a gripping adventure.

Dickinson has said on several occasions that he at first rejected the invitation to write his next children's book, *City of Gold and Other Stories from the Old Testament* (1980), a collection that made him the first author ever to win a Carnegie Medal in two consecutive years. He did so because he felt that Bible stories differed from the books already in his publisher's series – tales by Hans Christian Andersen and the Brothers Grimm. Such tales, he believed, were primarily for entertainment, whereas biblical stories always served a purpose. Furthermore, as Dickinson has explained in "The Oral Voices of City of Gold" (1989), previous retellings use either a "low style," a bland way of talking down to children, or a "high style," an inflated literary language never actually spoken by people. A children's version, he has said in "Time and Times and Half a Time," could result only in "Noddy in the Holy Land" or "Big Ears Meets Moses."

He changed his mind and accepted his publisher's commission, however, when he realized that he could develop a new approach by simulating the voices of those who orally transmitted the tales. As Dickinson indicated in "The Oral Voices of City of Gold," he believes that biblical tales "need to be written or spoken in the voice of someone who is trying to tell you something important, to instruct or persuade or explain." So for each of his tales, he developed a separate narrator and created a context that adds meaning to the story. Thus, a professional Hebrew entertainer who compares versions of the Flood story with a Babylonian rival simultaneously suggests the universality of the flood myth and indicates its importance as a cautionary tale reminding people of their duty to God. Similarly, because the father who tells his family about the twelfth plague with which God afflicted the Egyptians when they refused to release the Jews from bondage is himself hiding from persecution, the contrast provides a reason for the story's central position in Jewish tradition. Not all of the narrators are Hebrews. A hundred years after the event, a peasant fisherman tells an Egyptian official the story of the crossing of the Red Sea. His explanation of a mysterious monument celebrating Pharaoh's victory over the sea adds an ironic edge to the familiar tale.

These retellings, which Dickinson admits were influenced by Rudyard Kipling and by Robert Browning's monologues, are modern in form and language. Dickinson does not attempt to follow ancient storytelling practices, and he studiously avoids archaic language. The Babylonian sergeant who recounts the tale of David and Goliath as a training exercise for troops who might encounter slingers therefore speaks like a modern British soldier who constantly banters with his men. The one way in which Dickinson has followed a conventional pattern is in the order of the stories, one which follows that of the Bible. The narrative contexts, however, move backward and forward in time. Only at the end, when a Jew exiled to Babylon tells the story of the fall of Jerusalem, the city of gold that he translates into a symbol of the abiding faith of his people, does a pattern emerge. As the story's headnote reminds readers, in the same city on the same night, another Jew is telling the story of the Creation and Fall, and his account is the first story in the collection. Dickinson thereby suggests that the stories have developed separately over time before being integrated into a tradition. Dickinson has indicated that his original reservations about undertaking the project may have had some validity, for he notes that many people who claim to know his work do not know this one: just as literature teachers ignore it because it is shelved with books on religious instruction, religious education teachers probably feel that, because it is literature, it is not trustworthy. Both groups are mistaken. *City of Gold* is an informative, challenging, and entertaining introduction to Bible stories.

An Old Testament story also figures prominently in *The Seventh Raven* (1981), a thriller inspired by reactions to the 1979 hostage-taking at the American embassy in Iran, which the novel mentions several times. Narrated by seventeen-year-old Doll Jacobs and set in a middle-class London church, *The Seventh Raven* uses the staging of a children's opera about the dilemma of King Ahab as the center of physical and intellectual conflict. Succumbing to diplomatic pressure, the opera group adds to its cast Juan O'Grady, son of the Mattean ambassador to Britain. Four revolutionaries attempt to kidnap Juan during a rehearsal – to force the release of political prisoners and bring attention to the repression in their South American country. Frantically trying to locate Juan among the hundred costumed children and a small group of adults whom they take as hostages after their kidnapping plans fail, the revolu-

Frontispiece and title page for the book in which Dickinson develops pseudoscientific explanations for the traits of dragons

tionaries alternately terrorize and try to educate their hostages about political injustice and the need for revolutionary action. Their prisoners, however, spend their captivity rehearsing the play. After locating Juan, the revolutionaries reciprocate by staging their own drama, a show trial of narrator Doll Jacobs's mother that edges into reality when one revolutionary attempts to execute Mrs. Jacobs.

Dickinson brilliantly employs the opera as the thematic center of the novel. Based on the conflict between the prophet Elijah and Jezebel, the opera focuses on King Ahab – "the man in the middle," a king caught between the zeal of the revolutionary prophet and the traditions of his wife. This middle ground distinguishes almost every character of the novel. In many ways Doll is caught in the middle between the children, whom she is too old to join in the opera, and the adult "Mafia" that controls it; she also finds herself in the middle between the hostages, whom she wants to protect, and the revolutionaries, for whom she develops some sympathy. Doll's mother, a professional musician, is most dramatically in the middle. The terrorists insist that anyone not actively supporting them is an enemy, and they do not acknowledge that an artist can be dedicated only to art. Mrs. Dunnit, a lifelong Communist whose name suggests her status as someone

who has personally experienced all stages of revolutionary fervor, is forced into the middle of the action in a different way. She knows both the injustices that the current social organization promotes and the violation of justice to which revolutionary zeal leads. Her convincing defense of Mrs. Jacobs advances the idea that any society without a middle ground cannot have the liberty that revolutionaries claim to espouse.

As a novelist of ideas Dickinson gives both sides strong arguments. Doll notes throughout how important "gesture" or theatrical display is to a cause. Doll sees the female revolutionary constantly adopting intimidating but stereotypical poses that suggest her psychological attitude, and she realizes that the show trial, like an actual trial, is primarily a gesture dramatizing issues and proclaiming power. Dickinson does not completely resolve the issues. The novel clearly shows that revolutionaries are capable of oppressing and killing the innocent. At the same time, it shows victims developing sympathy for the revolutionaries' cause.

The Seventh Raven is a theatrical novel that succeeds, first of all, because it has some of Dickinson's most fully realized characters. Doll uses language appropriate for her social class and age and makes a convincing narrator; her development as a character is entirely plausible. Dickinson also succeeds in developing Danny, the dramatically gifted leader of the revolutionaries. He is less successful with the other three, but that may reflect the narrator Doll's inferior understanding of them. *The Seventh Raven* also succeeds as a vivid novel of manners showing the chaos of amateur theatricals and their petty factionalism. This comical infighting contrasts with the more serious political fights of the revolutionaries. Once these revolutionaries enter, the novel becomes a gripping thriller. It bogs down in lengthy speeches during the show trial, but Dickinson clearly communicates Doll's nerve-racking efforts to hide Juan and to understand and deal with each of the terrorists. Finally, *The Seventh Raven* dramatically spotlights the role of the arts and the political responsibility of artists, the psychology of the terrorist-hostage relationship, and the rival claims of dramatic gesture and violent action as tools of political reform.

Although more interesting in conception than either *The Gift* or *Annerton Pit,* which also display an interest in the paranormal, *Healer* (1983) is relatively weak in plot and characterization. Sixteen-year-old Barry Evans possesses a secret personality whom he calls "Bear" because it is emotional and aggressive. He sets out to rescue Pinkie Proudfoot, virtually a prisoner in the Foundation of Harmony run by her stepfather, John Freeman, who charges large fees to those seeking benefit from Pinkie's healing powers. *Healer* lacks the taut suspense necessary in an adventure, and it is only marginally better as a study of dualistic characters. Pinkie, desperate for attention and affection, is sometimes childishly wild but is more often prematurely wise – a sad, compassionate girl burdened by concern for the suffering of others. In spite of efforts to make her complex, Pinkie remains wooden.

Freeman is even less successful. For most of the novel, he is an ambiguous character, presented as both a Moses-like prophet of nonmedical cures and a charlatan, a crook who has married Pinkie's mother in order to exploit the daughter. By the time of the final confrontation, however, he seems just pathetically mad. Barry consciously wrestles with his dualism throughout, until he apparently achieves wholeness by making emotional "Bear" an integrated part of his personality. The novel coyly exploits ambiguity. Although Pinkie does not support Barry's interpretation of events, Barry is affected by knowing that she privately thinks of him as Bear. The conclusion is also ambiguous. It describes Barry as a bear awakening from hibernation and enjoying "the air of a world made new." Osten-

sibly he has heeded Pinkie's final cryptic advice about being happy, as the bears in a television show have been shown to be, but the image, particularly since it is the second description of Bear awakening from hibernation, may suggest not integration of the hidden personality so much as domination by it.

Dreams figure prominently in all but one of Dickinson's next books, *Giant Cold* (1984), *A Box of Nothing* (1985), *Mole Hole* (1987), and *Merlin Dreams* (1988). *Mole Hole,* the exception, is a toy book for preschoolers. It is a rhyming tale of a man who declares war on a gopher ruining his lawn, and its major interest lies in the design of the book: turning a wheel puts a new picture in the gopher holes on each page, and lifting a flap reveals the gopher's den, where the gopher is comically frustrating the man's plans.

Giant Cold, which began as a tale Dickinson told his children to keep them quiet during car journeys, describes in an unusual way a conventional dream. Dickinson uses what, on the jacket of the American edition, he calls a "curious second person singular grammar." The dream sequence, that is, refers to the central character as "you" but employs a standard third-person viewpoint in all descriptive passages. This gives an appropriately haunting, surrealistic quality to the prose, and to the allegorical story. In the dream a child who has been shrunk to the size of an elf is captured and exhibited for money. Feeling an intense call, he escapes and makes his way to Apple Island, a land of perpetual summer now locked in ice. Entering the frozen Giant Cold through its ear, the child journeys inside and discovers at its center the cause: the creature's own identity as a fearful, selfish person. Taking his hidden self by the hand, the child symbolically accepts both sides of his identity, becoming whole and ending the unnatural winter. Although the theme of wholeness is presented less ambiguously than in *Healer,* many children are likely to find the tale puzzling.

They will have no such difficulty with *A Box of Nothing,* a novel for middle readers. Although it teasingly suggests that its events are not a dream, its structure and themes are those of the conventional dream journey: a child who feels inadequate in some way comes to grips with his identity by dreaming about heroic adventures. In this case the adventures begin when James, a boy who has watched a television show about the beginning of the universe while he has struggled with a troublesome homework assignment, enters the Nothing Shop, a supposedly abandoned store across the street from the Burrough Dump. He buys a box of the original nothing that existed before the Big Bang that created the universe. Soon he discovers himself in a strangely transformed Dump, one inhabited by animated refuse and ruled by villainous rats. Like the boy in *Giant Cold,* he feels a call that takes him to the center of this Dump, where he empties his nothing into a black hole and thereby creates a new universe – into which all the Dump creatures are sucked. At the end James feels more confident of his understanding of the world and his ability to complete his difficult homework assignment. Though not a major work, *A Box of Nothing* combines meaningful adventure, comedy (Dickinson has great fun with scientific theory), and unusual characters such as the composite Dump Burra.

Merlin Dreams, which straddles the border between adult and juvenile literature, makes even more unusual use of dreams. Originally Dickinson planned to do for Arthurian stories what he had done for biblical stories in *City of Gold.* He changed his mind, he says in "Time and Times and Half a Time," because "Attempting to do anything like what you've done before is a recipe for failure" and because he felt that the two sets of myths were radically different: "By comparison the King Arthur stories are a complete frivolity." Although Dickinson, as in *The Weathermonger,* presents Merlin dreaming in a cave, these dreams do not affect the outer world. Instead they are influenced by events such as the changing seasons and by memories of Merlin's earlier years. The dreams are nine original stories inspired by the Arthurian world, and the most successful employ irony tellingly. In "Knight Errant" a disreputable knight completes a noble quest only because he is inferior in honor to others; in "Damsel" a novice knight undergoes strange adventures in which he succeeds not because of his knightly training but because he has a previously unknown ability to change shape. In "Enchantress" a hideous boy and a beautiful girl end the evil power of an enchantress who abducts beautiful children – but they do so only to find that people need their fears, and they therefore resurrect the enchantress through their fearful imaginings.

Dickinson returned dramatically to the poetry of ideas in *Eva* (1988), a science-fiction novel set in a bleak future dominated by the "shaper" corporations, futuristic television networks that, as the name implies, shape the minds and lives of their viewers. Thirteen-year-old Eva Adamson, severely injured in an automobile accident, is saved from death when doctors transfer her neuron map, the pattern of her identity, to the body of a chimpanzee. Through Eva's struggles to understand and accept

her situation, this sad and touching novel explores fundamental questions of what constitutes identity. Eva gradually learns that she is not a human mind trapped in a chimp's body but a whole being composed of mind and body. She learns to adjust to her new composite identity, unifying the impulses of her animal body and the intellectual abilities of her human mind.

Although it advances ethical, philosophical, and psychological questions of identity, *Eva* is also a highly suspenseful tale of ecological revolution that argues for the rights of animals to exist free from human control. Dickinson develops sympathy for the rights of animals through Eva's attempts to understand both her own impulses and the actions of the chimps with whom she finally decides to live. Eva plots to have the chimps, who are confined to a scientific sanctuary, released on a wilderness island. As her name symbolically indicates, Eva is a new Eve, promising a new beginning, a new future for an endangered species. Through her the chimps have a chance to develop new skills that will gradually help them evolve and thus enable them to survive on their own. The ecological message is particularly effective because our sympathies are with Eva, who experiences the entire life cycle of the chimp – from "birth" after her accident, through motherhood, to death in the wilderness. Because it makes its protagonist both human and chimp, the premise allows *Eva* to be a convincing psychological novel and yet to achieve the emotional identification of the anthropomorphic animal story.

Another revolution, this time a political revolution in the fictional African country of Nagala, is central in *AK* (1990), winner of the Whitbread Award. The title refers to the assault rifle carried by Paul, a twelve-year-old orphaned by war and adopted by a guerilla leader, Michael Kagomi. Paul initially defines himself by his gun: he is a warrior in a guerrilla army. He buries it once peace is declared, but, after a coup, he sets out to retrieve his gun and to rescue Michael, a prisoner of the military government. Like Tron's journey downriver in *The Blue Hawk,* Paul's trek resonates with mythic implications: in this case it is the quest for the father, for modern democratic values, and for a meaningful identity as well. The adventures also plausibly test Paul's determination, wit, and maturity. Thus, once he arrives in the capital, Paul recognizes that he can cause open warfare if he uses his AK rifle, and he therefore resists the urge to kill the thugs of the leader of the government. He further demonstrates his maturity by turning an organized, peaceful protest against the government to his own purpose of winning Michael's release.

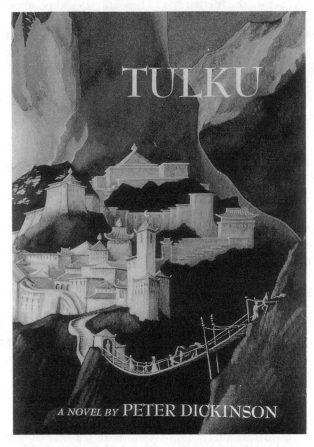

Dust jacket for Dickinson's children's novel set in China during the Boxer Rebellion

In addition to being a compelling adventure, *AK* is a powerful novel of political manners. Nagala, in all its colorful variety, is vividly presented, with its various scenes adding complexity to the conflict between a brutal dictatorship and repressed citizens. The scene in which government soldiers, who belong to a warlike tribe, murder the Fulu fishermen and burn their village highlights the issue of traditional tribal animosities. Scenes in the capital, with its rival urban gangs fighting to establish territorial rights, develop the contemporary incarnations of tribalism. Paul represents modern Africa and presents a new hope. He is often torn between the traditional claims of his "mother," – war, which constantly urges violence – and those of his foster father, who represents idealism and a desire for peace. Promoting nationalism to bridge ethnic divisions, Paul eventually sides with his father and the future. He demonstrates his choice graphically: he is persistent in obtaining first-rate medical care for Jilli, the Fulu girl who accompanies him on his trek, and he is instrumental in getting urban gangs to cooperate, at least temporarily, to defeat the government's thugs. The cooperating gangs and the gigantic crowd marching on the government palace suggest optimism about the future, but Dickinson qualifies this optimism in a pair of alternative endings set twenty years later.

The first, a romantic vision of wish fulfillment, intimates that the fight has been worthwhile and has led to a prosperous, democratic country. Paul, now a park warden, no longer requires his AK, which he has buried beneath a huge monument honoring his father. Contrasting with this is a more cynical conclusion that, because of its placement as the second of the two alternative endings, is especially disturbing. In it Paul is still a warrior fighting a corrupt government. Fellow guerrillas, whose defense of their own territory forms an ironic parody of tribalism, mistakenly kill him in an ambush. A young boy, reminiscent of Paul twenty years earlier, picks up Paul's AK and thereby reiterates the continuing cycle of violence that destroys the very people who dream of a better future. With its shocking and powerful alternate conclusions, *AK* is one of Dickinson's finest achievements, a novel that compounds the emotional pressures of an adventure story with the intellectual tensions of a novel of political manners.

Dickinson's native continent is also the setting of *Bone from a Dry Sea* (1992), a novel inspired by the controversial theories advanced by Elaine Morgan in such books as *The Descent of Woman* (1972) and *The Aquatic Ape* (1982). Dickinson's chapters alternate between parallel stories, one set four million years ago and one set in the present. The story in the past focuses on Li, an aquatic ape who stands apart from those in her small group because of her ability to observe and think. She learns, for instance, how to enlist the aid of dolphins in gathering food, although a male pushes her aside to claim credit. Following a tidal wave Li leads survivors to a new life. Four million years later Vinny, visiting her archeologist father on a dig in the now-dry bed of a primeval inland sea, is instrumental in discovering a fossil remnant from one of the aquatic apes. Like Li, Vinny is a thinker, the only one at the dig who is open-minded enough to consider seriously the possibility of aquatic apes. The alternation of these two stories sets up parallels between modern humans and their ape ancestors. For example, the bullying Dr. Hamiska has a laugh that sounds to Vinny like a bellow of challenge, a description that comically likens him to the bullying male ape. Li and Vinny are even more firmly connected by Vinny's dreams – which evoke scenes from Li's life – by bone imagery, and ultimately by the feeling each has of being in the center of a web or a set of forces.

The sections set in the past have considerable dramatic intensity, constantly detailing struggles for food, survival, and dominance in the group. They effectively portray the difficulties of an intellectually superior female among physically superior males. They also effectively suggest the rise of the religious impulse in Li's feelings about the dolphins who aid the apes – and in her feeling, after the tidal wave, that life is not purposeless. By contrast the family and professional conflicts in the contemporary sections lack power. Only at the end, when African troops depose the head of the archeological expedition, do conflicts achieve a comparable dramatic urgency. Furthermore, Vinny's intelligence does not adequately parallel Li's: Li develops ideas from observations and alters her group's culture and destiny, whereas Vinny repeats what she has read and fails to convert anyone to her thinking.

Structural novelty and a thematic concern with time are also evident in Dickinson's latest books. *Time and the Clockmice, Etcetera* (1993) is a lighthearted meditation on symbiotic relationships. The narrator is the elderly grandson of the man who built the celebrated Branton Town Hall clock. Because he alone possesses the plans for the elaborate clock, the town hires him to repair it. While exploring the clock, its bells, and its animated figures, he discovers a race of mice who can communicate by telepathy. He befriends the animals and later saves them from a scientist who wants to dissect them. The mice then assume the old man's role of preserving the secret of the clock's operation and of tutoring the new clock-keeper. Dickinson's narrative method makes this slight story amusing. The plot advances through a series of essays on such topics as mice, clocks, time, science, and people. Emma Chichester-Clark's drawings, to which the narrator makes frequent reference, are also integral to the exposition. The narrator tries to connect the various subjects by suggesting that the interdependence of the clock, mice, and people symbolizes the human situation on earth. This conclusion is strained, and many of the story's elements fail to cohere. Blind Cousin Minnie's concern with the moral qualities of bells nearly unbalances the plot, for example, because it involves an extremely eccentric notion of symbiotic relationships. Although adults will find this book mildly amusing, it is too droll and sophisticated to appeal to either children or adolescents.

Shadow of a Hero (1994), like *Bone for a Dry Sea*, alternates between stories set in the past and stories set in the present. The main story reflects the nationalistic fervor and the social chaos that followed the collapse of communism in eastern Europe. Thirteen-year-old Letta Ozolins is the granddaughter of Restaur Vax, the last democratic prime minister of the fictional country of Varina, which larger communist nations absorbed after World War II. Exiled in England, Restaur uses a primer to teach Letta the languages and legends of Varina. Chapters of this story alternate with chapters from the primer, complete with its linguistic and historical footnotes. The primer tells the romanticized story of Restaur Vax, the nineteenth-century liberator of Varina and an ancestor of the current Restaur. After the collapse of communism, the current Restaur visits Varina with his family. Letta soon realizes, however, that the ambitious Otto Vasa is using Restaur Vax because his name inspires those who long for Varina to become a united and independent country. After they are again exiled to England, Letta foils a plan to use her older brother as a terrorist. Eventually, the elderly Restaur Vax returns to Varina, where he dies. Otto Vasa's plan to turn a memorial service to his own benefit backfires, however, when Letta's brother informs the crowd that his grandfather distrusted Vasa.

Shadow of a Hero contains several brilliant elements: the legends are gripping tales, and their footnotes cleverly show how history is transformed to serve cultural needs. (The reader is given more information than Letta: the novel begins with a chapter missing from her copy of the legends.) The discussions between Letta and her grandfather establish the continuing cultural importance of such legends and the language that expresses them. Indeed, Dickinson's ingenious invention of two Varinian languages, a common one and a poetic one, makes the reader a pupil, along with Letta, in understanding the power of culture. Dickinson is also successful in showing how the shadow, or ghost, of the past haunts a country. Otto Vasa is thus ironically destroyed by the legendary name he cynically tries to exploit.

Despite its thematic brilliance and its success in developing the character of both the legendary and contemporary Restaur Vax, the novel falters. First of all, Letta, who is merely an observer with incomplete understanding during much of the novel, becomes active in a contrived and melodramatic situation. Second, although the inconclusive ending is politically and emotionally appropriate, it lacks dramatic power because events are narrated after the fact in a somewhat implausible conversation between Letta and her brother. Nevertheless, *Shadow of a Hero,* is a sensitive, intelligent novel.

Dickinson's most recent novels show him to be just as creatively vigorous as he was early in his career. That career itself is remarkable, for Dickinson has achieved distinction as a writer for both adults and children. As a children's author he has made notable contributions to various genres — thrillers, historical novels, fantasies, science fiction, and adventures. Dickinson's popularity with young readers comes from such thrillers as *The Gift* and *Annerton Pit,* but his critical reputation is likely to depend upon *The Dancing Bear, The Blue Hawk, Tulku, Eva,* and *AK.* In these Dickinson has shown that children's literature need not be formulaic or simpleminded to be highly readable.

Interview:

Jay Williams, "Very Iffy Books: An Interview with Peter Dickinson," *Signal,* 13 (January 1974): 21–29.

References:

David Rees, "Plums and Roughage: Peter Dickinson," in his *Painted Desert, Green Shade: Essays on Contemporary Writers of Fiction for Children and Young Adults* (Boston: Horn Book, 1984), pp. 153–167;

John Rowe Townsend, "Peter Dickinson," in his *A Sounding of Storytellers: New and Revised Essays on Contemporary Writers for Children* (New York: Lippincott, 1979; London: Kestrel, 1979), pp. 41–54.

Penelope Farmer

(14 June 1939 –   )

David L. Russell
Ferris State University

BOOKS: *The China People* (London: Hutchinson, 1960);

The Summer Birds (London: Chatto & Windus, 1962; New York: Harcourt, Brace & World, 1962);

The Magic Stone (New York: Harcourt, Brace & World, 1964);

The Saturday Shillings (London: Hamish Hamilton, 1965); republished as *Saturday by Seven* (London: Penguin, 1978);

The Seagull (London: Hamish Hamilton, 1965); republished as *The Sea Gull* (New York: Harcourt, Brace & World, 1966);

Emma in Winter (London: Chatto & Windus, 1966; New York: Harcourt, Brace & World, 1966);

Charlotte Sometimes (London: Chatto & Windus, 1969; New York: Harcourt, Brace & World, 1969);

Daedalus and Icarus (London: Collins, 1971; New York: Harcourt Brace Jovanovich, 1971);

Dragonfly Summer (London: Hamish Hamilton, 1971; New York: Scholastic, 1971);

The Serpent's Teeth: The Story of Cadmus (London: Collins, 1971; New York: Harcourt Brace Jovanovich, 1972);

A Castle of Bone (London: Chatto & Windus, 1972; New York: Atheneum, 1972);

The Story of Persephone (London: Collins, 1972; New York: Morrow, 1973);

William and Mary: A Story (London: Chatto & Windus, 1974; New York: Atheneum, 1974);

Heracles (London: Collins, 1975);

August the Fourth (London: Heinemann, 1975; Berkeley, Cal.: Parnassus, 1975); republished as *Long Ago Children's Omnibus* (London: Heinemann, 1976);

The Coal Train (London: Heinemann, 1977);

Year King (London: Chatto & Windus, 1977; New York: Atheneum, 1977);

The Runaway Train (London: Heinemann, 1980);

Standing in the Shadow (London: Gollancz, 1984);

Eve: Her Story (London: Gollancz, 1985; San Francisco: Mercury House, 1988);

Away from Home: A Novel in Ten Episodes (London: Gollancz, 1987);

Glasshouses (London: Gollancz, 1988);

Thicker Than Water (London: Walker, 1989);

Stone Croc. (London: Walker, 1991);

Snakes and Ladders (London: Little, Brown, 1993);

Penelope (London: Bodley Head, 1994).

OTHER: "Discovering the Pattern," in *The Thorny Paradise: Writers on Writing for Children,* edited by Edward Blishen (Harmondsworth: Kestrel, 1975), pp. 103–107;

"Jorinda and Jorindel and Other Stories," in *Writers, Critics, and Children,* edited by Geoff Fox and others (New York: Agathon, 1976), pp. 55–72;

Beginnings: Creation Myths of the World, compiled by Farmer (London: Chatto & Windus, 1978; New York: Atheneum, 1979);

Amos Oz, *Soumchi,* translated by Farmer (London: Harper, 1980).

Penelope Farmer's writings are widely varied: she has written books for children in the primary grades (including contemporary realistic fiction, historical fiction, and mythological retellings), fantasies for older children, and, most recently, novels for adults. Farmer confesses to a lifelong love of fantasy; as a child she loved to read – in addition to fairy tales – the works of Eric Linklater, Mary Norton, C. S. Lewis, Philippa Pearce, and Lucy Boston. Farmer notes that fantasy allows the writer to "make metaphors for life . . . turn it into narrative – and thereby get at the essences of life and death, which children need to be told no less than anyone." Although she has dabbled in several types of fiction, she invariably returns to fantasy, the genre of her most significant work.

Penelope Farmer was born in Westerham, Kent, on 14 June 1939 to Hugh Robert MacDonald and Penelope Boothby Farmer. She was the younger of fraternal twins, which perhaps led her, as one critic says, to "a lifelong preoccupation with estab-

Penelope Farmer

lishing a separate identity." Farmer was educated privately and then attended St. Anne's College, Oxford, where she earned a degree in history with second-class honors in 1960. In 1962 she received a diploma in social studies from Bedford College, London. Farmer taught in London from 1961 to 1963 but has devoted most of her adult life to writing. She married Michael John Mockridge, a lawyer, on 16 August 1962, and they had two children, Clare Penelope and Thomas. Divorced from Mockridge in 1977, she married a neurologist, Simon Shorvon, on 20 January 1984.

Farmer's first publication was *The China People* (1960), a collection of literary fairy tales for young people. They are suitably modernized and include a mixture of humor (something almost conspicuously absent from much of her later work), magic, and tantalizing wickedness. *The Summer Birds* (1962), her first full-length novel, grew out of a short story originally intended for *The China People,* which she removed before the book's publication as "It was too big an idea, too bony as a short story." The story

concerns a group of schoolchildren from a small English village who are taught to fly by a mysterious boy. He first appears to Charlotte Makepeace, a young girl who lives with her sister, Emma, and their grandfather Elijah at Aviary Hall, named for the bird images found throughout the house. Given the subject of the book, the name carries added symbolic significance, which some readers may find too heavy-handed.

Throughout the summer the children enjoy delightful afternoons flying about the countryside. Amazingly, no adults learn of this remarkable capability except their understanding teacher, Miss Hallibutt, who confesses her own childhood desire to fly and regrets that she is too old to join them. The children's pleasure is interrupted by a struggle of wills between the nameless boy and the irascible Totty, who insists on knowing the boy's secret. Battle lines are drawn and a mock medieval tournament ensues, with the boy emerging victorious. At the summer's end the truth is revealed: the boy – in reality a bird who has assumed human form – is playing the part of the Pied Piper, desiring to take the children with him to his home where they can fly forever.

He is more than the Pied Piper, however, for this tale is a variation on the Peter Pan story, with children tempted by the prospect of avoiding adulthood and grown-up responsibilities. It is Peter Pan without the sentimentality, however; one of the boys remarks, "Don't you think it'd be better to spend our lives flyin' than growin' up and goin' to work at eight o'clock every day? No more work, no nothin': just doin' what we like all day." The persuading argument, ultimately, is that they would all miss their families too much. One girl, a rather pathetic creature who lives with her neglectful uncle, nevertheless chooses to fly away with the boy. The ending is bittersweet, with necessity winning over the impossible dream. There is, of course, an unspoken reason for their remaining behind: that being human is ultimately more desirable than being a bird. Or, as Hugh Crago put it in *Children's Literature Review:* "Innocence, the openness to new experience, can only happen once, and it cannot be prolonged." It is the story of one enchanted summer as a symbol of childhood, which everyone must some day leave behind.

In *The Magic Stone* (1964) two girls, one from the upper class and one from the lower, are brought together by a magic stone. The "Arthur Stone" carries heavy associations with the legend of King Arthur; its magic is a heightening of the experiences of real life, resulting in a close relationship between the girls. Unfortunately, the stone is not an integral part of the story and is almost superfluous, since the friendship could have developed without it. Reviewers have found Farmer's imagery intrusive and her fantasy occasionally gratuitous – shortcomings that persist in many of her books.

Emma in Winter (1966) is a sequel to *The Summer Birds,* focusing on Emma Makepeace and a schoolmate named Bobby Frumpius, an outcast and a loner. Emma and Bobby share the same dream, recalling the summer when they flew as birds. The dream begins to overtake their lives, and they are swept back through time to the beginning of the world, where they encounter another Emma and Bobby threatening to overtake them. Bobby shouts at the illusory figures and drags Emma away; the children must then deliberately choose reality – which, despite its unpleasant features, is warmly familiar and preferable. Emma and Bobby, both outsiders at the beginning of the story, develop a warm relationship as a result of their adventures. The theme is similar to *The Summer Birds* in that children

are asked to choose between what often seems humdrum daily living in a familiar world and the promise of an exciting existence in some uncharted country. The book has been criticized for its slow pace and awkwardly devised fantasy scheme; it may also be too psychologically complex to appeal to some children.

Charlotte Sometimes (1969) is perhaps Farmer's best-known work. Its protagonist is that of *The Summer Birds,* Charlotte Makepeace. Through an unexplained enchantment, she changes places with another girl from the past. *Charlotte Sometimes* is in no way a sequel to *The Summer Birds* (as was *Emma in Winter*), and, curiously, no reference to Charlotte's earlier adventures is ever made. The focus of the book is the transposition of Charlotte with Clare, who attended the same boarding school and slept in the same bed forty years earlier. Charlotte goes to bed one night in 1958 as herself and wakes up in the same bed and the same place, but in 1918. Conversely, Clare wakes up forty years in her future. To readers who know Philippa Pearce's *Tom's Midnight Garden* (1958), this theme may have a ring of familiarity, and Farmer acknowledges that *Charlotte Sometimes* was partly an homage to Pearce's novel.

The exchange does not cause much of a disturbance, because both girls share a virtually identical appearance. They have no apparent control over their time travel, but they know that they exchange places on alternate days and that the bed is necessary for the magic to take place. Clare's experiences are not described – this is Charlotte's story – and the reader has no way of knowing how Clare copes (although Clare's story may have been the more interesting since her adaptation to the future would probably have been more dramatic). For Charlotte the exchange is perplexing, then exciting, and finally troubling. Events are complicated when Emily and Clare are to be moved from the school to private lodgings: the move occurs, to the dismay of the girls, on the day when Charlotte is in Clare's place, and without the bed Charlotte is unable to return to her own time. For several weeks Charlotte must play the role of Clare as the girls live in the home of the Chisel Browns, a rather depressing couple whose only son was killed in the Great War and who dominate their only daughter, Agnes, a repressed and diffident girl.

Farmer is good at establishing mood through physical description, and she piles up the images of decay when she writes of the drab Chisel Brown household. Farmer remarked in *Children's Literature Review* that "halfway through *Charlotte Sometimes* I realized that I was writing a book about identity." In this respect, the book reflects the author's deep awareness, from being a fraternal twin, of the necessity of maintaining a separate, distinguishable identity. Readers sense Farmer's personal involvement when she writes of Charlotte's dreams: "Charlotte began to dream she was fighting to stay as Charlotte, and one night woke from such a dream, struggling, even crying a little."

In a key scene near the conclusion of Charlotte's stay in the past, Emily assures her that "You're not really a bit like Clare," and although these words are uttered with an air of contempt, they are reassuring to Charlotte, who has lived for weeks as another person. But Charlotte's search for her identity broadens into another theme – into that of the whole question of reality, of what is important, of what purpose people serve. Critic David Rees has pointed out that *Charlotte Sometimes* is close to an adult book in its atmosphere and prevailing sentiment, its poignancy, its resignation, and its concern "with absence, loss, or death in action during war." It is not a novel of action but of contemplation, and it perhaps anticipates Farmer's eventual turn to the writing of adult novels.

Farmer's next major work was *A Castle of Bone* (1972). Rees remarks that this work "ought to have been [Farmer's] best book; its central idea is more strikingly original, the characters more vivid and varied, its potential, both serious and comic, greater." The critical consensus is that the book falls short of its promise. Nevertheless, readers cannot deny its originality: it opens with a pig bursting out of a cupboard in a bedroom, after which four children chase it downstairs and out of the house, until they ultimately lose it in a park. A flashback explains that the cupboard was found in a dilapidated secondhand shop and intended for the use of Hugh, the central character. The other principal characters are Hugh's sister, Jean, and their neighbors and friends, the siblings Penn and Anna. The cupboard is a magic cupboard, transforming whatever is put into it into an earlier stage of development; the pig was a consequence of placing an old pigskin wallet in the cupboard. A second story line focuses on the dreams Hugh experiences while the cupboard remains in his room: He finds himself in a strange land dominated by a great castle that appears to be made of bone.

The story reaches a crisis point when Penn, during a scuffle with his sister, is shoved into the cupboard and transformed into an infant. Some seriocomic scenes follow in which the three children attempt to care for a tiny baby while keeping his existence a secret from their parents. At last the children go to the shop where the cupboard was purchased and receive some cryptic advice from the old shopkeeper, who, as Farmer points out, began as a deus ex machina; he suggests Tiresias, the blind seer – although the author confesses that this reference had not consciously occurred to her during the writing.

Other symbols in the book include the trees, specifically a reference to the Celtic tree calendar, which assigns both a tree and a prevailing mood to each day of the week. References to light recur throughout the story as well. The principal themes of the story are, according to Rees, "growing up, growing awareness, maturing relationships." The Castle of Bone, Hugh ultimately realizes, is the symbol of himself and by extension of all humanity. Most critics agree that the image of the castle and Hugh's dreams do not always seem relevant and do not adequately sustain the reader's interest. Readers find the children and the events surrounding the cupboard much more engaging. But the book contains some unforgettable scenes and does reveal the quality of Farmer's imagination.

William and Mary: A Story (1974) concerns the daughter of a headmaster at a boy's school who is befriended by a boy during the holidays. Once again Farmer employs an intriguing and original fantasy element: William possesses a magic half shell and is seeking its other half. The children discover that by holding the shell and concentrating on something that relates to the sea they can be transported to a variety of wondrous places, where they can search for the matching half of the shell. They are first taken into a painting depicting the fall of Atlantis, and they eventually discover that a magazine photograph, a playbill, a song, or a poem about the sea can take them to another world.

Parallel with these adventures is an exploration of the developing friendship of the two children as they grow to understand their problems: Mary's loneliness and William's pain over the separation of his parents. The search for the shell becomes symbolic of William's desire to have his parents reunited, and it perhaps comes to represent the wholeness of William and Mary's friendship. Much like the nightly dream flights of *Emma in Winter,* the children's adventures bring them closer together, help them learn more about themselves, and move them yet another step closer to adolescence and away from childhood. Their excursions to exotic places proving fruitless, the children finally discover the shell's other half on the beach, virtually in their backyard. Although an intriguing idea, the fantasy element may strike many readers as lacking

The mysterious boy who teaches the children to fly; illustration by James
Spanfeller from Farmer's The Summer Birds *(1962)*

any real justification in the context of the story, and, perhaps even more seriously for young readers, lacking in sufficient excitement to carry a slow-moving plot.

Year King (1977) is clearly not for young children but for adolescents. It is the story of nineteen-year-old identical twins, Lan and Lew, as told from Lan's viewpoint. Once again Farmer draws on her experience as a twin and explores the question of identity that plagues many of her protagonists. Lan feels inferior to his brother in virtually all ways — academically, athletically, socially, and romantically. Lew has won a scholarship to Cambridge, and Lan remains home to study at a local university; it is their first separation. Inexplicably, Lan discovers that he is capable of mentally trading places with Lew, although he neither understands nor controls this power. These circumstances allow Lan to see things from Lew's point of view, but it is clear that Lew does not inhabit Lan's body — thus posing one of those perplexing problems often raised by Farmer's fantasies: in this case, what happens to Lew while Lan inhabits his body?

Lan is at one point convinced that Lew is attempting to kill him (or both of them) and eventually realizes that he has actually prevented Lew's apparent suicide attempt. As with *Charlotte Sometimes,* readers are likely to be troubled about some of the ramifications of the fantasy premise, and no explanation for the transmigration is ever attempted (although it is reasonable to assume that it has something to do with the special sympathy shared by twins). The sexual scenes, frank language, and a rather sophisticated exploration of character make this a book for older adolescents; it comes close to being a book for adults. Farmer, as quoted by Rees, remarked "I'm coming increasingly to wonder whether I actually write children's books and certainly feel I won't continue to do so much longer." *Year King* seems to be a transitional work that would take her into the realm of the adult novel.

In addition to the full-length novels, Farmer has written many shorter works for children, including contemporary novellas, retellings of classical myths, and historical fiction. In *The Seagull* (1965) Farmer departs from fantasy and writes the story of Stephen, a young boy who desires to keep as a pet a seagull whose wing he has mended. Stephen's grandmother gently attempts to dissuade him, but he stubbornly refuses to listen. Predictably, he relents and decides to give the bird its freedom. Although rather thin on plot and lacking in action, it is a sensitive portrayal of the relationship between Stephen and his grandmother.

In *Dragonfly Summer* (1971) Farmer reprises the character of Stephen, who is again on a visit to his grandmother, but this time he finds his cousin Peter also visiting. Stephen sees Peter as a rival for his grandmother's affections and companionship, and he imagines a conflict that exists only in his own mind. Peter is both noncompetitive and unaggressive – characteristics that Stephen finds difficult to grasp. Stephen eventually learns that "winning" over such an opponent carries no reward, and a friendship develops. Similar to *The Seagull,* the story is strong in character development, if weak in action, but the penetration of character and the sensitive exploration of theme have always been Farmer's long suits.

The introspective Stephen is typical of Farmer characters – the author is fascinated by the loner, the outsider, who is plagued by an almost tortuous self-examination and feelings of inferiority or inadequacy. The curative is inevitably human association and communion, a reaching out and accepting, a letting down of barriers and an embracing. Farmer seems to be saying that people discover their own identities through their impact on others, through the quality of their relationships with others, and through a willingness to become a meaningful part of the human community.

When Farmer set out to retell the classical Greek myths for children, she chose those myths that could best convey her vision of the world. The first of her retellings was *Daedalus and Icarus* (1971), describing Daedalus's life on Crete up to the tragedy of his son's fall into the sea, precipitated by his overweening pride in attempting to fly to the sun. For Farmer the message of the myth was far more important than the details, and her version has been criticized for its inaccuracy, as well as for its occasionally stilted or pseudoarchaic style. *The Serpent's Teeth: The Story of Cadmus* (1971) fared better with the reviewers, who praised it for its forceful and dramatic language. It also bears the mark of its time, for, as a review in *The New York Times* notes, "This myth contains some of the most fantastic antiwar propaganda in literature, plus a plug for conserving cities." Farmer's *The Story of Persephone* (1972) has been praised for its majestic prose, which seems appropriate when writing of the Olympian gods and goddesses – although some reviewers found her style occasionally ponderous. She does not forget, however, to stress the relevance of the story to the human condition. Her last retelling in this series of myths was *Heracles* (1975), which received reactions similar to the rest. The contradictions in critical judgment may be explained in part because the subject matter and the brevity of the books suggest an appeal to younger readers, whereas their style and themes seem to be quite clearly addressed to older children. Farmer later compiled a book of myths from around the world, *Beginnings: Creation Myths of the World* (1978). She has always remained enamored of both myths and folktales, which have inspired much of her work.

Farmer has also been inspired by history, particularly recent history, as suggested by the wartime setting of *Charlotte Sometimes*. She turned to a purer form of historical fiction in her short piece *August the Fourth* (1975), which begins with Meg's receiving the news that her brother has been killed in battle during World War I. Meg reminisces on the day, two years earlier, when Britain entered the war. On that day she and three friends had disobeyed their parents' orders to be home early and had enjoyed a carefree day in the village and neighboring countryside. Just beneath the surface, however, are the ominous signs of the end of a way of life. Farmer presents a fine portrait of the age, and, as with most of her books, atmosphere is more important than plot, human emotions more important than deeds.

Two more short works in the same vein followed: *The Coal Train* (1977) and *The Runaway Train* (1980). Both are period pieces set in the 1940s, and both are narrated by the daughter of a railway engineer, whose family lives in a trackside community bursting with energetic young children. Farmer has a keen fascination with the effects of war on the home front, as is also apparent in *Charlotte Sometimes* and *August the Fourth. The Coal Train* is the brief tale of a night during one cold postwar winter when a coal train derails, spilling its welcome contents into the village. The grateful people share in the unexpected bounty and are able to keep their homes truly warm for the first time since before the war.

BEGINNINGS
Creation Myths of the World

Compiled and Edited by
PENELOPE FARMER
Woodcuts by
ANTONIO FRASCONI

A Margaret K. McElderry Book
Atheneum   1979   New York

*Title page for the American edition of Farmer's compilation
of myths*

The children are able to thwart a plot by a greedy entrepreneur to confiscate the coal and sell it on the black market. *The Runaway Train* is the story of a postwar day excursion to the sea – the first to be enjoyed by the families of this little community since before the war. It is a day of carefree pleasures brought to an exciting climax when the engineer (the narrator's father) forgets himself in his euphoric state and gives his passengers a thrilling ride home. These stories were based on the memories of an acquaintance of Farmer's, who claimed that the incidents were both true. Always adept at evoking ambience, Farmer captures postwar Britain with its rationing, the people's search for simple pleasures, a strong sense of community values, and a pervasive belief in the common good.

For several years after *Year King,* it appeared that Farmer had turned her attention entirely to writing adult novels, but in 1989 she published *Thicker Than Water,* a collection of short stories for younger children. She remarked in a 21 February 1993 letter, "I propose to alternate adult and children's fictions from now on. There's an element of pure story telling in writing for children which I love." The author has also not abandoned her penchant for fantasy, and she has even used fantasy in her adult fiction, particularly in *Glasshouses* (1988), which employs a seventeenth-century ghost. In *Eve: Her Story* (1985) Farmer draws on her experience in retelling myths, this time fantasizing on the life of Eve as she might have told it – making for an interesting feminist tract.

Farmer's reputation in children's literature will undoubtedly be founded on her fantasies. Her fantasy elements are often highly original, if they are also occasionally contrived and even gratuitous to the essence of her stories. Her best fantasies are tales of wish fulfillment – the desire to fly, the desire to be someplace else, or to be someone else. Typically, she contrasts two different worlds, forcing her protagonists to make a commitment to one (always, of course, their own). Her protagonists are also alone in their problems; there is seldom recourse to adult help, and perhaps more significant, adults are typically unaware of a problem. This division between the world of the children and that of the adults, the complete failure of communication between the generations, is one of Farmer's most pointed contemporary commentaries.

Although there is little communication across the generations (Miss Hallibutt in *Emma in Winter* and Stephen and his grandmother in *The Seagull* are notable exceptions), Farmer makes it clear that human relationships of some sort are of primary importance. Her young protagonists learn the value of sympathetic understanding and of mutual interdependence. The problems Farmer's protagonists face are not the results of the ills of modern society, for Farmer is no social critic. Rather, they derive simply from the fact that good and evil reside and have always resided in the world. Charlotte Makepeace can learn as much about human nature and joy and sadness in the England of 1918 as she can in that of 1958. To survive in an indifferent world, Farmer's protagonists must look within themselves and dis-

cover their own courageous resolve. She is a writer of extraordinary range, and her works are the products of a lively imagination and penetrating mind.

Interview:

Cordelia Jones and Olivia R. Way, "Penelope Farmer," in their *British Children's Authors: Interviews at Home* (Chicago: American Library Association, 1976), pp. 76–84.

References:

Peter Dickinson, "A Bone from a Dry Sea," *Times Educational Supplement,* 14 August 1992, p. 20;

Margaret K. McElderry, "Penelope Farmer: The Development of an Author," *Elementary English,* 51 (September 1974): 798–805;

Flo Morse, "When Gods Were Human, All Too Human," *New York Times Book Review,* 27 August 1971, p. 24;

"Penelope (Jane) Farmer," in *Children's Literature Review,* volume 8, edited by Gerald Senick (Detroit: Gale, 1985), pp. 63–87;

David Rees, "The Marble in the Water: Penelope Farmer," in his *The Marble in the Water: Essays on Contemporary Writers of Fiction for Children and Young Adults* (Boston: Horn Book, 1980), pp. 1–13.

Jane Gardam

(11 July 1928 –)

Adrienne Kertzer
University of Calgary

See also the Gardam entry in *DLB 14: British Novelists Since 1960.*

BOOKS: *A Few Fair Days,* illustrated by Peggy Fortnum (London: Hamish Hamilton, 1971; New York: Macmillan, 1972);

A Long Way from Verona (London: Hamish Hamilton, 1971; New York: Macmillan, 1972);

The Summer After the Funeral (New York: Macmillan, l973; London: Hamish Hamilton, 1973);

Black Faces, White Faces (London: Hamish Hamilton, 1975); republished as *The Pineapple Bay Hotel* (New York: Morrow, 1976);

Bilgewater (London: Hamish Hamilton, 1976; New York: Greenwillow, 1977);

God on the Rocks (London: Hamish Hamilton, 1978; New York: Morrow, 1979);

The Sidmouth Letters (New York: Morrow, 1980; London: Hamish Hamilton, 1980);

Bridget and William, illustrated by Janet Rawlins (London & New York: Julia MacRae Books, 1981);

The Hollow Land, illustrated by Rawlins (London: Julia MacRae Books, 1981; New York: Greenwillow, 1982);

Horse, illustrated by Rawlins (London & New York: Julia MacRae Books, 1982);

Kit, illustrated by William Geldart (London & New York: Julia MacRae Books, 1983);

The Pangs of Love and Other Stories (London: Hamish Hamilton, 1983);

Crusoe's Daughter (London: Hamish Hamilton, 1985; New York: Atheneum, 1986);

Kit in Boots, illustrated by Geldart (London: Julia MacRae Books, 1986);

Through the Dolls' House Door (New York: Greenwillow, 1987; London: Julia MacRae Books, 1987);

Swan, illustrated by John Dillow (London: Julia MacRae Books, 1987);

Showing the Flag (London: Hamish Hamilton, 1989);

The Queen of the Tambourine (London: Sinclair-Stevenson, 1991; New York: St. Martin's Press, 1995);

Jane Gardam

Going into a Dark House (London: Sinclair-Stevenson, 1994);

The Iron Coast: Notes from a Cold Country (London: Sinclair-Stevenson, 1994).

OTHER: "Mrs. Hookaneye and I," in *The Thorny Paradise: Writers on Writing for Children,* edited by Edward Blishen (Harmondsworth: Kestrel, 1975), pp. 77–80;

"Jane Gardam," in *Something About the Author: Autobiography Series,* 9, edited by Joyce Nakamura (Detroit: Gale Research, 1990), pp. 169–181.

SELECTED PERIODICAL PUBLICATIONS –
UNCOLLECTED: "On Writing for Children:
Some Wasps in the Marmalade," part 1, *Horn
Book,* 54 (October 1978): 489–496;
"On Writing for Children: Some Wasps in the Mar-
malade," part 2, *Horn Book,* 54 (December
1978): 672–679.

Despite the enthusiastic critical response that
greeted the publication of Jane Gardam's first two
books and the many awards her eighteen books
have won, her work has received little scholarly attention. Given Gardam's satiric portrait of the
American scholar in *The Sidmouth Letters* (1980) and
equally satiric picture of children's literature circles
in *The Queen of the Tambourine* (1991), such scholarly
silence may relieve the author. It may also reflect
the ambiguous nature of her work. Her books are
not widely read in North America, perhaps not so
much because of her sensitivity to the nuances of
English class distinction (the feature her English reviewers tend to praise and about which American
reviewers feel ambivalent), as the fact that her work
resists easy labeling. Feminists tend to see her work
as too conservative, just as conservatives sense that
she is not quite one of the tribe. Similarly, reviewers
have trouble categorizing her: is she a children's
writer or not?

A Long Way from Verona (1971) won the
Children's Literature Association's 1991 Phoenix
Award, however, perhaps evidence of increasing
critical attention for Gardam's work. As Lissa Paul
noted, Gardam's resistance to categories makes her
an interesting and subversive writer. When Gardam
receives an unfavorable review, it is often because
the reviewer has trouble placing her work in a neat
category, finding her books either too sophisticated
for children or too simple for adults. Wanting to
track Gardam's development from children's writer
to author of adult short stories, reviewers often ignore the theoretical implications of Gardam's work.
Although in an essay for *Horn Book* Gardam claims
to write tame tales, her fiction is less predictable
than such a statement implies. Her "vicars' daughters" might imagine themselves to be the reincarna-
tions of Emily Brontë and are uncomfortable with
their assigned roles. Her protagonists, whether
young, adolescent, or middle-aged, are always on
the margins, simultaneously attracted and repulsed
by what they regard as the center.

This discomfort with assigned roles is shared
by Gardam. Denying that her works have any
moral or break any new ground in children's literature, Gardam has tended to dissociate herself from

what the narrator of *The Queen of the Tambourine* calls
tribes, whether she is wondering if she is indeed a
children's writer or satirizing feminists in her work
so that no one dare consider her a feminist. Despite
the satire, her sensitivity to details of class, male/
female relationships, mothers' voices, and interest
in the construction of marginality make her a writer
worth reading from a feminist position. Reviewers
such as Marcus Crouch have compared her to Jane
Austen, another writer who can be read as either a
conservative or a radical critic of women's place in
society: Austen's heroines cannot simply run away
from society; neither can Gardam's. Austen is
known for deliberately focusing on a small world;
similarly, Gardam is at her best when writing of
such small worlds, whether her stories are set in
Rhododendria, Jamaica, or Yorkshire.

Jane Gardam was born Jean Mary Pearson on
11 July 1928 in Coatham, North Yorkshire, a setting that reappears in her fiction. Although she
learned to read early and her father, William Pearson, was a famous schoolmaster, Gardam claims to
have had a bookless childhood. The social gulf between the background of her mother – Kathleen
Helm Pearson was a descendant of the de Bulmer
family, which has traced its roots back to the Norman Conquest – and that of her father appears in
Gardam's memory of her mother's disapproval
when Jane spoke Cumbrian, a dialect she learned
from summers spent at the paternal grandparents'
farm in West Cumberland. After attending Saltburn
High School for Girls, she received a scholarship
and attended Bedford College for Women, University of London, graduating with an honors degree
in English in 1949. She then did postgraduate work
in eighteenth-century literature for three years but
never completed her degree. After working for two
years as a traveling librarian with Red Cross hospital libraries, she married David Gardam on 20 April
1952 and continued to work until the birth of her
first child, initially as subeditor of *Weldons Ladies
Journal* (1952–1953) and then, more happily, as assistant literary editor of *Time and Tide* (1953–1955).
Altogether, the Gardams had three children, Timo-
thy, Mary, and Thomas.

Gardam did not publish until her children
were in school. In "Mrs. Hookaneye and I" (1975)
she describes how she would stop writing at 3:35
P.M. to pick up her child from school, wanting to
discuss her writing but knowing that she could not,
as a mother, do so. The anecdote is significant, for
it signals both her acceptance of the institution of
motherhood as well as her apparent frustration with
it, a double-edged response that she often explores

in her work. Gardam has written that the exhaustion of mothering, which prevented her from writing for ten years, was ultimately beneficial to her work. Once her third child was in school, she began publishing quickly, sending her first manuscript to Hamish Hamilton – the publisher of William Mayne, a writer she admired.

A Few Fair Days (1971), Gardam's first published book, is a collection of nine stories. Their protagonist, Lucy, is five years old at the book's beginning, eleven at the end. Lucy lives in the north of Yorkshire, in a world of seemingly timeless customs. When aunts come to tea, the menu is always the same, and when little girls go with their grandmother on visits, they are told how ladies dress and behave. Lucy's childhood faith in the unchanging nature of her world is reported with gentle irony – the adult narrator is aware of impending change, specifically the approach of World War II. Lucy and her friends may be delighted that the abandoned house where they play is not bought by strangers, but the book's last line indicates that their relief will be temporary, as soldiers will soon take over the house. Similarly, Lucy is free as a child to observe but pay little attention to the many signs of class, whereas the adult narrator constantly notes its power, as when the aunts dismiss newcomers from the south of England because they use paper napkins or when Lucy's mother is intimidated by her pretentious friend, Mrs. Binge-Benson. In addition, even if childhood offers some protection from the power of class, it also places Lucy in a marginal social position.

The book's title refers to a well-known local cake, called "Fair Days" after a favorite phrase of its baker. This attention to language, the mystery of how words are invested with meaning, also appears in Lucy's attempt to explicate a poem about Zoroaster (the sixth-century B.C. Persian prophet), her belief in the magic of naming herself the Princess of Cleves, her love of nonsense words, and her continual puzzlement over the way adults talk. Lucy suspects that she may be a bit mad, but in that she is just like the adults who most interest her: the elderly boarder, Mr. Crossley, and Auntie Kittie, both of whom are regarded as peculiar by other adults. Children and eccentric or mad characters have much in common in Gardam's fiction, as they struggle to live in a society that marginalizes them.

A Few Fair Days was well received, with many reviewers praising Gardam's characters, her comedy, and her spare, evocative language, although the occasional American reviewer suggested that the British flavor of Gardam's work might limit her appeal to American readers. Many reviewers read the stories autobiographically. Although Gardam has acknowledged that, like Lucy, her father was a schoolmaster; that she had a younger brother and many aunts; and that Thornby End is based on her grandparents' farm, she has denied that her fiction is autobiographical and has been careful to distinguish herself from her other heroines. In "Mrs. Hookaneye and I" Gardam describes *A Few Fair Days* as a tribute to her childhood landscape, but she insists that the characters are invented, stressing that memories – especially those of childhood – are always invented and that she can no longer distinguish which characters are based on real people.

Gardam's next novel, *A Long Way from Verona*, was her first book published in the United States. It was also the first of several by the author focusing on a female adolescent's experience. At thirteen Jessica is convinced that she is a writer, since she has been told so by a writer who has visited her school. Her teachers are not all equally impressed, however, and she struggles with their attempts to make her a lady as well as a more conventional writer. Ladies must exercise self-control, neither throwing chips in the train, nor writing forty-seven pages about the day *before* their summer holidays when the assignment specifically asked for an essay *on* their summer holidays.

The novel is structured in three parts: "The Maniac," who is the escaped Italian prisoner of war that Jessica meets; "The Boy," who is the first to hold her hand but is really more interested in discussing George Bernard Shaw with her socialist clergyman father; and "The Poem," which is never directly presented but is about Jessica's encounter with the maniac. The novel's plot, however, has little to do with the texture of Jessica's story. Jessica is an adolescent during the bombing of England. For much of the novel she takes the war for granted: for example, a gas mask is just something she must carry around. The war intrudes only occasionally, as when a favorite teacher dies or when Jessica must force herself to look at the bombed-out building where the teacher, Miss Philemon, died.

The appeal of *A Long Way from Verona* lies not in its plot, but in the energy of Jessica's narration: her ability to convey the rapid emotional shifts of adolescence; her ambivalence toward romance; her father's fame; and her mother's frustration at their newly impoverished state, a result of her father's career change from headmaster to clergyman. Since the novel is told from Jessica's point of view (and she implies that the novel is revenge for her mother's lack of attention), the reader does not

*Dust jacket for Gardam's story of a thirteen-year-old girl who
aspires to be a writer*

learn much about the mother, who is usually depicted dashing out the door on a church errand. This peripheral vision is itself revealing, both of the effect upon the mother of the father's new career and of the treatment of biological mothers in Gardam's adolescent fiction. The book was well received, named as one of the outstanding books of 1972 by *The New York Times Book Review*. The critical tradition of reading Gardam's fiction autobiographically also continued, with some reviewers claiming that the heroine was a slightly older Lucy. Gardam again rejected this autobiographical approach, cautioning that she never considered herself a genius as the heroine, Jessica Vye, does.

Athene Price, the protagonist of Gardam's next novel, *The Summer After the Funeral* (1973), is sixteen when her eighty-six-year-old father dies. Her mother sends Athene and her brother and sister to three different caretakers while she considers how they will survive. Mrs. Price is seemingly indiffer-

ent to her children and ignorant of their natures. She never suspects that Athene should not be left alone that summer, nor does she ever know how truly lonely the girl is. When Athene appears to be on the brink of committing suicide, Mrs. Price says that Athene is too well taught to follow through.

Despite Gardam's satire of Mrs. Price's questionable mothering, the character is right about her daughter. Fantasizing that she is the reincarnation of Emily Brontë, wondering whether she has lost her virginity in her sleep, becoming infatuated with a young man who resembles Heathcliff, and then falling in love with a married man, Athene does survive. It is a close call, however, for her relationship with her father has been intense (when she falls in love with the married man, he seems to be another version of her father), and her brother is sharply aware that the father's interest in his daughters was excessive. The other daughter (baptized Phoebe, nicknamed "Beams" after the reflection from her glasses) takes over the narration briefly in a first-person, comic account reminiscent of Jessica's voice. Beams's "ugliness," age (twelve), and interest in psychiatry produce a different perspective on the family situation and Athene's troubles in particular, for Beams senses that Athene's beauty and placidity have misled people to see her as the "perfect," silent female. Support for Beams's theory is found in both the novel's ending and the fact that this is the only adolescent novel by Gardam in which the heroine does not narrate her own story.

Although *The Summer After the Funeral* was named a *Boston Globe-Horn Book* Honor Book for 1974, critical response was less enthusiastic than it had been to Gardam's first two books. The shift from Jessica's comic voice to the Oedipal drama of Athene's story was not unanimously welcomed, but some reviewers continued to lavish high praise on Gardam's language, social commentary, and comedy. They also noted how Gardam's use of understatement allows adolescent readers freedom in interpreting Athene's relationship with her father.

As a result of her husband's work in international law, Gardam has traveled extensively. *Black Faces, White Faces* (1975) is ironically dedicated to Sandy Gully, a drainage ditch that was the subject of a legal case David Gardam conducted in Jamaica. Like all of the author's collections of short stories, this book challenges the distinction between children's and adult fiction. *Swan* (1987), first published as a children's book in the Redwing series, has since appeared in an adult collection of stories, *Showing the Flag* (1989), as has the ghost story "Bang Bang – Who's Dead," which was first published in a reader for adolescents. The title story of another adult collection, *The Pangs of Love and Other Stories* (1983), is a revision of Hans Christian Andersen's "The Little Mermaid."

One difference between Gardam's children's and adult fiction lies in their treatment of mothers: marginal and mocked in the adolescent fiction, they are often the subjects of the author's adult fiction (increasingly so in the more-recent collections of stories). In contrast to the portrait of Athene's mother is the sympathetic portrait in "The First Declension" of middle-aged Anne Shaw, who rejects the opportunity to travel with her husband to Jamaica so that she can stay home and supervise her children's homework – only to discover that the children do not need her as much as she thinks.

Gardam's work may challenge the distinction between children's and adult fiction, but the critical response to *Black Faces, White Faces* reveals how strongly reviewers insist on that distinction. *Black Faces, White Faces* won the David Higham Prize for the best first novel, although it was not the author's first book, nor, with its story structure, would some readers call it a novel. Ironically, the reviewer in the 28 September 1975 *Observer* suggested that the novel's "excess of craft" was the result of Gardam's having written too many children's books.

In her next book, *Bilgewater* (1976), Gardam returns to the first-person adolescent narrator that is her strength. Marigold Daisy Green, called "Bilgewater" because she is Bill's daughter, is a seventeen-year-old social misfit. Deprived of her mother at birth (the first thing she tells the reader), Bilgewater lives with her father, the housemaster, and Paula Rigg, the matron, at an old-fashioned boys' school.

Thinking herself ugly, the young woman longs for the attention of one young man, ends up in bed with another, and ultimately marries a third. The marriage becomes apparent only in the epilogue; as an adolescent who cheerfully admits her preadolescent lack of self-knowledge, Bilgewater is not aware that her life has any plot whatsoever. She grows through a series of set pieces that recur in Gardam's fiction: for example, the alienation produced by the weekend visit. In *Bilgewater* the country house turns out to be the home of Humphrey and Janice Rose, two socially inferior dentists. Bilgewater had not realized that the "superior neighbourhood" meant only that the house was on a hill.

Whenever Bilgewater is in a crisis, she longs for a fantasy mother who would know just what to say. But the events of the story, in particular the vulgarity of Janice Rose, a former friend of Bilgewater's mother, lead her to abandon this fantasy (she leaves the mother's amber beads in the dentist's china jar just before she escapes by climbing out the balcony window).

In addition, the behavior of other biological mothers – the headmaster's wife who runs off with the captain of the school, Terrapin's mother, who loaths her child – supports the Gardam pattern, which recognizes as the true mother the one who does the mothering – in Bilgewater's case, Paula Rigg. Paula reminds Bilgewater of a Thomas Hardy heroine, but Bilgewater is quick to point out that the Dorset-born Paula may look like Tess of the d'Urbervilles, may even sometimes sound like her, but would never simply lie down on Stonehenge and wait for her fate. The literary reference is characteristic of Gardam's subversive use of English fiction. As in *A Long Way from Verona*, Hardy is praised for his insight – "A novel . . . should say what ev-

Dust jacket for Gardam's 1981 book for younger readers, a collection of nine stories set in Yorkshire

erybody is thinking but nobody is saying" – and his work is then rewritten. Paula does not just accept her fate; she takes charge and saves the day. Similarly, Bilgewater, for all her unconventional behavior, or perhaps because of it, becomes the first woman principal of a Cambridge college.

In 1976 Gardam became a fellow of the Royal Society of Literature. In 1977 she described her work in a speech to the society (published in *Horn Book* in 1978). Reminding her audience of the C. S. Lewis maxim that "books enjoyed only by children are by definition bad books," she declared her desire to challenge the separation of children's literature from adult literature, a challenge that most reviewers ignored. Her next two books, *God on the Rocks* (1978), a runner-up for the Booker Prize, and *The Sidmouth Letters,* a collection of short stories, were reviewed as adult fiction. It is noteworthy that *God on the Rocks* gives the points of view both of an eight-year-old girl and her mother (of whose experience the child is pointedly kept ignorant) and that

The Sidmouth Letters includes several stories told from a mother's point of view, for example, "Lunch with Ruth Sykes." To have a mother admit that she does not like her daughter much, even if that daughter is an adult and even if the mother's actions demonstrate otherwise, appears by cultural consensus to make a work reviewers regard as inappropriate for children.

In the early 1980s Gardam left the adolescent heroine for a series of books for younger readers. *The Hollow Land* (1981), winner of the Whitbread Award for the best children's book, is set in Yorkshire, a setting that Gardam's own family still visited during vacations. Several readers for young children – *Bridget and William* (1981), *Horse* (1982), *Kit* (1983), and *Kit in Boots* (1986) – also use this setting. *The Hollow Land,* in nine stories set over a period of nineteen years, celebrates the growing friendship between the Yorkshire Teesdale family and the Bateman family, who are from London but are renting Light Trees, a home on the Teesdale farm. Eight-year-old Bell and five-year-old Harry become close friends, and the final story, "Tomorrow's Arrangements," set in 1999, concludes with Harry's becoming tenant of Light Trees for life.

In its own way *The Hollow Land* challenges categories: the urban London family can learn to appreciate the values of rural Yorkshire life; the young can engage in dialogue with the old (Harry in conversation with the dreaded Egg Witch's mother or Bell's grandfather, old Hewitson). In the final story an oil crisis necessitates a return to preindustrial ways of farming. Throughout the collection there is a strong sense of history, in the references to the bones of the Beaker People and to roads dating back to Roman times and in the ghost stories that Kendal, the chimney sweep, tells. It is noteworthy that when Kendal tells the story of a severed hand, Harry is asleep, but the adults are captivated, continuing evidence that for Gardam a good children's story must also interest adults.

Gardam's younger brother had become a farmer on the North York moors, and Gardam has acknowledged that the Yorkshire child protagonists of the readers are based on her nieces. Reviewers were struck by Gardam's ability in *Bridget and William* and *Horse* (meant for beginning readers), as well as *Kit* and its successor, *Kit in Boots* (intended as bridge books for slow readers), to simplify her art and yet not condescend. Reviewers praised Gardam's ability to challenge the language skills of the youngest readers and keep the treatment fresh, even when, as in *Bridget and William,* she was working with something as conventional as a horse story.

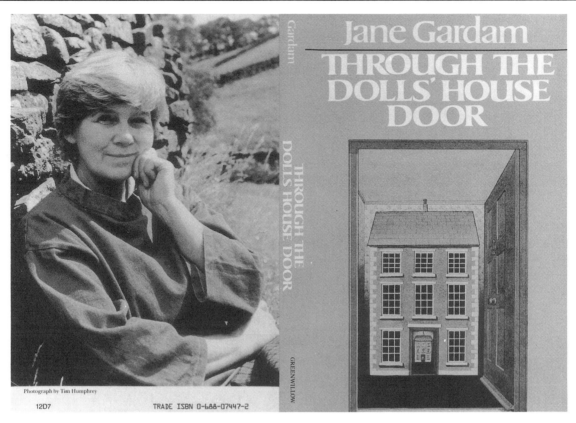

Dust jacket for Gardam's 1987 fantasy story about talking dolls

Reaction to *Crusoe's Daughter* (1985) and *Through the Dolls' House Door* (1987) has been more divided. *Crusoe's Daughter* was not even reviewed as a children's book even though in it Gardam returns to the first-person narrative of a young woman and focuses on Polly Flint's obsession with Daniel Defoe's *Robinson Crusoe* (1719), a text long appropriated by children's literature. Polly comes to live with her aunts in the Yellow House in 1904 when she is six; she dies there in 1986. She first mentions her obsession with *Robinson Crusoe* in connection with the day she first menstruates; in her Edwardian ignorance she thinks that she is dying. Crusoe teaches her paradoxically to accept her fate, that she too is stuck on an island and must learn to endure.

Yet *Crusoe's Daughter* is an ambivalent tribute to Defoe's novel. Gardam dedicated the novel to her mother and used an epigraph from Virginia Woolf, who appears as a character in the text. In her obsession with Defoe, Polly dismisses both the Brontës and Austen, but in many ways the novel Gardam writes is influenced as much by female novelists as by the male tradition. Even when Polly praises Crusoe's reason, she admits that the tradition of the English novel has not prepared her for

the knowledge of the female body, neither menstruation nor menopause. When she attempts to speak the language of female desire in letters to Theo Zeit, Theo rejects her and marries a woman who never wrote him letters. Polly never becomes a productive writer; instead she remains a female parrot of the male tradition, spending years engaged in a parody of scholarship as she translates *Robinson Crusoe* into German.

Polly's obsession is her unique way of dealing with the limited choices her society offers her, but the novel suggests that not all women were similarly stuck. Like all Gardam's adolescent heroines, Polly seems more affected by and aware of her father than her mother. The mother exists only in a faded photograph; the grandmother she dismisses as a typical Victorian battle-ax. Only in 1939, just before she becomes adoptive mother to Theo Zeit's German-Jewish refugee children and in this way finally ends her futile obsession with a male model, does Polly learn how her assumptions about her family, assumptions formed by her reading, have misled her. In fact, the real true heroine of the family was Polly's Victorian grandmother, Gertrude Younghusband, whose illicit love affair did not end in banishment and death, as prescribed by the traditional fiction that Polly reads. Fiction, then, molds the way readers see the world around them; perhaps by attempting to find a place for herself within the masculine tradition of the Robinsonnade, Polly loses sight of the lesson she intends to teach when she plans her lecture on the novel: "Every serious novel must in some degree . . . carry the form further."

In *Through the Dolls' House Door* Gardam continues to test the assumptions of reviewers. The novel is a fantasy about talking dolls, yet the intended reader does not appear to be a young child (and the book has been reprinted in a series for adolescents). Like *The Hollow Land* in its structure, (linked chapter-stories, each of which can stand on its own as a separate story), interest in history, and focus on family, *Through the Dolls' House Door* is framed by the voices of Mary and Claire, first as children and finally as mothers.

For much of the text the dolls to which the title alludes are abandoned, and the chapter titles — such as "Stuck," "Lost," and "Keeping Going" — indicate that the dolls are in a predicament similar to that of Polly Flint. Like Polly they survive through literature. In the night, for many years, when it appears that there is no chance of rescue, they tell each other stories. Bossy, the Dutch doll, relates revisionist history, a rewriting of a traditional legend from a marginalized point of view. In her version of the story of the boy who saved Holland, traditional history is itself marginalized and dismissed, as it is in the General doll's story of the Trojan War.

In an era of great expertise on children and professional interest in their reading, to question why children's fiction is separated from adult fiction and to note how this separation implies that children's fiction is not genuine fiction is to defy the experts. Anne Robin, a children's writer portrayed

in *The Queen of the Tambourine* (1991), is not sure that children read her books at all. To get an adult novel accepted, she writes under an assumed name and is instructed by her editor to add a masturbation scene. Eliza Peabody, the mad narrator, expresses contempt for Anne's children's books and the way they reveal her longing for another world. Yet Eliza also uses fiction — the stories she tells herself and the letters that she writes to an imaginary neighbor — as a way of dealing with the inadequacy of her world, specifically her inability to recover from a miscarriage and the subsequent hysterectomy. Like Anne, Eliza also suffers from the power of experts, in her case doctors, who tell her what she must be feeling. Like Polly Flint, Eliza's sanity depends on finding a way to mother freed of biological motherhood, an achievement that frees her to remember her mother's voice. Eliza questions whether there is a theory of children's literature at all; Jane Gardam's work challenges that theory to question any easy assumptions about the relationship between children and literature.

References:

M. S. Crouch, "The Tragicomedy of Being Young," *Junior Bookshelf,* 51 (December 1987): 260–265;

Lissa Paul, "Escape Claws: Cover Stories on 'Lolly Willowes' and 'Crusoe's Daughter,' " *Signal,* 63 (September 1990): 206–220;

Agnes Perkins, "What Books Should Be Sent to Coventry? – A Comparison of Recent British and American Realistic Fiction," in *Proceedings of the Sixth Annual Conference of The Children's Literature Association,* edited by Priscilla A. Ord (Villanova: Villanova University Press, 1980), pp. 155–164;

David Rees, "Caviare to the General: The Novels of Jane Gardam," *School Librarian,* 37 (February 1989): 5–8.

Leon Garfield

(16 July 1921 –)

Raymond E. Jones
University of Alberta

BOOKS: *Jack Holborn,* illustrated by Antony Maitland (London: Constable, 1964; New York: Pantheon, 1965);

Devil-in-the-Fog, illustrated by Maitland (London: Constable, 1966; New York: Pantheon, 1966);

Smith, illustrated by Maitland (London: Constable, 1967; New York: Pantheon, 1967);

Black Jack, illustrated by Maitland (London: Longman, 1968; New York: Pantheon, 1969);

Mister Corbett's Ghost, illustrated by Alan E. Cober (New York: Pantheon, 1968); enlarged as *Mister Corbett's Ghost and Other Stories,* illustrated by Maitland (London: Longman, 1969);

The Restless Ghost: Three Stories, illustrated by Saul Lambert (New York: Pantheon, 1969);

The Drummer Boy, illustrated by Maitland (New York: Pantheon, 1969; London: Longman, 1970);

The Boy and the Monkey, illustrated by Trevor Ridley (London: Heinemann, 1969; New York: Watts, 1970);

The God Beneath the Sea, by Garfield and Edward Blishen (London: Longman, 1970; New York: Pantheon, 1971);

The Strange Affair of Adelaide Harris, illustrated by Fritz Wegner (London: Longman, 1971; New York: Pantheon, 1971);

Child o' War: The True Story of a Boy Sailor in Nelson's Navy, by Garfield and David Proctor (London: Collins, 1972; New York: Holt, Rinehart & Winston, 1972);

The Captain's Watch, illustrated by Ridley (London: Heinemann, 1972);

The Ghost Downstairs, illustrated by Maitland (London: Longman, 1972; New York: Pantheon, 1972);

The Golden Shadow: A Recreation of the Greek Legends, by Garfield and Blishen (London: Longman, 1973; New York: Pantheon, 1973);

Lucifer Wilkins, illustrated by Ridley (London: Heinemann, 1973);

The Sound of Coaches, illustrated by John Lawrence (Harmondsworth: Kestrel, 1974; New York: Viking, 1974);

The Prisoners of September (Harmondsworth: Kestrel, 1975; New York: Viking, 1975); republished as *Revolution!* (London: Collins, 1989);

The Book Lovers: A Sequence of Love Scenes, Chosen and Arranged by Leon Garfield (London: Ward Lock, 1976; New York: Avon, 1978);

The Pleasure Garden, illustrated by Wegner (Harmondsworth: Kestrel, 1976; New York: Viking, 1976);

The House of Hanover: England in the Eighteenth Century (London: Deutsch, 1976; New York: Seabury, 1976);

The Lamplighter's Funeral, illustrated by Maitland (London: Heinemann, 1976);

Mirror, Mirror, illustrated by Maitland (London: Heinemann, 1976);

Moss and Blister, illustrated by Faith Jaques (London: Heinemann, 1976);

The Cloak, illustrated by Jaques (London: Heinemann, 1976);

The Valentine, illustrated by Jaques (London: Heinemann, 1977);

Labour in Vain, illustrated by Jaques (London: Heinemann, 1977);

The Fool, illustrated by Jaques (London: Heinemann, 1977);

Rosy Starling, illustrated by Jaques (London: Heinemann, 1977);

The Dumb Cake, illustrated by Jaques (London: Heinemann, 1977);

Tom Titmarsh's Devil, illustrated by Jaques (London: Heinemann, 1977);

An Adelaide Ghost (London: Ward Lock, 1977);

The Filthy Beast, illustrated by Jaques (London: Heinemann, 1978);

The Enemy, illustrated by Jaques (London: Heinemann, 1978);

The Confidence Man (Harmondsworth: Kestrel, 1978; New York: Viking, 1979);

Leon Garfield

Bostock and Harris; Or, The Night of the Comet,
    illustrated by Martin Cottam (Har-
    mondsworth: Kestrel, 1979); republished as
    *The Night of the Comet: A Comedy of Courtship Fea-
    turing Bostock and Harris* (New York: Delacorte,
    1979);

John Diamond, illustrated by Maitland (Harmonds-
    worth: Kestrel, 1980); republished as *Footsteps*
    (New York: Delacorte, 1980);

The Mystery of Edwin Drood, by Garfield and Charles
    Dickens (London: Deutsch, 1980; New York:
    Pantheon, 1981);

Fair's Fair, illustrated by Margaret Chamberlain
    (London: Macdonald, 1981); republished edi-
    tion, illustrated by S. D. Schindler (Garden
    City, N.Y.: Doubleday, 1983);

King Nimrod's Tower, illustrated by Michael Bragg
    (London: Methuen, 1982; New York:
    Lothrop, Lee & Shepard, 1982);

The House of Cards (London: Bodley Head, 1982;
    New York: St. Martin's Press, 1983);

The Writing on the Wall, illustrated by Bragg (Lon-
    don: Methuen, 1983; New York: Lothrop, Lee
    & Shepard, 1983);

Guilt and Gingerbread, illustrated by Wegner
    (Harmondsworth: Viking Kestrel, 1984);

The King in the Garden, illustrated by Bragg (London:
    Methuen, 1984; New York: Lothrop, Lee &
    Shepard, 1985);

Shakespeare Stories (London: Gollancz, 1985; New
    York: Schocken, 1985);

The Wedding Ghost, illustrated by Charles Keeping
    (Oxford: Oxford University Press, 1985; New
    York: Oxford University Press, 1987);

The December Rose (Harmondsworth: Viking Kestrel,
    1986; New York: Viking Kestrel, 1986);

The Empty Sleeve (Harmondsworth: Viking Kestrel,
    1988; New York: Delacorte, 1988);

The Blewcoat Boy (London: Gollancz, 1988); repub-
    lished as *Young Nick and Jubilee* (New York:
    Delacorte, 1989);

The Saracen Maid, illustrated by John Talbot (Lon-
    don: Simon & Schuster, 1991; New York:
    Simon & Schuster, 1994);

Shakespeare Stories II (London: Gollancz, 1994; Bos-
    ton: Houghton Mifflin, 1995);

Shakespeare: The Animated Tales (London: Heine-
    mann, 1994);

Sabre-Tooth Sandwich (Hemel Hempstead: Simon &
    Schuster, 1994).

Collections: *Adventures of the Boy and the Monkey*
    (Harmondsworth: Puffin, 1976) – comprises

The Boy and the Monkey, The Captain's Watch, and *Lucifer Wilkins;*

The Apprentices (New York: Viking, 1978; London: Heinemann, 1982) — comprises *The Lamplighter's Funeral; Mirror, Mirror; Moss and Blister; The Cloak; The Valentine; Labour in Vain; The Fool; Rosy Starling; The Dumb Cake; Tom Titmarsh's Devil; The Filthy Beast;* and *The Enemy;* republished as *Garfield's Apprentices,* 4 volumes (London: Pan, 1979).

OTHER: "The Cabbage and the Rose," by Garfield and Patrick Hardy, in *Miscellany Four,* edited by Edward Blishen (London: Oxford University Press, 1967), pp. 61–87;

"The Questioners," in *Winter's Tales for Children 5,* edited by M. R. Hodgkin (London: Macmillan, 1968), pp. 118–134;

"The Restless Ghost," in *The Restless Ghost and Other Encounters and Experiences,* compiled by Susan Dickinson (London: Collins, 1970), pp. 11–29;

Baker's Dozen: A Collection of Stories, edited by Garfield (London: Ward Lock, 1973); republished as *Strange Fish and Other Stories* (New York: Lothrop, 1974);

"Bookmaker and Punter," in *The Thorny Paradise: Writers on Writing for Children,* edited by Blishen (Harmondsworth: Kestrel, 1975), pp. 81–86;

"An Adelaide Ghost," in *A Swag of Stories: Australian Stories,* edited by Garfield (London: Ward Lock, 1977), pp. 35–44;

"An Evening with Leon Garfield," in *One Ocean Touching: Papers from the First Pacific Rim Conference on Children's Literature,* edited by Sheila Egoff (Metuchen, N.J.: Scarecrow, 1979), pp. 110–120;

Mervyn Peake, *Sketches from Bleak House,* selected and introduced by Garfield and Blishen (London: Methuen, 1984);

"Acceptance: 1987 Phoenix Award," in *Cross-Culturalism in Children's Literature: Selected Papers from the 1987 International Conference of the Children's Literature Association,* edited by Susan R. Gannon and Ruth Anne Thompson (Pleasantville, N.Y.: Pace University, 1987), p. 20;

"Historians and Storytellers," in *Travellers in Time: Past Present, and to Come* (Cambridge, Mass.: Children's Literature New England, 1990), pp. 22–26.

SELECTED PERIODICAL PUBLICATIONS – UNCOLLECTED: "And So It Grows," *Horn Book,* 44 (December 1968): 668–672;

"Writing for Childhood," *Children's Literature in Education,* 1 (July 1970): 56–63;

"Historical Fiction for Our Global Times," *Horn Book,* 64 (November–December 1988): 736–742;

"The Uses of Experience," *Canadian Children's Literature,* no. 54 (1989): 37–40;

"The Outlaw," *Horn Book,* 66 (March–April 1990): 1165–1170.

Described by John Rowe Townsend as "the richest and strangest" talent to emerge in British children's writing in the 1960s, Leon Garfield writes books that are simultaneously traditional and distinctive. Garfield claims that his goal is "to write the old-fashioned thing, the family novel, accessible to the twelve-year-old and readable by his elders." His novels relate page-turning adventures, often with wildly improbable action and eccentric characters. Their settings, appropriate to such old-fashioned narrative, are either eighteenth-century or Victorian England. Nevertheless, Garfield is neither a derivative writer nor an anachronism. Although frequently compared to Charles Dickens, Robert Louis Stevenson, and Henry Fielding, Garfield has his own flamboyant style and a sharp sense of the thematic possibilities of romantic adventure.

Leon Garfield was born on 16 July 1921 in Brighton, England, which, in an interview with Justin Wintle, the author described as "a very eighteenth-century town," and he was educated at Brighton Grammar School. His father was David Kalman Garfield, a flamboyant businessman who experienced frequent economic reversals, and his mother was Rose Blaumstein Garfield. Because his parents constantly fought, Garfield concluded that he had "a rather Dickensian background." More recently, in an interview with Roni Natov, he said that his one true resemblance to Dickens comes from the fact that his father, unable to afford the art studies his son had just begun, put him to work in a London office, which he hated.

At about this time, at the age of nineteen, Garfield entered his first marriage, which lasted three months. In 1940, after two or three months of office work, Garfield was called for military service. He served as a private in the Royal Army Medical Corps, which trained him in biochemistry and hematology, enabling him to qualify for work in hospitals after his discharge. Garfield's military service also included a stint on the War Crimes Investigation Team, a position he was given after he falsely claimed to be an interpreter so that he would not be sent to serve in the Far East. His work included a

The title character of Smith *(1967), a twelve-year-old pickpocket (illustration by Anthony Maitland)*

trip to Belsen, where he spent months digging up corpses to provide evidence for murder trials. Coupled with his laboratory training, this grisly experience provided Garfield with material that he worked into his books.

Discharged from the military in 1946, Garfield began work as a biochemical technician at Whittington Hospital, London. On 23 October 1948 he married Vivien Alcock, an artist whom he met while stationed in Belgium; he credits her with turning him from painting to writing. Alcock herself has become a respected writer for children and young adults. They have one daughter, Jane Angela, adopted in 1964 and named after the eighteenth-century novelist Jane Austen. In 1966 Garfield, having published two novels, began working part-time in various London hospitals. Since 1969 he has devoted himself full-time to writing; he has published voluminously, generally to good reviews, and he

has won several awards, including the Carnegie Medal in 1970 for *The God Beneath the Sea* and the Whitbread Literary Award in 1980 for *John Diamond.*

Marcus Crouch suggests in *The Nesbit Tradition* (1972) that Garfield "had no 'prentice period,'" but *Jack Holborn* (1964), Garfield's first published novel, belies that claim. The story of an orphan who escapes from his harsh life by stowing away, this derivative work relies heavily on the conventions of traditional boy's sea adventure: bloodthirsty pirates, mutiny, shipwreck, treasure hunting, hostile natives, and rags-to-riches success. Though the adventures are exciting and some of the characters are colorful, the story is ungainly and patently contrived.

Garfield's own accounts make it clear that he saw this as an apprentice work. In his essay "And So It Grows" (1968) Garfield claims that a reading

Frontispiece and title page for Garfield's novel about a boy who revives a hanged criminal

of Robert Louis Stevenson's *The Master of Ballantrae* (1889) inspired him to devise a story of good and evil brothers to illustrate two themes: "the dilemma of the good man in evil circumstances and the difficulty of telling good from evil." He chose the eighteenth-century setting that became the hallmark of his later work "unconsciously," after the setting of Stevenson's book, and he utilized conventional first-person narration by a young boy because he needed someone who could be bewildered by appearances and whose viewpoint would not require many political and social details.

Untrained in research, Garfield read voluminously and indiscriminately to acquire information. His discovery that Jonathan Swift and Daniel Defoe, whom he admired, had both depended on research for nautical information was, he says, "the most encouraging discovery I have ever made." Working out details as he went along, Garfield bogged down after describing a shipwreck; he was able to resume writing, he says in "Writing for Childhood" (1970), only after he discovered "a real essential of narrative," what he calls the "inner pace": "the excitement of not what was happening,

but what was going to happen." Finally, Garfield learned about acceptable length and complexity. The second publisher to examine the completed novel decided that it was a juvenile title; Garfield agreed to cut the book's length by about one-half.

Although Garfield claimed that *The Master of Ballantrae* was the only work by Stevenson that he had read, *Jack Holborn* bears a striking resemblance to Stevenson's *Treasure Island* (1883), a point noted by several critics. (More recently Garfield has said that he "plundered" the 1935 motion picture *Captain Blood*.) Like *Treasure Island,* Garfield's novel includes an unsuccessful mutiny, revenge enacted by someone pretending to be a ghost, a castaway who knows about a treasure, and a fever-producing jungle setting. Most of all, it resembles Stevenson's best-known work in its morally ambiguous characters. Jack Holborn, an orphan supposedly named after the parish in which he lives, is a more worldly wise version of Jim Hawkins. Jim's relationship with Long John Silver is partly a quest for an effective father figure, and Jack seeks relationships with men who exhibit equally questionable morality, including Pobjoy, who becomes demonic when drunk;

Solomon Trumpet, a more sinister castaway than Ben Gunn; and the Captain, who proves to be one of a pair of twins, one good and the other evil. The evil one promises Jack the secret of his birth if Jack saves him three times. After performing the requisite heroics (for the good twin) Jack discovers that the evil twin knows nothing of his origins.

The novel concludes with two set pieces that dispel all illusions: in the first, a trial scene, the evil twin is unmasked; in the second, Jack's reunion with his mother, he learns that he is not titled and that his name is truly Holborn. As Solomon Trumpet declares, "you've been yourself without knowing it!" Through Jack's discovery of self, Garfield suggests that the only meaningful nobility is nobility of conduct.

Encouraged by positive reviews, Garfield next wrote an adult novel, but he failed to find a publisher for it. Having accepted an advance to write a children's book, he mined parts of his rejected adult novel. The result, *Devil-in-the-Fog* (1966), won the first *Guardian* award for children's fiction. Although it seems more inspired by Dickens than Stevenson – especially in its Macawber-like character, Mr. Treet, the wandering player and self-proclaimed genius – this novel is very much a companion to the first.

It explores the question of identity – which, Garfield suggested in an interview with Wintle, may have been on his mind because he and his wife adopted their daughter at about this time – and the difficulty of penetrating appearances. The narrator, fourteen-year-old George Treet, receives what Jack desired, news of his noble birth. As the son of Sir John Dexter, he moves to an elegant home, where he tries to polish his rough edges in a vain effort to win respect from his new father and love from his new mother. George eventually discovers that Mr. Treet, his real father, "sold" him into riches to improve his lot in life.

Devil-in-the-Fog also relies on the contrivance of good and evil brothers. George at first believes Sir John to be the target of his evil brother, Richard, but he eventually discovers that Richard is good and Sir John villainous. These revelations are crammed into a mechanical ending that, together with the same forced suggestions of the supernatural employed in *Jack Holborn* and the hasty change in Lady Dexter's character, indicate an artist still in his apprenticeship.

Nevertheless, *Devil-in-the-Fog* reveals a growing mastery of symbolism; the pervasive fog symbolizes the difficulty in seeing identities and moral values, and Sir John's "diseased heart" suggests his evil na-ture. Second, Garfield, an admirer of Jane Austen, uses reactions to George's theatrical manners for comedy and social criticism, contrasting the haughtiness of the nobility with the humane warmth of the lower classes. Finally, he makes thematic use of the melodramatic confusions between good and evil. Thus, George displays maturity by abandoning his judgmental extremes and accepting his failed father; as Lady Dexter notes, there is something between the blackest villain and the brightest saint.

Smith (1967), one of Garfield's most popular and critically praised novels, marks a major advance in the author's art. Advised by his editor, Grace Hogarth, to abandon the first-person narration of the first two novels, Garfield switched to a subjective third-person voice that allows him to communicate both external appearances and emotional responses. The protagonist, Smith, is a twelve-year-old pickpocket in eighteenth-century London's underworld. Having stolen a document just before two men kill its bearer, Smith, pursued by the killers, tries to turn it to his advantage. This, however, requires that he somehow learn to read. A chance encounter with Mr. Mansfield, a blind magistrate whom he leads home, provides Smith with the chance to learn to read and to develop his understanding of himself and others.

Symbolism tends to allegory in this work: Smith, who judges spontaneously by his heart, leads the blind justice, who declares that "to me, devils and angels are one." The rigidly upright Mansfield finally develops compassion, telling a morally acceptable lie to protect Smith. The book owes much of its power to Garfield's simpler plotting, which uses vivid, tightly connected set pieces, some of which are among the best scenes he has written. These include a comical bath scene, in which layers of rotting clothes are peeled from the filthy Smith; pungently atmospheric scenes in Newgate Gaol; and Smith's symbolic trek through the snow with Mansfield.

Garfield's style includes several memorable phrases, such as the description of a tavern's patrons being "from all falls of life" or Smith's sister's warning that "Innocence is no excuse in the eyes of the Law." In spite of its tight thematic focus, its controlled humor, and its excitement, *Smith* shows signs of Garfield's continuing difficulty with closure. Despite effective irony, as when Billings, betraying his colleagues to avoid the gallows, is murdered by the hangman's father, the plot descends into an improbable treasure hunt. Furthermore, some of the symbolism is crude. Nevertheless, *Smith* merits praise as a vivid

Dennis Fast, who sells his childhood for a million pounds; illustration by
Anthony Maitland for Garfield's The Ghost Downstairs *(1972)*

celebration of humane feelings triumphing in an often callous and deceptive world.

Black Jack (1968) masterfully combines plot, character, and symbolism, subtly enriching Garfield's typical themes: identity, the search for a father figure, and the problem of distinguishing good and evil. The plot has two strands, each centered on a boy's relationship with a character who symbolizes a radical form of innocence. The first of these relationships forces the boy, Bartholomew Dorking, to walk away from his life as a draper's assistant. Having unwittingly resurrected the gigantic Black Jack, a hanged criminal, by removing a silver tube from his throat, Bartholomew accompanies him and repeatedly prevents him from murdering people. Bartholomew himself is reborn, a point symbolized when Black Jack renames him Tolly.

Tolly's subsequent adventures, like Jack Holborn's and Smith's, are partly a search for a father fig-

ure who will define his place in life. Tolly's adventures also develop a theme about good and evil. Black Jack is dressed as a monk, and he ironically commands Tolly, contemptuously called a saint, to "Lead me in the way of salvation." Tolly's example transforms Black Jack. In his interview with Natov, Garfield said Black Jack "was meant to represent the forces of nature; he's neither good nor bad. He's just brute strength." Tolly's commitment to love, however, leads Black Jack toward the salvation of humane feeling and moral action.

The second plot strand involves Tolly with the supposedly mad Belle Carter, a character based on Garfield's observation of a woman suffering from a rare form of encephalitis. As with Black Jack, Tolly resurrects Belle, leading her from living death to mature identity. Like Black Jack, she is also instrumental in changing Tolly. Through her, he sees that his intimidating uncle is not a fearful giant, but a comically small man. Unlike earlier Garfield heroes, Tolly rejects the father figure and sets out for the New World with Belle.

Black Jack is notable for an exciting plot that avoids the mechanical absurdities of Garfield's earlier books. Its climactic scenes – Black Jack's freeing of Belle from the madhouse and his rescue of Belle and Tolly from the crowds hysterically fleeing the earthquake of 1749 – thematically link the moral upheaval Black Jack creates in the madhouse and the social upheaval the earthquake causes in the wider world. The book is even more notable for its thematic groupings of Dickensian characters, especially the "religious" ones, through whom Garfield develops questions of good and evil. Black Jack storms the madhouse "like some ferocious monk off to do battle with the devil." In contrast, Corporal Mitchell, preaching doom, enslaves his listeners in hysteria. The avaricious Parson Hall victimizes the mad and their relatives. Hatch, rationalizing himself as "a kind of scourge," "God's punishment," victimizes everyone; in the end, fittingly, he falls into the "freezing fiery furnace" of the river, where a boat crushes his head. Another group consists of healers, such as the mercenary apothecary, the itinerant fairground huckster, Dr. Carmody, and the unscrupulous madhouse owner, Dr. Jones. Their actions contrast with Tolly's, for only he has compassion, and as a result, only he heals people. Finally, *Black Jack* deserves respect for the way it binds its plots and themes with symbols. Next to the religious references attached to Black Jack and Tolly, the most prominent symbolism is that developed by repeated images of the sea and sailing, which describe Dr. Carmody's troupe, occur in Belle's mad visions, and indicate Tolly's success in achieving an independent identity.

The Drummer Boy (1969) is both simpler and more ambitious than Garfield's previous novels. The simple plot is not completely free of the author's characteristic reliance on coincidence, but it supports a symbolism that is more sustained than that in *Black Jack*. As in earlier novels, the central concept in this novel of ideas concerns deceptive appearances. Charlie Samson, an army drummer repeatedly described as "the golden boy," must overcome social and personal illusions. Having gone to war "to find something to be worthy of," Charlie at first represents romantic innocence.

Garfield uses the present tense to give immediacy to Charlie's romantic idealism as he marches into battle, but he deftly switches to the past tense (after the troops are slaughtered in an ambush) to suggest the tarnishing of Charlie's romanticism. After the battle, which Sheila Egoff has called "one

of the most magnificent descriptions in children's literature," Charlie is joined by a motley crew of survivors, who loot the bodies of their dead. The portrait of Mister Shaw, the surgeon who gathers teeth from the corpses for use in dentures, is a macabre masterpiece, a forceful reminder that heroic death is an illusion. Charlie, however, struggles to maintain this illusion.

In England Charlie encounters contrasting figures who force him to go beyond appearances and to develop mature values. The most important of these are two young women. Sophia, daughter of the general, brings out his romantic illusions. Although her name means "wisdom," she is wise only in the ways of death. Dressed in red, the color of the army and its blood, she represents the diseased imagination; like a vampire, she feeds on the death of innocents. The smitten Charlie feeds her lies about her lover's brave death in battle and even corrupts himself by lying to save her father. In opposition to Sophia, representative of the head, is the aptly named servant, Charity, representative of the heart. Her perpetually visible white petticoat symbolizes both a wholesome carnality – a lust for life that Sophia lacks – and her moral innocence, for she is unable to hide what she is. Unlike Sophia, who admires Charlie's drum, symbol of his naive illusions, Charity despises it and suggests it be sold to a tinker.

Almost as important are the opportunists who seek to use Charlie, two men who also represent head and heart. The actions of the calculating general teach Charlie about the corruption of those who perpetuate illusions for their own benefit. Shaw, torn between homosexual desire and spiritual concern for Charlie, rises to moral nobility as Charlie's mentor, showing him both the hypocrisy of those who create illusions and the redeeming power of love. Having gone beyond his romantic illusions, a point symbolized when he breaks his drum while sounding an "Advance" into life, Charlie achieves maturity: he accepts Charity, the love she symbolizes, and reconciliation with his father.

With one notable exception, critical reaction to *The Drummer Boy* has been positive. Richard Camp calls it "so perfect a work of art" because of its "compression of complex ideas." David Rees, however, condemns it as "a total failure, almost unbelievably bad," and brands its style "self-indulgent and pretentiously inflated." Rees is severe, but his criticism suggests that lavish praise of this novel depends on ignoring the mixed nature of Garfield's achievement. As a novel of ideas, *The Drummer Boy* exhibits an almost visceral anger at social hypocrisy. At other times, its allegorical tendencies conflict with its realism. Its imagery, symbolism, and characterization make it one of Garfield's most stimulating and touching books. Reliance on easy irony and melodrama, however, undermines this seriousness, making the novel seem more pretentious than profound. In its mixture of brilliant and inept touches, *The Drummer Boy* accurately represents the strengths and limitations of Garfield's artistry.

From the beginning, Garfield used the supernatural to create atmosphere and tension. Pobjoy's disguise as Taplow's ghost, for example, is important to the revenge plot in *Jack Holborn*. With *Mister Corbett's Ghost* (1968), however, a dark, chilling story about the horrors of a guilty conscience, Garfield went beyond gimmicks. Benjamin Partridge, an apothecary's apprentice, undergoes a moral and emotional education when Mr. Corbett sends him out into the cold to deliver a prescription. Cursing his harsh master for denying him the New Year's Eve party he had hoped to attend, Benjamin enters into an agreement with a devilish old man to have his master die.

Ironically, his employer's death does not free Benjamin. Burdened first by Mr. Corbett's corpse, the symbol of his shame, and then by his ghost, the symbol of an unremitting conscience, Benjamin spends a surrealistically horrifying evening coming to terms with the destructive power of his hatred. After feeling compassion for his employer's family, he is given a second chance, and Mr. Corbett is brought back to life. Speaking of ghost stories, Garfield told Natov that "the ghost must arise from the person who sees it, usually as a projection of their guilt."

The title story of *The Restless Ghost: Three Stories* (1969) is remarkable only for the introduction of the characters Bostock and Harris, young rogues later featured in two superb comic novels. This tale of a guilty conscience, however, produces no supernatural thrills and contains no psychological depths.

The accompanying novella and short story, which were also included in the 1969 British edition of *Mister Corbett's Ghost and Other Stories,* are better examples of Garfield's cultivation of deliberate irony. In "Vaarlem and Tripp," a character study, a disreputable Dutch painter displays cowardice and artistic genius during a naval battle and crass opportunism afterward. Set aboard a ship carrying prisoners to Virginia, "The Simpleton" is more substantial. Sentenced to transportation for stealing, the naive Nicholas Kemp finds himself used by a fellow convict, the diabolical Bartleman. This Billy Budd-

like innocent not only survives a planned execution but triumphs over his enemies to win the heart of a lovely female passenger. In a satisfyingly ironic conclusion, the young gentlemen who had urged the protagonist to steal for them find themselves transported and become his indentured servants in Virginia.

Garfield's career took a new turn with *The God Beneath the Sea,* written in collaboration with Edward Blishen, as he moved outside the realm of historical fiction. The first of two volumes retelling Greek myths, *The God Beneath the Sea* originated in Garfield's aborted effort to write some linked creation myths commissioned for an anthology. When he decided, instead, to create a modern retelling of the most important Greek myths, Garfield enlisted the aid of Blishen. Their afterword outlines their aims: to select tales to form a continuous narrative re-creating a sense of the power the myths had for the original Greeks, and to do so by using what they called "the literary voice of our own time."

The God Beneath the Sea, which won the Carnegie Medal for Children's Literature, links tales through the story of Hephaestus, the ugly smith of the gods. Because of the disparate nature of the tales, the links are tenuous, but the authors structure the book poetically by beginning and ending with a description of Hephaestus falling from Olympus. The tales are organized in three sections, each including vivid episodes. The first, which presents the story of the creation out of Chaos, includes a suitably dark and horrifying tale of Cronus devouring his children. The short middle section, which recounts the creation of man, Prometheus's stealing of fire, and Pandora's opening of the box, is the most dramatically gripping – in the agonized questioning of Prometheus, it comes closest to giving a modern psychological bent to the tales. The final section includes an emotionally charged version of the Demeter and Persephone myth.

Controversy about Garfield's novels pales in comparison to that generated by *The God Beneath the Sea.* Although critics applauded the author's goals, they severely divided in assessing the book's execution. Style has been the focus of disagreement, with two well-known writers leading each critical camp. Alan Garner, in a scathing review, declared that "The prose is overblown Victorian, 'fine' writing at its worst, cliché-ridden to the point of satire, falsely poetic." Ted Hughes took the opposite position, praising the "authentic language and atmosphere" of the book and calling the tales "genuine imaginative retellings." Judgment of *The God Beneath the Sea* depends on taste: those who admire Garfield's theatrical flashiness find much to enjoy; others merely find it annoying and self-consciously literary.

Garfield and Blishen's second collection, *The Golden Shadow: A Recreation of the Greek Legends* (1973), created less controversy. Although the writing is more subdued, some critics still reacted negatively to its lush prose. In an otherwise laudatory review, Gerard Benson criticized it for including "a sub-Keatsian, orgasmic kind of writing, overladen with imagery." As in the first volume, the stories of one figure dominate. Garfield indicated to Wintle that he chose as the center of the book "a rather Dostoevskian figure," Heracles: "He's haunted by guilt and a desire to expiate." Consequently, the volume has a strong human focus, tracing the life cycle of this hero from childhood. Its concern is moral and psychological, probing the reasons for actions, including heroic ones. Another linking device is the nearsighted storyteller, a Homeric figure who wanders about the country seeking evidence of the gods and details of Heracles' life for inclusion in his stories. Always just too late to meet the gods or to see clearly what is happening, he shines a comic light in an otherwise dark book.

Like many professional children's writers, Garfield occasionally accepts commissions. His first such opportunity was for Heinemann's Long Ago Children series for readers seven to nine years old. To Garfield's credit, *The Boy and the Monkey* (1969), the first of three linked stories about Tim, an eighteenth-century urchin, and his monkey, is more than formulaic fiction; it is mainstream Garfield, and several reviewers criticized the writing as being too difficult for the designated audience. Tim, who uses his monkey to steal from rich people, is caught and transported rather than hanged when a compassionate jeweler refuses to value the stolen rings at their true worth. The didactic point about the financial value of a child's life is overdone, but the comic irony throughout is superb. *The Captain's Watch* (1972) continues Tim's adventures aboard the ship transporting him to Virginia. In the final volume, *Lucifer Wilkins* (1973), Tim and his monkey go to Brazil with Lucifer, an escaped slave. Placed together in a single volume in 1976, these slight tales provide a good introduction to Garfield's fictional world.

With *The Strange Affair of Adelaide Harris* (1971), Garfield produced something significantly different from his earlier fiction. The wit and humor that had been stylistic features take center stage in Garfield's most theatrical novel. A rollicking farce set in Regency Brighton, instead of the eighteenth-century London underworld that had become his trademark, *The Strange Affair of Adelaide Harris* features a large cast of comic eccentrics entangled in interwoven plots. These plots begin simply and improbably with two students at Dr. Bunnion's Academy who decide to expose a female infant in the manner of ancient Sparta. (Harris, confusing this custom with the story of Romulus and Remus, hopes to see his infant sister suckled by a vixen.) Enlisting the aid of Bostock, his dull, brawny friend, Harris steals his own sister, Adelaide, and leaves her on the Downs. The beautiful Tizzy Alexander finds Adelaide and, in bending down to pick her up, unwittingly escapes being thrown to the ground by unscrupulous Ralph Bunnion, son of the academy's owner.

Subsequent events grow naturally out of the humorous characters, each governed by a single trait. Thus, Major Alexander, Tizzy's distraught father, who "had a fiery and explosive sense of honor which he was inclined to lay like mines under friends and enemies alike," blusteringly challenges Ralph to a duel, which he spends the rest of the novel trying to avoid. Similarly, the hired detective, Selwyn Raven, convinced of his ability to spot evil, develops a conspiracy theory blaming everything on the innocent teacher, James Brett. Only one character develops: Brett, who is so lacking in confidence and force that he cannot refuse when asked to be a second by both parties in the duel. He ingeniously prevents the duel, makes way for a new teacher, saves Mrs. Bunnion's marriage, and, finally, declares his love for Tizzy, with whom he sails off to the New World, Garfield's symbol for happiness unburdened by personal history or class bias.

Critical reaction to *The Strange Affair of Adelaide Harris* has been almost unanimously positive. John Rowe Townsend, in *A Sounding of Storytellers* (1979), declares it to be "the happiest and in many ways the most enjoyable of all the novels," and Rhodri Jones has praised it as "a virtuoso performance." David Rees has gone further, calling it "a comic masterpiece, Garfield's finest novel." Garfield moves his busy cast of characters through intricate patterns without confusing his readers and creates genuinely funny episodes, such as the inept assaults of the lustful Ralph Bunnion. He further enlivens the novel with verbal humor, as in the scene in which Bostock declares that he is a hypocrite to give money to charity and his drunken recipient says that whatever his denomination, he is still a Christian to her.

Garfield returns to the characters and the comic manner of *The Strange Affair of Adelaide Harris* in a sequel, *Bostock and Harris; Or, The Night of the Comet* (1979), published in the United States as *The Night of the Comet: A Comedy of Courtship Featuring Bostock and Harris* (1979). Harris, having read about courtship in the animal kingdom, instructs Bostock in the proper way to attract a female. His efforts lead to a series of comical misunderstandings involving a small group of lovers. In keeping with the leitmotiv of the dance, the lovers repeatedly exchange partners until they end up with the appropriate ones. *Bostock and Harris; Or, The Night of the Comet* is not as intricate as its predecessor, and its central characters sometimes remain too long in the background. Nevertheless, it shares the virtues of *The Strange Affair of Adelaide Harris*. Neither is marked by the moral seriousness and biting social criticism characteristic of Garfield's other books, but they are engaging and funny novels, works that rank near the top of the author's achievements.

Although Garfield used historical settings throughout his career, he did not employ historical personages until *Child o' War: The True Story of a Boy Sailor in Nelson's Navy* (1972), the life story of Sir John Theophilus Lee, who at five became the youngest person ever to serve in the Royal Navy. Written in consultation with David Proctor, the book's twelve mock-epic chapters combine actual passages from Lee's autobiography with a fictional account of his bored family observing him while he dictates it. A pompous fool, always eager to court the rich and powerful, Lee remains on the edge of major events, scarcely recording details about them. In his interview with Natov, Garfield said that "anger is one of the strongest motives in writing, particularly social anger," and in this book Garfield repeatedly aims angry salvos at this toady and those he courts. Unfortunately, Garfield demolishes his target so early that repeated diatribes make his anger notable chiefly for its intemperance.

In "Writing for Childhood" Garfield declared that "we are the ghosts of what we were, and the phantoms of what we will become." Two years later he used this concept as the theme of a symbolic tale of the supernatural, *The Ghost Downstairs* (1972). Dennis Fast, whose name and actions suggest Faust, is possessed by the devils of envy and loneliness. When the diabolical Fishbane moves into the basement flat of the deceased Otto Hertz (German for "heart"), Fast sells seven years of his life for a million pounds. Believing he has cheated the devil by selling the first years of his life, Fast finds that he cannot enjoy his wealth because his childhood was the source of the dreams that make life worthwhile. The first part of the tale includes such characteristic

Garfield flourishes as a contract "Red in tooth and clause!" The second part, however, meanders in cryptic symbolism. Fast finally redeems himself when he stands in front of a locomotive driven by the ghost of his childhood. That ghost, in a scene suggestive of William Wordsworth's phrase "The Child is Father of the Man," kneels over the corpse, calling him "My son." Like many of Garfield's books, *The Ghost Downstairs* has a disappointing conclusion – in this case it is far too enigmatic.

The Sound of Coaches (1974) begins with vintage Garfield: a wild stagecoach ride and the death of a mysterious woman during childbirth. The baby, Sam, is raised by the morally rigid Chichesters, and as he grows older, he constantly wonders about his "other pa," his biological father. After Mr. Chichester is crippled, Sam carelessly wrecks the coach, and his embittered father drives him from his home. Sam joins a traveling theatrical troupe and discovers that the alcoholic actor Daniel Coventry is his father. As with Tolly and Black Jack, Sam determines to earn the respect of Coventry, who constantly upstages him. When Mr. Chichester attends a performance, however, Coventry performs poorly, whereas Sam shines. In an ironic twist on Garfield's theme of appearances, Sam never learns the truth about the roles people are playing. Coventry performs badly, not because of parental generosity but out of abject fear that Mr. Chichester will recognize him as the man who shot him years earlier. Conversely, Mr. Chichester is genuinely the protective father: his love bends his formerly inflexible commitment to truth, and he protects Sam's feelings by concealing his knowledge about his assailant.

Because its content and themes traverse familiar ground, some reviewers were highly critical of *The Sound of Coaches,* accusing Garfield of repeating himself. Such assessments do not take into account the subtle ways in which Garfield expanded his territory. *The Sound of Coaches* blends the mystery and occasional darkness of earlier works with the concern for manners developed in *The Strange Affair of Adelaide Harris*. The contrasting lives of the stagecoach drivers and the amoral theater company generate a probing, often ironic, exploration of the differences between appearance and reality, environment and heredity, youth and age, and rural and urban values. For example, Sam's search for his father, who he thinks may have been an outlaw, raises troubling issues about heredity. Sam's dramatic talent shows the force of inheritance, but the structure of the novel, which ends with his lover, the pregnant Jenny, taking the same journey his mother took, suggests that Sam has also been positively influenced by the moral environment of the Chichesters. Sam does not, as his father did, abandon the woman who loves him.

The novel does have some weaknesses, notably in the pretentiousness of the final section, which Garfield told Wintle was intended to be "a gloss on *The Tempest,* and the relationship of a Prospero to an Ariel." Nevertheless, it contains more psychologically complex characters than most of Garfield's work. Jenny, Garfield's first complex female character, for example, combines opportunism, devotion, sentimentality, and practicality. The novel's conclusion satisfies both the demands of romance, established by the fairy-tale opening "Once upon a winter's night," and the demands of realism, created by the portrayal of manners. In picturing the compromises and adjustments people make to maintain relationships, Garfield displays sentiment without being sentimental.

Even more impressive is *The Prisoners of September* (1975), republished in 1989 as *Revolution!,* an intricate book that traces the effect of the French Revolution on a wide cast of characters. The most important are two young Englishmen: Richard Mortimer, an aloof aristocrat and an idealist committed to the cause of democracy, becomes one of the Septemberers, radicals who massacred aristocrats in the prisons of Paris; Lewis Boston, son of a nouveau riche wine merchant, has none of his friend's intellectual passion, but he has a sentimental heart. While in Paris he sees Richard murder a young princess; overcome with revulsion, he helps a randomly chosen family of aristocratic prisoners escape to England. Unfortunately he discovers that the Latours are forgers, who continue their crimes in their new land. For his part, Richard is maddened by his experiences, returns to England, and commits a brutal murder. He ends up being murdered by British intelligence, which had recruited him in the first place, while Lewis agrees to wed the daughter of the criminals he saved.

In "Writing for Childhood" Garfield expressed a preference for "the discipline of classicism to the freedom of romanticism" and suggested that children's literature was the one place where a balance between the two was still possible. In *The Prisoners of September* he strikes that balance, creating a novel of ideas and feelings, of action and contemplation, and of comedy and tragedy. It is most obviously balanced in its characterization. The device of the good and evil brothers is reused, but here it is more than a plot contrivance. Although not literally related, Richard and Lewis symbolize different elements of a common identity. Richard symbolizes

the intellect on fire with ideas; he loves in the abstract, cherishing the idea of "the people," but he cannot love individuals. In contrast, Lewis symbolizes the heart; he impulsively reaches out to people. Garfield does not, however, make them mere allegorical figures. Both are naive, and almost everything they touch turns out ironically. Thus, Richard never discovers that he is a dupe of Dignam-Browne, the British agent who murders him. Similarly, Lewis performs two notable acts of public heroism, saving a countess in a runaway carriage and rescuing the Latours, but he learns afterward that those he has rescued are frauds.

Garfield is equally brilliant in setting up dialectical contrasts with other characters. Henrietta, Lewis's witty sister, and Gilberte, daughter of the forgers, are more believable and complex females than Jenny in *A Sound of Coaches.* They add depth to the novel's portrayal of domestic life, representing the extremes of romanticism and cynicism. Their reconciliation, complementing that of Richard and Lewis, marks the triumph of compassion combining with understanding, the heart working with the head. Garfield also adds a light touch to the intellectual debate between the claims of democracy and aristocracy through the portraits of Mr. Archer and Dr. Stump, two perpetually debating ideologues reminiscent of Thwackum and Square in Henry Fielding's *Tom Jones* (1749). Corporal Bouvet and Mr. Dignam-Browne provide an even starker contrast. The former is a mildly comic figure, a romantic idealist dreaming only of freedom in England; ironically, he ends up in an English prison. Dignam-Browne, on the other hand, is political cynicism personified, stirring up revolution to aid English financial interests. He conceals a loathsome disease ("from the neck down he was a mass of fearful corruption"), symbolizing the decay of morality and compassion. Such opposition and balances, which emphasize the disillusionment of the romantic, show that, operating alone, neither the intellect nor the heart is a good guide.

In addition to its intellectual balances, *The Prisoners of September* contains superb structural balances. Lewis's storybook rescue of the countess, resulting ironically in the public humiliation of her exposure as a thief, balances his rescue of the Latours, resulting in his private humiliation when he discovers that they are criminals. Light and dark episodes also balance. Henrietta fails to deliver Gilberte's letter of confession to the justice of the peace, thereby allowing Lewis to read it and accept her as morally reformed. Richard's letter to Dignam-Browne, in which he expresses fear that he will tell all he

Dust jacket for Garfield's 1978 collection of twelve linked stories

knows, gets delivered. Ironically, Richard decides after sending it that he did not mean it, but Dignam-Browne murders him because of it. Combining a slightly cynical romantic comedy of domestic manners with a tragic tale of political espionage and private disillusionment, *The Prisoners of September* avoids Garfield's previous lapses into mechanical resolutions.

In his interview with Natov, Garfield described his next novel, *The Pleasure Garden* (1976), as "a very odd book." Part murder mystery and part tangled allegory, it concerns various kinds of desire: desire for sex, for peace of mind, for purpose in life, for maternal comfort. The setting is the Mulberry Gardens, where children spy on the patrons to help the proprietor blackmail them. The murder mystery concerns efforts to discover who stabbed a youth in the gardens. As an allegory, the novel traces the battle between Dr. Dormann, a deathly figure in black, and Martin Young, a minister. Although at least part of the allegory is clear — they are referred to, respectively, as "the man possessed by a devil and the man possessed by an angel" — much is too overwrought to sort out. Reverend Young regularly goes to the Mulberry Garden to indulge in cheese-

cake, something that, given the novel's sly sexual innuendo, may or may not be symbolic. Dormann, the blackmailer, is one of Garfield's ambivalent figures, with a gift parallel to Young's, offering his victims confession, peace of mind, and a season's ticket. It is never clear why Garfield equates the comforts these two bring, thereby suggesting equally valid ways of coping with life. It is clear, however, that the garden is both an Eden (from which innocent children are driven) and one version of the *hortus conclusus* of pastoral tradition, the garden of earthly delights.

Townsend claims that the novel has "to be felt rather than to be fully comprehended," but that evades the issue of Garfield's ubiquitous symbolism. Adding to the difficulty is the author's copious style. Furthermore, although the theme involves sexual desire, the characters themselves are cold abstractions. The passages from the *Song of Songs* may suggest that Reverend Young has grown to accept Hebrew warmth, but it is not clear how this makes him different from the other patrons of the gardens. Young seems to find peace in acknowledging sensual desire, but it is difficult to see how this connects to his allegorical battle against Dr. Dormann.

Whether or not it is, as David Rees argues, "adult fiction trying to squeeze into the conventions of a children's book," *The Pleasure Garden* is a work in which Garfield seems unsure of both his audience and his message.

The question of audience is an important issue in two unusual books published in 1976, the same year as *The Pleasure Garden. The Book Lovers: A Sequence of Love Scenes, Chosen and Arranged by Leon Garfield* and *The House of Hanover: England in the Eighteenth Century* are at the upper end of suitability for adolescents, primarily because of subject matter. *The Book Lovers* is essentially an anthology of passages from such nineteenth-century writers as Dickens, Austen, Anthony Trollope, and Leo Tolstoy, framed by a plot in which a shy young man tries to ask a librarian for a date. Using passages from famous novels to communicate, they repeatedly misunderstand the purport of the messages and intentions of the other. Although mildly amusing for adults, its quiet wit is unlikely to appeal to adolescents.

The House of Hanover was commissioned for the Mirror of Britain series, books designed to introduce young readers to various historical periods. It also uses a clever device to create an unconventional view of history: its narrator walks through the National Portrait Gallery responding to the faces he sees and occasionally exchanging ideas with a talkative attendant. Garfield admits that he knows little about the politics of the eighteenth century but claims that such knowledge has been unnecessary in his fiction. In this work he ignores military and political leaders, concentrating instead on writers and artists. Reviewers did not respond favorably to the selection. Garfield's decision to emphasize some artists, such as Hogarth, and to treat others – such as Pope – only briefly, makes this a highly eccentric vision of artistic history.

The author's uneasy position between adolescent and adult literature is again apparent in *The Apprentices* (1978), a linked series of twelve stories originally published separately between 1976 and 1978. These stories of youths in the period of apprenticeship were published in England as thin books with large type and abundant illustration, suggesting that they were for young children. Reviewers repeatedly pointed out that this format was misleading. The American edition, in which the stories were first combined, was marketed as an adult book, without illustrations. Critics continue to argue the status of these stories, but although not for young children, they provide challenging reading for both adolescents and adults. As several reviewers of individual

tales suggested, some of them rank among the best of Garfield's writing.

Although these stories were originally published individually, Garfield, as he told Natov, intended "a novel in twelve self-contained chapters." The collection does not have the unity of a novel, but it is held together by the teeming squalor of London and by the focus on apprentices and their desires. Several devices also unite the work: each story involves a feast day and its customs; all the apprentices, except in the first story, bear birds' names, suggesting their vulnerability and their desire to soar; a lamplighter or a linkboy appears in each story, usually when illumination of some kind is necessary; every story contains a biblical quotation; and the central character of each story makes a cameo appearance in the next, creating, as Garfield said, "a sense of community and a particular time." Finally, the stories share a similar design. In each at least one character moves toward an epiphany, a moment of illumination in which his or her position in life becomes clear. In most cases, this episode involves the dropping of illusions and the achievement of harmony or peace, symbolized by a recognition of love.

Biblical imagery also underlies *The Confidence Man* (1978), which presents an actual event – the flight of a group of eighteenth-century Protestants from persecution in Catholic Germany – in terms of the exodus of the Jews from ancient Egypt. The story's major interest is in the shifting identity of Captain von Stumpfel, the group's leader, who is variously viewed as the devil, Grandfather Death, and a straw man. As the punning title suggests, though, von Stumpfel's major roles are as both a deceiver and a bringer of hope. He fulfills the first role when he disappears with the group's money and fulfills the second by giving confidence, even after he has disappeared, to the fourteen-year-old Hans Ruppert, an atheist who learns about faith. Later, in a preposterous coincidence, Hans learns that he has similarly affected von Stumpfel. In spite of some interesting narrative experimentation – Hans, in language realistically beyond him, reports the journeys, and an omniscient narrator describes the more static preparations – *The Confidence Man* never reconciles its realistic and symbolic elements.

In 1979 Garfield reestablished his position as a children's writer with *Bostock and Harris*. The next year, with *John Diamond,* titled *Footsteps* in the United States, he returned to the manner and themes of his early mysteries of identity. Narrated by a naive twelve-year-old, William Smith, this maturation tale uses the concept of footsteps in three

Giorgio and the princess; illustration by Fritz Wegner from Garfield's Guilt and
Gingerbread *(1984)*

ways: it represents the guilt of William's father, a swindler whose pacing William overhears even after his death; it suggests the pursuit of the murderous ruffians serving John Diamond, son of the man William's father swindled; and it symbolizes a journey toward understanding, for William's quest, which takes him to both the respectable and downtrodden areas of London, teaches him to look beyond appearances and to value his own life in the country. Although the plot involves a hidden treasure, Garfield suggests in the figures of John Diamond and the London thief Shot-in-the-Head that the true treasure is the heart, which can be brought from hatred or crime through love and acceptance. *John Diamond* has obvious faults: the writing is uneven, suffering from what Rees calls "excessive emotional straining"; the plot occasionally flags for set pieces of local color; and the theme of appearances and realities descends to sentimentality. Nevertheless, although it does not mark an advance over the early novels, it shares their attractions. Reviewers warmly welcomed it, and *John Diamond* won the Whitbread Award.

Garfield unambiguously entered the arena of adult writing by completing Charles Dickens's *The Mystery of Edwin Drood* in 1980. In 1981 he also entered a new area, that of the picture book. In *Fair's Fair,* a sentimental, Dickensian Christmas story, two waifs, a boy and a girl, are separately led to a deserted mansion, where they are lavishly and mysteriously fed. Because they believe in the rule of fairness, they clean the house and share their food with others. On Christmas Eve, after foiling burglars, they discover that everything has been designed as a test: one of the burglars is the owner of the house, and he adopts the children because they have displayed all the necessary virtues. Reviewers applauded the book as an appropriately warm seasonal tale.

They had distinctly mixed feelings, however, about Garfield's next picture books, three highly unusual adaptations of biblical stories. In *King Nimrod's Tower* (1982), *The Writing on the Wall* (1983), and *The King in the Garden* (1984), all illustrated by Michael Bragg, Garfield uses a subplot involving a child to give a new dimension to a biblical story. In

King Nimrod's Tower a boy tries to train an unruly dog at the site of the tower's construction. God confounds the workers with the confusion of languages in order to protect the boy, who would be injured if he simply destroyed the tower. The juxtaposition of the proud king's failure and the simple boy's success suggests both God's favoring of the meek and the need for humans to seek appropriate goals. In the second book Garfield shows Belshazzar brought low for arrogantly eating out of the holy bowl, while a humble kitchen boy who feeds a hungry cat escapes punishment because, as the prophet Daniel tells him, God punishes greed, not need. A little girl teaches a king his proper place in *The King in the Garden,* based on the biblical account of the madness of Nebuchadnezzar. For some critics these are fresh visions of the tales, but others have said that the subplots either distract from or distort the message of the original stories.

Garfield's last picture book during this period is aimed at an adolescent or adult audience. *The Wedding Ghost* (1985) emphasizes the theme of duality, which, in "An Evening with Leon Garfield," the author calls "the double life" of the man who has "the courage to awaken his dreams and his imagination." About to marry Jill, Jack embarks on a strange journey to the castle of Sleeping Beauty. Realizing that a failure to kiss her will mean his death, he awakens her and, at the time scheduled for his wedding to Jill, marches down a cathedral aisle to marry Sleeping Beauty. The cathedral dissolves into a country church, and Jack finds himself marrying Jill, but Sleeping Beauty is present as an invisible bride, showing that he will forever be haunted by desire. This story is notable for the drawings of Charles Keeping, which suggest that Jack has undertaken a psychological journey.

During the same period Garfield produced two other books outside the mainstream of his work. The first, *Guilt and Gingerbread* (1984), one of the author's favorites, is a rewriting of a rejected novel produced before the publication of *Jack Holborn.* Giorgio, a poor student who sets out to marry a rich princess, meets an old woman who promises him success if he will give her the princess's golden heart. In describing how Giorgio finds himself constantly replacing the princess's heart with inappropriate objects, this witty tale gives new meaning to the idea of touching someone's heart. In a satisfying conclusion, Giorgio learns that love is beyond the understanding of even his professors.

The second atypical book, *Shakespeare Stories* (1985), retells twelve plays. Although Garfield uses modern language to trace a clear line through the plots, he suggests the flavor of Shakespeare's work in the Elizabethan language of the dialogue. Garfield does more than "translate" Shakespeare: his selection of details and his abundant imagery make these generally well-received retellings interesting interpretations. He published a second collection, *Shakespeare Stories II,* in 1994.

Garfield's most recent efforts are unlikely to advance his reputation, although *The December Rose* (1986), the best of these, will not damage it. This novel began as a commission for a television script set in the Victorian era, on barges on the Thames, and Garfield reworked it for book publication. The central character, a chimney sweep named Barnacle, resembles Smith in many ways: Barnacle is an orphan taken in by a kindly stranger, who gives him a bath that begins his transformation from wild animal to sensitive human being; and he possesses valuable stolen property and is pursued by murderers. In Barnacle's case, however, the murderers are in the employ of corrupt government officials, who use the secret police for their own ends. The portrayal of the dedicated Inspector Creaker, who, Garfield has said, was based in part on Javert in Victor Hugo's *Les Miserables* (1862), is a memorable addition to Garfield's equivocal villains: he does evil deeds in the absolute conviction that he is serving the law. Creaker's destruction of the cynical ministers who deceived him ranks as among the most effective conclusions Garfield has devised because it is both psychologically and thematically appropriate. The sentimental ending of the main story, in which Barnacle purchases a barge for his kindly benefactor, is in striking contrast to this darker tale, but it is appropriate. Although *The December Rose* is not among Garfield's best books, its settings breathe life into overly familiar themes and patterns of action.

It is difficult to find any compensating merits in *The Empty Sleeve* (1988), an imperfect blending of Garfield's earlier stories. Like *Jack Holborn,* it concerns twins. Peter Gannet is supposedly slow and evil; Paul is bright and good, but with suggestions of moral ambivalence. Like *The Apprentices, The Empty Sleeve* uses birds' names for major characters, sprinkles religious imagery throughout, and works toward the moment when several characters, including Peter and Paul, have illuminations. Like *Mister Corbett's Ghost,* it invokes a ghost as a projection of guilt. The book fails to hold its disparate materials together. Inadequate characterization, an unconvincing plot, histrionic references to the ghost, a devil's mask worn by Paul, and a decaying ship that represents Peter's soul make this one of Garfield's least satisfying books.

In comparison, *The Blewcoat Boy* (1988), published in the United States as *Young Nick and Jubilee* (1989), is competent fiction. Commissioned as a book that would feature a National Trust property, it makes only incidental use of the famous charity school. Young Nick, a ten-year-old orphan concerned about making his sister, Jubilee, a desirable bride, decides to enroll her in school. Because they require a father's signature, they temporarily recruit a thief, the charming Christmas Owens, to play the role. Eventually, his love for Jubilee saves him from prison and he marries her. Garfield's style is troublesome: the narrative disconcertingly switches to an ungrammatical colloquial style. Otherwise, the work is predictable, sentimental fare, a gentle comedy without the violence typical of Garfield.

The Saracen Maid (1991) is an unremarkable addition to Garfield's oeuvre. It is the story of a simpleton, Gilbert Beckett, who is captured by pirates and freed by a Saracen maid, who later makes her way to London to marry him. Written like a simple folktale, the story ends with a joke few of its young readers will understand: Gilbert Beckett's son, Thomas, grows up to be a saint.

Garfield's recent books suggest that the bright talent of the early books may be fading. His best work is in *Black Jack; Mister Corbett's Ghost; The Strange Affair of Adelaide Harris; The Sound of Coaches; The Prisoners of September; Bostock and Harris;* and some of the tales in *The Apprentices.* These stand apart from most contemporary fiction for reasons more fundamental than their unfashionable historical settings. Full of humor and the delights of language, these are rich verbal structures that never insult the intelligence of young readers. They effectively combine adventure with philosophy or social criticism, and they symbolically explore questions of identity and meaning that are of concern to contemporary readers.

Interviews:

Justin Wintle, "Leon Garfield," in *The Pied Pipers: Interviews with Influential Creators of Children's Literature,* by Wintle and Emma Fischer (New York: Two Continents, 1975), pp. 192–207;

Roni Natov, "Re-Imagining the Past: An Interview with Leon Garfield," *Lion and the Unicorn,* 15 (June 1991): 89–115.

References:

Edward Blishen, "Greek Myths and the Twentieth Century Reader," *Children's Literature in Education,* no. 3 (November 1970): 48–51;

Marcus Crouch, *The Nesbit Tradition: The Children's Novel in England, 1945–1970* (London: Benn, 1972), pp. 34–38;

Sheila Egoff, *Thursday's Child: Trends and Patterns in Contemporary Children's Literature* (Chicago: American Library Association, 1981);

Alan Garner, "The Death of Myth," *Children's Literature in Education,* no. 3 (November 1970): 69–71;

Alethea Helbig, "Leon Garfield's Ghost Stories," in *The Phoenix Award of the Children's Literature Association,* edited by Helbig and Agnes Perkins (Metuchen, N.J.: Scarecrow Press, 1993), pp. 83–88;

Philip Holland, "Shades of the Prison House: The Fiction of Leon Garfield," *Children's Literature in Education,* no. 9 (Winter 1978): 159–172;

Ted Hughes, Review of *The God Beneath the Sea, Children's Literature in Education,* no. 3 (November 1970): 66–67;

Peter Hunt, "The Good, the Bad and the Indifferent: Quality and Value in Three Contemporary Children's Books," in *Signal Approach to Children's Literature,* edited by Nancy Chambers (Metuchen, N.J.: Scarecrow Press, 1981), pp. 225–246;

Rhodri Jones, "Leon Garfield," in *Good Writers for Young Readers,* edited by Dennis Butts (St. Albans: Hart-Davis, 1977), pp. 34–44;

Roni Natov, "History as Spiritual Healer: The Messianic Vision in Leon Garfield's *The Confidence Man," Lion and the Unicorn,* 15 (June 1991): 116–126;

Natov, *Leon Garfield* (New York: Twayne, 1994);

Natov, " 'Not the blackest of villains . . . not the brightest of saints': Humanism in Leon Garfield's Adventure Novels," *Lion and the Unicorn,* 2 (Fall 1978): 44–71;

"The 1987 Phoenix Award Winner: *Smith* by Leon Garfield," in *The Phoenix Award of the Children's Literature Association, 1985–1989,* edited by Alethea Helbig and Agnes Perkins (Metuchen, N.J.: Scarecrow, 1993), pp. 61–88;

Agnes Perkins, "Mystery and Melodrama: Three Novels by Leon Garfield," in *The Phoenix Award of the Children's Literature Association,* edited by Helbig and Perkins (Metuchen, N.J.: Scarecrow Press, 1993), pp. 71–74;

Taimi Ranta, "Retellings from Greek Mythology and Picture Book Stories by Leon Garfield," in *The Phoenix Award of the Children's Literature Association,* edited by Helbig and Perkins (Metuchen, N.J.: Scarecrow Press, 1993), pp. 77–82;

David Rees, "Blood, Thunder, Muck and Bullets: Leon Garfield," in his *What Do Draculas Do?: Essays on Contemporary Writers for Fiction for Children and Young Adults* (Metuchen, N.J.: Scarecrow Press, 1990), pp. 126–141;

John Stephens, "Intertextuality and *The Wedding Ghost*," *Children's Literature in Education,* no. 21 (March 1990): 23–36;

John Rowe Townsend, "Leon Garfield," in his *A Sounding of Storytellers: New and Revised Essays on Contemporary Writers for Children* (New York: Lippincott, 1979; London: Kestrel, 1979), pp. 66–80;

Mark I. West, "Comedy and Social History in Books by Leon Garfield," in *The Phoenix Award of the Children's Literature Association,* edited by Helbig and Perkins (Metuchen, N.J.: Scarecrow Press, 1993), pp. 75–76;

West, Ranta, Perkins, and Helbig, "Panel: Books of the 1987 Phoenix Award Winner, Leon Garfield," *Cross-Culturalism in Children's Literature: Selected Papers from the 1987 International Conference of the Children's Literature Association,* edited by Susan R. Gannon and Ruth Anne Thompson (Pleasantville, N.Y.: Pace University, 1987), pp. 21–29.

Alan Garner

(17 October 1934 –)

Roderick McGillis
University of Calgary

BOOKS: *The Weirdstone of Brisingamen: A Tale of Alderley* (London: Collins, 1960); republished as *The Weirdstone* (New York: Watts, 1961);

The Moon of Gomrath (London: Collins, 1963; New York: Walck, 1967);

Elidor (London: Collins, 1965; New York: Walck, 1967);

Holly from the Bongs, A Nativity Play, photography by Roger Hill, music by William Mayne (London: Collins, 1966);

The Old Man of Mow, photography by Hill (London: Collins, 1967; New York: Doubleday, 1970);

The Owl Service (London: Collins, 1967; New York: Walck, 1968);

Red Shift (London: Collins, 1973; New York: Macmillan, 1973);

The Breadhorse, illustrated by Albin Trowski (London: Collins, 1975);

Potter Thompson (London: Oxford University Press, 1975);

The Guizer: A Book of Fools, illustrated by V. Pritchard (London: Hamish Hamilton, 1975; New York: Morrow, 1976);

The Stone Book, illustrated by Michael Foreman (London: Collins, 1976; New York: Collins World, 1978);

Tom Fobble's Day, illustrated by Foreman (London: Collins, 1977; New York: Collins World, 1979);

Granny Reardun, illustrated by Foreman (London: Collins, 1977; New York: Collins World, 1978);

The Aimer Gate, illustrated by Foreman (London: Collins, 1978; New York: Collins World, 1979);

Fairy Tales of Gold, 4 volumes, illustrated by Foreman (London: Collins, 1979); republished as *Alan Garner's Fairy Tales of Gold,* 1 volume (London: Collins, 1980; New York: Philomel, 1980);

The Lad of the Gad (London: Collins, 1980; New York: Philomel, 1981);

The Stone Book Quartet (London: Collins, 1983);

Alan Garner's Book of British Fairy Tales, illustrated by Derek Collard (London: Collins, 1983; New York: Delacorte, 1985);

A Bag of Moonshine, illustrated by Patrick James Lynch (London: Collins, 1986; New York: Delacorte, 1986);

Jack and the Beanstalk, illustrated by Julek Heller (London: HarperCollins, 1992; Garden City, N.Y.: Doubleday, 1992);

Once Upon a Time, Though It Wasn't in Your Time and It Wasn't in My Time, and It Wasn't in Anybody Else's Time (Vancouver: Raincoast, 1993; New York: Dorling Kindersley, 1993).

OTHER: "Feel Free," in *Miscellany 4,* edited by Edward Blishen (Oxford: Oxford University Press, 1967);

The Hamish Hamilton Book of Goblins: An Anthology of Folklore, edited by Garner, illustrated by Krystyna Turska (London: Hamish Hamilton, 1969); republished as *A Cavalcade of Goblins* (New York: Walck, 1969); republished as *A Book of Goblins* (Harmondsworth: Puffin, 1972);

"The Fine Anger," in *Responses to Children's Literature: Proceedings of the Fourth Symposium of the International Research Society for Children's Literature, 1978,* edited by Geoff Fox and Graham Hammond (New York: K. G. Saur, 1980), pp. 1–12.

SELECTED PERIODICAL PUBLICATION – UNCOLLECTED: "Achilles in Altjira," *Children's Literature Association Quarterly,* 8 (Winter 1983): 5–10.

Alan Garner has become, through a relatively modest output, one of the most important writers for children since 1960. His work is carefully crafted, economic, and precise. His early works – *The Weirdstone of Brisingamen: A Tale of Alderley*

Alan Garner

(1960), *The Moon of Gomrath* (1963), and *Elidor* (1965) – rely on the type of fantasy popularized by J. R. R. Tolkien, parading its mythic structures openly through symbolic and allusive names, quotations, and even notes and prefaces. His work has become less derivative; its use of myth or overt fantasy has become naturalized in a manner reminiscent of the works of William Wordsworth: from *The Owl Service* (1967) to *The Stone Book Quartet* (1983), Garner has grounded his sense of the numinous firmly in the land, mostly the land of his childhood, and his characters have become figures in a landscape, figures that are integral parts of the land in which they grow.

Alan Garner was born on 17 October 1934. He comes from a family of craftsmen who have lived for generations near Alderley Edge in Cheshire, England, a place featured in many of his books. Garner's childhood was not easy. He suffered from several debilitating illnesses and proved clumsy in pursuing the craftsmanship traditional in his family. He was successful at school, except for the ridicule that his dialect attracted. In short, information about Garner's early years indicates a person of contrasts: weak health contrasted with ability in athletics; encouragement from teachers contrasted with their abuse of his speech; attachment to a place contrasted with his removal from this place through education.

Garner went to Manchester Grammar School and then to Magdalen College, Oxford, where he read classics. At age twenty-one he read William Golding's *Lord of the Flies* (1954) and resolved to become a writer. Leaving Oxford before taking his degree, Garner returned to Cheshire, to a medieval timber-framed house situated about eight miles from Alderley. On 4 September 1956 he began writing what would become his first work of fiction, *The Weirdstone of Brisingamen: A Tale of Alderley*. Since then his life as a writer has been a struggle to return emotionally and spiritually to the place of his childhood.

This "fusion with the land" has a biographical source. On more than one occasion Garner has recounted how the Education Act of 1944 not only allowed him access to an education at Manchester Grammar School that he might not otherwise have had because of his working-class origins but also

Alderley Edge in Cheshire, near Garner's childhood home. It is the setting of many of his books.

separated him from the discipline and strength of those origins. In his essay "The Fine Anger" (1980) he speaks of the "physical immobility" of his family as a means of overcoming "social classification": "On one square mile of Cheshire hillside, the Garners *are*. We know our place. And this sense of fusion with the land rescued me."

As Garner has grown closer to his roots, to his family, and its history in Cheshire, he has discovered an authentic voice, one that belatedly but strongly undertakes the Romantic quest to rediscover the mother tongue. In a 1978 interview with Aidan Chambers, Garner speaks of "the opportunity to reinstate a native English culture," an aim that bespeaks his authorial hope of preserving time-honored values related to language and the common people – a hope like that of such Romantic forbears as William Wordsworth. Garner also sees himself speaking a common language and preserving the passion and the truth that such a language contains.

Garner claims that his books contain "an instinctive searching out of the concrete culture that I had to be removed from in order to be educated." This searching has led him in *The Stone Book Quartet*

to the language of his Cheshire origins, northwest Mercian, a language he calls "direct and concrete." What he strives for, he says, is "to get back to the richness and freshness of a language which was beaten out of me by my teachers so that I could get on in the world."

In an interview published in *Children's Literature in Education* Garner claims, like Wordsworth, to provide his readers with "an emotional experience, not an intellectual one." Yet the experience one has in reading Garner's work is not without its intellectual dimension. In a 1981 interview with *Labrys* Garner puts it this way: "emotions have to be tightly controlled, since emotions are not linguistically structured. So, therefore, I am creating an emotional experience through the syntax, grammar and vocabulary. Words are originally poetic." He feels that he has achieved his aspirations in *The Stone Book Quartet,* a story he describes to Chambers as having been told "in a vocabulary I could taste – I could actually feel the words in my mouth." Such aspirations make Garner a writer who is heir to the traditions of high Romanticism.

Garner's education was in the classics; his pre-university training at Manchester Grammar had been at a school that he claims lacked an English department, and by the time he began to read English literature he found little in the canon of great works that was of relevance to him. There is a marked contrast, however, between Garner's statements on literature and influence (he has acknowledged that the three writers who have influenced him most are Homer, Aeschylus, and Euripides) and his intensely Romantic sensibility and practice. Garner has expressed his relief that his training was not in English, because most English graduates to whom he speaks have become journalists, despite their desire to be creative writers; he notes, "they were aware of the corpus of English literature and they felt there wasn't anything left to say." The anxiety hinted at in this statement is both one of influence and politics – the anxiety of a "first-generation grammar school boy from a working-class home."

Garner works toward a recovery of place in his books. Although nearly all his fiction (*The Owl Service* is the exception) is set near his childhood home of Alderley Edge, and although children or adolescents are invariably the main characters, only in *The Stone Book Quartet* does Garner break free of influence, discover his own voice, and recover his place and his childhood. Ironically, only in this work has he broken free of the children's-writer label, yet to write these books he drew from his childhood experiences for the first time.

As Garner has developed as a writer, his child characters have become stronger both as characters and as metaphors. Garner's children embody a vision of the world that can justly be called "Romantic"; they are both speaking features of Garner's mental and physical landscape and characters who intuitively grasp the paradox of similitude within dissimilitude. Garner's understanding of wholeness has taken shape in painful steps backward, from *The Weirdstone of Brisingamen* and *The Moon of Gomrath,* youthful pastiches of the twentieth-century pastoral fantasy most evident in the work of Tolkien and C. S. Lewis, to the apparently bleak wasteland visions of *Elidor, The Owl Service,* and *Red Shift* (1973), and finally to the lyrical balladry of the four stories of *The Stone Book Quartet.*

In these latter stories Garner not only connects with the genius loci of his Cheshire home, but in his child characters he also provides a vision of the possibility of hope. The beauty of Garner's *Stone Book Quartet* is that it is the creation of a writer wise enough to see things whole. The child, as Garner suggests as early as his description of the Children of Danu in *The Moon of Gomrath,* can never be "at the

end of what [he] undertakes[s]," nor can he or she be at the beginning. The child must always be between somewhere and nowhere, a true border figure, the guizer.

Placed in the midst of things, the child is at once human, natural, and divine; he or she is helpless and vulnerable as well as capable and strong. Garner remarks in "Coming to Terms" that childhood "is a period when we are at our most violent and we are at our most destructive and loving." Garner's children might be said to exist between two worlds, one past and irretrievable and the other that lies in the future yet is powerless to be born. In other words Garner's characters represent the limits of mortality. Some readers have found Garner's work dark and disturbing, but what Garner strives for is a vision that will both take into account the nightmares of history and offer hope.

The children who grope their way to such a vision grow progressively older from book to book: the four children in *Elidor* are anywhere from seven to thirteen or fourteen (Garner does not specify their ages; he refers to them only as "the children"), Roland being the youngest and Nicholas the eldest; the three children in *The Owl Service* are adolescents, perhaps fifteen and sixteen; and the two teenagers in *Red Shift* are seventeen or eighteen, old enough to think of leaving home and becoming independent. The children in *Elidor* experience a mysterious rite of passage in a borderland realm, neither in their own world nor in the fantastic land called Elidor. For a while they dwell in a liminal zone, a field of ritual activity.

Their experiences transport them from the playtime of childhood to an adult awareness of the delicacy and vulnerability of beauty, and of the violent struggle of power it initiates. As Roland and his brothers and sister throw the treasures, Grail symbols, back to Elidor at the end of the novel, Garner describes the shattering of magic casements and the acceptance of generations of the dead. The Grail symbols remain with the children, however, in the sense that the sexual selves of Helen, Roland, and the rest have been released.

The sexual frisson is not fully explored, but it is crucial to the lure of Elidor. Like his Romantic precursors, Garner uses sex as a metaphor for true and false desire, enmeshing and liberating nature. False desire generates illusory beauty, and true desire is a golden light flashed in the mind. Readers who find the end of *Elidor* inconclusive and dark fail to perceive Garner's latter-day Romanticism, in which he chronicles the violence and pain that accompany the loss of innocence. At the book's end reality disperses the illusions of romance, but the knowledge of the glorious vision holds. The children have come through an ordeal of consciousness. The book invokes Browning's "Childe Rowland to the Dark Tower Came," and like Browning's poem, *Elidor* gains strength from its ambivalence. Roland places the trumpet to his lips at the end of Browning's poem, and the children toss the treasures through the glass at the end of *Elidor.* Both acts are a defiance and a victory, partly sexual in quality. As always in Romantic art, energy is eternal delight; it mocks limitations and drives beyond romance.

Garner's *The Owl Service* won both the Carnegie Medal and the Guardian Award in 1967. In this novel contemporary adolescents live out their passions in the grip of an ancient Welsh legend, the legend of Blodeuwedd and Lieu Llaw Gyffes. In the source story, from the collection of fourteenth-century Welsh tales *The Mabinogian,* the characters Math and Gwydion fashion a woman from flowers and name her Blodeuwedd. She marries Lleu, the kinsman of Gwydion, but she falls in love with Gronw Peir. Disaster follows. Gronw "kills" Lleu, "an arrogant sungod." He returns and does the same to Gronw, who does not share Lleu's immortality.

In *The Owl Service* Gwyn and his mother, Nancy, live in a Welsh valley where Roger, his stepsister Alison and their parents come to holiday. The valley transmits its energy, its storehouse of passion, to Roger, Gwyn, and Alison, as it has done before to Nancy, to Huw Halfbacon (who is a handyman and gardener and considered by many in the valley to be half-baked, and who turns out to be Gwyn's father), and to Bertram (a cousin of Alison's mother). Throughout the book the three adolescents struggle in the grip of love, jealousy, and rivalry left to them from the past.

The valley is a center of energy that forces the characters to repeat the pattern set in the *Mabinogion* story. It is an omphalos where mind and nature are joined, bringing romance and reality, past and present, nature and supernature, the dark and the light together. Gwyn remarks that the valley "really is a kind of reservoir." A current connects the place to the characters and in so doing it disconnects the children from quotidian reality. Alison expresses this situation when she says: "Nothing's safe any more. I don't know where I am. 'Yesterday,' 'today,' 'tomorrow,' – they don't mean anything. I feel they're here at the same time: waiting."

Huw Halfbacon – handyman, gardener, and half-wit – understands this interpenetration of past,

present, and future. He is a poet, fool, and lover: in terms of the Welsh legend, he is both Gwydion and Lleu, magician and sufferer. He presides over the valley, and he cunningly prepares the children for the parts they must play. Although he owns nothing material, through an exquisite fitting to the land Huw owns "the ground, the mountains, the valley: I own the song of the cuckoo, the bramble, the berries: the dark cave is mine!" Huw holds the secret of the ages, and in his strangeness he is a threatening presence.

More often than not Huw is dismissed as dim; the children fail until the end of the novel to understand that he is a shaman, one who understands the boundaries. Gwyn's idea that he and Roger must "disconnect" Alison from the power that drives her is a failure to understand what Huw urges: "We have the blood. . . . And we must bear it." Huw realizes that the three adolescents – "the three who suffer every time" – must relive the ancient story of love, jealousy, desire, and destruction, because "we give this power a thinking mind. We must bear that mind, leash it, yet set it free, through us, so that no one else may suffer."

Poised between madness and sanity, past and present, nature and supernature, poverty and wealth, Huw represents an old order serving and offering itself as creative energy for a new order. Huw is both Gwydion, maker of woman from the powers of the broom, the oak, and the meadowsweet, and Lleu who slays Gronw (Bertram, in the novel). He carries the curse of "a great wrong," the death of Bertram. For Huw the past is eternally present: "There is a man being killed at that place . . . old time," he says at one point. For Huw the cycling of love and death perpetuates selfhood, the desire for power over nature that is always doomed to end in nature's power over man. He tries to communicate this to Gwyn and thus liberate him from selfhood so that Gwyn may grow up, since only by accepting the responsibility of maturity can Gwyn successfully meet the challenge the ancient story brings.

The children, from this perspective, work out the ancient pattern in order that others may be free of it. The centrality of the female to this pattern is that she comes to represent nature as a projection of male desire. Thus, as long she remains trapped within the ancient pattern, Alison will not be free to develop her own personality; she must be what others make her. Her obsession with owls, however, links her to the opposite mythic representation of womanhood: the dominating female. The active, destructive female finds prominent expression in the novel in Nancy (Gwyn's mother), Margaret

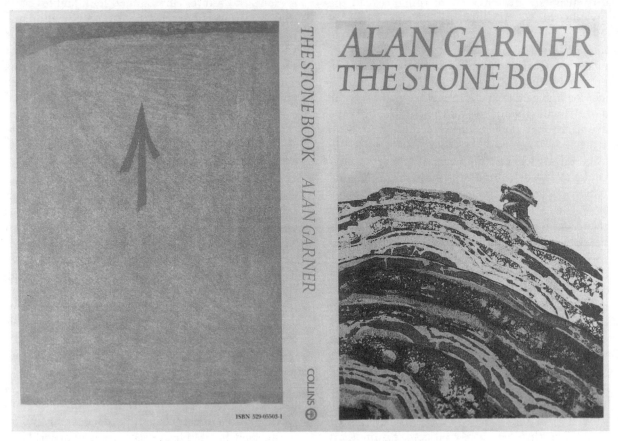

Dust jacket for Garner's 1976 novel about the visionary experiences of a young girl

(Alison's mother), and the Birmingham Belle (Roger's mother). They control those around them; their wills exert a power over men that leads to the men's diminishment. The prototype is Blodeuwedd, the woman created by a magician from flowers; once created she takes on a thinking mind, becomes independent of the man who created her, forsakes her husband for another man, and as punishment is changed into an owl. In short, Blodeuwedd is both beauty and beast, the femme fatale as well as the soulful woman. Which form she takes – flowers or an owl – depends on how men perceive her.

In *The Owl Service* a painting of Blodeuwedd appears on the billiard-room wall of the house Alison and her family inhabit. The spirit of this woman, as Huw tells the local people, is coming. In a variety of ways ancestors of the main characters have tried to "rid themselves" of Blodeuwedd by locking her away, in the pattern on a dinner service, or in a painting on a wall, or in a glass case, but these actions have proven futile. Blodeuwedd is loose, and her spirit enters Alison.

The most striking reflection of Blodeuwedd in Alison occurs when Alison sees from her window what she takes to be her image in the stone fish tank by the lawn. Gwyn also watches the reflection. Both see Blodeuwedd since, as Gwyn later explains, the angle and distance render it impossible that Alison's reflection appear in the pond. Alison begins as a victim, but she becomes overweening, suffocating: she turns from flowers to owl. Garner gives expression to the overweening woman in Alison's mother, Margaret, who wishes to turn Alison into herself, to perpetuate her dominion.

Alison's flowerlike beauty naturally attracts the male, Gwyn. To Gwyn, the Welsh working-class lad, Alison represents status and success. His desire for her takes the form of the will to dominate, the desire to prove himself worthy of her by conquering her, as in the scene in which Gwyn stands in a dark room watching Alison and her stepfather outside and wills Alison to look at him: "Look at me, girl. Look this way. Look. Look. Look. . . . I'll show you who's boss. You'll look. You will look." Gwyn's later claim that he only wants Alison to be herself is self-deceiving. She responds, "And what's that?. . . . What you make me? I'm one person with Mummy, and another with you. I can't argue: you twist everything I say round to what you want. Is this fair?" Alison is caught between the protective mother and the desiring male. Were Gwyn to realize that he is at odds with Alison because she is what he makes of her, and that making her in the image of his bitterness is simply perpetuating the human desire for power, for ownership, for possession, then he might act.

To act is not possible for Gwyn, however; he too is passive, a result of his ambivalence toward his Welsh background, which makes him an outsider in the sophisticated English educated class to which he aspires. Caught and immobilized between two worlds, Gwyn suffers a crisis of identity that manifests itself in anger, but because much of the book's action is focalized through Gwyn, who has wit and a desire for an education, the reader has sympathy for him.

Instead of Gwyn, however, it is Alison's stepbrother, Roger, who proves capable of comforting her. The novel's end, which has disturbed many readers, is sound: because of his confused bitterness, Gwyn can see only the "owl" side of Alison's nature, whereas the priggish Roger has an appreciation of beauty that allows him to respond to her "flowers." Roger, in the end, understands what Huw has been trying to communicate all along: Alison must be what others perceive her to be. Roger, who does not suffer an identity crisis, reaches out to Alison and encourages her to develop her beauty rather than her domineering side. Consequently, he saves her.

Garner deliberately overturns the reader's expectations: the middle-class snob Roger comes off better than the sympathetic working-class lad Gwyn. The daring volte-face at the end does not destroy the book's social commentary, however, which is embodied in Huw and the Welsh countryside. In the actions of Roger, Gwyn, and Alison, Garner effectively dramatizes the creative and destructive powers of human imagining and also the intensity of adolescent emotions.

Garner's next novel, *Red Shift,* is more openly a love story. The author weaves the stories of three sets of people in three times: the contemporary story of Jan, Tom, and the German wine grower; the seventeenth-century story of Margery, Thomas Rowley, and Thomas Venables; and the story of Roman Britain, centering on an unnamed female and Macey, who has a sense of his own double nature. By weaving the stories together, Garner suggests they are coterminous. The characters often speak the same words, share the same landscape, possess the same ax head, and sense their counterparts in the other stories. A spirit of place reaches across time to prevent the land's desecration. The landscape itself has a sacred power.

This sacred power is also manifest in the female characters; the girl in the Roman story is a corn goddess who protects and heals Macey; Margery in the civil war story protects the visionary Thomas; and Jan tries to protect Tom from his parents and from the knowledge of her sexual relationship with her German employer. All three females have a special feeling for the ax, and all three are associated with the land as sanctuary. Each is a nurse and a guide; each is at the center of things; and each is violated.

The violation of the land results in frenzy, as when Tom sells the "real and special thing" between him and Jan, the ax head, and rapes her: the result is the release of negative forces: "Five fiends have been in poor Tom at once: of lust, as Obidicut; Hibbidence, prince of dumbness; Mahu, of stealing, Modo, of murder; Flibbertigibbet, of mopping and mowing." These "fiends" plague Tom as they plague his counterparts in history; the young men wrestle with the fiends, and a sign of their struggle is the epilepsy each experiences. The seizures these characters suffer are not moments of joyful ecstasy but rather a sign of their isolation and uncertainty. On the other hand, Garner, in his essay "Inner Time," speaks of epileptics as manifesting "their symptoms under the control of their will, in the service of the community, to heal the sick and to communicate with God." The characters in *Red Shift* appear confused and uncertain, but they do break through to understanding; they discover their connection to the land and hence to the stream of life.

The modern-day Tom is crucial. He says that he sees yet "can't understand." He has no words to explain, but he senses his situation. In a strange but beautiful paragraph, Garner reveals Tom's incipient sense of Jan's significance to his understanding. The two of them are in the church about to climb the tower and about to hear the escapement wheel jerk. Tom explains how he needs a change — what he calls a "red shift" — because he has "all the right answers at none of the right times":

Jan wanted no more than to hold him. Her words vented. Meaning meant nothing. She wanted him to let the hurt go. He could talk forever, but not stop holding her. Each second made him less dangerous. And she's not even listening. Why can't I use simple words? They don't stay simple long enough to be spoken. I have not come to terms with her eyes or the smell of her hair.

The point of view here blends author and characters. The drive is to meaning beyond words, to a language both intellectual and instinctual. Tom senses that Jan and he, together, are the escapement, the mechanical wheel that moves time and rings bells. The moment, however, is lost. Not until the end of the book does Tom understand that Jan is not the voice of his own soul, but rather that she is the spirit of that which is not himself, the other. No single escapement wheel exists.

At the end of the novel the dialogue of the characters in all three stories interconnects, and in doing so it presents the girl from the Roman story reassuring present-day Tom (and also Thomas and Macey) that she is with him. His reply is: "I was wrong." Recognizing Jan for herself and not for what he wants her to be, Tom can overleap the bounds of selfhood. Jan becomes the spirit of place, Tom's "alma mater." In the final pages of the book, he rejoices that he has "found words. . . . For what I wanted to tell."

The book's themes of consciousness, understanding, place, and language are clarified in the final two pages of the book – unnumbered pages originally meant to be decorative endpapers. They consist of the coded message Tom slips into Jan's bag before she leaves at the end of the novel. The code, based on a system invented by Lewis Carroll, prevented Tom's mother from reading his letters from Jan, and the message is an epiphany revealing Tom's sensitivity and creativity. He finally has his own words, words that reconcile intellect and imagination, reason and emotion.

In *The Stone Book Quartet,* Garner perfects what he has learned. Each book recounts one day in the life of a child, an auspicious day in which the child learns that life is both rational and mysterious. Garner dramatizes visionary encounters without writing romances. In each book a child is the link that connects the past to the present through place. The books present the reader with rites of passage in which child, place, and history unite.

The first of the series, *The Stone Book* (1976), turns on three visionary encounters. Mary, the child-hero, climbs the church steeple to take her father, a stonemason, his lunch. While there she rides the golden weathercock and feels "only the brilliant gold of the bird spinning the air." Mary feels she is atop the world, at the center of things. Her father tells her she will remember this day for the rest of her life, and Mary replies, "I already have."

In the second visionary encounter, Mary experiences the past as present. Mary's father takes her to a deep cave where he sends her alone on a journey, traditionally taken by the eldest children of Mary's family. Mary descends deep into the ground until she can go no farther, while behind her she unwinds a silken thread. At the bottom she discovers a rock known as "Tough Tom," and on a wall of rock she sees her father's mason's mark on a "doubled bull." Near the bull is a carved hand the same size as her own. This secret place is both mysterious and clear: "all things led to the bull and the mark and the hand in the cave."

The final visionary moment in *The Stone Book* comes when Mary's father responds to her earlier request for a prayer book by giving her a stone rubbed and shaped to look like a book bound in blue-black calf skin. In this stone book, Mary, who has not learned to read, may read "all the stories of the world." It holds the mysterious history of the ages. In it Mary discovers a natural language, the language of her father and the wisdom of her past. The novel ends with Mary sitting by the fire reading her stone book.

The second book of the quartet, *Granny Reardun* (1977), introduces Joseph, Mary's illegitimate son, on the day when he realizes what craft he will study. On his final day of school, Joseph realizes the importance of the smith to the community; in a profoundly moving passage, he recognizes his métier. With his hand on the iron latch of the school door, Joseph turns about:

> The school porch showed the view, a stone arch around the world, and Grandfather had made that. It framed Saint Philip's steeple and the weathercock.
>
> And then Joseph knew.

The moment is an epiphany. The stonemason, Joseph's grandfather, is at the periphery, but the golden weathercock made of iron is at the center.

Opposing images of center and circumference, fluidity and fixity, time past and time present, change and permanence, and life and death ring through *The Stone Book Quartet* in a manner free of the tensions and anxieties of *The Owl Service* and *Red Shift*. The most striking image of these paradoxes is in *The Aimer Gate* (1978), the third book in the sequence but the final book to be published. It is unflinchingly visionary and offers no clear answers. The book is set during World War I, and the future of the child-protagonist, Robert, is uncertain.

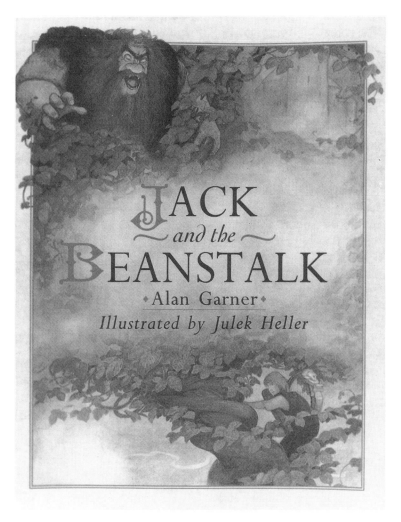

Dust jacket for Garner's version of a classic fairy tale

At the same time, Robert is what the future turns on; he is the escapement. In this book Garner elaborates the escapement metaphor, first introducing it in an oblique but beautiful passage early in the book. A crowd, including Robert, gathers at Leah's Hill to watch the cutting of the corn. Robert too watches. Before the cutting begins the three men who will cut the corn sharpen their scythes and the metal rings "like swords and bells" – the sounds of apocalypse, or the harmony of church and state. As Robert watches, the men stand in line and begin their swing.

It was a low swing, scythes and men like a big clock, back and to, back and to, against the hill they walked. They walked and swung, hips forward, letting weight cut. It was as if they were walking in a yellow water before them. Each blade came up in time with each blade, at Ozzie's march, for if they ever go out of time the blades would cut flesh and bone.

Like a great clock, the harvesters go "round the field, cutting a square spiral to the center."

In *The Aimer Gate* death threatens the forces of life. Craft, which began with the mason in *The Stone Book* and continued with the smith in *Granny Reardun,* now becomes destructive. Uncle Charlie is a British sniper in World War I; his craft is to kill. The rite of passage in this book takes place when Robert climbs up, as Mary in *The Stone Book* had climbed down, to his "secret cave in the air," high inside the chapel tower. He climbs as far as possible until he "was wearing the steeple. It fitted like a hat. He was wearing the steeple all the way to the earth, a stone dunce's cap."

Robert is thus portrayed as the fool, but without the fool's insight. Behind Robert stands his great grandfather, the stonemason in *The Stone Book,* and his father, the smith. Robert has arrived too late. His father tells him: "I don't know what there is for you to get aback of, youth." All Robert has is his secret, atop the church. If Robert is a disturbing character, it is because his vision is dreary, uncompromising; he puts the reader's sense of value to the test.

Robert's father teaches him how the chapel clock works. The complex mechanism of cogs and gears runs because of the escapement, the small wheel at the center that makes "so great a sound." "You couldn't have time without you had escapement," Robert's father says. He tells his son that the world needs a center: place, belief, family, whatever. "We're going at that much of a rattle, the whole blooming earth, moon and stars, we need escapement to hold us together."

Organic and mechanic metaphors join, but Robert does not understand that he *is* the escapement. Unlike his father and uncle he plays no instrument, but he sings; the music is internalized. He learns of death, and he learns he must get beyond death. His instincts are for fluency in giving, and the book ends with the tranquil after-image of escapement: father and uncle, smith and sniper, play their music while "the day swung in the chapel clock, escapement to the sun."

Robert's fate, however, remains a mystery. He does not make an appearance in the remaining book of the quartet, *Tom Fobble's Day* (1977). His absence, especially in light of his interest in becoming a soldier, is a reminder of discontinuity, as is the breaking of the stones of the Allman's house in *The Aimer Gate*. Indeed, war intrudes into these last two books of the sequence as a forceful reminder of death and disintegration. War not only kills or maims many of the men who wage it, but it also perverts crafts such as stonemasonry and smithing. Such perverting of craft leaves Robert with nothing to aspire to, no craft, no direction.

Tom Fobble's Day similarly offers its child-hero, William, no craft, but it chronicles a clear coming of age. At the beginning of the book, William is a child doing childish things. "Sledging" with Stewart Allman, William reveals that he is afraid to take his sledge down from the top of the great hill, and he allows the bigger boy to use and then to destroy his sledge. By the end of the book, William acquires a new sledge and with it the courage and confidence to overcome his fear of Stewart and the great hill. Even more powerful is William's putting aside childish war games for a sense of his own position in history. He learns that his responsibility is to preserve, not to break apart.

William's identity takes shape in his contact with his grandfather, Joseph, the young boy who set out to be a smith in *Granny Reardun*. He is rough and without sentimentality, but he fashions a sledge for William from bits of an old loom and an old forge. In dismantling the bellows handle from his forge, Joseph says goodbye to his craft; this is his day of retirement. In dismantling the old and unused loom, he is seemingly breaking something from the past, an object readers saw in *The Stone Book*. But Joseph's breaking of objects from the past does not signal disunity with that past. Instead, he fashions a sledge for his grandson from these fragments. His offering to William is a sledge of wood and iron that connects William to his ancestors. The sledge is a sacred object, and William senses this as he flashes down Leah's Hill:

> The line did hold. Through hand and eye, block, forge and loom to the hill and all that he owned, he sledged sledged sledged for the black and glittering night and the sky flying on fire and the expectation of snow.

This is the final paragraph of the book, and it rises to an apocalyptic pitch. The notion of ownership that it articulates is akin to that of Huw Halfbacon in *The Owl Services;* the land belongs to William because William belongs to the land. Fixity and movement, light and dark, fire and ice, all are brought into balance in an ecstatic night rite performed by William. Transmuted are the images of war, displaced by a grander vision of connectedness than the previous image of contention.

From the first pages of the book, war as contention and violence is evident both in the larger backdrop of the Battle of Britain (the time is 1941) and in the more local setting of boys' games. Three snowballs that strike William at the beginning of the book inaugurate the motif, and the boys also collect shrapnel that falls from the sky during air raids, with the most-prized pieces being those that are still hot. William even has an incendiary bomb. Late in the book, William rides his new sledge through the others on the hill, scattering them. As he does so, William pretends the sledge is a Spitfire and the others are enemy planes.

By the end of the book, however, both the real war and William's pretend war are transformed, precipitated by the death of Joseph, the grandfather who has been William's companion. Before he dies Joseph gives William the sledge, the key to the forge that has served Joseph for more than fifty years, the clay pipe that once belonged to Joseph's grandfather, and, after William, Tom Fobbles, the two horseshoes from inside Joseph's chimney. These objects are all talismans connecting the present with the past. Unlike the shrapnel and the incendiary bomb, they hold the meaning of family and community. They accomplish the transformation of war.

When William returns to his grandfather's home after his first ride on his new sledge, he discovers the house crowded with people. What's more, he sees that his grandfather is dying. This experience is not dark and despairing, rather it prompts William to empty his pockets of shrapnel, leaving the key and the pipe. To these he adds the horseshoes. Then he takes his sledge and goes back to Leah's Hill, where he sledges. The emptying of his pockets of shrapnel signals his putting away of childish things, and now the real war, as noted above, becomes the apocalyptic backdrop for his vision of connectedness.

In *The Stone Book Quartet,* Garner has gone far in polishing his craft. His desire was to get back to a language as pure as the spoken word of his forefathers and mothers. In *Tom Fobble's Day* the connection between Joseph the craftsman and Joseph the storyteller is clear. As he fashions the sledge for William, Joseph recalls anecdotes from his family history. At one point he tells William a story concerning old Robert, the owner of the clay pipe William has found. Joseph's language is as spare and tough as the sledge he makes, and his storytelling, as well as his making of the sledge, are analogous to Garner's craft.

Garner has produced no fiction since 1979 to compare with his major output. Instead, he has published several collections of folktales, a mark of his continued interest in both the preservation of artifacts from the past and the preservation of language at its purest. Garner says in the introduction to *The Lad of the Gad* (1980) that a folktale is "a collection of patterns to be translated with the skill, bias and authority of the craftsman, who, in serving his craft, allows that craft to serve the people." His desire is to preserve the tales in such a way that they carry with them the aura of the oral: "I have tried to place my literate ear in the way of a preliterate voice, so that, although the word in the air is not the same word on the page, the force may be recreated and felt." He says much the same in his introduction to *Alan Garner's Book of British Fairy Tales* (1983): "I have tried to get back, through the written word, to the sense of the spoken." From this perspective it is understandable why the dust jacket of his most recent book, *Jack and the Beanstalk* (1992), emphasizes the read-aloud quality of Garner's prose.

Garner's interest is in reanimating a tradition of British stories; he laments the passing of traditional fairy tales that were meant for the whole family, not just the children. The fairy tales he recreates are a link to the British past, and, as he

writes, "a healthy future grows from its past." Although he has compiled volumes of stories originating from outside the British isles — *The Hamish Hamilton Book of Goblins: An Anthology of Folklore* (1969) and *The Guizer: A Book of Fools* (1975), for example — he states in the introduction to the former volume that "Classical myth leaves me as cold as its marble." His abiding interest is in a pure northern air, and this interest has pushed his folktale writing to an extreme of ritualistic rhythms and repetitions. In content he gravitates to stories of the guizer, the fool, or the trickster figure who inhabits the borders of the real and the unreal, the lazy and the industrious, the foolish and the wise.

It is difficult to know how Garner's fiction will evolve, but a look at *The Breadhorse* (1975), one of Garner's few picture books, offers a clue. As Neil Philip suggests in *A Fine Anger: A Critical Introduction to the Work of Alan Garner* (1981), *The Breadhorse* is the story of a young boy's "flight back into humanity, through dreams." In the playground game of breadhorses, young Ned is always the horse, who has to carry the others on his back. His dream of riding a magnificent horse gives him the insight that the one who bears the others partakes of the magnificence of a great dream horse. This dream connects the story with Garner's conception of folktale, a type of story that records the dream of a community. Through connection with the dreams of the folk, readers receive a sense of identity, purpose, and security. Garner, after the anger of the early works up until *Red Shift,* has reached the point of accepting his craft as a national storyteller. He is recasting the sources of British culture through his retelling of British folktales.

Interviews:

"Coming to Terms," *Children's Literature in Education,* 2 (July 1970): 15–27;

Justin Wintle and Emma Fisher, "Interview with Alan Garner," in their *The Pied Piper: Interviews with the Influential Creators of Children's Literature* (New York: Paddington, 1975), pp. 221–235;

Cornelia Jones and Olivia R. Way, "Alan Garner," in their *British Children's Authors: Interviews at Home* (Chicago: American Library Association, 1976), pp. 94–100;

Aidan Chambers, "An Interview with Alan Garner," *Signal,* 17 (September 1978): 118–137;

"Interview," *Labrys,* 7 (1981): 80–87.

References:

Norma Bagnall, "An American Hero in Welsh Fantasy: *The Mabinogion,* Alan Garner, and Lloyd

Alexander," *New Welsh Review,* 2 (Spring 1990): 26–29;

Sarah Beach, "Breaking the Pattern: Alan Garner's *The Owl Service* and *The Mabinogion,*" *Mythlore,* 20 (Winter 1994): 10–14;

Michael Benton, "Detective Imagination," *Children's Literature in Education,* 13 (March 1974): 5–13;

Eleanor Cameron, "*The Owl Service*: A Study," in *Children's Literature: Criticism and Response,* edited by Mary Lou White (Columbus, Ohio: Merrill, 1976), pp. 191–200;

Emrys Evans, "Children's Novels and Welsh Mythology: Multiple Voices in Susan Cooper and Alan Garner," in *The Voice of the Narrator in Children's Literature,* edited by Charlotte F. Otten and Gary D. Schmidt (New York: Greenwood Press, 1989), pp. 92–100;

Peter J. Foss, "The Undefined Boundary: Converging Worlds in the Early Novels of Alan Garner," *New Welsh Review,* 2 (Spring 1990): 30–35;

Carolyn Gillies, "Possession and Structure in the Novels of Alan Garner," *Children's Literature in Education,* 18 (Fall 1975): 107–117;

Labrys, special issue on Garner, 7 (1981);

Maria Nikolajeva, "The Insignificance of Time: *Red Shift,*" *Children's Literature Association Quarterly,* 14 (Fall 1989): 128–131;

Philippa Pearce, "*The Owl Service,*" in *The Cool Web: The Pattern of Children's Reading,* edited by Margaret Meek, Aidan Warlow, and Griselda Barton (London: Bodley Head, 1977), pp. 291–293;

Neil Philip, *A Fine Anger: A Critical Introduction to the Work of Alan Garner* (London: Collins, 1981);

David Rees, "Hanging in Their True Shapes," in his *The Marble in the Water* (Boston: Horn Book, 1980), pp. 56–67;

Mavis Reimer, "The Family as Mythic Reservoir in Alan Garner's *Stone Book Quartet,*" *Children's Literature Association Quarterly,* 14 (Fall 1989): 132–135;

John Rowe Townsend, "Alan Garner," in his *A Sounding of Storytellers* (New York: Lippincott, 1979), pp. 81–94;

Victor Watson, "In Defense of Jan: Love and Betrayal in *The Owl Service* and *Red Shift,*" *Signal,* 41 (1983): 77–87.

Papers:

A collection of Alan Garner's manuscripts is held at Brigham Young University, Provo, Utah.

Rumer Godden

(10 December 1907 –   )

Patricia H. Ward
College of Charleston

BOOKS: *Chinese Puzzle* (London: Davies, 1936);

The Lady and the Unicorn (London: Davies, 1937);

Black Narcissus (London: Davies, 1939; Boston: Little, Brown, 1939);

Gypsy, Gypsy (London: Davies, 1940; Boston: Little, Brown, 1940);

Breakfast with the Nikolides (London: Davies, 1942; Boston: Little, Brown, 1942);

Rungli-Rungliot (Thus Far and No Further) (London: Davies, 1943); republished as *Rungli-Rungliot Means in Paharia, Thus Far and No Further* (Boston: Little, Brown, 1946; London: Macmillan, 1961);

A Fugue in Time (London: M. Joseph, 1945); republished as *Take Three Tenses: A Fugue in Time* (Boston: Little, Brown, 1945);

Bengal Journey: A Story of the Part Played by Women in the Province, 1939–1945 (London: Longmans, Green, 1945);

The River (London: M. Joseph, 1946; Boston: Little, Brown, 1946);

The Dolls' House, illustrated by Dana Saintsbury (London: M. Joseph, 1947; New York: Viking, 1948); republished, illustrated by Tasha Tudor (London: Macmillan, 1962); republished as *Tottie,* illustrated by Joanna Jamieson (Harmondsworth: Puffin, 1983);

A Candle for St. Jude (London: M. Joseph, 1948; New York: Viking, 1948);

In Noah's Ark (London: M. Joseph, 1949; New York: Viking, 1949);

A Breath of Air (London: M. Joseph, 1950; New York: Viking, 1951);

The Mousewife, illustrated by William Pene du Bois (London: Macmillan, 1951; New York: Viking, 1951); republished, illustrated by Heidi Holder (New York: Viking, 1982; London: Macmillan, 1983);

Kingfishers Catch Fire (London: Macmillan, 1953; New York: Viking, 1953);

Rumer Godden (courtesy of Macmillan Children's Books)

Hans Christian Andersen: A Great Life in Brief (New York: Knopf, 1954; London: Hutchinson, 1955);

Impunity Jane: The Story of a Pocket Doll, illustrated by Adrienne Adams (New York: Viking, 1954; London: Macmillan, 1955);

An Episode of Sparrows (New York: Viking, 1955; London: Macmillan, 1956);

The Fairy Doll, illustrated by Adams (London: Macmillan, 1956; New York: Viking, 1956); republished, illustrated by Pauline Baynes (London: Magnet, 1984); republished, illustrated by Penny Ives (New York: Philomel, 1995);

Mooltiki, and Other Stories and Poems of India (London: Macmillan, 1957); republished as *Mooltiki: Stories and Poems from India* (New York: Viking, 1958);

Mouse House, illustrated by Adams (New York: Viking, 1957; London: Macmillan, 1958);

The Greengage Summer (London: Macmillan, 1958; New York: Viking, 1958);

The Story of Holly and Ivy, illustrated by Adams (London: Macmillan, 1958; New York: Viking, 1958); republished, illustrated by Barbara Cooney (New York: Viking, 1985);

Candy Floss, illustrated by Adams (London: Macmillan, 1960; New York: Viking, 1960); republished, illustrated by Nonny Hogrogian (New York: Philomel, 1991);

China Court: The Hours of a Country House (London: Macmillan, 1961; New York: Morrow, 1961);

St. Jerome and the Lion, illustrated by Jean Primrose (London: Macmillan, 1961; New York: Viking, 1961);

Miss Happiness and Miss Flower, illustrated by Primrose (London: Macmillan, 1961; New York: Viking, 1961);

Little Plum, illustrated by Primrose (London: Macmillan, 1963; New York: Viking, 1963);

The Battle of the Villa Fiorita (London: Macmillan, 1963; New York: Viking, 1963);

Home is the Sailor, illustrated by Primrose (London: Macmillan, 1964; New York: Viking, 1964);

Two Under the Indian Sun, by Godden and Jon Godden (London: Macmillan, 1966; New York: Knopf & Viking, 1966);

The Kitchen Madonna, illustrated by Carol Barker (London: Macmillan, 1967; New York: Viking, 1967);

Gone: A Thread of Stories (New York: Viking, 1968); republished as *Swans and Turtles: Stories* (London: Macmillan, 1968);

In This House of Brede (London: Macmillan, 1969; New York: Viking, 1969);

Operation Sippacik, illustrated by James Bryan (London: Macmillan, 1969; New York: Viking, 1969);

The Tale of the Tales: The Beatrix Potter Ballet (London: Warne, 1971; New York: Warne, 1971);

Shiva's Pigeons: An Experience of India, by Godden and Jon Godden, photographs by Stella Snead (London: Chatto & Windus, 1972; New York: Viking, 1972);

The Diddakoi, illustrated by Creina Glegg (London: Macmillan, 1972; New York: Viking, 1972);

The Old Woman Who Lived in a Vinegar Bottle, illustrated by Mairi Hedderwick (London: Macmillan, 1972; New York: Viking, 1972);

The Peacock Spring (London: Macmillan, 1975; New York: Viking, 1975);

Mr. McFadden's Hallowe'en, illustrated by Ann Strugnell (London: Macmillan, 1975; New York: Viking, 1975);

The Butterfly Lions: The Story of the Pekingese in History, Legend, and Art (London: Macmillan, 1977; New York: Viking, 1978);

The Rocking Horse Secret, illustrated by Juliet Stanwell Smith (London: Macmillan, 1977; New York: Viking, 1978);

A Kindle of Kittens, illustrated by Lynne Byrnes (London: Macmillan, 1978; New York: Viking, 1979);

Five for Sorrow, Ten for Joy (London: Macmillan, 1979; New York: Viking, 1979);

Gulbadan: Portrait of a Rose Princess at the Mughal Court (London: Macmillan, 1980; New York: Viking, 1981);

The Dragon of Og, illustrated by Pauline Baynes (London: Macmillan, 1981; New York: Viking, 1981);

The Dark Horse (London: Macmillan, 1981; New York: Viking, 1982);

The Valiant Chatti-Maker, illustrated by Jeroo Roy (London: Macmillan, 1983; New York: Viking, 1983);

Thursday's Children (London: Macmillan, 1984; New York: Viking, 1984);

A Time to Dance, No Time to Weep (London: Macmillan, 1987; New York: Morrow, 1987);

A House with Four Rooms (London: Macmillan, 1989; New York: Morrow, 1989);

Fu-Dog, illustrated by Valerie Littlewood (London: MacRae, 1989; New York: Viking, 1989);

Indian Dust, by Godden and Jon Godden (London: Macmillan, 1989); republished as *Mercy, Pity, Peace, and Love* (New York: Morrow, 1989);

Coromandel Sea Change (London: Macmillan, 1991; New York: Morrow, 1991);

Listen to the Nightingale (London: Macmillan, 1992; New York: Viking, 1992);

Great Grandfather's House, illustrated by Littlewood (London: MacRae, 1992; New York: Greenwillow, 1993);

Pippa Passes (London: Macmillan, 1994; New York: Morrow, 1994).

Collections: *Four Dolls,* illustrated by Pauline Baynes (London: Macmillan, 1983; New York: Greenwillow, 1984) – comprises *Impu-*

nity Jane: The Story of a Pocket Doll, The Fairy Doll, The Story of Holly and Ivy, and *Candy Floss;*

Mouse Time: Two Stories, illustrated by Jane Pinkney (London: Macmillan, 1993) – comprises *The Mousewife* and *Mouse House.*

MOTION PICTURES: *The River,* screenplay by Godden and Jean Renoir, United Artists, 1951;

Innocent Sinners, screenplay by Godden and Neil Patterson, Universal Pictures, 1958.

OTHER: Carmen Bernos de Gasztold, *Prayers from the Ark,* translated, with a preface, by Godden, illustrated by Jean Primrose (New York: Viking, 1962; London: Macmillan, 1963); republished, illustrated by Barry Moser (New York: Viking, 1992);

Hans Christian Andersen, *The Feather Duster: A Fairy Tale Musical,* text adapted by Godden, music by Kai Normann Andersen (Chicago: Dramatic Publishing, 1964);

Carmen Bernos de Gasztold, *The Beasts' Choir,* translated, with a foreword, by Godden, illustrated by Primrose (London: Macmillan, 1965); republished as *The Creatures' Choir* (New York: Viking, 1965);

Round the Day: Poetry Programmes for the Classroom or Library, compiled by Godden, assisted by Margaret Bell (London: Macmillan, 1966);

Round the Year: Poetry Programmes for the Classroom or Library, compiled by Godden, assisted by Bell (London: Macmillan, 1966);

The World Around: Poetry Programmes for the Classroom or Library, compiled by Godden, assisted by Bell (London: Macmillan, 1966);

Olga S. Manders, *Mrs. Manders' Cook Book,* edited by Godden (New York: Viking, 1968);

Emily Dickinson, *A Letter to the World: Poems for Young Readers,* edited by Godden, illustrated by Prudence Seward (New York: Macmillan, 1968; London: Bodley Head, 1968);

The Raphael Bible, edited by Godden (London: Macmillan, 1970; New York: Viking, 1970).

SELECTED PERIODICAL PUBLICATIONS – UNCOLLECTED: "An Imaginary Correspondence," *Horn Book Magazine,* 39 (1963): 369–375;

"Beatrix Potter," *Horn Book Magazine,* 42 (1966): 391–398;

"The Will to Write," *Writer,* 98 (May 1985): 13–15, 46;

"A Little Tale That Anyone Could Write," *Horn Book Magazine,* 63 (1987): 301–307;

"Shining Popocatapetl: Poetry for Children," *Horn Book Magazine,* 64 (1988): 305–314;

"Hans Andersen, Writer," *Horn Book Magazine,* 66 (1990): 554–562.

A prolific writer of novels, short fiction, and nonfiction for adults as well as novels, stories, and poetry for children, Rumer Godden conveys in her works the plight and triumph of children separated from their parents, the difficulty of adjusting to new cultures and situations, the need for love and belonging, the importance of place and a stable home life, and the power and responsibility of the individual – adult, child, or animal – to solve problems and overcome obstacles. Her works for children include realistic fiction, doll stories, animal stories, ballet stories, and retellings of folktales. Her biographies of Hans Christian Andersen and Beatrix Potter, as well as various essays and speeches on the art of writing, emphasize the discipline involved in the production of exceptional children's literature.

Margaret Rumer Godden was born in Eastbourne, Sussex, on 10 December 1907, the second of four daughters. Her father, Arthur Leigh Godden, was a steamer agent stationed in India. Her mother, Katherine Norah Hingley Godden, came from a family of successful iron and steel manufacturers. When she was six months old, Godden's parents took her to India, where she remained until she was five. In 1913 her parents sent her and her older sister, Jon, back to England to be reared by their paternal grandmother and their aunt. During this period Godden was confronted for the first time with the differences between the indulged and almost princely life of Europeans in India and the strict, pious life of a traditional English home. The danger of raids in London precipitated the return of the sisters to India in November 1914.

Godden has described her childhood in India as "halcyon." As children she and her sisters were accustomed to making books – not simply writing stories but actually trimming the pages and sewing them together. Her only formal education in India was during the summer months when the family escaped the heat at various hill-country resorts. When she and her sisters were sent to school in England in 1920, the halcyon days were over. Godden attended five different schools in two years, finally completing her education at Moira House in Sussex, an unconventional school where she found "peace and opportunity" to write under the direction of her teacher and friend, Mona Swann. This difficult pe-

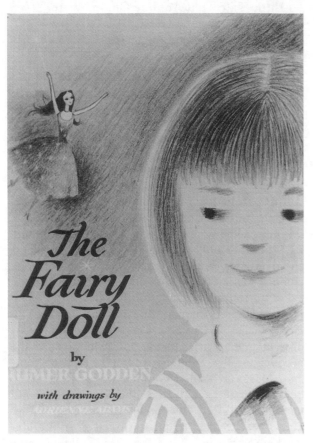

Dust jacket for one of Godden's popular doll stories

riod in the author's life is frequently paralleled in the lives of her young protagonists. After Moira House she studied ballet, and in 1928, three years after returning to India, she opened her own dancing school in Calcutta, which she ran for eight years. Away from family (her father had retired and the family moved to Cornwall) and restrictive English society, Godden became involved with a young stockbroker, Laurence Sinclair Foster; they married in 1934 in Calcutta after she discovered she was pregnant. The baby, David, died four days after his birth.

Godden's literary career began in 1935, when, on the same day she gave birth to a daughter, Jane, the novel *Chinese Puzzle* (1936) was accepted for publication. This book and her next novel, *The Lady and the Unicorn* (1937), were favorably reviewed but were not financial successes and have never been published in America. After the birth of her second daughter, Paula, in September 1938 at Godden's parents' home in Cornwall, her third novel, *Black Narcissus,* was published in January 1939 and achieved instant popularity on both sides of the Atlantic.

In 1939 Godden and her children returned to India to escape the war, and from September 1941 to March 1942 they lived at Jinglam, a bungalow on the Rungli-Rungliot Tea Estate in the Himalayas — the experience is the subject of her Himalayan diary, *Rungli-Rungliot (Thus Far and No Further)* (1943). With other army wives she and her children evacuated to the Kashmir region, where she lived in a remote mountain farmhouse with her children and nephew for almost three years; many of her experiences at Dove House were similar to those of Sophie Barrington Ward in *Kingfishers Catch Fire* (1953). Upon returning to Calcutta in 1944, Godden was asked by the Women's Voluntary Service to write a book about the contribution of Englishwomen to the war effort in India. Also at about this time, her husband's firm discovered that he had embezzled company funds. Without consulting Godden he joined the army and left her to repay his debts. The two later divorced.

Godden toured Bengal in 1945 and, while revisiting her childhood home of Narayangunj, began to write *The River* (1946). In her memoir *A Time to Dance, No Time to Weep* (1987), Godden recalls that the two treasures she brought back to England in 1945 were a precious Agra rug and the completed manuscript of *The River*.

After returning to England, Godden published her first children's novel, *The Dolls' House* (1947). As she admitted in an interview with Emma Fisher, it is the most sophisticated and satisfying of her doll stories. In *A House with Four Rooms* (1989) she comments, "I cannot judge my own books but I know I have not touched this standard since except perhaps in *The Mousewife*" (1951). In *The Dolls' House* Godden portrays in miniature human relationships and conflicts and emphasizes the necessity of inner strength, love, and sacrifice in confronting and overcoming the devastating forces of hatred and selfishness.

The story focuses on the relationships of four dolls of different composition and background who are brought together by their owners, sisters named Charlotte and Emily Dane. The protagonist of the story is Tottie Plantagenet, a small wooden Dutch farthing doll who has remained in the family of her present owners for a century and who provides a source of strength for the other dolls living in a shoebox with her: Mr. Plantagenet, the "father," an anxious doll who can never forget the abuse and neglect he suffered at the hands of previous owners; Birdie, the "mother," a light celluloid doll who is always cheerful but "not quite right in the head"; and Apple, the baby, who constantly gets into mischief.

Although the dolls cannot speak, they manage to communicate with each other, but they can only make their desires known to people by wishing very hard. Tottie teaches the Plantagenets to wish for a house, and eventually Charlotte and Emily receive a dusty Victorian dollhouse that had belonged to their Great-great-aunt Laura – a house in which Tottie used to live. Godden lavishly details the work of cleaning the house, fixing the furniture (even covering the sofa in petit point), and hanging real lace curtains. Charlotte and Emily finally move the doll family into the house, where the dolls intend to live happily ever after.

A conflict between good and evil ensues, however, when Tottie's old enemy, Marchpane, a beautiful and cruel china-and-kid doll, comes to live in the house. Although intimidated by Marchpane, Tottie claims strength from the hard wood of the tree she came from; she endures Marchpane's insults but suspects danger. When a burning candle almost sets Apple on fire as Marchpane smiles and watches, Birdie saves him but is herself destroyed. Although they never comprehend the whole story of conflict in the dolls' house, Charlotte and Emily realize that Marchpane has caused the tragedy, and they donate her to a museum where she can remain under glass to be admired but not touched. The Plantagenets mourn Birdie's demise, recognizing that "things come and things pass," but they still feel her presence in the house.

In *The Dolls' House* Godden establishes the rules followed in her other doll stories: dolls are meant to be played with and loved by children (that Marchpane does not want to be touched or played with reveals her defective doll nature); and dolls cannot do for themselves but are "done by" – unless a particularly sensitive and astute child hears their wishes, they are utterly powerless to effect change. Thus, the dolls' house mirrors the child's world and becomes an important metaphor for confronting and overcoming conflict.

In all of her stories Godden uses meticulous description, particularly of houses, furnishings, and objects; consequently she has been accused of caring more for things than for her characters. Hassell Simpson defends the author's use of description on the grounds that it contributes "emotional atmosphere" and affirms conventional ideals of "love and security, beauty and order, dignity and permanence." Related to Godden's love of detail is her attention to process – the process by which a dollhouse is restored or a conflict resolved; often the two are simultaneous.

In *The Dolls' House* and in most of her doll stories, the dolls' dialogue is in counterpoint to that of the humans; as Lois Rostow Kuznets has observed, this device is "suggestive of the silent, subterranean communication going on between the children and dolls." For example, when Charlotte asks Emily how they will make the money needed to furnish the dolls' house, the Plantagenets echo, "How?" Emily answers, "Somehow." In most of her children's books Godden also uses the device, as Fisher describes it, of having "characters break into the narrative and say something, as if the story was being told to them." Thus, in *Impunity Jane: The Story of a Pocket Doll* (1954), Godden describes the doll's first ride on a toy sailboat: "Most people would have been afraid and fallen overboard, like the lead sailor, but, 'Imp-imp-impunity,' sang Impunity Jane and reached the far side wet but perfectly safe." Godden claims that the device "gives enormous depth and naturalness to it; you suddenly see the person through another character's eyes." It is a device she uses frequently.

Godden has written seven doll stories since *The Dolls' House: Impunity Jane, The Fairy Doll* (1956), *The Story of Holly and Ivy* (1958), *Candy Floss* (1960), *Miss Happiness and Miss Flower* (1961), *Little Plum* (1963), and *Home is the Sailor* (1964). Acceptance, belonging, and learning to surmount obstacles are central to each; and in each, one or more dolls is instrumental in helping a child, and the doll and child are happier because of their relationship. In her interview with Fisher, Godden commented that her doll stories needed to have an ending in which good prevailed. Using *Candy Floss* as an example, she asserted, "one couldn't let Clementina Davenport win. . . . It is a story of conflict, and naturally you want the one you are involved with to win. Practically all good children's books have a very strong moral, even though you don't say it. I do believe a children's book must be ethical." All of Godden's children's stories have a strong, implicit moral. In addition, her best stories portray the triumph of an underdog protagonist – human, doll, or animal – through hard work, determination, and love.

Impunity Jane is the story of a doll who has been neglected by successive generations of little girls in the same family. As a sturdy and strongly jointed pocket doll who can be "dropped with impunity," she belongs not in a doll house on an uncomfortably beaded cushion but in the pocket of an adventurous child. She gets her wish – after more than fifty years – when Gideon spies Impunity Jane in his cousin Ellen's dollhouse and decides to steal her. In Gideon's pocket she shares his adventures,

The icon in Godden's The Kitchen Madonna *(1967), illustrated by Carol Barker*

but she senses her new owner's guilt in having stolen her and thus wishes to be returned to Ellen. When Gideon does return her, he finds that his cousin is getting rid of her dolls; he asks for Impunity Jane, who becomes his mascot. *Impunity Jane* is the simplest and most lighthearted of the doll stories, more the story of a doll who finally gets her wish than the account of a child who matures after many painful trials.

In the next of Godden's doll stories, *The Fairy Doll,* Elizabeth, who is the youngest of four siblings, never seems to do anything right. At age four she notices the fairy doll on top of the Christmas tree and believes it is alive. When, at seven, she still cannot do anything right, her great-grandmother tells her she needs a good fairy. Elizabeth appropriates the fairy doll, makes a fairy home for it, and begins to get "tings" in her head, presumably from the fairy doll's wand, as she learns to think for herself and solve her own problems. When the fairy doll is lost, Elizabeth believes she cannot act on her own, but with the encouragement of her

great-grandmother she finds that she can. The next Christmas, Elizabeth finds the fairy doll in its usual place with the other Christmas decorations, but she does not need it anymore, for the doll "has done her work." Unlike *Impunity Jane,* this story is concerned almost wholly with the rather painful experiences of a child learning to become independent. The doll helps the child much more than the child helps the doll, and the fairy doll's fate of being packed away once again is not portrayed as tragic.

The relationship between child and doll is more mutually rewarding in *The Story of Holly and Ivy.* It "is a story about wishing," but this time the doll, the child, and even an adult do the wishing. Holly, a Christmas doll in Mr. Blossom's village toy shop, wishes to have her own girl. Ivy is a lonely six-year-old orphan who is being sent by train to another orphanage to spend Christmas. Instead of going to the orphanage, however, Ivy goes in search of a grandmother. Mrs. Jones, a policeman's wife with no children of her own, trims her Christmas tree for the first time in years, hoping that she will be able to share it with a child. Through incredible coincidences, all three characters get their wish: Holly and Ivy get each other, and Ivy is adopted by the Joneses. Although the outcome is predictable, children can find satisfaction in the clear ways that the characters' needs and desires are realized.

Like *The Fairy Doll, Candy Floss* is about a doll's positive influence on a child. The plot reverses that of *Impunity Jane,* for although Impunity Jane waits fifty years to get her wish, Candy Floss has everything she could wish for at the beginning. Along with Cocoa the dog and Nuts the wooden horse, Candy Floss lives in a coconut shy (a throwing game at a fair) with a young man named Jack. Her life is perfect until they go to the biggest fair of all, near London. A spoiled rich girl, Clementina Davenport, spies Candy Floss and wants her, but when Jack will not sell, Clementina steals her. Since dolls can make no sounds, Jack does not hear Candy Floss's shrieks, and her wish to be returned is not immediately felt by Clementina. Clementina soon begins to feel guilty, however, and having accidentally broken the china doll, she throws Candy Floss down and tells her she is horrid. Clementina begins to feel horrid herself when she hears the music from the fairground, and she finally feels compelled to return the doll to Jack. Jack repairs Candy Floss and allows Clementina to work in the coconut shy. Thus, Candy Floss returns to her idyllic existence, and Clementina learns responsibility.

With *Miss Happiness and Miss Flower,* its sequel *Little Plum,* and *Home is the Sailor,* Godden returns to the novel form. Like *The Dolls' House,* these stories emphasize the interdependence of dolls and their owners, and once again conflicts arise that must be resolved through the dolls' wishes and human agency. Nona, a shy, motherless girl who has lived her eight years on her father's tea plantation in India, has been sent to live with relatives in England. Soon after arriving in England, Nona and her younger cousin Belinda receive two Japanese dolls from an American relative. The story depicts Nona's gradual and initially painful adjustment to a strange new place and culture as she attempts to build a Japanese dollhouse that will make Miss Happiness and Miss Flower feel more at home in their alien surroundings. In minute detail Godden includes all of the steps necessary in completing the house (a detailed house plan is even included), and at each step Nona has to overcome timidity and diffidence to accomplish her goal. When the house is finally finished after many obstacles, including interruptions from the demands of school and lack of funds to buy materials, Nona has completely adjusted to her new life. Similar to *The Fairy Doll* in its portrayal of the awkward adjustment of a shy child, *Miss Happiness and Miss Flower* also emphasizes the child's ability to solve her own problems. The striking parallelism between the plight of Nona and that of the Japanese dolls (both Nona and the dolls are sent away without being consulted), as well as a lack of a sentimental or contrived ending, makes *Miss Happiness and Miss Flower* the best of this group.

The period between *The Dolls' House* and *The Mousewife* brought many changes. In 1949 Godden married James L. Haynes-Dixon, a civil servant, and moved from London to Sussex. In autumn she made her first trip to America. In addition to publishing a narrative poem, *In Noah's Ark* (1949), and a novel adapting the plot of William Shakespeare's *The Tempest* (1623) as *A Breath of Air* (1950), Godden also traveled to India in 1949 and 1950 to oversee the filming of *The River,* for which she wrote the screenplay in collaboration with Jean Renoir.

Certainly one of Godden's best and most moving stories is *The Mousewife,* which is about striving for "something more" to bring meaning to ordinary life. A story that Godden claims to have written in fifty-five minutes, it conveys the theme that fulfillment in life requires courage and risk, but the rewards of such risk are knowledge, wisdom, and friendship. Inspired by an entry in Dorothy Wordsworth's journal about a mouse who befriends a caged dove, Godden's story begins with a description of the mousewife, who looks like other mice and does what they do but is "different from the rest": she wants more. She wonders about the world outside of Miss Barbara Wilkinson's house, where she lives. Sometimes she creeps up on the windowsill to look outside and wonders about what she sees. Her selfish husband is unsympathetic: "I think about cheese. . . . Why don't you think about cheese?"

After her husband is put to bed with indigestion from the currants in the Christmas cake, the mousewife is left to do all the foraging and cleaning. She goes to steal the peas and fat left untouched in the cage of a newly captured dove. Although initially scared away by the dove's movement and cooing, she ventures back. As she gets to know the dove and learns about his life outside the house, she no longer sees him as "large and strange and ugly" but feels genuine empathy for him. When her life is further complicated by a nestful of babies as well as her still-recuperating husband, she is not able to visit the dove for a while. When she is finally able to slip off for a visit, she finds that the dove is drooping from not eating and will die if he is not set free. She decides that night to release him, and as she watches him fly off she sees the stars, a gift "given to few mice." When the mousewife is very old, her great-great-great-grandchildren have great respect for her, because they suspect that even though she looks like other mice, "she knows something they do not." Although compared by critics to *The Dolls' House* because both have tiny protagonists, *The Mousewife* does not follow the typical pattern of Godden's doll stories. The mousewife is not a passive protagonist depending on a human being to carry out her wishes; she is capable of making and executing her own decisions, and as a result, her worldview is enlarged.

Godden's *Mooltiki, and Other Stories and Poems of India* (1957) is a collection of works that had been previously published in various periodicals. The publication of the adult novel *The Greengage Summer* (1958) followed, a work that has more recently been republished as a young adult novel. Like *The River* it is a coming-of-age story and draws heavily on the experiences of Godden, her sisters, and their mother while touring the battlefields of France after World War I. In the novel five children ranging in age from four to sixteen are left to fend for themselves at the Hotel des Oeillets when their mother becomes seriously ill. Reviewers and critics of Godden's adult novels have generally considered the book weaker than *Kingfishers Catch Fire,* which, along with *An Episode of Sparrows* (1955), *The Battle of the Villa Fiorita* (1963), and the children's novel *The*

Diddakoi (1972), employs what Simpson calls the "children adrift" motif, typically with a contrived, deus ex machina ending.

Godden returned to the children's novel with *The Kitchen Madonna* (1967), a moving story illustrating a child's ability to overcome personal barriers and accomplish a worthwhile goal. In this story Gregory, a quiet nine-year-old, is "oddly out of things at home." He is shy and withdrawn, but his younger sister Janet is pretty and outgoing. They discover that their Ukrainian housekeeper, Marta, is homesick for a "good place," a corner in the kitchen with a decorated Madonna and Child picture. Determined to make a good place for Marta, Gregory searches for an icon; after many attempts to find the perfect one, he discovers, quite by accident, a "dressed-up picture" of a Madonna called Our Lady of Czestochowa, Queen of Poland. Realizing that a decorated picture is what Marta had in mind, Gregory sets about to construct one for her.

The story details his efforts to obtain the fabrics, beads, and other decorations as well as the challenges and frustrations involved in constructing the picture – all efforts that force him to act independently. Marta is overwhelmed with joy by the picture Gregory makes, and Gregory's mother is touched that Gregory has opened his heart to another person. *The Kitchen Madonna* is similar to *Miss Happiness and Miss Flower* in characterization and plot development. The protagonists of both works mature as they face new challenges in accomplishing their goals. Like Nona in *Miss Happiness and Miss Flower,* Gregory has to overcome his diffidence to complete his task, and in the process he makes new friends.

Godden's next children's novel, *Operation Sippacik* (1969), is a departure from her earlier stories about dolls, mice, or lonely children; a recipient of the 1969 Children's Book of the Year Award from the Child Study Association, *Operation Sippacik* is an adventure story in which a boy and his donkey unexpectedly become heroes. It is set in Cyprus during a conflict between Greek and Turkish Cypriots. After United Nations British troops buy the donkey, Sippacik (meaning "very small donkey"), from twelve-year-old Rifat's grandfather, they spoil it so badly that they cannot make the donkey do any work. They hire Rifat to cajole the donkey into hauling their heavy equipment to their headquarters.

On one of these trips Rifat encounters a seriously wounded man who turns out to be his father, a Turkish soldier who had been forced into exile years earlier. With the help of Sippacik, Rifat attempts to smuggle his father through enemy lines. Although the UN forces must maintain their neutrality, the captain orders a "surprise night mission" to create a diversion so that Rifat can get through. As in all of her children's books, Godden pays careful attention to detail, but in this story her descriptions are more harshly graphic – the appearance of the father's wound, the smell of blood, the cuffings Rifat receives from his grandfather, and the blows Sippacik receives from a stick with a nail. *Operation Sippacik* is the first of Godden's children's novels to incorporate such starkly realistic details.

The Diddakoi reveals an unfortunate combination of realism and sentimentality. *Diddakoi* is a Sussex term for a half-Gypsy child. The novel is about Kizzy Lovell's difficult adjustment to the non-Gypsy ways of Amberhurst village after the death of her grandmother. She is bullied by the children at school and on one occasion is attacked and brutally beaten by a gang of "respectable" schoolgirls. With the help of her patient guardian, Miss Brooke, and the local lord of the manor, Adm. Sir Archibald Cunningham Twiss, Kizzy begins to accept her new life, and after one of the schoolgirls rescues her and Miss Brooke from a cottage fire, Kizzy becomes friends with the children at school. Miss Brooke and the admiral get married and adopt Kizzy.

As in her adult novels, Godden expresses an understanding and acceptance of an alien culture and a sympathy for Kizzy's plight, perhaps because the author had experienced a difficult adjustment when first sent to school in England. With the exception of Miss Brooke and the admiral, the adults in the novel, though well-meaning, are insensitive: they expect Kizzy to accept their ways unquestioningly and expect the other children to treat Kizzy well, but they do not try to understand her ways. Although the book received the 1972 Children's Book of the Year Award from the Child Study Association, the 1973 Whitbread Children's Book Award, and Holland's Silver Pen for the Children's Book of the Year, reviewers and critics have found fault with the story's contrived ending and excessive sentimentality. Of this abandoned-child story, Simpson comments, "Although the now familiar recipe is stirred up with fresh spices, nevertheless the ingredients are recognizable as having been measured out from other shelves in the Godden pantry."

The Old Woman Who Lived in a Vinegar Bottle (1972), a picture book for younger children, was the first of Godden's three folktale adaptations. Told on hair-washing nights for four generations in the Godden family, it is a story about the importance of gratitude and of not taking things for granted. The Old Woman lives a simple life in a "vinegar bottle" (oast house) with her cat, Malt. After finding a coin, the woman decides to buy a fish to eat, but she pities the fish and throws it back. The fish is a prince and grants her whatever she wishes. At first she asks only for a hot dinner for herself and Malt, and when she finds her wish has been granted, she immediately returns to say "thank you." The Old Woman soon asks for more, however – a cottage, furniture, clothes, a maid, and a car with chauffeur – and she forgets to thank the fish, which scolds, "You are a greedy ungrateful woman. . . . Go back to your vinegar bottle." When the woman returns later to apologize, the fish offers to restore everything she has asked for, but the woman realizes that she needs to fend for herself and asks only for an occasional hot dinner. The warmth and vividness for which Godden is known are evident in her attention to detail and dialogue in this adaptation. She has since published two other folktale adaptations, *The Dragon of Og* (1981) and *The Valiant Chatti-Maker* (1983).

In 1973 Godden's husband died from complications of diabetes and arterial sclerosis, and the following four years were difficult. Godden claims that her Pekingese dogs helped her in her grief and started her writing again. Of *The Butterfly Lions: The Story of the Pekingese in History, Legend, and Art* (1977) Godden comments, "I have not enjoyed writing any book more; it lifted me out of myself and so helped assuage the grief." A Pekingese is the narrator of her first novel, *Chinese Puzzle,* and a character in her picture book *Fu-Dog* (1989).

When Godden turned again to children's stories, she returned to familiar themes and plots. *Mr. McFadden's Hallowe'en* (1975) and *The Rocking Horse Secret* (1977) both convey the need for love and belonging and have neatly contrived endings. Indeed, both are merely a slight variation on the plot and theme of *The Diddakoi,* but of the two, *Mr. McFadden's Hallowe'en* is more successful at rising above its predictable story line. The protagonist, Selina Russell, is often in trouble and subject to rages. Although she is not an abandoned child, her best friend, Tim Scobie, is – like Kizzy in *The Diddakoi,* Tim is a Gypsy child who lives with and is later abandoned by an abusive aunt. Selina and her pony Haggis befriend the "thrawn old devil" Mr. McFadden, the largest landowner in the Scottish village of Menoock.

Conflict arises when Selina's Great-Aunt Emily leaves money to the village for a recreation center and park, but the only place for it is on

Dust jacket for Godden's story of a toy dog that turns into a real puppy

McFadden's land, which its owner refuses to relinquish. Although the rest of the village turns against McFadden, Selina's family helps him with his farm after his leg is injured in an accident, and when practical jokers stuff turf down McFadden's chimney on Halloween, Tim rescues McFadden from the smoking house. McFadden gives land to the village and adopts Tim. The park opens the following Halloween with a big celebration honoring Mr. McFadden. Although the plot is rather predictable, especially for readers of Godden's earlier works, the story is enlivened by engaging touches of humor and local color, including snatches of the Lowlands dialect. It received the 1975 Children's Book of the Year Award from the Child Study Association.

Godden returns to the picture-book format in five more recent children's stories: *A Kindle of Kittens* (1978), *The Dragon of Og, The Valiant Chatti-Maker, Fu-Dog,* and *Great Grandfather's House* (1992). Of these works *The Dragon of Og* and *Fu-Dog* have more intricate plots and more fully realized characters. The former was perhaps inspired by Godden's move to Scotland after the publication of *Five for Sorrow, Ten for Joy* (1979); it is a Scottish Lowlands tale of "long ago" about the enduring friendship of a timid dragon and Matilda, Lady of Castle Og, with the lesson that stinginess is costly. When Matilda's husband, Angus Og, hires a Norman knight to slay the dragon, because it eats two bullocks every month, but then refuses to pay the promised bag of gold, the knight allows the dragon's head and body to rejoin. Matilda nurses the dragon back to health from the castle's food stores until Angus agrees to let the dragon have its bullocks.

Fu-Dog is Godden's most fanciful story. It depicts the magical transformation of a toy fu dog into a real Pekingese puppy and teaches the importance of respecting one's cultural heritage. In the story seven-year-old Li-la, an English girl who is one quarter Chinese, receives a toy fu dog from her Chinese Great-Uncle. Fu-Dog speaks to Li-la, but her older brother Malcolm cannot hear him, presumably because he, like his father, dislikes all things Chinese. Li-la is the only one in her immediate family who looks Chinese, and she wants to learn more about the family and heritage that have been closed to her. When Fu-Dog whispers that she should go to London to find her Great-Uncle, Li-la convinces Malcolm to go as well. During their adventures Malcolm finally hears Fu-Dog's voice, but only as Fu-Dog is knocked out of Li-la's hand and carried away by a crowd during the Chinese New Year parade.

Great-Uncle consoles his niece by explaining that "Fu-Dog was a spirit dog . . . and spirits come and go." When Li-la asks if spirits also "go and come," he presents her with a Pekingese puppy, and Li-la hears Fu-Dog's voice. Great-Uncle also gives Malcolm his "dream bicycle," and when their parents come to London, Li-la's father finds that he likes his wife's Chinese relatives and their way of life. As in most of Godden's happy endings, the characters benefit both emotionally and materially, and the fairy-tale atmosphere of the story makes the ending seem less contrived.

With her recent children's novels *Listen to the Nightingale* (1992) and *Pippa Passes* (1994), Godden returns to one of her lifelong loves, the world of ballet. Godden's novels *A Candle for St. Jude* (1948) and *Thursday's Children* (1984) depict the rigors and joys of becoming a dancer and preparing for opening night, and in *Listen to the Nightingale,* ten-year-old Lottie must learn the discipline, sacrifice, and ultimately the rewards involved in becoming a prima ballerina. Lottie's aunt and guardian is the wardrobe mistress for Madame Holbein's ballet company, the same company depicted in *A Candle for St. Jude.* When Madame Holbein dies and the company dissolves, Lottie successfully auditions for Queen's Chase, the boarding school for the royal ballet. Because she can no longer care for her puppy, she regretfully gives it to Violetta, a wealthy, handicapped girl she has met in the park

while walking Prince. Violetta's brother, coincidentally, is also at Queen's Chase, and the two families grow closer as the children train for their first major performance. At the end of the novel the children and Prince have lead roles in "The Birthday of the Infanta," and Lottie's aunt marries Violetta's father, thus reuniting Lottie and Prince.

Although justly criticized for their contrivances of plot, Godden's books have enjoyed remarkable success. In her interview with Fisher, Godden remarked that most of her books have remained in print and many of her children's books continue to be republished, often with new illustrations. Musical scores have been arranged to accompany her translations of Carmen de Gasztold's poems, and her fiction, including *The Diddakoi* and *The Story of Holly and Ivy,* have been adapted for television.

Godden has often spoken and written of the humility and discipline involved in writing for children. She claims that excellent stories "never . . . have a big plot written down, but a little plot written up." She criticizes the attempts of modern editors to simplify the diction in children's stories, especially the classics. Her witty "An Imaginary Correspondence" (1963) depicts the attempts of an editor, Mr. V. Andal of De-Base Publishing, to convince Beatrix Potter's ghost to allow her tales to be published in enlarged books with simple words. Potter's reply is Godden's: "I have been told I write good prose. I think I write carefully because I enjoy my writing and enjoy taking pains over it. I write to please myself." In the seventh decade of her career, Godden is still writing. When asked what was unique about her books, she replied, "What makes my books different? They are written by me."

Interview:

Emma Fisher, "Rumer Godden," in *Pied Pipers: Interviews with the Influential Creators of Children's Literature,* edited by Fisher and Justin Wintle (New York: Paddington Press, 1974), pp. 285–294.

References:

Gwyneth Evans, "The Girl in the Garden: Variations on a Feminine Pastoral," *Children's Literature Association Quarterly,* 19 (Spring 1994): 20–24;

Lois Rostow Kuznets, *When Toys Come Alive: Narratives of Animation, Metamorphosis, and Development* (New Haven: Yale University Press, 1994), pp. 110–117;

Hassell Simpson, *Rumer Godden* (New York: Twayne, 1973).

Cynthia Harnett

(22 June 1893 – 25 October 1981)

Patricia B. Sigler
State University of New York – Oneonta

BOOKS: *David's New World: The Making of a Sportsman,* by Harnett and G. Vernon Stokes, illustrated by the authors (London: Country Life, 1937);

Junk, the Puppy, by Harnett and Stokes, illustrated by the authors (London: Blackie, 1937);

The Pennymakers, by Harnett and Stokes, illustrated by the authors (London: Eyre & Spottiswoode, 1937);

Velvet Masks, illustrated by Stokes (London: Medici Society, 1937);

Banjo, the Puppy, by Harnett and Stokes, illustrated by the authors (London: Blackie, 1938);

Mudlarks, by Harnett and Stokes, illustrated by the authors (London: Collins, 1940);

To Be a Farmer's Boy, by Harnett and Stokes, illustrated by the authors (London: Blackie, 1940);

Mountaineers, by Harnett and Stokes, illustrated by the authors (London: Collins, 1940);

Ducks and Drakes, by Harnett and Stokes, illustrated by the authors (London: Collins, 1942);

Bob-Tail Pup, by Harnett and Stokes, illustrated by the authors (London: Collins, 1944);

Sand Hoppers, by Harnett and Stokes, illustrated by the authors (London: Collins, 1946);

Getting to Know Dogs, illustrated by Stokes (London: Collins, 1947);

Two and a Bit, by Harnett and Stokes, illustrated by the authors (London: Collins, 1948);

Follow My Leader, by Harnett and Stokes, illustrated by the authors (London: Collins, 1949);

The Great House, illustrated by Harnett (London: Methuen, 1949; Cleveland: World, 1969);

Pets Limited, by Harnett and Stokes, illustrated by the authors (London: Collins, 1950);

The Wool-Pack, illustrated by Harnett (London: Methuen, 1951); republished as *Nicholas and the Woolpack* (New York: Putnam, 1953); republished as *The Merchant's Mark* (Minneapolis: Lerner, 1984);

Ring Out, Bow Bells!, illustrated by Harnett (London: Methuen, 1953); republished as *The Draw-*

Cynthia Harnett

bridge Gate (New York: Putnam, 1954); republished as *The Sign of the Green Falcon* (Minneapolis: Lerner, 1984);

The Green Popinjay, illustrated by Harnett (Oxford: Blackwell, 1955);

Stars of Fortune, illustrated by Harnett (London: Methuen, 1956; New York: Putnam, 1956);

The Load of Unicorn, illustrated by Harnett (London: Methuen, 1959); republished as *Caxton's Challenge* (Cleveland: World, 1960); republished as *The Cargo of the Madalena* (Minneapolis: Lerner, 1984);

A Fifteenth Century Wool Merchant, illustrated by Harnett (London: Oxford University Press, 1962);

181

Monasteries and Monks, illustrated by Edward Osmond (London: Batsford, 1963);

The Writing on the Hearth, illustrated by Gareth Floyd (London: Methuen, 1971; New York: Viking, 1973).

OTHER: *In Praise of Dogs: An Anthology in Prose and Verse,* edited by Harnett, illustrated by G. Vernon Stokes (London: Country Life, 1936);

"Cynthia Harnett," in *Third Book of Junior Authors,* edited by Doris De Montreville and Donna Hill (New York: Wilson, 1972), pp. 119–120.

Cynthia Harnett's unique contribution to children's literature relied on her ability to combine her talents for drawing and writing with an intense interest and absorption in British history. She won the Carnegie Medal in 1951 for *The Wool-Pack,* one of a series of major works involving the lives of ordinary people during significant historical periods. Her stories are the result of intensive scholarship and extensive research into all facets of daily life.

Cynthia Mary Harnett was born on 22 June 1893 in Kensington. The daughter of William O'Sullivan and Clara (Stokes) Harnett, she was educated at private schools and studied to be an artist, first at the Chelsea School of Art and later with her cousin, the artist and writer G. Vernon Stokes. During the 1930s they began a successful collaboration that produced several picture books about country life. In spite of their work with the censorship department, they continued to produce new titles throughout World War II.

Harnett's abiding interest in history began early. As she relates in an autobiographical sketch in the *Third Book of Junior Authors,* "In this swiftly changing world to have lived one's childhood in Queen Victoria's reign makes one almost a part of history." She also comments on how both she and Victoria had been born in Kensington and how, as a child, she often saw a little old lady dressed in black enjoying an afternoon drive in her carriage. She concludes, "I saw her often, loved her possessively, weeping genuine tears when shortly before my eighth birthday, they told me she was dead."

At about this time Harnett began to explore ruined castles and old churches with her older brother, who entertained her with stories as they made rubbings of medieval brasses and studied the coats of arms found on the tombs of knights. Writing stories was encouraged at school in Eastbourne, and at home Harnett received six pence for the ones she finished. Her real artistic ability was evident in

the books on which she collaborated with Stokes. *Bob-Tail Pup* (1944) and *Two and a Bit* (1948) were two in a series of attractive picture books popular with children, parents, and librarians. Although Harnett enjoyed this work, she still yearned to write about history.

In an article in *Horn Book* Harnett relates how a casual remark from a friend, who wondered "why there are so few historical novels about ordinary people," led to her writing historical novels for young people. Reflecting on her friend's question, Harnett found the direction she had been seeking. She had for some time been writing for children; she determined that she would write history for them, to instill in her readers the sense of place and events she had experienced many years before.

Her first historical novel for children, *The Great House* (1949), is the story of a late-seventeenth-century architect "practicing the new style in the days of William and Mary." A neighbor of Harnett's as well as several members of her family had been architects, and the historical period was chosen because it was a time of massive rebuilding. Much of London had been destroyed in the fire of 1666; among the many new architectural projects after the fire, Christopher Wren's rebuilding of St. Paul's was attracting particular interest. In the provinces many of the crumbling old medieval timber houses were being replaced by spacious and stately Italian-style dwellings built of brick. Finally, the story is set near Henley-on-Thames, which happened to be the location of Harnett's home.

The father in *The Great House* is engaged to plan a house at the fictitious "Ladybourne." He takes his children, Barbara and Geoffrey, along, and when the start of construction is delayed he leaves them in the care of Mrs. Jarvis at the local inn, Wheatsheaf. The children regret that the lovely old house is to be destroyed, and Geoffrey, who plans to be an architect like both his father and his hero, Christopher Wren, locates a better site for the new house. When the adults approve of his idea, Barbara is asked to live at the big house and Geoffrey is permitted to go to Oxford.

The story is relatively simple, but as a review in the October 1949 *Junior Bookshelf* pointed out, "it is set against a most painstakingly prepared and informative, yet never obtrusive background of domestic and village life." The various localities through which the story moves permit Harnett to contrast the noise and bustle of London with the peace and quiet of the countryside. Events take the characters from their London townhouse to the simple country inn and inside the elegant Ladybourne, as they re-create for the reader the sights and spirit of the time. The main characters are young girls and boys, and the center of attention is Barbara. Harnett's female characters are active, independent, and confident, often as strong and adventurous as the boys.

The artist in Cynthia Harnett causes her to emphasize the visual, and the background of her stories is also carefully developed. No detail is too minute to escape attention, and frequent illustrations help to support and extend the descriptions in the text. A significant feature of her writing in *The Great House* and later books is the importance of the setting; often more attention seems to be devoted to the development of the scenes than to the actors. Harnett exhibits a fascination with tools, implements, buildings, and the exact details of the daily life of the period. Her investigations took her to old houses, churches, museums, and wherever she could locate actual objects or historical maps and drawings. It is evident from the postscripts in several of her books that she enjoyed the search for these details, and once she had accumulated the pieces the stories appeared to have developed naturally. In spite of the time and effort devoted to locating and sketching these items, there is nothing artificial about their presence, as they are skillfully integrated into the events.

Although Harnett's historical novels deal with ordinary people, her characters tend to be rather affluent. Barbara and Geoffrey are children of an architect and therefore are among a privileged minority. Another common feature of Harnett's work is the presence of well-known historical figures to add an air of authenticity to the happenings. In this case, though he does not make an appearance, Wren is mentioned as a friend of their father's and a hero to Geoffrey. At the end of the book there is a postscript in which the artist points out many of the specific details of the illustrations, sharing with the reader her delight in the simple objects they portray.

Harnett's next project, *The Wool-Pack* (1951), is a story about a wool merchant from the Cotswold area during the period when the wool trade was prominent. The author remembered exploring the countryside with her brother and lying with their feet resting on a woolpack or a sheep as they made rubbings of the tombs of Cotswold merchants. The locale was farther from her home, however, and the proposed historical period, the 1490s, was also more distant than that of her first historical novel. To tell a realistic story set in that period required familiarity with the surroundings and the operations of the wool trade. As F. Phyllis Parrot points out in

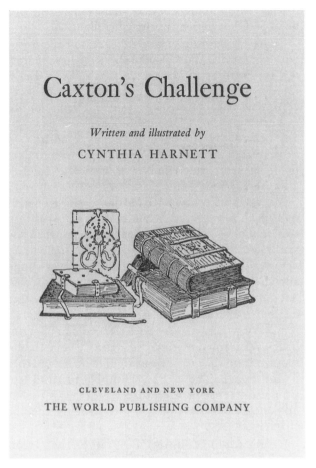

Title page for the American edition of Harnett's novel about the rivalries between printers and professional scriveners in fifteenth-century England

an essay for the *Library Association Record*, "In every detail *The Wool-Pack* shows evidence of a wide and accurate knowledge of history and of the Cotswold neighborhood." She notes that as a small child Harnett had spent long periods at her uncle's Cotswold rectory.

The story involves Nicholas Fetterlock, the twelve-year-old son of a wealthy merchant and a prominent member of the staple that controls the wool trade. There is an attempt to ruin Thomas Fetterlock by Lombard moneylenders, agents of the great Medici banking house in Florence, in conspiracy with Simon Leach, his packer. The story is carefully crafted, well paced, and exciting. Its action takes Nicholas from Burford to Newbury to meet his betrothed and ultimately to Southampton from which the wool is shipped. In researching the book Harnett had used old maps to work through the movements of the characters, and she includes a map at the end of *The Wool-Pack* depicting the major towns visited in the story, as well as including pictures and descriptions of story highlights.

In *The Wool-Pack* Harnett begins to experiment with characterization. Nicholas, the central character, is described in Margery Fisher's *Who's Who in Children's Books* (1975) as "a likeable, outspoken, confident boy." His background and behavior are in keeping with 1493, but his "character could fit any period." His bride-to-be, Cecily Bradshaw, is described in more detail. When Nicholas and Cecily first meet, she is hiding in a tree to catch a glimpse of him: "Her nose was turned up and bridged with freckles. Her fair hair, with a glint of gold in it, was parted in the middle and tied into two tight plaits. Her mouth was large, and when she smiled it was very large indeed. But the smile lit up her whole face, so that her small blue eyes shone and she radiated happiness." She becomes a principal in the later events. Harnett also includes some unsavory characters: Messer Antonio Bari; Bari's secretary, with a sallow, pockmarked complexion, little eyes framed by thick lids, and "a large flabby mouth"; and the treacherous double-dealing packer Simon Leach. These characters help to build tension and a sense of adventure. In Harnett's earlier books characters are often either strongly good or strongly evil.

In each of her historical novels Harnett incorporates information about the entertainment and diversions of the period. In *The Wool-Pack* the reader learns about the sport of falconry and about country fairs, the mood of which is captured and colorfully recounted, with many details of sights, sounds, and smells. *The Wool-Pack* is full of fascinating, accurate, and well-illustrated detail. For the high standard it achieved, the book won the Carnegie Award for 1951.

Harnett's next book, *Ring Out, Bow Bells!* (1953), is set in 1415 and chronicles the adventures of Dickon, apprenticed to his godfather, Master Mercer Richard Whittington; his older brother, Adam, apprenticed to his wealthy grocer grandfather; and his younger sister, Nan, who, along with her brothers, becomes involved in a dangerous plot. Much of the plot centers on the rivalry between various groups of apprentices. In rescuing a young fishmonger, Dickon incurs the enmity of an influential bully and through a series of misadventures finds himself accused of being a party to a treasonous plot. Lending an air of authenticity to the story, Harnett's cast also includes Dick Whittington and his cat, familiar through history and nursery rhyme. Whittington interacts especially with Nan but also with Grandfather, Dickon, and Adam. He is por-

trayed, in keeping with the character, as a generous and dearly loved hero.

Through her usual meticulous attention to detail, Harnett re-creates the City of 1415 and gives it life. The River Thames, the Tower, the city gates, buildings, and bridges play their part. The reader becomes immersed in the activities of everyday life: eating and drinking, walking through the crowded streets, taking a boat ride on the Thames, and dressing and sleeping. The daily routine of the apprentices contrasts to the grandeur and splendor of ceremonies marking holy days. In researching medieval London, Harnett found that the devastation caused by the bombing during World War II had uncovered much of the City as it was described in John Stow's *Survey of London* (1598), written during the reign of Queen Elizabeth I. Stow's book became a valuable resource as Harnett set out to rediscover early-fifteenth-century London. The author's scrupulous attention to detail is well illustrated in the map of "London in the time of King Henry," which appears at the end of *Ring Out, Bow Bells!* and which shows Dickon's London superimposed on a shaded drawing of modern London.

In a postscript to her next novel, *Stars of Fortune* (1956), Harnett describes the event that leads her to write the book: while visiting Sulgrave Manor, she discovered a book titled *The Washington Ancestry,* which included a ballad about a local legend of how Princess Elizabeth was hidden in Sulgrave Manor during the reign of Queen Mary. The challenge of where and when this could possibly have happened became the focus of Harnett's search. Although there is little evidence that the legend was true, it provided a springboard for an intriguing tale of the politics of power in the sixteenth century.

Once the idea began to take shape, Harnett followed wherever the trail led, carefully worked out the incidents, and found that the tale began to write itself. The author's illustrations include scenes of Sulgrave Manor sketched on location, key scenes of characters and events in the story, and the coats of arms of many of the families (her interest in heraldry was to find expression in several of the historical novels). The significance of the Washington "Stars and Stripes" symbolized the family's current fortunes and foreshadowed the role they were to play in the future.

Minor themes of the book include family conflicts, petty quarrels, and hidden treasure. As outlined in the *Times Literary Supplement* postscript, all of the main characters were real and the incidents either really happened or are plausible. Robert and

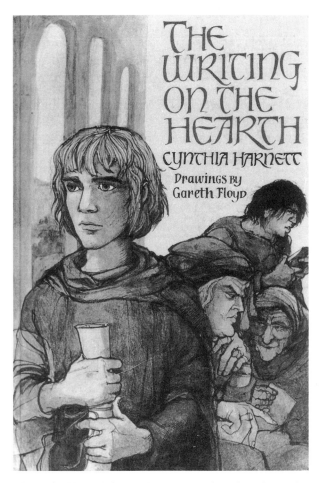

*Cover for Harnett's last book, an historical novel set during the
minority of King Henry VI*

Laurie Washington conspire to rescue Elizabeth from nearby Woodstock and smuggle her out of the country. Their sister, Anne, becomes involved in the scheme by helping them to conceal their activity from their parents. The authentic setting, convincing characterizations, and compelling events help convey the spirit of the times and make this book one of Harnett's most admired historical novels.

A pattern emerges in Harnett's career of books set in London alternating with those set in the country. *The Load of Unicorn* (1959) is one of the former and describes the rivalry between the printers and the professional scriveners of William Caxton's day. Benedict Goodrich, the son of a master scrivener, becomes apprenticed to Caxton, who has just introduced the printing press to England. The book's major theme concerns the reaction of the scriveners, who live by writing out documents longhand, to the perceived threat to their livelihood this invention represents. There is a plan to thwart

Caxton's work by diverting his supply of Unicorn, "an excellent paper for printing," but virtually useless for copybooks. Bendy not only assists the printer in obtaining an ample supply of paper but also in acquiring the complete manuscript of Sir Thomas Malory's *Le Morte D'Arthur*.

The settings include London and Westminster, Stratford-upon-Avon, and Newbold Revel. It is reasonable to assume that Harnett carefully studied each of these sites in the process of developing the historical evidence upon which the work rests. Her postscript to *The Load of Unicorn* describes the historical novel as the reverse of the detective story. The facts about real people and places, once uncovered, need to be woven together to create a believable story. People such as Caxton were there, and events surrounding them were recorded. It required a mind like Harnett's to determine what might have happened beyond these facts. She was extremely careful to inform the reader of what was true and what was fictional.

Harnett set her last novel, *The Writing on the Hearth* (1971), in Chiltern County during the minority of Henry VI. A reviewer in the February 1972 *Junior Bookshelf* observes that the book shows "an easy familiarity with the everyday life of country folk." One of its major themes is the folly of the war policy initiated by Henry V. Noble families plot to control the young king and take sides in the debate of whether or not to continue the war with France.

The story centers on Stephen, whose father died in France while defending his master, the earl of Suffolk. As a result Stephen is given the opportunity to learn to read and write and is promised a favor – rumored to be attendance at Oxford. The earl's wife, Alice, is the granddaughter of the poet Geoffrey Chaucer. The countess, whose monument is at Ewelme, is one of Harnett's best developed characters. A strong, gracious woman, Alice combines her roles of wife, household overseer, and benefactor to ordinary people such as Stephen.

The illustrations for *The Writing on the Hearth* were done by Gareth Floyd. Although they are interesting and, no doubt, done in close consultation with Harnett, they do not make the same contribution to the book that the author's illustrations had made to previous texts. Harnett's writing, however, shows the same devotion to detail and historical accuracy that was the hallmark of her previous work.

Cynthia Harnett's books continue to be read and enjoyed by children. *The Wool-Pack* has been reprinted in hardback eleven times, and the Puffin paperback is reprinted almost annually. In the United States six of her historical novels were republished by Lerner Publication Company in 1984. Her fascination with history led her to create tales of adventure set in accurately depicted periods. Through words and pictures she presented the reader with a vivid impression of everyday life set against a backdrop of actual events. Her enthusiasm, meticulous attention to detail, and high standards of research have left a legacy that helps children identify with and experience the past.

References:

Marcus Crouch and Alec Ellis, eds., *Chosen for Children: An Account of the Books Which Have Been Awarded the Library Association Carnegie Medal* (London: British Library Association, 1967), pp. 62–65;

Bertha Mahony Miller, *Illustrators of Children's Books 1946–1956* (Boston: Horn Book, 1958), p. 125.

Richard Hughes

(19 April 1900 – 28 April 1976)

Richard C. Rowland
Sweet Briar College

See also the Hughes entry in *DLB 15: British Novelists, 1930–1959.*

BOOKS: *Lines Written Upon First Observing an Elephant Devoured by a Roc* (London: Golden Cockerel Press, 1922);

The Sisters' Tragedy (Oxford: Blackwell, 1922);

Gipsy Night and Other Poems (London: Golden Cockerel Press, 1922; Chicago: Ransom, 1922);

Meditative Ode on a Vision (Plaistow: Curwen, 1923);

The Sisters' Tragedy and Other Plays (London: Chatto & Windus, 1924); republished as *A Rabbit and a Leg* (New York: Knopf, 1924); republished as *Plays* (London: Chatto & Windus, 1966; New York: Harper, 1966);

Ecstatic Ode on a Vision (Plaistow: Curwen, 1925);

A Moment of Time (London: Chatto & Windus, 1926);

Confessio Juvenis: Collected Poems (London: Chatto & Windus, 1926);

The Innocent Voyage (New York: Harper, 1928); republished as *A High Wind in Jamaica* (London: Chatto & Windus, 1929; New York: Harper, 1930);

Burial and The Dark Child (London: Privately printed, 1930);

Richard Hughes: An Omnibus (New York: Harper, 1931);

The Spider's Palace and Other Stories, illustrated by George Charlton (London: Chatto & Windus, 1931; New York: Harper, 1932);

In Hazard: A Sea Story (London: Chatto & Windus, 1938); republished as *In Hazard* (New York: Harper, 1938);

Don't Blame Me, and Other Stories, illustrated by Fritz Eichenberg (London: Chatto & Windus, 1940; New York: Harper, 1940);

The Administration of War Production, by Hughes and J. Dick Scott (London: H.M.S.O. & Longman, Green, 1955);

The Human Predicament: Volume I: The Fox in the Attic (London: Chatto & Windus, 1961; New York: Harper, 1961);

Liturgical Language Today (Penarth, Wales: Church in Wales Publications, 1962);

Gertrude's Child, illustrated by Rick Schreiter (New York: Harlan Quist, 1966; London: W. H. Allen, 1967);

Gertrude and the Mermaid, illustrated by Nicole Claveloux (New York: Harlan Quist, 1967);

The Human Predicament: Volume II: The Wooden Shepherdess (London: Chatto & Windus, 1973; New York: Harper, 1973);

The Wonder Dog: The Collected Children's Stories of Richard Hughes, illustrated by Antony Maitland (London: Chatto & Windus, 1977; New York: Greenwillow, 1977);

In the Lap of Atlas: Stories of Morocco, edited by Richard Poole (London: Chatto & Windus, 1979);

Fiction as Truth: Selected Literary Writings, edited by Poole (Bridgend: Poetry Wales Press, 1983).

PLAY PRODUCTIONS: *The Sisters' Tragedy,* London, Little Theatre, 31 May 1922;

The Man Born to Be Hanged, Portmadoc Town Hall, 1923;

A Comedy of Good and Evil, London, Royal Court Theatre, 6 July 1924; performed as *Minnie and Mr. Williams,* New York, Morosco Theatre, 21 October 1948.

MOTION PICTURES: *A Run for Your Money,* screenplay by Hughes, Charles Frend, and Leslie Norman, Ealing Studios, 1949;

The Divided Heart, screenplay by Hughes and Jack Whittingham, Ealing Studios, 1954.

RADIO: *Danger,* BBC, 15 January 1924.

OTHER: *Oxford Poetry,* edited by Hughes, Robert Graves, and Alan Porter (Oxford: Blackwell, 1921);

Richard Hughes in 1928

John Skelton, *Poems,* edited by Hughes (London: Heinemann, 1924);

"Physics, Astronomy and Mathematics," in *An Outline for Boys and Girls and Their Parents,* edited by Naomi Mitchison (London: Gollancz, 1932).

SELECTED PERIODICAL PUBLICATIONS –
UNCOLLECTED:

FICTION

"Home," *New Statesman,* new series 19 (9 March 1940): 303–304;

"The House Cow," *New Statesman,* new series 41 (6 January 1951): 8–9;

"Justice," *New Yorker,* 27 (29 September 1951): 31–32.

NONFICTION

"The Gentle Pirate," *Listener* (16 June 1938): 1268–1270;

"Tale-Telling for Children," *Graphic* (16 June 1938): 222–223;

"The Second Revolution: Literature and Radio," *Virginia Quarterly Review,* 23 (January 1947): 34–43;

"The Birth of Radio Drama," *Atlantic Monthly,* 200 (December 1957): 145–146;

"Eheu Fugaces . . . " *Virginia Quarterly Review,* 51 (January 1975): 258–263.

Readers of Richard Hughes may be surprised to find him categorized as a children's writer. Although he wrote several books of stories for children, his reputation is founded upon four novels for adults. The first and best-known of the four, *The Innocent Voyage* (1928), better known as *A High Wind in Jamaica* (1929), was quickly recognized as one of the most startling and impressive, though controversial, studies of childhood ever written. This book alone gives him a place of distinction in the history of children's literature, in the broader sense of that term.

Richard Arthur Warren Hughes was born in Surrey on 19 April 1900 to Arthur and Louise Grace Warren Hughes. All the standard reference works give his birthplace as Weybridge, but the biography by Richard Poole, who knew Hughes and his family, names it as Catenham. This discrepancy would not be worthy of notice save that it is symptomatic of a recurrent difficulty one finds in pinning down the facts of Hughes's life. He was the third child of the marriage, but his older brother died when Richard was eight days old, and his older sister when he was two. His father worked in the Public Record Office; when Richard was five his father died, leaving him in the care of his mother, who wrote magazine fiction to sustain them, and what he later described as "a rather grey synod of maiden aunts and great-aunts." Nevertheless, Hughes claims to have had a happy childhood.

He wrote from an early age, and his mother copied his poems out for him. One of them, long kept in print by the indefatigable anthologist Louis Untermeyer in successive editions of *Modern British Poetry,* was "An Invitation to the Muse," which Hughes swore late in life he had written at the age of six, though its last line, informing the Muse that she will not be well paid, seems precocious. He was seven when he wrote "Explanation on Coming Home Late," which concludes with a line of magical simplicity: pebbles on the bottom of the river had caught the speaker's eye; he adds, "It was their shining made us stay."

In 1913 Hughes went to Charterhouse School on a scholarship. He later wrote that the school "was not, just then, a particularly civilized place," but he claimed to have been very happy there, at least until his last year, when he became head boy (he disliked the responsibility) and was also working hard for an Oxford scholarship. At Charterhouse he met Robert Graves, whose view of the school in *Goodbye to All That* (1929) is considerably less benign. The year after he left school Hughes served in the army, though the war came to an end before he was sent to France. In January 1919 he went up to Oriel College, Oxford, with a scholarship.

The Oxford years were important to Hughes. He befriended Graves; met A. E. Coppard, T. E. Lawrence, W. B. Yeats, and John Masefield (at whose home on Boar's Hill he acted Theseus in Gilbert Murray's translation of *Hippolytus*); and wrote and published widely both in Oxford and London. He and a fellow-Carthusian, G. H. Johnston (later Lord Derwent), edited four issues of a magazine called *The Topaz of Ethiopia.* In 1921 Hughes, Graves, and Alan Porter jointly edited *Oxford Poetry.* In 1922 the undergraduate journal *The Isis* published Hughes's "A Heathen's Song," which so outraged Lord Alfred Douglas that he nearly persuaded the authorities to send its author down. By

the time he left Oxford, having switched from Classics to English and exiting with an undistinguished Fourth Class, Hughes had to his credit a play, *The Sisters' Tragedy* (1922), which had been produced on Boar's Hill and then in London, not without a flurry of near-censorship and consequent repercussion in Oxford, and published by Basil Blackwell; a collection, *Gipsy Night and Other Poems* (1922), published by the Golden Cockerel Press; and several reviews, poems, and stories published in London periodicals. This literary activity may well have had something to do with his lack of academic distinction.

Although the Hughes family had left Wales in Tudor days, Richard had always, like his father, felt himself to be a Welshman. (In later years he was to claim descent from King Lear through Goneril's line.) In his last year at Charterhouse he had visited the Graves family near Harlech. The father of the Graves brothers recorded in his diary that Hughes was "getting singing lessons and instructing the rest in considerateness." This is a striking early tribute to Hughes's sweetness of temper; all the evidence points to his being a loved and loving man. When Jenny Nicolson, following an unhappy love affair and a serious operation, had been rejected by her father, Robert Graves, the Hughes family volunteered to take her in. Only Lytton Strachey, meeting Hughes on 4 May 1931, found him "slightly sinister . . . but perhaps only timid under a mask."

Hughes rented a decayed cottage, once a dame's school, and settled in Wales. In 1921 his mother bought a slightly larger cottage close by, which they shared until his marriage, and Wales became his home for the rest of his life. Hughes's Welshness was less evident to the Welsh than to him, however; his upbringing had been strictly English, and there was a certain posturing in his assumption of a Welsh identity. One of his later uncollected stories, "Justice" (1951), shows his own comic awareness of this situation.

It was perhaps Hughes's sense of a limited experience that led to his eccentric lifestyle in these early years. He often walked home from Oxford to Wales, sleeping outdoors, meeting tramps, begging, or collecting money as a pavement artist. One summer he sailed via steerage to America, passing through Ellis Island, an experience vividly described in the diary "A Steerage Passenger," which appears in *A Moment of Time* (1926). When Hughes arrived in America he visited the family of the children's writer Margery Bianco in New Jersey.

Hughes's early writings brought him entrée to *Who's Who* at age twenty-four, though none of these

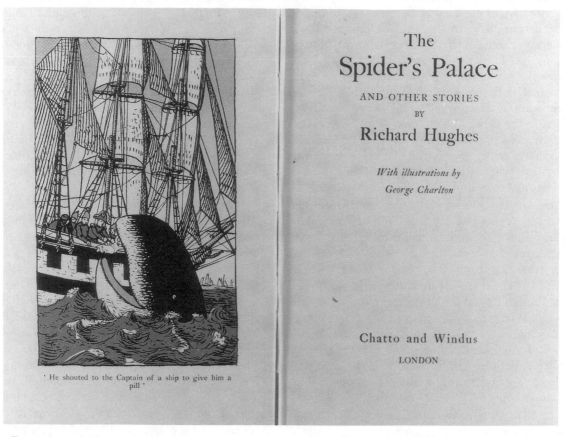

' He shouted to the Captain of a ship to give him a
pill '

The
Spider's Palace
AND OTHER STORIES
BY
Richard Hughes

*With illustrations by
George Charlton*

Chatto and Windus
LONDON

*Frontispiece and title page for Hughes's first book written specifically for children. The illustration shows a scene from the
story "Living in W'ales."*

works suggest his ultimate distinction. They do indicate his early interest in children, in the idea of innocence, in the ambivalence of good and evil in people's lives. *The Sisters' Tragedy* shows a small girl committing a mercy killing so that her older sister may be free to marry the man she loves, only to find that the lover will not marry the sister of a murderess. The best of the poems reflect the author's adventures on the road – with perhaps some imitation of W. H. Davies, whose poetry he had reviewed in the *Westminster Gazette* – and frequently cast a sharp eye upon the behavior of children, as in the title poem of *Gipsy Night* and strikingly in "The Horse Trough," which carefully describes a child killing a fly.

In 1922 Robert Graves wrote to Hughes urging him to grow beyond Graves's literary influence. It is true that the two poets had remarkably similar styles at this time. It is also significant that after this date Hughes produced very little poetry, instead turning his energies to prose, and when he published a volume of poetry it was called *Confessio Juvenis: Collected Poems* (1926).

The short stories Hughes wrote, many of them as an undergraduate, also show interest in the gap that divides children from their elders. "The Cart" reveals a child's terror of death; in "The Swans" malevolent children lure a baby away from its keeper. "Cornelius Katie" is a gypsy child who draws remarkably fine pornographic pictures. "Martha" is another child artist, exploited by a young man who steals her pictures to sell as his own and then, shamed by his own dishonesty, cruelly rejects her. In "Llwyd" the "mazed" child who sees fairies finds his own life made bleak by his father, a chapel preacher, who denies the fairies' existence; they are henceforward "lost forever." This work is perhaps the most successful of the author's short stories and a powerful picture of the brutal awakening of a child to the "real" world.

Equally significant on the path to *A High Wind in Jamaica* is *A Comedy of Good and Evil,* Hughes's only full-length play. It developed from a short story, "The Stranger," wherein a devil appears in human form upon the doorstep of a saintly Welsh clergyman and is taken in out of charity. In the story, however, the devil is a misshapen man, whereas in the play the devil is a beautiful child, Gladys, described in the stage directions as being "as young as is practical." She was first played by the young Hermione Baddeley and some years later by Robert Graves's fourteen-year-old daughter Jenny Nicolson, at a time when she was estranged from her father. Good and evil, innocence and experience, youth and age – these oppositions are at the heart of Hughes's writing.

After Oxford Hughes helped to found and manage the Portmadoc Players and wrote in a single sitting *Danger* (1924), the first play ever written specifically for radio (thus starting a lifetime relationship with the British Broadcasting Corporation). He also published and traveled widely: to the Balkans in 1922, to America in 1924, to the Adriatic and then to Morocco in 1926, and once more to America in 1928, where he completed his first novel, *A High Wind in Jamaica.* The novel was first published in the United States in 1928 under the title *The Innocent Voyage,* but in England it was given the title by which it has become generally known in both countries, though as late as 1944 a new edition with illustrations by Lynd Ward reverted to the earlier title. An argument can be made that the first title, though less arresting than the later one, points more effectively to the true content of the book.

A High Wind in Jamaica was an immediate success on both sides of the Atlantic and has never been out of print since. The novel was inspired by a genuine event. Hughes had stumbled upon an old woman's account of how she and her brothers and sisters, being shipped from Jamaica to England, had been intercepted by pirates, who transferred them to their own vessel while the captain of their ship was being roughly persuaded to surrender what valuables he was carrying. The children were then restored to their original craft and continued to England. Hughes wondered what might have happened if the children had remained aboard the pirate craft. His answer is that the unfortunate pirates would fall victim to the children; the absorbing story leads to the trial and execution of the pirates for a murder committed not by them but by Emily, the oldest daughter among the five Bas-Thornton children.

Emily, the central character, is a remarkable creation. Perhaps one of the book's most memorable episodes is when Emily suddenly realizes that she is herself; the experience is one of dawning sexual consciousness but also a kind of self-discovery that rings true to most readers. Hughes's Emily, having discovered that she is Emily, then moves on

more daringly to speculate on whether she may not in fact be God. Hughes's daughter Penelope, reading the book when she was ten, strongly identified with the character; she wrote, "It was as if I had been written before I was born." The book holds that sense of truth for many other young people and adults, though as a picture of the world of children it has created controversy ever since. Hugh Walpole, the author of three sensitive studies of a young boy, thought the book "a work of genius," while V. S. Pritchett rejected it flatly.

The children portrayed in the novel offended many adults; they have been described as evil and fiendish. In fact, they occupy a world different from that of adults, whether parents or pirates. They are not shocked by the violent actions of the pirates but are outraged when the pirates use the word "drawers" in scolding the children for sliding on the decks. When John, the oldest boy, disappears mysteriously, having fallen from a window on a misguided expedition ashore during a fiesta, the children quickly put him out of their minds; their blank response to questions when reunited with their family leads to further dark suspicions of the pirates. Penelope Hughes records her father as having responded to a question about what children needed most by saying, "Neglect. *Real* neglect – not neglect from behind a hedge or over a newspaper." In this novel children are given real neglect and oddly thrive on it, though Emily is nearly killed when her younger sister accidentally drops her "doll" (a marlinespike dressed in rags) upon her from a mast.

Hughes's aim was specifically to establish the difference between the world of children and that of adults while avoiding the sentimentality of the Victorian attitude. The sympathetic reader is equally touched by Emily, who cannot confess her crime, and by the pirates the children have learned to love, who feel themselves betrayed by the children they have cared for with awkward tenderness. Hughes was not the first writer to make such an attempt. Saki, for instance, in such stories as "Sredni Vashtar" and "The Open Window," viewed children with a determined detachment. Kenneth Grahame's *The Golden Age* (1895) stressed the gap between "the Olympians" (a term Hughes appropriated) and children. Hughes's mentor John Masefield also created boys who were neither angels nor heroes. Later, William Golding was to have a cult success with *Lord of the Flies* (1954), apparently written from the conviction that children *were* evil (certainly not Hughes's thesis). J. D. Salinger's equally stunning success with *The Catcher in the Rye* (1951) was based upon the unbridgeable gap between the young and

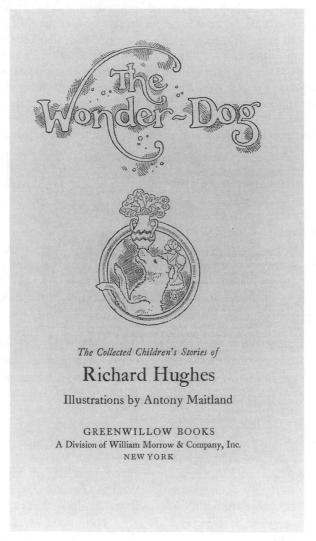

Title page for the first American edition of Hughes's collected children's stories

the old and won the devotion of the young of its generation for that reason.

When *A High Wind in Jamaica* proved successful, Harper hurried into print an omnibus edition of the four plays and many of the stories and poems that had not previously appeared in the United States. This volume includes a thirty-one-page "Autobiographical Introduction," a principal source regarding Hughes's early career. *A High Wind in Jamaica* was dramatized as *The Innocent Voyage* by Paul Osborn and ran for five weeks in New York in 1943. It became a film in 1965 under its other title, directed by Alexander Mackendrick. Both dramatizations had considerable merit, but both toned down the violence to make the story more acceptable.

The success of *A High Wind in Jamaica* led Hughes to withdraw to Morocco, where he bought a house in the Casbah of Tangiers for two donkeyloads of silver. It became a favorite retreat for the rest of the author's life, though he continued to have trouble finding it in the tumbled confusion of the twisting streets. Hughes's next publication, *The Spider's Palace and Other Stories* (1932), was the first of his books specifically written for children, a collection of twenty stories he had told, he later claimed, to the children of friends in readying himself to write about children in his first novel. He said that his method was to allow each child in the audience to choose an object to become part of the story, a technique which had been used with zest by the American writer Dorothy Canfield in *Made-to-Order*

Stories (1925). He also claimed that he forgot the stories as soon as he told them and that the children had to repeat them when he decided to write them down.

The stories are short and fantastic, with their own verbal logic. "Living in W'ales" puns on the title and is a robust comedy of a Jonah-like family of children whose comic climax comes when the host-whale goes solemnly shopping in Harrod's for the necessary furniture for his tenants. "Nothing" similarly plays on the grown-up admonition "Don't you touch nothing" to create a logical unreality. In "Telephone Travel," a child travels back and forth from house to house by the telephone connection. In "The School," when an unfortunate pupil goes down the drain with the bathwater, a stern schoolmistress says firmly, "She should have gotten out of the bath when she was told." In an essay written shortly before his death Hughes confirmed that fear of this misfortune was the one terror of his happy childhood.

A curious assignment soon came to Hughes. The publisher Victor Gollancz had planned a compendium of information for older children, to be titled *An Outline for Boys and Girls and Their Parents,* and had asked Naomi Mitchison to edit it. It clearly derived from H. G. Wells's enormously successful *Outline of History* (1920) and other works of popular instruction. Mitchison approached Hughes to write on the arts and was startled when he said that he wanted to write on mathematics. He produced a fifty-one-page essay, "Physics, Astronomy and Mathematics." Hughes's "Autobiographical Introduction" recounts how excited he had become by mathematics in his last years at Charterhouse: "I remember lying awake one night well into the small hours in a state of tense excitement, trying to visualize the three-dimensional projection of an object which should be bounded by eight cubes, thirty-two edges, and sixteen points! It was not till I succeeded that I was able to fall asleep."

The whole volume is a curious exercise: its contributors include Margaret Cole, Gerald Heard, Hugh Gaitskell, Clough Williams-Ellis, and W. H. Auden. Many of the contributors are condescending in tone and most of them are didactic, eager to shape the young person's views on religion or the family or the concept of nationalism, but not Hughes. His essay is subtitled "Beyond Common-Sense" and deals much of the time with the language of mathematics, showing it as a kind of parable not to be mistaken for fact; the "laws" of mathematics are like laws but open to sudden revision. Physics, astronomy, and mathematics are presented

almost as a kind of poetry. It is hard to believe that many boys or girls or their parents found much "useful" instruction in these pages, but some of them must have caught the writer's sense of wonder and excitement about space, time, and numbers.

Hughes married Frances Bazley, an artist, in 1932 after a whirlwind courtship. Amabel Williams-Ellis had sent Hughes to meet her at the railway station, and they soon announced that they were to be married the next Wednesday. When both families objected to the brevity of the notice, the day was changed to Thursday. The newlyweds honeymooned in Morocco and then established themselves in a dilapidated building known as "The Castle" because of some detached ruins, overlooking the Welsh fishing port of Laugharne. There in due course they produced a family of two sons and three daughters. They also became friends with Dylan and Caitlin Thomas, Hughes serving as godfather to the Thomases' first son and Frances putting up with Thomas's drunken excesses. Later the Hughes family established itself at Mor Edrin in Merionethshire on the water across from Portmadoc, where Richard had helped establish a theater and where he could indulge his lifelong enthusiasm for sailing; this remained their home for the rest of their life.

Hughes's second novel, *In Hazard: A Sea Story* (1938), was, like his first, based upon fact. He heard from an official of a shipping line the tale of a merchant ship, which had miraculously survived a ferocious hurricane in the Caribbean. Fascinated by the story Hughes obtained passage on such a ship as assistant purser to acquire the knowledge of life on a freighter, and his picture of the engine room of a steamship is precise and vivid. *In Hazard* is fully as remarkable as its predecessor. This time V. S. Pritchett joined in the praise. It has often been compared to Joseph Conrad's "Typhoon" (1903), for the story details the survival of a ship against all odds and of the varied human responses to extreme danger.

One of the more powerful episodes in the book is when a young junior officer, reaching out to arrest the young Chinaman suspected of leading the Chinese engine crew's near-mutiny, suddenly recognizes the other young man's humanity beneath his "otherness" and almost succumbs to it, then steadies himself to perform his duty. This theme – felt in the divisions in *A High Wind in Jamaica* between adult-child, upper class–lower class, respectable world–pirate world – was later to emerge clearly as Hughes's dominant concern.

The year after the appearance of *In Hazard* World War II began. Its first impact upon the

Hughes in later years

Hughes family came with the arrival of six young evacuees from the Midlands, which dramatically transformed and enlarged Hughes's captive audience for children's stories. His next publication was *Don't Blame Me, and Other Stories* (1940), a second and better collection of such tales. Some of the more-bizarre ingredients suggested by his listeners appear in "The Palace on the Rock," in which a king and queen keep their sixteen children in as many lobster pots; and in "The Elephant's Trunk," in which the elephant says, "Kindly pass the pepper; I want to unpack." "The Doll and the Mermaid" is about Gertrude, a wooden doll who drifts out to sea in a chamber pot and brings home a mermaid. Both Hughes and his daughter Penelope affirm that the story of the mermaid dripping all over the house cured one evacuee, a bedwetter, of her problem. Unfortunately, the overdelicate publishers changed the chamber pot to a pudding basin. The doll reappears in "Gertrude's Child," a distinguished contribution to the genre of "doll stories," in which Gertrude goes to the Child Shop to buy a child, an interesting variation on Hughes's theme of "otherness."

In 1940 the *New Statesman* published "Home," a short fable that presents things from the adult's point of view. In it a king and queen lose their way and, directed by an ancient Chinese sage, find themselves at a small farmhouse where three little children greet them as their missing parents. The queen sets one of them on her knee and says that they are glad to be back, "But at the same time she knew for certain she had never seen them before; and she had not the slightest idea of their names."

Once the evacuees had returned to their homes to face the dangers of urban life in wartime, Hughes was recruited by the Navy to serve in Bath as deputy principal priority officer, where he curbed his luxuriant beard, dressed uncharacteristically in formal civil-servant garb, and dodged bombs. In 1946 he was awarded the Order of the British Empire for this wartime work.

After the war Hughes worked for Ealing Studios writing film scripts, although the only one he wrote without a collaborator, "The Herring Farm," seems to have been too Welsh to have been produced. He also collaborated with J. Dick Scott on an official account of his war service, published as *The Administration of War Production* in 1955. In 1955 and 1956 he lectured at the University of London as Gresham Professor of Rhetoric; the lectures survive only in fragmentary notes. In 1956 he was awarded a D. Litt. by the University of Wales.

In the mid 1950s Hughes returned to his career as a novelist to embark on a projected trilogy called *The Human Predicament,* which was to cover the span from the end of World War I to the end of World War II. The first volume was published in 1961 as *The Fox in the Attic.* It is an ambitious work, following a large cast of characters through events in both England and Germany, and in the second volume there are interludes in America and Morocco. Its hero, Augustine Penry-Herbert, is Welsh and exactly Hughes's age. Much in the book must be autobiographical, but Hughes is canny at concealing which details are from his life and which are fictional. The book was admired but was by no means as popular as its two predecessors. As Hughes struggled on with the trilogy, reading German memoirs and histories, it became increasingly clear that three novels might not be enough. He said jokingly that as he had been born with the century he should be allowed to live until the year 2000 to finish it off. Later he decided that he would be about 140 when he finished the trilogy, a span of life he was not permitted.

In fact, only one other volume was completed, *The Wooden Shepherdess* (1973). The novel uses diaries and letters of Nazi leaders to document with considerable power the career of Adolf Hitler, who is a vivid and frightening presence in the novel. The primary emphasis is again on the duality of conflict — that of generations, of classes, of nations, and of faiths, both political and religious. The reader senses that the trilogy was to show Augustine's gradual awakening to a more understanding sense of the life of the less privileged, but *The Wooden Shepherdess* is in no sense a political novel; one remains unclear as to the author's specific politics as well as to his religion.

In 1970 Hughes published an essay, "Fiction as Truth," originally delivered when he was elected an honorary member of the American Academy of Arts and Letters. In it he states his belief that fiction is truer than what is called nonfiction, for it makes the effort to apprehend other people as persons, not things, that understanding the "Other" is the aim of fiction and the noblest of goals. He asserts, "It was the vast failure to learn that lesson which built the gas-ovens. The archetypal non-reader of Fiction was Hitler." This conviction seems to have become something close to an obsession.

Hughes did not live to bring this sequence to conclusion, but its direction is clear; its ideas are a development of the contrast between the child world and the adult world in *A High Wind in Jamaica* and between the young Marxist Chinese and the sheltered English boy of *In Hazard*. Though the two volumes of *The Human Predicament* are not books likely to find their way into the hands of even a ma-

ture child, children are still central to them. There is the haunting image of a dead child that begins the story (Hughes said this picture came to him in a dream, and he sat down and started the novel having no idea where it was to lead); there is the robust child Nora, who appears to have been intended to play a larger role in later volumes; there is the hero's profound bachelor devotion to his niece Polly, kept free of incest only by the inarguable purity of both characters; and there is Hitler's unsavory attraction to his own niece. Always, however, the gulf between adult and child is there.

In 1975 Hughes visited his younger son in New York and his youngest daughter in Canada but fell ill and returned to England in a wheelchair. He had leukemia. His old college, Oriel, had elected him an Honorary Fellow in spite of his earlier academic disgrace, and he visited Oxford for attendant festivities but was soon hospitalized. His wife, his elder son (a clergyman), and his eldest daughter (who had contemplated entering a convent but had married and was a mother) gathered to take turns reading to him as he steadily weakened. A touchingly comic story tells how the wife of the other old man who shared the hospital room was much relieved to discover that what they were reading was *Anna Karenina*; she had feared they were Jehovah's Witnesses sustaining him spiritually.

A further collection of Hughes's children's stories was being readied; a preface was needed. The author's children wrote one, but it was not what Hughes wanted, so he gathered his strength to write his last composition, the preface to *The Wonder Dog* (1977), the title story being the single example of his earlier writings for children to be included in the collection. He died on 28 April 1976.

Two more books by Hughes were published after his death, both edited by Richard Poole, who was later to become the author's first biographer. The first, *In the Lap of Atlas: Stories of Morocco* (1979), collected Hughes's stories about Morocco, some of them autobiographical, some of them tales he was told by the Arabs he met there. The latter have the deadpan extravagance of *The Arabian Nights* and might appeal to some children, unsuitable though the content may often be for young ears. The second, *Fiction as Truth: Selected Literary Writings* (1983), collects part of his critical writings. Among these essays is "Illogic and the Child," which reveals Hughes's devotion to Lewis Carroll and explains to some degree the tone of his own stories for children that sail over impossible aspects of events with such serenity.

Hughes's stories for children were neither written down to his audience nor written for adults.

He was aware that A. A. Milne's Christopher Robin stories and those of his old friend Margery Bianco, like most juvenile books, were aimed at the adults who bought the books. He tried to tell his stories to children as equals. Similarly, his adult books are full of children, not seen as doll-like figures but as complex personalities with serious problems. Hughes's ability to see children without condescension or sentimentality, even with a certain ruthlessness, gives his writing its staying power.

Biographies:

Penelope Hughes, *Richard Hughes: Author, Father* (Gloucester: Alan Sutton, 1984);

Richard Perceval Graves, *Richard Hughes: A Biography* (London: Deutsch, 1994).

References:

Victoria de Rijke and Ayeshea Zacarkiw, "Reading the Child Invention," *Children's Literature in Education,* 26 (September 1995): 153–169;

Richard Perceval Graves, *Robert Graves: The Assault Heroic: 1885–1926* (London: Weidenfeld & Nicholson, 1986; New York: Viking, 1987);

Paul Morgan, *The Art of Richard Hughes: A Study of the Novels* (Cardiff: University of Wales Press, 1993);

Morgan, "'A Moment of Time': The Short Stories of Richard Hughes," *New Welsh Review,* 1 (Autumn 1988): 57–63;

Richard Poole, *Richard Hughes: Novelist* (Bridgend: Poetry Wales Press, 1986);

D. S. Savage, "Richard Hughes, Solipsist," *Anglo-Welsh Review,* no. 68 (1981): 36–50;

Lance Sieveking, *The Eye of the Beholder* (London: Hulton, 1957);

Peter Thomas, *Richard Hughes* (Cardiff: University of Wales Press, 1973).

Ted Hughes

(17 August 1930 –   )

Michael Hennessy
Southwest Texas State University

See also the Hughes entry in *DLB 40: Poets of Great Britain and Ireland Since 1960.*

BOOKS: *The Hawk in the Rain* (London: Faber & Faber, 1957; New York: Harper, 1957);

Lupercal (London: Faber & Faber, 1960; New York: Harper, 1960);

Meet My Folks!, illustrated by George Adamson (London: Faber & Faber, 1961; Indianapolis: Bobbs-Merrill, 1973);

Selected Poems, by Hughes and Thom Gunn (London: Faber & Faber, 1962);

The Earth-Owl and Other Moon-People, illustrated by R. A. Brandt (London: Faber & Faber, 1963); published as *Moon-Whales and Other Poems,* illustrated by Leonard Baskin (New York: Viking, 1976); revised as *Moon-Whales* (London: Faber & Faber, 1988);

How the Whale Became and Other Stories, illustrated by Adamson (London: Faber & Faber, 1963; New York: Atheneum, 1964);

Nessie the Mannerless Monster, illustrated by Gerald Rose (London: Faber & Faber, 1964); republished as *Nessie the Monster,* illustrated by Jan Pyk (Indianapolis: Bobbs-Merrill, 1974);

The Burning of the Brothel (London: Turret, 1966);

Recklings (London: Turret, 1966);

Scapegoats and Rabies (London: Poet & Printer, 1967);

Wodwo (London: Faber & Faber, 1967; New York: Harper & Row, 1967);

Animal Poems (Crediton, Devon: Gilbertson, 1967);

Poetry in the Making: An Anthology of Poems and Programmes from Listening and Writing (London: Faber & Faber, 1967); abridged as *Poetry Is* (Garden City: Doubleday, 1970);

The Iron Man: A Story in Five Nights, illustrated by Adamson (London: Faber & Faber, 1968); republished as *The Iron Giant: A Story in Five Nights,* illustrated by Robert Nadler (New York: Harper & Row, 1968);

Ted Hughes (photograph by Layle Silbert)

Five Autumn Songs for Children's Voices, illustrated by Phillida Gili (Crediton, Devon: Gilbertson, 1968);

A Crow Hymn (Frensham, Surrey: Sceptre, 1970);

The Martyrdom of Bishop Farrar (Crediton, Devon: Gilbertson, 1970);

The Coming of the Kings and Other Plays (London: Faber & Faber, 1970); enlarged as *The Tiger's Bones and Other Plays for Children* (New York: Viking, 1974);

A Few Crows (Exeter: Rougemont, 1970);

Crow: From the Life and Songs of the Crow (London: Faber & Faber, 1970; New York: Harper & Row, 1971; enlarged edition, London: Faber & Faber, 1972);

Autumn Song, illustrated by Nina Carroll (Kettering, Northamptonshire: Steane, 1971);

Crow Wakes (London: Poet & Printer, 1971);

Poems, by Hughes, Ruth Fainlight, and Alan Sillitoe (London: Rainbow, 1971);

Shakespeare's Poem (London: Lexham, 1971);

Eat Crow (London: Rainbow, 1971);

The Coming of the Kings: A Christmas Play in One Act (Chicago: Dramatic Publishing, 1972);

Selected Poems 1957–1967 (London: Faber & Faber, 1972; New York: Harper & Row, 1973);

Sunday (Cambridge: Cambridge University Press, 1972);

Orpheus (Chicago: Dramatic Publishing, 1973);

Prometheus on His Crag (London: Rainbow, 1973);

The Story of Vasco (London: Oxford University Press, 1974);

Beauty and the Beast: A Play in One Act (Chicago: Dramatic Publishing, 1974);

Sean, the Fool, the Devil, and the Cats: A Play in One Act (Chicago: Dramatic Publishing, 1974);

The Tiger's Bones: A Play in One Act (Chicago: Dramatic Publishing, 1974);

Spring, Summer, Autumn, Winter (London: Rainbow, 1974); revised and enlarged as *Season Songs,* illustrated by Leonard Baskin (New York: Viking, 1975; London: Faber & Faber, 1976; revised and enlarged again, London: Faber & Faber, 1985):

Cave Birds (London: Scolar, 1975); revised and enlarged as *Cave Birds: An Alchemical Cave Drama* (London: Faber & Faber, 1978; New York: Viking, 1979);

Earth-Moon, illustrated by Hughes (London: Rainbow, 1976);

Eclipse (Knotting, Bedfordshire: Sceptre, 1976);

Gaudete (London: Faber & Faber, 1977; New York: Harper & Row, 1977);

Chiasmadon (Baltimore: Charles Seluzicki, 1977);

Sunstruck (Knotting, Bedfordshire: Sceptre, 1977);

Moon-Bells and Other Poems (London: Chatto & Windus, 1978; enlarged edition, London: Bodley Head, 1986);

A Solstice (Knotting, Bedfordshire: Sceptre, 1978);

Orts (London: Rainbow, 1978);

Moortown Elegies (London: Rainbow, 1978);

The Threshold (London: Steam, 1979);

Adam and the Sacred Nine (London: Rainbow, 1979);

Remains of Elmet (London: Rainbow, 1979); revised as *Remains of Elmet: A Pennine Sequence* (London: Faber & Faber, 1979; New York: Harper & Row, 1979);

Four Tales Told by an Idiot (Knotting, Bedfordshire: Sceptre, 1979);

Moortown (London: Faber & Faber, 1979; New York: Harper & Row, 1979);

Henry Williamson: A Tribute (London: Rainbow, 1979);

A Primer of Birds (Lurley, Devon: Gehenna, 1981);

Under the North Star, illustrated by Leonard Baskin (London: Faber & Faber, 1981; New York: Viking, 1981);

Selected Poems 1957–1981 (London: Faber & Faber, 1982); republished as *New Selected Poems* (New York: Harper & Row, 1982);

River (London: Faber & Faber/James & James, 1983; New York: Harper & Row, 1984);

What Is the Truth?: A Farmyard Fable for the Young, illustrated by R. J. Lloyd (London: Faber & Faber, 1984; New York: Harper & Row, 1984);

Ffangs the Vampire Bat and the Kiss of Truth, illustrated by Chris Riddell (London: Faber & Faber, 1986);

Flowers and Insects: Some Birds and a Pair of Spiders (London: Faber & Faber, 1986; New York: Knopf, 1986);

Tales of the Early World, illustrated by Andrew Davidson (London: Faber & Faber, 1988; New York: Farrar, Straus & Giroux, 1991);

Moortown Diary (London: Faber & Faber, 1989);

Wolfwatching (London: Faber & Faber, 1989; New York: Farrar, Straus & Giroux, 1991);

A Dancer to God: Tributes to T. S. Eliot (London: Faber & Faber, 1992; New York: Farrar, Straus & Giroux, 1993);

Rain-Charm for the Duchy and Other Laureate Poems (London: Faber & Faber, 1992);

Shakespeare and the Goddess of Complete Being (London: Faber & Faber, 1992; New York: Farrar, Strauss & Giroux, 1992);

The Iron Woman: A Sequel to "The Iron Man" (London: Faber & Faber, 1993); republished as *The Iron Woman* (New York: Dial, 1995);

Winter Pollen: Occasional Prose, edited by William Scammell (London: Faber & Faber, 1994; New York: Picador, 1995).

OTHER: *Five American Poets,* edited by Hughes and Thom Gunn (London: Faber & Faber, 1963);

Keith Douglas, *Selected Poems,* edited, with an intro-
    duction, by Hughes (London: Faber & Faber,
    1964; New York: Chilmark, 1965);
A Choice of Emily Dickinson's Verse, edited, with an in-
    troduction, by Hughes (London: Faber &
    Faber, 1968);
Seneca, Oedipus, adapted by Hughes (London: Faber
    & Faber, 1969; Garden City, N.Y.: Double-
    day, 1972);
*With Fairest Flowers While Summer Lasts: Poems from
    Shakespeare,* edited, with an introduction, by
    Hughes (Garden City, N.Y.: Doubleday,
    1971); republished as *A Choice of Shakespeare's
    Verse* (London: Faber & Faber, 1971);
"Myth and Education," in *Writers, Critics and Chil-
    dren,* edited by Geoff Fox, Graham Hammond,
    Terry Jones, Frederick Smith, and Kenneth
    Sterck (New York: Agathon, 1976; London:
    Heinemann, 1976): 77–94;
Sylvia Plath, *Collected Poems,* edited, with an intro-
    duction, by Hughes (London: Faber & Faber,
    1981; New York: Harper & Row, 1981);
Plath, *Journals,* edited by Hughes and Frances
    McCullough (New York: Dial, 1982);
The Rattle Bag: An Anthology of Poetry, edited by
    Hughes and Seamus Heaney (London: Faber
    & Faber, 1982);
Sylvia Plath's Selected Poems, selected by Hughes (Lon-
    don: Faber & Faber, 1985);
The Essential Shakespeare, selected, with an introduc-
    tion, by Hughes (New York: Ecco, 1992).

SELECTED PERIODICAL PUBLICATION –
UNCOLLECTED: "Myth and Education,"
    Children's Literature in Education, 1 (1970): 55–
    70;

Ted Hughes's poetry for adults has made him
one of the most important British writers in the second half of the twentieth century. When his work
first appeared in the late 1950s, it struck many readers as a bold departure from the urbane and under-
stated poetry that dominated the English literary
scene. Using powerful, evocative language, Hughes
wrote about the elemental forces of nature and the
relation of the human to the nonhuman world,
often tapping into the dark recesses of the psyche.
During the past four decades he has broadened the
themes of his early work, producing a richly varied
body of poetry for adults. He has also become an
accomplished writer of children's books – stories,
plays, and several volumes of poetry. These books,
like his adult writing, often explore darker aspects
of the self and the physical world, though less

Hughes with Sylvia Plath

fiercely and with more humor and playfulness. The
quality and variety of his work for young readers
assure him an important place among British children's writers.

Ted Hughes was born Edward James Hughes
on 17 August 1930, the youngest child of William
Henry Hughes, a carpenter and veteran of the
Great War, and Edith Farrar Hughes, a descendant
of Nicholas Farrar, founder of the seventeenth-
century Anglican community at Little Gidding.
Hughes spent his first seven years in the town of
Mytholmroyd, deep in the Calder Valley of West
Yorkshire, a region of steep cliffs and desolate
moors. This landscape of stark contrasts instilled in
Hughes an abiding respect for the vastness and
power of the natural world. Hunting and fishing expeditions with an older brother also stirred a passionate, lifelong interest in animals; beast, fish, and
fowl inhabit nearly all his books.

When he was eight, Hughes's family moved to Mexborough in South Yorkshire, where he attended the local school. With encouragement from his teachers, he developed an interest in writing poetry and published several pieces in the Mexborough school magazine, *Don and Dearne*. In 1948 Hughes won an Open Exhibition to Cambridge University but delayed his enrollment for two years to serve in the Royal Air Force. He was assigned to a remote station in East Yorkshire, where he worked as a radio mechanic and, in his spare time, read extensively. After completing his service Hughes entered Pembroke College, Cambridge, to study English but switched in his final year to anthropology. His reading in this subject has had a lasting influence on his poetry, which draws frequently on ritual, myth, and folklore. In the two years following his graduation in June 1954, Hughes published several poems in Cambridge literary magazines and supported himself by working as a schoolteacher, gardener, night watchman, and zoo attendant.

In February 1956, at a party to celebrate the launching of a Cambridge poetry magazine, Hughes met Sylvia Plath, who was studying at Newnham College as a Fulbright fellow; within four months they were married. While finishing her M.A. at Cambridge and working on her own writing, Plath promoted her husband's career, typing his poems and sending them to magazine editors. In October of that year she encouraged him to enter a collection of forty poems in a contest sponsored by the Poetry Center of the Young Men's and Women's Hebrew Association in New York. The judges selected Hughes's manuscript from nearly three hundred submissions, and his first book, *The Hawk in the Rain* (1957), soon appeared in England and America. By this time Hughes and Plath had moved to Massachusetts, where for two years they taught and wrote before returning to England in December 1959. During his American sojourn Hughes met Leonard Baskin, the artist who later illustrated many of his books.

The Hawk in the Rain and Hughes's second book for adults, *Lupercal* (1960), quickly established him as a strong presence in contemporary poetry. Reviewers singled out his vivid, often chilling, descriptions of animals, his vigorous style, and his bold treatment of universal themes. Shortly after these early successes, Hughes launched his career as a children's writer, publishing four books for young people in the early 1960s: *Meet My Folks!* (1961), *The Earth-Owl and Other Moon-People* (1963), *How the Whale Became and Other Stories* (1963), and *Nessie the*

Mannerless Monster (1964). Hughes's writing for children may have been triggered by changes in his domestic life. His daughter, Frieda Rebecca, was born in April 1960, and in the summer of the following year he and Plath moved from London to rural Devon, seeking solitude for their writing and a larger home for their growing family. A son, Nicholas Farrar, was born in January 1962.

While notably lighter in tone than Hughes's earliest collections for adults, his first four books for children are considerable achievements. In two different essays titled "Myth and Education" (1970; 1976) he argues for the power of children's literature to transform readers' lives. Such literature, he explains, is therapeutic and magical. It can invigorate the imagination of a young reader and counteract the corrosive effects of the modern technological world, which places its trust solely in objectivity and scientific certitude. According to Hughes, the machine age insulates people from both the physical world and the inner world of the psyche; the children's writer can awaken and develop an "imagination which embraces both outer and inner worlds in a creative spirit."

In *Meet My Folks!* Hughes promotes the kind of imaginative revitalization that he speaks of in his "Myth and Education" essays. The book is a collection of poems about a bizarre comical family, described by one of its children. The paternal grandmother knits compulsively: "Her shrubs have scarves and pullovers, / Her birds have ear-muffs over their ears." The father is an "inspector of holes," and his wife is a cook whose specialties include "Sautéed Ant Eggs on Champagne Alligator." Uncle Dan is an inventor of various devices, including a "roll-uppable rubber ladder" and a "bottomless glass for ginger beer," while Sister is "nothing but a great big crow." These family portraits have something of the inventiveness and comic appeal found in Shel Silverstein's poems or in Edward Lear's nonsense verse, but they generally lack the sharp, memorable language of these poets. Keith Sagar points out that the "rhythms and rhymes are fitful" and that the poems, though "fresh and engaging, are often shapeless."

"My Own True Family," the final — and best — poem in *Meet My Folks!*, moves beyond the range of the comic portraits in the rest of the book. The "family" in this case is a stand of oak trees that addresses the child-speaker in a frightening dream: "We are chopped down, we are torn up, you do not blink an eye. / Unless you make a promise now — now you are going to die." The child agrees to plant two oak trees for each one that he sees felled. Saved

As the animals enjoy themselves, Toto the Turtle weeps with shame;
illustration by Rick Schreiter from Hughes's How the Whale
Became and Other Stories *(1963)*

from death, he returns from his dream to the ordinary world but is profoundly altered by his experience: "When I came out of the oakwood, back to human company, / My walk was the walk of a human child, but my heart was a tree." This poem, a kind of ecological parable, introduces Hughes's notion of the interconnectedness of the human and the nonhuman worlds, a recurrent theme in his writing. The poem urges respect for the natural world, the larger, "true" family of which the child is a member.

Hughes's second collection of children's poems, *The Earth-Owl and Other Moon-People,* resembles his first one in its inventiveness, but its creative force comes from the realm of nightmare. The poems in *Earth-Owl* describe a bizarre moon-world of extravagant creatures, grotesque in form and ominous in behavior. This world engaged Hughes's interest for many years; in 1976, more than a decade

after *Earth-Owl* appeared, he published a limited-edition collection of all new poems called *Earth-Moon. Moon-Whales and Other Poems,* which gathers most of the pieces from the two previous volumes, also appeared in 1976.

All told, Hughes has produced more than fifty moon poems, creating an eerie world whose geography resembles the actual moonscape, complete with extinct volcanoes, craters, and barren wastes, but whose inhabitants come from the dark recesses of the psyche. There are disembodied Moon-Shadow Beggars who pursue their victims across "the frontier from dark to light," desperately clutching after a body to invade. The shadows "reach after you with arms of elastic length, / They screech, sob and suffer." Those who pity them are lost forever: "they will pour / Into you through the wide open door / Of your eye-pupil, and fill you up." In another poem the reader (addressed again as "you") wakes to find footprints of giant "Moon-Walkers" on the ceiling; the end hints that only the light of day keeps these creatures at bay.

Some critics find poems such as "Moon-Shadow Beggars" and "Moon-Walkers" inappropriately fearsome for young readers. John Adams, for example, writing in *Signal,* criticizes Hughes's "obsession with animal energy" and finds his poetic vision dark and narrow. Others counter that Hughes's aim is not merely to shock but to confront real childhood fears that contemporary culture tries to repress or ignore.

In any event, the darkness of the moon poems is not unrelentingly bleak. Hughes undercuts his own grimness with humor and whimsy, suggesting that children can face their fears by developing a healthy sense of the absurd. Thus, those stricken with horrible diseases such as "lunar galloping cactus" or "moon-cloud grip" experience dreadful symptoms at first but are cured by unlikely remedies – by sighing for a whole day in one case. In addition, the most unearthly of beasts, such as the "silver white" moon-ravens, sometimes turn out to be helpful. Others creatures, if not exactly benevolent, inspire wonder more than fear. The eerie and massive moon-whales "plough through the moon stuff / Just under the surface / Lifting the moon's skin / Like a muscle."

Hughes's other book of children's poetry from the early 1960s has a notably lighter tone than the moon poems. *Nessie the Mannerless Monster* is a picture book about the lonely, unappreciated Loch Ness monster, who is "disgusted to find herself dismissed as a myth." Hughes wrote the story in a slack, uneven doggerel, imitating the style of the Scots poet William McGonagall. Although some readers have criticized the work's awkward versification, Hughes believed, according to Keith Cushman, that the sprawling manner "would be delightful to a young listener."

In the poem Nessie travels to Edinburgh, then south through Yorkshire, and finally to London, trying to convince the disbelieving world that she exists. Most people cannot or will not see her. Some mistake her for "a huge cat" or a "fox as long as a brass band." In London a scientist at the Kensington Museum, where Nessie goes to view a dinosaur skeleton, says: "Imposter! You are impossible! If you were extinct and no more / Indeed I would say you were a Plesiosaur." Nessie's quest ends happily: a Scots poet named Willis recognizes her, takes her to Buckingham Palace, and speaks to the Queen, who declares her Vice Regent; the monster returns to reign contentedly in her lake.

Nessie the Mannerless Monster appears at first to be a fanciful, humorous adventure story, but considered in light of Hughes's assertion that the modern world insulates children from the vitality of the physical and psychic realms, it becomes a moral tale. The scientist who denies Nessie's existence speaks for the analytical, antimythological bias of contemporary culture. The poet Willis, by contrast, speaks for the imagination, showing the reason-bound world that Nessie does exist. Poetry thus triumphs over science, affirming the child's power to imagine. On a more fundamentally emotive level, young readers can also identify with Nessie's sense of being unappreciated and unloved, sharing vicariously in the recognition she achieves at the end of the book.

The last of the four children's books Hughes published in the early 1960s is *How the Whale Became,* a collection of eleven prose fables explaining how various animals acquired their present forms and identities. All creatures, a prefatory note asserts, were "pretty much alike" in the beginning. Most practiced being what they wanted to be until they succeeded, but some – such as the fox, hyena, bee, and donkey – "came about in other ways." One of the best fables in the book is the story of Bombo, a large creature who cannot decide what to become. After the more self-assured animals laugh at him, Bombo retreats to live in isolation until a great fire sweeps the land; he saves the other animals, carrying them from the fiery edge of the river to the safety of his island. Thereafter Bombo becomes an elephant. His heroic behavior makes him what he is – a shy and modest creature admired for his cleverness and silent strength.

With their fanciful accounts of animal origins, the fables in *How the Whale Became* engage children's natural curiosity about the physical world. In a note to one of his adult poetry collections, *Rain-Charm for the Duchy and Other Laureate Poems* (1992), Hughes describes his own "boyhood obsession with the animal kingdom." That obsession is apparent throughout his poetry, both in his strikingly realistic descriptions of animals and in his mythological transformations of various creatures. Like his animal poems, some of the fables in *How the Whale Became* expose children to the raw and violent power of the natural world. The first story, for example, portrays the owl as a bloodthirsty trickster who convinces other birds to become his prey: "'This is better than rats and mice and beetles,' said Owl, as he cleaned the blood from his beak." Other fables, like the tale of the polar bear, are more clearly in the tradition of Aesop, using animals to teach lessons about human behavior.

*Dust jacket for the volume of poems based on Hughes's
experiences while he was in rural Devon*

During the years when his first children's books were appearing in print, Hughes's personal life became increasingly turbulent. After the birth of Nicholas in January 1962, his wife's mental state began to deteriorate. Long subject to depression, Plath had attempted suicide nine years earlier and began suffering from a recurrence of her psychological problems. That summer Hughes entered an affair with Assia Gutman Wevill, which helped precipitate the failure of his already shaky marriage. The following autumn Hughes and Plath separated, both returning to London, where Plath rented a flat for herself and the children. Her situation worsened, and on 11 February 1963 she took her own life. Plath's suicide profoundly affected Hughes, who subsequently edited much of her work and promoted her posthumous reputation as a poet. After her death, with help from family and friends, Hughes took an active role in rearing Frieda and Nicholas.

In the years immediately following Plath's suicide, Hughes wrote few new poems. *Wodwo,* a collection of his writing for adults from a period of roughly eight years, appeared in 1967, as did a book for children, *Poetry in the Making,* a series of radio scripts he wrote during the 1960s for the BBC series "Listening and Writing." These talks give advice for young people "aged between ten and fourteen" who wish to write poetry. Hughes's emphasis throughout is on content rather than form, on "How to try to say what you really mean" rather than on emulating a particular "stylistic ideal." Reviewers of the book enthusiastically endorsed this approach, contrasting it with the more prescriptive methods found in creative writing textbooks. Thomas Lask, in *The New York Times Book Review,* praised Hughes for "asserting once again that there are no poetic subjects, that the stuff of poetry comes out of the stuff of living."

In keeping with Hughes's emphasis on content, most of the chapters of *Poetry in the Making* focus on writing about a particular topic. Each talk is amply illustrated with poetry by Hughes and others, and most chapters end with a gathering of verse suited for younger readers, making the book an anthology of poetry as well as a guide to writing. For adult readers the book offers an added advantage: Hughes's autobiographical and critical comments provide insight into his own poetic methods (he draws, for example, a telling comparison between writing poetry and capturing animals, a favored activity of his youth). Two chapters, "Meet My Folks" and "Moon Creatures," specifically discuss poems from his earliest collections for children.

Hughes's next book for young readers, *The Iron Man: A Story in Five Nights* (1968), is a prose tale about two "monsters" – the giant title character and a "space-bat-angel-dragon," which, in the latter part of the tale, threatens the earth with destruction. In the first chapter, the Iron Man, "taller than a house," arrives mysteriously at the top of a cliff and accidentally steps over the edge, breaking into pieces as he crashes on the rocky beach below. The next morning his detached hand and eye slowly gather the other shattered pieces of his body and reassemble it.

The second and third chapters detail the Iron Man's confrontation with local farmers. First spotted by Hogarth, a farmer's son, the Iron Man begins to eat tractors, farm equipment, even barbed-wire fences – anything made of iron or steel. With Hogarth's assistance the farmers trap and bury the mechanical monster. Later, after the Iron Man emerges from the ground, Hogarth convinces him to live peaceably at the local scrap yard, where he enjoys an endless supply of discarded metal.

In the fourth and fifth chapters, which form a new story loosely connected to the first three, Hughes introduces the gigantic "space-bat-angel-dragon," drawn to earth by the war cries of humanity. Vicious and warlike, the creature demands to be fed living beings. Hogarth again saves the day by convincing the Iron Man to face the space-creature in a test of endurance. In the end the defeated creature agrees to fly around the earth at night singing a "strange soft eerie space-music," which causes humanity to stop making weapons and to live in peace.

Like the earlier story of Nessie, *The Iron Man* has an ingenious plot and is an imaginative exercise for young readers. The story also taps into children's fears of the unknown. Like the earlier moon creatures, however, the two monsters in *The Iron Man* turn out to be less fearful than they first

seem. The story symbolically integrates the darker forces of the psyche into the daylight world of ordinary human experience. Young Hogarth heroically faces his fears and uses his ingenuity to help overcome the two monsters; he even makes one of them his friend. The Iron Man is a hero of larger proportions. Sagar calls him "the hero of myth who voluntarily undergoes the most terrible trials, agonies, purification, and, having given everything, miraculously redeems the world."

Along with the poetry and fiction he produced during the 1960s, Hughes wrote several children's plays that were first broadcast on radio and later gathered in *The Coming of the Kings and Other Plays* (1970). Based on folktales and myths and written largely in verse, these plays develop themes found in Hughes's stories and poems from the same period, notably his distrust of rational, scientific solutions to human problems and his belief in imagination as a tool of psychic regeneration. Some reviewers argued that the plays push their messages too insistently, that didacticism overshadows theater. Although Hughes sometimes strains to establish his point, the plays also have a richness of plot, character, and language that sharpens their dramatic appeal.

The first play of the collection, *The Coming of the Kings,* retells the biblical story of the Magi, focusing initially on an innkeeper and his wife whose materialism blinds them to the events played out around them. The pair are crudely comic figures, always bickering and hopelessly inept at their trade. A minstrel's prediction of a royal visit gives the couple hope of reviving the failing inn. Greed gets the best of them, however, and they mistake a shady businessman, a power-hungry priest, and a ruthless police inspector for the true kings. They turn away Joseph and Mary, directing them to a nearby stable. When the true kings arrive, the innkeeper and his wife are baffled; the kings ignore them and turn toward the couple in the stable.

The ending highlights the play's contrast between two fundamentally different outlooks: the worldly materialism of the self-seeking company gathered at the inn (representatives of the established order) and the imaginative, otherworldly viewpoint of the minstrel (a poet) and the three kings (spiritual seekers). Hughes develops this contrast not only through character and action but in the language of the play itself. The speeches of the "materialists" are comic, bombastic, or pompous; the minstrel and the kings, by contrast, speak in moving, stately verse: "He will be born to the coughing of animals / Among the broken, rejected objects / In the corner that costs not a penny / In the darkness of the mouse and the spider."

Although poetic language is less conspicuously a factor in *The Tiger's Bones,* the second of Hughes's children's plays, its themes are similar to those of *The Coming of the Kings.* At the center of the drama is a scientist named Master whose aims are purely materialistic and self-serving. With the help of three comic sycophants – Jitterwit, Dully, and Von Gonktop – he proves in the most irrefutably scientific manner that a meteor is soon to crash into the earth and destroy it. Later Master sets out to "civilize" a tribe of "savages," but his introduction of capitalism destroys those he had hoped to "save."

Like the scientist in *Nessie the Mannerless Monster,* the Master in *The Tiger's Bones* is blinded by his unquestioning trust in the rational. His prediction of the end of the world, it turns out, is based not on astronomical observations but on a mistaken speck of dust in his telescope. Likewise, his scheme to improve humanity, workable in theory, fails in practice. In the end he is destroyed by his greatest act of intellectual arrogance: he gives life to the bones of a tiger, but the life he creates eats him. The play thus becomes a satire on the excesses of rationalism and the modern reverence for science: as in many of Hughes's stories and poems, scientific certitude gives way to events beyond human control.

The other three plays in Hughes's collection are less overtly satiric than *The Tiger's Bones,* but they are no less forceful in developing his theme that the irrational must be acknowledged rather than repressed; the cultivation of imagination is a route to that acknowledgement. In *Beauty and the Beast,* a variation on the traditional folktale, the irrational takes the form of a bear who steals away Floreat, a sickly and melancholy girl whose wealthy father had tried to cure his daughter with various "scientific" remedies. The bear, a horrifying monster in the eyes of the overprotective father, turns out to be gentle creature whose love returns Floreat to spiritual health. In *Sean, the Fool, the Devil, and the Cats,* the questing hero faces dark, irrational forces to find regeneration for himself and for the girl he marries. Finally, in *Orpheus* (added to an enlarged 1974 American edition of Hughes's plays), the hero of classical myth enters the fearsome darkness of the underworld to recover the soul of his beloved wife, Eurydice. In each of these plays the protagonist braves the unknown for the sake of love, risking danger, even death, to affirm life. Fred Rue Jacobs points out that in Hughes's work, "when the

monster is released it is seen to be love, and the light it has been inhibited from shedding, and which has become a twisted, killing force . . . is love veiled."

Hughes's personal life, relatively uneventful in the years following Plath's suicide, was shattered again in March 1969, when Assia Gutman Weevil, his companion since 1962, killed herself. In August 1970 Hughes married Carol Orchard, and two years later he purchased Moortown, a cattle farm in Devon, which he subsequently farmed with his father-in-law, Jack Orchard. During this time, and throughout the 1970s, Hughes produced a remarkable number of poetry collections for adults, starting with *Crow: From the Life and Songs of the Crow* (1970), an unrelentingly dark exploration of the primitive, violent forces of nature. Other major trade editions include *Selected Poems: 1957–1967* (1972), *Cave Birds* (1975), *Gaudete* (1977), *Remains of Elmet* (1979), and *Moortown* (1979). This last book includes poems based on Hughes's work as a farmhand; they strike a new tone in his work – acceptance, even celebration, of the cyclical patterns of nature mirrored in the routine of farm life.

The gentler tone of *Moortown* is also evident in *Spring, Summer, Autumn, Winter* (1974), revised and enlarged as *Season Songs* (1975), a volume of children's poems drawn from Hughes's experiences in rural Devon. The songs fall into four sections, one for each season, making the book a record of the annual pattern of generation, life, and death in the natural world. Hughes actually composed the first of the poems, the autumn sequence, as lyrics to be sung at a harvest festival at Little Missenden; they were collected in a limited-edition volume, *Five Autumn Songs for Children's Voices* (1968). The spring, summer, and winter poems came later – some of them, it appears, after Hughes had begun working at his Moortown farm. Reading a selection of the poems for BBC radio, he explained that his "only concern" in *Season Songs* was "to stay close to simple observation" and to keep "within hearing of children." Most reviewers of the book agree that Hughes successfully achieved his aim, and many note that the book is also of considerable interest for adult readers.

The most salient feature of *Season Songs* is its directness, its refusal to adorn nature or to sentimentalize farm life. In strikingly spare language, Hughes celebrates birth and the coming of spring: "Lambs bounce out and stand astonished / Puss willow pushes among bare branches / Sooty hawthorns shiver into emerald." But he also reminds the

*The animals fleeing from "Poor Thing"; one of Andrew Davidson's
illustrations for "The Shawl of the Beauty of the World," in
Hughes's* Tales of the Early World *(1988)*

reader, just as directly, that a newborn lamb can die
unaccountably:

> Death was more interesting to him.
> Life could not get his attention.
> So he died, with the yellow birth-mucous
> Still in his cardigan.
> He did not survive a warm summer night.

Other poems in the volume record pleasurable or
unsettling images of the natural world: the musical
rush of a March river overflowing its banks, a
sensuous haying season when the grass is "wooed
by the farmer," an autumn day ominously wringing
the "neck" of summer and rolling away the sun "till
he's cold and small," and a dead salmon floating in
an icy river. As these images suggest, *Season Songs*
often moves outside the boundaries of children's
verse; in challenging young readers with subtle,
sophisticated language, Hughes asks them to stretch
their imaginations and to look at the world in fresh
ways.

Moon-Bells and Other Poems (1978) is an equally
challenging book – a selection of children's poems
from earlier volumes combined with several new
pieces close in style and content to Hughes's work
for adults. John Moles, writing in the *Times Literary
Supplement,* called the book "a young person's guide
to Ted Hughes." Indeed, though it has something of
a miscellaneous quality, *Moon-Bells* is a good introduction to Hughes's poetry. The volume reprints
seven "moon poems," an excerpt from *Nessie the
Mannerless Monster,* and pieces published in books for
adults, suggesting again Hughes's willingness to
blur the distinction between younger and older
readers.

The new material in *Moon-Bells* consists mainly
of nature poems, most of them about animals, wild
and domesticated. Some poems are grim and frightful, closer to the dark vision of *Crow* than to anything found in the author's earlier collections for
children. "Horrible Song," for example, describes
the crow as a "subtle" and "lusty" creature who, "If

he can't get your liver," will "find an old rat / Or high-way hedgehog hammered flat, / Any old rubbish to make him grow." There is also, in "Pets," a frightful badger, a "striped-faced rusher at cats," who crunches the "bones and meat of a hare." Other poems give less ominous views of nature. "The Birth of Rainbow," for example, movingly describes a cow and her newborn calf: "She was licking her gawky black calf / Collapsed wet-fresh from the womb, blinking his eyes / In the low morning dazzling washed sun."

Hughes's fascination with animals also illuminates *Under the North Star* (1981), a collection of twenty-four poems about wild creatures who inhabit northern regions. Unlike *Moon-Bells,* this collection has an impressive unity of tone, which Cushman describes as "the same poise and equilibrium, the same inner stillness, that is discernible in *Season Songs.*" But whereas *Season Songs* details the rhythms that link humans with the world of nature, *Under the North Star* presents the nonhuman world in all its otherness. The reader experiences the particularity of mammals, birds, and fish, but those creatures also become part of a larger cosmic order. Many poems suggest mythical origins for the animals or link them to the vast forces of nature. In an age guided by the certainties of technology, such images conjure up the vast perspective of nature, which becomes, in Hughes's terms, a source of awe and imaginative regeneration.

While the thematic implications of *Under the North Star* are vast, the poetry is generally accessible for young readers. The imagery, for one thing, gives the writing a strong visual appeal: "The Brooktrout, superb as a matador, / Sways invisible there / In water empty as air." There is also a strong aural dimension, including extensive use of traditional rhythms and stanzaic patterns – rhymed couplets and quatrains, for example. This degree of poetic regularity is unusual in Hughes's later work, but it seems appropriate here given the mythic, incantatory quality of many poems. The book's use of humor further broadens its appeal. Several creatures, including the moose, the black bear, and the woodpecker, are treated comically, counterpointing the dark, often violent, imagery found in other poems.

Under the North Star and *Season Songs* contain Hughes's most accomplished and sophisticated poetry for children; it is not surprising that he included selections from these books in his 1982 volume for adults, *Selected Poems 1957–1981.* In the same year, he and the Irish poet Seamus Heaney edited *The Rattle Bag,* an anthology of English and American poetry "suitable for younger people." Three new books of Hughes's poetry for adults also

appeared during the 1980s: *River* (1983), *Flowers and Insects: Some Birds and a Pair of Spiders* (1986), and *Wolfwatching* (1989).

In his recent work for children Hughes has returned to storytelling. *What Is the Truth?: A Farmyard Fable for the Young* (1984) and *Ffangs the Vampire Bat and the Kiss of Truth* (1986) are book-length stories in verse. *Tales of the Early World* (1988) is a collection of ten prose fables. Readers of Hughes's earlier work for children will recognize in these books a number of familiar features: inventive, often wildly fanciful plots; the use of myth and fable; an acute interest in the natural world; and an ear for the beauty of language. These works also illustrate Hughes's notion that literature should expose children to vital, mysterious, and sometimes fearsome realms of experience that have been largely dismissed in the age of technology.

In *What is the Truth?,* for example, the "Truth" is not a scientifically discernible abstraction but a recognition that the divine lives in the creatures of the earth. This lesson is implicit in the poems of *Season Songs* and *Under the North Star,* but here, in fable form, it becomes overt. The action of the story is initiated when God's Son wants to visit earth to learn from mankind. Although God counsels his Son to "Be satisfied with Heaven," the pair descend to the earth in the middle of the night and begin to question the spirits of several sleeping mortals in a farming village. At God's request these spirits describe their farm animals and the wild beasts of the countryside, delighting God's Son with their poems and songs. But God, unimpressed, explains that none of the spirits has spoken the "Truth." To humans, he says, animals are merely "toys": "Some they keep, some they break. How many escape unbroken? Not even the swiftest." At the end of the fable, God reveals the "Truth": he and the animals are one and the same. The divine infuses the ordinary world, but humans, in their own limited perspectives, fail to recognize this "Truth." While Hughes makes the moral clear, the text leading up to it is long and cumbersome. The villagers' poems, often rich and moving in themselves, fail to define their speakers as distinct characters. Finally, while the plot of the fable is ingenious, its development is slight, making the story little more than a framework for the poetry.

If *What Is Truth?* lacks plot development, *Ffangs the Vampire Bat and the Kiss of Truth* has it in abundance. The book is a wildly inventive fantasy in loose, sometimes rambling verse, about the adventures of Ffangs, a "failed vampire" who "can't stand the sight of blood, let alone the taste of it." He sets out from Vampire Island for London, determined to become human. After a series of comic misadventures, Ffangs ends up at Buckingham Palace to see the Queen. The frightened London authorities attack him with guns, tank shells, missiles, and a nuclear bomb, all to no avail. They finally hire the noted vampire hunter Thomas Squarg of Transylvania to do the job. Before Squarg can destroy Ffangs, a beauty queen named Sweety Crisp (used as a decoy) discovers that the vampire is harmless. The Queen immediately "commands the Lord Mayor of London / To set up Ffangs / In a Restaurant," where he eats strawberries and cream all day. These extravagant events occur in the first two chapters of Hughes's book. The remaining three chapters introduce a new series of adventures – mainly the activities of Squarg and Sweety Crisp – linked rather tenuously to the main story. The book ends with Ffangs's magical transformation into a boy, Bright Lad, after he is kissed by "truth" in the form of a green snake.

Thematically and technically, *Ffangs the Vampire Bat* resembles *Nessie the Mannerless Monster.* Like Nessie, Ffangs is an outsider, a creature seeking acceptance in a hostile world. Fearing the "monster," society excludes him from the daylight realm of ordinary experience. But in Hughes's scheme, individual and social well-being demand that the monster be confronted and integrated, not excluded. This theme, which recurs throughout his work, appears again at the end of Ffangs's quest when he is restored to human form by the kiss of a horrible snake. This snake, another "monster" from the dark recesses of the psyche, turns out to be the regenerating power of love. *Ffangs the Vampire Bat,* despite its fractured, disjointed plot, manages to explore its central theme in a fresh way, and while the story line may baffle some children, the book has compensating virtues, most notably its inventiveness and its often absurd humor.

Hughes's third story book from the 1980s, *Tales of the Early World,* is one of his most successful works of fiction. In language at once colloquial and richly poetic, he evokes a world in the throes of creation, with God giving shape to some of his most daring animal inventions. The ten stories in the book resembles Hughes's earlier collection of creation fables, *How the Whale Became,* but the newer volume has a broader imaginative appeal, with a colorful, fully developed cast of divine and human characters – God, his mother, Man, Woman, Boy, and Girl – along with an assortment of fascinating animals. All these characters are on friendly terms; humans and animals ask favors of God, and he coop-

erates by repairing flaws in his work. In one story, he takes away the parrot's beauty and bewitching voice in order to resolve a conflict between Man and Woman.

Some of God's creations, such as fleas and newts, appear spontaneously, the products of natural forces beyond his control. Others, such as the horse, come about through acts of God's supreme artistry. Most often, however, a combination of chance and artistry bring new creatures into existence. In "The Shawl of the Beauty of the World," for example, Boy and Girl steal into God's workshop and meddle with one of his unfinished works – a featherless, headless, footless bird called Poor Thing – giving it a dreadful voice and the feet of a demon. God's mother, taking pity on the naked creature, puts her magnificent, multicolored shawl over it. The result is the first peacock. All the tales show God as a powerful, benevolent maker, a protector of his creatures. At the same time, he is an engaging divinity who laughs, gets angry, argues, eats sausages, and sometimes bungles his creations.

The friendly mood in *Tales of the Early World* is consistent with the tone of much of Hughes's writing for children since *Season Songs.* It should be noted, however, that the raw violence of the natural world, its capacity for death and destruction, is never far below the surface in Hughes's work. Some critics have objected to this violence, finding it gratuitous or overly intense for children, but others have praised Hughes for refusing to patronize young readers and for confronting both the creative and destructive forces of nature. From this perspective, his work calls readers to see anew the sanctity of the physical earth and to face the "monsters" inside and outside themselves in order to live vitally rather than mechanically.

In recent years Hughes has written mainly for adult readers. He has also produced a new book of juvenile fiction, his first in five years. *The Iron Woman: A Sequel to "The Iron Man"* (1993) borrows its central premise – an iron giant come to life – and some of its central characters from Hughes's earlier story. In the more recent book the Iron Woman emerges from a polluted marsh near a waste-disposal factory, seeking vengeance for humanity's destruction of the environment. Lucy, the protagonist, joins forces with Hogarth and the Iron Man to save the country from the enraged creature. The Iron Woman's actions force the people to acknowledge the damage they have done to the natural world.

Thematically, the book recalls not only Hughes's fables about the powers of science and technology run amok but also his broader theme of the unity of the human and nonhuman worlds. This concern is central throughout the author's work. In *Meet My Folks!,* for example, the concluding poem describes a boy who redeems himself through an act of reverence for the natural world. Hughes was writing children's literature with an environmental message long before it became fashionable to do so.

Hughes has received many honors for his children's writing, including the Kurt Maschler Award, the Guardian Award for Children's Fiction, and, on three occasions, the Signal Poetry Award. His achievements as a writer for adults have also brought him distinctions, among them a Guggenheim Fellowship, the Queen's Gold Medal for Poetry, the Somerset Maugham Award, and the Hawthornden Prize. In 1977 he was awarded the Order of the British Empire, and in 1984 he succeeded Sir John Betjeman as poet laureate of England. In assessing Hughes's contributions as a children's writer, Keith Cushman notes the continuity between his work for younger and older readers, especially in recent years, when poetry for children has been an integral part of his overall artistic achievement. Cushman writes, "The effort to reach the child's imagination with poetry, to nurture it, to preserve it and keep it whole, must be recognized as being of paramount importance to the literary faith of Ted Hughes."

Bibliography:

Keith Sagar and Stephen Tabor, *Ted Hughes: A Bibliography 1946–1980* (London: Mansell, 1983).

References:

Keith Cushman, "Hughes' Poetry for Children," in *The Achievement of Ted Hughes,* edited by Keith Sagar (Athens: University of Georgia Press, 1983), pp. 239–256;

John Gough, "Experiencing a Sequence of Poems: Ted Hughes's Season Songs," *Children's Literature Association Quarterly,* 13 (Winter 1988): 191–194;

Fred Rue Jacobs, "Hughes and Drama," in *The Achievement of Ted Hughes,* edited by Sagar (Athens: University of Georgia Press, 1983), pp. 154–170;

Olivia Bottum Lenz, "Landscape of Our Dreams: Ted Hughes's *Moon-Whales and Other Moon Poems,*" *Children's Literature Association Quarterly,* 13 (Spring 1988): 22–25;

Brian Morse, "Poetry, Children, and Ted Hughes," in *The Signal Approach to Children's Books,* edited by Nancy Chambers (Metuchen, N.J.: Scarecrow Press, 1981), pp. 109–125;

Keith Sagar, *The Art of Ted Hughes,* second edition (Cambridge: Cambridge University Press, 1978);

Sagar, *Ted Hughes* (London: Longmans, 1972);

Leonard M. Scigaj, *Ted Hughes* (Boston: Twayne, 1991).

Mollie Hunter

(30 June 1922 –)

Joel D. Chaston
Southwest Missouri State University

BOOKS: *A Love Song for My Lady* (London: Evans Brothers, 1962);

Stay for an Answer (New York: French, 1962);

Patrick Kentigern Keenan, illustrated by Charles Keeping (London: Blackie, 1963); republished as *The Smartest Man in Ireland* (New York: Funk & Wagnalls, 1965);

Hi Johnny, illustrated by Drake Brookshaw (London: Evans Brothers, 1963);

The Kelpie's Pearls, illustrated by Keeping (London: Blackie, 1964); republished with illustrations by Joseph Cellini (New York: Funk & Wagnalls, 1966); republished with illustrations by Stephen Gammell (New York: Harper & Row, 1976);

The Spanish Letters, illustrated by Elizabeth Grant (London: Evans Brothers, 1964; New York: Funk & Wagnalls, 1967);

A Pistol in Greenyards, illustrated by Grant (London: Evans Brothers, 1965; New York: Funk & Wagnalls, 1968);

The Ghosts of Glencoe (London: Evans Brothers, 1966; New York: Funk & Wagnalls, 1969);

Thomas and the Warlock, illustrated by Keeping (London: Blackie, 1967); republished with illustrations by Cellini (New York: Funk & Wagnalls, 1967);

The Ferlie, illustrated by Michal Morse (London: Blackie, 1968); republished with illustrations by Cellini (New York: Funk & Wagnalls, 1968);

The Bodach, illustrated by Gareth Floyd (London: Blackie, 1970); republished as *The Walking Stones,* illustrated by Trina Schart Hyman (New York: Harper & Row, 1970);

The Lothian Run (New York: Funk & Wagnalls, 1970; London: Hamish Hamilton, 1971);

The Thirteenth Member (London: Hamish Hamilton, 1971; New York: Harper & Row, 1971);

The Haunted Mountain, illustrated by Trevor Ridley (London: Hamish Hamilton, 1972; New York: Harper & Row, 1972);

Mollie Hunter

A Sound of Chariots (New York: Harper & Row, 1972; London: Hamish Hamilton, 1973);

The Stronghold (New York: Harper & Row, 1974; London: Hamish Hamilton, 1974);

A Stranger Came Ashore (London: Hamish Hamilton, 1975; New York: Harper & Row, 1975);

Talent is Not Enough: Mollie Hunter on Writing for Children (New York: Harper & Row, 1976);

The Wicked One (London: Hamish Hamilton, 1977; New York: Harper & Row, 1977);

A Furl of Fairy Wind: Four Stories, illustrated by Gammell (New York: Harper & Row, 1979);

The Third Eye (London: Hamish Hamilton, 1979; New York: Harper & Row, 1979);

You Never Knew Her as I Did! (London: Hamish Hamilton, 1981; New York: Harper & Row, 1981); republished as *Escape from Loch Leven* (Edinburgh: Canongate, 1987);

The Dragonfly Years (London: Hamish Hamilton, 1983); republished as *Hold on to Love* (New York: Harper & Row, 1984);

The Knight of the Golden Plain, illustrated by Marc Simont (London: Hamish Hamilton, 1983; New York: Harper & Row, 1983);

I'll Go My Own Way (London: Hamish Hamilton, 1985); republished as *Cat, Herself* (New York: Harper & Row, 1986);

The Three Day Enchantment, illustrated by Simont (New York: Harper & Row, 1985);

The Mermaid Summer (London: Hamish Hamilton, 1988; New York: Harper & Row, 1988);

The Pied Piper Syndrome and Other Essays (New York: Harper & Row, 1992);

Day of the Unicorn, illustrated by Donna Diamond (New York: HarperCollins, 1994);

Gilly Martin the Fox, illustrated by Dennis McDermott (New York: Hyperion Press, 1994).

OTHER: "The Last Lord of Redhouse Castle," in *The Thorny Paradise: Writers on Writing for Children,* edited by Edward Blishen (Harmondsworth: Kestrel, 1975), pp. 128–139;

"Mollie Hunter," in *Something About the Author – Autobiographical Series,* volume 7, edited by Joyce Nakamura (Detroit: Gale Research, 1988), pp. 139–154.

SELECTED PERIODICAL PUBLICATIONS – UNCOLLECTED: "One World," *Horn Book,* 51 (December 1975): 557–563;

"One World, Part II," *Horn Book,* 52 (February 1976): 32–38;

"If You Can Read, Part I," *Horn Book,* 54 (June 1978): 257–262;

"If You Can Read, Part II," *Horn Book,* 54 (August 1978): 431–437;

"A Need for Heroes," *Horn Book,* 59 (April 1983): 146–154.

Mollie Hunter is one of the most popular and influential twentieth-century Scottish writers of fiction for children and young adults. Her work, which includes fantasy, historical fiction, and realism, has been widely praised and has won many awards and honors, such as the Carnegie Medal, the Phoenix Award, a *Boston Globe–Horn Book* Honor Award, and the Scottish Arts Council Award. There has also been great interest in Hunter's views about writing fiction, and she has published two collections of essays and speeches on the subject. Hunter's portrait hangs in the Scottish National Portrait Gallery, and her papers and manuscripts are preserved in the Scottish National Library. Her books have been as popular in the United States as in the United Kingdom, and most are still in print. Critic Peter Hollindale has gone so far as to assert that Hunter "is by general consent Scotland's most distinguished modern children's writer."

Maureen Mollie Hunter McVeigh was born on 30 June 1922 in Longniddry, East Lothian, Scotland, the third of five children born to William George McVeigh, an Irish motor mechanic, and Helen Eliza Smeaton Waitt. Hunter has written that her childhood environment provided her with a sense of history and that her first language, Doric, which she describes as a poetic peasant dialect, contributed to her connection with the past. She grew up in a family of readers and had access to her grandfather's large library. Hunter, her sisters, and her brother inherited something of their mother's dramatic flair and often acted out the stories she told them. As a child Hunter heard many of the tales of Scottish history and folklore that she later used in her writing. While attending Preston Lodge School, where the only subject that really interested her was English, Hunter enjoyed writing essays in which she could play with language. When a teacher asked what Hunter wanted to be when she grew up, she responded, "A kennel maid." The teacher, calling the answer "nonsense," predicted that Hunter would grow up to become a writer.

Hunter had a special relationship with her father, whom she has described as a penniless World War I veteran, "a man of strong social conscience, always on the side of the underdog." Hunter was devastated when he died in 1931 from aftereffects of his war wound. Years later she was finally able to describe some of her intense feeling of loss in the autobiographical *A Sound of Chariots* (1972).

After her father's death Hunter gained a keener awareness of herself and the world around her, which prompted her to try to write poetry. First, however, she decided that she needed to obtain a good education. Although Hunter had to leave school when she was fourteen to work in one of her grandfather's flower shops in Edinburgh, she took night-school classes and studied independently at the National Library. She developed a

Dust jacket for Hunter's story of a farmer who decides that he can outwit the magical sídhe

deep interest in comparative religion, the history of Scotland, and folklore.

At the age of eighteen Hunter became reacquainted with Thomas "Michael" McIlwraith, who at the age of twenty was drafted into the armed forces. On 23 December 1940, after a year in the navy, McIlwraith married Hunter while he was on leave. While separated from her husband during World War II, Hunter continued to read and study, and she became involved in politics, giving speeches during the general election. At the end of the war McIlwraith returned home, and he and Hunter tried to begin a family. Their first child, a boy, was born prematurely and died. The doctor told Hunter she could not have more children, but she set out to prove him wrong and eventually gave birth to two healthy sons, Quentin Wright in 1951 and Brian George in 1953.

In 1952 the McIlwraiths moved to the Scottish Highlands, first near Inverness and later to The Shieling, in a village near Loch Ness. Although her husband bought her a typewriter and encouraged her to write, much of Hunter's time was taken up with helping him get established in his career in hospital catering. Eventually Hunter began to publish newspaper articles, short stories, and some historical research; some of her essays on Scottish history appeared in *The Glasgow Herald* and *The Scotsman*.

Hunter and her family have also been involved with Inverness Cathedral, where she joined a drama group called the Cathedral Players. Hunter has also done stage directing, partly because of her husband's singing in a local opera company, and acting. In 1961 her one-act play *A Love-Song for My Lady* was produced at the Empire Theatre, Inverness. In the same year another one-act play, *Stay for an Answer,* was presented by the Cathedral Players of Inverness in the Scottish Drama Association's Drama Festival. Both plays were published in 1962.

Stay for an Answer is of special interest because it looks forward to some of Hunter's historical novels. The play, set in July 1747, involves a family taking part in the Jacobite rebellion. Like many of the heroes of Hunter's historical fiction, the play's protagonist, Mistress Jean McLachlan, has divided loyalties. As in Hunter's novels, the play personalizes historical events by focusing on their effect on an individual.

When their children were still young, Hunter's husband suggested that she write a novel. During the next two years she worked on a long manuscript, but it was not accepted for publication. Hunter's next attempt at writing fiction grew out of a group of stories she told her children about an Irishman named Patrick Kentigern Keenan. Hunter's older son, Quentin, suggested that she make a book out of the "Patrick" stories so that he could read them, and Hunter decided to try. She would read installments of the work in progress to her sons; on one such occasion she discovered one of the boys weeping over the story. Those tears, Hunter later wrote, convinced her more than ever that she should become a writer. She further explains that her choice of form allowed her to synthesize her two loves, her writing and her children. Hunter completed the book and sent it off to the publisher Blackie and Son, which published it in 1963 as *Patrick Kentigern Keenan;* it was published as *The Smartest Man in Ireland* (1965) in the United States.

The basic plot of *Patrick Kentigern Keenan* is one that Hunter employs in many of her literary folktales: a stubborn, cocky person stands up against and eventually vanquishes an antagonistic supernatural force. As in traditional folktales, the novel's protagonist, Patrick, has some basic character flaws that almost cost him his life. He is lazy and both stubborn and proud, determined that he can outwit the local fairies or leprechauns. He tries to trick the fairies by paying for a pair of their boots with false gold; in retribution they kidnap his son, and he must slave away to pay them back.

Patrick steals a fairy's crown to win a hundred head of fairy cattle, then returns it when humans think the cattle are merely a swarm of flies. Patrick is temporarily transformed into a hare by a fairy woman and chased by his own dog. Later he tries to steal a fairy horse and searches for fairy gold, only to be diverted from his quest by a fairy woman in disguise. During his various adventures Patrick collects several fairy objects that help him rescue his son, Kieron, who is kidnapped a second time by the fairies. This time Patrick imprisons the fairies in their underground kingdom.

Much of the book focuses on Patrick's gradual change in character. While both he and his son remain stubborn to the end, he learns to value his wife's common sense, realizing that there are things more important than fairy gold and magical objects. In the end Patrick can finally prove the truthfulness of one of his supernatural encounters and earns the title "the smartest man in Ireland." The only one of Hunter's books to draw on her Irish heritage, *Patrick Kentigern Keenan* established the author's ability to breathe life into folk sources and convince readers that the fantastic might be possible.

Hunter's next book was her first historical novel. Although she originally wanted to write poetry, Hunter explains that she finally realized that her studies of Scotland's past and its folklore had been training her to write fantasy and historical fiction. *Hi Johnny* (1963) is set in Edinburgh of 1540 and concerns Lady Margaret Setoun, who has been kidnapped by the laird of Hepburn. The novel's main character, a peddlar called "Hi Johnny," attempts to save her and finds himself in conflict with the laird.

The novel features exotic characters and a series of plot twists. Peter Hollindale describes *Hi Johnny* as the first of Hunter's three historical "romances," which also include *The Spanish Letters* (1964) and *The Lothian Run* (1970). Their emphasis, he explains, "is on the vigorous development of stirring blood-and-thunder plots," rather than a serious exploration of historical events.

The Kelpie's Pearls (1964) is a literary folktale about a seventy-two-year-old woman, Morag Macleod, who helps a kelpie caught in the pool near her house. Eventually she befriends the water sprite

and young Torquil Mac Vinish, who Morag believes has "King Solomon's Ring," the power to attract and befriend animals. Morag begins to spend her afternoons telling Torquil stories, and her evenings talking with the kelpie.

When a trapper named Alisdair tries to steal a string of pearls the kelpie has given Morag, she uses a chant she has learned from her grandmother to protect Alisdair from the kelpie, who takes the form of a wild horse. Morag's neighbors and the press dub her "The Witch of Abriachan," and people come from all over to catch a glimpse of her. With the help of her grandmother's book of magic, she raises a three-day storm to drive away the tourists and, as a result, attracts even more publicity and tourists. In the end, Morag departs with the kelpie for Tir-nan-Og, the land of eternal youth, leaving Torquil a note of comfort prompting him to go work for a naturalist.

The main theme of *The Kelpie's Pearls* is that special gifts, magical ones such as those of Morag or more natural ones such as those of Torquil, are often misunderstood and unappreciated. At times, too, there is a price for making one's gifts known. As the kelpie tells Morag, because of her gift she can no longer be the woman she once was. Morag, Torquil, and the kelpie, however, find happiness through their friendships and individuals who value them.

The Kelpie's Pearls was named as an American Library Association Notable Book and was on the *Horn Book* Honor List. Reviews noted Hunter's gift of balancing economic dialogue and fine prose and called it a "spellbinder." Almost ten years later children's writer Eleanor Cameron listed it as one of Hunter's two best books. More than *Patrick Kentigern Keenan*, *The Kelpie's Pearls* looks forward to the smooth, seemingly effortless feeling of Hunter's later literary folktales.

The Spanish Letters, Hunter's second historical novel, is again set in her favorite century, the sixteenth, and her favorite city, Edinburgh. Critics noted the novel's credibility and Hunter's good sense of time and place. In "The Last Lord of Redhouse Castle" (1975) Hunter has written that in *The Spanish Letters* she chose to write about a street boy in order to challenge the traditional use of middle-class heroes in historical novels. The book's fifteen-year-old protagonist, Jamie Morton, is a member of the "caddies," who hire themselves out as messengers and porters. Like many of Hunter's young heroes, Jamie is headstrong, impetuous, and a romantic. He dreams of being trained in fencing, and,

*Dust jacket for Hunter's fictionalized account of her childhood
and her father's death*

through an unusual set of circumstances, he gets his wish.

This is the first of several of Hunter's novels in which historical events are presented from the point of view of a teenage boy who helps a more mature, heroic man save the country. Partly through the persuasion of John Forbes, the local fencing master, Jamie agrees to help English government agent Roger Macey, who is trying to capture a group involved in a Spanish plot against Britain and Scotland. Through several exciting plot twists, Jamie helps find the body of another English government agent and discovers that Forbes's daughter, Marie, has been abducted to an underground tunnel.

Eventually Macey and Jamie discover the traitor's gold, rescue Marie, and recover the "Spanish Letters," which reveal a plot against King James. There is a suspenseful climactic scene at the Edinburgh prison, the Tolbooth, in which King James is saved and the earl of Huntley's betrayal is exposed. The novel ends with Macey and Marie's wedding.

Jamie, who is to be trained in fencing and join Macey in the service of Elizabeth I, has undergone a transformation, learning to control his impetuous nature and discovering a focus and purpose for his life.

A Pistol in Greenyards, another historical novel, followed in 1965. This book, set in the nineteenth-century Scottish Highlands, grew out of a single incident in which a boy pulled a pistol on a "Sherriff-Officer" who was serving his people a writ of eviction. In preparation for this book, Hunter read many diaries and letters and interviewed elderly people who were familiar with Crofting. In order to convey the emotions of her story, Hunter uses a first-person narrator for the first time.

The narrator, Connal Ross, is a fifteen-year-old boy from the Scottish Highlands whose people are brutally forced off the property that they have farmed for centuries. The Highlanders take a stand against their evictors, partly because of landowner Alexander Munro's false promises. The whole town, including the children, watches for those who might try to force them off their land. As in many of her later novels, Hunter endows one of her characters, an elderly blind man named John Chisholm, with a prophetic "second sight." Chisholm, one of the village's "bodachs," or old men, foresees a confrontation in which Connal's mother and older sister, Katrine, are injured.

During an altercation between the people of Greenyards and Sherriff-Officer Dugald McCaig, Connal prevents McCaig from killing his mother by pulling a pistol on him. Eventually the people of Greenyards are attacked, and some, including children, are killed. Connal is forced to hide in a cave for six months, and his mother is arrested. Connal and his sister are helped by a lawyer, who manages to get the charges against their mother reduced. At the end Connal and Katrine are safely on board the *Good Chance,* sailing for America. Their mother, serving a twelve-month prison sentence, hopes to join them thereafter.

In this novel Hunter explores the unwarranted violence perpetrated against the people of Greenyards and the tension between Highlanders and Lowlanders, which is partially eased when Katrine marries Dr. Hamilton, a Lowlander. The author makes several heartfelt laments for the Highlanders, whose ancient culture is being destroyed. Because Hunter develops a complex and sympathetic narrator, this book seems more personal and moving than either *Hi Johnny* or *The Spanish Letters.* Several reviews noted the novel's vividness, commenting on its brutal, gripping story.

Hunter's next book, *The Ghosts of Glencoe* (1966), is also a fictionalized account of a massacre of Scottish Highlanders – in this case the February 1692 killing of seventy-eight members of the Mac-Donald Clan by a military regiment of their enemies, the Campbells. As presented in the novel, the massacre is planned without King William's knowledge by the secretary of state and the earl of Bredalbane and is put into action by Capt. Robert Campbell of Glenlyon. Before attempting to exterminate the MacDonalds, Glenlyon's regiment sets up camp in Glencoe for twelve days, gaining the clan's trust and enjoying its hospitality.

The massacre is only partially successful, however, because of the rebellion of several of the regiment's officers, including the novel's narrator, the sixteen-year-old ensign Robert Stewart. Stewart finds himself torn between his desire to become a great military officer and his own growing appreciation of the MacDonalds. Ultimately he helps some of the clan escape, even returning to Glencoe to try to rescue a young boy who has been left behind.

Stewart emerges a hero, is reinstated into the military, and comes across the now renegade Campbell, who is still haunted by the "ghosts of Glencoe," those people he helped kill.

Hunter does not spare details when describing the massacre, which is the novel's climax. As a result, the book contains some of her most suspenseful and powerful writing. In creating the protagonist, Hunter drew from stories told by survivors of the Glencoe massacre. Hunter's husband also helped her map out and explore the terrain depicted in the novel.

With *Thomas and the Warlock* (1967), Hunter returned to fantasy. The novel, which explains why there are no more witches or warlocks in Scotland, is similar to *Patrick Kentigern Keenan* in that its protagonist, Thomas the blacksmith, endangers his family by believing that he can outwit the supernatural. The novel suggests that only through unselfishness and community cooperation can evil can be vanquished. When Hugo Griffith, a warlock, kidnaps Thomas's wife, Janet, because her husband has been poaching on his land, the whole town bands together to rescue her. The warlock is defeated only when Thomas, his son, the minister, the sheriff, and the laird work together. When first published, *Thomas and the Warlock* was commended for both its humor and original characters, which are more developed than those of Hunter's first fantasy.

The Ferlie (1968), yet another fantasy, was chosen as a Child Study Association of America Book of the Year. A fairly simple story, it celebrates the power of music, as well as the triumph of two oppressed children over their selfish masters. The main character, Hob Hazeldene, lives on the Scottish side of the border between England and Scotland. He has been brought up by Goody Cunningham, a witch, who sends him to herd cattle for Big Archie Armstrong and his wife, Mistress Kate. It soon becomes clear that Hob is a talented musician. He carves a whistle or flute from a reed and learns to play a mystical melody that he has heard in his dreams.

Archie and his sons steal some cattle belonging to the "ferlies" or fairies, but Hob frees them when they turn into frogs. Forced by Archie, Hob reluctantly brings back the herd by playing his flute, but they escape in the form of rats. On Midsummer's Evening, Hob follows the ferlie band to their underground kingdom, where he is captured. He escapes from the ferlies with the help of a horseshoe, ultimately finding love with another servant, Marget, and leaving Archie for a new master. While this is one of the simplest of Hunter's literary

Hunter with the Carnegie Medal she won for The Stronghold *(1974)*

folktales, it has remained popular and was broadcast on BBC radio as "The Enchanted Whistle."

Another fantasy about the supernatural, *The Bodach* (1970; published in the United States as *The Walking Stones*), was named a Child Study Association of America Book of the Year. Once again, critics noted its believability and strong narrative. It focuses on ten-year-old Donald Campbell and his parents, Ian and Kitty, all friends of "the Bodach," an elderly storyteller who allegedly has second sight. As the novel begins, the Bodach foretells the coming of three men, each named Rory. This prophecy is fulfilled, and the three men announce that they are going to build a power station and flood the glen where the Campbells and the Bodach live.

Donald soon learns that, like the Bodach, he can conjure up his Co-Walker, a double of himself that can do his bidding. When the Bodach saves Donald from the supernatural Washer at the Ford, who brings death to anyone she touches, the old man bequeaths his powers and staff to the boy. When the Bodach dies, it is up to Donald to see that, before the glen is flooded, thirteen ancient

stones have their chance to walk about as they do every hundred years.

Like many of Hunter's fantasies, *The Bodach* celebrates the value of old traditions and customs. It is important to the Bodach that there be someone who can pass on the story of the stones after he has gone, and Donald learns that stories are valuable. As the Bodach tells him when his family acquires a television, only through oral tales will he learn of the Great Gray Man who haunts the slopes of Ben MacDhui or of the Great Stones themselves. Like many of Hunter's books, *The Bodach* also stresses the value of imagination. Donald's ability to create his own Co-Walker, which he uses to trick the men at the power station, is linked to his ability to use his creative abilities.

The Lothian Run, Hunter's next historical novel, was named as an honor book in the Children's Spring Book Festival sponsored by *Book World,* but it received mixed reviews. Of all of Hunter's historical novels, *The Lothian Run* most closely resembles the works of Sir Walter Scott, to whom her autobiographical character Bridie Mc-

Shane pays homage in *The Dragonfly Years* (1983). Some of the historical events and characters of *The Lothian Run* recall Scott's *Heart of Midlothian* (1818): both books feature the hanging of John Porteous by the smuggler Geordie Robertson, who disguises himself as a woman, as well as the ensuing riot at the Tolbooth prison.

Like Edward Waverley of Scott's *Waverley* (1814), sixteen-year-old Sandy Maxwell of *The Lothian Run* wants an exciting romantic profession instead of the one that he seems destined to pursue. In 1736 Sandy is apprenticed to an Edinburgh lawyer, Mr. Wishart. Sandy's demand to be released to pursue some other profession coincides with a visit to Wishart's office by Deryck Gilmour, an officer from the Special Investigations Branch of the Customs Service. After Gilmour engages Wishart to help apprehend the smuggler Geordie Robertson, Sandy is sent home to Prestonpans, a coastal village, to make inquiries about Robertson, who used to frequent the area.

Sandy finally realizes that he wants to become an investigator for the customs service. As the novel progresses Sandy discovers the need for education in his new line of work, demonstrating his courage by surviving an assassination attempt, helping to capture a group of smugglers, and assisting in putting down the famous Porteous riot. The climactic riot scenes are extremely well written, although the book as a whole lacks the depth of some of Hunter's other historical novels.

Hunter's *The Thirteenth Member* (1971) is a revised version of her first (unpublished) book. The novel, which begins in July of 1590, is told mostly from the point of view of a sixteen-year-old stablehand, Adam Lawrie, who accidentally discovers a coven of witches near his Scottish village, Tranent. Initially Adam trusts no one and feels little compassion for Gilly Duncan, a kitchen maid who has been forced by her mother to become the thirteenth member of a witches' coven. Partly at the instigation of his mentor, a local alchemist named Master Grahame, Adam decides to help rescue Gilly from the coven and oppose the witches' plan to destroy King James VI.

It is difficult for Adam to know whom to trust because he cannot tell which ones are witches. In the end Adam helps unmask the man who has been masquerading as the devil, Master Grahame's twin brother, and successfully defends Gilly when they are both brought before King James. Unselfishly Adam gives up the opportunity to become a soldier and to receive land, the reward for helping expose another of the earl of Bothwell's plots against the

king. Instead, he bargains for Gilly's freedom and they start a new life together.

The book, as Hunter discusses in *Something About the Author – Autobiographical Series* (1988), was carefully researched over a long period of time. To her original unpublished manuscript, however, she added the notion "that one would be better off dead than tamely accepting that evil would eventually triumph." In *Talent is Not Enough* (1976) Hunter adds that the story finally came together when she was able to personalize it through the characters of Adam and Gilly. This particular book is one of Hunter's favorites, despite the fact that it has not won the awards many of her other novels have received.

In 1972 Hunter published two books that were well received. The first, *The Haunted Mountain,* was awarded the Scottish Arts Council Literary Award and was a *New York Times* Outstanding Book of the Year and an American Library Association Notable Book. Robert Nye in *The New York Times Book Review* lauded the book for taking fantasy seriously, and *The School Librarian* suggested that it would appeal to both older readers as well as to children. In many respects *The Haunted Mountain* resembles *Patrick Kentigern Keenan.* Once again, the main character, MacAllister, is a stubborn man who is convinced that he can beat the fairies – who in this book are called "sídhe" (pronounced "she"). As a result, he decides to reclaim his Goodman's Croft, the part of his farm that, according to local custom, was to be left for the sídhe.

Once again pride and stubbornness create problems for Hunter's characters, but, as in many traditional tales, the love of a child for a parent helps defeat the antagonists. The novel is more suspenseful and takes itself more seriously than *Patrick Kentigern Keenan,* and MacAllister is more complex than the earlier Patrick and more quick to recognize that his predicament has resulted from his own actions. As in most of her later fantasies, Hunter allows a child to defeat creatures that threaten adults.

A Sound of Chariots, Hunter's fictionalized account of her childhood and her father's death, had been written in 1963, then put in a drawer, where it remained for eight years until an editor accidentally heard of it. Hunter was surprised that the editor considered the manuscript a children's book, as she had not intended it for that audience. The novel focuses on Bridie McShane, Hunter's alter ego, who is devastated when her father, Patrick, dies. The book's title comes from a line in Andrew Marvell's poem "To His Coy Mistress," which expresses Bridie's fear of death: "But at my back I always

*Dust jacket for Hunter's 1979 novel about a fourteen-year-old
girl who must come to terms with painful memories*

hear, / Time's wingèd chariot hurrying near." Unlike some other popular children's books about death, such as Katherine Paterson's *Bridge to Terabithia* (1977), the major death in *A Sound of Chariots* occurs in the first chapter. Only then does Bridie, through a series of flashbacks, explore her relationship with her father.

Bridie idolizes her father, a Socialist concerned with making a better life for himself and the other war veterans in his neighborhood. This creates problems with Bridie's mother, an extremely religious member of the "Brethren" who dislikes Patrick's contention that Christ was a revolutionary. Bridie's memories of her father are recounted in the novel's first eight chapters, grouped as part 1. Bridie struggles to keep her father's acceptance, especially when her younger brother is born and her mother suggests that she has now lost her "place in the sun." Bridie remains her father's favorite, however, a feeling separating her from her three elder sisters, whom she calls "The Others."

When Bridie discovers the love letters her parents wrote while courting, she also begins to appreciate her mother and the strong bond between her parents. Partly because of these letters, Bridie decides she wants to become a writer.

Part 2, comprising the novel's last nine chapters, begins with the death of Bridie's father, tracing its effect on the McShanes over several years. Bridie's brother, William, slowly begins to understand the meaning of death when his pet rabbit, Bluey, dies. Bridie's mother is forced to do menial work to make money, and the sisters' education is cut short so they can work for a living. For Bridie, this means that she cannot go to the university but must take a position working in one of her grandparents' flower shops. She determines, however, that the situation will not prevent her from becoming a writer.

Most important, the death of her father has a strong psychological, even spiritual effect on Bridie. She grows out of the nightmares she has after his death, developing what she describes as a clarity of vision about the world. She also is able to express her grief for her father, bursting into tears after performing a song at a Christmas party for the children of World War I veterans. She also gradually discovers her love for her mother. After an attempt to show her mother her love by bringing her a bouquet of birthday violets, she braves the weather and local aristocracy to bring her mother her coat. The novel ends with Bridie maturing and leaving home. Through the advice of her English teacher, Dr. McIntyre, Bridie determines to live life to the fullest, at least partly in honor of her father.

A Sound of Chariots has been the subject of a great deal of critical attention from scholars and children's writers. Geraldine DeLuca sees the book as a "remarkable departure" from Hunter's other work and praises its uniqueness and authenticity, arguing that it "captures the mind of a young adolescent the way few adolescent novels do." Eleanor Cameron, who calls this book one of Hunter's best, finds in it an increase in the author's "fine fierce ability to go directly to the heart of a scene, to wring from it the final drop of meaning" and a "skillful interweaving of sights, sounds and feelings as these would be experienced by a child during a moment that will change the child's life forever." *A Sound of Chariots* was on the *Horn Book* Honor List and was a *New York Times* Outstanding Book of the Year and an American Library Association Notable Book. It won the Children's Book Award from the Child Study Association of America and received the 1992 Children's Literature Association's Phoenix Award, which is given for an outstanding book published twenty years before.

Hunter was awarded the Carnegie Medal in 1974 for *The Stronghold,* a historical novel set in the first century B.C. on the Orkney Islands, which Hunter visited while researching the book. One evening she stood in one of the ancient first-century brochs described in the novel in order to try to understand her characters' feel for the supernatural. She claimed, "I felt as if my body was being drained of life and I became quite hollow. I turned and ran back to the car. Never have I been so glad of my little modern box of glass and steel."

The Stronghold explores life among a tribe of people known as "The Boars," who become divided when their tribal chief, Nectan, and the chief of the islands' priesthood of Druids, Domnall, disagree on how they should handle the Roman slave traders who attack them yearly. In the ensuing struggle between Nectan and Domnall, Hunter creates characters who are torn among loyalty to their leader, reli-

gious superstition, a desire for power, and dreams of safety and security. The novel's protagonist, eighteen-year-old Coll, is intensely loyal to his foster father, Nectan, but feels that if he were permitted to realize his long dream of building stone towers or strongholds, then the Boar could fight off the Romans and the rift between Nectan and Domnall would be healed.

As depicted by Hunter, the Boars are a believable group of people beset with very human problems. Many of them are easily manipulated, either through their anger, their religious fervor, or their desire to dominate others. By learning to control his emotions and focus on his dream, Coll creates edifices that will last for centuries. The book includes some of Hunter's most vivid writing and effectively incorporates historical detail into an extremely credible narrative.

In 1975 Hunter produced one of her strongest and most popular fantasies, *A Stranger Came Ashore,* which was named a *Boston Globe–Horn Book* Award Honor Book. It was also a Child Study Association of America Book of the Year, a *New York Times* Outstanding Book of the Year, a *School Library Journal* Best Children's Book, a Library of Congress Book of the Year, and an American Library Association Notable Book.

In *The Pied Piper Syndrome and Other Essays* (1992) Hunter confesses that after working on *A Stranger Came Ashore* for six months, she tore up the manuscript because she had produced "nothing more than a good guidebook to Shetland." The final result, perhaps her best fantasy, is indeed filled with the culture of the Shetland Islands, north of Scotland, including the post-Christmas festival, Up Helly Aa; a traditional Shetland funeral; and riddles and folktales. It also includes some of Hunter's best descriptive writing, in particular the climactic battle between Nicol Henderson and Finn Learson and Robbie's encounter with the seal pups in the voe.

One version of the novel's plot is recounted in the last chapter: "A stranger had come ashore to Black Ness, and there he had fallen in love with Elspeth Henderson. Then there had been a fight between him and Elspeth's young man, and the stranger had taken off in a huff." Robbie Henderson, Elspeth's eleven-year-old brother, suspects the stranger, Finn Learson, of being "the Great Selkie," a seal who has come to shore and taken human form. Fed by the stories of his "Old Da" (grandfather), Robbie becomes increasingly suspicious of Finn Learson. After his Old Da dies, Robbie seeks the help of the schoolmaster, Yarl Corbie, who practices magic and, purportedly, can transform himself into a raven. In the end, Finn Learson, blinded in one eye by Yarl Corbie, returns to the sea as a bull seal.

The book draws on Shetland folk beliefs, presenting the struggle between good and evil as a battle between the son of the sea god, Finn Learson, and the earth god, who temporarily manifests himself in the form of "the Skuddler," Nicol Henderson. The novel's major themes deal with courage, perception, and the value of the imagination. Robbie is afraid of the water, the dark, his schoolmaster, and supernatural creatures called "trows." Nevertheless, he faces his fears and stands up to the Great Selkie.

One of the book's strengths is that its language is carefully ambiguous. It can be read as a true account of Robbie's interactions with the supernatural or merely a story he tells when he grows up and becomes an "Old Da" himself. All of the real magic happens out of Robbie's sight. Robbie never sees Finn Learson or Yarl Corbie transform themselves, and even the description of the fight between Finn Learson and Nicol Henderson uses the words *seems* and *appeared,* casting doubt on the reality of what is happening.

In April and May of 1975 Hunter traveled to the United States as the May Hill Arbuthnot Lecturer. In 1976 Hunter was sponsored by the British Council, the International Reading Association, and the education authorities of New Zealand and Australia to tour New Zealand and Australia. Several of Hunter's lectures were subsequently published in *Talent is Not Enough: Mollie Hunter on Writing for Children.* This collection of essays has been popular with readers and was on the *Horn Book* honor list and was a Child Study Association of America Book of the Year. Hunter's essays are filled with autobiographical anecdotes and allusions to her own works, as well as those of others, and are important contributions to the growing body of criticism about literature for children and young adults.

For her fantasy *The Wicked One* (1977), Hunter was awarded her second Scottish Arts Council Literary Award. The book was also named by the *School Library Journal* as one of the Best Books for Spring 1977 and was an American Library Association Notable Book. The first half of the novel deals with Colin Grant, who cannot control his temper. As a result he becomes a prime target for the Grollican, or "Wicked One," a monstrous invisible creature that creates misfortune for its victims. Toward the end of the novel, Colin, his wife, Anna, and youngest son, Ian, emigrate from their home in the Scottish Highlands to the United States, where

they defeat the Grollican by rendering it visible with a bag of flour. As children's novelist Natalie Babbitt has noted, " 'Grollican,' comes perilously near to being a perfect anagram for 'Colin Grant,' and is in fact an incarnation of Colin's fiery temper." In the end Colin frees himself from the Grollican by learning to control himself. As a character Colin is much like Patrick Kentigern Keenan in Hunter's first novel, a man with both passion and common sense.

Most of the second half of the book is devoted to Colin's son, Ian, who has a crooked back. Ian develops a great love for a magical pony, which Colin brings back from the underground home of the fairies. Through Ian's kindness to the Grollican, he frees the pony from a spell and it turns into a girl named Flora, whom he later marries. While Hunter uses traditional types of folk characters, the Grants are not merely caricatures but struggle with genuine emotions.

Hunter followed *The Wicked One* with a collection of literary folktales, *A Furl of Fairy Wind: Four Stories* (1979), which was a Child Study Association of America Book of the Year. Each of the four stories in this volume treats themes and motifs present in Hunter's longer fantasies. In "The Brownie" a farmer's wife learns that it is impossible to cheat a Brownie out of his bowl of hot porridge. "The Enchanted Boy" tells of a young boy who is enchanted by a fairy queen always to look to the past, and "Hi Johnny" (not to be confused with Hunter's novel by this name) is about a peddlar who decides not to cheat the fairy people when he sells them wares made of iron. "A Furl of Fairy Wind" deals with a girl named Margaret who learns how to smile after she helps defeat a changeling and rescues a baby and its mother from the fairies. Each of these stories evokes the tone and style of traditional folktales.

The Third Eye (1979) was the first of several later books specifically intended for young adults; it was named to the *Horn Book* honor list. Hunter has suggested that with *The Third Eye* she began to project herself more and more through female characters. Up until this time virtually all of her books, except for *The Kelpie's Pearls* and *A Sound of Chariots,* had featured male protagonists.

In structure, tone, and setting *The Third Eye* is strongly reminiscent of *A Sound of Chariots,* and Jinty Morrison is closely related to Bridie McShane. The novel is a compelling look at the town of Ballinford, West Lothian, during the early 1930s. It is structured as a series of flashbacks as fourteen-year-old Janet "Jinty" Morrison waits to give evidence in the

*Dust jacket for the American edition of Hunter's novel featuring
a group of itinerant Scots known as "travellers" or "tinkers"*

death of the most powerful man in her community, the earl of Ballinford. Only toward the end of the book does it become apparent that the earl has committed suicide and that Jinty feels responsible to keep that fact a secret. Through flashbacks Hunter explores her favorite themes in a series of interconnected episodes involving Jinty's family and the people of Ballinford.

Much of the book deals with learning to perceive things as they really are. Jinty is gifted with what her art teacher calls "The Third Eye," a special ability to perceive things that others cannot. Unlike the "second sight" depicted in some of Hunter's other novels, there is nothing magical or mystical about Jinty's ability. It is, as Archie Meikle tells her at the end of the novel, merely that she "can see things . . . whole and clear." Nevertheless, Jinty only gradually comes to see those around her clearly.

The novel explores the fine line between social classes, particularly the difference in lifestyles between the Morrisons and the Ballinfords. This difference is heightened when Jinty spends a sum-

mer working as a kitchen maid in Ballinford manor. Her mother is obsessed with seeing that all three of her daughters go to the university and is incensed when the eldest, Meg, marries Dave Ferguson, a garage mechanic, and the next oldest, Linda, schemes her way into the hotel business.

Like *A Stranger Came Ashore,* this novel also explores the tension between old customs (such as pagan harvest festivals, corn dollies, and "anvil" marriages) and modern Christianity (as represented by the minister, Mr. Elphinston). Jinty is intrigued by the past. The novel also chronicles Jinty's growth into adulthood, which involves encounters with death. In the end, like Cat's "second sight" in *I'll Go My Own Way* (1985), Jinty's third eye tells her not to try to be like anyone but herself.

In 1980 Hunter was a writer in residence at Dalhousie University, Halifax, Nova Scotia. In 1981 *You Never Knew Her as I Did!* (republished as *Escape from Loch Leven,* 1987), a historical novel about Mary, Queen of Scots, was published, and critics praised the book for presenting a balanced view of the controversial queen. *You Never Knew Her as I Did!* was a Notable Children's Trade Book in the Field of Social Studies and was one of the New York Public Library's Books for the Teenage, 1982.

Hunter has stated that all of her books are about conflict and that her historical fiction always involves individuals choosing sides in order to take a stand. This is one of the main issues in *You Never Knew Her as I Did!,* in many ways one of Hunter's finest and most carefully structured historical novels. The story is narrated by Will Douglas, the illegitimate son of Sir William Douglas, the hereditary keeper of Lochleven Castle. Most of the action takes place in 1567, the year in which Will turns seventeen and Mary is held captive at Lochleven. Will, who is a page, has always liked Mary, who once nicknamed him "my little orphan" to soften the fact that others call him "bastard." Will, however, is related to her enemy, James, Earl of Moray, who becomes the regent when Mary is forced to abdicate. The novel recounts Will's part in two attempts to free Mary from the castle. The first fails and results in Will's banishment, but the second is successful. Although the novel takes a sympathetic view of the queen, it also paints her as a complex and powerful woman who easily attracts Will's love and devotion.

Will is also a complex character with definite faults, including a penchant for gambling away his savings and a desire for excitement and mischief. Through the course of the novel, however, Will matures, learning about loyalty and love. One important idea in the novel is the function of role-playing in surviving the political intrigues that surround the characters. Like many of Hunter's other novels, the book culminates in the celebration of a holiday, in this case a festival in honor of May Day and Will's birthday, during which Will plays "The Lord of Misrule," pretending to be a fool. His wild antics become a cover for the queen's escape, which does not, however, prevent her eventual death years later.

In an interview in *Top of the News,* Hunter explains that her readers had wanted a sequel to *A Sound of Chariots* but that she was loath to return to the subject matter because it was so painful. *The Dragonfly Years* finally appeared in 1983, however. In the eyes of some readers, this sequel does not compare well to *A Sound of Chariots.* Several American reviewers called the book unsatisfying and decried its "mushy" ending. In many respects, however, the book is a satisfying continuation of the original. As in the first book, Hunter is clearly relating her own biography, from her time working in her grandfather's chain of flower stores to her

courtship and marriage during World War II. At the beginning of the novel, Bridie is still struggling with her father's death but is beginning to reach out to other people. As the book progresses she gains empathy for a cleaning woman, a traveling tinker woman, a Jewish jeweler, and an unmarried co-worker who becomes pregnant. She also regains faith in God, but not for her mother's religious group, the Brethren.

Like Hunter, fifteen-year-old Bridie spends her spare time reading at the National Library. Bridie still wants to become a poet, although in a scene set near a monument to Sir Walter Scott, her friend Peter McKinley helps her see that, with her interest in Scotland's past, she should try her hand at historical fiction. While Peter admires Bridie, he also tells her that she sends out "ideas like dragonflies darting all over the place. And catching even one of them is like trying to catch a dragonfly." She feels, however, that someday she will get past these "dragonfly years" and learn to weave a net that will capture all her dragonfly ideas.

In many ways the last part of the novel is a traditional romance, depicting Bridie's growing love for Peter. Their path toward marriage, which takes place while Peter is on leave from the navy, is rocky. Bridie's dying grandmother paves the way for her marriage, reiterating one of the novel's major themes when she tells Bridie that her family has always cared too much about money and pleads, "Oh, Bridie girl, hold on to love!"

At this point in her career, Hunter wrote two picture books, *The Knight of the Golden Plain* (1983) and *The Three Day Enchantment* (1985), both of which were illustrated by Caldecott Medalist Marc Simont. Both mock some of the conventions of traditional hero tales. In each of the stories Sir Dauntless, the Knight of the Golden Plain, spends a Saturday on a quest. The introduction, the illustrations, and hints in the texts reveal that the knight is really a contemporary boy who is imagining his adventures. In 1994 Hunter wrote a third adventure featuring the knight, *Day of the Unicorn,* this time illustrated by Donna Diamond.

In *The Dragonfly Years* Bridie McShane meets two tinkers and contemplates writing a book about one of them. In *I'll Go My Own Way* (republished as *Cat, Herself* (1986) in the United States) Hunter wrote the book that Bridie imagines. Like *The Third Eye,* it is a novel written specifically for young adults. While it is a mostly realistic work set in Scotland in the 1970s, it shares themes and motifs with some of Hunter's fantasies, in particular *The Wicked One.*

The novel focuses on Cat McPhie, a young member of a group known as "travellers" or "tinkers," itinerant Scots who differentiate themselves from Gypsies. The travellers spend their days roaming Scotland, except for the winter, when they camp so their children can receive schooling, and they survive by poaching and begging. They believe that formal education is virtually useless and that people should learn by doing things. They do not feel bound by many of their country's laws and do not have legal or formal wedding ceremonies. They also have strong notions about gender roles, and Cat is in danger of being labeled a "split mechanic" because she desires to hunt and fish like her father.

Like many young adult novels, *I'll Go My Own Way* explores a girl's changing attitudes toward herself, her family, and society. The novel follows Cat's life from age eleven to age sixteen, when she decides that, despite reservations, she wants to remain a traveller for life. Gradually Cat learns to value her heritage, including the "second sight" she has inherited from her mother and grandmother. She determines, however, that she will go her own way; she challenges the travellers' attitudes toward women and learns to fish and hunt like her father. Cat also forces Charlie Drummond to ask for her hand in marriage, rather than allowing him to "mark her down" as his bride without consulting her.

Two of the novel's most important themes are the persecution of those who are perceived as different and the value of folk traditions. The group must move frequently, and its members are mistreated by many of the nontravelers they meet. Toward the end of the novel, their campsite is destroyed by firebombs and several characters are killed. The novel, however, depicts a few nontravellers such as Mr. Brownlee and Dr. Ballantyne, who fight for the group's fair treatment. Hunter clearly sympathizes with the travellers, presenting their antagonists as irrational bigots. She is, however, careful to point out faults in the travellers and does not glorify them. As in most of Hunter's books, folk beliefs are also important in *I'll Go My Own Way*. Cat is entranced by her grandmother's stories, which include a romantic folktale about a man who, like Patrick Kentigern Keenan and Colin Grant, tricks the fairies. Cat also discovers the value of her "gift," as well as the traditions of her family.

A few reviewers noted that Cat is similar to Bridie McShane. The book demonstrates Hunter's ability to write for older readers and to portray obscure groups of people successfully. *I'll Go My Own Way* was a Child Study Association of America

Book of the Year, an American Library Association Best Book for Young Adults for 1986, and a *School Library Journal* Best Book for Young Adults.

In 1987 Hunter spent time as a teacher of creative writing at Aberlour Summer School for Gifted Children. The following year she wrote another fantasy, *The Mermaid Summer,* which was listed in Editor's Choices of the American Library Association Booklist and received a starred review in *The Bulletin of the Center for Children's Books*. Once again Hunter treats the interaction between mortals and supernatural beings. In this case the magical antagonist is a malevolent mermaid who has become angry at a Scottish fisherman named Eric Anderson.

The book is filled with depictions of folk customs and lore, such as the Herring Festival at which Anna is chosen queen and the Thanksgiving service when the villagers have been saved from the sea. Most of the difficulties the characters face result from Eric's boastfulness and the children's impulsiveness and stubbornness. It is Anna and Jon's strong wills and their love for their grandfather, however, as opposed to the mermaid's pride, that help them defeat her. Like the folktales from which it is drawn, the novel is well structured with a suspenseful climax. The novel does not, however, have the depth or the ambiguity of *A Stranger Came Ashore,* nor are its characters as well developed. Nevertheless, the depiction of the Herring Festival and the children's confrontations with the mermaid are vivid and represent Hunter at her best.

In 1992 Hunter traveled to Hartford, Connecticut, where she accepted the Phoenix Award from the Children's Literature Association for *A Sound of Chariots*. Later that year she produced a second collection of critical essays, *The Pied Piper Syndrome and Other Essays*. Like *Talent is Not Enough,* some of the essays in this volume had been published previously and most of them treat the art of writing for children and young adults.

In 1994 Hunter again turned to Scottish folklore for inspiration in creating a picture book, *Gilly Martin the Fox,* a retelling of an old Scottish folktale first published in English in John Francis Campbell's *Popular Tales of the West Highlands* (1860). The story describes the prince of Alban's quest for the Blue Falcon in order to break a spell placed on him by the Witch of Alban. The prince is accompanied by a fox named Gilly Martin, who helps him complete a variety of tasks in order to secure the falcon. *Gilly Martin the Fox,* illustrated by Dennis McDermott, retains the simplicity and humor of the original tale, once again demonstrating Hunter's power as a storyteller.

Few writers have produced a body of work appealing to such a wide audience and treating such diverse topics as Mollie Hunter. In addition, virtually all of Hunter's books have been critical successes. Any one of her later books would have secured her well-deserved reputation as one of Scotland's best writers for children and young adults. Hunter is a gifted storyteller, grabbing her readers from the beginning of each story or novel, sharing her own "third eye," which allows her to see her culture with clarity and sympathy. As a whole Hunter's books manage to keep the promise that in *The Pied Piper Syndrome and Other Essays* she ascribes to good books for the young: "a promise of magic that will not turn to disappointment, of pleasure that will not turn sour—because that promise, too, is one that has been made in all honesty, and has been just as faithfully fulfilled."

Interview:

"Mollie Hunter: An Interview," *Top of the News,* 41 (Winter 1985): 141–146.

References:

Natalie Babbitt, "The Wicked One," *New York Times Book Review,* 26 June 1977, p. 23;

"Breaking the Rules: Engagement and Extravaganza in Never-Never-Land," *Times Literary Supplement,* 26 November 1964, p. 1081;

Eleanor Cameron, "At Her Back She Always Heard," *New York Times Book Review,* 5 November 1972, p. 6;

Joel Chaston, "Cat, Herself," in *Beacham's Guide to Young Adult Literature,* volume 6, edited by Kirk Beetz (Washington, D.C.: Beacham, 1994), pp. 2910–2917;

Stanley Cook, "Mollie Hunter," *School Librarian,* 26 (June 1978): 108–111;

Susan Cooper, "Strains of Mark Twain," *Christian Science Monitor,* 1 May 1974, p. F5;

Geraldine DeLuca, "Unself-Conscious Voices: Larger Contexts for Adolescents," *Lion and the Unicorn,* 2 (Fall 1978): 92–96;

Patricia Dooley, "Profile: Mollie Hunter," *Children's Literature Association Newsletter,* 3 (Autumn 1978): 3–6;

Paul Heins, Introduction to Hunter's *Talent is Not Enough: Mollie Hunter on Writing for Children* (New York: Harper & Row, 1976), pp. ix–xiii;

Janet Hickman, "Profile: The Person Behind the Book – Mollie Hunter," *Language Arts,* 56 (March 1979): 302–306;

Mary Hoffman, "Scottish Story Weaver," *Times Educational Supplement,* 13 January 1984, p. 39;

Peter Hollindale, "World Enough and Time: The Work of Mollie Hunter," *Children's Literature in Education,* 8 (Autumn 1977): 109–119;

Charlotte Huck, Introduction to Hunter's *The Pied Piper Syndrome and Other Essays* (New York: Harper & Row, 1992), pp. ix–xviii;

Roni Natov, "The Truth of Autobiographical Fiction for Children," *Children's Literature in Education,* 17 (Summer 1986): 112–125;

J. S. Ryan, "The Spirit of Old Scotland: Tone in the Fiction of Mollie Hunter," *Orana,* 20 (May 1984): 93–101; (August 1984): 138–145;

George Shannon, "The Work of Keeping Writing Play: A View Through Children's Literature," *Children's Literature in Education,* 21 (March 1990): 37–43;

M. Sarah Smedman, "Springs of Hope: Recovery of Primordial Myth in 'Mythic Novels' for Young Readers," *Children's Literature,* 16 (1988): 91–107.

Diana Wynne Jones

(16 August 1934 –)

Donna R. White
Clemson University

BOOKS: *Changeover* (London: Macmillan, 1970);
Wilkins' Tooth, illustrated by Julia Rodber (London: Macmillan, 1973); republished as *Witch's Business* (New York: Dutton, 1974);
The Ogre Downstairs (London: Macmillan, 1974; New York: Dutton, 1975);
Eight Days of Luke (London: Macmillan, 1975; New York: Greenwillow, 1988);
Cart and Cwidder (London: Macmillan, 1975; New York: Atheneum, 1977);
Dogsbody (London: Macmillan, 1975; New York: Greenwillow, 1977);
Power of Three (London: Macmillan, 1976; New York: Greenwillow, 1977);
Charmed Life (London: Macmillan, 1977; New York: Greenwillow, 1977);
Drowned Ammet (London: Macmillan, 1977; New York: Atheneum, 1978);
Who Got Rid of Angus Flint?, illustrated by John Sewell (London: Evans, 1978);
The Spellcoats (London: Macmillan, 1979; New York: Atheneum, 1979);
The Magicians of Caprona (London: Macmillan, 1980; New York: Greenwillow, 1980);
The Four Grannies, illustrated by Thelma Lambert (London: Hamish Hamilton, 1980);
My Brother and I Like Cookies, by Jones and Anna L. Carlson, illustrated by Jones (Lynnwood, Wash.: Karwyn Enterprises, 1980);
The Homeward Bounders (London: Macmillan, 1981; New York: Greenwillow, 1981);
The Time of the Ghost (London: Macmillan, 1981);
Witch Week (London: Macmillan, 1982; New York: Greenwillow, 1982);
Warlock at the Wheel and Other Stories (London: Macmillan, 1984; New York: Greenwillow, 1984);
Archer's Goon (London: Methuen, 1984; New York: Greenwillow, 1984);
The Skiver's Guide, illustrated by Chris Winn (London: Knight, 1984);
Fire and Hemlock (London: Methuen, 1985; New York: Greenwillow, 1985);

Diana Wynne Jones

Howl's Moving Castle (London: Methuen, 1986; New York: Greenwillow, 1986);
A Tale of Time City (London: Methuen, 1987; New York: Greenwillow, 1987);
The Lives of Christopher Chant (London: Methuen, 1988; New York: Greenwillow, 1988):
Chair Person, illustrated by Glenys Ambrus (London: Hamish Hamilton, 1989);
Wild Robert, illustrated by Emma C. Clark (London: Methuen, 1989; Boston: G. K. Hall, 1992);
Castle in the Air (London: Methuen, 1990; New York: Greenwillow, 1991);
Black Maria (London: Methuen, 1991); republished as *Aunt Maria* (New York: Greenwillow, 1991);

A Sudden Wild Magic (New York: Morrow, 1992);

Yes, Dear, illustrated by Graham Philpot (London: HarperCollins, 1992; New York: Greenwillow, 1992);

Hexwood (London: Methuen, 1993; New York: Greenwillow, 1994);

The Crown of Dalemark (London: Mandarin, 1993; New York: Greenwillow, 1995);

Everard's Ride (Framingham, Mass.: NESFA, 1995).

Collection: *Stopping for a Spell: Three Fantasies,* illustrated by Joseph A. Smith (New York: Greenwillow, 1993) – includes *Chair Person, The Four Grannies,* and *Who Got Rid of Angus Flint?.*

PLAY PRODUCTIONS: *The Batterpool Business,* London, Arts Theatre, October 1968;

The King's Things, London, Arts Theatre, February 1970;

The Terrible Fisk Machine, London, Arts Theatre, January 1971.

OTHER: *Hidden Turnings: A Collection of Stories through Time and Space,* edited by Jones (London: Methuen, 1989; New York: Greenwillow, 1990);

Fantasy Stories, edited by Jones (London: Kingfisher, 1994; New York: Larousse Kingfisher Chambers, 1994).

SELECTED PERIODICAL PUBLICATION –
UNCOLLECTED: "The Heroic Ideal – A Personal Odyssey," *Lion and the Unicorn,* 13 (June 1989): 129–140.

Contemporary children's fantasy has its own conventions and standards, often unacknowledged but recognized by those who write or publish fantasy. Diana Wynne Jones has built her reputation on challenging those conventions, standing them on their heads, and openly criticizing them. Instinctively hostile to rules, Jones employs her unbounded inventiveness to create fantasy worlds that break the conventions and show her readers the world from a new and imaginative angle. Jones specializes in surprising plot twists and slapstick humor, which she combines with scenes of serious drama. Like Margaret Mahy, Jones believes that fantasy is the ideal medium to unveil psychological truth.

Diana Wynne Jones was born in London on 16 August 1934, the first child of Richard Aneurin Jones and Marjorie Jones. At the outbreak of World War II in 1939, Jones and her younger sister Isobel were evacuated to their grandmother's house in Wales, where they were soon joined by their mother and newborn sister, Ursula. Although the family stayed in Wales for only a year, Jones fell in love with the Welsh language – an affection that has influenced her writing. The rich, rolling Welsh polysyllables haunted her dreams even in adulthood and provided an accompaniment to her creative writing.

In 1940 the family moved to the Lake District, where Jones and her sisters went to school with other young evacuees. Here they encountered two famous children's authors – Arthur Ransome and Beatrix Potter – who objected to having their quiet lives invaded by noisy, rambunctious children. Potter went so far as to strike Isobel for swinging on the farm gate. Authors, Jones perceived, were old and grumpy and selfish.

Because of difficulties with neighboring children, Marjorie Jones moved her family again in 1941. After a brief stay in Yorkshire, they returned to London in 1942. The worst of the blitz was over, but the Germans were still making bombing runs on London. The wail of the air-raid sirens, the whistle of falling bombs, the muffled explosions, and the rat-a-tat of the anti-aircraft guns made a deep impression on Jones as she huddled with her family behind blackout curtains. Reading provided an escape from this frightening reality. Despite her early negative impression of authors, Jones decided at age eight that she would be a writer when she grew up. Her parents laughed off her announcement; writing was not an appropriate vocation for a dyslexic child.

In 1943 Richard and Marjorie Jones moved their family to the village of Thaxted in Essex to run a cultural residential center and summer school for young people. Jones and her sisters were housed alone in a hastily converted shack and left to their own devices for the next decade. Richard and Marjorie were too busy with the school to attend to their daughters' needs. Neglected and emotionally abandoned, the sisters turned to one another for support and companionship and learned that laughter was a superb coping skill.

Village life was a shock after London; there was little to do. Jones entertained herself by haunting the local church and climbing on roofs, hoping to learn to fly. But the worst aspect of country life was the absence of books. Since her father was too stingy to buy books for his children, Jones turned to the only reading material at hand – the myths and legends on the school's bookshelves. Jones immersed herself in the Greek myths, John Bunyan's *Pilgrim's Progress* (1678, 1684), Homer's *The Iliad* and

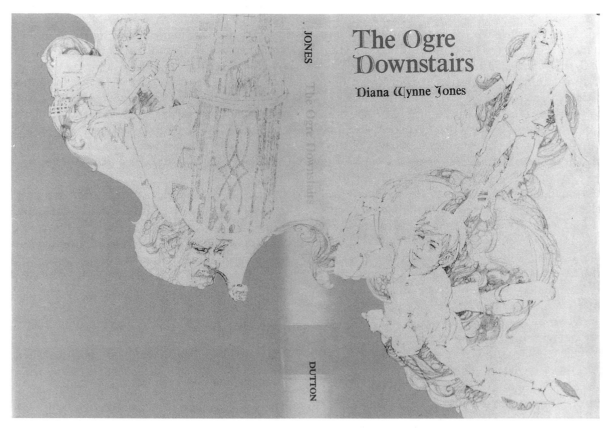

Dust jacket for Jones's second book for children, a fantasy critics have compared to the work of E. Nesbit

The Odyssey, Sir Thomas Malory's *Le Morte d'Arthur* (1485), and a volume of medieval romances given to her by her sympathetic grandmother. Once a year – at Christmas time – Richard Jones would unlock the cupboard that contained a highly treasured set of Arthur Ransome books and allow his children to choose one volume to share between the three of them. When she was nine, Jones received a bowdlerized version of *The Arabian Nights* and discovered a heroine, Scheherazade, with whom she could identify. Married to a murderous king, Scheherazade had to tell stories in order to preserve her life. Jones began to tell stories, too – to entertain her sisters when they ran out of reading material. Between the ages of twelve and fourteen Jones composed two massive epics that filled twenty exercise books; she read these heroic adventures out loud to her sisters at night.

Thanks to a near photographic memory, Jones excelled in school and was eventually accepted at St. Anne's College, Oxford, in 1953. This was the heyday of the Inklings, a group of writers whose most famous members included C. S. Lewis and J. R. R. Tolkien. Jones attended lectures by both

men and, like other future fantasy writers, was influenced by their ideas.

In 1956 Jones received her B.A. from Oxford and married John A. Burrow, a scholar of Middle English whom she had met years before at her parents' school in Thaxted. For the next few years she was busy raising children: Richard was born in 1958, Michael in 1961, and Colin in 1963. Her husband and sons taught her what a normal family life was like, and she began to understand how abnormal her own childhood had been. Jones was determined that her sons would not lack for literature, but she soon discovered that there was a dearth of good contemporary fantasy for children. To fill that gap she began to write. Her first efforts were not successful; her style was too quirky and individualistic for children's publishing in the 1960s. Not until her youngest son was in school was she able to devote full attention to her writing. Finally, in 1972 literary agent Laura Cecil convinced Macmillan to publish *Wilkins' Tooth.*

Although it seems shallow compared to many of her later works, *Wilkins' Tooth* (1973) shows the unflagging inventiveness and sense of humor characteristic of Jones's style. The story is about two children who go into the revenge business and find themselves tangling with an unpleasant bully and the local witch. Jones's second book for children, *The Ogre Downstairs* (1974), provoked comparisons to Edwardian fantasist E. Nesbit. As in Nesbit's domestic fantasies, events go unaccountably awry when children interact with magic. There are, in fact, five children (Nesbit's usual number), but they are from two different families. Caspar, Gwinny, and Johnny's mother has just married Douglas and Malcolm's father – the Ogre of the title. When the hated stepfather gives chemistry sets to Johnny and Malcolm, interesting events ensue: toffee bars come to life, Greek-speaking warriors spring from the ground, and the children even learn how to fly. In order to cope with various magical mishaps, the children must form an alliance with one another, and eventually with the Ogre himself. An immensely funny book, *The Ogre Downstairs* also explores two of Jones's pervading themes: displacement and alienation. Most of the early reviews were favorable.

Jones's neglected childhood provides a thread that runs throughout her novels. The Ogre is the first of many unreasonable father figures in her books, although events prove him to be merely misunderstood. Fathers do not fare well in Jones's fantasies; her own father could not provide a model for a caring adult. In her imagined worlds fathers are usually ineffective, selfish, neglectful, unloving parents. Mothers, while not portrayed as negatively as fathers, often ignore their children's needs to pursue their own desires.

The three books Jones published in 1975 – *Eight Days of Luke, Cart and Cwidder,* and *Dogsbody* – extended her exploration of adult/child alienation. David, the young hero of *Eight Days of Luke,* receives abominable treatment at the hands of his adult relations, who expect him to be grateful for their neglectful care. After a series of alarming but often hilarious adventures with the Norse gods, David ends up under the benign care of his cousin's abandoned wife. Like many of Jones's other heroes David suffers from a poor self-image until he takes a successful hand in the supernatural events surrounding him. These young heroes usually initiate the magic, often unknowingly, and learn either to control it or to work within it.

Dogsbody tells the story of Sirius, a powerful stellar being framed for murder and sentenced to live on Earth as a dog. The dog in question is based on Jones's family dog, and she captures his character with affection and humor. Although the story is primarily told from Sirius's viewpoint, there is a neglected child in the figure of Kathleen, a young girl forced to live with and work for a hateful aunt while her father, an Irish terrorist, is in prison. Kathleen's love for the dog, Sirius, enables him to unmask the real murderer and reclaim his powerful heritage. Kathleen, however, is a tragic figure who loses everyone and everything she loves, although there is a small hope at the end of the book that she and Sirius may someday be reunited. *Dogsbody* was recommended for the Carnegie Medal but did not win the award.

Dogsbody introduces another recurring figure in Jones's works: the beautiful, calculating, and unscrupulous sorceress who seeks total power – who appears in this case as Sirius's old girlfriend. This figure seems to be modeled after Morgan le Fay. She appears in a younger guise in *Charmed Life* (1977), as a fairy queen in *Fire and Hemlock* (1985), and as the dreaded Witch of the Waste in *Howl's Moving Castle* (1986); she is also a supporting player in many other books. Sometimes she receives the just rewards of her wickedness by being killed, as she is in *Dogsbody,* but often she gets away with her evil deeds.

Cart and Cwidder is the first in a four-book series about a mythical medieval land called Dalemark. It tells the story of Moril, a member of a family of gypsylike troubadours who travel between the oppressed earldoms of the South and the free lands of the North. After Moril's father is murdered and his mother immediately remarries, Moril and his siblings carry out their father's last request to transport a young nobleman to the North. Along the way Moril learns to play a magical lutelike cwidder. His adventures help Moril realize that his beloved father was both a spy and a selfish autocrat and his mother a dutiful but unloving caregiver.

The Dalemark series represents a more conventional kind of fantasy than Jones usually writes – almost High Fantasy. There is less humor, more violence, and heroics on a grand scale. The series continues with *Drowned Ammet* (1977), *The Spellcoats* (1979), and *The Crown of Dalemark* (1993). In *Drowned Ammet,* Mitt, a young freedom fighter, discovers the power of the old gods. *The Spellcoats* is a prequel about a seemingly human family who become gods themselves. The most recent volume unites the heroes of *Cart and Cwidder* and *Drowned Ammet* in a search for the lost crown of Dalemark.

Part of the pleasure of writing a series like Dalemark is the challenge of creating a fully realized other world. While Jones's fantasies are usually set either in the contemporary world or in a magical

Dust jacket for the first of Jones's four books set in medieval Dalemark

world that impinges on that world, Dalemark is a medieval world with its own mythology and legends. It is a product not only of Jones's imagination but also of her childhood reading of Greek epics and medieval romance and her adult appreciation of Tolkien's *The Lord of the Rings* (1954–1955). In order to re-create the high seriousness of the old heroic epics, she had to abandon her usual humor and skewed angles of vision for a loftier style and a straightforward narrative. The change in tone threw reviewers off balance: those who appreciated her earlier books found Dalemark to be second rate and emotionally unconvincing, while early detractors were won over by this more conventional fantasy.

Jones returned to her complicated and humorous style for *Power of Three* (1976), which contains one of her most surprising and successful twists of viewpoint. Three children with supernatural abilities join with their people's traditional enemies to save their beloved moorland. When the children encounter the mythical Giants, the reader suddenly realizes that the Giants are normal human beings and the child heroes are actually fairies. Reviewers praised Jones's inventiveness but cautioned readers that the book was demanding, as indeed are most of

her works. Jones believes that children have no trouble following her plots; only adults find them confusing. *The Power of Three* was runner-up for the prestigious *Guardian* Award for 1977.

Charmed Life is the first book in a loosely linked series. The link is provided by the excessively polite, handsome, nine-lived enchanter Chrestomanci, who reappears in *The Magicians of Caprona* (1980), *Witch Week* (1982), and *The Lives of Christopher Chant* (1988), as well as in a number of short stories. In *Charmed Life* Chrestomanci becomes guardian of his young relatives Gwendolyn and Cat and eventually discovers that Gwendolyn has been using her brother's nine lives to power her own selfish magic. Like the other books in the series *Charmed Life* abounds in high comedy, fast-paced adventure, and convoluted plots. Yet even in the midst of the comedy, the theme of alienation and abandonment sounds a mournful note. *Charmed Life* succeeded in charming the reviewers, and few reviewers found anything negative to say about the Chrestomanci books. The first of the series was recommended for the Carnegie Medal and won the 1978 *Guardian* Award.

The Magicians of Caprona is a tribute to both *Romeo and Juliet* and Italy's commedia dell'arte, and it contains one of the few happy families in all of Jones's books. The feuding Montana and Petrocchi families must combine their magic to save their city from invasion. Again Jones combines slapstick humor and puns (for example, there is a magician named Mario Andretti who drives a sleek white car) with terrifying moments like the live Punch and Judy show that nearly kills the reluctant participants.

Witch Week also contains moments of hilarity and terror as the children at a boarding school try to hide their magical talents from a world that burns witches. The fledgling witches' attempts at magic produce some funny moments. For example, when Charles tries to find his missing pair of shoes he accidentally conjures up every shoe in the school. The book contains at least one autobiographical note: Nan's compulsive and stomach-turning description of a school lunch was inspired by an essay Jones wrote in school.

The Lives of Christopher Chant, which tells the story of Chrestomanci's boyhood, maintains the tone of the series. Christopher is another neglected child of selfish parents. Desperate for affection he allows his wicked uncle to abuse his magical powers, although he does not realize the extent of the abuse until he is removed to the guardianship of another nine-lived enchanter. Despite such serious overtones this book, like its predecessors, abounds in comedy. It also contains private jokes and references to Jones's childhood: an elderly witch knits Christopher a long, colorful scarf that would be instantly recognizable to fans of the British science-fiction show *Dr. Who,* and Christopher and his school chums enjoy an unexpurgated version of *The Arabian Nights* rather than the bowdlerized edition of Jones's youth.

Two of Jones's most powerful novels were written back to back and published in 1981. *The Homeward Bounders* explores more deeply the theme of displacement. When young Jamie discovers that his world and many parallel worlds are gameboards for a super race he calls *Them,* he becomes a discard, bumped from one reality to another with each move of the game and surviving on the slim hope that he will find his way home again. The ending is heartbreaking: since his own home no longer exists in time, Jamie elects to walk the bounds between worlds forever, anchoring everyone else's realities. By using the timeless legends of the Wandering Jew, the Flying Dutchman, and Prometheus, Jones evokes the emotions of displaced persons in a powerful, believable way – no doubt because of her own childhood experiences as an evacuee.

The Time of the Ghost moves from Jones's evacuee years to her life in Thaxted. The most autobiographical of her novels, this is the story of four neglected sisters living in a converted shack attached to a boys' boarding school. One of the sisters appears to be a ghost who is trying to save herself from an evil spirit the girls have accidentally raised. Jones has admitted that one of the sisters is a self-portrait. It could be sloppy, overweight Cart; prissy, hysterical Sally; theatrical Imogen; or feral, dwarflike Fenella. The parents are more shocking figures than the evil spirit: Phyllis is uncaring, and Himself is a sarcastic, unfeeling monster. Neither parent notices that one of their daughters is missing, and neither visits her when she lies near death in a hospital. *The Time of the Ghost* is the only one of Jones's novels that has not been published in an American edition; its acute Englishness makes it nearly inaccessible to most American readers.

Having perhaps exorcised a few personal demons, Jones turned again to her more lighthearted style in *Archer's Goon* (1984). Unlike most of Jones's heroes, Howard Sykes has loving parents (although he does turn out to be adopted). Howard and his family are swept up in the machinations of the seven wizards who secretly run the town. The publication date is no accident; the book is Jones's tribute to George Orwell's *1984* (1949). *Archer's Goon* provides a humorous and quite literal take on "Big Brother is Watching You." It was a Boston Globe–Horn Book honor book in 1984.

A picture Jones owned inspired *Fire and Hemlock,* her most challenging book for adolescents. Ostensibly the story of Polly's friendship with the musician Thomas Lynn, the book makes sudden shifts from present to past and between Polly's two sets of conflicting memories. Echoes of the folk ballads "Tam Lin" and "Thomas the Rhymer" resound throughout the tale, along with hints of *The Odyssey,* T. S. Eliot's *Four Quartets* (1943), and the myth of Cupid and Psyche. Jones purposefully arranged the female characters in triads to reflect the ancient Celtic triple goddesses. *Fire and Hemlock* is a powerful, demanding book that examines deep and conflicting emotions.

Jones's next book, *Howl's Moving Castle,* is a brilliant pastiche of fairy tales – Jones's best work to date. More outrageously funny than her other fantasies, this book overflows with memorable and original characters: Sophie Hatter, a timid and self-defeating girl who learns to assert herself after she is turned into an old woman; Calcifer, the grouchy fire demon who sings Welsh rugby songs; Michael, the diffident sorcerer's apprentice; and the

Dust jacket for Jones's fantasy with Jungian overtones

sly, slippery, vain, cowardly, and thoroughly engaging Wizard Howl. Jones recalls laughing so hard while writing the book that she fell off the sofa, and that laughter reverberates throughout the story. Sophie's adventures with a pair of "seven-league boots" provide several of the funniest passages in children's literature. This was the second of Jones's books to be named a Boston Globe–Horn Book honor book. Jones later wrote a sequel to *Howl's Moving Castle,* built on her love for *The Arabian Nights. Castle in the Air* (1990) tells the story of a daydreaming carpet seller and his adventures with a princess, a genie, a magic carpet, and several hostile jinn. Sophie, Calcifer, and Howl appear in disguise. While not quite as brilliant as the first novel, the sequel is highly entertaining.

A Tale of Time City (1987) touches again on Jones's childhood evacuation. In a case of mistaken identity Vivian Smith is kidnapped from an evacuation train by a pair of overeager young time travel-

ers. Stranded outside history, she helps them save Time City from destruction. Inspired by her own dietary restrictions (and perhaps by a phrase in a Beatles' song) Jones invented a delicious treat called a butter-pie, which she describes in mouth-watering detail. A capering ghostly harlequin who disrupts Time City is carried over into *Black Maria* (1991) in the figure of the newly exhumed Antony Green. *Black Maria* is a darker fantasy – really a horror story – featuring werewolves and zombies and a man who is buried alive. Again there is a selfish, ineffective father, but young Mig's mother rises to heroism on behalf of her children and Antony Green.

Jones's most recent novel for young adults is *Hexwood* (1993), which attempts to play with time in a manner similar to *Fire and Hemlock.* Like *The Homeward Bounders* and *A Tale of Time City,* Hexwood is as much science fiction as fantasy. Jones resurrects the war-gaming plot of *The Homeward Bounders* as well as the Big Brother theme of *Archer's Goon*. Although Ann Stavely is the nominal heroine, Jones creates an ensemble cast of characters and constantly shifts scenes and points of view. Most of the action occurs in a mysterious wood that draws all the characters together and pits them against one another. No one is quite what he or she appears to be; identity and age are mutable traits. The novel has strong Jungian overtones; in fact, five of the characters are Jungian archetypes, and the purpose of the strange events is to synthesize them into a balanced whole.

Although most of Jones's fantasies are written for preadolescents and young adults, she has also written four books for younger readers – all in a strongly humorous vein – one picture book, and an adult science fiction novel. In *Who Got Rid of Angus Flint?* (1978), an unwelcome houseguest meets his comeuppance when the household furniture revolts. A magical machine transforms *The Four Grannies* (1980) into one supergranny who retains all the faults of the originals. *Chair Person* (1989) comes alive when a magical chemical spills on an old armchair. *Wild Robert* (1989) is the ghost of a spoiled young wizard who returns to claim his family home. The picture book *Yes, Dear* (1992) is about a little girl who finds a magic leaf but cannot get her busy parents and siblings to listen to her. *A Sudden Wild Magic* (1992) is an adult science fiction novel published in the United States; however, it is not too

adult for sophisticated adolescents. *Everard's Ride* (1995) is a limited American edition that mixes adult stories with stories for younger readers.

By reworking her own childhood emotions and experiences, Diana Wynne Jones has created lively, original fantasies built on a foundation of psychological realism. Her neglected young heroes always find personal strength and are usually left in the care of at least one loving adult. Because Jones writes for her own entertainment (and for that of the literature-starved child she once was), she is able to amuse her readers as well, even while challenging them to keep up with her fast-paced, convoluted plots.

Interviews:

Fiona Lafferty, "Realms of Fantasy: An Interview with Diana Wynne Jones," *British Book News Children's Books* (Winter 1987): 2–5;

Kit Alderdice, "Diana Wynne Jones," *Publishers Weekly*, 238 (22 February 1991): 201–202.

References:

Sally Holmes Holtze, ed., "Diana Wynne Jones," in *Fifth Book of Junior Authors* (New York: Wilson, 1983), pp. 166–167;

Gillian Spraggs, "True Dreams: The Fantasy Fiction of Diana Wynne Jones," *Use of English*, 34 (Summer 1983): 17–22.

Penelope Lively

(17 March 1933 –   )

Alan McLay
Carleton University

See also the Lively entry in *DLB 14: British Novelists Since 1960.*

BOOKS: *Astercote,* illustrated by Anthony Maitland (London: Heinemann, 1970; New York: Dutton, 1971);

The Whispering Knights, illustrated by Gareth Floyd (London: Heinemann, 1971; New York: Dutton, 1976);

The Wild Hunt of Hagworthy, illustrated by Juliet Mozley (London: Heinemann, 1971); republished as *The Wild Hunt of the Ghost Hounds* (New York: Dutton, 1972);

The Driftway (London: Heinemann, 1972; New York: Dutton, 1973);

The Ghost of Thomas Kempe, illustrated by Maitland (London: Heinemann, 1973; New York: Dutton, 1973);

The House in Norham Gardens (London: Heinemann, 1974; New York: Dutton, 1974);

Boy Without a Name, illustrated by Ann Dalton (London: Heinemann, 1975; Berkeley, Cal.: Parnassus, 1975);

Going Back (London: Heinemann, 1975; New York: Dutton, 1975);

A Stitch in Time (London: Heinemann, 1976; New York: Dutton, 1976);

The Stained Glass Window, illustrated by Michael Pollard (London: Abelard-Schuman, 1976);

Fanny's Sister, illustrated by John Lawrence (London: Heinemann, 1976; New York: Dutton, 1980);

The Presence of the Past: An Introduction to Landscape History (London: Collins, 1976);

The Road to Lichfield (London: Heinemann, 1977; New York: Grove, 1991);

The Voyage of QV66, illustrated by Harold Jones (London: Heinemann, 1978; New York: Dutton, 1979);

Nothing Missing But the Samovar, and Other Stories (London: Heinemann, 1978);

Penelope Lively (photograph by Jerry Bauer)

Fanny and the Monsters, illustrated by Lawrence (London: Heinemann, 1979);

Treasures of Time (London: Heinemann, 1979; Garden City, N.Y.: Doubleday, 1980);

Fanny and the Battle of Potter's Piece, illustrated by Lawrence (London: Heinemann, 1980);

Judgement Day (London: Heinemann, 1980; Garden City, N.Y.: Doubleday, 1981);

The Revenge of Samuel Stokes (London: Heinemann, 1981; New York: Dutton, 1981);

Next to Nature, Art (London: Heinemann, 1982);

Perfect Happiness (London: Heinemann, 1983; New York: Dial, 1984);

According to Mark (London: Heinemann, 1984; New York: Beaufort, 1985);

Uninvited Ghosts and Other Stories, illustrated by Lawrence (London: Heinemann, 1984; New York: Dutton, 1985);

Corruption and Other Stories (London: Heinemann, 1984);

Dragon Trouble, illustrated by Valerie Littlewood (London: Heinemann, 1984; New York: Barron, 1989);

Pack of Cards: Stories 1978–86 (London: Heinemann, 1986; New York: Grove, 1989);

Moon Tiger (London: Deutsch, 1987; New York: Grove, 1988);

Debbie and the Little Devil, illustrated by Toni Goffe (London: Heinemann, 1987);

A House Inside Out, illustrated by David Parkins (London: Deutsch, 1987; New York: Dutton, 1988);

Passing On (London: Deutsch, 1989; New York: Grove, 1990);

City of the Mind (London: Deutsch, 1991; New York: HarperCollins, 1991);

Judy and the Martian (London: Simon & Schuster, 1992);

Cleopatra's Sister (London: Viking, 1993; New York: HarperCollins, 1993);

The Cat, the Crow and the Banyan Tree, illustrated by Terry Milne (London: Walker, 1994; Cambridge, Mass.: Candlewick, 1994);

Oleander Jacaranda: A Childhood Perceived (London: Viking, 1994; New York: HarperCollins, 1994);

Good Night, Sleep Tight, illustrated by Adriano Gon (London: Walker, 1994; Cambridge, Mass.: Candlewick, 1995).

TELEVISION SCRIPTS: *Boy Dominic* series, 3 episodes, 1974;

Time Out of Mind, 1976.

OTHER: Ivy Compton-Burnett, *Manservant and Maidservant,* introduction by Lively (Oxford: Oxford University Press, 1983).

SELECTED PERIODICAL PUBLICATIONS –
UNCOLLECTED: "Children and Memory," *Horn Book,* 49 (June 1973): 400–407;

"The Ghost of Thomas Kempe," *Junior Bookshelf,* 38 (June 1974): 143–145;

"Children and the Art of Memory: Part I," *Horn Book,* 54 (February 1978): 17–23;

"Children and the Art of Memory: Part II," *Horn Book,* 54 (April 1978): 197–203;

"Bones in the Sand," *Horn Book,* 57 (August 1981): 641–651; reprinted in *Innocence and Experience:*

Essays and Conversations on Children's Literature, edited by Barbara Harrison and Gregory Maguire (New York: Lothrop, Lee & Shepard, 1987), pp. 13–21.

Penelope Lively has achieved popular success and high critical acclaim for her books for children written in the 1970s and for her later novels and short stories for adults. She is regarded today as one of Britain's most respected writers. She has written twenty children's books and thirteen books of fiction for adults, a remarkable achievement in just twenty-three years. Her work has received high praise for her wit, shrewd insight, and elegant style.

Central preoccupations in Lively's writing, whether for children or for adults, are the importance of place and a sense of continuity, both personal and collective, between past and present. In her June 1973 article for the *Horn Book,* "Children and Memory," she writes perceptively of her reasons for writing for children and the effect she hopes her books may have upon her readers: "It is the perception, often startling, that places have a past, that they are now but also were then, and that if peopled now, they were peopled then. "It is a step aside from self, a step out of the child's self-preoccupation, and therefore a step toward maturity." She writes primarily to entertain her young audience but at the same time to engage their imaginations about their own lives and the lives of other people. "Children need to sense that we live in a permanent world that reaches away, behind and ahead of us, and that the span of a lifetime is something to be wondered at, and thought about, and that – above all – people evolve during their own lives."

The role of the novelist is not to teach didactic lessons about the past but to open up an imaginative landscape for the reader, to share the pictures that the writer carries about in her own head. In an article in the August 1981 *Horn Book,* "Bones in the Sand," she asserts, "The one thing we all share is the capacity to remember; the novelist tries to convey the significance and the power of that capacity in fictional terms, to make universal stories out of that particular story that we each carry in our own head. At its grandest, this theme is the most compelling in all literature; it is the means whereby we, as writers for children, hope to introduce them to larger and more exciting worlds – to talk about what it is like to be human."

Penelope Margaret Green was born and raised in Cairo, Egypt, the only child of Roger Low and Vera Green. She received no formal schooling but

Lively and her father in Egypt, circa 1940

was educated by a governess, who read to her the Bible, Greek and Norse mythology, Charles Dickens, and *The Arabian Nights,* "a marvellous basis of narrative," she said in a 1988 interview. Remembering the years of World War II in "Bones in the Sand," she recalls being taken to the desert by an archaeologist at the age of eight or nine and being shown a skeleton thousands of years old. "Within the depression, curled like a fetus, is the delicate structure of a skeleton: backbone, ribs, leg bones, the tracery of a hand." In the background were armored cars, lorries and petrol cans of the desert war. These unusual experiences as a child undoubtedly contributed to her nascent interest in history.

At the end of the war in 1945 Green was sent back to England to live in London with her grandmother. In "Bones in the Sand" (1981) she recalls visiting the bombed-out areas around Saint Paul's Cathedral and seeing the exposed layers of London's history in the rubble. "I am excited; I am lifted out of the prison of my own head and glimpse something larger. Imagination reaches out." Although the cold northern climate of England was a shock after the hot, dry landscape of Egypt, she came to love the lush green countryside of her new

home. "I have grown my own roots, and an attachment to the landscape and atmosphere of midland England that is perhaps the stronger for being acquired."

Her three years in a boarding school were deeply unhappy, "an absolutely appalling purgatory," she asserted in 1988. It was a school that emphasized athletics and tried to discourage her love of reading. A rooted dislike of boarding schools is reflected in *Going Back* (1975) and *Passing On* (1989). In 1951 she entered Saint Anne's College, Oxford, where she spent three happy years studying modern history. After receiving her B.A. degree in 1954, she became a research fellow and met Jack Lively, a research fellow at Saint Antony's College. They were married on 27 June 1957. Their daughter, Josephine, was born in 1958 and a son, Adam, in 1961. The Livelys commute between their home in London and an old rectory in Oxfordshire. Jack Lively is a professor of politics at the University of Warwick and the author of several books on political theory.

Before becoming a writer Lively reviewed children's books in newspapers and magazines and presented a program on children's literature on

BBC radio. She became fascinated by the history and folklore of Oxfordshire, an interest that helped to inspire her first three stories for children. The themes and structures of all three novels are similar, combining a realistic contemporary setting, a historical dimension, and an element of fantasy linking past and present. All three demonstrate the author's central concern with continuity and memory.

In *Astercote* (1970) Lively explores the power of old legends and beliefs in a quiet Cotswold village. After the last inhabitant of Astercote died of the Black Death six hundred years ago, the village was surrounded by forest and almost forgotten except for one link with the past – a chalice, buried in the earth and guarded by the Tranter family of World's End Farm. When the chalice is stolen the villagers in Charlton Underwood fear that the plague will return, and they barricade their village against all outsiders. The story illustrates the continuity of collective memory underlying the present, just as the lost village of Astercote lies buried deep in the wood.

Peter and Mair Jenkins, children of the new schoolmaster, are drawn into the wood where they meet Goacher, a retarded young man who lives there with his two dogs and wild hawk. Goacher shows them the stone foundations of the old cottages and church and reveals where the chalice is buried. In the wood Mair can hear the chiming of bells, the sound of voices, and the movement of animals – echoes of the past – whereas Peter hears nothing unusual. The children assist in tracking the thief, a young mechanic, and recovering the chalice in a dramatic pursuit. The narrative is exciting and fast-paced, the descriptions of the village and countryside vivid, and the haunted atmosphere of the wood effectively conveyed. Though an apprentice work, *Astercote* introduces a distinctive new voice.

The Whispering Knights (1971), according to Lively in "Children and Memory," illustrates "the strange mystique attached to standing stones" and the legends that cling to certain places. The setting was suggested by the circle of standing stones near Great Rollright in North Oxfordshire. Three children, playing at reproducing with modern substitutes the witches' brew from William Shakespeare's *Macbeth* (1623), inadvertently conjure up Morgan le Fay, an archetypal evil witch who represents the "bad side of things." As she grows in power she becomes a powerful destructive force that the children must combat with the assistance of Miss Hepplewhite, a wise old lady with magic power of her own. As the new wife of Mr. Steel, an elderly factory owner, Morgan threatens to divert the plans for a new motorway through their village. She also kidnaps Martha, who must be rescued by William and Susie. As the children escape they are pursued by Morgan in a driverless limousine across the countryside. The conflict ends in an apocalyptic battle between the forces of evil, Morgan, and those of good, Miss Hepplewhite and the Whispering Knights – the standing stones who rise to defeat the enemy. Once again Lively combines fantasy and realism in an exciting adventure that rises to a dramatic (perhaps melodramatic) climax.

In *The Wild Hunt of Hagworthy* (1971) Lively turns again to folklore for the legend of the phantom horsemen who ride the skies after a battle. The legend is associated with Exmoor in West Somerset, the setting for the novel. When the Vicar of Hagworthy decides to revive the Horn Dance for the village fete in August, the older villagers murmur grim warnings that it may bring back the Wild Hunt. As the antler-wearing boys practice the dance they are taken over by a primitive and violent power. They find a target for their bloodlust in Kester Lang, another villager, who goes out of his way to taunt and provoke his former comrades as if compelled to be the victim in the reenactment of some ancient sacrifice. Suspense is built up by the hot, sultry weather, the electrically charged atmosphere before a thunderstorm, and by the ominous signs that the ghost hunt has come back. Fortunately, at the end of the novel tragedy is averted; the thunderstorm passes, and village life returns to normal.

The Wild Hunt of Hagworthy is the most successful of these first three novels. It is a tightly constructed adventure story that creates an awareness of dark, powerful forces in human nature. Village life with its undercurrents of fear and tension is convincingly portrayed. There is greater depth of characterization in this novel in the sometimes strained relationship between Kester Lang and the protagonist Lucy Clough. They share idyllic moments of friendship, but Lucy becomes increasingly concerned by Kester's sudden changes of mood and his perverse attempts to harass the dancers. She is deeply disturbed by the impending outbreak of violence, which she can foresee but apparently can do little to prevent. Lucy's concern for Kester's safety and her intervention in the final pursuit break the spell and release the boys from their role as hunters. Kester and Lucy watch in awe as the ghost hunters and hounds ride overhead, but the storm is passing and the real threat has been dispersed.

In her fourth novel, *The Driftway* (1972), Lively continues the theme of continuity between past and present but experiments with a different

Dust jacket for Lively's 1973 book, a humorous ghost story

narrative technique. The first chapter begins like a realistic problem novel. Paul, resenting his father's remarriage and rejecting his stepmother's attempts to take the place of his dead mother, decides to run away with his younger sister, Sandra, when they are accused of a minor theft. The children set out on the road to Cold Higham where their grandmother lives. The rest of the novel is concerned with Paul's experiences along the way in the company of Old Bill, a traveler with a horse and cart. On the journey Paul sees visions and hears voices, messages from the past that show him that people in every age and time of life have difficulties far greater than his own. Old Bill explains: "That's what the Driftway is: a place where people have left messages for one another."

The novel alternates between the slow, steady pace of horse and cart and the stories told by figures from the past: an Anglo-Saxon boy fleeing the Danes who have killed his family; a youth escaping from the battle at Edgehill in 1642; a stableboy in the eighteenth century who pretends to be the highwayman, Driftway Jim, only to be robbed by the real Driftway Jim. The stories that he has heard and the wise comments of Old Bill help Paul to realize the futility of running away. By entering into the experiences of other people, he is better able to come to terms with his own inner conflicts. After the tense realism of the first chapter, the pace of the journey is leisurely, and the descriptions of the pastoral landscapes along the way are lyrical and impressionistic. Though the voices from the past are clearly realized and their stories memorable, the loose, nondramatic structure and slow movement reduce tension and relax the reader's interest. It is an interesting experiment in narrative technique, but not entirely successful.

The Ghost of Thomas Kempe (1973) was quickly recognized as a masterpiece of comic exuberance and invention that treats the ghost story with remarkable originality. It reveals a sureness of touch and a robust humor that were only intermittently present in Lively's earlier books. The ghost is a useful literary device for introducing the protagonist James Harrison (and the reader) to the history of the cottage and the village of Ledsham. James is an active, adventurous ten-year-old boy, accustomed to getting into trouble. When a poltergeist makes his presence known, James is naturally blamed for the disturbances because, as he admits, they are just the sort of things he does himself. He does not even believe in ghosts, but he is forced to the conclusion that his room is haunted. "'Nobody believes in him except me,' said James. 'And I wouldn't if I didn't have to.'"

Thomas Kempe is not a frightening ghost but a comic figure. A "cunning man," or sorcerer, during the reign of King James, he tries to practice his arts of sorcery, alchemy, and astrology in an age that no longer believes in them. He is cranky, arrogant, and bad-tempered, expressing his displeasure by rattling windows, slamming doors, breaking vases, and writing notes in an antique script to his apprentice James. The ghost's actions become more serious, however, when he smashes the village surgery, accuses the Harrisons' neighbor (Mrs. Verity) of being a witch, and finally sets fire to her cottage. Thomas Kempe represents the malice and superstition of the seventeenth century and must be exorcised. James must take responsibility for the ghost and for himself and learn to control his own potential for evil. With the assistance of Bert Ellison, local builder and exorcist, James finally succeeds in returning the ghost of Thomas Kempe to the vault where his tomb lies.

James also learns about the past in a Victorian diary that he rescues from the rubbish heap. It is a sprightly and charming account by Miss Fanny Spence describing a visit by her nephew Arnold Luckett during the summer holidays. Arnold is a boy like James who loves food, swimming, and climbing trees. Arnold, too, had lived in James's attic room and had been haunted by the ghost of Thomas Kempe. James feels a special comradeship with Arnold over the century or more that separates them. He can talk to Arnold and tell him jokes. The elderly Mrs. Verity recalls a visit to the village by the prosperous Arnold Luckett, then an old gentleman. Mrs. Verity is a living link between the young Arnold of the diary, Arnold as an old man, and the young James. James has learned a great deal about the layers of time of which people and places are composed. "Time reached away behind and ahead and back to the crusading knight, and Thomas Kempe and Aunt Fanny, and Arnold; and forward to other people who leave their names in this place,

look with different eyes on the same streets, rooftops, trees."

The theme of continuity and the layers of time is explored even more subtly and complexly in *The House in Norham Gardens* (1974), a brilliant fusion of fantasy, history, and realism focused on the delicate transition from childhood to maturity of fourteen-year-old Clare Mayfield. Clare lives with her great-aunts Susan and Anne in a large Victorian house in North Oxford. On the realistic level the story provides sensitive and sympathetic insight into Clare's thoughts and feelings during three months between December and the end of February. Clare is a fully rounded character – thoughtful, affectionate, and imaginative. Secure in the love of her great-aunts, she is content with her routine of school, study, cooking, shopping, and household duties; her everyday life does not change, and nothing much happens. This state of dormancy is reflected in the winter weather outside – the cold, freezing winds, barren gardens, and snow.

Built near the turn of the century by Clare's great-great-grandfather, a famous anthropologist and university professor, the house and the Oxford setting represent one historical dimension. Although the house is now shabby, its dignity and grandeur reflect the prosperity of the age when it was built. It is a relic of a bygone age but also a museum, a storehouse of artifacts brought from Africa and Asia. The great-aunts also are relics of the past when women were first admitted as students at Oxford, but they belong to Clare's present as well. Another dimension of time is provided in the brief paragraphs at the beginning of each chapter, describing the life of a primitive people in a remote valley in New Guinea. Their experiences reflect the traumatic effect of the twentieth-century world on the timeless world of the aboriginal tribe.

When Clare finds a wooden shield in the attic storeroom, she is drawn into the world of the New Guinea valley in her dreams. She meets little brown people who seem to ask her for something, but she does not understand what they want. In later dreams the brown people appear near the river Cherwell in Oxford and in her garden. Clare is deeply disturbed by these haunting dreams. She does not sleep well, looks weary and pallid, and catches a cold. Her dreams are curiously related to her growing anxiety about her aunts. She has taken for granted that they will always be there, but she is aware that they are becoming old and frail. When she comes home from school one day to find the house empty, she rushes off on her bicycle on the icy streets and is knocked down by a car. In the hos-

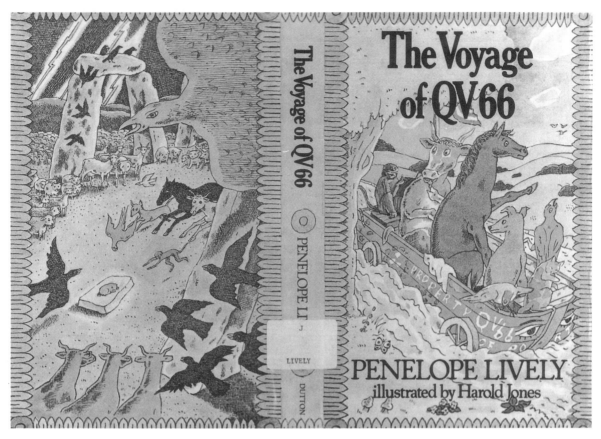

Dust jacket for Lively's story of six animals' adventures in a future world without humans

pital she dreams of the brown people. In the dream she brings back their sacred tamburan but discovers that they have forgotten its symbolic meaning and do not want it. Clare is freed from her own obsession and fears. Her strange, haunting dream life suggests a parallel between the difficult transition of a primitive people to the science and technology of the modern world and the equally difficult period of adjustment in adolescence between the security of childhood and the stresses of life as an adult.

When Clare returns home the change to clear skies, sunshine, and early signs of spring mirrors the change in her. She is no longer obsessed by the tribe's tamburan and donates it to the Pitt-Rivers museum. In a moment of inspiration she buys a copper beech sapling as a birthday present for Aunt Susan, a gift that looks to the future rather than to the past. As she thinks of all the people and possessions in the house, she realizes that they will all continue in her memory: "Where they will be, in a peculiar way, is inside my head." Clare has come to terms with herself and her life and can go confidently into the future.

In *Going Back* Lively experiments further with the stream-of-consciousness technique. The first-

person narrative uses the voice of a grown-up, Jane, happily married with children of her own, who has returned to Medleycott after the death of her father. The title refers literally to the journey back to the farm where she had grown up, but metaphorically it means going back in time, through memory, into the past. The narrative structure is similar to Nina Bawden's *Carrie's War* (1973), but in *Going Back* the reader is constantly aware of the adult voice interpreting and commenting on her experiences as a child. Jane is aware of the uncertainty, the selectivity, in the process of memory: "Remembering is like that. There's what you know happened, and what you think happened. And then there's the business that what you know happened isn't always what you remember. Things are fudged by time; years fuse together."

The events of the past are described in flashbacks, as Jane remembers growing up with her brother, Edward, during the years of World War II. Medleycott was a paradise for the children while their father was away in the army. They enjoyed the long summer days and the sense of freedom. The war brought the land-girls (a type of farm laborer) Pam and Susie, the conscientious objector

239

Mike, the soldiers, and dances. The house was full of warmth, excitement, and laughter until their father came home on leave and banished the dog, Samba, to the stables, ordered the housekeeper not to take the children to dances, and later refused to allow Mike the "conchie" in his house. The tension between the children and their harsh, rigid father comes to a head when he sends Edward to a boarding school. Deeply unhappy at school, Edward decides to run away from home when he returns on mid-term leave. Jane runs away with him, and they reach Mike on the farm. Although he accepts that he must go back to the school, Edward has won a battle: "I think he felt he'd won something within himself, though, rather than with father, or school, or anything."

From the beginning the narrative is tinged with sadness and melancholy, not merely nostalgia but the knowledge that Edward was later killed in Korea. Jane's memories of their childhood during the war years are suffused with a sense of sorrow and loss. The author's concern with memory and regret points forward to the adult novels she was later to write. In a preface to the recent issue of *Going Back* (a Penguin edition for adults) Lively writes: "reading it now, I see that it is only tenuously so a children's book; the pitch, the voice, the focus are not really those of a true children's book. Looking at it fifteen years later, I see it quite differently, and recognize it as a trial run for preoccupations with the nature of memory, with a certain kind of writing with economy and allusion."

A Stitch in Time (1976) returns to a more conventional structure for a children's book, but it explores with wit and humor the same themes of time, past and present, and the continuity of memory. Central to the story is the setting of Lyme Regis, famous as a seaside resort and for the abundant fossils along its cliffs and beaches, which suggest the eons of geological time that went into the formation of the layers of rock underlying the town. Maria Foster, a quiet, introspective girl of eleven, carries on conversations with petrol pumps, portraits, and an amusingly sardonic cat, whom she finds more rewarding than most people. She is the only child of a staid, conventional couple. Although the holiday threatens to be boring, Maria acquires new friends and interests during her stay in Lyme Regis. There is a comic contrast between her family and the boisterous activities of the Lucas family next door. She becomes friends with Martin Lucas, and they go to the Lyme Regis Museum to study the fossils and displays of geology; she also accompanies the Lucases to a medieval joust.

Maria is introduced to another dimension of time when she meets old Mrs. Shand, the owner of a Victorian cottage, whose room is filled with photographs and mementos of her family. Maria is attracted to a sampler made in 1865 by a ten-year-old girl, Harriet Polstead. The sampler is a picture of the old cottage and ilex tree. The title of the novel puns upon the familiar proverb but also alludes to the stitched sampler made in 1865 and Maria's imaginative link with Harriet. Intrigued by the sampler, Maria wrongly leaps to the conclusion that Harriet died at the age of ten and later assumes that Harriet died in a landslide more than a hundred years ago.

From the beginning Maria is haunted by a sense of mystery. When she first arrives at the cottage she hears a dog barking and a swing creaking, but there is neither a dog nor a swing. Later she and Martin find an old swing and set it up. Her fears reach a climax on a picnic outing by the Foster and Lucas families when she hears the sound of a dog barking excitedly and is convinced that the landslide will happen again. She experiences a nervous breakdown and has to be carried home. It is never quite clear whether Maria has invented it all because of an overactive imagination or whether she did indeed hear messages from the past as did Mair in *Astercote*. The fantasy element remains ambiguous for the reader. Maria discovers from Mrs. Shand that Harriet did not die in the landslide but grew up, married, and went to Australia. Maria's wrong assumptions led to her erroneous conclusion, and she learns that it was the dog that died in the landslide in 1865. Again, there are layers of time in the novel: the present time of Maria's holiday in Lyme Regis, the past of the cottage and the Polstead family, and the geological prehistory of the fossils. Maria makes important discoveries about all these layers and about herself.

The Voyage of QV66 (1978) is a radical departure from all of Lively's earlier books. Set in the future after some major disaster has caused widespread flooding and destroyed the human race, it is an animal fable in which animals talk, read and write, and behave much like human beings. Though not harsh political satire like Jonathan Swift's *Gulliver's Travels* (1726) or George Orwell's *Animal Farm* (1945), it views human nature and civilization from a wry, ironic perspective. There are clear parallels to the story of the Flood and Noah's Ark, but the human family has been replaced by a motley group of six animals who have come together by chance. On their odyssey the animals encounter many new situations, some comic and some threatening, that help to forge them into a cohesive family unit. The story is narrated by Pal the dog, a practical and good-natured animal, but the central figure is Stanley the monkey, the most humanlike in shape and intelligence of all the animals. He has brilliant ideas and lofty ambitions, and he makes up wonderful stories – a poet, artist, inventor, and philosopher – but he is easily excitable, egotistical, and at times bad-tempered. He is like a child trying to imitate the grownups without quite understanding what he is doing.

In order to discover what he is and who he is, Stanley has set out on a journey to London with his companions on the flat-bottomed boat QV66. It is for the most part a leisurely voyage through pastoral landscapes from Carlisle in the north through the Lake District and Midlands to London in the south. Readers are invited to laugh at the ways in which the animals imitate human behavior but are also exposed to the caustic comments made about humans, especially their habits of eating animals and killing one another with sharp sticks. There are satirical portraits of the packs of dogs in Manchester who are trying to establish a fascist police state and the crows who have appointed themselves high priests of a pagan religion that requires blood sacrifices on midsummer's dawn at Stonehenge.

When the animals finally reach London, they find the zoo has been taken over by monkeys of all sizes, shapes, and dispositions. They have established committees, regulations, work parties, and other activities that mirror the human world of government bureaucracy. Stanley, too much of an individualist to fit into this kind of society, recognizes that his true friends are his traveling companions, not his own kind. The voyage of the QV66 will continue; the journey of life is open-ended. The story is full of comic inventiveness and surprises, of jokes and sly allusions, such as the apt quotations from the King James Bible which Offa the pigeon pronounces. Readers see the human world from a different point of view, not often flattering. The little group of animals on the QV66, however, represents the virtues of friendship, loyalty, and community and offers hope for the future.

The Revenge of Samuel Stokes (1981) returns to the formula of the ghost story used in *The Ghost of Thomas Kempe.* In both novels the ghost of a proud and quarrelsome man of the past enters the life of a family in the present and causes a maximum of confusion. The Thorntons have just moved into a house in a new housing estate when strange events begin – odd smells of cooking, a box hedge growing in a vegetable garden, bad television reception. The

situation becomes more serious as brick walls appear, the supermarket is flooded, and a greenhouse turns into a Greek temple overnight. Tim Thornton and Jane Harvey form an alliance with Tim's grandfather, who enjoys gardening, cooking unusual recipes, and telling long stories.

When a strange figure appears on their television set, the children recognize Samuel Stokes, the eighteenth-century landscape designer who laid out Charstock Park, the site of the housing estate. He threatens to remove the houses and restore his park. As irascible as Thomas Kempe, Stokes gives them peremptory orders and instructs Tim's grandfather in gardening. He later telephones Tim and utters further threats. After a new house collapses, a garden is transformed into an eighteenth-century grotto, and the whole estate is flooded, Tim, Jane, and Grandpa tempt the ghost of Samuel Stokes with a lavish banquet cooked on an open fire in Grandpa's backyard. The device succeeds as the voice of Samuel Stokes suddenly appears on the radio to give instructions on the proper preparation of sauces. Grandpa cunningly persuades him to take an interest in the council's designs for a new park and playground instead of the housing estate. The ruse is successful as the lake disappears and the houses return to normal.

The novel succeeds as entertaining social comedy and fires some good-humored satirical shafts at residents' associations, developers, and council members. Samuel Stokes is a haughty, overbearing personality with almost godlike powers. While the situations and characters are similar to *The Ghost of Thomas Kempe,* there is always fresh invention and witty flourishes. The reemergence of the eighteenth-century landscape illustrates Lively's recurrent theme of a child's awakening to a sense of history and continuity.

In addition to the major novels for children, Lively has also written several shorter books for beginning readers, ages eight to ten, and two collections of short stories. *Boy Without a Name* (1975) is the story of a nameless and homeless orphan in the mid seventeenth century who is sent back to the village where he was born. Here he finds a home and work with a kindhearted stonemason, is given a name, and learns the trade of shaping stone. It is a universal story of a boy finding his identity and a place in the world and is narrated in a simple, economical manner. In *The Stained Glass Window* (1976) a medieval love story is brought to life in the imagination of a young girl as she looks at the twin portraits of a crusader and his wife in a stained glass window. It is a tender story of love, separation, and a miracle that reunites the lov-

*Dust jacket for Lively's collection of short stories combining
elements of fantasy and humor*

ers, rich in colors like the stained glass. Both stories offer young readers some awareness of the rich tapestry of English history.

Fanny's Sister (1976) is the first of three stories about Fanny Stanton, a spirited and independent young girl, the eldest child of a large Victorian family. When another infant is born, Fanny feels resentful of the new baby and in church wishes that it would go back to God. Suddenly afraid that her prayer will be granted, she decides to run away; when she asks the vicar for employment he puts her to work washing dishes and making tea. Fanny begins to realize the long hours and hard work of kitchen maids. The vicar is a wise old gentleman with a good sense of humor. He assures Fanny that God has no intention of changing his mind about the baby. By the time he takes her home, they have become good friends who share a secret. In *Fanny and the Monsters* (1979) Fanny's ambition is to become a paleontologist. When she is taken to the Crystal Palace, she runs off by herself to see the prehistoric monsters, statues of dinosaurs on an island

lake, and meets a young and enthusiastic paleontologist from the British Museum. In a quarry near her home Fanny discovers the exposed skeleton of an iguanadon where the men have just blasted the cliff face, and she sends for Dr. Halliday. The story touches lightly on the controversy over the geological discoveries and theories of evolution in the mid nineteenth century. Mr. Stanton will not have Charles Darwin mentioned in his house, but he is impressed that his daughter is acquainted with Dr. Halliday and has made a scientific discovery of her own. *Fanny and the Battle of Potter's Piece* (1980) ignores questions of religion and science and describes a territorial battle between the Stanton children and their new neighbors, the Robinsons, over a stretch of open ground between their gardens. After a series of battles the children discover that it is more fun to play together than separately. It is a story about family rivalries and imaginative play in the manner of E. Nesbit's Bastable stories.

Uninvited Ghosts and Other Stories (1984) is Lively's first collection of short stories for children.

They are humorous, sometimes hilarious stories that share a delightful touch of fantasy, involving unexpected (and usually unwanted) visitors. In the title story Marian and Simon Brown discover that the house they have just moved into is inhabited by a family of resident ghosts with irritating and disagreeable habits, such as knitting, sucking peppermint drops, singing hymns, and telling interminable stories. These are comic ghosts, drearily domestic in their habits, who "love kiddies" and follow the children everywhere. Finally, Marian and Simon persuade the ghost family to move down the street, where twin babies live. In "Time Trouble" a nine-year-old boy discovers that he cannot manipulate time when he makes a deal with a grandfather clock. In "The Dragon Tunnel" a legendary dragon comes back to life and has to be fed by two brothers. In "A Flock of Gryphons" pigeon eggs turn into pigeon-sized griffins on Westminster Abbey and become a great tourist attraction. Demonstrations are held to turn the Embankment into a griffin sanctuary or to keep British griffins in Britain, until the griffins fly away like migrating swallows. In "The Great Mushroom Mistake" the Hancocks' house is infested with mushrooms until they are defeated by a dose of Aunt Sadie's homemade cough mixture.

Dragon Trouble (1984) is a light, amusing story for beginning readers. While Peter is visiting his grandfather in Cornwall, he buys a Victorian glass dome with two eggs inside for his grandfather's birthday. The eggs hatch into little dragons, which they feed with fish fingers. They even enter the dragons in the annual village pet show and win first prize in the miscellaneous category. As the dragons grow and their appetite increases, Peter and his grandfather decide that they can keep them no longer and release them on the cliffs. *Debbie and the Little Devil* (1987) is a comic tale of an encounter between eight-and-a-half-year-old Debbie and a little devil who appears at the end of her bed prodding her with a long black fork – an amusing version of the folktale theme of outwitting the devil. Debbie, a strong-minded little girl, rejects the devil's proposals of mischief as pathetic, stupid, and nasty. She defeats him in games of Scrabble, Snap, and Rummy and uses a calculator to beat him in arithmetic; the devil is so enraged that he howls, gnashes his teeth, and disappears.

A House Inside Out (1987) is a series of stories concerning the Dixon family and their pet dog, Willie, a family of mice, and several thousand insects who share their household. These are lighthearted, amusing stories of domestic life seen from the unconventional point of view of these small, usually inconspicu-

ous creatures. Willie is the hero of several stories – a lazy, mischievous, but lovable pet whose chief pleasures in life are eating, sleeping, and chasing the cat next door. He worships Mrs. Dixon and tries to tell her how much he loves her, but of course she cannot understand what he is saying. He is always getting into trouble through his own greed or foolishness and receives many scoldings, even a spanking or two, but he is always forgiven.

Another hero is Sam the mouse, father of a family of thirty-nine mice; he lives with his wife, Doris, in a cardboard box under the stairs. Sam is adventurous and boastful, and he likes to show off. In one story he is imprisoned in a teapot and has to be rescued by the other mice. On another occasion he is caught in the carrier of a motorbike and taken for a hair-raising ride. In a third story he climbs up on Mr. Dixon's shoulder while he is sleeping in front of the television. When Mr. Dixon suddenly awakes Sam is caught in his handkerchief and stowed in his pocket, and again the other mice have to rescue him. Each adventure becomes an even better story for Sam to tell. A third hero is Nat the pill bug, a creature with a shell like an armadillo and fourteen legs. Nat is an individualist who asks questions and keeps his thoughts to himself; he forms an unlikely friendship with a spider. All three heroes are like small children for whom every day is an adventure, full of difficulties and dangers but also rewards.

Lively's best written work for children is unquestionably the five novels from *The Ghost of Thomas Kempe* to *The Voyage of QV66*, which illustrate her originality and artistry at its best. Although she continued to write stories for children throughout the 1980s, it is evident that her creative energy has been directed into the writing of fiction for adults. In 1988 she admitted: "I don't get the ideas any more, and I'm crowded with ideas for adult writing, so I have rather abandoned my children's books. . . . I began to feel that I was in danger of writing the same children's book over and over again. More than that, I'd exhausted the ways in which I could explore my own preoccupations and interests within children's books." Most of her books for children are still in print, either in hardcover or paperback editions, and most are readily available in public libraries for a new generation of readers.

In 1994 Lively published *Oleander Jacaranda: A Childhood Perceived,* an autobiographical account of her experiences as a child growing up in Egypt before and during World War II. She recounts the sensations and emotions she experienced as a child and explores the differences in perspective and understanding between the child and the adult who tries to recover the immediacy of the past through memory. In this memoir, as in her fiction for children and adults, Lively explores the layers of past and present in consciousness and the essential continuity of self.

Penelope Lively has received the highest accolades for her writing: the Carnegie Medal for *The Ghost of Thomas Kempe* in 1974; the Whitbread Award for *A Stitch in Time* in 1976; the Southern Arts Literature Prize for *Nothing Missing But the Samovar and Other Stories* (1978) in 1979; the National Book Award for *Treasures of Time* (1979) in 1980; and the Booker Prize for *Moon Tiger* (1987) in 1988. In 1985 she became a fellow of the Royal Society of Literature, and in 1991 she was awarded the Order of the British Empire for her contribution to literature.

Interview:

Amanda Smith, "*PW* Interviews Penelope Lively," *Publishers Weekly,* 223 (25 March 1988): 47–48.

References:

Judith Armstrong, "Ghosts as Rhetorical Devices in Children's Fiction," *Children's Literature in Education,* 9 (Summer 1978): 59–66;

Eleanor Cameron, "The Eternal Moment," *Children's Literature Quarterly,* 9 (Winter 1984–1985): 157–164;

Nicholas Le-Mesurier, "A Lesson in History: The Presence of the Past in the Novels of Penelope Lively," *New Welsh Review,* 2 (Spring 1990): 36–38;

David Rees, "Time Present and Time Past: Penelope Lively," in his *The Marble in the Water* (Boston: Horn Book, 1979), pp. 185–198;

Louisa Smith, "Layers of Language in Lively's *The Ghost of Thomas Kempe,*" *Children's Literature Quarterly,* 10 (Fall 1985): 114–116;

John Rowe Townsend, "Penelope Lively," in his *A Sounding of Storytellers: New and Revised Essays on Contemporary Writers for Children* (New York: Lippincott, 1979), pp. 125–138;

Virginia L. Wolf, "From the Myth to the Wake of Home: Literary Houses," *Children's Literature,* 18 (1990): 53–67;

Pierre Yvard, "*Pack of Cards:* a Theme and a Technique," *Journal of the Short Story in English,* 13 (Autumn 1989): 103–111.

Jill Paton Walsh

(29 April 1937 –)

Rosanne Fraine Donahue
University of Massachusetts, Boston

BOOKS: *Hengest's Tale,* illustrated by Janet Margrie (London: Macmillan, 1966; New York: St. Martin's Press, 1966);

The Dolphin Crossing (London: Macmillan, 1967; New York: St. Martin's Press, 1967);

Fireweed (London: Macmillan, 1969; New York: Farrar, Straus & Giroux, 1970);

Wordhoard: Anglo-Saxon Stories, by Paton Walsh and Kevin Crossley-Holland (London: Macmillan, 1969; New York: Farrar, Straus & Giroux, 1969);

Farewell, Great King (London: Macmillan, 1972; New York: Coward-McCann, 1972);

Goldengrove (London: Macmillan, 1972; New York: Farrar, Straus & Giroux, 1972);

Toolmaker, illustrated by Jeroo Roy (London: Heinemann, 1973; New York: Seabury, 1974);

The Dawnstone, illustrated by Mary Dinsdale (London: Hamish Hamilton, 1973);

The Emperor's Winding Sheet (London: Macmillan, 1974; New York: Farrar, Straus & Giroux, 1974);

The Butty Boy, illustrated by Juliette Palmer (London: Macmillan, 1975); republished as *The Huffler* (New York: Farrar, Straus & Giroux, 1975);

The Island Sunrise: Prehistoric Britain (London: Deutsch, 1975; New York: Seabury, 1976);

Unleaving (London: Macmillan, 1976; New York: Farrar, Straus & Giroux, 1976);

Crossing to Salamis, illustrated by David Smee (London: Heinemann, 1977);

The Walls of Athens, illustrated by Smee (London: Heinemann, 1977);

Persian Gold, illustrated by Smee (London: Heinemann, 1978);

A Chance Child (London: Macmillan, 1978; New York: Farrar, Straus & Giroux, 1989);

The Green Book, illustrated by Joanna Stubbs (London: Macmillan, 1981; New York: Farrar, Straus & Giroux, 1982);

Babylon, illustrated by Jenny Northway (London: Deutsch, 1982);

A Parcel of Patterns (London: Kestrel, 1983; New York: Farrar, Straus & Giroux, 1983);

Lost and Found, illustrated by Mary Rayner (London: Deutsch, 1984);

Gaffer Samson's Luck, illustrated by Brock Cole (New York: Farrar, Straus & Giroux, 1984; London: Viking Kestrel, 1985);

Lapsing (London: Weidenfeld & Nicolson, 1986; New York: St. Martin's Press, 1987);

Five Tides (Cambridge: Green Bay, 1986);

Torch (London: Viking Kestrel, 1987; New York: Farrar, Straus & Giroux, 1988);

Birdy and the Ghosties, illustrated by Alan Marks (London: Macmillan, 1989);

A School for Lovers (London: Weidenfeld & Nicolson, 1989);

Can I Play Jenny Jones, illustrated by Jolyne Knox (Oxford: Bodley Head, 1990);

Can I Play Queenie, illustrated by Knox (Oxford: Bodley Head, 1990);

Can I Play Wolf, illustrated by Knox (Oxford: Bodley Head, 1990);

Grace (London: Viking Kestrel, 1991; New York: Farrar, Straus & Giroux, 1992);

Matthew and the Sea Singer (Hemel Hempstead: Simon & Schuster, 1992; New York: Farrar, Straus & Giroux, 1993);

When Grandma Came, illustrated by Sophie Williams (New York: Viking, 1992);

Pepi and the Secret Names (New York: Lothrop, Lee & Shepard, 1994);

Knowledge of Angels (Cambridge: Green Bay, 1994; New York: Houghton Mifflin, 1994);

A Piece of Justice (New York: St. Martin's Press, 1995).

Collection: *Children of the Fox* (New York: Farrar, Straus & Giroux, 1978) – comprises *Crossing to Salamis, The Walls of Athens,* and *Persian Gold.*

Jill Paton Walsh

OTHER: "History is Fiction," *Horn Book,* 48 (February 1972): 17–23;

"Seeing Green," in *The Thorny Paradise: Writers on Writing for Children,* edited by Edward Blishen (Harmondsworth: Kestrel, 1975), pp. 58–61;

"The Art of Realism," in *Celebrating Children's Books,* edited by Betsy Hearne and Marilyn Kaye (New York: Lothrop, Lee & Shepard, 1981);

"Writers and Critics: A Dialogue Between Jill Paton Walsh and John Rowe Townsend," *Horn Book,* 58 (October 1982): 498–504 (December 1982): 680–685.

Jill Paton Walsh explores basic human concerns – love, death, and maturation – in novels that appeal to readers of all ages. In addition to the historical novels for which she is best known, she has written two realistic contemporary novels, two futuristic works, several fantasies, and several folklore adaptations. Paton Walsh's preferred subjects are in the large area of human experience that adults and children have in common. She explains

that she writes for children largely from a belief that a book should be as simple and as readable as the writer can make it – which is to say that it ought to be for children. Paton Walsh dislikes the idea that something written for children is necessarily inferior; she points out that no one thinks a children's doctor need not be so competent as his colleagues, or that a carpenter who makes toys can manage with shoddy joinery. Her governing principle is to make whatever she is doing as simple and accessible as possible.

Gillian Bliss was born on 29 April 1937 to John L. and Patricia D. Bliss in London. She received her early education (1943–1955) at St. Michael's Convent, a day school in North Finchley, London. She earned a diploma in education and an M.A. in English from St. Anne's College, Oxford (1955–1959). From 1959 to 1962 she taught English at Enfield Girls' Grammar School. In 1961 she married Antony Paton Walsh, a chartered secretary, and started to raise her family. Her husband continued in his career while she stayed at home with the

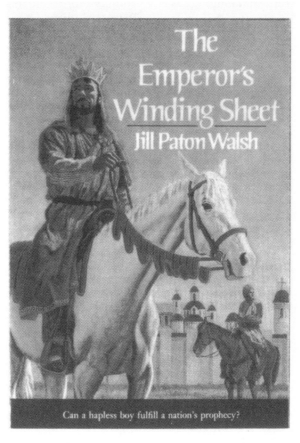

Dust jacket for Paton Walsh's novel set during the final days of the Byzantine Empire

children: Edmund Alexander, Margaret Ann, and Helen Clare. Paton Walsh started to write shortly after the arrival of her first child.

The often painful experience of maturing from adolescence to adulthood is a common theme in Paton Walsh's books. She has said that she is fascinated by the relationship of child and adult and the process — never completed, always in critical stages of advance and change — by which one becomes the other. This fascination, combined with her belief that what *really* happened long ago is bound to make the best story possible, has produced some fine historical novels. In her 1972 "History is Fiction" article, Paton Walsh defends and defines the historical novel. In discussing the nature of historical fiction she considers two opposing criticisms: the partisans of fiction who adopt a high aesthetic tone and argue that the creative imagination should not be adulterated with the dross of history, and historians who put on the armor of truth and object to the mingling of fictional elements with the pure ore of historical fact.

Children's historical fiction is, like all historical fiction, an interpretation of the past, the people,

and the events that have had an effect on our lives. Historical fiction should portray these people and events in a way that not only re-creates what is known but goes a step further and imagines characters' emotions and everyday experiences as well. Paton Walsh asserts that, if the novel has anything to say about history, it must say it through the story, through character and event, not merely through setting.

Paton Walsh defines a historical novel as being wholly or partly about the significant public events and social conditions of a past time. She draws connections between the events of the past and those of the present, allowing her young reader to journey along with the protagonist through a society that is different and strange, as in *The Emperor's Winding Sheet* (1974). Paton Walsh makes the past relevant through likable and credible characters: the protagonist in conflict with and alienated from the adult world is a universal and timeless subject. The world the protagonist experiences may differ from that of the reader, but Paton Walsh evokes recognition from her reader while at the same time maintaining historical authenticity.

Believing that to write historical novels one must be as good at history as any historian, Paton Walsh has produced works that are both historically and psychologically true. She is mindful of the distinction between historical fiction and historical fact and operates in the realm of the possible while never crossing over into the false. In the prologue of her first novel, *Hengest's Tale* (1966), she states, "I am not a scholar, but I like this story, and so I have put it together as best I can, and filled the gaps with new bits of my own and written it down for you to read."

Hengest, a mid-fifth-century ruler of Kent and one of the first of the successful Saxon invaders, lies dying as he admits that he is an oath-breaker and a murderer. In an attempt to die in peace he tells the story of his youth and how he came to Britain with Jutish warriors to aid Vortigern, including his complex and ultimately tragic friendship with the king's son, Finn. The central plot shows Hengest trying to balance his admiration of Finn against his loyalty to his own people. Hengest witnesses and participates in many battles and feuds as he grows to adulthood; he learns violence, revenge, and anger as a way of life and finally kills his friend Finn. Hengest never recovers from killing Finn and confronts his unresolved feelings only when he is at the point of death. Hengest, Finn, and the various minor characters are surprisingly three-dimensional for a first-time writer. There are enough differences in thought pattern and action to make them believable as people of the Dark Ages, but at the same time they have enough similarities to modern people to be understandable. David Rees in his article "Types of Ambiguity" observes, "In spite of a complicated plot which appears to be unpromising material for a writer making her debut, Walsh makes a rattling good story." Paul Heins in a 1966 *Horn Book* review comments, "The balance between stirring events and strong characterization – combined with the authentic details – makes a memorable historical narrative."

Paton Walsh's debut as a writer of historical fiction was viewed as promising; however, her next two novels disappointed some critics. *The Dolphin Crossing* (1967) and *Fireweed* (1969) are stories about World War II and the differences imposed by class structure. In *The Dolphin Crossing*, Pat Riley, an evacuee living in a derelict railway carriage, and John Aston, a boy from a wealthy family, would never have met and become partners except for the war. The two boys sneak out in the middle of the night

and take John's boat across the channel to help the British soldiers who have been stranded at Dunkirk. They skirt close to the shore and take eight men at a time to the large ship, *Wakeful*. After John and Pat bring home the last eight men they are able to save, Pat sneaks back to try to rescue more, unable to bear the thought of men still left there. He does not return, and as the book ends it is assumed that he has died in a valiant but irresponsible attempt.

Fireweed introduces Bill and Julie, two teens of divergent backgrounds who, like John and Pat, would never have met, much less formed a relationship, if it were not for the war. A lower-class evacuee, Bill has already been on his own for some time when he meets Julie, a member of a wealthy family, who is a survivor from a ship that had been torpedoed on the way to Canada. Alone in the London Blitz, they manage to survive and, in fact, take in an abandoned child, Dickie. Together they form a sort of family in an empty house; Bill goes out in the morning to look for food and work, while Julie stays home and tries to clean the house and take care of Dickie. There are times when fifteen-year-old Bill wants a grown-up around to take over responsibility for Julie and Dickie, but at other moments he feels welcome in coming home for the first time in his life. Although Julie and Dickie are saved when the house collapses, the little family splits up when Julie and Dickie go to the hospital. Bill does visit Julie in the hospital and meets her mother and brother, but after this visit they never see each other again.

Critics have found fault with Paton Walsh's characterizations in both novels, but the characters are not what matters most in these stories. In *Dolphin Crossing* the heroism of the British is the main focus; the *Oxford Companion to Children's Literature* observes, "When Walsh is talking about the battle itself she demonstrates a gift for rendering in words some of the great moments of history, vividly portraying the heat of the battle in all its chaos, glory, and horror. The quality of the prose rises to a finer level, and the handling of detail never obscures the general outlines." John Rowe Townsend, while noting improbabilities in *Fireweed,* states that it "is a book to be read, remembered, and reread." *Fireweed* won the *Book World* Festival Award for 1970.

Paton Walsh's fourth novel, *Goldengrove* (1972), along with her 1976 novel, *Unleaving,* are perhaps her most ambitious and popular works. Both deal with loss, with adolescent emotion, and with memory. The titles are taken from the second line of Gerard Manley Hopkins's poem "Spring and Fall":

Dust jacket for Paton Walsh's novel of time travel and social commentary on the treatment of children

Margaret, are you grieving
Over Goldengrove unleaving?

In *Goldengrove* readers meet Madge Fielding in the spring of her life; she is coming alive to new experiences and adventures daily, while leaving her childhood behind. The novel tells the story of Madge and Paul, a younger boy she knows as her cousin, who spend two weeks every summer at their grandmother's house in Cornwall. As this particular summer starts, things are different. Not only have they arrived later in the year than usual but they have to sleep in separate rooms for the first time. Madge is older and more sensitive than Paul; even though she still cares very much for him, she is starting to do things alone. She keeps meaning to work on the boat with Paul, but her intentions go astray. In an effort to keep peace, she offers to read to Professor Ashton, a blind professor staying at Gran's cottage, and the time she does spend with Paul is not quite as rich and as satisfying as in the past.

Madge finds her reading sessions with the professor special. Even when she reads something she doesn't understand, like William Empson's *Seven Types of Ambiguity* (1930), she is gratified to be helping. The more she recites and learns from Jane Austen, Lewis Carroll, John Donne, and John Milton, the more she wants to know. She starts to imagine herself as Jane Eyre and the professor as Mr. Rochester, and she spends as much time as possible with him. When she finds out that Paul is actually her brother, she feels betrayed by her parents. She goes to the professor and tells him she is going to stay; she will read to him forever. He does not want her to stay, for with time she will only grow bitter and resent him. His first wife having abandoned him means he will never trust again. Madge tells him that feeling that way is far worse than his blindness. He explains that lack of trust is not unique with him: these feelings merely represent growing up. Madge runs away sobbing uncontrollably, goes to the beach, climbs into the boat, and heads to the lighthouse, almost drowning in the process. She is rescued, but it is not clear whether she will live.

In *Unleaving,* Madge's grandmother has left her the beloved Goldengrove. Again it is summer, and Madge is about to enter college. She is deciding to rent the house to two Oxford professors and their philosophy students for a reading party, though she still misses her grandmother and is not sure that she wants strangers in Gran's house. The story is told through the eyes of young Madge as she listens to the reading groups and observes their findings with interest. A second distinct voice narrating events is that of a grandmother, apparently staying with a daughter's family at Goldengrove at a different time. Though it is not at first obvious, the two narrators are one and the same: the grandmother is Madge Fielding sixty years later.

Professor Tregeagle has brought his family to Goldengrove: his son, Patrick, moody and private, who rejects the philosophical discussions; and his severely retarded daughter, Molly, an embarrassment to the professor. The professor may be a good teacher, but he does not appear to be a good father. Madge starts spending more and more time with Patrick, who begins to share himself with her. The relationship is slow in building, but the foundation appears solid. Patrick is extremely sensitive and thinks deeply and constantly; he obsesses over Molly's happiness but realizes there will always be someone to laugh at her, or be repelled by her, or even hurt her. The issue of mercy killing arises when Molly dies as she and Patrick climb the cliffs. Whether Patrick pushed her is not clear in the description of the event:

Up the path on the brink scramble Molly and Patrick. She is picking the thrift at the edge, brightly visible in her emerald green dress. Patrick points; she leans out, stooping over the outermost clump of flowers; and behind them both Paul and Madge see Patrick's arm suddenly lifted, see him stretch out towards her as she falls.

Nor is it clear after the death of Molly what really did happen. Madge initially thinks that Patrick pushed her; Paul thinks that he was reaching out his arm to grab her. Patrick himself is confused. He wants her safe, not dead. Once the reader realizes that the grandmother who is telling the interwoven stories is actually Madge sixty years later, it becomes clear that Madge and Patrick did marry, have a daughter, and live at Goldengrove.

Paton Walsh spent time at her grandmother's house in St. Ives, the model for Goldengrove, when she was evacuated from the dangers of wartime London. Many reviewers have commented on the similarities between Walsh's *Goldengrove* and *Unleaving* and Virginia Woolf's *To the Lighthouse* (1927). All three novels are set in St. Ives, use the same type of house as a background to the sea and cliffs, have a lighthouse as a recurring motif, and even share some similarities in Walsh's and Woolf's language. The similarities were not intentional on Walsh's part, however, for she did not know that Woolf had lived in St. Ives.

Goldengrove and *Unleaving* have been especially praised for their evocation of place. *The New York Times Book Review* terms Paton Walsh's description of the English seaside around Cornwall "masterly." She has also received praise for her handling of the difficult subject matter of *Unleaving.* Too wise to attempt answers about growing, living, dying, or ethical choices, she exalts the mystery, the unknowing itself. Though Paton Walsh's books are generally well liked and widely read in the United States, *Unleaving* is the only one to receive a major American award, the *Boston Globe–Horn Book* award for 1976.

Paton Walsh left her memories of St. Ives to go back to the Stone Age in *Toolmaker* (1973), a book about a young boy, Ra, in a forest tribe who tries to juggle building a hut, hunting for food, and gathering flint for spearheads. His mother has recently died, and he cannot afford to buy himself a wife. He goes hungry until his friend Yul offers to gather food in exchange for a spearhead for hunting. Ra is uneasy because new things frighten him; he only knows the way of the tribe, that every man does everything for himself. At first Ra feels like a woman when the other men go off to hunt and he stays behind to make spearheads, but soon he is making weapons for all the men. Deserted during a famine, Ra finds a village where there is plenty of food and where his skill is appreciated. He makes curved knives for cutting grass, round-ended tools to crush and grind grain, and scrapers for cleaning skins, as well as axes and fishhooks. However, he cannot understand the tribe's language. Summoned by his repentant friends, Ra eventually goes back to his tribe. Working together is one of Paton Walsh's recurring themes. In *Toolmaker* she demonstrates how every member of the group has specific duties. The best toolmaker should make the arrows and spears; the best hunter should hunt; the best fisherman should fish; the best animal skinner should skin the animals; and, most important, everyone should share. The book has suffered in comparison to other books about prehistory, such as Henry Treece's *The Dream-Time* (1967) and especially the works of Rosemary Sutcliff.

The Emperor's Winding Sheet, one of Paton Walsh's most ambitious works, portrays the end of the Byzantine Empire. The protagonist, Piers Barber – called Vrethiki, meaning lucky – is a naive slave boy who has been chosen to be constantly at the Lord Constantine's side. Because Vrethiki is so naive, everything has to be explained to him by his more worldly friend Stephanos, a technique that allows the reader to understand the background of the story and its characters, especially Emperor Constantine. (Vrethiki is genuinely an outsider; conveniently – if perhaps somewhat implausibly – he is British.) As the young protagonist starts to understand why the Greek Church is resisting any effort to ask Rome for help, the reader can see the impossible predicament of Constantine. The empire is being threatened by the Turks; unless Constantine can reunite the churchmen, he can expect no help from the Pope. Despite valiant attempts to hold them off, the Turks storm the gates and sack the city, killing Constantine. In Vrethiki's two years with the emperor, his emotions have gone from anger and hate to admiration and love. Although he never understood why the emperor risked his life for a hopeless cause, now that the emperor is dead he risks his life to save the emperor's body from desecration.

As Stephanos tells Vrethiki, what cannot be avoided in life must be accepted with dignity. Men are not judged by the fate God appoints for them; rather, they are judged by the manner in which they meet that fate. The theme of doing the best one can in spite of obstacles and appearances is woven throughout *The Emperor's Winding Sheet*. Constantine's kindness to his subordinates, his loyalty to his empire, and his friendship to his peers show him to be a good man. While he is depicted as more comfortable on the battlefield than at the head of an army, his nobility is shown again and again as he fights in the best way he can for what he knows may be hopeless. Rees, who has criticized Walsh for her depiction of working-class characters, says, "Nobody, not even Rosemary Sutcliff, can do a siege or a naval engagement on a crowded battlefield as well as Jill Paton Walsh." This ability is what makes *The Emperor's Winding Sheet* one of the most appealing of modern historical novels for children. Its action, complex themes, and evocation of a little-known historical setting earned its author the Whitbread Award of the Booksellers' Association.

The Butty Boy (1975), published in America as *The Huffler,* depicts another child from a wealthy background meeting children from the working class. Harry is bored and unhappy with her new home; her nursemaid, Susan, has been sent away because Harry is getting too old to have one. When Harry is made to go outside for some fresh air, she wanders down to the canal, where she sees two boats being drawn by a horse on the tow path. Fourteen-year-old Bess and her eleven-year-old brother, Ned, are trying to bring both boats loaded with coal to the paper mill. Harry leads them to believe that she is a mistreated servant girl, and the two take her on as a "huffler" for the journey. As the three travel along the canal, the Jebb children worry that adults may discover their older brother is not on board. Harry first worries about being found, then wonders why no one is looking for her. As Bess helps Harry wash, she wonders why Harry's back is not marked from beatings, like a typical servant girl's; she and her brother are also surprised that Harry can read.

The main theme of *The Butty Boy* is the superficiality of class differences. Until her trip down the canal Harry never knew about the lives of the people who made many of the things she used daily. Harry can read and write, but only because she has been taught. In two days she is able to teach Bess and Ned not only to write their names but to decipher other words. Many years later Harry still clutches a ticket with a message of hope and friendship written on the back.

While realizing that Paton Walsh is attempting to show "that working class life in the nineteenth century was hard and the people ill-fed, overworked, and underpaid," Rees argues that the bargers "are somewhat too jolly and rosy-cheeked: it's the past distorted by nostalgia. . . . In every incident there's something comforting taking the edge off what it was really like." It is unusual for Paton Walsh to receive criticism as thoroughly negative as this, but her failure to create convincing characters among the working class is a continuing concern among critics. As in *Dolphin Crossing* and *Firewood* Paton Walsh appears to be concerned with other matters than the critics. The pervasive metaphor of reading (Harry can read words but Bess and Ned can read the evidence on her body; each learns something of the other's reading skills) suggests that the novel is more about perceptions and preconceptions than about working-class life as such. That Paton Walsh took these criticisms to heart, however, is shown in the grimness of her next Victorian story, *A Chance Child* (1978).

Paton Walsh's first adult novel, *Farewell Great King* (1972), portrayed Themistokles and the struggle with Persia, and she returned to this figure in several juvenile titles. In *Crossing to Salamis* (1977), the story of Themistokles' famous trick of sending a false message (that the Greeks were going to flee

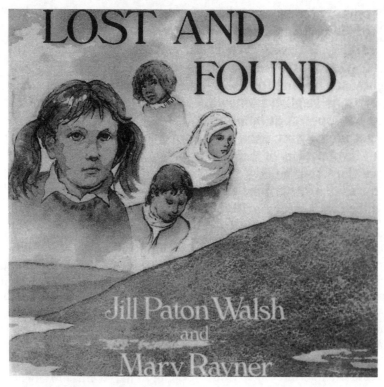

*Dust jacket for Paton Walsh's book about the experiences of four children who
are asked to deliver gifts to their grandparents*

Athens again) to the king of Persia is the main focus. When the Persian ships crowd into the narrow channel between Salamis and Athens, they are defeated by the ready and waiting Athenians. But despite the authentic detail and description, the story is actually about Aster, a sheltered girl who boldly risks everything most important to her in order to warn the general of possible treason.

The Walls of Athens (1977) shows Themistokles taking the lead in building the walls surrounding Athens. Again, the real focus of the story is on a young adult who comes forward to help. Demeas, a shepherd boy, stretches his endurance and resolution to their limits in order to carry the crucial message that may decide the future of the city. In *Persian Gold* (1978) Themistokles is rejected by both the Athenians and the Spartans. He throws himself on the mercy of the king of Persia and subsequently is befriended by Lala and her brother, Perdiccas, the children of Amyntas, the king of the Molossians. Lala, knowing the customs of the Molossians, tricks her father into helping Themistokles to escape. In all three of the stories, the actions of Themistokles are historically accurate, but the emphasis in each is on the child. Without a thought for their own safety, Aster, Demeas, and Lala all try to make a

difference. None of the children does anything extraordinary, but a hero need only be an ordinary person who does what he or she believes is right. In 1978 the three Themistokles stories were issued together under the title *Children of the Fox*.

Paton Walsh's next novel combines fantasy with a historical approach to child-labor practices in the nineteenth century – a combination in the tradition of Charles Kingsley's *Water Babies* (1863), though Paton Walsh writes with passion and indignation about working conditions for children in factories rather than about the circumstances of young chimney sweeps. *A Chance Child* is a novel of time travel in which a young boy, locked away in a closet, neglected and unloved, escapes from his world to the past, where he finds children who are treated as badly as he is. Since the only name he has ever known is Creep, that is the name he chooses for himself during his journey aboard a boat that takes him down the canal from twentieth-century to nineteenth-century England.

Creep's first stop is at a mine where it becomes apparent to the reader that not everyone can see him. At first he is seen only by children, but as the novel progresses it becomes clear that he is seen by the kind and the innocent. At the mine Creep meets the first of the children he travels with; he hears a horrible scream and sees young Tom Moorhouse hurled against the wall, then left to lie there groaning. Creep offers to help Tom run away, and they pull the boat into the open water where it again goes of its own accord. The next time that the boat stops they are at the edge of an iron factory where Tom finds work. Here they first see Lucy: a little girl hanging on a loop of sooty rope from the rooftree, treading the handle of a bellows blowing the fire of a furnace. Lucy is called Blackie, because the whole side of her face is a black scar from an earlier fall into the fire.

The three children run away first to a pottery, where they are temporarily employed, and then to a coal mine where only Tom finds work. Creep and Blackie set out on their own and end up at a cotton mill where Blackie finds work as a piecer. As in the other jobs, conditions are appalling. There is an overseer walking up and down carrying a whip; it is not unusual for the children at the mill to be beaten. At the cotton mill Creep finally becomes a real person to be seen by all. He leaves Blackie at the mill and goes to work building canals.

Meanwhile, Creep's half-brother, Christopher, searches for him in the twentieth century. Christopher is the one person in the present day who loves Creep; he used to sneak him food in the closet and talk to him. When he finally realizes that Creep has gone into the past, he does some research and finds a reference to him in the Parliamentary Papers. Creep married Lucy, Christopher discovers, and they had ten children, of which four lived. He learned how to read and write and worked as a printer; the four of his children who survived infancy never worked in a factory.

There have been some negative reviews about the unrealistic depiction of the working-class children in *A Chance Child*. But while Walsh apparently cannot create convincing characters for everyone, her talent for creating realistic detail and description is often applauded. In *The New York Times Book Review* Jane Langton observes, "Walsh's splendid descriptive power seems to blow the hot sparks of the forge in our faces and the choking lint of the mill into our lungs. Our ears ring with the fall of the massive hammer in the ironworks; they catch the huge sighing that sweeps the valley from the great bellows fanning the smelter fire; and at last they hear even the inaudible cries of the beaten children in the mill."

It is perhaps unsurprising that an accomplished historical novelist like Paton Walsh should try her hand at a science-fiction novel, but one could say that in *The Green Book* (1981) she follows the line of history into the future. The novel records the story of a community that immigrates to a distant planet when Earth is about to disintegrate. The families who have to flee Earth have been handpicked; they are sophisticated and literate and have the necessary knowledge not only to survive but to prosper in a new environment. But the settlers have no margin for error. They have enough seed for one harvest, and if that fails they will take the pills of last resort and die. Unfortunately, the world of Shine (so named by Patti, the youngest colonist) has a different cellular structure from that of earth. The grass of Shine kills earth-bred rabbits; the soil of Shine changes the molecular structure of the grains the colonists sow. The fear of the settlers is that they will be unable to eat what they have grown.

Paton Walsh pursues her familiar themes in *The Green Book*. For instance, even in this futuristic setting, class distinctions remain, at least in the minds of the adults. The children, however, do not recognize class distinctions among the colonists and resist perpetuating them. Regardless of whose perception is truer, Paton Walsh stresses one of her recurrent themes: The individual's self-perception can be distorted, even crippled, by the dominant societal attitude. This familiar theme goes hand in hand with Paton Walsh's much used topic of the individual's usefulness to society as an originator of ideas. *Toolmaker* was set in prehistory; *The Green Book* can be said to be set in posthistory. But both worlds recognize the vital role played in any society by the person who can see things in a new light.

The Green Book also shows the difference between adults' and children's abilities to cope with problems, and it greatly respects the child's vision. When the adults have virtually resigned themselves to starvation, the children find the candy trees; when the adults are sure the wheat they have grown is deadly, the children make flour from it and eat bread baked from it. The willingness of the children to take chances saves all their lives. Finally, a child's choice, condemned as foolish by all the adults, proves to be the wisest choice of all. Patti chose to bring the green book, an empty journal, with her to Shine. She fills it with their story, the history of the colony. The adults, who find themselves hungry for stories, realize at the end that Patti in saving their story has been truly wise.

Paton Walsh explores the power and persistence of memory in *Babylon* (1982). As three black children, Dulcie, David, and Lesley, walk along an abandoned viaduct, they can see cracked, black chimneys over the whole city. Dulcie imagines that they are all in Babylon, and all three children start to sing a song learned at the Sunday mission. As they walk and sing, they think back to their earlier homes in Jamaica, reminiscing about the food and the sights they left behind.

A Parcel of Patterns (1983) concerns spiritual struggle and change during the Great Plague of 1665. Parson William Momphesson is sent by the Restoration Church to the village of Eyam in Derbyshire to replace Parson Thomas Stanley, the Puritan minister. Parson Momphesson does not send Parson Stanley away as he is supposed to but rather lets him live in the village, where he continues to preach the Puritan faith while slandering the new way. The mostly Puritan village, where decoration (of clothing or anything else) is deemed unacceptable, is struck with the Black Death after a packet of patterns arrives for the tailor, who ordered the material to make Parson Momphesson's wife, Catherine, some pretty clothes.

The strong-willed Puritans are seen through the eyes of Mal Percival, a teenage girl whose faith and courage are tested with each new death. The villagers voluntarily quarantine themselves to keep the disease from spreading, but Eyam loses within a year 267 of its 350 people. When her best friend, Emmot, dies without ever having known the joy of Roland's arms, Mal decides that Emmot should have slept with Roland first and made a marriage later, like the girls of the poor who would go to the altar swelling with sin and full of happiness. Though she has always tried to please God, near the end of the book Mal questions her faith because she does not understand him.

Parson Stanley symbolizes the familiar, while Parson Momphesson represents the unknown. The two parsons, likable but different, join together to comfort the sick and the bereaved. When Mal starts to question the Puritan faith, the reader is aware that the new religion will welcome her. Neil Philip notes in a *New York Times* review, "*A Parcel of Patterns* is a most dreadful, moving story, and it is related by Jill Paton Walsh with a quiet, unerring restraint which will disturb and possess the reader long after the frenzy aroused by a sensational approach would have died away." The novel won the Universe Prize for 1984.

In *Lost and Found* (1984) Paton Walsh tells the stories of four children, each asked to bring a prized possession to a grandparent. All four children – being children – forget their purpose and lose the possession. Little Ag loses an arrowhead made by his father for his grandfather. As he looks to find the misplaced arrowhead, he finds a stone with a hole in it; the grandfather calls it a ring stone meant to bring good luck. Sweet Alysoun loses a jug of fresh cream, and as she looks for it she finds a stone, sharp at both ends and along both sides. Alysoun brings this to her grandmother who calls it an elfshot, a fairy arrowhead that brings good luck. In the third story Peterkin loses a sixpence that his mother owes his grandfather. He finds a funny jug that he brings instead. The grandfather needed the sixpence to buy a jug to carry home his ale and he actually likes the ancient jug better. In the last story Jenny is supposed to be bringing scissors to her grandmother for her birthday. Instead, she finds an old coin. The grandmother is quite happy with the sixpence and shows Jenny the picture of King George on the coin. The many years between Ag losing the arrowhead and Jenny losing the scissors show that childhood is timeless and universal.

In *Gaffer Samson's Luck* (1984) a small boy copes with problems that result when his father relocates after losing his job. James dislikes having to leave his friends and his home in the Yorkshire Dales to move to the Peterborough Fens. On the Fens one can see for miles; there are no trees, and everything is flat and lonely. James's new house is small, with no land for a garden. At school the students are divided into estate kids and village kids, and he belongs with neither group; he lives in the wrong area to be an estate kid, and one must be born a villager. The one person in school who seems to care about him is Angey, who lives in a van and is not accepted by either group.

James gains acceptance in the rigid clan structure of the village through his relationship with Gaffer Samson. James tries to find the Gaffer's lost luck, a stone given to the old man by a gypsy. While trying to complete the mission for the Gaffer, James must outmaneuver the village gang. Needing to borrow the gang member Terry's boat, James agrees to take whatever dare Terry wants in exchange. Terry dares him to cross the Rymers, a dangerous weir. However, it is Terry who is nearly drowned trying to cross. James crosses the Rymers in the middle of the night while Terry lies in critical condition; when the Gaffer gives James his luck, James goes to the hospital and slips it into Terry's hand before his operation. This deceptively simple story about belonging, change, courage, and generosity won the Smarties Prize Grand Prix in 1985.

The timeless materials from folktale, myth, and tradition which Paton Walsh chooses to deal with in *Five Tides* (1986), a collection of stories for adults, and later in *Birdy and the Ghosties* (1989) express some overarching interests and themes typical

Jill Paton Walsh

Gaffer Samson's Luck

Pictures by
Brock Cole

Will James find the Gaffer's luck in time?

Dust jacket for Paton Walsh's novel about a small boy who must
cope with his family's relocation after his father loses his job

of her work. The strangeness and the wonder of human love and human self-denial are as clearly expressed in *Five Tides* as in *Fireweed*. The unrelenting savagery of the sea is no less clearly demonstrated in *Five Tides* than in *The Dolphin Crossing*. *Five Tides* consists of retold ballads and folktales about dwellers near the sea at the time of Oliver Cromwell. Paton Walsh recaptures ancient times and gives a flavor of the beliefs of the era. The message of all five tales is that the sea gives back the bones of the dead and that those left behind are taken care of. *Five Tales* is notable also as the author's first publication from Green Bay Press, which she set up in 1986 with John Rowe Townsend.

Torch (1987) is set in a postnuclear world where industrial civilization has long ago been destroyed. Unlike *The Green Book,* there is no historical memory whereby people are able to learn by others' mistakes. The value of hindsight is extremely important in this novel; it becomes apparent only midway through the book that what the children carry

is the torch used to start the Olympic Games. Because of the nuclear war, technological expertise and other forms of knowledge have been completely lost. The torch that the children carry symbolizes what is missing in the world. Togetherness, as in teamwork and in friendship, is the theme of *Torch.* The values of truth, goodness, and beauty are interwoven throughout the travels of the children and are symbolized by both the torch and the children. The torch burns brightly when all is well, and it ceases to burn when the motives of an individual or a society are dishonest or self-serving. The torch goes out at different times during the journey – when someone tries to misuse it – but it always relights when the children are being unselfish, caring, and, most important, unknowing.

The theme of a future world is treated differently in *Torch* than in *The Green Book.* Both novels take place after man's destruction of the world. In *The Green Book* the families who have to flee Earth have the technological ability to be comfortable on a strange planet. In *Torch* people with no knowledge of the past are struggling along, knowing nothing, having almost nothing. The common thread in both of these novels is the death of literature. In *The Green Book* few have thought to bring books; they find out that they no longer have the goodness they needed. In *Torch* it becomes apparent that the destruction of the world occurred because people stopped learning new ways to do things. The children have never heard of books before meeting the scholar who may be the only person able to read in this new world. Through reading the scholar has learned how to perform some simple medical procedures in order to help others. Paton Walsh shows that reading not only helps human beings learn new things, it also tells them what and how much they still need to know; it forces them to think differently. The debates about literature and literacy will continue, but it is important that writers continue to impress upon children the importance of literature.

Birdy and the Ghosties is another of Walsh's highly successful ventures into the literary folktale. Birdy; her mother; and her father, the ferryman, live at the river's mouth, where her father rows travelers across the river. One day a penniless old woman begs the ferryman to take her across the river. When they reach the other side, the old woman tells the ferryman to take good care of Birdy because she has second sight. In the days that follow, Birdy thinks a lot about having second sight, finding that the world does indeed appear different.

In a later episode the ferryman tells Birdy that he is worried by not being able to see what is in the boat with them. Birdy sees three hideous ghosts — a great, rotting slimy man; a woman hinged and "scaled" like a crawfish; and a child feathered like a cormorant, holding a bleeding and rotting fish in its claws. But when her father asks her to describe what she sees, she does not want to alarm him. Instead, she describes the ghosts as a king with a wise face, a queen with a kind face, and a prince with black hair and a smiling face, all dressed in gold and finery. As they arrive at the island, Birdy takes two more looks at the ghosts, and on the second look they are indeed wise and fair to look upon. They explain: Birdy's vision of them has now replaced the terrible way a frightened fisherman had seen them a century before.

To reward Birdy, the three ghosts offer her a farm, but she sees only seaweed-covered rocks; Birdy asks to lose her second sight, but the ghosts refuse. In the end her reward is the boy ghost's cuddle-toy, really a net full of mussel shells. But the mussel shells merit a second look; each contains a pearl. Paton

Walsh creates a moment of great perception when Birdy suddenly realizes that the "one-strand river" is anything in life that one never gets over.

Paton Walsh returned to historical novels with *Grace* (1991), a fictionalized account of a true story set in 1838. *Grace* depicts a young girl, Grace, and her father, Mr. Darling, risking their lives to save the survivors of a wrecked ship. As they are trying to keep the survivors warm and fed in the small lighthouse, the rescue-ship crew arrives, angry that their reward has been snatched from their hands. Because of the weather conditions neither Mr. Darling nor the rescue crew believed that the other could reach the wreck. Mr. Darling and Grace would have preferred to leave the rescue in the hands of the men who performed such acts as an accustomed thing. Because Grace, a young working-class girl, was involved in the rescue, the public showers her with gifts, and the men who also risked their lives in trying to save the survivors are virtually ignored; they come to feel resentment and even loathing for the Darlings.

Paton Walsh tells the story of this conflict between a heroic action and the resentment aroused by that action in the voice of Grace Darling. Portrayed as a brave and well-meaning young woman, Grace finds her life taken over by the pressures of the public and the arrogance of the aristocrats who choose to make themselves her sponsors. In Grace Darling's sad fate Paton Walsh reveals the worst elements of class distinction: As a working-class girl Grace could not hope to marry a gentleman; yet, having acquired wealth above her station, she could not expect the poor fisherman who loved her to marry her and be known as a man who married for money. Once the aristocracy became interested in Grace, she had little choice about the disposition of her own goods and her own person. As much for her father's sake as for her own, she had to please the duke of Alnwick and to appear grateful when all she wished was to be left alone.

Paton Walsh also uses Grace's story to show the religion of the time as an oppressive tool to keep the people in their proper place. Grace becomes increasingly tormented by the question of whether or not she performed her heroic deed selflessly or out of a desire for reward. She has thought on the matter so much that she can no longer recall what was really in her mind on the actual occasion. But she is aware — the ministers she has consulted have all said so — that a good deed done for an evil reason has no merit. She is tormented by nightmares about scrabbling for gold coins on the sea-wet rocks, and she comes to consider the very action for which most people praise her a terrible sin. The same public that has elevated her to such stature gives her no peace and can turn upon her quickly. Her correspondents rebuke her for not replying quickly. A proposed visit to the circus at Edinburgh brings severe reprimands from total strangers who would not have their heroine thus exposed to the public eye.

When Grace develops a serious illness she can see that those around her expect her to die; she becomes obsessed with remembering what she was thinking of the morning of the wreck, to know whether she performed the rescue for reward. Slipping from her sister's house, where she is supposed to be resting, Grace climbs up to the castle at night to look at the rocks out at sea where the wreck took place. There she meets Mr. Tulloch, one of the survivors, who tells her "It doesn't matter! ... It doesn't matter a grout why you did it! If you did it for rage and spite and greed, am I the less living for that?" His insistence that the reason does not matter frees Grace's mind; the next day she dies. Although it may relieve Grace to hear that her motives do not matter, the reader is not similarly relieved. It seems enormously unfair that anyone should believe that Grace Darling could have foreseen the outpouring of wealth and public admiration that followed her deed and could therefore have devised a plot. Such injustice in the minds of her fellow creatures is not adequately redressed by "It doesn't matter." *Grace* ends on an unrelievedly unhappy note.

In addition to writing fiction for all ages Paton Walsh has been Whitall Lecturer at the Library of Congress (1978) and an accomplished critic. She has contributed to reference works, including essays on Nina Bawden, Lucy M. Boston, Penelope Farmer, and Ursula K. LeGuin for the 1994 first edition of *Twentieth Century Young Adult Writers* as well as earlier essays in *Twentieth Century Children's Writers*. And she continues to write outstanding children's literature. Most recently Paton Walsh has written three short fiction pieces for younger readers and two novels for adults. The juvenile titles are *Matthew and the Sea Singer* (1992), a folktale adaptation; *When Grandma Came* (1992), a contemporary story; and *Pepi and the Secret Names* (1994), set in ancient Egypt. *Matthew and the Sea Singer* was named an American Library Association Notable Book for its year. Her two novels, *Knowledge of Angels* and *A Piece of Justice,* are mystery thrillers.

References:

David Rees, "Types of Ambiguity," in his *The Marble in the Water* (Boston: Horn Book, 1990), pp. 141–154;

John Rowe Townsend, "Jill Paton Walsh," in his *A Sounding of Storytellers: New and Revised Essays on Contemporary Writers for Children* (New York: Lippincott, 1979), pp. 153–165.

Philippa Pearce

(23 January 1920 –   )

Judith Gero John
Southwest Missouri State University

BOOKS: *Minnow on the Say,* as A. Philippa Pearce, illustrated by Edward Ardizzone (Oxford: Oxford University Press, 1954); republished as *The Minnow Leads to Treasure* (Cleveland: World, 1958);

Tom's Midnight Garden, as A. Philippa Pearce, illustrated by Susan Einzig (Oxford: Oxford University Press, 1958; Philadelphia: Lippincott, 1959);

Still Jim and Silent Jim (Oxford: Blackwell, 1960);

Mrs. Cockle's Cat, illustrated by Antony Maitland (London: Constable, 1961; Philadelphia: Lippincott, 1962);

A Dog So Small, illustrated by Maitland (London: Constable, 1962; Philadelphia: Lippincott, 1963);

The Strange Sunflower (London: Nelson, 1966);

The Children of the House, with Brian Fairfax-Lucy, illustrated by John Sergeant (Philadelphia: Lippincott, 1968; Harmondsworth, Middlesex: Longman Kestrel, 1968); republished as *The Children of Charlecote* (London: Gollancz, 1989);

The Elm Street Lot, based on stories for the British Broadcasting Corporation 1969, enlarged edition, illustrated by Peter Rush (Harmondsworth, Middlesex: Kestrel, 1979);

The Squirrel Wife, illustrated by Derek Collard (Ipswich, Suffolk: Cowell, 1971; New York: Crowell, 1972);

Beauty and the Beast, illustrated by Alan Barrett (New York: Crowell, 1972; Ipswich, Suffolk: Cowell, 1972);

What the Neighbours Did and Other Stories, illustrated by Faith Jaques (Harmondsworth, Middlesex: Kestrel, 1972; New York: Crowell, 1973);

The Shadow-Cage and Other Tales of the Supernatural, illustrated by Ted Lewin (New York: Crowell, 1977; Harmondsworth, Middlesex: Kestrel, 1977);

The Battle of Bubble and Squeak, illustrated by Alan Baker (London: Deutsch, 1978);

Philippa Pearce

The Way to Sattin Shore, illustrated by Charlotte Voake (Harmondsworth, Middlesex: Kestrel, 1983; New York: Greenwillow, 1984);

A Picnic for Bunnykins, as Warrener (Harmondsworth, Middlesex: Viking, 1984);

Two Bunnykins Out for Tea, as Warrener, illustrated by Glenys Corkery (Harmondsworth, Middlesex: Viking, 1984);

Bunnykins in the Snow, as Warrener, illustrated by Walter Hayward (Harmondsworth, Middlesex: Viking, 1985);

Lion at School and Other Stories, illustrated by Caroline Sharpe (New York: Greenwillow, 1985;

Harmondsworth, Middlesex: Viking Kestrel, 1985);

Who's Afraid? and Other Strange Stories (Harmondsworth, Middlesex: Kestrel, 1986; New York: Greenwillow, 1987);

Emily's Own Elephant, illustrated by John Lawrence (London: MacRae, 1987; New York: Greenwillow, 1988);

The Tooth Ball, illustrated by Helen Ganly (London: Deutsch, 1987);

Freddy, illustrated by David Armitage (London: Deutsch, 1988);

Old Belle's Summer Holiday, illustrated by William Geldart (London: Deutsch, 1989);

In the Middle of the Night (London: BBC, 1990);

Here Comes Tod!, illustrated by Adriano Gon (London: Walker, 1992).

OTHER: Harold Scott, *From Inside Scotland Yard,* adapted for children by Pearce (London: Deutsch, 1963; New York: Macmillan, 1965);

"The Writing of *Tom's Midnight Garden,*" in *Chosen for Children: An Account of the Books Which Have Been Awarded the Library Association Carnegie Medal,* edited by Marcus Crouch and Alec Ellis (New York: Library Association, 1967);

"The Writer's View of Childhood," in *Horn Book Reflections: On Children's Books and Reading, Selected from Eighteen Years of "The Horn Book Magazine 1949–1966,"* edited by Elinor Whitney Field (Boston: Horn Book, 1969), pp. 49–53;

Stories from Hans Christian Andersen, edited, with a preface, by Pearce, illustrated by Pauline Baynes (London: Collins, 1972);

"Writing A Book: *A Dog So Small*" in *The Thorny Paradise: Writers on Writing for Children,* edited by Edward Blishen (Harmondsworth, Middlesex: Kestrel, 1975), pp. 140–145;

"The Sins of Miss Halliday," in *Writers of East Anglia,* edited by Angus Wilson (London: Secker, 1977), pp. 191–196;

George Sand, *Wings of Courage,* translated and adapted by Pearce, illustrated by Hilary Abrahams (Harmondsworth, Middlesex: Kestrel, 1982);

"Face to Face," in *A Sporting Chance,* edited by Margaret Cameron (London: Bodley Head, 1985);

"The Nest Egg," in *Once Upon a Planet* (Harmondsworth, Middlesex: Puffin, 1989);

"The Making of Stories for Children," in *After Alice: Explaining Children's Literature,* edited by Morag Styles, Eve Bearme, and Victor Watson (London: Cassell, 1992), pp. 25–35;

"The Writer, the Children, and Box B," in *New Readings: Contributors to an Understanding of Literacy,* edited by Keith Kimberley, Margaret Meek, and Jane Miller (London: Black, 1992).

SELECTED PERIODICAL PUBLICATIONS – UNCOLLECTED: "The Nest," *Cricket,* 3 (August 1976): 30–35;
"The Rope," *Fiction,* 5 (July 1986).

Philippa Pearce entwines realistic and imaginary landscapes and characters to create some of the most memorable fantasy of modern times. Her prevalent theme of the importance of friendship is explored through believable adventure plots. Secrets – happy, sad, adventurous, or horrible – dominate her stories and bring the reader insight into the power and necessity of communication. Images of loneliness and the ways human beings (and occasionally animals) combat loneliness complement the motif of secrecy in Pearce's fiction.

Ann Philippa Pearce was born in Great Shelford, five miles south of Cambridge. She was the fourth and youngest child of a miller, Ernest Alexander Pearce, and his wife, Gertrude Alice (Ramsden) Pearce, and grew up in a mill house on the banks of the River Cam. The river, the house, and the garden of Pearce's childhood appear in *Minnow on the Say* (1954), *Tom's Midnight Garden* (1958), and several other works. According to Pearce, "the midnight garden and its house are based closely on the mill-house garden and the mill house as [my] father – who was born there – knew them as a boy."

Pearce was educated at the Pearse Girls' School in Cambridge and then attended Girton College, Cambridge, where she read English and history, completing the B.A., with honors, in 1942. She joined the School Broadcasting Department (Radio) of the BBC in 1945, as a scriptwriter and producer, and worked there until 1958. Many of her stories, especially those collected as *The Elm Street Lot* (1979), were originally produced by the BBC.

For a short while Pearce worked as an editor in the educational department of the Clarendon Press in Oxford, but in 1960 she returned to London to work as a children's editor at André Deutsch. Although she worked there only part-time, her name became associated with several of the books she edited. Some, such as Harold Scott's juvenile edition of *From Inside Scotland Yard* (1963) and *Stories from Hans Christian Andersen* (1972), Pearce does not feel should be listed with her other works, for they are primarily examples of her editing skills. Other books, such as her adaptation of *Beauty and*

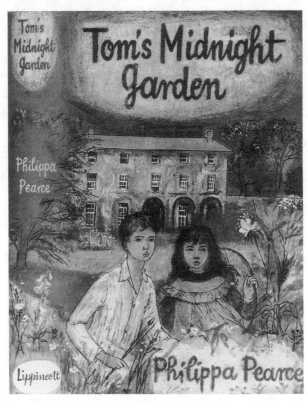

*Dust jacket for Pearce's second novel, a Carnegie Medal winner
that John Rowe Townsend has called "nearly perfect"*

the Beast (1972), her translation and adaptation of *Wings of Courage* (1982), and her collaboration with Brian Fairfax-Lucy on *The Children of the House* (1968), are more properly placed within the body of her original work.

While at André Deutsch, Pearce was also writing and producing radio programs for both children and adults, as well as reviewing children's books for the *Guardian* and the *Times Literary Supplement*. In 1963 she met and married Martin Christie, a fruit grower; they had a daughter. Her husband died in 1965 soon after their daughter was born, and Pearce remained in London doing freelance writing until 1973, when she and her daughter moved back to Great Shelford.

Because her daughter loved animals, they kept, as Pearce recalls, "minnows, snails, leeches, tadpoles, goldfish, gerbils, hamsters, cats, dogs, poultry, goats, and ponies." Pearce's own interest in animals is apparent in some of her stories, most obviously *The Battle of Bubble and Squeak* (1978) and *A Dog So Small* (1962). She includes animals in her sympathetic portrayal of secret lives, and animals appear in her fantasy stories, such as *Mrs. Cockle's Cat* (1961), and stories that bridge fantasy and real-

ity, such as *Old Belle's Summer Holiday* (1989). Pearce continues to reside in Great Shelford.

Pearce's first novel, which recalled life along the banks of the Cam and was initially published under the author's full name, was *Minnow on the Say*. David Moss, who lives in the village, finds an old canoe, which he dubs "The Minnow"; a flood and his search for the owner lead him to Adam Codling, heir to his family's estate, but the Codlings have fallen on hard times. The boys hope to recover the family fortune before the estate is sold and Adam must move away. When the treasure fails to be where the clues lead them they are ready to give up, but they confide their failures to Adam's aunt. In revealing their secret search, they find sympathy and comfort, and eventually a solution: in an intriguing plot twist, the aunt recovers the treasure and sets the family right. The family home is saved, and the aunt is the real hero.

The book was well received by critics. As a runner-up for the Carnegie Medal, it was applauded for its freshness and imaginative qualities. It was also placed on the 1956 honor list of the International Board on Books in Great Britain. Under its American title, *The Minnow Leads to Treasure,* it was named an honor book in the *New York Herald Tribune* Spring Book Festival in 1958 and received the Lewis Carroll Shelf Award in 1959. The book, for all of its vivid and realistic images, is certainly a fantasy. While the plot might seem to be too fantastic for its realistic setting, its twists and turns provide a welcome relief from the formulaic stories common in the 1950s.

The true genius of the story is in Pearce's ability to create scenes. While recovering from tuberculosis in the summer of 1951, the author transported herself in her imagination to the Cam River of her childhood. In setting the book's scenes, Pearce used minute details from childhood experiences to help her reader visualize the protagonists as they scrape and varnish the canoe, hang precariously over bridges, and fight over Adam's beautiful cousin. The fantasy of the plot is made more plausible by the re-creation of scenes and details that draw the reader into a fantasy world.

Pearce's second novel, *Tom's Midnight Garden,* has received high praise. A Carnegie Medal winner, the book was called "nearly perfect" by John Rowe Townsend, and most critics would agree. It is set in East Anglia and begins with Tom Long (symbolic of all of the longing in the book) being sent away during the summer holidays because his brother, Peter, has been stricken with measles. He finds himself with his Aunt Gwen and Uncle Alan, occupying a flat in a converted house owned by Mrs. Bartholomew, who lives upstairs. Tom misses his brother and the garden they had planned to play in during the holidays. Between the petting by his childless aunt and the boredom of his environment, Tom finds himself even more unhappy than he had expected.

One night when a strange grandfather clock in the flat strikes thirteen, Tom discovers a beautiful garden attached to the house – the problem is that the garden only exists in the past. At night, while the rest of the world dreams, Tom goes into the garden and makes friends with Hatty, a child of the Victorian era. Hatty seems to be the only one in the past who can see Tom. He visits Hatty's world frequently, and time passes much more quickly for the girl, who grows into a young woman during Tom's stay with his aunt and uncle.

The idea of characters meeting across time was inspired by J. W. Dunne's *Experiment in Time,* and while Pearce does not attempt to understand or explain Dunne's theory, his book provided a base on which she could build. Dreams and time offer characters in *Tom's Midnight Garden* an opportunity to grow, heal, and bridge gaps.

On the last night of his stay Tom returns to the garden to find only a cement slab, part of the present-day house. In his sorrow and terror Tom screams Hatty's name, and the next day he hears that a neighbor, Mrs. Bartholomew, wants an apology for the noise in the night. When he goes to apologize, Tom discovers that Mrs. Bartholomew is Hatty and that her dreams and her loneliness had called him into the garden.

Throughout the story Tom shares his secret adventures with his brother through letters. One night when Tom forgets to write, Peter himself is briefly transported to Hatty's world. Because he is able to share his secret world with Peter, Tom is able to draw him into time at almost the same moment when he is about to lose Hatty to adulthood.

As Hatty grows, as Peter frets at being forgotten, and as Tom longs for the garden and the little girl he first met there, the three characters converge in the past near a cathedral. On a memorial stone near the cathedral another inscription addresses the issue of time. The stone is for a Mr. Robinson, "who had exchanged Time for Eternity," and new possibilities open in Tom's mind. The dream, the clock, the memorial stone, and even the garden and Hatty invoke movement and growth, and inevitably death. Time barriers are not the only ones to disintegrate; barriers between sexes and between ages also crumble. Tom longs for Peter's company and then follows Hatty's cousins through the garden, but it is Hatty who sees him and asks him to play. At the end of the story Tom, the child, and Hatty, now grown old and known as Mrs. Bartholomew, will continue to cross the barriers time usually erects between generations. Although many important children's books have been written since *Tom's Midnight Garden,* it continues to be the guidepost by which modern fantasies and modern literature for children is judged.

Mrs. Cockle's Cat is Philippa Pearce's first picture book (Antony Maitland's illustrations earned it a Kate Greenaway Award in 1961). Although the pictures are what made the book an award winner, the story's themes and motifs are clearly Pearce's, and the work reveals the author's considerable storytelling skill. Friendship, adventure, fantasy, and secret lives are intricately woven into this tale of an old woman and her fickle cat, Peter. Mrs. Cockle lives in London (Pearce moved to London in 1960) at the top of an old building. Peter loves her company, but he loves fish even more. When Mrs. Cockle has no fish for Peter, he leaves. Mrs. Cockle is lonely, but on one particularly windy day she finds herself flying through the air until she lands

Pearce in the garden at the Mill House, the inspiration for Tom's Midnight Garden

beside a small fishing boat containing a fisherman, his catch of fish, and Peter. Mrs. Cockle suggests that she could stay and keep house for the fisherman, and, since his cat seems to like her company, he agrees.

Pearce next turned her talent to a novel-length study of a young boy and his love for animals in *A Dog So Small*. Ben Blewitt is the middle child in a family of five and often feels left out and lonely. For his birthday he believes his grandfather will give him a dog. Ben, like Mrs. Cockle, lives in London, in an area where he could not have a dog; in addition, the grandparents could not afford to give dogs to all of their grandchildren. His practical grandmother sends a picture of a chihuahua that her son (now dead) had brought to her from Mexico. Ben is deeply affected by the picture and begins keeping company with an imaginary dog, "so small you can only see it with your eyes closed."

Ben's secret friend begins to affect his real existence; following his dog, Chiquito, into the street one day, Ben is hit by a car and receives a concus-

sion and three broken ribs. His nightmares following the accident are filled with three dogs – the picture-dog, which has been lost; Chiquito, who disappeared when Ben was hit by the car; and "no-dog." In each nightmare, the result is the same – Ben ends up with no-dog.

As Ben recovers, his grandfather's dog, Tilly, has a litter of puppies. Conveniently, Ben's family moves to a part of London where Ben can have a dog, but the happy ending is not so simple. Ben assumes that the small puppy at his grandfather's house will remain small, but by the time he receives his long-awaited gift, the dog, Brown, has grown and is no more clever or brave than any other dog. He tries to chase it away but suddenly he realizes that without Brown all he will have left is the no-dog of his nightmare. Ben calls, and when Brown returns, the boy gains the partner he has needed throughout his life.

The book won the 1963 Spring Book Festival Award, given by the *New York Herald Tribune*. As with Pearce's other novels it is a careful blending of realistic setting, a sympathetic protagonist, and fantasy elements resulting in a happy ending. In this story, however, the child's imagination marks his escape from reality into a secret world where he loses himself. The happy ending is achieved by returning the boy to the reality of his world and the frightened young dog who will love him.

The need of a child to be loved is an overwhelming theme in *The Children of the House*, co-authored with Brian Fairfax-Lucy, in which four children feel the pain of neglect but delight in their relationship with each other. The story of Laura, Thomas, Hugh, and Margaret Hatton is more realistic and sadder than most of Pearce's writing. The protagonists are from an aristocratic family and are not allowed to have friends. Their parents, or at least their father, is too concerned with money to be concerned with his children's welfare, and their mother is too weak – except where her land and her horses are concerned – to be effectual. The parents give precedence to maintaining their large house and estate, and thus willfully neglect to provide their children with clothes for school, or any but the barest of necessities. In the end both the heir-apparent and his brother die in the war, and Laura dies of a fever as a nurse; only Margaret remains, and she becomes estranged from her parents.

The main plot is Fairfax-Lucy's, but the details – the means the children devise to have fun and adventures in spite of their parents – probably derive from the imagination of Pearce. In 1989 the book was republished as *The Children of Charlecote*, and Alice Fairfax-Lucy wrote a new foreword; in it she confirms that "the account of life at Charlecote was always autobiographical and authentic; at the same time, there had to be inventions, elaborations and a professional shaping to make a finished story." She credits Pearce with creating the story from her husband's account of his life.

Although Pearce was editing for Andre Deutsch and writing on her own, she had not lost touch with the BBC. In 1969 she wrote a series of stories produced by the BBC for their *Jackanory* series. The stories, "Mr. Crackenthorpe's Bath," "A Hamster at Large," "Rooftop," "Kite Crazy," and "Miss Munson and the Festival of Arts, Crafts, Athletics, Pets, Gardens and Inventions," were collected, along with a new one, "Old Father Time," as *The Elm Street Lot.* The title refers to both a group of children who live in the neighborhood and the name of the lot where they often meet. Through the thin veil of memory separating the child from the adult, Pearce offers her readers a taste of another time and place.

In "Mr. Crackenthorpe's Bath" the children not only solve the mystery of the missing bath but are also able to trick the thieves into returning it. This is the kind of poetic justice and heroic behavior that appeals to children, who often feel they have little or no power. Other stories are also reassuring since, in spite of the problems the children face, the endings always prove satisfactory. "Miss Munson and the Festival of Arts, Crafts, Athletics, Pets, Gardens and Inventions" begins with a brag, a bet, and a broken window but ends by showing the children helping Miss Munson to have a more beautiful garden and to overcome her shyness. "Old Father Time" involves the older children on the block and a one-eyed cat for whom the story is named. In all of the stories the adults, except for a few who are childlike, have little to do with the children. Secrets are shared within the group and the camaraderie within the neighborhood underscores the friendship and emotional security the children find among themselves.

Although Pearce's love of her childhood home influences her work with realistic settings, the world of fantasy also has a profound influence on the author. After the realistic and somewhat nostalgic world of *The Elm Street Lot,* Pearce turned to a completely new venture, resulting in a tale that invokes the oral tradition. *The Squirrel Wife* (1971) was an honor picture book in the 1972 *New York Herald Tribune* Spring Book Festival. The simple story is enlivened by the brilliant linocuts of Derek Collard, but the story has a sparkle all its own.

Employing the Cinderella motif, *The Squirrel Wife* concerns a young man who is sadly mistreated by his older brother but bears his sorrow patiently. His patience and his kindness to the "Green People" of the forest is rewarded when he is promised a wife who has knowledge of the secrets of the forest. In the spring he places a small ring around the arm of a newborn squirrel; she grows into a woman with wild eyes and becomes his wife. The unkind brother returns and causes them trouble, but the squirrel wife is finally transformed into a real woman, and the couple live out their lives happily in the town. Although their secret life initially causes problems (no one trusts his wife while she is still part-squirrel because of the wild look in her eyes, and the older brother pursues his sibling beyond all reason), their loyalty and love enable them to overcome their problems and to prevail.

As though she had not quite purged her need to get back to her fairy-tale roots, Pearce wrote a picture-book adaptation of *Beauty and the Beast* and collected and edited her favorite *Stories from Hans Christian Andersen* before returning to realistic settings.

In 1972 she collected some of her favorite stories into the book *What the Neighbors Did and Other Stories,* a British honor book for the Hans Christian Andersen Award and a 1974 honor book in the International Board on Books for Young People. *What the Neighbors Did and Other Stories* is another loosely connected group of eight stories of children living in a Cambridgeshire village; these stories share setting and themes but not characters.

The title story, "What the Neighbors Did," is told by a young boy who observes the infantile behavior of his neighbor, Mr. Macy, who is retired and is often locked out of the house by his domineering wife. He tries to hide a dog in his shed, but when it is discovered he is forced to turn it out. Dirty Dick, a trash collector who lives next door to the Macys, sees the dog and takes it home with him. Mr. Macy, heartbroken, longs for his dog now that it is on the other side of the fence. Finally, he announces to the neighbors that Dirty Dick, who had been hiding money in a sock, has been robbed. When no fuss is made, and when Dick does not call the police, Macy asks the narrator to return secretly the sock of money, which Macy himself had stolen. Afterward, Dick leaves with the dog, never to return. The youngster who became unwittingly involved is left with the awareness of how childish grown-ups can be.

It is obvious in this group of stories that Pearce has moved away from fantasy happy end-

Dust jacket for Pearce's story of a family brought together by their experiences with pet gerbils

ings. These stories emphasize the notion that not everything can be resolved. "The Tree in the Meadow" tells the story of a huge elm tree that is slowly dying. When it is to be pulled down, Ricky and his friends leave school during their lunch hour to watch. The workmen have left a rope in the tree, and the boys successfully pull the tree down, almost killing themselves in the process. The next day they feel like conquering heroes and spend the afternoon swaggering in the tree's branches. Ricky wakes up that night and finds that he is crying; his feeling about the death of the tree and his part in it remains a secret sadness that he is not sure he understands. The ending, abrupt and uncertain, triggers in the reader memories of those times when we do not feel what others think we should feel.

"Fresh," later published separately as an illustrated book, is the tale of a country cousin, Dan, and a city cousin, Laurie, who search for "collectibles" in the stream behind Dan's house during Laurie's visits. On this visit they find a rare, live freshwater mussel, which Laurie names "Fresh." Dan has always willingly shared findings with his cousin, but this time he tries to let the mussel escape before Laurie can take it home. Like Ricky he is inexplicably sad at the end of the story – not so much

jealous of Laurie as sad to see the mussel being removed from its home. Dan also holds the secret of his feelings and of his nighttime journey.

This is a collection of loss-of-innocence stories, of stories about growing up. In "The Great Blackberry Pick," Val compares her father's behavior to that of a new young father with his wife and baby. Her father insists on everyone picking blackberries, gets angry that she loses his handkerchief, and is irate that he has to waste a day looking for it. The young couple who help her when she is lost and hungry enjoy each other's company and their new baby, and Val becomes painfully aware of her own father's shortcomings. In "Lucky Boy," Pat is also growing up, no longer wishing to play with baby Lucy who had once been his favorite companion. When there is a danger she might drown, he recognizes her absolute trust in him and feels ashamed. The near tragedy will be their secret, but the darker secret for Pat is his desire to be away from the child.

"Still Jim and Silent Jim" brings to mind the brilliance of *Tom's Midnight Garden*. Once again the barriers between the very young and very old are blurred, as young Jim grows up at his grandfather's feet. Their furtive but exhilarating trip to Little Barley to measure the grandfather's tombstone and prove to the other children that modern is not always the best helps cement their friendship. The final story, "Return to Air," is a symbolic story celebrating life. Sausage, a heavyset boy, concerned with what others will think if he cannot duck-dive down to recover a brick, gains a new perspective on life as he struggles through the water to return to air.

The effect of dark secrets on the human psyche and the need to free the soul from their hold make up the connections between the strange stories in *The Shadow-Cage and Other Tales of the Supernatural* (1977). The book, awarded a Carnegie commendation in 1977, was Pearce's first after she moved back to Great Shelford. While not all of the stories stress the evil side of the supernatural, the power of dark secrets to terrorize recurs consistently in this collection.

"The Shadow Cage" concerns the aftermath of townspeople's unkindness to an old woman suspected of witchcraft. After her death they burn her body and her house; a small bottle found near her house lures a young boy into danger. "Miss Mountain" is the story of a child's secret sadness that haunts her even after she is an old woman. Again, the connections between young and old, the present and the past, are intricately woven into the story. "Her Father's Attic" follows the same premise as "Miss Mountain," exploring a long-ago child's mistreatment and its effects. "The Running-Companion" deals with the secret hatred of one brother for another.

More in the realm of fantasy, "Guess" plays with the idea of a wood nymph dislocated when her tree is toppled by a storm. Netty Barr gives her the location of another forest, and in return, the nymph lets Netty into her mind. "The Dog Got Them" mingles humor with sadness as Andy Potter's uncle, Capt. Joel Jones, retires from the sea, takes up the bottle, and dies from a case of delirium tremors. "The Strange Illness of Mr. Arthur Cook" focuses on the single-mindedness of some old people. "At the River-Gates" and "Beckoned" deal with death and family loyalty, and "The Dear Little Man with His Hands in His Pockets" deals with a different kind of loyalty and with magic.

In *The Battle of Bubble and Squeak,* a Carnegie commendation book and a Whitbread Award winner, Pearce creates a story about a child trying to convince a tired mother that gerbils should be allowed in her house. Sid Parker is given two gerbils and tries hard to convince his mother to let him keep them. Sid's stepfather, Bill Sparrow, tries to intervene, but the mother finally succeeds in giving

them away. When the gerbils come back, returned by another tired mother, Sid's mother begins to get used to them. They accidentally escape, and the neighbor's cat catches and injures Bubble. Afterward, Sid's mother is the only one who can hold the gerbil while Sid administers his medicine. When the boy who moved away returns to claim his gerbils, the family convinces him to buy new ones.

On the level of story, *The Battle of Bubble and Squeak* is accessible for children. From the squeaking of the wheel on the first page to the bite Sid receives when he tries to capture the escaped creatures and the fun the gerbils have playing in the tubes scattered on the table, the story's details are vivid and entertaining. Beyond the hide-and-seek of the gerbils, however, is a story of family, love, and trust that grows between the children and their new stepdad, Bill, and the new appreciation for life gained by their mother, Alice.

After writing a story in which pets help bring a family together, Pearce turned to the subject again with a slightly more serious attitude. *The Way to Sattin Shore* (1983) won both a Carnegie commendation and a Parent's Choice award in literature. Its protagonist, Kate Tranter, lives with her mother, grandmother, and two older brothers. All of her life she has been told that her father died on the day she was born and that terrible knowledge, combined with many family problems, leaves her feeling strange and alienated. In a compelling search for herself, Kate discovers new information that helps her reunite her family. Again a happy ending, complete with the return of Kate's father, impedes the realistic qualities of the book, but her search is compelling.

The dark secret that had torn Kate's family apart touches her on two levels: first, the fear that her father might have killed her uncle, whose death caused her mother to go into labor (although Kate was not born until the next day); and second, her indecision about her course of action after she discovers the true murderer, Arnie West. When her reunited family prepares to move to Australia, Kate feels she must warn her paternal grandmother that the man who is going to care for her is the murderer, but she finally realizes that her Granny already knows this. Readers of the novel are likely to be haunted by the secret knowledge they share with the young protagonist and her grandmother. But like the dark secrets held by characters in other Pearce stories, Arnie West's secret has caused him more pain than it has caused anyone else, and Kate, along with the reader, learns that there is no escape from the past.

Themes of loyalty and love are contrasted with images of betrayal and abandonment. Kate learns of the various kinds of attachments that hold people together. Her maternal grandmother, who has dominated Kate's mother and has grown to despise her grandchildren for the signs of their father she observes in them, clings to her family out of fear. Her paternal grandmother, on the other hand, cares for the man who murdered her son because he is the only one left for her to care for and because he is unable to love himself. Struggling with these realizations, Kate is able to find herself, her family, and her own identity.

One project about a family from which Pearce wishes to distance herself is a short series of books about the Bunnykins family. *A Picnic for Bunnykins* (1984), *Two Bunnykins Out for Tea* (1984), and *Bunnykins in the Snow* (1985) were to be the first books in a long series written under the pseudonym of "Warrener." The series was never completed, and the individual books are difficult to locate. They are about simple things – playing in the snow, having tea with grandmother, and the kinds of childhood crises every child experiences, such as losing a favorite cup or ruining a favorite toy. The books lack the depth exhibited in Pearce's other work, but they are pleasant stories nonetheless.

In writing the Bunnykins stories, Pearce discovered that she wanted to do something for younger readers, so she wrote a group of short stories for a younger audience. Most of the stories in the collection *Lion at School and Other Stories* (1985) had originally been published as a part of the BBC *Listening and Reading* series: "The Lion at School" (1971), "The Great Sharp Scissors" (1977), "Hello Polly" (1977), "Runaway" (1979), and "Secrets" (1979). The stories deal with fears and problems that children are faced with every day. "The Lion at School" deals with a small child's troubles with bullies at school. "Runaway" is about fear of punishment and the consequences related to fear. "The Manatee" reflects on a child's fear of the dark and of the unknown. Some of the stories, "Brainbox" for example, are silly but delight children. "Secrets," on the other hand, is closer to Pearce's other work in tone. The premise is a simple one: a family stops on the road for tea and the daughter goes off in search of the restroom. Instead of a restroom she finds a young boy who shows her his secret spying place, from which they can watch the family; when she returns she avoids a trap they had planned for her in her absence. The youngest child outwitting the family recalls the oral-tale motifs Pearce frequently uses in her stories.

"The Executioner" is an animal story that underscores the author's knowledge of animal and human behavior. At a rented holiday house a young boy discovers a mouse; his father also discovers the mouse and leaves a trap for it. The boy springs and later hides the mousetrap. It is the child's point of view that makes the real impact on the reader. The boy must make his own choices and live with the secret knowledge of what he has chosen to do. It is precisely because he struggles and chooses that he evokes the reader's respect.

The stories collected in *Who's Afraid? and Other Strange Stories* (1986) have dark undertones, but they are less haunting than Pearce's earlier supernatural collection. "A Christmas Pudding Improves with Keeping" suggests that hate might be instilled in an inanimate object. Conversely, Mr. Hurrel fills an inanimate object with love in "Mr. Hurrel's Tallboy." In "Samantha and the Ghost" a young girl visiting her grandparents convinces a noisy ghost to leave. "Auntie" is a gentle tale, in which a child's great-aunt saves him from being run over by a car, even though she knows that it will cost her her life. In "The Yellow Ball" two children, Con and Lizzie, find an old yellow ball in a tree in the meadow. Whenever a human hand holds the ball, a ghost dog comes to play; after a series of interactions, the ghost dog is contented and Con, who has always been afraid of animals, is ready for a real dog of his own. "The Road It Went By" concerns a wonderful plant that grows along the root of the ground elder, and a man named Percy's fascination with the plant. His young nephew does not understand this fascination, but he knows intuitively how special it is. When the uncle dies, the child knows the ground elder that his aunt plants on the grave would please his uncle.

The rest of the stories are darker. "Black Eyes" plays with popular modern images of toys that are deadly. The horror of some family relationships is examined in "His Loving Sister." "The Hirn" is a story of nature fighting against progress as a stand of trees ringing some black water frighten away and nearly kill a young man who does not understand what everyone else seems to be aware of – that the trees have a life of their own. "A Prince in Another Place" is the story of a man who is befriended by the devil because of his own wickedness. Although these stories do not have the power of Pearce's first set of ghost stories, they may be more appropriate for children, as they stress human emotions over supernatural events.

In 1987 Pearce published *The Tooth Ball,* another story that she had written for the BBC. It was soon followed by *Emily's Own Elephant* (1987) and *Freddy* (1988). With these books Pearce seemed to be heading in a new direction, with stories more appropriate for picture books and aimed at younger readers than were her early books. Still working with typical childhood experiences – a loose tooth, a trip to the zoo, and needing a blanket in order to get to sleep – Pearce manages twists of fantasy to make the stories more delightful than real life. Although the solution of having two blankets in *Freddy* is simple enough, the idea of Emily owning an elephant enlarges on the zoo experience and creates a new world of fun for the imaginative child. "The ToothBall" is much grander than stories of the tooth fairy, as a little boy is able to get not just a quarter but a group of friends in return for his lost tooth wrapped in foil and paper.

As if to allay fears that her power as a storyteller might be fading, Pearce wrote *Old Belle's Summer Holiday.* Many of her strengths as a storyteller are underscored in this story of Belle, a mill cat who decides to enter the mill house for the first time in her life. When the mill shuts down for a summer vacation, Belle's routine is disrupted, and she is not comfortable with the silence. She has a new litter of kittens and is not sure that they are safe, so she finds her way into the empty mill house. She carries the kittens inside, leaving traces of her visit as she goes. When the family returns, she has moved back out of the house; all that is left are the signs that someone or something has been inside.

The story's scenes bring back the sights and sounds of the mill, the river, the house, and the surroundings of Pearce's childhood. Belle is a realistic cat and yet fantastic also. The blending of realism and fantasy, the secrets that will never be told, the mystery left to be solved all point to Pearce's finest works. Even the tie between the kittens and old Belle with one blind eye are consistent with Pearce's imagery.

Pearce tried something new with *Here Comes Tod!* (1992), which bridges the gap between children's picture books and children's novels. Like *The Elm Street Lot* and some of her other collections of short stories, *Here Comes Tod!* is a series of episodes about a little boy as he discovers the world. The chapter titles suggest the nature of the experiences he encounters: "Tod and the Surprises," "Tod and the Enormous Orange," "Tod and the Desperate Search," "Tod and the Visitor," "Tod and the Birthday Present," and "Tod and the Wildest Country in the World." The protagonist learns about life; he is allowed to examine and surprise others.

The majority of Pearce's work is clearly written for children, but the author neither talks down to her audience nor talks over their heads. Her work invites the reader to peel back the layers and examine the human emotions she describes. Because Pearce works from the top of her head and does not keep a notebook, it is difficult to say whether she will write another novel. She has always loved to write short stories and continues to place her stories in periodicals. Whether or not Pearce produces another novel, she will undoubtedly continue to write the short stories that peek into the souls of characters and reveal the secrets they hide.

References:

Raymond E. Jones, "Philippa Pearce's *Tom's Midnight Garden:* Finding and Losing Eden," in *Touchstones: Reflections on the Best in Children's Literature,* volume 1, edited by Perry Nodelman (West Lafayette, Ind.: Children's Literature Association, 1985), pp. 212–221;

David Rees, "Achieving One's Heart's Desires," in his *The Marble in the Water: Essays on Contemporary Writers of Fiction for Children and Young Adults* (Boston: Horn Book, 1980), pp. 36–55;

John Rowe Townsend, "Philippa Pearce," in his *A Sense of Story: Essays on Contemporary Writers for Children* (London: Longman, 1971), pp. 163–171;

Townsend, *Written for Children: An Outline of English-Language Children's Literature* (New York: HarperCollins, 1990), pp. 236–237, 247–249.

K. M. Peyton

(2 August 1929 –   )

Gwyneth Evans
Malaspina University College

BOOKS: *Sabre: the Horse from the Sea,* as Kathleen Herald, illustrated by Lionel Edwards (London: A. & C. Black, 1947; New York: Macmillan, 1963);

The Mandrake, as Kathleen Herald, illustrated by Lionel Edwards (London: A. & C. Black, 1949);

Crab the Roan, as Kathleen Herald, illustrated by Peter Biegel (London: A. & C. Black, 1953);

North to Adventure (London: Collins, 1959; New York: Platt, 1965);

Stormcock Meets Trouble (London: Collins, 1961);

The Hard Way Home, illustrated by R. A. Branton (London: Collins, 1962); republished as *Sing a Song of Ambush* (New York: Platt & Munck, 1964; revised edition, Aylesbury, Buckinghamshire: John Goodchild, 1986);

Windfall, illustrated by Victor Ambrus (London: Oxford University Press, 1962); republished as *Sea Fever* (Cleveland: World, 1963);

Brownsea Silver (London: Collins, 1964);

The Maplin Bird, illustrated by Ambrus (London: Oxford University Press, 1964; Cleveland: World, 1965);

The Plan for Birdsmarsh, illustrated by Ambrus (London: Oxford University Press, 1965; Cleveland: World, 1966);

Thunder in the Sky, illustrated by Ambrus (London: Oxford University Press, 1966; Cleveland: World, 1967);

Flambards, illustrated by Ambrus (London: Oxford University Press, 1967; Cleveland: World, 1968);

Fly-by-Night, illustrated by Ambrus (London: Oxford University Press, 1968; Cleveland: World, 1969);

The Edge of the Cloud, illustrated by Ambrus (London: Oxford University Press, 1969; Cleveland: World, 1970);

Flambards in Summer, illustrated by Ambrus (London: Oxford University Press, 1969; Cleveland: World, 1970);

K. M. Peyton

Pennington's Seventeenth Summer, illustrated by Peyton (London: Oxford University Press, 1970); republished as *Pennington's Last Term* (New York: Crowell, 1971);

The Beethoven Medal, illustrated by Peyton (London: Oxford University Press, 1971; New York: Crowell, 1972);

A Pattern of Roses, illustrated by Peyton (London: Oxford University Press, 1972; New York: Crowell, 1973);

Pennington's Heir, illustrated by Peyton (London: Oxford University Press, 1973; New York: Crowell, 1974);

The Team, illustrated by Peyton (London: Oxford University Press, 1975; New York: Crowell, 1976);

Prove Yourself a Hero (London: Oxford University Press, 1977; New York: Collins World, 1978);

The Right-Hand Man, illustrated by Ambrus (London: Oxford University Press, 1977; New York: Oxford University Press, 1979);

A Midsummer Night's Death (London: Oxford University Press, 1978; New York: Collins, 1979);

Marion's Angels, illustrated by Robert Micklewright (London & New York: Oxford University Press, 1979);

Dear Fred (London: Bodley Head, 1981; New York: Philomel, 1981);

Flambards Divided (London: Oxford University Press, 1981; New York: Philomel, 1982);

Going Home, illustrated by Chris Molan (London: Oxford University Press, 1982; New York: Philomel, 1982);

Free Rein (New York: Philomel, 1983); republished as *The Last Ditch* (London: Oxford University Press, 1984);

Who, Sir? Me, Sir? (London: Oxford University Press, 1983);

Froggett's Revenge, illustrated by Leslie Smith (London: Oxford University Press, 1985);

The Sound of Distant Cheering (London: Bodley Head, 1986);

Plain Jack (London: Hamish Hamilton, 1988);

Downhill All the Way (Oxford & New York: Oxford University Press, 1988);

Darkling (London: Corgi, 1989; New York: Dell, 1989);

Skylark (London: Oxford University Press, 1989);

No Roses Round the Door (London: Methuen, 1990);

Poor Badger (London: Doubleday, 1990; New York: Delacorte, 1992);

Late to Smile (London: Methuen, 1992);

Apple Won't Jump (London: Hamish Hamilton, 1992);

The Wild Boy and Queen Moon (London: Doubleday, 1993);

Snowfall (London: Scholastic, 1994).

OTHER: "On Not Writing a Proper Book," in *The Thorny Paradise: Writers on Writing for Children,* edited by Edward Blishen (London: Kestrel, 1975), pp. 123–127;

The Puffin Book of Horse and Pony Stories, edited by Peyton (London: Puffin, 1993; New York: Viking, 1993).

Prolific and versatile, K. M. Peyton has written successful adventure stories, historical fiction, pony stories, romances, and, recently, short fiction for young children. She writes equally well about male and female characters in their struggles to find a place for themselves in the world, in their discovery of love, and in their exasperation with parents or authorities. Peyton never condescends to her readers or glamorizes youthful rebellion; she depicts adolescence with honesty and compassion. She is best known for two trilogies: the Flambards books, about a girl growing up in a country house before and during World War I; and the Pennington series, about a concert pianist from a working-class background. Peyton is skilled in evoking action and movement, and her protagonists are passionately involved with sailing, flying, music, or horses. Her style keeps her readers similarly involved, a skill developed partly through her apprenticeship in writing serial fiction.

Peyton was born Kathleen Wendy Herald on 2 August 1929 in Birmingham, England, to William Joseph and Ivy Kathleen Herald. As a child she wanted a pony, but instead she had to sublimate her longing into writing. She began to write at age nine and published her first story while a student at the Wimbledon High School. Her first novel, *Sabre: the Horse from the Sea,* was illustrated by Lionel Edwards and appeared in 1947; it was followed by two other horse stories. Although her parents wanted her to attend university, Kathleen chose the Manchester School of Art and received her Art Teacher's Diploma in 1951, a year after having run away to marry a fellow art student, Michael Peyton. Michael's energy, enthusiasm for adventure, and love of sailing heavily influenced Peyton's early writing, and they collaborated on several books in the first years of their marriage. In her early life, however, can be found many of her subjects and themes: the longing for a horse of one's own, a longing that so stirs Ruth in *Fly-by-Night* (1968) and *The Team* (1975) and Jenny in *Darkling* (1989); and the need to rebel against parental domination and make independent choices, a need that drives Tim in *A Pattern of Roses* (1972) and Jonathan in *Prove Yourself a Hero* (1977) and *Free Rein* (1983).

After her marriage Kathleen taught art briefly at Northampton High School (1953–1955) until her first daughter was born; the difficulty of being both a committed teacher and a mother is the subject of one of her few adult novels, *No Roses Round the Door* (1990). To help the family's finances, she collaborated with Michael on adventure serials, which they signed as "K. and M. Peyton." When the stories were to be issued in book form and the publishers preferred the name of a single author, the Peytons amalgamated their initials and became "K. M. Peyton." In these early novels Kathleen's maturing skills were aided by her husband's enthusiasm for adventure and knowledge of seafaring life. With characteristic modesty she described the process in a 1974 interview in *The Pied Pipers* as one in which Michael "thought up all the plots and I wrote them down. I didn't know what was going on half the time." Kathleen was, however, acquiring sailing experiences of her own as the Peytons sailed off the Essex coast, where they settled in an old cottage. These experiences with boats, and later with horses, stimulated Peyton's writing and, although she retained the collaborative initials "K. M." as part of her pen name, the novels soon became her work alone.

The serial origins of *North to Adventure* (1959), *Stormcock Meets Trouble* (1961), and *The Hard Way Home* (1962) — all written for *Scout Magazine* — are evident in the rapid pace of the action, broadly sketched characters, and obligatory cliff-hanging climax at the end of each chapter. *North to Adventure* is a stirring adventure that owes, and acknowledges, a considerable debt to Robert Louis Stevenson's *Treasure Island* (1883). Sixteen-year-old Nick joins a crew sailing the Arctic Ocean off Greenland in search of a ship that has mysteriously disappeared. An escape by night, a wild dog-team chase across a glacier, and a siege in a snowbound fort maintain the breathless pace, which rarely slackens for description, reflection, or character analysis. Key elements of the plot such as Nick's discovery of a fellow crew member's treacherous plans, the encounter with a survivor from the missing ship, and the discovery that the contested treasure has been moved recall *Treasure Island*. Nick is as eager and rash as Stevenson's Jim Hawkins, but Nick's friendship with an Inuit youth and his recognition of the different values and way of life of the Inuit add another dimension to this story of danger and survival in a bleak, dramatic landscape.

The Canadian north is the setting for *The Hard Way Home* (published in 1964 in the United States as *Sing a Song of Ambush*), in which resourceful English Sea Scouts rescue a popular American singing star (with the remarkable name of Colly Highball) from his kidnappers. Again the action is fast-paced, but characters and situations do little to distinguish this novel from other conventional adventure stories. Peyton produced one more such novel, *Brownsea Silver* (1964), on commission for the centenary of the Scout movement, but with her need for money less pressing, Peyton decided to please herself and write "a proper book." Having been rejected by her previous publisher, Collins, the resulting manuscript was sent by Peyton to Oxford University Press. Oxford accepted it and has subsequently published more than twenty Peyton novels, many of them illustrated, like this one, by Victor Ambrus. *Windfall* (1962) again evokes the seafaring life, this time in the familiar environment of the Essex coast where the Peytons had settled. Set in the late nineteenth century, the novel is more reflective and descriptive and more thorough in exploring complex relationships than the previous books.

Matt, fifteen, must support his mother and four brothers and sisters after his father drowns. His good-heartedness and his knowledge of the treacherous coastline win him the friendship of a boy whose wealthy father hires Matt to work on his racing yacht. Matt's courage and seamanship eventually enable him to triumph over a bullying uncle and the vicious enmity of a fellow sailor; in the end he has earned the money for a new fishing boat. The friendship between two boys of different backgrounds is more fully developed in this novel than in the previous adventure books, and the story concludes realistically with the boys' recognition that this friendship is unlikely to outlast the circumstances that have thrown them together. Peyton effectively conveys the discomforts and danger of the fisherman's life. Like the villains of the earlier books, however, Beckett is a stock figure of selfishness and brutality. Peyton's growing maturity as a novelist can be seen by contrasting him to the antagonist of another Essex fishing novel, *The Maplin Bird* (1964), published two years later.

Many similarities exist between *Windfall* and *The Maplin Bird*: nineteenth-century settings; working-class, fatherless young people from fishermen's families encountering privileged, upper-class people who sail for amusement; and plots set in motion by a vessel in distress. The chief character of *The Maplin Bird* is, however, a girl. Spirited and keen on seafaring, Emily is obliged to become a housemaid after she and her brother run (or, literally, sail) away from a bullying guardian. Although full of action and adventures at sea, *The Maplin Bird* is also concerned with emotions and with the ambiguous relationships between family members as well as between servants and masters. Against her better judgment Emily develops strong feelings for Adam, the

Cover for the second novel in Peyton's Flambards series

daredevil son of her employer, and she and her brother become involved in helping him escape the consequences of his activities as a smuggler. Peyton offers no pat solutions for Emily, and she must come to terms with the conflict between common sense and emotion. Certainly Adam is a more complex and interesting antagonist than Peyton had previously created. His charm and his boredom with his mother's staid household partly excuse him to Emily and the reader, but a callous and ruthless side to his nature is also revealed, and Emily and Toby recognize that they are lucky to escape relatively unharmed from their involvement with him. Adam, less lucky, is captured and jailed, and Emily feels a poignant regret along with her recognition that he has earned his fate.

The central character of *The Plan for Birdsmarsh* (1965) is a boy quite unlike the awesomely competent heroes of Peyton's early books, one whose interior life is as much the concern of the book as are

the sea races and rescues. Paul is a dreamy, introspective farmer's son who has little interest in boats. He expects to be happy farming Birdsmarsh, his family's land on the Essex coast, and puts his ancient smack in the water only to please his friend Gus, who has a passion for sailing. Paul and Gus are more believable characters than Peyton's previous paired heroes. Gus's enthusiasm for boats and engines is accompanied by a determination schooled by lifelong conflict with his unsupportive family. Paul, despite a happy family life, feels ineffectual in contrast to others. The "plans for Birdsmarsh" proposed by a London developer are to turn the farm of Paul's family into a yacht basin, with hotel and parking lot for a thousand cars. Gentle, nature-loving Paul is appalled; Gus hopes for congenial employment; Paul's physicist brother Chris is indifferent, wholly absorbed in designing an exposure suit. In the double climax of the book, Paul is shipwrecked and puts his brother's exposure suit to an unplanned test by spending thirty-three hours floating in the North Sea. Chris, meanwhile, risks his own life in confronting an unprincipled yachtsman trying to steal his design for the exposure suit.

As these exciting events are resolved, something is accomplished on a deeper level as well, since Paul's ordeal gives him a more positive perspective. Amid the rejoicing of the final scenes the novel preserves a sense of irony and realism. Chris is so absorbed in his invention that he is virtually unaware of what his brother has endured, and Birdsmarsh falls prey to the developers. During the crisis Gus has momentarily seen the world through Paul's eyes and come to a new appreciation of his friend. Both he and Paul lose things they care about deeply, but they mature in the process. The plot has been criticized as somewhat unfocused, but it could be said that the structure of the novel reflects one of its major themes. Each of the unheroic though likable characters is preoccupied with his own concerns and thus only partly aware of what is happening around him; one person's major life crisis may appear to another as merely a fit of the sulks. The setting unifies the book: like almost all of Peyton's novels, this one describes the Essex landscape, which she knows intimately. Other elements in the book also come from her own experience: the impromptu test of the exposure suit reflects a personal experience with a suit invented by a friend, and her husband, Michael, now a successful commercial artist, provided information about industrial espionage and theft of designs.

Thunder in the Sky (1966) is a clearly focused novel set during World War I, about the conflict of loyalties experienced by fifteen-year-old Sam when he realizes that his brother, Gil, may be carrying messages for a spy ring. The setting is again the southeastern English coast, but the sailing vessels this time are barges supplying the Allied troops in France. Sam is naive and headstrong, a more obviously limited character than most of Peyton's heroes, but his dilemma is explored with depth and insight. The other members of the spy ring remain stock villains, but Gil himself, seen through Sam's anguished speculation, is presented sympathetically. The plot of *Thunder in the Sky* is simpler than those of most of Peyton's previous novels, and its focus is clearly on Sam's moral predicament. There are still many exciting action scenes, notably the zeppelin attack near the end of the novel, but they provide the context for the moral conflict rather than being ends in themselves.

Windfall, The Maplin Bird, The Plan for Birdsmarsh, and *Thunder in the Sky* form a quartet of novels about young people and the seafaring life off the coast of Essex from the early 1800s to the present day. The protagonists of all four books are unremarkable adolescents from working-class families; diligent and well-intentioned, they confront more-privileged characters who make use of their skills and abuse their trust. When these efforts are foiled, mostly through the protagonists' reliance upon their own strengths, the young people return to their own ways of life, with some renewed sense of their own worth.

Flambards (1967) represents a new direction in Peyton's fiction, moving away from the adventure story and toward the romance. Christina, an orphan, is as resilient and self-sufficient a heroine as Emily of *The Maplin Bird*, but she comes from a different social class and will inherit a fortune when she turns twenty-one. Freed of the grim necessity to work for her food and lodging, Christina has opportunities denied to Emily and can expect to be sought in marriage by the men she encounters, rather than having to struggle against entanglements with them as Emily did. Peyton's concern for the situation of the servant girl, however, is still evident in the character of Violet — who is "ruined" by Mark, one of the cousins in whose country house, Flambards, Christina is sent to live. Mark resembles his father, Christina's Uncle Russell, in his arrogance, vitality, obsession with horses and hunting, and disregard for the feelings of other people. While *Flambards* concerns members of a more privileged social class than the previous novels do, it does not idealize their lives by ignoring the social inequities that make them possible.

The story of the Flambards series, consisting of three books published in close sequence — *Flambards, The Edge of the Cloud* (1969), and *Flambards in Summer* (1969) — and a fourth volume, *Flambards Divided* (1981), published twelve years later, concerns Christina's relationship to the life of Flambards and three young men who live there. When she is sent to the country at the age of twelve, Christina is surprised by the disorder of the Flambards household. Since her aunt's death, the house and garden have deteriorated, while what little money remains from Uncle Russell's depleted fortune goes to maintaining the stables and horses. His enjoyment of the hunters is now vicarious, as Russell has been seriously injured in a riding accident some years before. *Flambards* opens with the description of another serious hunting accident in which Christina's younger cousin, Will, falls and breaks his leg. Christina and the injured Will arrive at Flambards almost at the same time, and Christina's compassion is at once aroused by Will's suffering and the indifference of his father and brother. Despite this harsh introduction, Christina discovers that she loves riding under the patient instruction of the gentle groom, Dick. Will, however, loathes it so much that Christina finds him deliberately damaging his injured leg further so that he will not have to ride again. Christina also learns of his fascination with the developing endeavor of aviation, and she compares Will's intellectual and moral courage with Mark's bravado on the hunting field.

Handsome, self-confident Mark has been chosen by the older family members to be Christina's future husband so that her fortune can save Flambards, but as the novel progresses, Mark's selfishness and irresponsibility become increasingly evident. When his reckless riding injures Christina's favorite mare, he and his father order the horse shot and fed to the foxhounds. Christina persuades Dick to help her save the mare secretly, but this results in Dick losing his job. The consequences are revealed to be grave indeed, as Dick has been supporting a sick mother and the Russells prevent him from getting any other job in the area. Dick had known the risk but had been willing to do anything for Christina. She is distressed and guilt-ridden about Dick's fate but helpless to alter it. Moving into her eighteenth year, she finds herself increasingly absorbed by Will and his activities. He inadvertently disrupts a cross-country horse race when his rickety biplane crash-lands near the finish line, and Uncle Russell is so enraged by this dramatic revelation of what Will has been doing that he is determined to send this unsatisfactory son to exile in British Columbia. *Flambards* dramatizes the conflict between the traditional life of the country gentry in its golden Edwardian sunset, embodied in Uncle Russell and Mark, and the emerging world envisioned by Will, with its changing social order and transforming technology of car and airplane. Christina, seeing Flambards as "dying" and repelled by the narrowness and brutality of her uncle and Mark, refuses Mark's proposal and flees from the Hunt Ball with Will in a borrowed Rolls Royce. They drive to London and sanctuary at her Aunt Grace's, where Christina can wait for Will to get a job in the new aeronautics industry and then marry her.

The Edge of the Cloud picks up Christina's story on the same fateful evening with which *Flambards* concludes. As she drives off with Will on the last page of the first novel, Christina thinks, "It's starting," and this second novel goes on to reveal that "it" represents a new life for Christina, both in her external circumstances and in the emotional turmoil of her developing love for Will. Christina has learned from the circumstances of her girlhood to conceal her feelings; Will, who is obsessed with his work on aircraft, tests her stoic resolution repeatedly by endangering himself (and sometimes her) in flying the flimsy, dangerous aircraft of the period. Christina learns to control her fears for Will's safety and also learns to realize that his love for her will never equal his passion for flying. As *Flambards* considered different kinds of physical and moral courage, *The Edge of the Cloud* concerns how people respond to fear, danger, and grief. Undergoing agonizing surgery to reset his leg in this novel, Will is an intrepid pilot and faces physical pain uncomplainingly. Although naturally a gentle person, he is still a Russell and brooks no opposition. In a striking parallel to his father's behavior, Will simply cannot conceive that Christina might not share his enthusiasms and bullies her appallingly. His insensitivity to her fear of flying, as well as to the social conventions governing their relationship, causes Christina much grief; almost always she must compromise and pretend to have interest and pleasure she does not feel.

Though Will at first has some difficulty getting a job in aeronautics and has to work his way up gradually, he advances from mechanic to exhibition pilot and designer. Uncle Russell has forbidden their marriage until they come of age at twenty-one, and so to be near Will, Christina finds a job at a hotel near the airfield. Traditional class and gender relationships are erased at the airfield, where an easy, classless camaraderie based on common enthusiasm for the new technology foreshadows changes that will come to British society after the war. As the shadow of World War I falls over the ending of *Flambards*, the war becomes a fact of life at the end of *The Edge of the Cloud:* accompanied by Mark on horseback in a scene neatly paralleling the end of *Flambards*, Christina and Will drive to their wedding – but it is 1914, and Will has just enlisted in the Royal Flying Corps. First Will's mentor and then Will's flying partner die in aircraft accidents; then Uncle Russell dies also, and the novel ends with Will about to embark on a flying adventure far more dangerous than any exhibition stunts.

The Edge of the Cloud was awarded the Carnegie Medal for 1969, an honor for which several of Peyton's earlier books had been runners-up. The selection aroused some controversy; Dominic Hibberd, in a 1972 essay for *Children's Literature in Education*, charged that the book was commercially rather than artistically motivated, that its prose style was inferior, and that it failed to present a

Pennington's parents; illustration by Peyton for Pennington's Seventeenth Summer *(1970)*

thorough and detailed analysis of social and economic conditions in Britain during the period. Colin Ray, chairman of the selection committee, responded by pointing out that the medal criteria include, in addition to literary merit, "its potential impact on the young reader, its ideas, its chances of being read, its individual aspects which make it stand out from the rest." Peyton's popularity with young readers has not endeared her to academic critics; awards committees, however, have appreciated the energy of her writing, her sense of landscape and history, her gift for evoking physical activity, and above all her empathy for young people. In 1970 Peyton received the Guardian Award for the Flambards trilogy.

The concluding volume of the trilogy, published in the same year as *The Edge of the Cloud,* suggests by its name, *Flambards in Summer,* that some flowering and fulfillment will occur in the lives of Christina and of the old house that is clearly her true home. At the opening of the novel, all is sorrow and decay. World War I has brought both personal and national devas-

tation. Will has been killed in France; Mark is missing and supposed dead; and Christina returns to Flambards. Left in the hands of two elderly and dispirited servants, the house and farm have decayed further, and the war has drained the pool of agricultural laborers who might have helped make it a working farm again. Nonetheless, with the same determination that in the earlier volumes she gave to learning to ride and to loving and supporting Will, Christina sets about to bring Flambards back to life. She is strengthened by the discovery that she had become pregnant just before Will's death. Persistent inquiries lead her to Violet, the former kitchen maid, who is persuaded by a sum of money to give up to Christina, her child by Mark. Although the neighborhood is scandalized by Christina's bringing Mark's illegitimate son to Flambards, the presence of Tizzy and her own baby, Isobel, help Christina begin to realize her vision of the house as once more full of the people and animals she loves. Also to the horror of her neighbors Christina employs a German prisoner of war, but her efforts to make Flambards a working farm come within reach of achievement only when she makes another journey to London to find Dick, the groom who had lost his job years before. When Dick, who has been invalided out of the army, returns to manage the farm, he and Christina work together to bring the estate back to life.

Just as the crops are being harvested and Flambards seems to be becoming the pastoral idyll of Christina's vision, serenity is shattered by the unexpected return of Mark. As the rightful owner of Flambards, he takes over, renews his suit to Christina, charms Tizzy, and threatens to dismiss Dick. A complex sequence of events brings the novel to a climax. Tizzy, misunderstanding the hostilities among the adults and threatened in his newly found happiness, sets fire to the farm buildings, and Dick and Mark must strive together to stop the fire from spreading. Soon afterward Mark learns from the lawyer that the debts he has inherited with Flambards are so heavy that he must sell the property; Christina, who has come of age and has been restoring the farm with her own wealth, offers to buy it and make Tizzy her heir. Fearing a relapse in Dick's health, she makes her love for him public (and again scandalous) knowledge. The novel ends with the resilient Mark engaged to a wealthy girl, and Christina secure in her work of bringing Flambards back to life.

Christina is a strong and memorable personality whose courage and determination help to account for the great popularity of the Flambards trilogy. *Flambards in Summer* shows what Christina can do when she is in charge, and what she accomplishes is impressive. She is unswayed by local prejudices, self-disciplined, able to command as well as sympathize, energetic and efficient in her work, and life-affirming in the ends to which she chooses to put her money and energy. While her purchase of Tizzy from Violet has raised eyebrows, Peyton makes it clear that Tizzy and his Violet have no great love for each other, while Christina quickly becomes devoted to him. Christina's toughness in claiming Tizzy, like her decision to make him sleep alone in Mark's old bedroom with the alarming foxes' masks on the wall, is part of the character that readers have seen develop through the often harsh experiences of the three novels, and her actions and decisions – while not always admirable – are much in keeping with her character and her time.

In the Flambards trilogy Peyton shows rural England at a turning point in history, as the old order of fox-hunting landowners begins to give way to a new society based on the technology of automobile and airplane and on the easing of class distinctions. While these changes seem somewhat remote in *Flambards,* the new order is vividly present in the airfield setting of *The Edge of the Cloud,* and in *Flambards in Summer* the ravages of World War I inaugurate a new order in which Flambards is successfully farmed by a collection of people who have never worked on the land. The hereditary squire must marry a hotel owner's daughter in order to preserve his lifestyle, and the heiress Christina may marry her former groom. While the old servants and the traditionalists complain, Peyton through her heroine seems to accept these changes as a good thing; the recognition of merit in Dick rather than of caste in the self-centered Mark and the transformation of Flambards into a productive farm rather than a center for foxhunting represent a movement deeply satisfying to most readers.

The important role of the horses in the Flambards books shows a renewal of Peyton's old interest in horses, and during the composition of her two major trilogies, the Flambards and Pennington books, Peyton also wrote the pony story *Fly-by-Night,* returning to the genre with which she began her career. As its heroine Ruth Hollis is only twelve at the start of the story and fourteen at the end, the book has a younger intended readership than that of the trilogies. *Fly-by-Night* and its sequel *The Team* are, however, directly related to the Pennington trilogy and to the later series of books about Jonathan Meredith (*Prove Yourself a Hero, A Midsummer Night's Death* [1978], and *Free Rein*) by sharing major characters in common among them. The latter two Pennington books are told largely from Ruth's point of view, and she is seen again in *Marion's Angels* (1979); *The Team* concerns four young people on an equestrian team including Ruth, Jonathan, and their friend Peter – who also plays a major role in three of the other books. This linking of different groups of novels through common characters adds an interesting dimension to Peyton's work. *Fly-by-Night* is also the first of a group of books that Peyton illustrated herself, with expressive and humorous line drawings. The forlorn stance of Ruth watching the fortunate children with ponies, Mrs. Meredith scolding Jonathan, or Ruth and Pennington having their first good look at each other certainly add to readers' understanding of those characters, and while other illustrators may show more technical skill, one perhaps may regret that Peyton did not illustrate more of her own writing.

In an interview in *The Pied Pipers,* Peyton dismissed *Fly-by-Night* as "minor." In this case her tendency to disparage her own achievements has not dissuaded readers from finding *Fly-by-Night* as admirable a work within its genre as some of the other more "serious" books in theirs. Several reviewers noted that *Fly-by-Night* was one of the few pony stories that captured their interest. Marcus Crouch in *The Nesbit Tradition: The Children's Novel in England 1945–1970* (1972) calls it perhaps "the very last of the pony books" and "certainly one of the best." It offers rich evidence of Peyton's lively sense of humor, both in the physical comedy occasioned by Ruth's misadventures in riding her unschooled New Forest pony and in the verbal banter of her affectionately insulting brother, Ted. The Peytons themselves had purchased a New Forest pony and undergone similar experiences in training it, and the novel is dedicated to their daughter Hilary and the pony, Cracker. *Fly-by-Night* is as much a family story as a pony story, since Ruth's scheme to buy a pony with her savings and keep it in the backyard is at all points linked with the lives of her parents and brother. Often stories in this genre dispense with parents by leaving them as invisible sources of the wherewithal to maintain the ponies and keep the riders in sandwiches and dry jodhpurs. In this novel the concerns and reactions of the parents are important to the story. Although Ruth draws an unfavorable contrast between her parents and the sheepskin-jacketed adults she sees at the Pony Club events, Ruth's family supports her in her obsession as far as finances will allow. She envies her schoolmate Peter, who lives at his father's horse-training stable. When Peter is driven to run away from home by the harsh demands of his father, however, Ruth comes to appreciate the merits of her own family.

Jumping back chronologically from the period of Ruth's life in the Pennington books that were published earlier, *The Team* continues the stories of Ruth and Peter. Ruth is still the center of interest, the story following her purchase of another unlikely pony when she has outgrown Fly-by-Night, her difficulties learning to manage it, and her eventual success on the Pony Club Area Trials team. The other members of the team, however, also have important roles in this novel: the descriptions of the riding events are set in the contexts of family life and the nonequestrian troubles that each adolescent has to face. Wealthy, handsome Jonathan has problems with his mother, a domineering, competitive, yet inspiring Pony Club leader for whose creation Peyton drew upon her own experience as a local Pony Club secretary. Peter's father is still dictatorial and insensitive, while Thea, who has lost both father and brother in a car accident, must bear the responsibilities shirked by her vague, eccentric mother. The adult world is seen here from the perspective of the teenager – not unkindly, but acutely aware of its deficiencies. As in *Fly-By-Night,* the disrespectful humor of Ted helps to keep the intensity of the equestrians in perspective and to connect their rather narrow world to the rest of life.

Pennington's Seventeenth Summer (1970; published in 1971 in the United States as *Pennington's Last Term*) also gives an adolescent's view of the world around him, but Patrick "Penn" Pennington is a more troubled and more gifted youth than Peyton had previously created. Shouted at or ignored by his slovenly parents and regarded as the despair of most of his teachers, Penn at seventeen is a tall and athletic lout with long hair and a notoriously uncooperative attitude toward virtually everyone. He is also, however, a gifted pianist, and the action of the novel centers on the efforts of his school music teacher, Crocker, to get him to practice for an important competition. Penn is himself more interested in feuding with a fellow student, playing the harmonica, avoiding the police, and irritating another teacher, Mr. Marsh, or "Soggy." The novel is told largely from Penn's perspective, but a few scenes show the teachers debating how to cope with him; the music and athletics teachers want to direct his talents into constructive or at least socially approved channels, while Soggy is simply determined to get revenge. The characters and their activities are presented in an exaggerated way befitting Penn's own outlook. Although a rebel, Penn is generally well-intentioned, but because of his appearance and his reputation as a troublemaker, his behavior is often misinterpreted by adults. Trying to help, Penn usually ends up in worse trouble than ever.

At the climax of the novel, major obstacles are placed in Penn's way to prevent him from performing at the piano competition. Soggy canes him brutally on the hands; a hostile classmate locks him in a boat cabin; and he finds Crocker drifting, unconscious, in another boat and has to row off for help just when he should be appearing at the competition. Worst of all, a girl for whom he feels a mute passion urges him to attend the Folk Festival on the same afternoon as the competition. Adversity, however, always rouses Penn's spirit. The caning makes him determined to play after all, in defiance of Soggy, and the trials of getting to the competition provoke him into giving his best performance. Showing up very late – in squelching Plimsolls and borrowed, paint-besmattered clothing, his hands in

Dust jacket for Peyton's novel about a boy who is kidnapped and the emotional problems he faces after he is ransomed

agony – he plays as he has never played before and wins first prize: "he played to warm poor Crocker's soul and to damn Soggy and to lift the Mendelssohn melody out of the County Council piano into the cold dome of the Council Chamber to stab the alien heart of Mr. Smythe-Potter with its vigour and beauty." In a humorous anticlimax Penn visits the home of the girl of his dreams and is asked to play the piano. Irritated, he plays so loudly as to arouse the interest of a famous piano teacher who happens to be visiting next door. The teacher invites Penn to study with him in London and intervenes to rescue him from the local police, who want to send Penn to a correctional institution.

The fortunate sequence of events might seem somewhat overdone, but it is entirely convincing as one reads it. The gripping descriptions of action that Peyton always excels in presenting, the terse and slangy dialogue, and the undercutting of Penn's heroism by his ludicrous misfortunes and the surly suspicion with which he greets success – all help the reader accept the ending. Peyton based the character of Penn and his friends on a group of schoolboys she observed regularly sitting near her on a bus, and she defends her plot by noting in Edward

Blishen's *The Thorny Paradise* (1975) that "the real-life Pennington spectacularly sav[ed] a man from drowning in the river during a Force 8 gale." Pennington is certainly far from the conventional image of a refined, effete classical musician, and much of the charm and energy of the novel comes from the contrast between Penn's present role as a rather thuggish schoolboy and his potential role as a concert pianist.

In *The Beethoven Medal* (1971) the contrasting worlds to which Pennington belongs are further thrown into conflict, as he, after two years of studying music in London, has grown to take his music seriously. Spending the summer in his home village of Northend and driving a baker's van, Penn comes to the attention of Ruth Hollis, now sixteen, who turns with her usual single-minded devotion from horses to this remarkable boy. Ruth knows nothing of Penn's life and achievement as a musician, and the novel is a moving study through Ruth's eyes of what music can mean in the life of someone as gifted as Penn, and what it requires of him in turn. This novel and its sequel, *Pennington's Heir* (1973), are told largely from the perspective of Ruth, a character with whom Peyton perhaps feels more at ease, but both continue to focus on Penn's struggle to resolve the anger at and resentment of authority that he has stored up all his life and that now endangers his career as a musician. Penn's moodiness and the heavy discipline of his practice schedule, enforced even in absentia by the spirit of Professor Hampton, create difficulties in the relationship between Ruth and Penn. Deeply thrilled by his musicianship, she is also frightened by the violence that has already earned him three months in prison for hitting a fellow music student. Despite her mother's disapproval and her own sense of insecurity, Ruth lives for the brief times she can spend with him, and her dreamy absorption in her love affair is depicted with kindly humor. On one of his infrequent outings with her, Penn loses his temper and strikes a policeman; he is sent to Brixton but is released briefly, through the Professor's intervention, to play a Rachmaninoff concerto with a famous German orchestra and to substitute for an ailing pianist at the Proms in the Albert Hall. In contradiction to Penn's behavior is the despair of people who care for him, and Ruth allies herself with Professor Hampton to keep faith with him during the months Penn will have to spend in prison. Ruth's mother, sad and anxious, accepts Ruth's choice of Penn, and the novel ends in a mood of sober hopefulness.

Pennington's Heir opens with Penn's release from prison and Ruth's consciousness of the tension between herself and the Professor, who she feels is concerned with Penn only as a performer, whereas she loves him as a human being. Carried away by emotion following his release, Penn and Ruth make love, and Ruth becomes pregnant. The shock of this news, delivered minutes before an important audition, causes Penn to play badly, lose a significant opportunity, and break with the Professor. Marrying Ruth, he is uncertain whether he really loves her and is desperately anxious about what he is doing to his career, but their near-penniless life together proves more enjoyable than Ruth's parents had gloomily prophesied, and Penn begins to get some work. His former girlfriend recovers her interest in Penn, and Ruth's feelings of inferiority revive. In one of Peyton's characteristic multiple climaxes, Ruth has labor pains backstage while Penn has a memory lapse in the middle of a Liszt sonata. The baby, nicknamed Lud for Beethoven, is a great joy to Ruth but distracts Penn from his work. When the former girlfriend attempts to seduce Pennington, Ruth and Penn quarrel and, flinging a heavy mug at him, she breaks a bone in his hand. In desperation Ruth appeals for help to the Professor, who rushes Penn to a Harley Street surgeon who

saves his hand and his career. Reconciliation with the Professor reverses Penn's fortunes, and the trilogy ends with Penn, sullen and courageous, launched on a great career.

In these last two volumes of the trilogy Ruth plays much the same role as Christina in *The Edge of the Cloud,* devoting herself to a young man who has a passion for something else. While this traditional feminine role is rather unfashionable, Peyton makes clear its demands and difficulties and shows both young women experiencing satisfaction as well as frustration in their lives. Christina moves on after Will's death to a more independent existence, but Ruth's nature as it develops through four novels seems to be one of dogged determination and devotion without strong personal ambition. Ruth's limitations are suggested, often humorously, and her indignation with her disapproving mother does not keep the reader from suspecting, contrary to Ruth's own view in *The Beethoven Medal,* that she will indeed become "like her own mother when she [is] forty." This trilogy conveys Peyton's tolerant understanding of both the baffled, well-intentioned parents' point of view and the adolescents' exasperation with it, as it fails to meet the adolescents' idealism about what their own lives should be.

A Pattern of Roses, published between the second and third volumes of the Pennington trilogy, also deals with a troubled young man but represents a significant change of genre for Peyton by presenting a time-slip fantasy. This fantasy is one of Peyton's most serious novels, dealing with social injustice and the necessity to recognize and pursue self-fulfillment, as well as with the conflict between parents and young people. Tim Ingram, nearly sixteen, is convalescing from glandular fever in his new home, an Essex cottage to which his parents are adding an expensive addition. When some old drawings dated 1910 and signed with Tim's own initials are found concealed in the chimney, Tim initiates a search for the artist, assisted by the Vicar's daughter, Rebecca. Unlike Rebecca, Tim is not particularly forthright or determined, and his lassitude comes not only from his illness but also from his reluctance to fulfill his parents' expectations by working hard at school and then entering his father's advertising business. Tim begins more and more to identify with the Tom Inskip of 1910, who died at Tim's age just after having completed the drawings. The life of Tom's rural Edwardian England is evoked with beauty and accuracy, but the socially prescribed limitations on the farm laborer, even a youth as intelligent as Tom, and the rigid class divisions create in Tim a sense of injustice and waste.

Tim's paranormal experiences culminate in a scene on the frozen lake where Tim and Rebecca learn that Tom drowned in an attempt to rescue a hound belonging to the Vicar's niece. From this death, however, comes a new life for Tim, as he finds the courage to tell his parents that he wants to use his art for self-expression rather than put it to commercial use in the family firm. He plans to stay in the village, work for the smith, and perhaps eventually become a craftsman in wrought iron.

In *The Right-Hand Man* (1977) Peyton returns to straightforward historical fiction, this time set in the early nineteenth century. Although the subject matter seems different from that of her previous novels, the novel employs several of Peyton's recurrent themes such as the choice of a career, the power imbalance created by class distinctions and privilege, and the ambivalent feelings of two young men who are both friends and rivals. The terrain is again Essex, and horses play a prominent role in the fast-paced action – which is, however, balanced with descriptive passages and reflections by the central character. Young Ned has been little given to reflection during his life as a stagecoach driver, at which his skill and charm have made him highly successful, but he is tricked into going to work for the equally young and charming but much more reckless Lord Ironminster, whose obsession with driving fast horses both fascinates and endangers Ned. Inevitably Ned ends up in Newgate prison, where he is threatened with hanging for murder, but he is saved by the combined efforts of Ironminster and a girl Ned had once befriended.

Set in the coaching inns, country estates, and London streets of the Regency period, the novel sketches its historical background lightly but convincingly. Peyton always lets the context indicate what a "curricle" or a "wheeler" might be, with no whiff of didacticism. She does, however, give a vivid sense of the rough side of life as lived by the servant class in 1818: Ned has a compassionate heart, but he drinks and brawls readily, and the cold, lice, and hard labor of his station in life are not glossed over. Extended passages describing a carriage accident in which a horse is killed and another maimed, the brutal ungloved fistfight between Ned and one of Ironminster's cousins, and the horrifying squalor of the Common Felons' ward at Newgate Prison are powerful counterbalances to the evocation of Regency elegance and the charm of old coaching days.

A strong theme of this novel, rooted in both class and gender relationships, appears in the way the powerful use those under them, usually in a casual and unthinking way. As Ned treats Matty's affections lightly, Ironminster and his friends get Ned into a fight without allowing him to think what it will cost him. The injustice is partially redressed when the penitent Ironminster purchases Ned's freedom by agreeing to marry the judge's daughter, but the novel is clear in its implications that life is often unfair. In the moral world of *The Right-Hand Man* violence and trickery are used by both sides, although the "good" characters do not initiate the skulduggery and their actions permit a just if not legal resolution of the conflict.

Between 1977 and 1984 Peyton published three adventure stories about Jonathan Meredith, stories involving more vigorous and violent action – kidnapping, shooting, drowning – than the quieter novels of her Flambards and Pennington period. Jonathan's difficulties with his mother (earlier depicted in *The Team*) and his attempts to live up to her standards give him almost as many problems as Pennington. While the first half of *Prove Yourself a Hero* is mainly an adventure story hearkening back to Peyton's early boys' books with a yacht race, kidnapping, and the threat of death, after Jonathan's release the novel concentrates on his psychological reactions to his experience. Feeling himself a failure for not having resisted his kidnappers more effectively and feeling guilty about his parents' loss of the £500,000 ransom, Jonathan has nightmares and is sent home from his boarding school. Confinement with his tough-minded mother, who is bitter about the criminals' escape with her money, makes him feel worse than ever, but fortunately she has the insight to suggest that Jonathan take a job as stable hand and rider with Peter Macnair and his father. The hard physical work cures the nightmares, but Jonathan's guilt and anxiety persist. A chance meeting with the slow-witted groom who had assisted his abductors brings him the astonishing but welcome news that his captors had considered him remarkably courageous. Although he is shot and seriously injured in this encounter, the physical injury is far less meaningful to him than the emotional release from his guilt and sense of failure. His mother recognizes that her attitude has been hard on him, and she shows the love that underlies her often unreasonable demands. Mrs. Meredith is one of the most interesting adult characters in Peyton's work, and the reader is made in this book, as in *The Team,* to share the young people's mixed feelings of exasperation and admiration toward her.

Jonathan has a second encounter with criminal adult behavior in *A Midsummer Night's Death,* but this time the criminal is not a stranger but his favorite teacher, a man whose sophistication and skill as a mountain climber have made him Jonathan's idol. The atmosphere of an expensive boarding school and the interaction of the boys and masters is well conveyed. An effete English teacher apparently throws himself into a river after conducting a particularly unsuccessful class on Shakespeare's *A Midsummer Night's Dream* (1600). Jonathan's roommate blames himself, but Jonathan begins to suspect that the suicide may have been murder. The characters are, for the most part, convincing, but the rapidity of events prevents Peyton from developing character and theme as fully as she has elsewhere. Hugo is by no means a stock villain, and the ambiguities of his conduct — as well as Jonathan's response to it — make the novel more complex than the standard mystery-thriller, the genre to which it does, however, clearly belong.

The final novel about Jonathan, entitled *The Last Ditch* (1984) in England and *Free Rein* in the United States, is a sober study of further conflict between Jonathan and his mother, this one occasioned by the pregnancy of a schoolmate, Iris, who has seduced Jonathan after deceitfully assuring him that she has been using birth control. Jonathan is unjustly given the entire blame by his headmaster and by his mother, who takes in Iris to live with them. Humiliated at school and unable to return home, Jonathan finds Peter Macnair, who has an unsatisfactory job at a stable. Driving an antiquated hearse and pulling a horse box containing Dogwood, a horse that Peter hopes to ride in the Grand National, the two young men go off to seek their fortunes.

They "squat" in a derelict mansion, and Jonathan trains Dogwood while Peter — aided by Pip, a local girl who is the opposite of Iris and in whom Jonathan recognizes his ideal of an empathetic and capable companion — works with other horses. An injury prevents Peter from riding in the Grand National, and Jonathan must take Dogwood around the grueling course. The novel ends on hopeful notes with Jonathan returning home, his parents recognizing his right to make his own decisions, Jonathan feeling a spark of interest in his new daughter when Iris suggests "Dogwood" as a middle name, and Iris (again falsely) assuring Jonathan that she no longer loves him — so that he is free to pursue a relationship with Pip. Apart from the exciting action of the horse races and a few scenes of rather black humor, *Free Rein* is a thoughtful, unromanticized account of a young man at a turning point in his life.

While Peyton was publishing her novels about Jonathan Meredith, she was also writing others that take up a new subject: the problems of early married life. This is an important theme in the later part of *Pennington's Heir,* and it is taken up again in the continuation of his story in *Marion's Angels,* when Pennington and his life with Ruth are viewed from the perspective of a twelve-year-old girl. Marion is an odd, isolated child, happy when alone or with her widowed father but criticized by the village women and ostracized by her schoolmates for her eccentric behavior and emotional outbursts. Marion's angels are medieval wood carvings on the interior of the roof of a fifteenth-century church near the site of a music festival where Penn is playing. The roof is in danger of collapse, but since only a miracle, it seems, could raise the money needed to restore it, Penn, who appreciates Marion's intense reactions to music, advises her to pray for a miracle. She does so and is rewarded by the immediate appearance of a famous American violinist who offers to raise money through a series of concerts with Penn as accompanist. However, the new opportunities in the United States that this arrangement creates for Penn distress Ruth.

She bitterly resents Penn's total absorption in his work and knows that touring would separate them even further. Marion gradually becomes aware of a growing attraction between Ruth and Marion's father, Geoff, which may develop into much more if Penn goes to America. As Marion prays for a solution during a storm, she sees, as if in one of her visions, one of the angels swooping down toward her, and its body shields her as the church tower collapses. Penn misses his plane and injures his hands while helping Geoff to rescue her from the rubble, and Ruth comes to him; the situation is at least temporarily resolved. Like *A Pattern of Roses, Marian's Angels* ventures beyond Peyton's usual terrain of realistic fiction to involve experiences on the verge of the supernatural. Since characters in each novel do offer nonsupernatural explanations for what Tim and Marion believe to be mystical or psychic experiences, Peyton leaves readers free to make their own interpretations.

Quasi-supernatural phenomena also appear in *Dear Fred* (1981), as does a real-life character, the 1880s jockey Fred Archer, long one of Peyton's heroes. Laura, a young girl at the start of this novel, has a passion for Fred Archer, who sometimes visits the training stables of her Uncle Harry near the racing town of Newmarket. Tiger, a stable boy, has the gift of "second sight" and through dreams and visions can foretell the future, including the names of major horse-race winners. Like the child in D. H.

*Dust jacket for Peyton's story of a girl who works at a stable to
be near the horse she loves*

Lawrence's "The Rocking-Horse Winner" (1926), Tiger finds his gift a burden, and Laura and Harry keep it secret and try to protect Tiger from his exploitative family. Laura's awakening response to Tiger's physical attraction echoes the passion of Laura's mother, Cecily, for her husband's brother. Cecily preserves a chilly and withdrawn demeanor to match that of her husband, a designer whose work and whose person she despises, but she reveals her true self to the horseman, Harry. On her first outing with Tiger, Laura witnesses with horror and fascination the lovemaking of her mother and Harry. Through her own sexual initiation with a cousin, she tries to find the ecstacy she has seen on her mother's face, but Laura cannot find fulfillment until she marries Tiger, a marriage delayed by his foreknowledge of a terrible death for the idolized Fred Archer.

The exciting racing scenes that Peyton so often uses to bring the disparate elements of a novel together in its climax do not quite succeed in *Dear Fred,* and Archer's story, always darkened by Tiger's unspeakable vision of its end, seems awkwardly related to the rest of the book. Thematic echoes of D. H. Lawrence's story appear not only in the boy's dreaming of horse-race winners but in the novel's opposition of the sensual, passionate life to the frigid aestheticism of Cecily's husband and the artistic circle of William Morris, an aestheticism treated with surprising hostility by the usually generous-spirited Peyton. The death of Cecily from meningitis, during her husband's absence on erotic adventures, also has literary echoes of Aldous Huxley's *Point Counter Point* (1928), in which a mother blames herself for the death of her child (from the same disease) while she makes a secret visit to her lover. Even though *Dear Fred* is not altogether successful, the exploration of new territory by including historical figures and by writing frankly about the sexual experiences of both adolescents and adults indicates Peyton's continuing willingness to experiment.

Flambards Divided offers a further exploration of conflict and unhappiness in marriage. The glow that lay over the first three Flambards novels, published more than a decade earlier, is gone from this later volume, although the setting and main characters are virtually identical. Christina – having met Mark, Will, and Dick in the first book, loved Will in the second, and learned to love Dick in the third – marries Dick at the beginning of this fourth book but soon finds that she truly loves Mark; she is about to marry *him* at the end of this novel. This tale of changing partners is concluded with a realistic exploration of discord that may result from a rash and convention-defying marriage in this fourth volume. The differences in social position, background, and interests that friends and relatives warned Christina and Dick about do indeed prove harder to ignore than Christina's socialist views (learned from Will) and Dick's idealistic devotion to her had allowed them to admit. Dick is tradition-bound, and his injured pride makes him apt to withdraw from social life rather than be rejected as an upstart, while Christina is always prepared to challenge tradition and badly misses the lively social interaction with her peers whom she had known while engaged and married to Will. Farming alone cannot hold them together, and when Christina foolishly has a road race with Mark and loses the baby whom she and Dick had hoped would heal their marriage, Dick turns from her to a servant, while Christina resumes her former social life and awaits Mark's divorce. The atmosphere of the book, characteristic of depictions of the 1920s, is one of regret at the failure of initial postwar idealism and a sense of the impermanence of love relationships.

In *The Sound of Distant Cheering* (1986), the first of Peyton's novels written specifically for adults, and *Darkling,* another young adult novel, Peyton offers different versions of the same story. In each, a good-hearted and hardworking girl, employed as a stable "lad" in order to be near a horse she loves, falls in love with a more privileged young man working at the same stable. A young horse she has raised becomes a winning racer, and the aloof young man accepts her love, but complications arise from the girl's concern for a needy elderly person. Interestingly, the adult novel comes to a fairly straightforward happy ending, but *Darkling* ends less conventionally: Jenny renounces a trip to America with her lover in order to stay home with her dying grandfather, and she is consoled by the return of her illegitimate half brother to support her. Jenny of *Darkling* is still in school when the novel begins, while Rosy in *The Sound of Distant Cheering* is nearly thirty. Both girls are intensely loyal, unassuming, tolerant of defects in those they love, and good at developing the best qualities of the young horses they raise. Peyton's humor appears in her description of the secretive begetting of Rosy's foal, accomplished without the knowledge of the stallion's owner, and of Jenny's purchase of a wild Irish colt and her attempt to conceal its stable.

Like several of Peyton's books, although *Darkling* is ostensibily an animal story, it is more about the people involved with the horses than about the horses. The Peytons purchased a share in a racehorse, and like Jenny and Rosy they became familiar with the passions and heartbreaks of serious racing. In this novel the Newmarket world of jockeys, trainers, owners, and stable lads is vividly created through the physical life and labor of the stables and the complex distinctions of class and position among the denizens of that world. It is the environment of *Dear Fred* exactly one century later. Jenny and Rosy, like Ruth and Pennington, are outsiders in the wealthy, competitive world of horse racing, but these Cinderellas try very hard, and eventually their innate goodness receives recognition and reward. *Darkling* celebrates Jenny's patience, kindness, and loyalty – virtues that are not glamorous or fashionable but that are presented here as genuine and of great value. Jenny's half brother, Straw, and her charming and disreputable grandfather also display these qualities in their love and care for their animals. In this novel goodness may not necessarily carry all before it, but it is recognized and honored, and while the book is not moralistic, it conveys clearly what its author believes are the qualities which really matter.

Like *The Sound of Distant Cheering,* Peyton's two other novels for adults – *No Roses Round the Door* and *Late to Smile* (1992) – explore the subjects of love and marriage within the familiar context of a horse-racing community, but from the perspectives of older characters rather than the adolescent protagonists of most of her books. The boundaries between adult and young adult fiction, however, may blur in the case of a writer like Peyton. The Flambards stories, both in book form and as a thirteen-part series made for Yorkshire television, have been popular with adults as well as young people, and both *Marion's Angels* and *Dear Fred* address subjects of marital incompatibility outside the usual range of adolescent fiction.

In some of her recent children's books, however, Peyton deliberately addresses a younger audience. Written in a matter-of-fact manner from the perspective of a ten-year-old girl, *Going Home* (1982) is an account of two children running away from foster parents on holiday in central France and finding their way back to England. Milly is as resourceful and responsible as Peyton's older heroines, and the story sympathetically presents the pressures and anxiety she feels in caring for her six-year-old brother, as well as her pleasure in independence and achievement. *Plain Jack* (1988) is an engaging fable of two horses: Fire of England, "the horse with a great talent who never used it"; and Plain Jack, "the horse with little talent who used it all." This picture book is a blunt and kindly distillation of several major concerns of Peyton's fiction — the relationship between racehorses and their owners, caring or exploitative; the influence that differences in training and riding can make in a horse's performance; and the triumph of the earnest, wholehearted effort of the underdog over a glamorous and privileged competitor.

Another horse story for young readers, *Apple Won't Jump* (1992), alternates between the perspective of young Penny, who dreams of a pony that would win medals for jumping, and that of Apple, the pony she is given, who sensibly wonders why he should jump when it is easier to go around. A dramatic accident leads to a happy ending and compromise between Penny and Apple.

Two other books for younger children, *Froggett's Revenge* (1985) and *Skylark* (1989), open with a sense of mystery. Denny Froggett and Ben each know that something or someone is hiding in the woods near their house, and by courageously overcoming his anxiety each boy makes an important friend. Denny's mysterious neighbor turns out to be a gigantic dog, which, though friendly, terrifies the bully who has been making Denny's life a misery. Eventually a suitable home for the dog is found on a hill farm with an eight-foot-tall former schoolmate of Denny's father, and the lighthearted story ends satisfactorily for all concerned.

The resolution of *Skylark* is not so tidy, as the story of its two lonely children is altogether more realistic. The mysterious inhabitant of Ben's woods turns out to be Elfrieda ("Elf"), a fourteen-year-old runaway who, while hiding from her mother in an unused summerhouse and waiting for her sailor father's ship to return, has been keeping herself comfortable by adroit shoplifting and general competence. Ben, some years younger, is neglected by his actress mother and his frivolous nanny Mitzi, who leaves him to his own devices. The children befriend each other, but Elf's situation seems hopeless

until Ben's Uncle Brownjohn arrives and takes charge. He takes Elf to her father and dismisses the police, whom Mitzi has summoned in hopes of getting the £1,000 reward offered for Elf's return. By deciding to move in with Ben, replacing the incompetent Mitzi with his own kindly and sensible housekeeper, and taking Ben to the Battersea Home for Dogs to choose a pet for himself, Uncle Brownjohn transforms Ben's life for the better. The story implies, however, that Elf's problems may not be so readily resolved, and there is a touch of sadness in the ending of this fine book.

A strong vein of humor that has always been present in Peyton's work is the dominant feature of two novels written about a group of young adolescents in Sam Sylvester's comprehensive school class. Comedy in *Who, Sir? Me, Sir?* (1983) and its sequel *Downhill All the Way* (1988) comes from the misadventures of an ill-assorted and likable group of characters faced with athletic challenges that seem hopelessly beyond their capabilities and from the slapstick consequences of their efforts. The stories are told in a high-spirited and colloquial style that effectively suggests how the characters think and speak of each other. In *Downhill All the Way* Sam, who manages to break both a leg and a wrist without even getting onto his skis, is viewed by his students with a kindly pity.

In *Who, Sir? Me, Sir?* Sam enters some of his most unlikely students in a tetrathalon competition against a private boys' school. Nutty, a four-square and determined girl, is a capable rider but cannot swim or run; Jazz, a handsome Sikh boy who wears a turban in all the events, can swim but fears riding; Hoomey is a natural pessimist and weakling who is terrified of all the events; and Nails, whose usual recreation is stealing cars, may not be released by the police and social workers in time to participate. None of the team knows anything about the fourth skill, shooting. Their horses have been destined for the knacker. The team has virtually no place to practice and cannot afford trainers. As in *Plain Jack,* however, determination and hard work eventually triumph over privilege — or at least tie with it. The resolution is satisfying but somewhat unconventional in that both teams cheat (the antagonists do so first, however, just as those of Peyton's earlier *The Right-Hand Man* do). Sam's motley group of students gains self-esteem in the process. Nails particularly finds a sense of belonging and purpose for the first time in his life, through his discovery of a passion for horses.

Most of the same characters reappear in *Downhill All the Way,* when Sam takes his class skiing in

Dust jacket for Peyton's book about the athletic misadventures of
Sam Sylvester and his classmates

the French Alps. The second novel is perhaps less tightly organized than the first, with more emphasis on slapstick humor – as afforded by an improbable plot to pass off Hoomey as the son of the owner of Harrods and by Hoomey's unintended participation in a downhill race and ski jump. The experiences of self-discovery undergone by Jean and David are less fully integrated into the rest of the story than were the changes that the tetrathalon competitors experienced through their training. Yet *Downhill All the Way* conveys an equally engaging portrayal of the attitudes, language, and humor of its adolescent characters.

The character-building value of team competition is again a theme in *The Wild Boy and Queen Moon* (1993), in which Sandy, the main character, is not chosen for the riding team and has to do stable chores on the sidelines while her friends gallop round the course. This novel focuses not on the race scene or on the horses, although Sandy runs a livery yard on her father's farm, but on relationships among the young riders and within Sandy's extended family. Dependable Sandy is more sensitive than her stolid exterior reveals, and her sufferings from family problems and exclusion from the racing team are counterbalanced by her romantic admiration of the mysterious "wild boy" and his horse, Queen Moon. Some loose ends in the plot are laft dangling, but the novel is gripping and often funny.

Peyton returns to the setting of the Alps in *Snowfall* (1994), a historical romance. Charlotte, the protagonist, is an attractive girl whose affections are engaged by different young men of contrasting social backgrounds. The exhilaration of climbing in the high mountains confirms Charlotte's determination to escape from the stultifying though kindly life of the vicarage in which she was raised. She moves to England, where she lives communally with a group of young Oxford graduates. Friends of a charming aristocrat named Milo, they work with him at restoring a neglected country estate, but they assume the clothing and manner of his servants when outsiders visit so as to hide the true nature of their community. An unexpected visit by the Prince of Wales, an avalanche, and a plot to kidnap a racehorse provide abundant action, but the focus of the novel remains on the fluctuations of Charlotte's feelings.

In published interviews Peyton is disarmingly candid about her literary aims and models. Like Anthony Trollope's notorious account of his writing practices in his *Autobiography* (1883), Peyton's unpretentious references to her own writing have encouraged some critics to underestimate her mastery of her art. The early books were written to order and to make money. Since the mid 1960s, however, her impressive output is that of a writer who, while born to her work, has developed and matured while she has at the same time retained her clear sense of the concerns and interests of the young people about and for whom she writes. Critical attention has focused on the novels of the late 1960s and early 1970s, but both the lighter adventure stories and the more serious novels of the 1980s and afterward have maintained Peyton's popularity with readers of different ages. Her style – although it can be overlush and can slip into cliché, particularly in the romantic novels – can be spare and precise, and she has a fine ear for the cadences and idiom of colloquial speech. Training as an artist undoubtedly contributes to the sharpness and depth of her visual images and descriptions. Strong patterns are observable in her work: the pairing of characters from contrasting social backgrounds, the repetition of certain names, and the use of a competitive event such as a boat race or horse race or a piano competition as the climax toward which many of her plots build. Nonetheless, each of the stories is distinct; historical settings are varied and accurate, and the different landscapes and seascapes of Essex are sensitively evoked.

Peyton's outstanding gift, however, is her ability to bring to life any activity in which she has an interest, an ability that comes from her own kinetic understanding of it. She can convey to the reader a remarkably vivid sense of what it feels like to sail a boat in a high wind, guide a horse over a brush jump, or play a Liszt sonata. Peyton has done all of these many times – she learned to play the piano while working on the Pennington books, though she may not have managed Liszt – and is able to make the reader feel with her characters the thrill of accomplishing something difficult. While in *Marion's Angels* Ruth's baby fills someone's boots with potatoes, Peyton notes approvingly of him, "Lud was a doer." Peyton too is a doer, one with the rare gift to write about the doing and to share its excitement with her readers.

Interviews:

Emma Fisher, "K. M. Peyton," in *The Pied Pipers,* by Justin Wintle and Emma Fisher (London & New York: Paddington, 1974), pp. 263–276;

Cornelia Jones and Olivia R. Way, "K. M. Peyton," in their *British Children's Authors: Interviews at Home* (Chicago: American Library Association, 1976), pp. 127–136.

References:

Marcus Crouch, *The Nesbit Tradition: The Children's Novel in England 1945–1970* (London: Benn, 1972), pp. 152–154;

John Rowe Townsend, "K. M. Peyton," in his *A Sounding of Storytellers: New and Revised Essays on Contemporary Writers for Children* (New York: Lippincott, 1979), pp. 166–178.

James Reeves

(1 July 1909 – 1 May 1978)

Constance Vidor
The Cathedral School, Cathedral of Saint John the Divine

BOOKS: *The Natural Need* (Deyá, Majorca: Seizin Press, 1935; London: Constable, 1935);

The Imprisoned Sea (London: Editions Poetry London, 1949);

The Wandering Moon, illustrated by Edward Ardizzone (London: Heinemann, 1950; New York: Dutton, 1960);

XIII Poems (London: Privately printed, 1950);

Mulcaster Market: Three Plays for Young People, illustrated by Dudley Cutler (London: Heinemann, 1951); republished as *The Peddler's Dream and Other Plays* (New York: Dutton, 1963);

The Blackbird in the Lilac: Verses, illustrated by Ardizzone (London: Oxford University Press, 1952; New York: Dutton, 1959);

The Password and Other Poems (London: Heinemann, 1952);

Man Friday: A Primer of English Composition and Grammar (London: Heinemann, 1953);

English Fables and Fairy Stories, Retold, illustrated by Joan Kiddell-Monroe (London: Oxford University Press, 1954; New York: Walck, 1966?);

The King Who Took Sunshine (London: Heinemann, 1954);

Pigeons and Princesses, illustrated by Ardizzone (London: Heinemann, 1956);

The Critical Sense: Practical Criticism of Prose and Poetry (London: Heinemann, 1956);

A Health to John Patch: A Ballad Operetta (London: Boosey, 1957);

Prefabulous Animiles, illustrated by Ardizzone (London: Heinemann, 1957; New York: Dutton, 1960);

Mulbridge Manor, illustrated by Geraldine Spence (London: Heinemann, 1958);

The Talking Skull (London: Heinemann, 1958);

Teaching Poetry: Poetry in Class Five to Fifteen (London: Heinemann, 1958);

James Reeves

Titus in Trouble, illustrated by Ardizzone (London: Bodley Head, 1959; New York: Walck, 1960);

Exploits of Don Quixote, Retold, illustrated by Ardizzone (London: Blackie, 1959; New York: Walck, 1960);

Collected Poems 1929–1959 (London: Heinemann, 1960);

Ragged Robin, illustrated by Jane Paton (London: Heinemann, 1961; New York: Dutton, 1961);

Hurdy-Gurdy: Selected Poems for Children, illustrated by Ardizzone (London: Heinemann, 1961);

Fables from Aesop, Retold, illustrated by Maurice Wilson (London: Blackie, 1961; New York: Walck, 1962);

A Short History of English Poetry 1340–1940 (London: Heinemann, 1961; New York: Dutton, 1962);

Sailor Rumbelow and Britannia, illustrated by Ardizzone (London: Heinemann, 1962); published as *Sailor Rumbelow and Other Stories,* New York: Dutton, 1962);

The Strange Light, illustrated by Lynton Lamb (London: Heinemann, 1964; Chicago: Rand, McNally, 1966);

The Story of Jackie Thimble, illustrated by Ardizzone (New York: Dutton, 1964; London: Chatto & Windus, 1965);

Three Tall Tales, Chosen from Traditional Sources, illustrated by Ardizzone (London & New York: Abelard-Schuman, 1964);

The Questioning Tiger (London: Heinemann, 1964);

The Pillar Box Thieves, illustrated by Dick Hart (London: Nelson, 1965);

The Road to a Kingdom: Stories from the Old and New Testaments, illustrated by Richard Kennedy (London: Heinemann, 1965);

Understanding Poetry (London: Heinemann, 1965; New York: Barnes & Noble, 1968);

The Secret Shoemakers and Other Stories, illustrated by Ardizzone (London & New York: Abelard-Schuman, 1966);

Rhyming Will, illustrated by Ardizzone (London: Hamish Hamilton, 1967; New York: McGraw-Hill, 1968);

The Cold Flame, Based on a Tale from the Collection of the Brothers Grimm, illustrated by Charles Keeping (London: Hamish Hamilton, 1967; New York: Meredith Press, 1969);

Selected Poems (London: Allison & Busby, 1967; revised edition, 1977);

The Trojan Horse, illustrated by Krystyna Turska (London: Hamish Hamilton, 1968; New York: Watts, 1969);

Mr. Horrox and the Gratch, illustrated by Quentin Blake (London: Abelard-Schuman, 1969; Chicago: Wellington, 1991);

The Angel and the Donkey, illustrated by Ardizzone (London: Hamish Hamilton, 1969; New York: McGraw-Hill, 1970);

Subsong (London: Heinemann, 1969);

Commitment to Poetry (London: Heinemann, 1969; New York: Barnes & Noble, 1969);

Heroes and Monsters: Legends of Ancient Greece Retold, illustrated by Sarah Nechamkin (London: Blackie, 1969);

Gods and Voyagers (London: Blackie, 1969; New York: Two Continents, 1978);

Inside Poetry, by Reeves and Martin Seymour-Smith (London: Heinemann, 1970; New York: Barnes & Noble, 1970);

Islands and Palaces (London: Blackie, 1971); republished as *Giants and Warriors* (London: Blackie, 1977; New York: Two Continents, 1978);

Maildun the Voyager, illustrated by John Lawrence (London: Hamish Hamilton, 1971; New York: Walck, 1972);

How the Moon Began, illustrated by Ardizzone (London: Abelard-Schuman, 1971);

How to Write Poems for Children (London: Heinemann, 1971);

The Path of Gold, illustrated by Turska (London: Hamish Hamilton, 1972);

Poems and Paraphrases (London: Heinemann, 1972);

The Forbidden Forest and Other Stories, illustrated by Raymond Briggs (London: Heinemann, 1973);

The Voyage of Odysseus: Homer's Odyssey Retold (London: Blackie, 1973);

A.D. One: A Masque for Christmas (London: Privately printed, 1974);

The Lion That Flew, illustrated by Ardizzone (London: Chatto & Windus, 1974);

Two Greedy Bears (Persian folktale), illustrated by Gareth Floyd (London: Hamish Hamilton, 1974);

Collected Poems 1929–1974 (London: Heinemann, 1974);

More Prefabulous Animiles, illustrated by Ardizzonne (London: Heinemann, 1975);

The Clever Mouse, illustrated by Barbara Swiderska (London: Chatto & Windus, 1976);

Quest and Conquest: Pilgrim's Progress Retold, illustrated by Joanna Troughton (London: Blackie, 1976);

The Reputation and Writings of Alexander Pope (London: Heinemann, 1976; New York: Barnes & Noble, 1976);

The Writer's Approach to the Ballad (London: Harrap, 1976);

Arcadian Ballads, illustrated by Ardizzone (Andoversford, Gloucestershire: Whittington Press, 1977);

The Closed Door (Sidcot, Somerset: Gruffyground Press, 1977; Brookston, Ind.: Twinrocker, 1977);

Eggtime Stories, illustrated by Colin McNaughton (London: Blackie, 1978);

The James Reeves Storybook, illustrated by Ardizzone (London: Heinemann, 1978); republished as

The Gnome Factory and Other Stories (London: Penguin, 1986);

A Prince in Danger, illustrated by Floyd (London: Kaye & Ward, 1979);

Snow White and Rose Red, illustrated by Jenny Rodwell (London: Andersen Press, 1979).

Collection: *Complete Poems for Children,* illustrated by Ardizzone (London: Heinemann, 1973).

OTHER: *The Quality of Education: Methods and Purposes in the Secondary Curriculum,* edited by Reeves and Denys Thompson (London: Muller, 1947);

The Poets' World: An Anthology of English Poetry, edited by Reeves (London: Heinemann, 1948); revised and republished as *The Modern Poet's World* (London: Heinemann, 1957);

The Writer's Way: An Anthology of English Prose, edited by Reeves (London: Christophers, 1948);

Orpheus: A Junior Anthology of English Poetry, 2 volumes, edited by Reeves (London: Heinemann, 1949–1950);

Dialogue and Drama, edited by Reeves and Norman Culpan (London: Heinemann, 1950; Boston: Plays, 1968);

D. H. Lawrence, *Selected Poems,* edited by Reeves (London: Heinemann, 1951);

Speaking Oak: English Poetry and Prose: A Selection, edited by Reeves (London: Heinemann, 1951);

John Donne, *Selected Poems,* edited by Reeves (London: Heinemann, 1952; New York: Macmillan, 1958);

Heinemann Junior Poetry Books, 4 volumes, edited by Reeves (London: Heinemann, 1954);

The Bible in Brief: Selections from the Text of the Authorised Version of 1611, edited by Reeves (London: Wingate, 1954); republished as *The Holy Bible in Brief* (New York: Messner, 1954);

John Clare, *Selected Poems,* edited by Reeves (London: Heinemann, 1954; New York: Macmillan, 1957);

The Merry Go Round: A Collection of Rhymes and Poems for Children, edited by Reeves, illustrated by John Mackay (London: Heinemann, 1955);

Gulliver's Travels: The First Three Parts, edited by Reeves (London: Heinemann, 1955);

Gerard Manley Hopkins, *Selected Poems,* edited by Reeves (London: Heinemann, 1956; New York: Macmillan, 1957);

Robert Browning, *Selected Poems,* edited by Reeves (London: Heinemann, 1956; New York: Macmillan, 1957);

"James Reeves," in *A Puffin Quartet of Poets,* edited by Eleanor Graham, illustrated by Diana Bloomfield (London: Penguin, 1958), pp. 51–96;

A Golden Land: Stories, Poems, Songs New and Old, edited by Reeves, illustrated by Gillian Conway and others (London: Constable, 1958; New York: Hastings House, 1958);

The Idiom of the People: English Traditional Verse from the Manuscripts of Cecil J. Sharp, edited by Reeves (London: Heinemann, 1958; New York: Macmillan, 1958);

The Selected Poems of Emily Dickinson, edited by Reeves (London: Heinemann, 1959; New York: Barnes & Noble, 1966);

Samuel Taylor Coleridge, *Selected Poems,* edited by Reeves (London: Heinemann, 1959);

The Personal Vision . . . , edited by Reeves (London: Poetry Book Supplement, 1959);

The Rhyming River: An Anthology of Verse, 4 volumes, edited by Reeves (London: Heinemann, 1959);

Over the Ranges, edited by Reeves and William Vincent Aughterson (Melbourne: Heinemann, 1959);

The Everlasting Circle: English Traditional Verse, edited by Reeves (London: Heinemann, 1960; New York: Macmillan, 1960);

The War 1939–1945, edited by Reeves and Desmond Flower (London: Cassell, 1960); republished as *The Taste of Courage* (New York: Harper, 1960);

Stephen Leacock, *The Unicorn Leacock,* edited by Reeves (London: Heinemann, 1960);

Great English Essays, edited by Reeves (London: Cassell, 1961);

Selected Poetry and Prose of Robert Graves, edited by Reeves (London: Hutchinson, 1961);

A First Bible: An Abridgement for Young Readers, edited by Reeves, illustrated by Geoffrey Fraser (London: Heinemann, 1962);

Georgian Poetry, edited by Reeves (London: Penguin, 1962);

Frantisek Hrubin, *Primrose and the Winter Witch,* translated by Reeves, illustrated by Jirí Trnka (London: Hamlyn, 1964);

Gulliver's Travels: Parts I–IV, edited by Reeves (London: Heinemann, 1964);

The Cassell Book of English Poetry, edited by Reeves (London: Cassell, 1965; New York: Harper, 1965);

Jonathan Swift, *Selected Poems,* edited by Reeves (London: Heinemann, 1967; New York: Barnes & Noble, 1967);

A New Canon of English Poetry, edited by Reeves and Seymour-Smith (London: Heinemann, 1967; New York: Barnes & Noble, 1967);

The Christmas Book, edited by Reeves, illustrated by Raymond Briggs (London: Heinemann, 1968; New York: Dutton, 1968);

One's None: Old Rhymes for New Tongues, edited by Reeves, illustrated by Bernadette Watts (London: Heinemann, 1968; New York: Watts, 1969);

An Anthology of Free Verse, edited by Reeves (Oxford: Blackwell, 1968);

The Reader's Bible, edited by Reeves (London: Tandem, 1968);

The Sayings of Dr. Johnson, edited by Reeves (London: Baker, 1968);

Homage to Trumbull Stickney: Poems, edited by Reeves and Seán Haldane (London: Heinemann, 1968);

Alexander Pushkin, *The Golden Cockerel and Other Stories,* translated by Reeves, illustrated by Jan Lebis (London: Dent, 1969; New York: Watts, 1969);

Poets and Their Critics 3: Arnold to Auden, edited by Reeves (London: Hutchinson, 1969);

The Poems of Andrew Marvell, edited by Reeves and Seymour-Smith (London: Heinemann, 1969; New York: Barnes & Noble, 1969);

Chaucer: Lyric and Allegory, edited by Reeves (London: Heinemann, 1970);

A Vein of Mockery: Twentieth-Century Verse Satire, edited by Reeves (London: Heinemann, 1973);

Thomas Gray, *Selected Poems,* edited by Reeves (London: Heinemann, 1973); republished as *The Complete English Poems of Thomas Gray* (New York: Barnes & Noble, 1973);

Five Late Romantic Poets, edited by Reeves (London: Heinemann, 1974);

Marie de France, *The Shadow of the Hawk and Other Stories,* translated by Reeves, illustrated by Anne Dalton (London: Collins, 1975; New York: Seabury Press, 1977);

The Springtime Book: A Collection of Prose and Poetry, edited by Reeves, illustrated by McNaughton (London: Heinemann, 1976);

Selected Poems of Walt Whitman, edited by Reeves and Seymour-Smith (London: Heinemann, 1976);

The Autumn Book: A Collection of Prose and Poetry, edited by Reeves, illustrated by Watts (London: Heinemann, 1977);

Selected Poems of Thomas Hardy, edited by Reeves and Robert Gittings (London: Heinemann, 1981).

James Reeves brought a poet's imagination and a scholar's seriousness to his writing for children. Respected as a critic, educator, and scholar, he achieved an honorable reputation as an author for both adults and children. Frequently compared with Walter de la Mare's work, Reeves's prose and poetry for children exemplify a wide knowledge of traditional forms and folktale themes, a love of nonsense and whimsy, and an understanding of the musical and rhythmic capacities of the English language.

Reeves was born in the London suburb of Harrow-on-the-Hill to Albert John and Ethel Mary Reeves and soon moved with his parents to the more rural environment of Buckinghamshire. He was educated at Stowe School, Buckinghamshire, then at Jesus College, Cambridge University, where he received his M.A. in English language and literature. He married Mary Phillips in 1936 and had three children: Stella, Juliet Mary, and Gareth Edward.

Reeves taught in state schools and colleges from 1933 to 1952, becoming a full-time author and editor in 1952. He had been writing poetry since 1920 but did not begin writing for children until the age of forty-one, well after his career as an author for adults was established. As quoted in the *Third Book of Junior Authors* (1972), he credited his "bad eyesight" as an important influence, stating that "I have never read anything I have written, but I have listened to every word of it. Any appeal my writing has for children, therefore, is to some extent due to its being written as much for the ear as for the eye." Indeed, much of Reeves's writing has the spare quality of oral folk traditions. Possibly owing to his previous experience as a writer for adults, Reeves began and continued his career as a children's writer on an even plateau of excellence, adhering to the forms, themes, and techniques that define his style. Although best known as a poet, he also wrote novels, short stories, and plays, edited poetry and traditional literature, translated folktales, and retold a wide variety of classic and traditional stories for young readers.

With *The Wandering Moon* (1950), his first book of verse for children, Reeves set a high standard for his subsequent work. These poems evoke an innocent and benign world where waiting for a party to begin, collecting sea shells, and wondering how to spend "a farthing and a penny" are the characteristic pleasures of childhood. Poems like "Roundabout," "Little Fan," and "Queer Things" show ordinary situations becoming suddenly and humorously magical. A cast of colorful, nonsensical char-

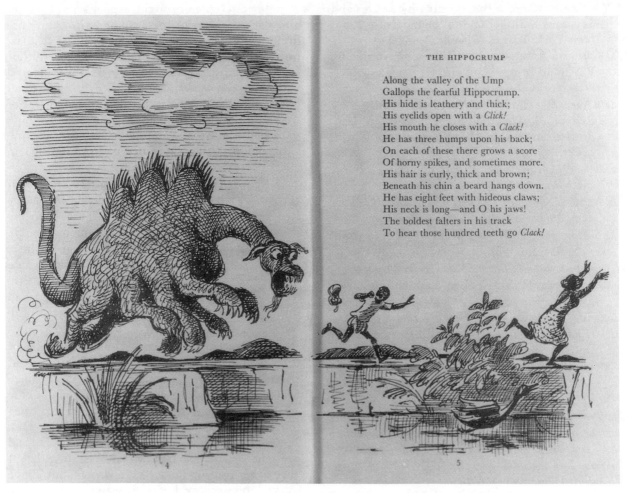

THE HIPPOCRUMP

Along the valley of the Ump
Gallops the fearful Hippocrump.
His hide is leathery and thick;
His eyelids open with a *Click!*
His mouth he closes with a *Clack!*
He has three humps upon his back;
On each of these there grows a score
Of horny spikes, and sometimes more.
His hair is curly, thick and brown;
Beneath his chin a beard hangs down.
He has eight feet with hideous claws;
His neck is long—and O his jaws!
The boldest falters in his track
To hear those hundred teeth go *Clack!*

Pages from Reeves's Prefabulous Animiles *(1957), with one of Edward Ardizzone's whimsical illustrations*

acters makes its appearance in poems such as "Mr. Tom Narrow," who pushes his grandmother around in a wheelbarrow, and "Mrs. Utter," who eats no butter. The more lyrical poems such as "Grim and Gloomy" use the musical resonances of spoken words to suggest both the sights and the sounds of nature:

Oh, grim and gloomy,
So grim and gloomy
Are the caves beneath the sea.
Oh, rare but roomy
And bare and boomy,
Those salt sea caverns be . . . [.]

In *The Wandering Moon*, as in most of his other works, Reeves can be found at both his weakest and strongest. Occasionally, his love of nature and enchantment becomes a sickly parade of hackneyed "fairy-tale" images, as in "Musetta of the Mountains," but poems such as "Stocking and Shirt" are

paradigms of dancing rhythm and concrete sensory imagery:

Stocking and shirt
    Can trip and prance,
Though nobody's in them
    To make them dance.
See how they waltz
    Or minuet,
Watch the petticoat
    Pirouette . . .
'Stop!' Cries the housewife,
    But all too late,
Her clothes have passed
    The furthest gate.
They are gone for ever
    In the bright blue sky,
And only the handkerchiefs
    Wave good-bye[.]

In 1952 Reeves became the general editor for the Poetry Bookshelf series published by William

Heinemann of London. He left teaching in 1952 to become a full-time writer and editor, and from 1960 he was the general editor for Unicorn Books, London.

The Blackbird in the Lilac: Verses (1952) continues the themes and techniques introduced in *The Wandering Moon.* "Giant Thunder," "Run a Little," and "Time to Go Home" exemplify Reeves at his most eloquent, creating sensory, rhythmic evocations of childlike delight in the natural world. The 10 May 1959 *New York Herald Tribune Book Review* commented that the "poems [were] as carefully wrought as Milne's using traditional meters."

Pigeons and Princesses (1956) marked Reeves's entry into children's fiction. He had already produced a volume of retellings, *English Fables and Fairy Stories, Retold* (1954), and he continued the direct, simple, action-driven style of folktale narration in the short stories of *Pigeons and Princesses.* "The Discontented King" and "Eleven White Pigeons" are whimsical stories that play with traditional fairy-tale motifs by featuring royal characters who behave with an engaging lack of dignity. "The Discontented King" is a well-constructed narrative that uses repetition to underscore the humor in a king's petulant search for a perfect castle. The royal family in "Eleven White Pigeons" must travel in a laundry cart and support themselves as musicians when a coup forces them from the castle.

Resourcefulness is the keynote of "The Old Woman and the Four Noises" and "The Stonemason of Elphinstone," both of which are patterned on well-known stories from folklore. In the former, an old woman discovers that a squeaking door and other household noises are actually the voices of several elves and a friendly mouse. She then cleverly prevents her well-meaning neighbor from doing the repair work that would deprive her newfound friends of their homes. The protagonist of "The Stonemason of Elphinstone" is a talented but lazy artisan who makes a rash bargain with an elf in order to finish a job on time. The stonemason then eludes payment by discovering the elf's name and thereby turning it to stone.

"Little Monday," the collection's most compelling tale, features a homeless waif who is adopted by a kind baker's family. Reeves contrasts the complacent ordinariness of the baker's family to the wildness of the mischievous Monday, vivacious and charming, who is disastrously in love with trouble. She breaks crockery, starts arguments, and leaves hurt feelings and messy rooms in her wake. When the bakehouse burns down, the family suspects Monday is the arsonist, and she runs away from

their anger. Eventually, the real culprits are caught, and Monday returns home just as the family realizes how much they miss their exasperating adoptee.

With *Prefabulous Animiles* (1957) Reeves returned to poetry and received a cordial critical reception. The reviewer for the December 1960 *Horn Book* thought that Reeves was at his "teasing fanciful best" in this collection of nonsense verses describing fantasy beasts such as the "Hippocrump," the "Catipoce," and the "Chickamungus." Edward Ardizzone illustrated this book, as he had Reeves's previous original works for children, but for the first time the illustrations assumed equal prominence with the text. *Prefabulous Animiles* exemplifies the best of what Reeves and Ardizzone were capable of achieving throughout their long artistic association. The forceful black-and-white illustrations curl around the text in flowing designs on double-page spreads. Dark shadows and thick lines bring out a mysterious element in the poems, and the creatures' eyes stare out from the pages with unnerving intensity. Reeves commented in the preface to *The James Reeves Story Book* (1978) that he gave Ardizzone "a lot of trouble with some of the creatures . . . where his imagination was severely but delightfully stretched." Ardizzone's illustrations, however, also stretch the poems, adding a provocative hint of menace to their bouncing whimsy.

Mulbridge Manor (1958) was Reeves's first sustained piece of fiction for young readers. The quickly moving plot features a group of village children who tumble into and out of various adventures. Poetic touches are judiciously added to set a scene or introduce a character, but action dominates this innocent and enjoyable story. At the time of publication it evoked a familiar, if unusually coincidence-filled, world; it now suggests a poignantly remote and pastoral era.

The publication of *Exploits of Don Quixote, Retold* (1959) established Reeves as an important contributor of retold stories to children's literature. He had already published *English Fables and Fairy Stories, Retold,* which is still in print today, and he continued to produce skillful retellings until the year of his death. Reeves's tales from classic, folkloric, and mythic literature comprise a veritable survey of the major elements of storytelling in the Western world. Although uneven in quality, as a group they envision a child readership that has the intelligence to comprehend and the curiosity to discover the breadth and depth of the literary canon.

Writing in the 24 February 1977 *Times Educational Supplement,* Audrey Laski found *Fables from*

Aesop, Retold (1961) and *Giants and Warriors* (1977) "dreary and flat," and indeed, many of Reeves's retellings cannot stand comparison with the exciting illustrations and vivid narrative style that young readers of the 1970s were beginning to expect. More successful at the time of publication and deserving of lasting attention are *Quest and Conquest: Pilgrim's Progress Retold* (1976), *Exploits of Don Quixote, Retold,* and *The Cold Flame, Based on a Tale from the Collection of the Brothers Grimm* (1967). Both *Quest and Conquest: Pilgrim's Progress Retold* and *Exploits of Don Quixote, Retold* are judicious abridgments that retain a sense of the original versions' poetry and character. The August 1969 *Horn Book* congratulated Reeves for "plausibly develop[ing] physical and emotional experiences to extend the meaning of the original" and for the "DeJong-like intensity" of *The Cold Flame.* (Reeves commented, however, in the *Third Book of Junior Authors* that *The Cold Flame* was in fact intended for adults and was only published on a children's list at the publisher's insistence.)

Although Reeves's fourth book of poetry for children, *Ragged Robin* (1961), joins *Mr. Horrox and the Gratch* (1969) and *Complete Poems for Children* (1973) as his only original works that have remained in print, it is the least indicative of the three of his talent. The February 1962 *Horn Book* was muted in its praise: "Although there are some faltering lines and the book doesn't seem somehow necessary, the right ring of poetry sounds often enough." *Ragged Robin* is structured on the alphabet, with a poem for each letter. "Avalon," "Castles and Candlelight," and "Heroes on Horseback" suggest the prevailing subject matter, the promise of which is often betrayed by slack rhythms and sentimental musings. Although the sheer music of words is more subdued in this work, it nevertheless reveals through its imagery the charm and variety of Reeves's imagination.

In *Sailor Rumbelow and Other Stories* (1962) Reeves again used folktale motifs in original short stories told in a traditional idiom. "Sailor Rumbelow" is the poignant story of a tiny sailor in a ship in a bottle and a miniature maiden named Britannia inside a crystal globe who fall in love as they gaze at each other from inside their unbreakable containers on opposite sides of a parlor. "The Gnome Factory," which is one of his few stories that is set in modern times, sounds a favorite theme of humility rewarded. In a typical mood of sympathy for pastoralism and simplicity, Reeves contrasts Midas Pike's greedy ambition to erect "great blocks of offices" in the place where his tenant Mr. Turnbull operates a garden-ornament factory that doubles as a playground for the orphans living next door. Reeves also wrote "Foo the Potter" and "The Prince's Hunt" for this collection, but the remaining stories are all reprints from *Pigeons and Princesses*.

The Strange Light (1964) speaks to the book-loving child who would enjoy entering into a metaphorical speculation about the creative process and the ontology of fictional characters. In this longer novel for middle-grade readers, young Christina discovers a parallel world inhabited by people who are waiting to become characters in books. A violet light suffuses the faces of people who are being considered by writers in the "real" world, and acceptance by an author for inclusion in a story is seen as the fulfillment of their patient existence in a limbo where nothing much happens or changes from day to day. Conflict arises when a bully and his gang try to lead a strike, but Christina neutralizes the ruffians by persuading her uncle to write them into a story, thus removing them from the world of would-be characters. The concept carries the story, which moves swiftly from one event to another. Atmosphere and character development are neither attempted nor necessary to this clever and amusing narrative.

Also in 1964 Reeves published *The Story of Jackie Thimble* (1964), a story told in verse that features a sixteen-inch-tall boy who discovers a way to improve his family's desperate fortunes by singing for coins from inside a pillar box. The small size of the book complements the hero's small dimensions and combines with the shadowy black-and-white pictures to create an intimate experience for the reader. Ardizzone's illustrations reveal a virtuoso use of cross hatchings to cast a textured veil over each scene, underscoring the story's surreal qualities. Reeves's verse races along in time to the quick plot turns, despite one or two metrical missteps.

In the preface to *The James Reeves Story Book* Reeves credits Ardizzone for the idea that led to the publication of *Rhyming Will* (1967): "I treasured the idea and let it ripen in the back of my mind until it could be harvested." Will is a boy who speaks only in rhyme. Chased from his birthplace by philistine villagers, he runs off to London, where he attracts the Lord Mayor's attention. Commanded to recite an "Ode" for a visiting "Nabob," Will unexpectedly loses his poetic ability and instead presents a short, straightforward welcoming speech in prose. Reviled by the Lord Mayor and other guests, Will's unpretentious good sense is nevertheless rewarded by the ode-hating Nabob. The large picture-book format gives ample scope for Ardizzone's flowing lines and soft colors that emphasize the story's humor.

*Dust jacket for Reeves's young-readers' version of Miguel de
Cervantes's classic*

Pretentiousness is likewise gently mocked in *Mr. Horrox and the Gratch*. A fashion-conscious art dealer — appropriately named Mr. Smart — asks the unassuming middle-aged Mr. Horrox to stop painting "farmyards and cottage doors with roses around them" in order to accommodate the market's changing tastes. Obligingly, Mr. Horrox moves to a cottage in Scotland with the intention of painting "waterfalls, Highland cattle and pine trees in the sunset." Fortunately for his career, a mischievous spirit called a Gratch also lives in the cottage and begins to decorate Mr. Horrox's "lifelike" pictures with exciting scribbles. At first, the artist is annoyed, but his mood changes when Mr. Smart arrives and expresses delight. "But they're most *interesting* . . . I like that nervous line, and your tone values are strong." Mr. Horrox, whose lack of artistic inspiration is paralleled by his lack of vanity, is now pleased to hand over his creative tasks to the Gratch and assists him by choosing colors, supplying materials, and adding titles, which are in his accustomed realistic mode: "Harvest at Glen Barra," "Storm over the Loch," and the like. As in many other of Reeves's stories, humility earns its reward. Mr. Horrox begins to copy the Gratch's paintings and eventually surpasses his invisible teacher. His resulting exhibition "caused great excitement in the art world." Quentin Blake's cartoonlike illustrations capture the comically counterpoised expressions of the characters in moments of self-importance, bemusement, excitement, and contentment.

Complete Poems for Children reminded the public of Reeves's poetic accomplishments. It contains no new verses but brings together all the poems from *The Wandering Moon, The Blackbird in the Lilac, Prefabulous Animiles, Ragged Robin,* and *The Story of Jackie Thimble.* The 22 November 1973 *Times* hailed it for its "rhythms that sing in the memory and feelings that speak straight to the heart." Many of Ardizzone's illustrations from the original editions are included, and his work replaces the original illustrations by Evadne Rowan in *The Wandering Moon* as well as Jane Walsh's illustrations for *Ragged Robin.* Reeves finished his career as a children's poet with *More Prefabulous Animiles* in 1975. He and Ardizonne continued in the vein as *Prefabulous Animiles,* again sounding the delightful notes of nonsense, mischief, and wordplay.

Ardizzone's illustrations are largely responsible for the entrancing atmosphere that suffuses the picture book *The Lion That Flew* (1974). Two children living in Venice obtain a magic ring, climb on the back of a statue of a winged lion, and wish themselves into flight. They travel to London, intercept an art theft, and take the stolen painting back to Venice. There they turn the painting over to a British ambassador who returns it to London. Since the artwork is by the Venetian artist Canaletto, there is an ironic triple reference in the notion of stealing: the painting has in all probability been stolen from Italy by the British, is again stolen by a common thief, is stolen by the children from the thief, and is finally stolen back at the end — albeit with Italian acquiescence — by the British. The mood and emphasis of both text and pictures, however, is one of windswept magical delight, as the children swoop over radiantly majestic landscapes.

Like so much of Reeves's prose, *The Clever Mouse* (1976) evokes a folktale environment, set in "Persia long ago." It features a plucky mouse named Susa, who tricks a lazy gardener into killing a dragon that has taken over her favorite garden bower. Susa's titular cleverness turns out to involve considerable self-reliance and physical courage in this short, entertaining plot. The reader's enjoyment of Susa's resourcefulness, however, is puzzlingly undercut by the story's concluding lines. Susa exults, "Even if you aren't very big, you can often win by being clever." But her mother shakes "her wise head from side to side and [says] nothing." Barbara Swiderska's sweeping double-page illustrations wrap around and overlay the text, making this Reeves's most sophisticated-looking publication in terms of page design.

The James Reeves Story Book is a retrospective of Reeves's prose, reprinting stories selected from *Pigeons and Princesses, The Secret Shoemakers and Other Sto-* ries (1966), and *Three Tall Tales, Chosen from Traditional Sources* (1964). Although source notes are absent, it appears that some of the stories are retellings of traditional folk material, while others are original narratives in traditional style. "Rhyming Will" and "Sailor Rumbelow and Britannia" are also included, but unfortunately many of the original illustrations are omitted. Illustrations for many of the other stories, however, are produced in larger sizes, and indeed the evidence of Reeves's long and fruitful association with Ardizzone is apparent in the overall design of the book. The reviewer for the 29 September 1978 *Times Literary Supplement* praised it for its "musicality and precision of language, skilful construction of dramatic narrative, and unfailing ability of the writer to produce, in parallel with simple-seeming text, the resonances and reverberations appropriate to the folk idiom."

James Reeves died at the age of sixty-eight on 1 May 1978. The 9 May 1978 *Times* obituary praised him for "never produc[ing] a shoddy piece of work" and for setting himself "high standards . . . whether he was writing adult poems, children's books or anthologies of other poets' work." In a more stringent judgment, Martin Seymour-Smith, writing in *Contemporary Poets* (1975), remarks that "Reeves' poetry requires rigorous selection." Both comments are apposite to Reeves's writing for children. As a reteller, editor, and translator, he made an enormous amount of literature available to young readers, choosing his materials carefully and treating them always with respect, sometimes with brilliance. His prose and poetry styles mirror the values they espouse: craftsmanship, humor, and simplicity. As a collaborator with one of the twentieth century's greatest illustrators, he helped to demonstrate the imaginative eloquence that can result from the combination of complementary talents. Although his oeuvre has some weak moments, the best of his poems attain perfection in their musical declamation of nonsense, pastoral lyricism, and strong, sparkling imagery.

Ian Serraillier

(24 September 1912 – 28 November 1994)

Lois Rauch Gibson
Coker College

BOOKS: *Three New Poets,* by Serraillier, Roy Mc-
Fadden, and Alex Comfort (Billericay, Essex:
Grey Walls Press, 1942);

The Weaver Birds, illustrated by Serraillier (London:
Macmillan, 1944; New York: Macmillan,
1945);

Thomas and the Sparrow, illustrated by Mark Severin
(London: Oxford University Press, 1946);

They Raced for Treasure, illustrated by C. Walter
Hodges (London: Cape, 1946); abridged and
republished as *Treasure Ahead* (London:
Heinemann, 1954);

Flight to Adventure, illustrated by Hodges (London:
Cape, 1947); abridged and republished as
Mountain Rescue (London: Heinemann, 1955);

Captain Bounsaboard and the Pirates, illustrated by Michael Bartlett and Arline Braybrooke (Lon-
don: Cape, 1949);

The Tale of the Monster Horse, illustrated by Severin
(London: Oxford University Press, 1950);

There's No Escape, illustrated by Hodges (London:
Cape, 1950; New York: Scholastic, 1973);

The Ballad of Kon-Tiki and Other Verses, illustrated by
Severin (London: Oxford University Press,
1952);

Belinda and the Swans, illustrated by Pat Marriott
(London: Cape, 1952);

Jungle Adventure, illustrated by Vera Jarman (London: Heinemann, 1953);

The Adventures of Dick Varley, illustrated by Jarman
(London: Heinemann, 1954);

Beowulf the Warrior, illustrated by Severin (London:
Oxford University Press, 1954; New York:
Walck, 1961);

Making Good, illustrated by Jarman (London:
Heinemann, 1955);

Everest Climbed, illustrated by Leonard Rosoman
(London: Oxford University Press, 1955);

Guns in the Wild, illustrated by Shirley Hughes (London: Heinemann, 1956);

The Silver Sword, illustrated by Hodges (London:
Cape, 1956; New York: Criterion, 1959); re-

Ian Serraillier

published as *Escape from Warsaw* (New York:
Scholastic, 1963);

Katy at Home, illustrated by Hughes (London:
Heinemann, 1957);

Poems and Pictures, illustrated by Severin, Hughes,
and others (London: Heinemann, 1958);

A Puffin Quartet of Poets, by Serraillier, Eleanor
Farjeon, James Reeves, and E. V. Rieu, edited
by Eleanor Graham, and illustrated by Diana
Bloomfield (London: Penguin, 1958);

Katy at School, illustrated by Hughes (London:
Heinemann, 1959);

The Ivory Horn: Retold from the Song of Roland,
illustrated by William Stobbs (London: Oxford University Press, 1960);

The Gorgon's Head: The Story of Perseus, illustrated by
Stobbs (London: Oxford University Press,
1961; New York: Walck, 1962);

The Windmill Book of Ballads, illustrated by Severin
and Rosoman (London: Heinemann, 1962);

The Way of Danger: The Story of Theseus, illustrated by Stobbs (London: Oxford University Press, 1962; New York: Walck, 1963);

Happily Ever After: Poems for Children, illustrated by Brian Wildsmith (London: Oxford University Press, 1963);

The Clashing Rocks: The Story of Jason, illustrated by Stobbs (London: Oxford University Press, 1963; New York: Walck, 1964);

The Midnight Thief, music by Richard Rodney Bennett, illustrated by Tellosa (London: BBC, 1963);

The Enchanted Island: Stories from Shakespeare, illustrated by Peter Farmer (London: Oxford University Press, 1964; New York: Walck, 1964); abridged and republished as *Murder at Dunsinane* (New York: Scholastic, 1967);

The Cave of Death, illustrated by Stuart Tresilian (London: Heinemann, 1965);

Fight for Freedom, illustrated by John S. Goodall (London: Heinemann, 1965);

Ahmet the Woodseller, music by Gordon Crosse, illustrated by John Griffiths (London: BBC, 1965);

A Fall from the Sky: The Story of Daedalus, illustrated by Stobbs (London: Nelson, 1966; New York: Walck, 1966);

The Challenge of the Green Knight, illustrated by Victor Ambrus (London: Oxford University Press, 1966; New York: Walck, 1967);

Robin in the Greenwood, illustrated by Ambrus (London: Oxford University Press, 1967; New York: Walck, 1968);

Chaucer and His World (London: Lutterworth, 1967; New York: Walck, 1968);

The Turtle Drum, music by Malcolm Arnold, illustrated by Charles Pickard (London: BBC, 1967);

Havelok the Dane, illustrated by Elaine Raphael (New York: Walck, 1967); republished as *Havelok the Warrior* (London: Hamish Hamilton, 1968);

Robin and His Merry Men, illustrated by Ambrus (London: Oxford University Press, 1969; New York: Walck, 1970);

The Tale of Three Landlubbers, illustrated by Raymond Briggs (London: Hamish Hamilton, 1970; New York: Coward-McCann, 1971);

Heracles the Strong, illustrated by Rocco Negri (New York: Walck, 1970; London: Hamish Hamilton, 1971);

The Ballad of St. Simeon, illustrated by Simon Stern (London: Kaye & Ward, 1970; New York: Watts, 1970);

A Pride of Lions, music by Phyllis Tate, illustrated by Joanna Troughton (London: Oxford University Press, 1971);

The Bishop and the Devil, illustrated by Stern (London: Kaye & Ward, 1971; New York: Warne, 1971);

Have You Got Your Ticket?, illustrated by Douglas Hall (London: Longman, 1972);

Marko's Wedding, illustrated by Ambrus (London: Deutsch, 1972);

The Franklin's Tale, illustrated by Philip Gough (London: Kaye & Ward, 1972; New York: Warne, 1972);

I'll Tell You a Tale: A Collection of Poems and Ballads, illustrated by Charles Keeping and Renate Meyer (London: Longman, 1973; revised edition, London: Kestrel, 1976);

Pop Festival, illustrated by Hall (London: Longman, 1973);

Suppose You Met a Witch, illustrated by Ed Emberley (Boston: Little, Brown, 1973);

The Robin and the Wren, illustrated by Fritz Wegner (London: Kestrel, 1974);

How Happily She Laughs and Other Poems (London: Longman, 1976);

The Sun Goes Free (London: Longman, 1977);

The Road to Canterbury, illustrated by John Lawrence (London: Kestrel, 1979);

All Change at Singleton: For Charlton, Goodwood, East and West Dean (London: Phillimore, 1979);

Goodwood Country in Old Photographs, by Serraillier and Richard Pailthorpe (Gloucester: Sutton, 1987);

The Mouse in the Wainscot, illustrated by Giora Carmi (Chicago: Contemporary Books, 1988).

OTHER: *The New Windmill Series,* more than 400 volumes to date, edited by Ian and Anne Serraillier (London: Heinemann, 1950–   );

Selina Chonz, *Florina and the Wild Bird,* translated by Ian and Anne Serraillier, illustrated by Alois Carigiet (London: Oxford University Press, 1952);

Wide Horizon Reading Series, 4 volumes, edited by Serraillier and Ronald Ridout (London: Heinemann, 1953–1955);

"Ian Serraillier," in *Third Book of Junior Authors* (New York: Wilson, 1972);

"Poetry Mosaic: Some Reflections on Writing Verse for Children," in *The Thorny Paradise: Writers on Writing for Children,* edited by Edward Blishen (Harmondsworth: Kestrel, 1975), pp. 97–102;

*Beowulf battles Grendel's mother; illustration by Mark Severin from
Serraillier's* Beowulf the Warrior *(1954)*

"Ian Serraillier," in *Something About the Author Autobi-
    ography Series,* volume 3 (Detroit: Gale Re-
    search, 1987), pp. 247–262;

"Greats, English and Appendicitis," in *Hall-Memoirs
    of St. Edmund Hall Graduates 1920–1980,* edited
    by Alan Jenkins (London: Farrand, 1989), pp.
    47–50.

Ian Lucien Serraillier enjoyed a long career as
a respected writer, editor, and reteller of tales for
children. He is frequently praised in histories and
textbooks of children's literature for bringing renewed life and vigor to the myths and legends of
Greece, Rome, and England. His poetry and prose
retellings are recommended for their subtle, sophisticated style and their enticing readability. First
published as a poet and later known primarily for
those highly praised children's versions of classical
hero tales, Serraillier has a reputation that now rests
even more solidly on the award-winning book *The
Silver Sword* (1956), a tale of four Polish children
surviving World War II.

Serraillier was born in London on 24 September 1912, the first child of Lucien and Mary Rodger
Serraillier. He began school near Hampstead Heath,
where his family lived, but his father died in the
great influenza epidemic of 1919. Soon afterward he
went to a boarding prep school in Sussex, and by
1926 he and his brother Antony were both boarders
at Brighton College, also in Sussex. Serraillier has
said in autobiographical essays that he never liked
being a boarder and that he did little reading as a
child. Yet he always knew he wanted to be a writer,
in spite of the steady diet of what he calls "dry and

rather indigestible" Greek and Latin verse he was made to read and write at school.

Meanwhile, his mother, who suffered from asthma, had begun to spend much of the year in the Swiss Alps. The children joined her for school holidays. As the oldest, Serraillier was responsible for taking his younger siblings – Antony, Rosemary, and Michael – through France by train to Switzerland. In her afterword for the 1993 Puffin Modern Classics edition of *The Silver Sword* Serraillier's daughter Jane Serraillier Grossfeld reports that these trips filled her father with great anxiety; they may well have been his source for Ruth Balicki's feelings in *The Silver Sword* as she leads her siblings on the difficult wartime journey from Poland to Switzerland.

But the Swiss holidays brought great joy and relief to the Serraillier children. Not only were they free of the eternal Greek and Latin, but also their mother allowed them much independence. They loved the mountains, and both "mountain walking" and skiing long remained favorite pastimes for Serraillier. In his 1987 *Something About the Author Autobiography Series* essay he notes that, though he no longer climbed the Matterhorn, he was "content with the view from lesser hills nearer to home."

Serraillier first climbed the Matterhorn at age sixteen with his fifteen-year-old brother, Antony, and a guide. Soon afterward he wrote an account of this experience for a climbing magazine; he adapted that article for his 1987 autobiographical essay. As vivid and exciting as any of his fictional adventure tales, it also reads exceedingly well aloud.

Though Serraillier may have felt constrained by the rigid curriculum of his boarding-school days, he admitted that it gave him "an excellent formal training and a sound discipline in language structure, particularly verse technique." It also no doubt helped develop a feel for language that makes his prose as appealing as his verse to the ear.

Serraillier's ear for language also led him to clarify the pronunciation of his unusual surname. At the end of an autobiographical sketch in the *Third Book of Junior Authors* (1972) he tells readers, "My name, Serraillier, is pronounced: SER (as in *ser*pent), and if you rhyme the rest with *Australia* you won't go far wrong."

Though his classical education laid the foundation for his future career as poet and reteller of ancient tales, Serraillier abandoned his study of classics in favor of English shortly after entering Saint Edmund Hall, Oxford. He relished the new freedom of university life, explored diverse paths in life and thought, and discovered the literature of his own country – to which he had had minimal exposure before. These studies led later to his children's versions of the tenth-century Old English poem *Beowulf,* Geoffrey Chaucer's tales, William Shakespeare's plays, and the earlier legends and romances of Gawain, Havelok, and Robin Hood.

He continued to spend holidays in Switzerland, and his first job after completing his degree was teaching English at an international school on Lake Geneva. He continued teaching English for many years thereafter at various schools in England. His first permanent position (1936–1939) was at Wycliffe College, a boys' boarding school in Gloucestershire. In 1940 he moved to Dudley Grammar School in industrial Worcestershire, where he met his future wife and editorial collaborator, Anne Margaret Rogers. She and her younger sister, daughters of the physics master, were students at a nearby girls' school. Later Anne studied French and German at Cambridge; upon her return to Worcestershire in 1944, she and Serraillier were married at the Quaker Meeting House in Stourbridge.

As a Quaker and a pacifist, Serraillier refused to fight in World War II. On 5 November 1940 Serraillier convinced a government tribunal of the sincerity of his convictions and was granted conscientious-objector status, providing that he perform Air Raid Precautions work, loan his car to the Friends Ambulance Unit, and continue teaching English.

During his years at Dudley, Serraillier also published his first books of poetry. In *Three New Poets* (1942) Serraillier's work appeared with that of Roy McFadden and Alex Comfort in a collection for adults. In 1944 he published his first book of poems for adults and children, *The Weaver Birds.* Several poems from that collection have since appeared as parts of picture books such as *The Ballad of St. Simeon* (1970) and *The Bishop and the Devil* (1971), both illustrated by Simon Stern and generally reviewed as sophisticated fare for reading aloud to stretch children's minds and vocabularies.

After the birth of their first child, the Serrailliers in 1946 moved to Sussex, which became the family's permanent home. Serraillier taught until 1961 at Midhurst Grammar School, where his four children – Helen, Jane, Anne, and Andrew – were educated. By then his success as a writer and editor allowed him to devote himself fully to those occupations.

Between 1946 and 1961 Serraillier established himself as a poet, a masterful reteller of classics, and a writer of original adventure stories. In addition to his 1942 and 1944 poetry collections Serraillier published *The Tale of the Monster Horse* (1950) for children, inspirational poems for older children and adults in *The Ballad of Kon-Tiki and Other Verses* (1952), and a collection of children's narrative poetry called *Belinda and the Swans* (1952). (A poem in this last collection became the basis for the 1973 Ed Emberley picture book, *Suppose You Met a Witch.*) In 1958 Serraillier's work was included in *A Puffin Quartet of Poets,* which is described on its back cover as including selections from "four of our finest writers of children's verse."

In 1954 Serraillier produced what would become one of his most enduring contributions to children's literature, a retelling in blank verse of the Old English epic poem *Beowulf.* Admired by scholars and publishers, it remains available on both sides of the Atlantic. Focusing on the three battles between Beowulf and the monsters (Grendel, Grendel's mother, and the fire dragon), Serraillier captures the grandeur and the precariousness of existence in the human world of Danes, Geats, and Swedes. Using alliteration, metaphor, and vivid imagery, Serraillier brings to life the magnificence of King Hrothgar's court: the mead hall, with its "gleaming roof / Towering high to heaven − strong to withstand / The buffet of war"; Queen Wealtheow, in her "gown of broidered gold . . . behind her / a long train, dark as the night, / Illumined with galaxy of stars that, as she glided / Forward to greet her guests, trembled in the torchlight"; and finally Hrothgar's riches − "bright hangings of woven gold," "jeweled goblets," and "soft couches, pillow-strewn, / With fleeces of thick wool."

Serraillier also creates tension and excitement in each of the battle scenes as he describes the terrifying monsters. As Grendel's mother batters Beowulf before he defeats her, Serraillier writes:

In a trice, up she reared
Her shaggy frame and, grappling, squashed him
    down.
Then, like a dizzy sailor trapped in the shrouds
When sea and heaven swing sickening past
As a sudden wave, topheavy, grinds him down
Into the whirl clinging madly, yet struggling
All the while to fight free − so Beowulf
Under the whelming monster was prisoned fast.

The story is riveting; Serraillier's version − a retelling, not a translation − eliminates most of the historical matter yet captures the essence of the original. Lydia Reynolds reported in the Spring 1994 *In Review* that she held the rapt attention of children as

Dust jacket for Serraillier's version of the Greek myth of Perseus

young as four years old during several read-aloud sessions.

Many of Serraillier's other retellings of classics are in vivid, readable prose. The words *strong, forceful, vigorous, clear, direct,* and *lively* resound in critical descriptions of such prose retellings as *The Gorgon's Head: The Story of Perseus* (1961), *The Clashing Rocks: The Story of Jason* (1963), *A Fall from the Sky: The Story of Daedalus* (1966), and *Havelok the Dane* (1967).

In addition to retelling classical adventures Serraillier wrote some original adventure tales. The first, *They Raced for Treasure* (1946), Serraillier himself calls tightly plotted but "conventional"; in its sequel, *Flight to Adventure* (1947), Serraillier makes an exception to his usual practice and incorporates into his adventure some of his childhood experiences in the Swiss Alps. *There's No Escape* (1950) is also set in the Alps, in a fictitious country called Silvania, into which young hero Peter Howarth is sent by parachute to rescue a brilliant older scientist before the enemy can force him to reveal secrets. Somewhat banal by modern standards, all three of the books are exciting nonetheless. But with the fourth in this series, Serraillier achieved the greatest success of his career.

The Silver Sword is a well-crafted, sensitive historical novel that has been translated into at least a dozen languages and continues to appear in new editions. It was dramatized by the BBC (1957) and by Stuart Henson, whose *The Play of the Silver Sword* was first performed at the Coliseum Theatre in Oldham in 1983. Many school and professional productions have followed.

This story of the Balicki family of Warsaw documents their struggle to survive and to reunite during and just after World War II. When the story begins, Joseph Balicki, a schoolmaster like Serraillier, has been taken away by the Nazis for having turned Hitler's picture to the wall during a scripture lesson. Soon troopers also come for his Swiss wife, Margrit, leaving Ruth (thirteen), her brother, Edek (eleven), and their three-year-old sister, Bronia, to fend for themselves.

The novel took Serraillier five years to complete. When he began his research in 1951 he was still teaching at Midhurst, so he wrote only during holidays, taking great care to make his details accurate. Though he had not left England during the war, he collected descriptions of events and people from contemporary sources such as the *Picture Post,* a popular British photographic magazine featuring pictures of war-devastated cities and countrysides, as well as the Pestalozzi children's village for war orphans in Switzerland. He also studied Red Cross case histories of refugees and UNESCO publications about the effects of the war on children. His child characters were based on the experiences of real people in these files, though the originals were not real-life siblings. According to Serraillier's daughter Jane, her father used as a plot book a hard-backed school notebook into which he had taped magazine articles about ruined cities; children stealing food from goods trains or living in abandoned cellars; and other children whose drawings, like Bronia's, depicted the scenes around them. Also in the plot book are sketches of war zones and of canoes, perhaps remembered from his own prewar trips along the Danube.

Despite its realism, or perhaps because of it, the book was not immediately popular. Early critics wondered if it was too harsh for children. When it was made into a BBC television series in 1957, some viewers complained that war in general – and this war in particular – was not appropriate television fare for children. But in his 1987 autobiographical essay Serraillier quotes the German artist Horst

Loreck, whose firsthand experiences led to authentic, moving illustrations in a German edition of *The Silver Sword:* "Those were terrible times, and we must never allow them to happen again." Serraillier adds, "The war and its devastating aftereffects, including the suffering of families separated from their loved ones, are always there in my story. But so are courage, hope, humour, resourcefulness and human kindness."

Several generations of readers have agreed. Despite its complex narrative, the story's tale of love and determination in the face of overwhelming obstacles has maintained its status as one of the foremost World War II books for children. The narrative begins with Joseph Balicki's story and follows him through his daring escape from a prison camp to a return to Warsaw, a chance meeting with the orphan boy/pickpocket Jan, and his departure for Switzerland to seek his wife. Then it shifts to the story of his children, from the time that their mother is taken from them, through their struggles to survive, and to their chance meeting with Jan, whose eventually awakened memory of meeting Joseph starts them on their quest to find their parents in Switzerland.

In telling the story of the Balicki family Serraillier interweaves pain and joy, fatigue and determination, and a panoply of other conflicting emotions. These contribute to his convincing portrayal of a wartime life that demands acceptance of ordinarily unthinkable deprivations and humiliations but also produces calmly heroic acts. Soup kitchens, garbage bins, and begging are the children's preferred sources of food, but they also steal from the Nazis, a dangerous last resort. Edek begins helping peasants smuggle food to the black market; after he is caught and sent away, Ruth and Bronia must struggle alone amid increasing devastation and fear for their brother. Ruth organizes a school for war orphans in an abandoned cellar and is forced to turn children away, so hungry are so many for a semblance of normalcy. Throughout, the children remain determined to endure – and to reunite their family.

This determination increases after they adopt the boy Jan, a complex creation of this war: simultaneously a wily pickpocket, a pugnacious hater of all in uniform, and a vulnerable child, Jan elects himself Ruth's protector and considers her his mother after she nurses him to health. When they recognize the small paper silver sword among Jan's treasures, Jan remembers receiving it from Joseph Balicki, a memory that the struggle to survive has temporarily erased. The knowledge that their father has gone to

Switzerland in search of their mother renews their hope and reopens their quest.

Jane Serraillier Grossfeld suggests that the search for the father is a recurrent theme in her father's work, perhaps a result of his own early loss. Certainly it is a central concern in *The Silver Sword.* Edek, Ruth, and Bronia ultimately find their parents, but Jan must substitute their parents for his own, of whom all trace is lost.

Several of the book's most humorous and most moving scenes involve Jan. His love of animals leads him to tame an escaped chimpanzee in a funny and heartwarming episode; his scrawny pet rooster's death in a children's stampede for a morsel of spilled food hovers between pathos and tragedy. But neither Jan nor the reader has time to linger over this sorrow, as the children discover their lost brother, Edek, among the hungry throng.

Neither their finding of Edek nor other seeming coincidences undermines the book's realism, because all such "luck" comes after many setbacks, much hard work, and relentless ingenuity. Even the "happy ending" in Switzerland comes only after a near-death encounter with a storm and the sacrifice of Jan's dog. Furthermore, all of the children must heal gradually after the war: Edek must recover from tuberculosis (though the child on whom he was modeled had died); Ruth must learn to have a mother after having been one for so long; and Jan must learn to stop stealing, hurting, and hating.

Perhaps the greatest strength of *The Silver Sword* is Serraillier's realistic portrayal of complex events and people. Despite hunger some people continue to share; and, though the Nazis are the enemies, the loving German farm couple who rescue the children explain that their own two sons, who were not evil people, had nonetheless died as Nazi soldiers.

When *The Silver Sword* was first published in the United States, it was retitled *Escape from Warsaw,* lest people mistakenly assume it is set in the Middle Ages. Under either title it remains among the most profound children's novels about war. If Serraillier's goal as a Quaker was to underscore the sense-

lessness and immorality of war, and the ability of the human spirit to prevail, he has succeeded admirably.

Though *The Silver Sword* and *Beowulf the Warrior* remain Serraillier's best-known publications, many of his other books frequently reappear in print. In 1988 an early poem, "The Mouse in the Wainscot," was illustrated under that title in board-book form for toddlers, and many of his classical retellings remain widely available.

In 1950 Serraillier and his wife founded and began coediting the New Windmill series, an enterprise in which his wife remains involved for Heinemann Educational Books. The series makes available to schools affordable hardback editions of novels of such caliber as John Steinbeck's *Of Mice and Men* (1937) and Erich Maria Remarque's *All Quiet on the Western Front* (1929). Serraillier's daughter Jane has described this series as one of her parents' most valuable literary contributions.

Serraillier continued to live in Sussex until his death on 28 November 1994, from complications of Alzheimer's disease. Among his last literary enterprises were books of local history for adults, *All Change at Singleton: For Charlton, Goodwood, and East and West Dean* (1979) and *Goodwood Country in Old Photographs* (1987), the latter of which he wrote with Richard Pailthorpe. But future generations of children are likely to know him as poet, teller, and reteller of tales – and his lasting reputation as a distinguished writer for children remains secure in *Beowulf the Warrior* and *The Silver Sword.*

References:

Marcus Crouch, *The Nesbit Tradition: The Children's Novel in England 1945–1970* (London: Benn, 1972), pp. 26–30, 180;

Carolyn T. Kingston, *The Tragic Mode in Children's Literature* (New York: Teachers College, 1974), pp. 102–105;

John Rowe Townsend, *Written for Children: An Outline of English-Language Children's Literature* (New York: Lothrop, 1965), pp. 114–117.

Margery Sharp

(25 January 1905 – 14 March 1991)

Elizabeth C. Overmyer

BOOKS: *Rhododendron Pie* (London: Chatto & Windus, 1930; New York: Appleton, 1930);

Fanfare for Tin Trumpets (London: Barker, 1932; New York: Putnam, 1933);

The Nymph and the Nobleman (London: Barker, 1932);

The Flowering Thorn (London: Barker, 1933; New York: Putnam, 1934);

Sophy Cassmajor (London: Barker, 1934; New York: Putnam, 1934);

Four Gardens (London: Barker, 1935; New York: Putnam, 1935);

The Nutmeg Tree (London: Barker, 1937; Boston: Little, Brown, 1937);

Harlequin House (London: Collins, 1939; Boston: Little, Brown, 1939);

The Stone of Chastity (London: Collins, 1940; Boston: Little, Brown, 1940);

Three Companion Pieces (Boston: Little, Brown, 1941);

Lady in Waiting: A Comedy, play adaptation of *The Nutmeg Tree* (New York: French, 1941);

Cluny Brown (London: Collins, 1944; Boston: Little, Brown, 1944);

Britannia Mews (London: Collins, 1946; Boston: Little, Brown, 1946);

The Foolish Gentlewoman (London: Collins, 1948; Boston: Little, Brown, 1948);

The Foolish Gentlewoman: A Play in Three Acts (London: French, 1950);

Lise Lillywhite (London: Collins, 1951; Boston: Little, Brown, 1951);

The Gipsy in the Parlour (London: Collins, 1953; Boston: Little, Brown, 1954);

The Tigress on the Hearth (London: Collins, 1955);

The Eye of Love (London: Collins, 1957; Boston: Little, Brown, 1957); republished as *Martha and the Eye of Love* (London: New English Library, 1969);

The Rescuers: A Fantasy (London: Collins, 1959; Boston: Little, Brown, 1959);

Melisande (London: Collins, 1960; Boston: Little, Brown, 1960);

Something Light (London: Collins, 1960; Boston: Little, Brown, 1961);

Miss Bianca: A Fantasy (London: Collins, 1962; Boston: Little, Brown, 1962);

Martha in Paris (London: Collins, 1962; Boston: Little, Brown, 1962);

The Turret (Boston: Little, Brown, 1963; London: Collins, 1964);

Martha, Eric, and George (London: Collins, 1964; Boston: Little, Brown, 1964);

The Sun in Scorpio (London: Heinemann, 1965; Boston: Little, Brown, 1965);

Lost at the Fair (Boston: Little, Brown, 1965; London: Heinemann, 1967);

Miss Bianca in the Salt Mines (London: Heinemann, 1966; Boston: Little, Brown, 1966);

In Pious Memory (Boston: Little, Brown, 1967; London: Heinemann, 1967);

Rosa (London: Heinemann, 1969; Boston: Little, Brown, 1970);

Miss Bianca in the Orient (London: Heinemann, 1970; Boston: Little, Brown, 1970);

Miss Bianca in the Antarctic (London: Heinemann, 1970; Boston: Little, Brown, 1971);

The Innocents (London: Heinemann, 1971; Boston: Little, Brown, 1972);

Miss Bianca and the Bridesmaid (London: Heinemann, 1972; Boston: Little, Brown, 1972);

The Lost Chapel Picnic, and Other Stories (London: Heinemann, 1973; Boston: Little, Brown, 1973);

The Magical Cockatoo (London: Heinemann, 1974);

The Children Next Door (London: Heinemann, 1974);

Margery Sharp

The Faithful Servants (London: Heinemann, 1975;
Boston: Little, Brown, 1975);

Bernard the Brave: A Miss Bianca Story (London:
Heinemann, 1976; Boston: Little, Brown,
1977);

Summer Visits (London: Heinemann, 1977; Boston:
Little, Brown, 1978);

Bernard into Battle (Boston: Little, Brown, 1978; London: Heinemann, 1979).

PLAY PRODUCTIONS: *Meeting at Night,* London,
Globe Theatre, 14 June 1934;

Lady in Waiting, adapted from the novel *The Nutmeg
Tree,* New York, Martin Beck Theatre, 27
March 1940; produced as *The Nutmeg Tree,*
London, Lyric Theatre, 9 October 1941;

The Foolish Gentlewoman, London, Duchess Theatre,
23 February 1949.

Margery Sharp was a writer who successfully
challenged the line that so often divides children's
books from adults'. She had been writing for adults
for more than thirty years before her first book for
children, *The Rescuers,* was published in 1959. It was
reviewed for both adults and young readers and

was followed by eight more volumes, which together became known as the Miss Bianca series.
The heroine of these fantasies is the elegant white
mouse Miss Bianca, who leads her cohorts in the
Mouse Prisoners' Aid Society to daring rescues
around the world. The books were popular in both
children's and general collections of public libraries
and can still be enjoyed by readers of all ages who
relish their scenes of high adventure, witty characterization, and social commentary.

Margery Sharp was born on 25 January 1905
in Malta, the third daughter of J. H. Sharp. In a
brief article published in the March 1958 *Ladies'
Home Journal* she remembers having blotted her
copybook in kindergarten: "I was kept in to write
twenty times, 'I must not play with ink.' I have been
playing with ink ever since." Her first work was
published before she entered the university, as she
recalled her earliest efforts for interviewer Roy
Newquist in 1964:

I started writing in the classic way – poetry, or rather
verse – and I can remember that my first published
poem was on that extremely classic subject, "The
Moon." I was in the sixth form in high school (that is,
here, the top form). I used to write these verses to fill up

magazines. You know, a short story very rarely ends exactly at the bottom of a page. There's a gap of three or four inches, and the editors at that time were always willing to buy a poem to fill in. I was paid ten and sixpence, half a guinea, for each. For a high school student this is a very rewarding sum, at least it was when I was doing it.

Sharp graduated from Streatham Hill High School and attended Bedford College, London University, where she received a B.A. degree with honors in French. Like Miss Bianca, who also speaks flawless French, the young Margery Sharp traveled widely and in 1929 was a member of the first women's debating team from the British universities to visit the United States. In her obituary reminiscence quoted in the London *Times* Sharp describes herself as the team's third speaker, the one who "made her audiences laugh, where the opening speakers tended to be . . . weighty." This was the first of several trips to the United States, where she has always had a strong readership. Although a few of her books appeared first in the United States, most were published simultaneously in both the United States and Great Britain.

In the year after her debating team trip Sharp's first novel, *Rhododendron Pie* (1930), was published. In 1938 she was married in New York to Maj. Geoffrey L. Castle, who became an aeronautical engineer after World War II. Except for a brief stint during the war, when Sharp was a teacher for the Armed Forces Education Program and her husband an artillery major, she continued to be a fulltime writer living in London. They had no children.

Sharp's work for adult readers reached a large audience in both the United States and Great Britain. Her short stories appeared frequently in both American and British magazines such as *Harper's Bazaar, Collier's, Saturday Evening Post, Ladies' Home Journal, Good Housekeeping, Strand,* and *Punch.* Her novels *Cluny Brown* (1944), *The Foolish Gentlewoman* (1948), and *The Gipsy in the Parlour* (1953) were serialized in American women's magazines. During the 1940s *Cluny Brown, Britannia Mews* (1946), and *The Foolish Gentlewoman* were Book-of-the-Month Club selections – and the first and last of these three, along with *The Nutmeg Tree* (1937), were adapted for motion picture production. In 1934 Sharp's first play, *Meeting at Night,* was produced in London, and both *The Nutmeg Tree* and *The Foolish Gentlewoman* also appeared as play productions.

Sharp's adult novels were known for their quirky and endearing heroines such as Cluny Brown, whose hobby is plumbing, and Julia, who in *The Nutmeg Tree* first appears singing in the bath –

to which she has retreated to avoid bill collectors. Sharp's gift for deft and witty writing was accompanied by a perceptive view of people, and her adult novels and stories not only entertain but comment tartly on society.

These qualities are equally evident in the Miss Bianca books, the first of which, *The Rescuers: A Fantasy,* was published in 1959. It was apparently written for adults, for its *Booklist* review comments: "Published as an adult book, this beguiling fantasy is likely to be most enjoyed by children and adults reading to children." Virginia Haviland, writing in *Horn Book,* also notes that "Many line drawings . . . make this volume look like a children's book; the text . . . has no audience limitation." However it was originally perceived, there was never any doubt that it would attract a dual readership. Critics recognized that the subject matter and (in the American edition) the enchanting illustrations by Garth Williams made it a natural choice for family readalouds, while the sophistication of the language and Miss Bianca's sharp observations would delight adults. In a 1964 interview Sharp described her own delight and authorial aims in writing her Miss Bianca books:

> I enjoy writing them immensely because they are a complete release of the imagination. The first of the Miss Bianca series was called *The Rescuers.* It was about the Prisoners' Aid Association of Mice – mice are traditionally the prisoner's friend, you know – so I described how the organization works with all its branches in different countries, the basic idea being the cheering of prisoners in their cells. You might say that it's national service stuff all mice go through. But there are adventures when they feel prisoners have been wrongly imprisoned and should be released. It's fascinating to me, and I hope to the people who read the books.

Sharp establishes in this first Miss Bianca book a framework that would prove flexible enough to serve her well for the rest of the series. The Mouse Prisoners' Aid Society (M.P.A.S.) has a daring first mission – to rescue a young Norwegian poet from the grim Black Castle. To direct this mission, the Society turns to an unexpected figure: Miss Bianca.

> Everyone knew who Miss Bianca was, but none had ever seen her.
>
> What was *known* was that she was a white mouse belonging to the Ambassador's son and lived in the schoolroom at the Embassy. Apart from that, there were the most fantastic rumors about her: for instance, that she lived in a Porcelain Pagoda; that she fed exclusively on cream cheese from a silver bonbon dish; that she

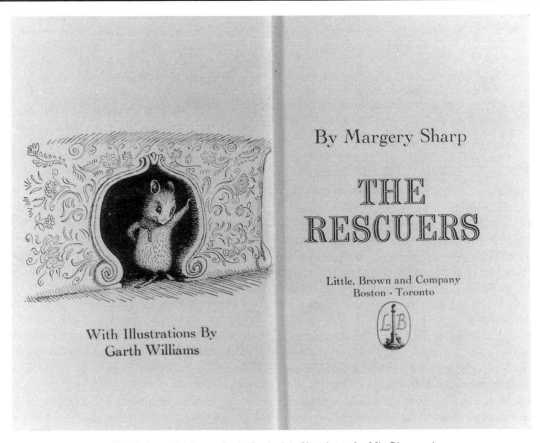

Frontispiece and title page for the first book in Sharp's popular Miss Bianca series

wore a silver chain round her neck, and on Sundays a gold one. She was also said to be extremely beautiful, but affected to the last degree.

Most of these rumors are true, but Miss Bianca also has a great capacity to rise to the occasion, whether it be a social challenge, a physical hardship, or both. In *The Rescuers* her initial response to the rescue plan is to faint, but upon recovering, she not only uses the diplomatic pouch to travel to Norway and recruit a Norwegian mouse, Nils, but accompanies him and the stalwart M.P.A.S. volunteer, Bernard, on the perilous trip. The escape is hair-raising to the end, but Sharp also provides periods of relief — as when the three mice settle into domesticity, inside the only mousehole in the castle, and hold regular meetings of the Prisoners' Aid Society. Miss Bianca's impeccable manners and her penchant for writing poetry stand in sharp contrast to the hardships of the trip and the roughness of her companions: Bernard is a humble pantry mouse, and Nils a rough-and-tumble adventurer. The relationship between Miss Bianca and Bernard is one of the enduring features of the series,

for as it continues Bernard remains loyal and hopeful, Miss Bianca ever more unattainable.

The stylish plot is distinguished by equally stylish writing: its inventive details of rescue, sharpness of dialogue, and skillful combination of anthropomorphic and truly mouselike characterizations are maintained to a surprising degree throughout the series. The writing is formal; Sharp selects her words as precisely as Miss Bianca approaches her projects. While children will relish the robust adventure and such details of mouse life as postage-stamp carpets or wallpaper made from chewing-gum wrappers, the books are also full of more-sophisticated humor. Literary and historical allusions abound, both in the dialogue (Madam Chairwoman quotes Suckling) and in Miss Bianca's own poems. The social interactions of the characters are affectionately described, yet with an appreciative eye for their humor.

While the Heinemann edition is illustrated by Faith Brooks, readers of all ages have appreciated the Garth Williams illustrations for the Little, Brown edition published in the United States, and Williams's illustrations appeared in both the English and American editions of the next three Miss Bianca series titles. As Margery Sharp remarked to Newquist,

> I think a great deal of the success has been due to Garth Williams' illustrations. His technique is marvelous, but he shows the most wonderfully sympathetic imagination. For example, in one place I describe the chairman's chair as being made from walnut shells, so Garth Williams carpentered a walnut shell into a chair and then drew it. . . .

Sharp's comments were overly modest. Even without Garth Williams's illustrations, *The Rescuers* was placed on the Commended List for the Carnegie Medal and in the United States on the honor list by *Horn Book*. The book was generally well received by critics. Writing in the *San Francisco Chronicle* on 20 November 1959, William Hogan hailed it as "a 'mouse book' the way Kenneth Grahame's *The Wind in the Willows* was a 'mole book' or a 'rat book.' " Dan Wickenden for the *New York Herald Tribune* commented in a 27 December 1959 book review that "Perils beset the writing of such a work, but Miss Sharp accomplishes her mission. She has no trouble in persuading us to suspend belief; her mice, despite their human characteristics, remain intrinsically mouselike, and are engaging individuals as well; the pitfalls of archness on the one hand or pretentious symbolism on the other are nimbly avoided. We read with delight, and even with excitement, a good tale told for its own sake."

In the next year Margery Sharp published two more titles, one of which, *Melisande* (1960), is occasionally listed as a children's book. However, despite its extensive illustrations, it is a curiosity for adults. The wordless novel is told in double-page, black-and-white, cartoonlike illustrations by Roy McKie, and Sharp's only contribution is in the four-page foreword, which fills in details of the plot. Melisande is a dog who progresses from selling violets outside an opera hall to performing successfully six months later in the role of Mimi in Giacomo Puccini's *La Bohème* (1896). Retiring early, she finds happiness singing on the streets with a Salvation Army band. Poking obvious fun at the 1956 musical *My Fair Lady,* the brief text and more than seventy pages of pictures are full of knowing references to the opera and other high-society interests.

After the success of *The Rescuers,* Sharp waited two years before publishing a sequel, *Miss Bianca: A Fantasy* (1962). Its child readers find a sympathetic victim in eight-year-old Patience, who has been pressed into service by a cruel Grand Duchess. Through a masterful combination of flattery and manipulation, Miss Bianca rouses the Ladies' Guild of the Prisoners' Aid Society to join the rescue party. The drilling of the ladies under the stern and bracing leadership of the games mistress is memorably depicted, and wonderfully witty scenes show the games mistress trying to save face when the Ladies' Guild returns alone, leaving Miss Bianca alone to effect the rescue. None of the mice is particularly thrilled about rescuing a little girl, for "little girls are fond of kittens."

As in the first Miss Bianca book, much of the humor comes from the contrast between large and small. Although Miss Bianca is compared to Napoleon and the Duke of Wellington in formal, mock-heroic style, the reader is never allowed to forget that she and her supporters are mice. The heroics are not allowed to become too tiresome, as practicality is as much an earmark of the rescue as bravery – a good counterbalance to Miss Bianca's extraordinary good manners, her practice of which occasionally passes from diplomacy to affectation. (As Nils had remarked to Bernard in the preceding *The Rescuers,* "She *can,* you know, be just a bit of a nuisance.")

Characterization is achieved largely through Sharp's gift for humorous and revealing dialogue. Miss Bianca sways an audience by eloquence, often expressing her deepest feelings in slightly pretentious but touching verse. Bernard is eminently down-to-earth and usually sticks to the facts, as when he comes to Miss Bianca's aid before a doubting audience by reciting the guidebook descriptions of the Diamond Palace and the Grand Duchess: "Born in 1883 . . . only d. and sole issue of the late Grand Duke Tiberius." Secondary characters also speak in distinctive voices, while the narrative gives Miss Bianca an ironic editorial voice in comments to herself and asides to Bernard: "Miss Bianca, however, again glanced anxiously at the Secretary, and he knew exactly what she was thinking: that their common adventure had given mice an unfortunate taste for *flamboyance* in welfare work."

Critical reviews show that the books were sometimes more enthusiastically received in the United States than in England. Reviewer Aileen Pippett wrote in *The New York Times,* "Only Margery Sharp has the secret of how to tell this kind of tale. She spreads the fantasy thick but does not let it cloy. Her invention never flags; her wit is neat, and her feeling for children and animals is genuine. She has the courage of her gaiety. Her book is a trifle, but it is delicious." By contrast, a British reviewer for the *Times Literary Supplement,* while acknowledging the charm of the book, pointed out that it "has a

Sharp in 1951

slight flavour of patronage." Yet *Miss Bianca: A Fantasy* was named as one of the American Library Association's Notable Books for Children.

Before the next Miss Bianca story, *The Turret* (1963), was published, one of Sharp's short stories was adapted for motion pictures, and another adult novel was published. In *The Turret* Miss Bianca and Bernard find new allies in the Prisoners' Aid Society Boy Scout troop, a ragtag lot of six young mice held together by the half-Irish Shaun, who becomes Miss Bianca's confidant when Bernard refuses to help. Miss Bianca is really on her own this time, because the new Madam Chairwoman of the M.P.A.S. (the formidable games mistress) is more interested in improving the physical condition of the members than in leading rescues – and the membership is easily dissuaded from offering any help to the turret's unpopular prisoner, Mandrake. As the adventure unfolds with its usual verve and hair-raising interruptions, the knowledgeable reader enjoys seeing the M.P.A.S. nearly disintegrate under the bullying of the games mistress, while Bernard at home faces his own peril: he is encouraged to marry the games mistress to save the Society. For adults, the possibility is a joy to contemplate, as are the points Sharp makes at the expense of rabid calorie-counters.

In 1965, two years after *The Turret,* Margery Sharp published a very different children's book – an easy reader, *Lost at the Fair.* Its sixty-four pages make it a long easy reader, and it seems a surprisingly plodding work. There is much repetition of word and phrase, a common device in beginning readers, but here it soon becomes tedious. The story is slight, and the characters, a young brother and sister and their dog, are forgettable. Hope McGrady, in a review for *Library Journal,* wrote that "The idea of this story is appealing, but much is lost in the telling. Vocabulary is on a first-grade level, but poorly constructed sentences . . . and sentences which continue from one page to another are confusing to beginning readers."

The challenge of writing a popularly and critically successful series is to acknowledge the affection of readers for familiar characters and situations and yet to introduce novelties that allow readers to deepen their acquaintance with the characters. Sharp returned to her mice in 1966, and in the remaining series novels rose to this challenge in a variety of ways. *Miss Bianca in the Salt Mines* (1966) takes her heroine to a most exotic locale, a vast network of salt mines reachable only by an accident-plagued railroad line. Accompanying Bernard and

Miss Bianca on this trip are a pair of highly unlikely companions, two elderly and often cranky professors who, unlike the previous energetic and patriotic assistants, are helpful only in spite of themselves. This book is full of classic Sharp touches, including several tart remarks at the expense of higher education. As ever, the mice remain mice. The mittens which the Ladies' Guild knits for the child prisoner, Teddy-Age-Eight, are an enormous undertaking, involving much piecing together of countless quarter-inch squares. When the gloves are finished, their transportation is another challenge since they are so big that they form "a sizable bale," but, marvelously, they come in very handy. Bernard's appreciative response to the natural beauty of the salt mines lake is to compare it to the top of a tin of tongue. The end of the book seems more contrived than most: an accident wrecks the train at the scene of a great picnic, where the Boy's tutor immediately recognizes Miss Bianca and Teddy-Age-Eight, his own nephew.

During the next four years Sharp published two more adult novels and a few short stories. The fifth Miss Bianca tale, *Miss Bianca in the Orient* (1970), is the first to be set almost entirely beyond Miss Bianca's own unidentified country. Sharp's target in this book is the self-indulgent luxury of the beautiful Ranee, who demands constant entertainment and happiness from her countless servants and indulges in careless cruelty toward those who displease her. Bernard's role is diminished in this story, as he passes his time in the stables with bachelor mice who teach him to play polo (the mouse version, of course, in which the mice take part in a game by clinging to the tails of the horses). Less satisfying than the previous books, this adventure presents characters hard to distinguish and suspense milder than usual. Erik Blegvad's black-and-white illustrations are more delicate than Garth Williams's but have a humor and elegance that is as distinctive and suited as Williams's work.

Miss Bianca in the Orient was followed immediately by the sixth in the series, *Miss Bianca in the Antarctic* (1970), which also takes the mice to foreign shores. In a clever double deception, the prisoner to be rescued is initially a familiar figure, the Norwegian poet from *The Rescuers,* but the prisoners soon become none other than Bernard and Miss Bianca. The cold, the endless expanses of white (against which Miss Bianca almost completely disappears) and a new set of creatures (penguins and polar bears), along with the novelty of the rescuers' need to rescue themselves, sustain the reader's interest. An interlude in which the two mice are kept as pets by a young polar bear offers an opportunity for whimsy, as Miss Bianca entertains the cub with storytelling. Miss Bianca also faces the evil Emperor Penguin, who, like Sharp's other villains, is a ruler who misuses power. The denouement is contrived. Catherine Storr, writing in the 12 November 1971 *New Statesman,* found this book "patronizing and coy," while American reviewers were less critical.

During an intervening year between Miss Bianca stories an adult novel, *The Innocents* (1971), was published; the number of short stories Sharp wrote was greatly decreasing. With her return to Miss Bianca and Bernard in *Miss Bianca and the Bridesmaid* (1972), Sharp discontinued her trend of choosing exotic locales and set her story deep within the walls of the Ambassador's home, where a wedding is about to take place and the bride's six-year-old sister, Susan, has disappeared. Miss Bianca and Bernard face peril from two directions – the evil associated with a wooden doll which seems to have lured Susan from her bedroom, and the dangers of the main drain into which the search takes them.

Although there are some fine details, such as the selection of an M.P.A.S. gift for the bride and a chance to eavesdrop on such old friends as Shaun and the two professors, this book – like *Miss Bianca in the Orient* – spends more time than the earlier books did with its human characters, and it is less interesting for that reason. The sinister wooden doll seems out of place, and the adventure is slighter than usual since the victim really finds herself. The book concludes with these ultimately misleading words: "And on what better note to end this last tale of Bernard and Miss Bianca and the M.P.A.S.?" The *New Yorker* review of 2 December 1972 admitted that this was "not quite up to snuff," although a writer for the *Times Literary Supplement* on 3 November 1972 had regretted that this might be the last in the series.

The next two books for children, both published in 1974, were very different – and disappointing. *The Children Next Door* is a short novel for middle readers. A family of three motherless children are the only youngsters in a London high-rise. When summer vacation arrives, they decide to invent a set of "children next door." A series of very mild adventures ends, incredibly, with the arrival next door of actual children who are almost identical to the imaginary ones.

What a difference there is between this family and the ever-resourceful and exquisitely cultured Miss Bianca, who would have found much to enjoy in London! The flatness of the writing is accentu-

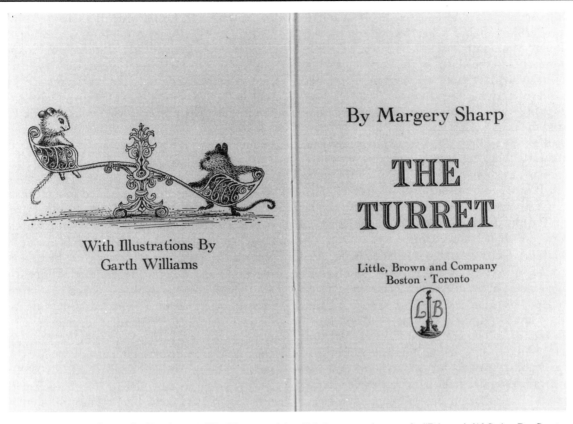

With Illustrations By
Garth Williams

By Margery Sharp

THE TURRET

Little, Brown and Company
Boston · Toronto

Frontispiece and title page for Sharp's 1963 Miss Bianca novel, in which the protagonist meets the "Prisoners' Aid Society Boy Scout Troop," a group of six young mice

ated by the sharp disparity between country and city. The subtleties in characterization that distinguish the best of Sharp's work are here entirely missing, as the children seem indistinguishable from each other except in gender. For the grandeur of the Prisoners' Aid Society adventures, Sharp has substituted the smallest of domestic stages, and the result is a tame and lackluster story.

Also published in 1974, *The Magical Cockatoo* is a Victorian adventure in which the Miss Bianca conventions seem to be reversed, with the child performing a brave deed to rescue a young prince and redirect the course of history. This seventy-five-page novel is much more developed than *The Children Next Door,* although eleven-year-old Lally, alone with her grandparents and their stuffy household, seems even better at feeling sorry for herself than the children of that previous book. She meets a porcelain cockatoo who comes to life by moonlight and challenges her to several undertakings which eventually make her more resourceful. In her greatest adventure she returns an icon to a young prince in exile, the victim of a coup d'état.

The Magical Cockatoo is a second-rate adventure when compared to the Miss Bianca books. The smaller scale upon which it is drawn reduces it to a mannered and predictable tale peopled by broadly drawn and often stereotyped characters. A hint of didacticism, which is unusual for Sharp, also appears: Lally's growth from a sulky child to a girl whose bravery impresses even her brother may satisfy the cockatoo but is slightly oppressive to the reader. A reviewer in the 5 July 1974 *Times Literary Supplement* notes that "the elegance of the writing and the production cannot disguise final failure." Neither *The Children Next Door* nor *The Magical Cockatoo* was published in the United States. It is interesting that the three stories written exclusively for children — *Lost at the Fair, The Children Next Door,* and *The Magical Cockatoo* — have proven to be much less successful than the fantasies which started for adults and drew readers of all ages.

Margery Sharp was seventy-two when a new Miss Bianca story came out. *Bernard the Brave: A Miss Bianca Story* (1976) actually stars Bernard, who fills in for Miss Bianca while she is vacationing with the Boy. A decrepit reprobate of a mouse, Nicodemus, has requested help in launching a search for his missing mistress, an heiress who has disappeared on the eve of her critical eighteenth birthday. Accompanied by an effete teddy bear, Algernon, Bernard makes a harrowing trip to the Wolf Range Mountains, where he discovers the lost Miss Tomasina in the clutch of the very same gang of bandits who have been terrorizing the resort where Miss Bianca has been vacationing. Algernon is a touching buffoon, not quite the equal of Bernard, and the teamwork is less satisfactory than that of Miss Bianca and Bernard, although Bernard fills Miss Bianca's shoes admirably in making such pronouncements as "You know little of the principles of the M.P.A.S. . . . A prisoner's to be rescued, like it or not!" Sharp has two new illustrators, Leslie Morrill for the Little, Brown edition and Faith Jaques for the Heinemann edition.

Margery Sharp's final Miss Bianca book, *Bernard into Battle,* was published in 1978, and in this tale Miss Bianca appears again in a less active role. The locale is once more the Ambassador's house, and an open main drain again starts the plot moving. This time it allows entrance by a fierce band of rats determined to spread dirt and disease throughout the Embassy. With the Ambassador and his family away, the mice fight back under Bernard's leadership. Their most inventive weapon is a large supply of Gorgonzola cheese, the use of which effectively ends an attempted siege of the M.P.A.S. meeting place, the Moot House:

> 'Twas indeed a gallant cheese. Its fumes proved so deadly, the rats succumbed as before a gas-attack. Those in front fell sideways from their hunkers with all four feet in the air, and even the rearmost ranks choked and spluttered but a moment before following suit, and within a moment more all were *hors de combat* (which is French for being down and out). Even Hercules [the head rat] was *hors de combat,* he the foremost of all having received the Gorgonzola's full blast absolutely *nez a nez* (which is French for head on), and lay senseless upon what should have been his field of victory!

Bernard's troops are also well-armed with the Ambassador's supply of pen-nibs, and in the fierce Battle of the Cellar Steps many mice lose their lives. (The former scout, Shaun, appears lifeless but revives spectacularly during the funeral ceremonies.) Sharp's depiction of the mice on their own gives the reader a new perspective on life at the Embassy, another example of her impressive ability to give each book a fresh twist. The ending is again anticlimactic, but the final battle scenes do bring the series to a fittingly heroic close. Miss Bianca's erudition, here seen in her stroll through the graveyard as she meditates on Thomas Gray's "Elegy Written in a Country Church-Yard" (1751), seems forced and lacking in child appeal. Leslie Morrill illustrated both the British and the American editions, and her depictions of Miss Bianca fully clothed are unexpected and seem out of character. Reviewers were not enthusiastic. Marjorie Lewis in the March 1979 *School Library Journal* wrote that "Those who have enjoyed the Englishness and literary fantasy of the Bianca books . . . will not be put off by the archly precious quality of this latest adventure; others will find it exceedingly pretentious."

This was Margery Sharp's final book, although her older titles continued to appear in new editions. In 1977 Walt Disney Productions produced a motion picture, *The Rescuers,* which was based on *The Rescuers* and *Miss Bianca.* According to Sharp's obituary, this motion picture became one of the five most popular videos for children in the United States. It certainly provoked new interest in Miss Bianca and her friends, although the motion picture contains much that comes from Walt Disney's writers rather than from Margery Sharp, and it also provided the impetus for the Miss Bianca series to be reprinted in paperback. In 1990 Walt Disney released a sequel to *The Rescuers* with the title *The Rescuers Down Under,* a motion picture that was not based on a particular Miss Bianca title.

While the individual books seem to weaken after the first four, the series as a whole is notable for its integrity. Sharp continued to find new settings, new characters, and new angles to explore. She allowed her main characters, Miss Bianca and Bernard, to develop and to age over the course of the novels, and she rewards her readers by acknowledging the connections between the books. The main drain, for example, thoroughly explored in *Miss Bianca and the Bridesmaid,* is a richer source of peril in the final book because of its familiarity. It is also satisfying to meet in different situations such minor characters as the water rat who helped ferry Miss Bianca in *The Turret* and who then reappears guarding the drain in *Miss Bianca and the Bridesmaid.* The knowledgeable reader also enjoys the deft characterizations of the changing Madam Chairs and the chances to follow such groups as the Ladies' Guild and the Scouts, who continue to be mentioned after their more prominent adventures are over. During the course of the books Sharp began inserting translations of most of her French phrases, but she never "wrote down" for a child audience: her last book includes a reference to "a cake of gamboge," and a tightly-knit hedge of holly is described as a "cheval de frise."

Margery Sharp was, above all, a superb storyteller. Her books yield real pleasure to those readers willing to appreciate subtleties of language and characterization. Through the more than fifty years in which she wrote, many titles, including the Miss Bianca series, were translated into other languages – including German, Italian, Norwegian, Hebrew, and Portuguese – and Sharp recalled that "foreign companies have told me that the stories are written in such good English they are a pleasure to translate." In the late 1980s they were also republished in different formats, such as with large print and in paperback.

Margery Sharp died in London on 14 March 1991 at the age of eighty-six, one year after the death of her husband. She had suffered a stroke five years previously and, although remaining vigorous, had not written since then. Although her children's books number fewer than one-fourth of her production (and far fewer if one were to count all her short stories), the Miss Bianca series is today better known than her exclusively adult work. In those nine Miss Bianca works Sharp told rousing stories in which etiquette is as important as might, and human nature is ultimately good despite the existence of villainy. The heroic tone of these stories is unspoiled by pretense. With an eye for revealing detail, they delight readers by presenting nothing more and nothing less than good narratives developed with clever characterization and intelligent insight. Readers who discover *The Rescuers* and its sequels will appreciate Margery Sharp's ability to ignore the usual pedagogical age-level divisions and, in the tradition of the best animal fantasies, to poke gentle fun at human foibles.

Interviews:

C. S. Forester, "Margery Sharp," *Book of the Month Club News* (July 1946): 4–5;

Archibald G. Ogden, ". . . No Wonder Her Characters Are Real!," *Book of the Month Club News* (June 1948): 5–6;

Roy Newquist, "Margery Sharp," in his *Counterpoint* (New York: Simon & Schuster, 1967), pp. 538–542.

References:

Margery Blount, "Lilliputian Life: The Mouse Story," in her *Animal Land: The Creatures of Children's Fiction* (New York: Morrow, 1975), pp. 152–169;

Margery Fisher, "Miss Bianca," in her *Who's Who in Children's Literature: A Treasury of the Familiar Characters of Childhood* (New York: Holt, Rinehart & Winston, 1975), pp. 227–229;

Louisa Smith, "The Miss Bianca Series," in *Survey of Modern Fantasy Literature,* volume 3, edited by Frank N. Magill (Englewood Cliffs, N.J.: Salem, 1983), pp. 1037–1039.

Papers:

A collection of Margery Sharp's manuscripts is at the Houghton Library of Harvard University. It includes manuscripts of various novels and stories, including the Miss Bianca books, *The Innocents, The Rescuers, Martha in Paris,* and *Bernard the Brave,* as well as notes and early drafts, revised typescripts, printer's copies, and galley proofs.

Barbara Willard

(12 March 1909 – 18 February 1994)

Steven Engelfried

BOOKS: *Love in Ambush,* by Willard and Elizabeth H. Devas (London: Howe, 1930);

Ballerina (London: Howe, 1932);

Candle Flame (London: Howe, 1932);

Name of the Gentleman (London: Howe, 1933);

Joy Befall Thee (London: Howe, 1934);

As Far as in Me Lies (London: Nelson, 1936);

Set Piece (London: Nelson, 1938);

Personal Effects (London: Macmillan, 1939);

The Dogs Do Bark (London: Macmillan, 1948);

Portrait of Philip (London: Macmillan, 1950); revised as *He Fought for His Queen* (London: Heinemann, 1954; New York: Warne, 1954);

Proposed and Seconded (London: Macmillan, 1951);

Celia Scarfe (London: Appleton-Century, 1951);

Echo Answers (London: Macmillan, 1952);

One of the Twelve (London: French, 1954);

Fit for a King: A Nativity Play in One Act (London: J. G. Miller, 1955);

Snail and the Pennithornes, illustrated by Geoffrey Fletcher (London: Epworth Press, 1957);

Winter in Disguise (London: M. Joseph, 1958);

Snail and the Pennithornes Next Time, illustrated by Fletcher (London: Epworth Press, 1958);

Son of Charlemagne, illustrated by Emil Weiss (Garden City, N.Y.: Doubleday, 1959; London: Heinemann, 1960);

The House with Roots, illustrated by Robert Hodgson (London: Constable, 1959; New York: Watts, 1960);

Snail and the Pennithornes and the Princess, illustrated by Fletcher (London: Epworth Press, 1960);

The Dippers and Jo, illustrated by Jean Harper (London: Hamish Hamilton, 1960);

Eight for a Secret, illustrated by Lewis Hart (London: Constable, 1960; New York: Watts, 1961);

The Penny Pony, illustrated by Juliette Palmer (London: Hamish Hamilton, 1961);

If All the Swords in England, illustrated by Robert M. Sax (Garden City, N.Y.: Doubleday, 1961; London: Burns Oates, 1961);

Stop the Train!, illustrated by Harper (London: Hamish Hamilton, 1961);

The Summer with Spike, illustrated by Anne Linton (London: Constable, 1961; New York: Watts, 1962):

Duck on a Pond, illustrated by Mary Rose Hardy (London: Constable, 1961; New York: Watts, 1962);

Hetty, illustrated by Pamela Mara (London: Constable, 1962; New York: Harcourt, Brace, 1963);

Augustine Came to Kent, illustrated by Hans Guggenheim (Garden City, N.Y.: Doubleday, 1963; Kingswood, Surrey: World's Work, 1964);

The Battle of Wednesday Week, illustrated by Douglas Hall (London: Constable, 1963); republished as *Storm from the West* (New York: Harcourt, Brace, 1964);

The Dippers and the High-Flying Kite, illustrated by Maureen Eckersley (London: Hamish Hamilton, 1963);

The Suddenly Gang, illustrated by Lynette Hemmant (London: Hamish Hamilton, 1963);

The Pram Race, illustrated by Constance Marshall (London: Hamish Hamilton, 1964);

A Dog and a Half, illustrated by Jane Paton (London: Hamish Hamilton, 1964; New York: Nelson, 1971);

Three and One to Carry, illustrated by Douglas Hall (London: Constable, 1964; New York: Harcourt, Brace, 1965);

Sussex (London: Batsford, 1965; New York: Hastings House, 1966);

The Wild Idea, illustrated by Douglas Bissett (London: Hamish Hamilton, 1965);

Charity at Home, illustrated by Hall (London: Constable, 1965; New York: Harcourt, Brace, 1966);

Surprise Island, illustrated by Paton (London: Hamish Hamilton, 1966; New York: Meredith Press, 1969);

The Richleighs of Tantamount, illustrated by C. Walter Hodges (London: Constable, 1966; New York: Harcourt, Brace, 1967);

The Grove of Green Holly, illustrated by Gareth Floyd (London: Constable, 1967); republished as

Barbara Willard

Flight to the Forest (Garden City, N.Y.: Doubleday, 1967);

The Pet Club, illustrated by Hemmant (London: Hamish Hamilton, 1967);

To London! To London!, illustrated by Antony Maitland (London: Longman, 1968; New York: Weybright & Talley, 1968);

Hurray for Rosie!, illustrated by Floyd (London: Hutchinson, 1968);

Royal Rosie, illustrated by Floyd (London: Hutchinson, 1968);

The Family Tower (London: Constable, 1968; New York: Harcourt, Brace, 1968);

Junior Motorist: The Driver's Apprentice, by Willard and Frances Howell, illustrated by Ionicus (London: Collins, 1969);

The Toppling Towers (London: Longman, 1969; New York: Harcourt, Brace, 1969);

The Pocket Mouse, illustrated by Mary Russon (London: Hamish Hamilton / New York: Knopf, 1969);

Priscilla Pentecost, illustrated by Doreen Roberts (London: Hamish Hamilton, 1970);

The Reindeer Slippers, illustrated by Tessa Jordan (London: Hamish Hamilton, 1970);

Chichester and Lewes, illustrated by Graham Humphreys (London: Longman, 1970);

The Lark and the Laurel, illustrated by Floyd (London: Longman, 1970; New York: Harcourt, Brace, 1970);

The Sprig of Broom, illustrated by Paul Shardlow (London: Longman, 1971; New York: Dutton, 1972);

The Dragon Box, illustrated by Jordan (London: Hamish Hamilton, 1972);

A Cold Wind Blowing (London: Longman, 1972; New York: Dutton, 1973);

Jubilee!, illustrated by Hilary Abrahams (London: Heinemann, 1973);

The Iron Lily (London: Longman, 1973; New York: Dutton, 1974);

Harrow and Harvest (London: Kestrel, 1974; New York: Dutton, 1975);

Bridesmaid, illustrated by Paton (London: Hamish Hamilton, 1976);

The Miller's Boy, illustrated by Floyd (London: Kestrel, 1976; New York: Dutton, 1976);

The Eldest Son (London: Kestrel, 1977; New York: Dell, 1989);

The Country Maid (London: Hamish Hamilton, 1978; New York: Greenwillow, 1980);

The Gardener's Grandchildren, illustrated by Gordon King (London: Kestrel, 1978; New York: McGraw-Hill, 1979);

Spell Me a Witch (London: Hamish Hamilton, 1979; New York: Harcourt Brace Jovanovich, 1981);

A Flight of Swans (London: Kestrel, 1980; New York: Dell, 1989);

The Keys of Mantlemass (London: Kestrel, 1981);

Summer Season (London: Julia MacRae, 1981);

Famouse Rowena Lamont (London: Hardy, 1983);

The Queen of the Pharisees' Children (London: Julia MacRae, 1983);

Smiley Tiger, illustrated by Laszlo Acs (London: Julia MacRae, 1984);

Ned Only (London: Julia MacRae, 1985);

The Farmer's Boy (London: Julia MacRae, 1991);

The Ranger's Daughters (London: Julia MacRae, 1992).

OTHER: *Hullabaloo! About Naughty Boys and Girls,* edited by Willard, illustrated by Fritz Wegner (London: Hamish Hamilton, 1969; New York: Meredith, 1969);

"I . . .": An Anthology of Diarists, edited by Willard (London: Chatto & Windus, 1972);

Happy Families, edited by Willard, illustrated by Krystyna Turska (London: Macmillan, 1974);

"The Thorny Paradise," in *The Thorny Paradise: Writers on Writing for Children,* edited by Edward Blishen (Harmondsworth: Kestrel, 1975), pp. 158–162;

Field and Forest, edited by Willard, illustrated by Faith Jaques (London: Penguin, 1975);

Bunshu Iguchi, *Convent Cat,* translated by Willard (London: Hamish Hamilton, 1975; New York: McGraw-Hill, 1976);

Max Bollinger, *The Giants' Feast,* translated by Willard, illustrated by Monika Laimgruber (London: Hamish Hamilton, 1975).

Barbara Willard is best known as the author of the Mantlemass series of historical novels, but in the course of writing more than fifty books for children she successfully explored a rich variety of fiction. She had the ability to create unique and complex characters in a subtle and economical manner, and her books are notable for their vividly rendered settings, conveyed without overly extensive description. The common thread running through Willard's writing concerns interactions between family members and often among many families within one community. Her most memorable characters are strong willed but far from perfect. Learning and growing because of their mistakes, Willard's charac-

ters remain real and important to the reader through both their triumphs and failures.

Born in Sussex on 12 March 1909, Barbara Willard grew up with a strong interest in the theater, since her father was a fairly well-known stage actor. Her love of theater and literature was encouraged by the headmistresses of two schools she attended. She often toured with her father and attempted a stage career herself for a few years after leaving school. She draws upon her experiences as an actress in a few of her novels, most notably *The Country Maid* (1978) and *Summer Season* (1981).

As her prospects as an actress dimmed, Willard turned to writing. She lived in London and during the 1930s published eight of her thirteen mildly successful adult novels while working as a script reader for American films. Her brother, Christopher, born when Willard was twelve, was killed in World War II. As the war ended, Willard left London and returned to the Sussex region, sharing a small house with a journalist named Frances. After many rejections she published her first novel for children, *He Fought for His Queen* (1954), adapted from her adult book *Portrait of Philip* (1950). She would continue in the field for more than thirty years.

During the first decade or so of her career as a writer for children, Willard produced a variety of excellent books, including mysteries, animal stories, and historical novels. In some way, though, most of her work centered around family dynamics. Margery Fisher in a December 1969 article in *School Librarian* proclaimed Willard "a virtuoso when it comes to family relationships." Her works are also notable for their craftsmanship. In her sketch for the *Something about the Author Autobiography Series* Willard names the necessary elements for a good children's book: "good plotting, sharp characterisation, and above all else, economy."

Though Willard developed into a fine historical novelist, her early efforts in that area were unexceptional. *If All the Swords in England* (1961), for instance, is clearly a different sort of book than the later Mantlemass titles. Centered around the great feud between King Henry II and Thomas Becket, the archbishop of Canterbury, the story unwinds through the eyes of twin brothers: Edmund serves as a page in the king's household, while Simon becomes a secretary to Becket during the archbishop's exile in France. Full of action and historical drama, the novel nevertheless lacks the resonance of Willard's later work, and the mixture of fact and fiction is sometimes awkward. *If All the Swords in England* turns out to be more Thomas Becket's story

Dust jacket for the first novel in Willard's Mantlemass series

than Simon's and feels more like a history lesson than a novel.

In *A Dog and a Half* (1964), which is aimed at younger readers, Willard's sense of family and community overshadow the conventions of a typical animal story. Brandy is the "dog and a half," a friendly Saint Bernard adopted by Jill and Limpet. Brandy's owner, the delightful Mrs. Remnant, must give up her pet when she is forced to leave her home. The dog eventually helps to catch a crook, but finding a proper home for Mrs. Remnant, where she can keep her dog and her new friends, is the significant triumph that concludes the story. Jill, Limpet, and Brandy return in a sequel, *Surprise Island* (1966).

Both of the Jill and Limpet books feature conventional plots, with slightly contrived events. As with much of Willard's work, however, intriguing characters help to raise the stories above the ordinary. In *A Dog and a Half,* for example, Jill easily convinces herself that her parents will be delighted to have a Saint Bernard pet, though she actually knows better. When her mother suggests that Jill

should have known better, the girl admits, "I knew it too quietly," a perfect sample of Willard's perceptive economy of language.

Like much of Willard's earlier work, *Three and One to Carry* (1964) is essentially a family story with a bit of romance and mystery thrown in. The attraction lies mainly in the author's ability to create believable and endearing characters. The likable members of the Lodge family must struggle to keep their home, and the happy resolution of this battle concludes the novel. The heart of the book, however, centers around Simon and Prue and their amusing efforts to endure a summer looking after the insufferable Arthur. The relationship among the three develops in a warm and subtle manner while the mystery involving the Lodges' home unravels. When some sort of mutual respect and friendship emerges, it is especially convincing because it occurs despite the intentions of the children. *Three and One to Carry* is a pleasant novel without a great deal of drama, but because the characters are so endearing the action is still suspenseful.

In *Charity at Home* (1965) concerns about a family relationship clearly drive the novel's action. Fourteen-year-old Charity Carrington belongs to a loving family, for though her parents are long dead, her aunt and uncle have treated Charity as their own daughter. When she discovers an unexpected artistic talent Charity begins to think of herself as different from those around her. Spurred by Derek, a sympathetic but slightly cynical teenage boy, Charity begins to doubt her own history. In an exciting climax Charity helps thwart a robbery at a neighbor's estate and is forced to recognize the happy truth of her background.

The robbery itself moves the plot along in an artificial manner, but Charity's emotions and reactions always ring true. Her doubts about her origins and her final recognition of the true value of her home and family are convincing. Charity's self-acceptance is not that different from Jill's in *Surprise Island* or even Cecilia Highwood's in *Harrow and Harvest* (1974), but the three heroines, like the three novels, differ greatly in setting, tone, and subject matter.

The Richleighs of Tantamount (1966) are a different sort of family than those found in most of Willard's books. Four rich children, rather spoiled and quite sure of themselves, find themselves abandoned in a decaying mansion by the sea. A friendship with two poor children and the discovery of a smuggling operation, which is run from their own ancestral home, combine to force the Richleighs to learn valuable lessons about the world. The plot is contrived and melodramatic but absorbing nonetheless, and the oceanside setting with Tantamount looming above provides a vivid background for the action, one of many examples of the author's skill at conveying a distinctly visual element in her novels. Willard states in her *Something About the Author* sketch that the planning of scenes for her 1970 novel *The Lark and the Laurel* "became . . . almost filmic." Dramatically visual moments run through much of her work.

The Family Tower (1968) and *The Toppling Towers* (1969) represent Willard's most ambitious attempts in the family novel, in part because the family involved is simply so large and complex. In her autobiographical sketch Willard states that she had hoped to write one "long book about a very big family" but wrote it in two parts at her publisher's request. The novels received mixed reaction. A June 1968 review in *Junior Bookshelf* suggested that to meet all of the family members "in the space of 140 pages is confusing." On the other hand, the jumble of personalities and various friendships and rivalries seem quite appropriate for such a large, self-contained family. It is hard to keep track of all the characters, but Jo Tower is a strong enough protagonist to hold the reader's interest. She manages to come to terms with her rival Emily's special qualities without sacrificing her own strong personality. Jo Tower may be Willard's most memorable character outside of the Mantlemass series.

After living in Ashdown Forest for more than a decade, Willard finally decided to use it as the setting for a historical novel. *The Grove of Green Holly* (1967) introduces many of the elements that would later make the Mantlemass books so successful. Set in the mid 1600s just after the Great Rebellion, the story is seen through the eyes of young Rafe Finch, but Rafe's grandfather, Gregory Trundle, dominates the action. An aging actor who played with Shakespeare himself, Gregory can no longer perform his art because of the strict tenures of Puritanism. When Charles II needs to flee England in secret, Gregory uses his actor's skills with makeup successfully to disguise the young king.

Later, after fleeing to a different part of the forest, Rafe's grandfather continues to practice his trade, though to no other audience than a grove of holly trees. In a vivid climax an inflamed mob of Puritans find Gregory there, name him a blasphemer, and kill the old man. Through Gregory Trundle, Willard shows what a powerful effect theater can have, both as entertainment and as social expression. His fate demonstrates how the sweeping social changes of government and religion can have a tragic impact on ordinary people who seem in many ways far removed from the great events of the times.

Willard expands such themes with her magnificent family saga, the Mantlemass series, beginning with *The Lark and the Laurel* in 1970. The seven main books cover nearly two centuries of English history, from 1485 to 1644. During this time England saw the beginning of the Tudor reign, sweeping religious reforms, the defeat of the Spanish Armada, and the Great Rebellion, among other momentous changes. Through eight generations of the Medley and Mallory families, whose fates are both intertwined with the Mantlemass estate, Willard shows the effects of great events on the lives of the forest folk of Sussex. Though great historical changes are central to each plot, the books are especially memorable because the portrayal of the characters is so strong. Having already written successful family novels and historical novels, Willard found a perfect framework to do both at once in the Mantlemass books.

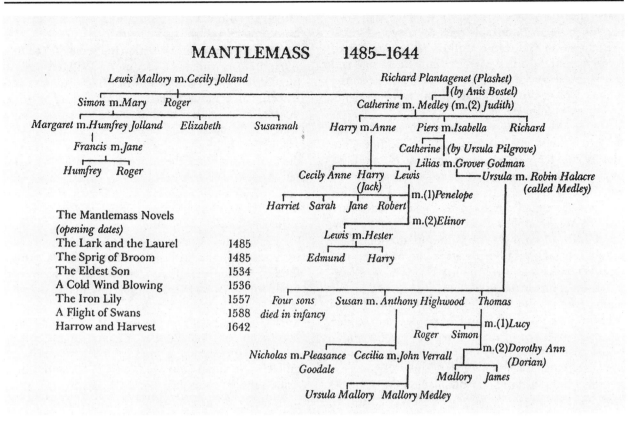

Genealogical chart from Harrow and Harvest *(1974) showing the descendants of Lewis Mallory*

Another strength of the Mantlemass series is Willard's use of language. In all of the Mantlemass books she manages to inject well-chosen samples of Sussex dialect without confusing the reader. As she states in the *Something about the Author* sketch, "No one could suppose that *stoachy* means anything other than *muddy*." Her rich use of language captures the flavor of the forest population of the time.

The Lark and the Laurel introduces the series and Cecily Jolland, one of many memorable Mantlemass heroines. The spoiled daughter of a scheming lord who switches allegiances during the Wars of the Roses, Cecily is sent to stay in Sussex when her father flees to France. Unprepared for the roughness of country life, she stubbornly refuses to accept her fate as anything less than temporary. Her aunt Elizabeth, however, is even more stubborn and gradually earns Cecily's respect and affection. Dame Elizabeth is the first of a long line of Mantlemass matriarchs whose typical qualities include forthright honesty (often at the expense of accepted manners), an iron will, and true kindness beneath the intimidating exterior. Meanwhile, Cecily's friendship with Lewis Mallory, a neighbor of Mantlemass, blooms into love. By novel's end,

Cecily has embraced the country life and gathered enough strength and self-assurance to defy her father.

Cecily's development from an unthinking puppet of her father into a caring and willful young woman is handled expertly. She learns much from her aunt and from Lewis, but her own exuberant personality surprises them both. Willard's plot is carefully conceived, as Cecily's discoveries about herself lead to knowledge about her own past which appears to prevent her from staying in Sussex and marrying Lewis. In an ironically satisfying twist the arranged marriage that she half remembers turns out to have been with Lewis.

The main action of *The Sprig of Broom* (1971) takes place one generation after that of *The Lark and the Laurel* and concerns the Medley family and their great secret. In a vivid opening chapter a boy named Richard learns that the king of England, about to die in battle, is his true father. Twenty years later Richard has settled near Mantlemass and has a child named Medley. After inquisitive strangers appear at the home of Richard Plashet, Richard disappears, leaving Medley and his mother alone. Medley eventually searches for his father, hoping to learn more about his past. If Richard's history proves to be an honorable one, Medley will be allowed to wed Catherine Mallory, the daughter of Cecily Jolland. When Medley finds his father and learns the secret of his royal heritage, he rejects the temptations of possible kingship for the country life he knows and loves.

Since the reader knows Medley's true heritage from the start, his father's actions are not completely mysterious. Of more interest is Medley's own growth. He loves Catherine and would gladly wed her, but he needs to know his father's secret for his own sense of identity, not just to earn her father's approval. His decision to embrace the honest dignity of country life is an affirmation more than a refusal, and in many ways a stronger choice than his father's attempt to bury the past.

Amid all of the great family drama, Willard manages to instill fascinating details of historical authenticity. In one of many examples the reader learns how Richard made a window in his small house, using glass from the ruins of a chapel, and how this unusual feature allows Medley to read during the winter, a rare and valuable luxury. Like *The Lark and the Laurel*, *The Sprig of Broom* was a runner-up for the Guardian Award.

A Cold Wind Blowing (1972) jumps another generation to Piers, the second of Medley's three sons (the other two brothers are Harry, the oldest, and Richard). When Dom Thomas, Piers's kindly uncle, is killed, the young man vows to take care of Isabella, a silent young woman whom Thomas died protecting. Piers struggles with his own feelings and with the mystery behind Isabella's past, but eventually the two are married. When Isabella finally remembers that she had once been a nun and that their marriage may be construed as blasphemous, the two leave Mantlemass. After the birth of her child, Isabella takes her own life, convinced that she will be damned for breaking her vow. The novel's conclusion is appropriately bleak, showing what a devastating effect the great events of the world can have upon ordinary people. Initially Dom Thomas cannot easily convince the Medleys that church persecution could actually affect life at Mantlemass. "We have been so quiet and undisturbed here," says Master Medley. "Can all this truly touch us?"

Willard refuses to take easy sides when dealing with history. Isabella's death comes at her own hand because of the strength of her convictions, rather than being caused by a powerful villain like Robin Halacre, Piers's heir, or an angry mob. Rather than urging the reader to take sides on religious or political matters, Willard focuses on indi-

viduals who must try to get along as best they can in a complex and intrusive world.

Lilias Godman, the title character of *The Iron Lily* (1973), stands out as one of Willard's most memorable creations. Cast out of her home at age fifteen, Lilias gains a place as a servant in a lord's manor. Through her healing skills she earns favor, which leads to a marriage that her crooked shoulder would surely have denied her. When her husband dies Lilias becomes the supremely competent master of his iron foundry. Guided by a ring which her mother had left her, Lilias suspects that the Medleys of Mantlemass have some mysterious connection with her long-dead mother, so she opens a new foundry in the same forest. The Medleys treat her with respect, and Lilias's daughter Ursula grows fond of Robin, Piers's adopted son. Lilias has other plans for her daughter, though, having arranged a marriage to expand her iron empire. When she learns that Piers may be her own father, Lilias sends Ursula away, fearing that a marriage to Robin would be incestuous as well as impractical. Robin and Ursula finally do wed, and Piers and Lilias trade secrets. Piers learns that Lilias is in fact his daughter, and he reveals the family connection to the Plantagenet line for her to pass on to one member of the next generation.

Other characters play large roles in this novel, but Lilias dominates with her stubborn will and sometimes blind ambition. More than any other Medley, she epitomizes the qualities of boldness and determination that run through the generations. She greatly impresses Richard and Piers Medley by standing up with both wit and bravery to a mob of foresters who protest her use of foreign laborers. Lilias's moments of tenderness are few and subtle but have just enough impact to move the reader to empathize with her. *The Iron Lily* won the Guardian Award for fiction.

Harrow and Harvest takes place during the Great Rebellion of the 1640s, when Nicholas Highwood is temporary master of Mantlemass. Since his position descends through the female line, Nicholas knows he will not retain Mantlemass for himself. The true heir is his young cousin Edmund, who surprisingly appears after fleeing from the Parliament troops who killed his father. Nicholas finally proclaims himself a supporter of Parliament, much to the joy of his neighbors, and Edmund eventually agrees. Dorian Medley, cousin to Nicholas and his sister Cecilia, ultimately betrays the rest of the family to Royalist sympathizers, resulting in the death of Edmund and the burning of Mantlemass. While Nicholas decides to make a new start in America, his sister decides to stay in England. After sharing her knowledge of Medley history with her future husband, Cecilia destroys the records but retains the ring that had been passed down through generations.

Willard captures the horror of civil war most vividly in her account of the death of Advent Goodale. A vocal supporter of Parliament, Goodale comes to the aid of Parson Lovet, his political rival, who is threatened by a troop of soldiers. The soldiers then hang Goodale instead, naming him a hypocrite. This senseless death of one man has more immediate impact on the people of Mantlemass than any descriptions of impersonal battles or massacres might. As always, Willard manages to bring history alive by personalizing it.

Harrow and Harvest completes the Mantlemass series, but some of Willard's other books fit in as well. *The Miller's Boy* (1976), shorter and less complex than the major books about Mantlemass, returns to the time period of *The Lark and the Laurel.* The title character, Thomas Welfare, is fit to be a friend to Lewis Mallory as a youth, but both have too much pride to accept the unequal relationship that would inevitably follow when they reach adulthood. Willard followed *The Miller's Boy* with two more major Mantlemass works.

The Eldest Son (1977) fits seamlessly into the family chronicle, with part of the action occurring at the same time as *A Cold Wind Blowing.* Strong willed and single-minded, Piers's older brother Harry is convinced that future Medley fortunes lie in iron rather than horses. He becomes a good husband and father but still longs impatiently for freedom. Asserting his will over his younger brother, he impulsively purchases a strange miniature horse for his daughter. The horse carries the farcy, a form of plague, and Harry's daughter tragically dies from it. Forced to burn Ghylls Hatch to the ground, the Medley family is taken in by the Mallorys at Mantlemass. The guilt-ridden Harry finally decides to leave his home and make a fresh start with an iron foundry in another forest far away.

Willard's heroes are never perfect, and Harry is perhaps least perfect of all. Certainly he is less endearing than his youngest brother, Richard, or his father, Medley, yet the reader cannot help but empathize with his actions. Though his conflicts with Medley are unfortunate, they seem inevitable. Willard insightfully shows how two such strong-willed characters may ultimately be better off separate.

The "siege" of Ghylls Hatch is one of Willard's most riveting scenes. As the Medleys endure the agonizing process of burning their horses and possessions in order to prevent the spread of disease, the neighboring foresters surround their land, making sure they follow every procedure. Master Medley hopes to stop short of destroying his house, but the foresters' leader, Old Grover, insists that he take this step. Despite the strong wills and deep feelings of the Medleys, they bow to the foresters' wishes, showing how deep the roots of community reach.

A Flight of Swans (1980) follows the events of *The Iron Lily* and the marriage of Ursula Godman and Piers's heir, Robin. Ursula is made to realize that her choice of Robin was a poor one. He never fulfills the promise that others saw in him as a young man, mismanaging Piers's horses and frequently spending unexplained time away from Mantlemass. When he hears rumors that Piers may have caused his true father's death, Robin turns to treachery, betraying ironworking secrets to Spanish spies. One of the spies is Humfrey Jolland, the older brother of Roger, a distant cousin who is being raised by Ursula at Mantlemass. When he learns of his brother's actions, Roger offers Humfrey a chance to escape, which Humfrey takes, rather than turning him in immediately.

The treachery of Robin and Humfrey is based on political gain, since the secrets they steal go toward the Spanish war effort. Their motives, especially in Robin's case, are based more on personal bitterness than on any lack of patriotism and have a personal impact on Ursula and Roger that far outweigh other considerations. The circumstances of the war with Spain have undeniable effects on the characters of Mantlemass but serve only to illuminate their strengths and flaws, rather than cause or create them. The reader has no doubt that Robin's flaws would inevitably have become apparent to Ursula in some manner.

Like *The Eldest Son, A Flight of Swans* should be considered as one of the seven major Mantlemass works even though it was written after *Harrow and Harvest.* Ideally, perhaps, the reader should follow the order of historical events rather than that of publication date. Willard returned to Mantlemass twice more in the 1980s. *The Keys of Mantlemass* (1981) is a collection of short stories that fill in some of the gaps in the family histories of Medley and Mallory. *The Queen of the Pharisees' Children* (1983) takes place in the area around Mantlemass twenty years after the destruction of the manor.

Willard's attachment to the region she wrote about was celebrated by a "Happening to Remember Barbara Willard," held at Ashdown Forest Centre on 14 May 1994. Although Willard's career continued into the 1990s, the Mantlemass books stand out as her highest achievement. While each novel is memorable in its own right, the series is even more impressive when looked at as a whole. Willard created dozens of vivid, original characters in a fully realized setting. Many of her characters share qualities of strength and determination, but each is unique. Cecily Jolland, Lilias Godman, and Cecilia Highwood, for example, are all strong-willed leaders yet possess vastly different personalities. Showing the effects of significant events on ordinary people, the plots are compelling and often quite exciting to read, as action, romance, and adventure are woven seamlessly into the historical framework. Though much of her other work is noteworthy, the Mantlemass series is clearly Willard's finest work and earns her a place alongside such authors as Rosemary Sutcliff, Leon Garfield, and K. M. Peyton as a leading writer of British historical fiction for children.

Interview:

Cornelia Jones and Olivia R. Way, "Barbara Willard," in their *British Children's Authors: Interviews at Home* (Chicago: American Library Association, 1976), pp. 167–176.

Reference:

Margery Fisher, "Barbara Willard," *School Librarian,* 17 (December 1969): 343–348.

Books for Further Reading

Adamson, Lynda G. *A Reference Guide to Historical Fiction for Children and Yound Adults.* New York: Greenwood, 1987.

Avery, Gillian, and Julia Briggs, eds. *Children and Their Books.* Oxford: Oxford University Press, 1989.

Barker, Keith. *In the Realms of Gold: The Story of the Carnegie Medal.* London: Youth Libraries Group, 1986.

Bathurst, David. *Six of the Best! Being an Affectionate Tribute to Six of the Most Significant School Story Writers of the Twentieth Century.* Chichester: Romansmead, 1994.

Bator, Robert, ed. *Signposts to Criticism of Children's Literature.* Chicago: American Library Association, 1983.

Berger, Laura Standley, ed. *Twentieth Century Children's Writers,* fourth edition. Detroit: St. James Press, 1995.

Berger, ed. *Twentieth Century Young Adult Writers.* Detroit: St. James Press, 1994.

Blishen, Edward, ed. *The Thorny Paradise: Writers on Writing for Children.* Harmondsworth: Kestrel, 1975.

Blount, Margaret. *Animal Land: The Creatures of Children's Fiction.* London: Hutchinson, 1974.

Butts, Dennis, ed. *Good Writers for Young Readers.* London: Hart-Davis Educational, 1977.

Butts, ed. *Stories and Society: Children's Literature in Its Social Context.* Basingstoke: Macmillan, 1992.

Cadogan, Mary, and Patricia Craig. *You're a Brick, Angela! The Girls' Story, 1839–1985.* London: Gollancz, 1986.

Carpenter, Humphrey, and Mari Prichard. *The Oxford Companion to Children's Literature.* New York: Oxford University Press, 1984.

Chambers, Aidan. *Booktalk: Occasional Writing on Literature and Children.* London: Bodley Head, 1985; New York: Harper & Rowe, 1985.

Chambers, Nancy, ed. *The Signal Approach to Children's Books: A Collection.* London: Kestrel, 1980.

Chester, Tessa Rose. *Children's Books Research: A Practical Guide to Techniques and Sources.* Stroud, Gloustershire: Thimble Press/Westminster College, 1989.

Cox, Jack. *Take a Cold Bath, Sir! The Story of the Boy's Own Paper.* London: Lutterworth, 1982.

Crouch, Marcus. *The Nesbit Tradition: The Children's Novel in England, 1945–1970.* London: Ernest Benn, 1972.

Crouch and Alec Ellis, eds. *Chosen for Children: An Account of the Books Which Have Been Awarded the Library Association Carnegie Medal, 1936–1975,* third edition. London: Library Association, 1977.

Dixon, Bob. *Catching Them Young,* 2 volumes. London: Pluto, 1977.

Donelson, Kenneth L., and Alleen Pace Nilsen. *Literature for Today's Young Adults,* fourth edition. New York: HarperCollins, 1993.

Dusinberre, Juliet. *Alice to the Lighthouse: Children's Books and Radical Experiments in Art.* London: Macmillan, 1987.

Egoff, Sheila. *Thursday's Child: Trends and Patterns in Contemporary Children's Literature.* Chicago: American Library Association, 1981.

Egoff. *Worlds Within: Children's Fantasy from the Middle Ages to Today.* Chicago: American Library Association, 1988.

Egoff, G. T. Stubbs, and L. F. Ashley, eds. *Only Connect: Readings on Children's Literature.* Toronto & New York: Oxford University Press, 1969.

Fisher, Margery. *The Bright Face of Danger.* London: Hodder, 1986.

Fisher. *Intent upon Reading: A Critical Appraisal of Modern Fiction for Children,* second edition. London: Brockhampton, 1964.

Fisher. *Matters of Fact: Aspects of Non-Fiction for Children.* London: Brockhampton, 1972.

Fox, Geoff, Graham Hammond, Terry Jones, Frederic Smith, and Kenneth Sterck, eds. *Writers, Critics, and Children: Articles from* Children's Literature in Education. London: Heinemann Educational Books, 1976.

Gose, Elliott. *Mere Creatures: A Study of Modern Fantasy Tales for Children.* Toronto: University of Toronto Press, 1988.

Harvey Darton, F. J. *Children's Books in England: Five Centuries of Social Life,* third edition, revised by Brian Alderson. Cambridge, London & New York: Cambridge University Press, 1982.

Haviland, Virginia, ed. *Children and Literature: Views and Reviews.* Glenview, Ill.: Scott, Foresman, 1973.

Hearne, Betsy, and Marilyn Kaye. *Celebrating Children's Books: Essays on Children's Literature in Honor of Zena Sutherland.* New York: Lothrop, Lee & Shepard, 1981.

Helbig, Alethea, and Agnes Perkins, eds. *The Phoenix Award of the Children's Literature Association: 1985–1989.* Metuchen, N.J. & London: Scarecrow Press, 1993.

Hendrickson, Linnea. *Children's Literature: A Guide to the Criticism.* Boston: G. K. Hall, 1987.

Hildick, Wallace. *Children and Fiction: A Critical Study in Depth of the Artistic and Psychological Features Involved in Writing Fiction for and about Children,* revised edition. London: Evans, 1974.

Hindle, Roy. *Oh, No Dear! Advice to Girls a Century Ago.* London: David & Charles, 1976.

Hollindale, Peter. *Choosing Books for Children.* London: Elek, 1974.

Hollindale. *Ideology and the Children's Book.* Stroud, Gloustershire: Thimble Press, 1988.

Howarth, Patrick. *Play Up and Play the Game: The Heroes of Popular Fiction.* London: Eyre Methuen, 1973.

Hume, Kathryn. *Fantasy and Mimesis: Responses to Reality in Western Literature.* New York & London: Methuen, 1984.

Hunt, Peter L. *Children's Literature: The Development of Criticism.* London: Routledge, 1990.

Hunt. *Criticism, Theory, and Children's Literature.* Oxford: Blackwell, 1991.

Hunt. *An Introduction to Children's Literature.* Oxford & New York: Oxford University Press, 1994.

Hunt and Dennis Butts. *The Oxford Illustrated History of Children's Literature.* London & New York: Oxford University Press, 1995.

Hunt, Beth Humphries, and Sarah Wikinson. *Children's Book Research in Britain,* revised edition. Cardiff: University of Wales, 1982.

Hunt, ed. *Further Approaches to Research in Children's Literature.* Cardiff: University of Wales, 1982.

Inglis, Fred. *The Promise of Happiness: Value and Meaning in Children's Fiction.* Cambridge: Cambridge University Press, 1981.

Jackson, Rosemary. *Fantasy: The Literature of Subversion.* London & New York: Methuen, 1981.

Kohl, Herbert. *Should We Burn Babar?: Essays on Children's Literature and the Power of Stories.* New York: New Press, 1995.

Leeson, Robert. *Children's Books and Class Society: Past and Present.* London: Writers & Readers Publishing, 1977.

Leeson. *Reading and Righting: The Past, Present and Future of Fiction for the Young.* London: Collins, 1985.

Lesnik-Oberstein, Karín. *Children's Literature: Criticism and the Fictional Child.* Oxford: Clarendon Press, 1994.

Lewis, Naomi. *Fantasy Books for Children,* revised edition. London: National Book League, 1977.

Lurie, Alison. *Don't Tell the Grown-Ups: Subversive Children's Literature.* Boston: Little, Brown, 1990.

Lynn, Ruth Nadelman. *Fantasy for Children and Young Adults: An Annotated Bibliography,* fourth edition. New York: R. R. Bowker, 1995.

May, Jill P., ed. *Children and Their Literature: A Readings Book.* West Lafayette, Ind.: Children's Literature Association, 1983.

Meek, Margaret, Aidan Warlow, and Griselda Barton, eds. *The Cool Web: The Pattern of Children's Reading.* London: Bodley Head, 1977.

Morag, Bearne, and Watson. *The Prose and the Passion: Children and Their Reading.* London: Cassell, 1994.

Nikolajeva, Maria. *Children's Literature Comes of Age: Toward a New Aesthetic.* New York: Garland, 1995.

Nodelman, Perry. *The Pleasures of Children's Literature,* second edition. New York & London: Longman, 1996.

Quigly, Isabel. *The Heirs of Tom Brown: The English School Story.* London: Chatto & Windus, 1982.

Rees, David. *The Marble in the Water: Essays on Contemporary Writers of Fiction for Children and Young Adults.* Boston: Horn Book, 1980.

Rose, Jacqueline. *The Case of Peter Pan: Or, the Impossibility of Children's Literature.* London: Macmillan, 1984.

Salway, Lance. *Reading about Children's Books: An Introductory Guide to Books about Children's Literature.* London: National Book League, 1986.

Saxby, Maurice, and Gordon Winch, eds. *Give Them Wings: The Experience of Children's Literature,* second edition. Melbourne: Macmillan Australia, 1991.

Shavit, Zohar. *The Poetics of Children's Literature.* Athens: University of Georgia Press, 1986.

Smith, Karen Patricia. *The Fabulous Realm: A Literary-Historical Approach to British Fantasy, 1780–1990.* Metuchen, N.J. & London: Scarecrow Press, 1993.

Special Collections in Children's Literature: An International Directory, third edition. Chicago: American Library Association, 1995.

Stephens, John. *Language and Ideology in Children's Fiction.* London & New York: Longman, 1992.

Stones, Rosemary. *Pour out the Cocoa, Janet: Sexism in Children's Books.* London: Longman, 1983.

Styles, Morag, Eve Bearne, and Victor Watson. *The Prose and the Passion: Children and Their Reading.* London: Cassell, 1994.

Styles, Bearne, and Watson, eds. *After Alice: Exploring Children's Literature.* London: Cassell, 1992.

Townsend, John Rowe. *A Sounding of Storytellers: New and Revised Essays on Contemporary Writers for Children.* London: Viking Kestrel / New York: Lippincott, 1979.

Townsend. *Written for Children: An Outline of English-Language Children's Literature,* fourth edition. New York: HarperCollins, 1992.

Trease, Geoffrey. *Tales Out of School: A Survey of Children's Fiction,* revised edition. London: Heinemann, 1964.

Tucker, Nicholas. *The Child and the Book: A Psychological and Literary Exploration.* Cambridge & New York: Cambridge University Press, 1981.

Tucker, ed. *Suitable for Children? Controversies in Children's Literature.* London: Sussex University Press, 1976.

Turner, E. S. *Boys Will Be Boys: The Story of Sweeney Todd, Deadwood Dick, Sexton Blake, Billy Bunter, Dick Barton, et al,* revised edition. London: M. Joseph, 1975.

Vandergrift, Kay E. *Child and Story: The Literary Connection.* New York: Schuman, 1980.

Vandergrift. *Children's Literature: Theory, Research and Teaching.* Littleton, Colo.: Libraries Unlimited, 1989.

Waggoner, Diana. *The Hills of Faraway: A Guide to Fantasy.* New York: Atheneum, 1978.

Wall, Barbara. *The Narrator's Voice: The Dilemma of Children's Fiction.* London: Macmillan, 1991.

Warner, Philip. *The Best of British Pluck: The Boy's Own Paper.* London: Macdonald & Jane's, 1976.

Wintle, Justin, and Emma Fisher. *The Pied Pipers: Interviews with the Influential Creators of Children's Literature.* New York: Paddington, 1975.

Zipes, Jack. *Fairy Tales and the Art of Subversion: The Classical Genre for Children and the Process of Civilization.* London: Heinemann, 1983; New York: Wildman, 1983.

Contributors

Joel D. Chaston..*Southwest Missouri State University*
Sarah V. Clere ....*Mount Olive College*
Rosanne Fraine Donahue ....*University of Massachusetts, Boston*
Catherine L. Elick ....*Bridgewater College*
Steven Engelfried...*West Linn, Oregon*
Gwyneth Evans...*Malaspina University College*
Lois Rauch Gibson...*Coker College*
Michael Hennessy ....*Southwest Texas State University*
Judith Gero John ....*Southwest Missouri State University*
Raymond E. Jones..*University of Alberta*
Adrienne Kertzer ....*University of Calgary*
Charles E. Matthews ....*College of Charleston*
Roderick McGillis ....*University Of Calgary*
Alan McLay..*Carleton University*
Elizabeth C. Overmyer ....*Berkeley, California*
Kathy Piehl...*Mankato State University*
Richard C. Rowland...*Sweet Briar College*
David L. Russell ....*Ferris State University*
Patricia B. Sigler ....*State University of New York — Oneonta*
Louisa Smith...*Mankato State University*
Jon C. Stott...*University of Alberta*
Constance Vidor......................*The Cathedral School, Cathedral of Saint John the Divine*
Virginia A. Walter ....*University of California, Los Angeles*
Patricia H. Ward ....*College of Charleston*
Donna R. White ....*Clemson University*

Cumulative Index

Dictionary of Literary Biography, Volumes 1-161
Dictionary of Literary Biography Yearbook, 1980-1994
Dictionary of Literary Biography Documentary Series, Volumes 1-13

Cumulative Index

DLB before number: *Dictionary of Literary Biography,* Volumes 1-161
Y before number: *Dictionary of Literary Biography Yearbook,* 1980-1994
DS before number: *Dictionary of Literary Biography Documentary Series,* Volumes 1-13

B

E

G

M

Q

Y